THE ROUTLEDGE COMPANION TO RELIGION AND SCIENCE

The field of religion and science is one of the most exciting and dynamic areas of research today. This Companion brings together an outstanding team of scholars to explore the ways in which science intersects with the major religions of the world and religious naturalism. The collection provides an overview of the field and also indicates ways in which it is developing. Each topic is presented in a clear, readable fashion, ideal for scholars but also useful for upper-level undergraduates.

James W. Haag is a Lecturer in the Philosophy Department at Suffolk University, USA.

Gregory R. Peterson is a Professor in the Philosophy and Religion Department at South Dakota State University, USA.

Michael L. Spezio is Assistant Professor of Psychology and Neuroscience at Scripps College and Visiting Faculty at the California Institute of Technology, USA.

THE ROUTLEDGE COMPANION TO RELIGION AND SCIENCE

Edited by
James. W. Haag, Gregory R. Peterson, and Michael L. Spezio

LONDON AND NEW YORK

First published in 2012
by Routledge
2 Park Square, Milton Park, Abingdon, Oxon OX14 4RN

Simultaneously published in the USA and Canada
by Routledge
711 Third Avenue, New York, NY 10017

Routledge is an imprint of the Taylor & Francis Group, an informa business

British Library Cataloguing in Publication Data
A catalogue record for this book is available from the British Library

Library of Congress Cataloging in Publication Data
The Routledge companion to religion and science / edited by James. W. Haag, Gregory R. Peterson, and Michael L. Spezio.
p. cm.
Includes bibliographical references.
1. Religion and science. I. Haag, James. W. II. Peterson, Gregory R., 1966- III. Spezio, Michael L.
BL240.3.R685 2011
201′.65–dc22
2011011491

ISBN: 978-0-415-49244-7 (hbk)
ISBN: 978-0-203-80351-6 (ebk)

Typeset in Goudy Old Style
by Taylor & Francis Books

Printed and bound in Great Britain by
CPI Antony Rowe, Chippenham, Wiltshire

CONTENTS

PART II
Scientific and religious models of the world

CONTRIBUTORS

Nancy Ellen Abrams is a lawyer (J.D., University of Michigan) with a B.A. from the University of Chicago in history and philosophy of science. She specializes in the role of science in a new politics. She is an award-winning writer and co-authored, with Joel R. Primack, *The View from the Center of the Universe: Discovering our Extraordinary Place in the Cosmos* (Riverhead, 2006). Abrams and Primack gave the Terry Lectures at Yale in October 2009 on "Cosmic Society: the New Universe and the Human Future"; their book based on those lectures will be published by Yale University Press, spring 2011.

Nathaniel F. Barrett is a postdoctoral research fellow at the Institute for the Biocultural Study of Religion. His research interests include cognitive and evolutionary theories of religion, the Chinese traditions of Daoism and Confucianism, and philosophy of nature. He has published articles in *Process Studies*, *International Journal for Philosophy of Religion*, and *Journal for the American Academy of Religion*.

Whitney A. Bauman is Assistant Professor of Religion and Science at Florida International University. His book *Theology, Creation and Environmental Ethics* (Routledge, 2009) won the Templeton Award for Theological Promise. He is co-editor with Rick Bohannon and Kevin O'Brien of *Grounding Religion: A Field Guide to the Study of Religion and Ecology* (Routledge, 2010) and *Inherited Land: The Changing Grounds of Religion and Ecology* (Wipf and Stock, 2011). He is currently working on his second manuscript, tentatively entitled *Religion, Nature and Queer Theory: Opening Spaces for Dialogue*.

Jesse M. Bering is the Director of the Institute of Cognition and Culture and a Reader in the School of History and Anthropology at Queen's University, Belfast, Northern Ireland. A research psychologist by training, he writes the popular weekly column "Bering in Mind," a featured blog for the *Scientific American* website. In addition, he has published over sixty professional scientific articles, nearly all in the area of human social evolution. He was awarded the 2010 "Scientist of the Year Award" by the National Organization of Gay and Lesbian Scientists and Technical Professionals, a division of the American Association for the Advancement of Science.

Donald M. Braxton is the J. Omar Good Professor of Religious Studies at Juniata College. He received his PhD from the University of Chicago in 1993. He has worked at De Paul University, Indiana University, St Norbert College, and Capital University. His work focuses on the scientific study of religion from evolutionary and cognitive perspectives. Since 2002, his work has focused on computational simulations of religious behavior. His work has been published in various journals including *The Journal of Religion*, *The Journal of Cognition and Culture*, *Zygon* and *the Global Spiral*.

C. Mackenzie Brown is a historian of religions specializing in the Hindu tradition. He is the author of a number of books on medieval Hindu theology, but more recently he has focused on the relationship of Hinduism and modern science. He has written several articles on Hindu interpretations of evolution and creationism, and is currently working on a book, *Hindu Perspectives on Evolution: Darwin, Dharma, and Design* (Routledge, 2011). He teaches in the Religion Department at Trinity University in San Antonio, Texas.

Brian Burkhart, Ph.D. is Assistant Professor of Philosophy (Institute of Transdisciplinary Studies) at California State University Northridge. He grew up on the Navajo nation in Arizona and is also from the Cherokee tribe of Oklahoma, where he still has a lot of family. He wrote his doctoral dissertation at Indiana University on environmental ethics and indigenous philosophy, and is in the process of having a book published by SUNY Press entitled *Respect for Kinship: Toward an Indigenous Environmental Ethics*. His essay "What Coyote and Thales Can Teach Us: An Outline of American Indian Epistemology" can be found in *American Indian Thought* (Blackwell, 2004).

Charlene P. E. Burns, Ph.D. is Professor, Department of Philosophy & Religious Studies, University of Wisconsin-Eau Claire. Her research centers on issues in theology and the sciences, with special focus on rethinking Christian theological claims in light of psychology and the cognitive sciences. Her publications include *Mis/Representing Evil: Evil in an Interdisciplinary Key* (Inter-disciplinary Press, 2009), *More Moral Than God: Taking Responsibility for Religious Violence* (Rowman & Littlefield, 2008), and *Divine Becoming: Rethinking Jesus and Incarnation* (Fortress Press, 2002).

Geoffrey Cantor is Professor Emeritus of the History of Science at the University of Leeds and Honorary Senior Research Fellow at University College, London. His publications on science and religion include *Michael Faraday: Scientist and Sandemanian* (Macmillan, 1991), *Quakers, Jews, and Science* (Oxford University Press, 2005), and, with John Hedley Brooke, *Reconstructing Nature: The Engagement of Science and Religion* (the 1995–96 Gifford Lectures at Glasgow; T& T Clark, 1998; Oxford University Press, 2000). His most recent book offered a reinterpretation of the Great Exhibition and was entitled *Religion and the Great Exhibition of 1851* (Oxford University Press, 2011).

Tyrone Cashman holds master's degrees in ancient Greek, medieval European and modern European philosophy, and a Ph.D. from Columbia University in the philosophy of science. He has done research as a medical technician, worked with ecosystem biologists, engineers and neuroscientists, and has lectured at over twenty universities and colleges. He has served as CEO of the American Wind Energy Association and publisher of the *Whole Earth Catalog*. His articles and a book explore various aspects of systems dynamics and complexity.

Christopher Key Chapple is Doshi Professor of Indic and Comparative Theology at Loyola Marymount University in Los Angeles. He is the author of several books, including *Karma and Creativity* (1985), *Nonviolence to Animals, Earth, and Self* (1994), *Reconciling Yogas: Haribhadra's Array of Views on Yoga* (2003), and *Yoga and the Luminous: Patanjali's Spiritual Path to Freedom* (2008). He has edited several books on religion and ecology, including *Ecological Prospects* (1993), *Hinduism and Ecology* (2000), *Jainism and Ecology* (2002), and *Yoga and Ecology* (2008). He is editor of the journal *Worldviews: Global Religions, Culture, and Ecology*.

Rabbi Shai Cherry, Ph.D. is the Education Director of Tifereth Israel Synagogue in San Diego, California. He also teaches at the Thomas Jefferson School of Law. Cherry is the author of *Torah Through Time: Understanding Bible Commentary from the Rabbinic Period to Modern Times* (Jewish Publication Society, 2007) and several essays on Judaism and Darwinism.

Francisca Cho is an Associate Professor of Buddhist studies at Georgetown University. Her research focuses on the aesthetic expression of Buddhism in East Asia. She is the author of *Embracing Illusion: Truth and Fiction in the Dream of the Nine Clouds* (SUNY Press, 1996) and *Everything Yearned For: Manhae's Poems of Love and Longing* (Wisdom Publications, 2005). She is currently working on a book that addresses the conflict between religion and science through the Buddhist philosophy of language.

Ronald Cole-Turner holds the H. Parker Sharp Chair in Theology and Ethics at Pittsburgh Theological Seminary. His research focuses on religious perspectives on new or emerging technologies. He is the author or editor of seven books, including most recently *Design and Destiny: Jewish and Christian Perspectives on Human Germline Modification* (MIT Press, 2008) and *Transhumanism and Transcendence* (Georgetown, 2011). He is a founding member of the International Society for Science and Religion, serving as a vice president and a member of the executive committee.

Terrence W. Deacon is Professor of Anthropology and Neuroscience at the University of California, Berkeley. His current work focuses on the mechanisms underlying the emergence of major synergistic innovations in evolution. He is author of *The Symbolic Species: The Coevolution of Language and the Brain* (W.W. Norton, 1998) and *Mind from Matter: The Emergent Dynamics of Life* (W.W. Norton, 2011).

Chris Doran is an Assistant Professor of Religion at Pepperdine University in Malibu, California. He received a bachelor's degree in biology and a Master of Divinity from Pepperdine, and a Ph.D. in Systematic and Philosophical Theology from Graduate Theological Union in Berkeley, California. He has two primary areas of research interest. As a participant in the science and religion dialogue, he is involved with Christian responses to evolutionary theory, particularly examining why intelligent design is incompatible with Christian theology. He also has recently begun writing on Christian understandings of sustainability and environmental justice.

Noah Efron is the founding chairman of the Program in Science, Technology and Society at Bar Ilan University. He has served as President of the Israeli Society for History and Philosophy of Science, and serves on the executive committee of the International Society for Science and Religion. Efron has been a member of the Institute for Advanced Study in Princeton, and a Fellow at MIT and Harvard University. He is the author, most recently, of *Judaism and Science: A Historical Introduction* (Greenwood, 2006). Efron is a member of the City Council of Tel Aviv-Jaffa, where he lives with his wife, daughter, son, and various animals.

Gary B. Ferngren is Professor of History at Oregon State University. He has written extensively on the history of medicine in the ancient world, and on the historical relationship of science and religion. His publications include *The History of Science and Religion in the Western Tradition: An Encyclopedia* (Garland, 2000), of which he is General Editor; *Science and Religion: A Historical Introduction* (Johns Hopkins, 2002), of which he is Editor; *From Athens to Jerusalem: Medicine in Hellenized Jewish Lore and Early Christian Literature* (Erasmus, 2000), of which he is Co-Editor; and *Medicine and Health Care in Early Christianity* (Johns Hopkins, 2009).

Ellison Banks Findly is Professor of Religion and Asian Studies at Trinity College, Hartford, CT. She teaches courses in Hinduism, Buddhism, Indian Art, Indian Philosophy, and Theories of Non-Violence. Her books include *Dana: Giving and Getting in Pali Buddhism*, *Women's Buddhism, Buddhism's Women*, and *Plant Lives: Borderline Beings in Indian Traditions*. She is currently at work on a manuscript entitled *Spirits in the Loom: Religion and Design in Lao-Tai Textiles* that explores the environmental, historical, and religious influences on shamanic textile design, as well as the impact of shamanic rituals on animal sacrifice.

Joshua W. Fost is an Assistant Professor at Portland State University in Portland, Oregon, and is the author of the 2007 book *If Not God, Then What?: Neuroscience, Aesthetics, and the Origins of the Transcendent* (Clearhead Studios, 2007). His teaching interests are in the history and philosophy of science and the implications of a naturalistic worldview, especially with respect to neuroscience and the mind, and his research focuses on neurophilosophy and the pedagogy of science and critical thinking. Dr. Fost earned his Ph.D. in psychology and neuroscience from Princeton University in 1996.

Robert M. Geraci is Associate Professor of Religious Studies at Manhattan College, where he studies religion and technology. He is the author of *Apocalyptic AI: Visions of Heaven in Robotics, Artificial Intelligence, and Virtual Reality* (Oxford, 2010) and the recipient of a National Science Foundation grant to study meaningful and transcendent experiences in virtual worlds (2010–2012).

Jonathan C. Gold is Assistant Professor in the Department of Religion at Princeton University. His research focuses on Indian and Tibetan Buddhist intellectual traditions, especially theories of language, translation, and learning. He is author of *The Dharma's Gatekeepers: Sakya Pandita on Buddhist Scholarship in Tibet* (SUNY Press, 2007), which places this great thirteenth-century Tibetan philosopher in dialogue with contemporary thought on the nature of language and the role of the scholar in the formation and preservation of knowledge. His current interests include the Indian Buddhist philosopher Vasubandhu and the modern history of the doctrine of non-violence.

Mehdi Golshani holds a Ph.D. in physics from the University of California (at Berkeley). He is Distinguished Professor of Physics at Sharif University of Technology, in Tehran, Iran, and heads the Philosophy of Science Department of that university. His research interests include particle physics, cosmology, foundations of quantum mechanics, and science & religion. Among his recent books are *From Physics to Metaphysics* (1997), *Issues in Islam and Science* (2004), *Can Science Dispense with Religion?* (2004), and *The Holy Qur'an and the Sciences of Nature* (2008).

Ursula Goodenough is Professor of Biology at Washington University. She earned a Ph.D. at Harvard. She teaches cell biology and co-teaches 'The Epic of Evolution' with a physicist and a geologist. Her research covers the cell and molecular biology of the green alga *Chlamydomonas*. Her book *The Sacred Depths of Nature* (Oxford University Press, 2000) offers religious responses to scientific understandings of nature. She has served as president of the American Society for Cell Biology and the Institute on Religion in an Age of Science. She is a member of the American Academy of Arts and Sciences. She has five children and five grandchildren.

Charles Goodman is Associate Professor of Philosophy and Asian and Asian-American Studies at Binghamton University. He is the author of *Consequences of Compassion: An Interpretation and Defense of Buddhist Ethics* (Oxford University Press, 2009) and of several articles on Indian and Tibetan Buddhist ethics, metaphysics, and epistemology. Goodman holds a Ph.D. in Philosophy from the University of Michigan, Ann Arbor, and a BA in Physics from Harvard University.

Aubrey D. N. J. de Grey is a biomedical gerontologist based in Cambridge, UK, and is the Chief Science Officer of SENS Foundation, a California-based charity dedicated to combating the aging process. He is also Editor-in-Chief of *Rejuvenation Research*. His research interests encompass the characterization of all the side-effects of metabolism ("damage") that constitute mammalian aging and the design of interventions to repair and/or obviate that damage. He has developed a comprehensive plan for this, termed Strategies for Engineered Negligible Senescence (SENS), which breaks aging down into seven major classes of damage and identifies detailed approaches to addressing them.

James W. Haag is Lecturer in Philosophy at Suffolk University in Boston. He is author of numerous publications on science, philosophy, and religion, as well as the book *Emergent Freedom: Naturalizing Free Will* (Vandenhoeck and Ruprecht, 2008). Haag is currently Assistant Editor for the journal *Religion, Brain & Behavior* and is co-chair of the Science, Technology, and Religion Group of the American Academy of Religion.

David Harnden-Warwick is a doctoral student at Queen's University, Belfast. His research, made possible by the generous aegis of the John Templeton Foundation, seeks to integrate findings from cognitive archeology with a workable empirical program that can shed light upon the earliest expressions of supernatural-agent belief in genus *Homo*. David also holds a B.A. in philosophy and religious studies from Bethany College (WV) and a Master of Theological Studies from Emory University's Candler School of Theology.

Noreen Herzfeld is the Nicholas and Bernice Reuter Professor of Science and Religion at St. John's University in Collegeville, Minnesota. She holds degrees in Computer Science and Mathematics from The Pennsylvania State University and a Ph.D. in Theology from The Graduate Theological Union, Berkeley. Herzfeld is the author of numerous articles in both academic journals and the popular press as well as several books, including *In Our Image: Artificial Intelligence and the Human Spirit* (2002), *Technology and Religion: Remaining Human in a Co-Created World* (2009), and *The Limits of Perfection in Technology, Religion, and Science* (2010).

Lee Hester (Thurman Lee Hester Jr.) is a citizen of the Choctaw Nation of Oklahoma, born and raised in Oklahoma. He is active in the Indian community of central Oklahoma and has served as a Chairman of the Board, Cultural Committee Chair and President of the OK Choctaw Tribal Alliance. In the national Indian community, he has served on the American Philosophical Association's Committee on American Indians in Philosophy and as a National Caucus member of the Wordcraft Circle of Native Writers and Storytellers. A philosophy Ph.D., Lee has taught Indigenous Philosophy and Native American Law and Policy at universities in Canada and the United States.

Antje Jackelén is Bishop of the Diocese of Lund in the Church of Sweden and Adjunct Professor of Systematic Theology/Religion and Science at the Lutheran School of Theology at Chicago, USA, where she taught 2001–07. She was director of the Zygon Center for Religion and Science 2003–07. Dr. Jackelén currently serves as president of the European Society for the Study of Science and Theology. She is the author of *Time & Eternity* (Templeton Press, 2005), *The Dialogue between Religion and Science* (Pandora Press, 2004) and numerous articles published in various languages.

Gregg Jaeger is Associate Professor of Natural Sciences and Mathematics at Boston University. He holds a Ph.D. in Physics from Boston University, and B.Sc. degrees in Mathematics, Philosophy, and Physics from the University of Wisconsin. He works in quantum information theory and the foundations of physics. He has published books including *Quantum Information* (2007), *Entanglement, Information, and the Interpretation of Quantum Mechanics* (2009), and *Philosophy of Quantum Information and Entanglement* (2010), more than forty scientific articles, and two patents (in quantum computing).

William R. Jordan, III was the founding editor of "Ecological Restoration," and a founding member of the Society for Ecological Restoration International. He is co-director of the Institute for Nature and Culture at DePaul University and director of the New Academy for Nature and Culture, a think tank that explores the relationship between humans and their environment and provides a critical perspective on environmental thinking and practice. His books include *The Sunflower Forest: Ecological Restoration and the New Communion with Nature* (University of California Press, 2003) and *Making Nature Whole: A History of Ecological Restoration* (Island, in press).

Stephen Kaplan is Professor of Religious Studies at Manhattan College (Bronx, N.Y.). In addition to *Different Paths, Different Summits: A Model for Religious Pluralism* (Rowman & Littlefield, 2002), his other publications focus on Indian religious thought in a comparative context, frequently engaging the neurosciences. Holography, as a heuristic device, has often been an important element in his publications, including *Hermeneutics, Holography and Indian Idealism* (Motilal Banarsidass, 1987). Kaplan has been involved in the educational reform movement of the N.Y.C. public schools and, for example, the establishment of Bronx New School and the Jonas Bronck Academy.

Livia Kohn, Ph.D. is Professor Emerita of Religion and East Asian Studies at Boston University. Her specialty is the study of the Daoist religion and Chinese long life practices. She has written and edited over twenty-five books, including *Taoist Meditation and Longevity Techniques* (1989), *Laughing at the Dao* (1995), *Daoism Handbook* (2000), *Cosmos and Community* (2004), *Daoist Dietetics* (2010), and *Sitting in Oblivion* (2010). She is also executive editor of the *Journal of Daoist Studies*.

Gerald James Larson is Professor Emeritus, Religious Studies, UC Santa Barbara, and Tagore Professor Emeritus of Indian Cultures and Civilization, Indiana University, Bloomington. Dr. Larson is the author or editor of some twelve books and well over 100 scholarly articles on South Asian studies. His most recent publication is Volume XII of the *Encyclopedia of Indian Philosophies*, entitled *Yoga: India's Philosophy of Meditation* (Motilal Banarsidass, 2008). A collection of essays has been published in his honor, *Theory and Practice of Yoga: Essays in Honour of Gerald James Larson*, edited by Knut A. Jacobsen (Brill, 2005).

Karen Lebacqz holds her Ph.D. from Harvard University and has taught at Yale, McGill University, and in the Graduate Theological Union, Berkeley, CA. Ordained in the United Church of Christ, she is the author of more than eight books and numerous articles in bioethics, theories of justice, and feminist theology. She has served on numerous national organizations dedicated to the link between science and religion.

B. Andrew Lustig holds the Holmes Rolston III Chair in Religion and Science at Davidson College. He has published widely on issues in bioethics and in Catholic social ethics. His current research focuses on ethical questions raised by developments in synthetic biology.

Derek F. Maher received his M.A. and Ph.D. from the University of Virginia in the history of religions, with an emphasis on Indo-Tibetan Buddhism. His recent publications include his annotated translation of the classic two-volume *One Hundred Thousand Moons: A Political History of Tibet by Tsepon Shakabpa* (Brill, 2010), and, with Calvin Mercer, the co-edited volume *Religion and the Implications of Radical Life Extension* (Palgrave Macmillan, 2009). His background in physics enlivens his interest in the relationship between religion and science. At East Carolina University, Maher is the director of the Religious Studies Program.

Ebrahim Moosa is associate professor of Islamic Studies in the Department of Religion at Duke University. His interests span modern and classical Islamic law, theology, and Muslim ethics. His interests include debates in Muslim family law and bioethics. Apart from his work on the eleventh-century Muslim thinker al-Ghazali, Moosa explores the epistemological shifts in modern Muslim ethical thought and the way it challenges tradition.

Timothy O'Connor is Professor and Chair of the Department of Philosophy at Indiana University Bloomington. He has published numerous articles in metaphysics, philosophy of mind and action, and philosophy of religion. He is the editor of *Agents, Causes, and Events: Essays on Indeterminism and Free Will* (Oxford University Press, 1995); and co-editor of *Philosophy of Mind: Contemporary Readings* (Routledge, 2003), *Downward Causation and the Neurobiology of Free Will* (Springer, 2009), *Emergence in Science and Philosophy* (Routledge, 2010) and *A Companion to the Philosophy of Action* (Blackwell, 2010). He is the author of *Persons and Causes* (Oxford, 2000) and *Theism and Ultimate Explanation* (Blackwell, 2008).

Richard K. Payne is Yehan Numata Professor of Japanese Buddhist Studies, and Dean, Institute of Buddhist Studies, Berkeley. The Institute is affiliated with both the Graduate Theological Union, Berkeley and Ryukoku University, Kyoto. His specialization is the ritual traditions of Japanese tantric Buddhism. He is developing a cognitive theory of ritual based on the study of these and similar ritual traditions. He is also working on the issues of the psychologization of Buddhism in contemporary popular religious culture. He is Editor in Chief of the Oxford Bibliographies Online/Buddhism, and of *Pacific World: Journal of the Institute of Buddhist Studies.*

Ann Milliken Pederson is Professor of Religion at Augustana College in Sioux Falls, South Dakota. She teaches Christian theology, with particular emphasis on religion and medical sciences, feminist theologies, and Lutheran constructive theology. She is also an Adjunct Associate Professor in the Section for Ethics and Humanities at the Sanford School of Medicine of the University of South Dakota. Dr. Pederson has written three books, entries in the *Oxford Handbook of Religion and Science*, and numerous articles in *Zygon*, *Word and World*, and other periodicals. Her current research explores embodiment and incarnation in light of the medical sciences and biotechnologies.

Ted Peters is Professor of Systematic Theology at Pacific Lutheran Theological Seminary and the Graduate Theological Union in Berkeley, California, USA. He co-edits the journal *Theology and Science* (published by Routledge for the Center for Theology and the Natural Sciences). He is author of *Science, Theology and Ethics* (Ashgate, 2003), *Playing God? Genetic Determinism and Human Freedom* (Routledge, 2nd edn, 2002), and *Anticipating Omega* (Vandenhoeck & Ruprecht, 2008). He is co-author of *Theological and Scientific Commentary on Darwin's Origin of Species* (Abingdon Press, 2009) and co-editor of *Bridging Science and Religion* (SCM & Fortress, 2002).

Gregory R. Peterson is Professor and Program Coordinator in the Philosophy and Religion Department at South Dakota State University. His primary work has engaged the intersection of philosophy, theology, and science, especially in areas pertaining to human nature and ethics. He is the author of *Minding God: Theology and the Cognitive Sciences* (Fortress Press, 2002).

Scott L. Pratt is Professor and Head of Philosophy at the University of Oregon. Pratt is author of two books: *Logic: Inquiry, Argument and Order* (Wiley-Blackwell, 2010) and *Native Pragmatism: Rethinking the Roots of American Philosophy* (Indiana University Press, 2002), and has also co-edited four volumes including *American Philosophies: An Anthology* (Blackwell, 2002) and *The Philosophical Writings of Cadwallader Colden* (Humanity Books, 2002). He has published articles on the philosophy of pluralism, Dewey's theory of inquiry, Josiah Royce's logic, and the intersection of American philosophy and the philosophies of indigenous North American peoples.

Joel R. Primack is distinguished professor of physics at the University of California, Santa Cruz. After working on what is now called the standard model of particle physics, he helped to start the field of particle astrophysics. He and his colleagues developed the Cold Dark Matter theory, which is the basis for the standard modern theory of cosmology and galaxy formation. Primack also helped start the Congressional Science and Technology Fellowship Program, the American Physical Society Forum on Physics and Society, and the AAAS Program on Science and Human Rights. He chaired the AAAS Committee on Science, Ethics, and Religion 2000–02.

Ahmed Ragab is a lecturer on the history of science at Harvard University. He works on the cultural and intellectual history of the Middle East with special emphasis on science, medical theory and practice, and the relation between science and religion in the Middle East from the medieval to contemporary period. His publications focus on epistemic and intellectual authority in Islamic and scientific domains, and on the progress of the social perception of science in the Middle East.

Varadaraja V. Raman, Emeritus Professor at the Rochester Institute of Technology, is a philosopher, writer, and physicist. He holds a Ph.D. in Theoretical Physics from the University of Paris. He has authored books and articles on the historical and philosophical aspects of science, as well as on aspects of Indic culture. His recent book is *Truth and Tension in Science and Religion*, and his forthcoming book is *Indic Visions in an Age of Science*. He is a Senior Fellow at the Metanexus Institute, a fellow of the International Society for Science and Spirituality, recipient of the

Raja Rao Award from the Jawaharlal Nehru University, Delhi, and of the Academic Fellow Award of the Institute of Religion in an Age of Science of which he is the current president.

Daniel S. Rizzuto, Ph.D. manages the research program at the Swedish Neuroscience Institute in Seattle, WA. He completed his doctorate in neuroscience at Brandeis University and his postdoctoral training in brain–machine interfaces at the California Institute of Technology. Dan is also a long-time practitioner of *vipassana* (insight) meditation.

Holmes Rolston, III is University Distinguished Professor and Professor of Philosophy Emeritus at Colorado State University. He was Templeton Prize laureate in 2003. He gave the Gifford Lectures, University of Edinburgh, published as *Genes, Genesis and God* (Cambridge University Press, 1999). His *Science and Religion: A Critical Survey* was re-published in 2006 (Templeton Press), a new edition after twenty years. His most recent book is *Three Big Bangs* (Columbia University Press, 2011). He has lectured on all seven continents.

Michael Ruse is the Lucyle T. Werkmeister Professor of Philosophy and Director of the Program in the History and Philosophy of Science at Florida State University. He is the author of many books on Darwin and his revolutionary ideas about evolution. He has long been interested in the relationship between science and religion, and his most recent book, *Science and Spirituality: Making Room for Faith in the Age of Science* (Cambridge University Press, 2010) is an attempt to show the limits of science and whether there is then a possible place for a religion such as Christianity.

F. LeRon Shults is professor of theology and philosophy at the University of Agder in Kristiansand, Norway. He is the author of several books, including *Christology and Science* and *Reforming the Doctrine of God*, and over forty articles on themes related to religion and science. Shults is also the general editor of the Brill book series "Philosophical Studies in Science and Religion."

Michael L. Spezio is Assistant Professor of Psychology and Neuroscience at Scripps College and Visiting Faculty in Social and Affective Neuroscience at the California Institute of Technology. He is a social neuroscientist, investigating the psychology and neuroscience of emotional communication, empathy, compassion, political decisions, and moral action, and how Christian contemplative practices influence these processes. He is a Senior Fellow with the Mind and Life Institute, a member of the Editorial Board for *Theology & Science*, and a past member of the Scientific Advisory Board of the John Templeton Foundation. He is also an ordained minister in the Presbyterian Church (U.S.A.).

William R. Stoeger, S. J. is a staff scientist for the Vatican Observatory Research Group at the University of Arizona, Tucson. His present research includes theoretical cosmology and gravitational theory, and interdisciplinary studies bridging the natural sciences, philosophy and theology. He has been a key contributor to the Vatican Observatory's and Center for Theology and Natural Science's project and series 'Scientific Perspectives on Divine Action.'

J. Jeanine Thweatt-Bates holds a Ph.D. from Princeton Theological Seminary in Theology and Science. She is the author of *Cyborg Selves: A Theological Anthropology of the Posthuman* (Ashgate, forthcoming) and currently serves as an instructor for the Science for Ministry Institute.

Hava Tirosh-Samuelson is Irving and Miriam Lowe Professor of Modern Judaism and Director of Jewish Studies at Arizona State University. She writes on Jewish intellectual history, Judaism and ecology, and Judaism and science. She is the author of *Happiness in Premodern Judaism: Virtue, Knowledge and Well-Being* (2003); and editor of *Judaism and Ecology: Created World and Revealed Word* (2002) and *The Legacy of Hans Jonas: Judaism and the Phenomenon of Life* (2008). She is currently completing a monograph on conceptions of nature in Judaism and editing a book on transhumanism.

Rabbi Lawrence Troster is Director of the Fellowship program and Rabbinic Scholar-in-Residence for GreenFaith, the interfaith environmental coalition in New Jersey. Rabbi Troster is one of the U.S.A.'s leading Jewish eco-theologians and religious environmental leaders. He has published numerous articles and has lectured widely on eco-theology, bio-ethics, and Judaism and modern cosmology. He received his B.A. from the University of Toronto and his M.A. and rabbinic ordination from the Jewish Theological Seminary of America in New York City.

Grace Wolf-Chase is an Astronomer at the Adler Planetarium and Senior Research Associate in the Department of Astronomy and Astrophysics at the University of Chicago. She received her bachelor's degree in physics from Cornell, and her Ph.D. in astronomy from the University of Arizona. Prior to her current appointment, she was awarded a National Research Council postdoctoral fellowship at NASA Ames Research Center and a University of California President's postdoctoral fellowship at the University of California at Riverside. Her research emphasis is star formation, which she integrates with citizen science programs that enlist the public to assist scientific discovery.

Laurie Zoloth, Ph.D. is a McCormick Professor of Religion, and of medical humanities and bioethics, at Northwestern University, where she directs the Brady Program in Ethics and Civic Life, and the Center for Bioethics, Science and Society. She is a past president of the American Society for Bioethics and Humanities, a vice-president of the Society for Jewish Ethics, and the founding chair of the Howard Hughes Medical Institute Bioethics Advisory Board. Her books reflect her research interests in justice and moral philosophy, healthcare, and the Jewish philosopher Emanuel Levinas. She has received numerous awards, including both NASA and ASBH's highest awards for service in the field.

INTRODUCTION

James W. Haag, Gregory R. Peterson, and Michael L. Spezio

This volume is an edited collection of essays by scholars in theology, religious studies, philosophy, and the sciences, addressing the ways in which science intersects with the major religions of the world and religious naturalism. It is a further and, in important respects, novel contribution to ongoing scholarship in what is sometimes referred to as "religion-and-science."[1] A defining mark of scholarship in this field has been a concern to rethink the relation between science and religion beyond the confines of the conflict model typically instantiated in public debates in the United States and elsewhere. This requires re-evaluation of the historical record, rethinking of theological categories, and questioning of how the sciences are more generally understood to impact theological and philosophical claims. Tracing its roots to Ian Barbour's *Issues in Science and Religion* and to the establishment of *Zygon: Journal of Religion and Science*, both first published in 1966, the field has since been considerably deepened and broadened. Indeed, the explosion of literature on religion and science topics over the past two decades has made it challenging even for experts to keep pace with these developments – thus the need for this volume.

Any volume claiming to be a "Companion" to a field of work has the significant challenge of reaching a wide audience. This includes undergraduate and graduate students who may be completely new to the topics covered, but for whom the study of religion-and-science is of no small importance. In addition, active religion-and-science scholars and related professionals also make up the diverse listeners we must keep in mind. In developing this volume, we have endeavored to serve both audiences, seeking a balance between accessibility and expertise that can provide a useful resource for both. Striving to meet this challenge, we have also sought to bring together essays that serve to develop a new model for scholarly engagement, and by doing so, to help move the field forward in new and promising directions.

New voices in established contexts

The structure and conceptual depth of a Companion volume, partly due to its intended audience, is different from most other edited books. That is, as a Companion, this text is required to maintain a sustained association with the field to which it relates. The scholarship and research that motivates the creation of a Companion already has a structure – the volume must be a "companion" to something. For the past fifty years or so, the religion-and-science field of scholarship has evolved in a way that is reflected in the organization of this volume. This body of scholarship has made significant strides in understanding possible relationships between science and religion, often providing new insights on traditional problems, and engaging material and ideas that had not been previously considered. It would be inappropriate for a Companion volume simply to relate to a field in name only, while failing to echo the discipline's historical composition. That is, an utterly innovative tactic would not only be immensely difficult (since it would entail constructing an entirely new approach to the field) and undesirable (with the result of trying to reinvent what had already been done), but would also run counter to the integrity of Routledge's Companion series.

Having said this, it is also important that a Companion push the field in new directions. The major contribution of this volume is its multicultural breadth and scientific rigor on topics that are, and will be, compelling issues in the first part of the twenty-first century and beyond. In this regard, we have expanded the "religion" side of religion-and-science. The history of religion-and-science scholarship has been dominated by considerations of the compatibility or incompatibility of tenets in Christian theology with specific scientific theories. Or scholars have emphasized reconceptualizations of the historical relation of the Christian religion with science in a way that moves beyond a simplistic warfare model. Although this endeavor has generated a significant body of scholarship that is widely respected and of high quality (e.g. Polkinghorne 1994; Barbour 2000; Numbers and Lindberg 2003) there is a real and deep need for other religious traditions to be considered as well.

This deliberate effort to expand the conversation comes with many challenges, including the actual structure of the volume. To date, the vast majority of work accomplished in religion-and-science has come from scholars representing Western traditions of thought, which is problematic as the conversation continues to become global. In keeping with the intention that this volume should be a useful companion to the field at present, its organization includes topics that are critical to the current religion-and-science literature. We acknowledge that this will have a "Western-looking" structure, but there are straightforward and historical reasons for this. While it is a significant challenge to agree quickly on conceptual categories across religious traditions, there exists a standard way of categorizing fields in the sciences. While it would be a mistake to assume that such categories are neutral or natural (as some of the contributing essays will reveal), they are at least cross-cultural, even if limitedly so, in a way that other category schemes are not. However, instead of merely rehearsing the typical views, we have solicited a diverse group of authors who can comment on how the suggested topics are relevant or irrelevant to their particular tradition. We believe this approach will provide a needed contribution precisely on the issue of why religion-and-science has been developed almost exclusively in the West, as well as a potential source of critique by those outside of this tradition.

Accordingly, this volume has contributions from scholars who can speak authoritatively about differing religious traditions, including Buddhism, Christianity, Hinduism, Islam, Judaism, Native American Spirituality, Daoism, and Religious

Naturalism. We have not pigeonholed "non-Western" voices into a small section entitled "World Religions," as has been typical for other comprehensive review texts on religion-and-science. This more accurately captures the nature of the field and exemplifies the direction in which the field should move – and it represents a genuinely novel contribution. While there exist texts that pursue the interaction of differing religions and their stance toward the sciences (e.g. Peters *et al.*, 2003), these texts are few in number and typically limited to consideration of two or three religious traditions. This Companion is the first to offer such a wide and comprehensive range of perspectives on the key issues where religion and science meet.

Engaging science beyond critique

There is another historical trend that we diligently try to counterbalance – the importance of engaging the content of science, rather than simply talking about "science in general" at a safe distance. Under one kind of religious studies approach, one might study and develop social critiques of how scientists construct their theories, and do so in a way that "protects" religion as something distinct from, and independent of, the sciences. One might call this approach an anthropology of science, a sociology of science, or a psychology of science. While these approaches are important, they rarely candidly engage the substance of science. Alternatively, the history of theology's interaction with science has been with the explicit intention of addressing the very data and theories that scientists accept on a daily basis. In line with the history and general method of religion-and-science, the authors in this volume are asked to actively relate the content of religious understandings directly to scientific theories. It is not our intention in any way to say that there are absolute claims made by scientists that we must accept without question. Rather, we acknowledge that there are some key positions in the various sciences that are widely accepted. (A popular example is the encounter between scientists and members of the intelligent design movement. While there may be some "in-house" disagreements between scientists – for instance, the differing positions on evolution taken by Richard Dawkins and Stephen Jay Gould – these differences are technical details that disappear in the scientists' united rejection of intelligent design.) Outwardly contesting claims made by scientists, based on social grounds – while a worthwhile task and one that appears in abbreviated form in certain articles within this Companion – is but one approach to engaging the sciences, typically leaving much else to be said.

For this reason, the scientific chapters in our volume serve several purposes. It is important for a book on religion-and-science to have articles *by scientists* about the *content of the science* of their respective fields. This is a feature that clearly distinguishes the current volume from other edited volumes currently available. In addition, the religious diversity in this volume is mirrored by the representation of assorted scientific fields. Second, one of the main audiences for a Companion volume is undergraduates. In addition to the central purpose of educating students about religion-and-science, when this text is used in learning environments, it can serve a more basic function of increasing science literacy. It is important that students interested in religion-and-science have access to material that accurately describes the current content of the scientific fields being engaged simply in order to understand what the issues are. Surprisingly, this is important even for science students, who are typically narrowly trained in one field without ever developing competence in other fields of science. A student in chemistry may know little, if anything, about Big Bang cosmology or sub-atomic particle physics, and even less about evolutionary theory and neuroscience. For this reason, the scientific chapters offer the reader access to the scientific content pertinent for responsible interdisciplinary reflection. It is scientific reflection written by scientists.

This type of structure is different from the standard religious studies and theological critiques of the sciences; instead, it challenges authors and readers to take seriously the substance of the various sciences. We view this as an approach that combines lucidity with an organic connection to the subject matter. Religion-and-science as the subject matter cannot be ignored for what we might like it to be, but must be engaged directly as it currently stands.

It is these two features that principally distinguish this volume from other, recent contributions to the field, such as Philip Clayton and Zachary Simpson's (2006) *The Oxford Handbook of Religion and Science* and Peter Harrison's (2010) *The Cambridge Companion to Religion and Science*. Both of these are important and fine contributions to understanding religion-and-science, but both reveal the limitations in approach beyond which this volume seeks to go. While both volumes have a number of quality articles by scientists, all are focused not on the science itself, but on relating the science to specific theological concerns. Of the two works, only Clayton and Simpson's brings some attention to non-Christian traditions, and then only in seven articles set at the beginning (including one on atheism and one on religious naturalism).

Readers of this volume will quickly see the difference in emphasis, although this raises two further questions. The first of these concerns representation. Although the religion essays are far more diverse than in any previous multi-author work, readers will still note a larger representation of essays speaking about or from branches of the Christian tradition and Western religious and philosophical thought generally. Further, some decisions have also had to be made regarding the specific religions and the extent to which they are represented. While parity has been the editorial ideal, scholar availability has in most cases been the reality To a significant extent, the existence of inequalities in representation in this volume reflects the level of scholarly engagement with science by English-speaking religion scholars generally. In this respect, this volume is part of an ongoing conversation, one that has seen growing and significant diversity, but that still aspires to greater inclusion of multiple traditions and perspectives in the coming years.

A second question concerns the message that may be understood to be sent by including such a wide range of voices. Some readers may search in vain for a concluding chapter that seeks to distill the variety of perspectives into one unified view, or tries to synthesize the shared religious wisdom found at the base of all the religious traditions included in the volume, and by doing so supersede them. The current work does not seek such a unified voice, nor is that its goal. Rather, the goal is to give the diversity of voices their full expression, reflecting to some extent the real diversity of value and religious expression found in the world today. Despite this, the observant reader will quickly find recurring patterns of argumentation and interpretation across this diversity, and we submit that the reader who pays attention to such dynamics will be richly rewarded.

Overall, this Companion describes and assesses the historical development of the field of religion-and-science; it notes the ethos of the present-day discussion and elaborates its central themes; by employing the use of multicultural voices, it attempts to expand the dialogue for future generations of scholars.

Structure of the volume

The volume is organized into three parts: I Epistemology and history; II Scientific and religious models of the world; III Religion and science, values and public policy. Each part is then separated into smaller and specific sections.

Part I Epistemology and history

(i) Frameworks and methods

This section explores the differing ways in which one can and should relate the fields of religion and science, and reveals how disciplinary setting makes a difference in the ways basic questions of frameworks and methods are understood. F. LeRon Shults examines these issues from the perspective of a Christian theologian, noting the complex history of Christianity and science, and indicating the importance of theological categories of relationality and contextuality. Francisca Cho, a religious studies scholar who has focused on Buddhism and science, explores definitional questions and the role the language of science has played in explaining religion, relating this to internal frameworks of Buddhism to speak of religion itself as a form of empiricism. Geoffrey Cantor provides a history of the history of science, noting the move away from traditional conflict models of religion-and-science, and increasing awareness of the distinctive interactions of Jews and Muslims with science. Concluding the section, Brian Yazzie Burkhart brings forth a Native perspective, addressing the complexities and possibilities when encountering both of the Western categories, religion and science.

(ii) Historical overviews

The interaction between religion and science is not merely a recent phenomenon, but has deep historical roots, and understanding these roots is often key for understanding current debates and possibilities. The first selection, by Ahmed Ragab, provides a thorough overview of science and Islam, beginning with the influence of Greek thought and the complex interplay between political realities, science, and Islamic thought in the nineteenth and twentieth centuries, when the relationship to science becomes intertwined with the relationship to the West. Gary Ferngren, by contrast, traces the interaction of Christianity and science, noting the importance of Augustine's "handmaiden" metaphor in the ancient period and the complex reception of Aristotle by medieval theologians, before moving on to the importance of the scientific revolution, the rise of the new theories of Charles Lyell in geology and Charles Darwin in biology in the nineteenth century, and the new physics of Albert Einstein and Werner Heisenberg (among others) in the twentieth. Noah Efron notes the very different history of Jews, Judaism, and science. This history is much longer, with roots in the Old Testament period, and – in addition to noting the importance of such figures as Moses Maimonedes and Baruch Spinoza – examines the Talmud's complex and plural attitude towards natural wisdom. Efron concludes with a brief study of the rise to prominence of Jews in science, not only in Western Europe but in the Soviet Union and Israel as well.

Part II Scientific and religious models of the world

(i) Cosmologies and cosmogonies

Cosmology, on the one hand, is the naturalistic account of the universe in its entirety. Cosmogony, on the other, is a theoretical account of the beginnings of the universe. Scientific accomplishments have contributed immensely to our current understandings. Furthermore, many religions make claims about, and find significance in, the origin and nature of the cosmos. Joel Primack and Nancy Abrams lead the section with an overview of scientific cosmology, briefly tracing the history of cosmological theories from ancient roots through the rise of Big Bang theory to the current science of the "double dark" universe that includes both dark matter and dark energy. The essay of Primack and Abrams is complemented by that of Grace Wolf-Chase, who helps the reader focus on the immense scales of space that astronomy works with, as well as surveying two important and more recent fields: the study of exoplanets and astrobiology, both building on prior work in planetary astronomy. Gerald Larson's essay recapitulates some of the classic Hindu texts on cosmogony, noting that the complex understanding of time in Hindu thought might parallel modes of thinking in scientific cosmology. Donald Braxton takes the article by Primack and Abrams as a launching point for discussing the possibilities of religious naturalism and, in particular, whether it even makes sense for a philosophical naturalist to also be religious. Working from the perspective of a Christian theologian, Antje Jackelén concludes the section by addressing the challenges scientific cosmology and astronomy raise both for the Genesis account of creation and for theories of divine action, and notes the resources in *logos* theology for thinking about these issues.

(ii) Quantum theoretical approaches and causality

The broader implications of quantum mechanics have been of significant interest not only to scientists, but also to many religious scholars, who have found insight and opportunity for theological and religious reflection when engaging this fundamental account of nature. Quantum mechanics raises many issues, but especially pertinent to religious concerns are the notions of causation and determinism, and questions of the interconnectedness of things. Gregg Jaeger begins with an overview of quantum mechanics and its implications for basic philosophical questions of realism, reductionism versus holism, the role of observation in measurement, and understandings of freedom and determinism. V.V. Raman follows this, noting the many possible parallels between quantum mechanics and themes of Hindu thought, from accounts of karma and causation to understandings of the subject–object relation. William Stoeger takes up the relation between quantum mechanics and Catholic thought, arguing that while Catholic theology makes no claims on what quantum mechanics ought to say, it does take an interest in rival philosophical interpretations of quantum mechanics. Mehdi Golshani notes the long history of Muslim thought embracing strong conceptions of causality and the challenge that quantum mechanics brings to this embrace, raising for some the possibility of returning to weaker understandings of causality found in the Asharite school, a move that has theological implications.

(iii) Complexity, emergence, and eliminativism

This field has been slowing expanding over the past thirty years. The popular expression "The whole is more than the sum of its parts" continues to interest those opposed to overly reductionist accounts on the one hand, and unnecessarily dualist ones on the other. Reality is not simply about the smallest parts or the most complex wholes that make up the universe – snowflakes, minds, and societies are significant because they epitomize a unique interaction between parts and wholes. In addition, many religious scholars have been attracted to the idea of emergence because it appears to offer a way to genuinely affirm that which religion seeks to explain. Terrence Deacon and Tyrone Cashman provide an introduction to the concept of emergence in philosophy and science, emphasizing their own dynamic account of emergence that promises to reconcile scientific accounts of being and causation with agential accounts of freedom. Timothy O'Connor amplifies consideration of the philosophical significance of emergence and how it might contribute to understanding the metaphysical status of such topics as consciousness and agency. James Haag considers the relevance of emergence theories for Christian theology, examining the role of the concept in the thought of three recent theologians: Philip Clayton, Arthur Peacocke, and Gordon Kaufman. Charles Goodman notes that parallels exist to emergence theories in the *Abhidharma* literature of Buddhism, and argues that the form of emergence theory developed by Deacon and Cashman has important relevance for *Madhyamaka* approaches.

(iv) Evolutionary biology and suffering

Darwin's theory of evolution has been a focus of debate and interpretation since its inception, and has been used both to attack and to promote religious world-views. Although conflict has been a primary motif in American popular culture, the reception of evolution has varied considerably among the world's religious traditions and even within religious traditions. Ursula Goodenough begins with a biological framework for understanding suffering, including an evolutionary account of why organisms suffer and how suffering came to be. Providing a philosopher's perspective on pain and suffering, Holmes Rolston III argues for a cruciform account of evolution and suffering that takes into consideration the phenomenology of suffering as well as its physical correlates. Lawrence Troster traces the evolution of Jewish thought on suffering from its origins in scriptural accounts to post-Holocaust thought. Troster gives particular attention to the persistence, but eventual demise, of demonic/theurgic accounts, and finds especial insight in the writings of Hans Jonas. Writing from the perspective of Christian theology, Ted Peters contemplates the apparent wastefulness of the evolutionary process from the perspective of the theology of the cross and the promise of a new creation.

(v) The cognitive sciences and religious experience

The relationship of mind and body, reason and emotion, religious experience, and the basic meaning of what it is to be human are raised by developments in such fields as neuroscience and artificial intelligence. An overview of the field and some of the research on religious experience is provided by Michael Spezio. Richard Payne seeks to unmask the question of religious experience by noting its specifically Western roots, and indicates the very different route of reflection that occurs when one starts with Buddhist categories of understanding mental properties in relation to the goal of awakening. Charlene Burns analyzes the shortcomings of neurotheology and, resisting forms of non-reductive physicalism, argues for an embodied, relational account of human becoming consistent with the teachings of the New Testament. Stephen Kaplan concludes the section with a consideration of the relation of cognitive science to Hindu concepts of consciousness, cognition, and perception, and suggests ways in which cognitive science and Hindu thought may positively interact.

(vi) Ecology and the integrity of nature

The relationship between human beings and the non-human world has been of importance to both religion and science. Almost all religions, from diverse times and places, weave narratives concerning human interaction with the wider world, both animate and inanimate. Increased knowledge, over the past forty years, about the detrimental human impact on the world's ecosystem situates the religious scholar and theologian in a unique position. Nathaniel Barrett and William Jordan begin with a challenge to environmentally oriented religion scholars, charging that religious ecological reflection has not kept up with the science of ecology and that it suffers from an overly sentimental understanding of the natural world. Hava Tirosh-Samuelson in turn challenges the underlying categories of Barrett and Jordan's overview, and after surveying the history of Jewish thought concerning the natural world, evolution, and ecology, emphasizes the role that responsibility plays in Jewish reflection. Christopher Chapple provides an overview of the complex diversity of the representations of nature in the religions of South and East Asia, connecting these to the rise of environmental movements in India in the twentieth century. Drawing broadly on Western religious and philosophical thought, Whitney Bauman connects religion to meaning-making, encouraging the reader to see the way in which religions, institutions, and ethical systems "materialize" the natural world.

Part III Religion and science, values, and public policy

(i) Origins

In the public sphere, the primary mode of interaction between religion and science has been one of conflict, often about issues of origins. In the United States, this has manifested itself primarily in debates over evolution and attempts to install first creation science, and more recently intelligent design, into the public classroom. Michael Ruse begins by charting the history of Darwinian evolution and its complex reception by Christian communities in Europe and America. Scott Pratt provides an overview of contemporary Native American understandings of creation and the role that origin stories play in Native American thought. C. Mackenzie Brown surveys the diversity of early Hindu creation accounts, and delineates the role of colonialism in nineteenth-century Hindu accounts, as well as more recent Hindu forms of anti-evolutionary creationism. Chris Doran provides an overview of recent and conflicting responses to evolution in the form of the intelligent design movement and theistic evolution, also noting the important questions that evolution can raise for Christian thought. Shia Cherry shows that Jewish reactions to evolution have been similarly diverse, but also notes the very different history of understanding and interpreting the text of Genesis 1 in earlier Jewish thought.

(ii) Biotechnology and justice

As scientists continue to expand knowledge of human biology, important questions will need to be clarified. These questions deal with stem cell research, genetic engineering, and trait enhancement, among others. They overlap significantly with topics pertinent in theological anthropology and ethics. Ronald Cole-Turner surveys several of the important advances in biotechnology-related research, from genetic engineering and the Human Genome Project to issues surrounding stem cells and their potential. Karen Lebacqz provides a Protestant perspective, and notes that despite the diversity of Protestant denominations, agreement can frequently be found in the concern for distributive justice, the poor, and the ways in which power is implemented. Ebrahim Moosa notes the "glocal" character of biotechnology in the Muslim world, where access is uneven and controversies remain in some countries over issues, such as organ transplantation, that most Westerners consider settled. Andrew Lustig provides an understanding of biotechnologies from a Catholic perspective, noting a rootedness in principles of natural law and in more recent developments such as that of Vatican II. Laurie Zoloth, confronting biotechnology as a means of industrial production and employing a careful reading of biblical texts, argues for an ethic based in faithfulness to relationships in the face of an uncertain reality, and an understanding of hospitality that concentrates on the needs of the poor.

(iii) Non-human cognition: animal cognition and artificial intelligence

In the Western theological tradition, there has often been a presumption of human uniqueness, often embodied in the doctrine of the image of God. In recent years, this presumption has faced serious challenges from studies of animal cognition and intelligence. David Harnden-Warwick and Jesse Bering begin with an overview of the extensive literature on theory of mind in primate studies, and speculate on its implications for thinking about the emergence of religion. Ellison Banks Findly notes how Hindu understandings of animals are linked to doctrines of *karma* and *samsara*, and she provides perspective on *Samkhya* theorizing on other minds and the roles of animals in Hindu narrative. Gregory Peterson surveys Christian understandings of humans and animals, noting the historical importance of the doctrine of the image of God for thinking about the issue, and linking the literature on animal cognition and theory of mind to questions of ethics, suffering, and redemption. Jonathan Gold notes the challenges in speaking of a theory of mind in the context of Buddhist doctrines of no-self, and relates this to the broader Buddhist minimizing of human distinctiveness embodied in understandings of *karma* and reincarnation and exemplified in the *Jataka* tales of the Buddha's past lives.

(iv) Aging and life extension

One of the themes most prevalent in religious traditions has to do with the beginning and end of life. Technology advancements have now made end-of-life issues more difficult to assess. Is the extension of life a religious issue? Aubrey de Grey provides a succinct overview of the science of aging and the research strategies with promise to significantly prolong life, noting that the goal of such efforts must not be simply the prolongation of frailty, but a true regenerative medicine. Derek Maher gives a Buddhist perspective, noting that, for Buddhists, longevity is not a good in and of itself, but is linked to how a life is conducted. Further, Maher points out that issues of justice loom large for Buddhists, many of whom are in the developing world and lack access to adequate healthcare while money is spent prolonging the lives of the wealthy. Livia Kohn surveys some of the basic ethical issues concerning longevity science, and compares the current science of longevity to traditional Daoist techniques of longevity in context of its valuation of immortality. Ann Pederson challenges the Enlightenment values behind the anti-aging movement, providing instead a Christian theological account of human embodiment and the awareness of death informed by the philosophy of science developed by Donna Haraway.

(v) Transhumanism and artificial intelligence

Exploration of cyborgs and the integration of machine and organism have long been staples of science fiction. Recent and potential advances suggest that this may no longer be the case. Dan Rizzuto and Joshua Fost begin by making the case for transhumanism, arguing that cognitive and biological enhancements are but the next stage of human evolution, and that such enhancements can contribute to a just and good society. Robert Geraci traces the history and diverse forms of transhumanism, arguing that it takes the form of religion in many of its key commitments. Taking a more critical view, Noreen Herzfeld contends that a Christian understanding of embodiment and human sinfulness suggests a much more cautious approach to programs of enhancement than that advocated by transhumanists. Thurman Lee Hester, Jr. concludes the section, reflecting on transhumanism from American

Indian perspectives and arguing for the importance of the principles of respect and circularity when thinking about the technologies that transhumanists seek to develop and use.

How to use this Companion

Using a volume of this size can be daunting. Generally, each chapter can function as a stand-alone contribution to religion-and-science. However, some will prove more valuable when read alongside others. More specifically, chapters in Part I are historical and methodological overviews that do not reference other chapters in the volume. Parts II and III are structured slightly differently. In this area of the volume, we have included scientific "introductions" on the various topics selected for our Companion. Following these are religious "responses" from differing religious traditions. Our suggestion, when looking at chapters in the latter part of the book, is to read both the scientific introductions as well as the religious response(s) that interest you. While some of the response chapters deal implicitly with the introductions, others are explicit and a lack of familiarity with the introductory submissions could prove problematic.

Consequently, we envision a number of ways in which the volume could be used in a classroom context. The most basic and obvious approach is to use it as a primary text for a course on science and religions, possibly supplemented by original readings in select areas. The text is well designed for this purpose, and instructors should find sufficient integrity in sections, and flow across sections, to stimulate students' interest and participation. Although the entire volume could be used for such a course, the size of the book will no doubt suggest selecting those sections most pertinent to the character of the course and students' needs, and the fact that each section can stand alone should facilitate this. Alternatively, many instructors will no doubt wish to use the text more selectively. Two likely possibilities would be to select chapters for a course that emphasizes monotheistic traditions (Judaism, Christianity, and Islam) or the religions of South and East Asia, using the chapters on Hinduism, Buddhism, and Daoism. A course emphasizing historical and ethical approaches may focus on Parts I and III of the volume. A unique element of the text is inclusion of Native American perspectives, and some instructors may wish to use these as a starting point. As already noted, since the essays in Parts II and III are written in dialogue with the science summary articles, it will typically be most effective to assign the science readings along with the relevant religion readings for a given section. Other possible combinations will no doubt suggest themselves to readers as they progress through the volume.

Note

1 Use of the hyphenated "religion-and-science" follows Philip Hefner's lead to identify "a collective noun–not […] two separate entities" (Hefner 2006: 562). This phrasing attempts to designate "the field" of religion and science interactions.

References

Barbour, Ian (2000) *When Science Meets Religion*, New York: HarperOne.

Clayton, Philip and Zachary Simpson (eds) (2006) *The Oxford Handbook of Religion and Science*, New York: Oxford University Press.

Harrison, Peter (ed.) (2010) *The Cambridge Companion to Religion and Science*, Cambridge: Cambridge University Press.

Hefner, Philip (2006) "Religion-and-Science," in *The Oxford Handbook of Religion and Science*, Philip Clayton and Zachary Simpson (eds), New York: Oxford University Press, 562–76.

Numbers, Ron and David Lindberg (2003) *When Science and Christianity Meet*, Chicago, IL: University of Chicago Press.

Peters, Ted, Muzaffar Iqbal and Syed Nomanul Haq (eds) (2003) *God, Life, and the Cosmos: Christian and Islamic Perspectives*, Aldershot, UK: Ashgate.

Polkinghorne, John (1994) *Science and Christian Belief*, London: SPCK.

Part I

EPISTEMOLOGY AND HISTORY

(i) Frameworks and methods

1
RELIGION AND SCIENCE IN CHRISTIAN THEOLOGY

F. LeRon Shults

The meaning and use of the terms "religion" and "science" are contested and contentious, as the other chapters in this section of the Companion amply demonstrate. This chapter focuses on the challenges and opportunities that shifts within late modern philosophy of science and the study of religion have created for contemporary Christian theology, by altering the conceptual and pragmatic playing field within which interdisciplinary engagement can occur. These shifts also have broader intellectual and social implications because the Christian religion no longer plays the same political and cultural role that it once did in the West.

I begin by pointing briefly to the complex relation between the *Christian* religion and the emergence of early *modern* science, which is an important first step toward understanding our current context. Second, I trace some key developments in late modern philosophy of science that have contributed to the renewal of positive and concrete interaction between scientific and theological disciplines. The third part describes Ian Barbour's influential taxonomy of ways of relating religion and science, and some of the responses to it by philosophers and theologians in the Christian tradition. I conclude by suggesting that Christian theologians in the "science and religion" field ought to complement their interaction with the sciences with a more rigorous engagement with developments in the study of *religion* (or *religions*), especially the increased interest in attending to otherness and difference.

Christian religion and early modern science

The year 2009 marked the 400th anniversary of Galileo's first use of the telescope and the 200th anniversary of the birth of Charles Darwin. The controversies around these two figures stand out in the public imagination as primary examples of what appears to be a basically negative relationship between science and Christianity. Indeed, discoveries and theoretical developments in the scientific disciplines they represent (cosmology and biology), as well as others, have clearly threatened traditional Christian views of the world and the place of humanity within it. During the middle ages, Christian theology could be articulated within a relatively stable understanding of the cosmos as a set of concentric spheres with the Earth fixed at its center and of human persons as immaterial souls housed within (or enlivening) material bodies. A mixture of Platonic and Aristotelian assumptions played a regulative role in shaping Christian doctrines such as creation and providence, sin and redemption. The undermining of these cosmological and anthropological assumptions by Galileo and Darwin, among many others, weakened the formulations that had been shaped by them.

In the nineteenth and early twentieth centuries, many historians interpreted the role of the church in the Galileo and Darwin affairs simply as (failed) ecclesial attempts to suppress enlightened scientists. In the latter part of the twentieth century, however, historical research into these (and other) episodes has shown that the "warfare" reading of the relationship between science and the Christian religion was too simplistic. As John Hedley Brooke (1991) has pointed out, there were several ways in which Christianity positively sponsored the development of the early modern sciences; for example, providing presuppositions (about order and causality), as well as sanctioning and even motivating empirical study of the world (as God's good creation). There were Christians on both sides of the debates over the proposals of Galileo and Darwin (Lindberg and Numbers 1986; McMullin 2005). In cosmology and anthropology, as well as other sciences, deeper philosophical and broader cultural concerns were at play in the ongoing struggle to interpret human experience within the world.

Nevertheless, something radical happened to the Christian religion during the early modern period. "Why was it virtually impossible not to believe in God in, say, 1500, in our Western society, while in 2000 many of us find this not only easy, but even inescapable?" (Taylor 2007: 25). The answer to this question is complex, but the rise of early modern science, which challenged the hegemony of the Christian interpretation of the world, clearly played an important role in this shift. Pre-modern people reflected on the world and themselves, and imaginatively attempted both to make sense and to make use of the forces that shaped their experience. But what we today call "science" emerged as part of *modernity*. Pre-modern people attended to their fears and desires in relation to that which they understood as ultimately conditioning the world and themselves, and developed ways of trying to orient themselves appropriately to that reality. However, the construction and segregation of what came to be called "religion" as a sphere of human life separated from other spheres was also a distinctly *early modern* phenomenon. The social and religious reformations of the sixteenth century, the ending of the Thirty Years' War with the treaty of Westphalia in 1648, and the growing independence and fragmentation of scientific inquiry in the eighteenth century all contributed to the separation between the sacred and the mundane, the religious and the secular.

For the purposes of this brief survey, we can focus on some of the key philosophical factors that shaped these developments. The dichotomy between "science" and "religion" is connected to dualisms of other kinds, both metaphysical and epistemological. In the early seventeenth century, Descartes argued for a strong distinction between extended thing (*res extensa*) and thinking thing (*res cogitans*). His assertion "I think, therefore I am," which was intended as an indubitable foundation for the construction of rational knowledge of the world, was tied to an anthropological dualism between the immaterial soul and the material body. Intellectual certainty was the goal and mathematics was the ideal. By the end of the seventeenth century, the success of Newton's laws of mechanics – the mathematical measurement of extended material bodies – had reinforced the growing sense that the study of "immaterial" things would require some other indubitable foundation (the Bible, the Church?) and some other methodological principles. In the eighteenth century, many theologians continued attempting to prove the existence of God based on causation or order in the external world, but others (as diverse as Jonathan Edwards and Charles Wesley) began to focus their energy on religious affections and the internal conviction of the soul as the basis for knowledge of immaterial (spiritual) realities.

The religious sphere might be passionate and subjective, but science should be neutral and objective. This attitude contributed to the rise of positivism as well as the academic division between the "natural" sciences and the "human" sciences in the late nineteenth century. Where did these developments leave theology? Charles Hodge tried to emulate the natural sciences (deducing propositions from "data" posited in the Bible), while Ernst Troeltsch refigured theology as a kind of human science (interpreting the social teaching of the Christian church). Others gave up on the idea that theology was a "science" at all: Religion has to do with *faith* and science has to do with *reason*, and never the twain shall meet. Each of these decisions impacted the way in which the task of (or need for) acquiring, formulating, and defending "knowledge" about religious issues was understood and executed. These epistemological dualisms, however, were inherently linked to early modern metaphysical dualisms, both of which have been challenged by developments within late modern philosophy and science. As we will see in Part III, these shifts have opened up new possibilities for the interaction between Christian theology and contemporary science.

Late modern philosophy of science and Christian theology

The "philosophy of science" deals with what counts as academic knowledge (*scientia*) and how it is properly acquired, formulated and defended. It explores the relations among, and self-understanding of, organized fields of human inquiry, analyzing the nature, process, and outcome of inquiry itself. This requires attending to broader epistemological and hermeneutical issues that reach across different fields. Two developments in the late modern philosophy of science are particularly relevant for understanding the resurgence of interest in the positive interaction between religion and science among Christian theologians in the early third millennium.

The first is a shift toward using *relationality* as a constitutive and generative category in both metaphysics and epistemology. Despite their differences, Plato and Aristotle both privileged the category of *substance* over relation. First and foremost, knowledge (*episteme*, *scientia*) of some thing requires identifying its substance (or essence); the way in which the thing is dynamically related to other things is secondary. The valorizing of inertial "substances" was still evident in much early modern cosmology and anthropology. Over time, however, the inadequacy of theories of being and knowing that failed to attend sufficiently to the relations between things became increasingly clear. By the end of the eighteenth century, Kant would argue that the concepts of substance and accidents are sub-categories "Of Relation." The story of the philosophical turn to relationality is too complex to repeat here (cf. Shults 2003), but the outcome is evident in the role played by the category of "relation" in the dominant scientific cosmologies and anthropologies of the twentieth century. We can point, for example, to Einstein's theories of relativity in physics and to Klein's object relations theory in psychology.

Classical Christian theology had relied on the category of substance for most of its doctrinal formulations: For example, the Trinity is one substance but three persons; the Incarnation is a union of divine and human substances; and spiritual Redemption bears on the immaterial substance of the soul. For much of the Western tradition, theological knowing (*scientia*) was primarily about defining these substances; the "problem" was dealing with the relations inherent in each of these doctrines. Although many theologians have continued to hold onto the categories of substance metaphysics and the predication theories associated with it, others have actively participated in the turn to relationality that has transformed contemporary models of knowing and being. Perhaps the most obvious example is the revival of trinitarian doctrine in the twentieth century, in which relational and dynamic concepts of divine life have played a dominant role. It is no surprise that many of the Christian theologians who contributed to this doctrinal revival were also actively engaged in dialogue with contemporary philosophy and science.

A second development that is relevant to our topic is the shift toward accepting the *contextuality* of all knowledge. Much early modern philosophy of science (anachronistically speaking) idealized knowledge that was putatively universal – objective and certain knowledge accessible to any and all neutral observers who, dispassionately following the rules of logic, could deduce apodictic conclusions from rationally or empirically self-evident foundations. Increasingly, however, late modern philosophers of science have come to recognize that this ideal is not only impossible, but also undesirable. Like all human inquirers, scientists' search for knowledge is embodied by and embedded in particular contexts, shaped by pre-understandings, and motivated by more or less passionate interests. Moreover, each science has its own disciplinary context that is guided by paradigms (Kuhn) or research programs (Lakatos). The positivists tried to separate evaluation from fact-finding; for them, scientists ought not to allow their subjective values to hinder the neutral observation of the posited data. Most post-positivist philosophers of science agree that, regardless of the phenomena under investigation, data are always and already theory-laden.

This can appear to force a choice between absolutism and relativism, and many Christian theologians have embraced one or other of these options. However, the appeal to contextuality has also opened up new opportunities in theology. The diversity and richness of the discourse has been enhanced by a growing recognition of ways in which the interpretative categories and embodied practices of other contexts can lead to creative insights and new possibilities for understanding one's own context. Moreover, this philosophical shift has opened up conceptual space for overcoming the early modern dualism between faith and reason that hardened as "religion" and "science" drifted apart. If knowing something or someone requires some level of commitment within a context – a fiduciary connection to that which is known – and believing something or trusting someone requires some contextualized knowledge of that thing or person, then "faith" and "reason" are interwoven within every contextualized pursuit of knowledge. The dynamics of the dialectic between participation and distanciation may vary in accordance with each context, but human inquiry requires both faithful commitment and rational judgment.

The appeal of relationality and the appeal to contextuality have together contributed to a growing appeal for *interdisciplinarity* within and across the sciences. The dichotomy between the natural and human sciences was reinforced by other dualisms, including the metaphysical separation of reality into extended things and thinking things, and the epistemic division between "explaining" the former through nomological deduction and "understanding" the latter through ideographic description. The further fragmentation of the sciences and increased specialization was also encouraged by the ideal of detailed analysis of discrete phenomena. This methodological reduction, which is quite appropriate and often fruitful in various contexts, has sometimes been transmuted into a material reductionism that eclipses the value of other disciplines. This tendency is still dominant in some circles, but growing awareness of the relational complexity of the world and the contextual limitations of each field of inquiry has led to an increased openness toward interdisciplinary engagement. This is the context within which Christian theologians can now explore new possibilities for clarifying and enhancing the relation between religion and the scientific disciplines.

Ways of relating science and religion

During the latter part of the twentieth century, there was a surge of interest in "science and religion," especially among Christian theologians and scientists. Ian Barbour's *Issues in Science and Religion* (1966) is often considered largely responsible for initiating a new and creative phase in the relation between the fields. Several other founding figures contributed to the burgeoning conversation (cf. Torrance 1969; Peacocke 1971; Pannenberg 1976), and during the last quarter of the century, several societies and journals were founded on both sides of the Atlantic in order to facilitate this rapidly growing interdisciplinary discussion. The first volume of Barbour's Gifford lectures – *Religion in an Age of Science* (1990) – set out a taxonomy of ways of relating science and religion that has been the starting point for methodological debate ever since. He distinguishes between four general types of relation: conflict, independence, dialogue, and integration.

Barbour uses examples of "scientific materialism" and "biblical literalism" to illustrate the first way of relating science and religion. Although these two positions are opposed at so many levels, they also have a great deal in common methodologically. He argues that their shared belief that religion and science are necessarily in conflict is based on a shared misunderstanding of the nature of science. Both approaches assume that sciences such as evolutionary theory are inherently atheistic, which leads to a forced choice: either science or (theistic) religion. The scientific materialist's move from specific explanations of a phenomenon to broad claims about reality and knowledge, and the biblical literalist's move from a particular reading of scripture to a general declaration about nature are both philosophically naïve. In this way of understanding the relation, each side of the "conflict" begins with its own allegedly sure foundation as the basis for making rival statements about the same domain, such as the history of nature.

In the second type, which Barbour calls "independence," religion and science are understood as having contrasting methods that deal with different domains, or as simply having different languages that are used for distinctive purposes. Barbour illustrates this model with three examples: neo-orthodoxy, existentialism, and linguistic analysis. For Karl Barth and many of his followers, theology is based on self-authenticating divine revelation alone, while science is based on human observation and reason; each is valid but should not interfere with the other. Some existentialists (whether theistic or atheistic) separate the fields by saying that science has to do with "how" questions and religion has to do with ultimate "why" questions. Finally, George Lindbeck's cultural linguistic approach minimizes the role of truth claims about reality in theology, arguing that religious language functions within a way of life, forming particular practices. Against such models, which attempt to immunize or isolate theology from science in some way, Barbour calls for a critical realist epistemology in which the fields can be brought into constructive dialogue.

Barbour's third way of relating the fields is "dialogue." In this model, science and religion meet and discuss significant shared concerns, such as boundary questions and methodological parallels. On the one hand, religious and scientific reflection can interact around questions regarding the contingency conditions of the order and causality of the cosmos (e.g. the "Big Bang"). Within this kind of dialogue, Barbour observes a variety of theological attitudes: from a neo-orthodox or neo-Thomist resistance to reformulating doctrine as a result of the dialogue, to a correlational or revisionist openness to such reformulation. Another form of the "dialogue" approach to the relation focuses on methodological similarities between the disciplines. For example, both religion and science can be seen as guided by paradigms or traditions, and as appropriately including the personal participation of the observer. However, Barbour emphasizes the importance of noting the differences between the fields and of moving beyond merely methodological discussions toward creative interaction.

The final type of relation within Barbour's taxonomy is "integration." Here the concrete content of theology and science are brought into explicit engagement. He suggests there are three distinct versions of this model: natural theology, theology of nature, and systematic synthesis. As an example of the first, he points to attempts to prove the existence of God based not on revelation, but on appeals to human reason based on scientific findings (e.g. order or apparent purposiveness). Rather than moving unilaterally from science to God, a theology of nature begins within a religious tradition but reformulates its doctrines in light of contemporary science. Within such approaches, one finds a wide variety of ways of balancing the authoritative weight of the biblical tradition and scientific interpretations of human experience of the world. Finally, Barbour outlines the way of relating science and religion that he himself prefers: a systematic synthesis in which both fields contribute to the development of a comprehensive and coherent world-view. He views process philosophy as the most promising candidate for fulfilling this ideal integration.

Barbour's overview of the options has been critically engaged by several participants in the international science and religion conversation. In *Rethinking Theology and Science* (1998) Niels Gregersen and Wentzel van Huyssteen acknowledged the value of Barbour's taxonomy, but suggested that the complexity of our pluralistic context required a diversity of approaches. The contributors to that book offered six different models for rethinking the relation: post-foundationalism, critical realism, naturalism, pragmaticism, complementarity, and contextual coherence theory. Mikael Stenmark (2004) has pointed to the importance of recognizing the different dimensions (social, teleological, epistemological, and theoretical) of science and religion as we go about understanding and facilitating their interaction. Robert Russell (2008) has proposed a "creative mutual interaction" model of the relation between theology and science, arguing that each field ought to offer something of intellectual and constructive value to the other. His own attempts at pursuing such a creative engagement have focused on issues such as finitude (contingency) and time (eschatology). These methodological and material issues continue to generate lively discussions among theologians and scientists in the Christian tradition.

Religion, science, and the limits of theology

In fact the emerging academic field of "science and religion" has for the most part been dominated by scholars from the Christian tradition. Representatives from other traditions have increasingly been invited and incorporated into the conversation, and this diversity has been enriching. The majority of non-Christians participating and publishing in the main conferences and journals of the field, however, are still from monotheistic traditions (Judaism, Islam). The ongoing conversation will be enriched as more members of other religious traditions (whether theologians or scientists) enter it, and as more Western Christian theologians and scientists listen to, and participate in, conversations going on elsewhere. In this final section, I want to suggest that this process can be facilitated and enhanced by attending to ways in which developments in the late modern philosophy of science have also shaped the academic study of religion or, better, the sciences of *religions*. In an increasingly pluralistic world, Christian theology will need to improve its intellectual dexterity as it learns to tend to its own limits *vis-à-vis* other religious traditions as well as other scientific disciplines.

The philosophical turn to *relationality* has also had a significant effect on a variety of sciences that study religion, fostering holistic neuropsychological theories of religious experience and paleoanthropological theories of the emergence of religious symbolism. In the academic field of religious studies, this shift has also played a role in shaping interpretations of encounters with otherness within and across religions. Many early approaches to religious "pluralism" focused on identifying that which is the same within the essence of the world's religions. Increasingly, however, the category of difference has come to play a generative role in theory construction and dialogical practice among religious scholars. This shift from attempting to define the (identical) essence of religion to attending to the constitutive and regulative function of relations to "the other" has been shaped by what we might call a philosophical turn to *alterity*. This has implications for the reconstruction of formulations of

Christian doctrine that were articulated under the dominance of the category of sameness (such as the Symbol of Chalcedon, which uses the phrase "the same" eight times in a single sentence).

This shift has another, perhaps even deeper, implication for Christian theology. The interaction between theology and other scientific disciplines should not ignore the fact that "the" Christian tradition is not an essence, isolated and protected by clear boundaries and limits. Its very "identity" is always and already being constituted by its ongoing (negative and positive) tensive relations with "other" traditions. Christian theologians cannot simply observe the relation between science and religion from the outside and consider possible ways in which they might be related. All of our considering is from within our particular experience of a traditioned field of inquiry. But the reason for this limitation goes even deeper. The differentiation among religious traditions is not "accidental" to their "substance." Our identities are mediated to us through our differences; the alterity of the Christian tradition is partially constituted by its differentiated relations to other traditions – even and especially when these relations are alienated or alienating.

This brings us to the importance of *contextuality* in late modern philosophy of science, which has also affected the study of the religions. Here, too, the danger of relativism can appear to loom large on the horizon, but this is not the only option besides absolutism. If we think of the "religious" dimension of human life as that sphere of mutual engagement in which persons tend to their fascination with, and fear of, ultimate boundedness, which shapes and is shaped by all the other dynamic modes of social binding and being bound (*re-ligere*), then we can see how the notion of limits can play a constitutive material role as well as a regulative methodological role in theological reflection. Scholars of religion are interested both in the finite tensive dynamics of proximate social realities and in people's interpreted engagement with that which they understand as ultimate reality (or as the ground of ultimate meaning and value). Much of the late modern philosophical discourse about alterity has appealed to the idea of "the infinite" as a generative limit-notion.

The way in which persons are bound together and engage their various contextual boundaries is shaped by their experience of sociality and their encounter with infinity, both of which have to do with the existential experience of being limited. The dynamics that hinder or facilitate engagement across disciplinary and religious boundaries are related to our fear of our own limitations (finitude) and our desire to be cared for without limits. All social interaction (including the engagement between religionists and scientists) is structured by both our longing for, and dread of, being bound to one another. Our ways of attending to disciplinary and traditional boundaries emerge within the complex, dynamic field of human sociality, which is constituted by these binding forces of fear and desire that characterize our struggle within and against our being limited by and for others.

Attending to these relational, contextual dynamics within the interdisciplinary field of "science and religion" raises questions about the role of theologians (including those from the Christian tradition) within this ongoing conversation. Like other disciplines, theology ought humbly to recognize and clarify its own limitations – its (inter)dependence upon other modes of human inquiry. But it can and should also confidently contribute to the discourse what only it can offer. Broadly speaking, theology involves inter-traditional discourse about infinity. People's interpretations of their sense of an ultimate world-constructing boundary (or the conditions of contingency) shape their understanding and practice of empathy for religious (and disciplinary) others. Theological discourse in this broader sense deals with the significance of limitation itself, with existential negotiations of the ultimately significant limit: being limited by the infinite as the ultimate condition for any and all finite limitation whatsoever.

Talking about "ultimate" conditions and "the infinite" can feel intimidating, especially in light of the way in which certain ways of binding beliefs about ultimate reality can be (and have been) used in terrible ways – inciting terror throughout the world. It is important to remember that inter-traditional discourse about infinity does not escape the conditions of sociality. Like all inquiry, it is embedded within particular relational contexts. But this kind of inquiry often awakens intense anxiety and longing, leading to a tension between nervously protecting and passionately teasing the boundaries of one's habitations. This is why attending to the dialectic between fear and desire is so important as we attempt to understand and facilitate healthy interaction across and within the bounds that limit us. It is relatively easy for Western Christian theologians to talk to Western Christian (or non-Christian) scientists. In our pluralistic world, it will become increasingly important to complement such inter-disciplinary dialogue with more rigorously empathic inter-religious engagement.

References

Barbour, Ian (1966) *Issues in Science and Religion*, New York: Harper & Row.

——(1990) *Religion in an Age of Science*, San Francisco, CA: Harper Collins.

Brooke, John Hedley (1991) *Science and Religion: Some Historical Perspectives*, Cambridge: Cambridge University Press.

Gregersen, Niels Henrik and J. Wentzel van Huyssteen (eds) (1998) *Rethinking Theology and Science: Six Models for the Current Dialogue*, Grand Rapids, MI: Eerdmans.

Lindberg, David C. and Ronald L. Numbers (eds) (1986) *God and Nature: Historical Essays on the Encounter between Christianity and Science*, Berkeley, CA: University of California Press.

McMullin, Ernan (ed.) (2005) *The Church and Galileo*, Notre Dame, IN: University of Notre Dame Press.

Pannenberg, Wolfhart (1976) *Theology and the Philosophy of Science*, F. McDonagh (trans.), Philadelphia, PA: Westminster Press.

Peacocke, Arthur (1971) *Science and the Christian Experiment*, London: Oxford University Press.

Russell, Robert J. (2008) *Cosmology: From Alpha to Omega*, Minneapolis, MN: Fortress Press.

Shults, F. LeRon (2003) *Reforming Theological Anthropology: After the Philosophical Turn to Relationality*, Grand Rapids, MI: Eerdmans.

Stenmark, Mikael (2004) *How to Relate Science and Religion: A Multidimensional Model*, Grand Rapids, MI: Eerdmans.

Taylor, Charles (2007) *A Secular Age*, Cambridge, MA: Harvard University Press.

Torrance, T.F. (1969) *Theological Science*, London: Oxford University Press.

Further reading

For a general introduction to the key methodological and material issues that have shaped the late modern discourse among Christian theologians about the relation between religion and science, see the essays in W. Mark Richardson and Wesley Wildman, eds, *Religion and Science: History, Method, Dialogue* (New York: Routledge, 1996) and Christopher Southgate, ed., *God, Humanity and the Cosmos: A Companion to the Science–Religion Debate*, 2nd edn (London: T& T Clark, 2005). Arthur Peacocke's *Theology for a Scientific Age* (Minneapolis, MN: Fortress, 1993) is considered one of the classics in the field. Important contributions by other leading figures in the discussion include Philip Clayton, *God and Contemporary Science* (Grand Rapids, MI: Eerdmans, 1997), Willem Drees, *Religion, Science and Naturalism* (Cambridge: Cambridge University Press, 1999), George Ellis and Nancey Murphy, *On the Moral Nature of the Universe* (Minneapolis, MN: Fortress, 1996), John Haught, *God After Darwin*, 2nd edn (New York: Westview Press, 2007), John Polkinghorne, *Exploring Reality: The Intertwining of Science and Religion* (New Haven, CT: Yale University Press, 2007), and Holmes Rolston, *Genes, Genesis and God* (Cambridge: Cambridge University Press, 1999). For treatments of ways in which contemporary science impacts particular Christian doctrines, see Philip Hefner, *The Human Factor* (Minneapolis, MN: Augsburg, 2000), F. LeRon Shults, *Christology and Science* (Aldershot, UK: Ashgate, 2008), and Denis Edwards, *Breath of Life: A Theology of the Creator Spirit* (Maryknoll, NY: Orbis, 2004).

2
EMPIRICISM, CONCEPTUAL CLEAVERS, AND THE DISCOURSE ON RELIGION AND SCIENCE

Francisca Cho

This essay uses the concept of "empiricism" to demonstrate a way of connecting religion and science that gets around the enormous problem of defining them. I use the term empiricism not as a definition, but as a scalpel to carve religion and science into manageable entities that can be related to each other. I pick empiricism in particular because of the way it re-envisions religion within the framework of religion and science. By turning to the example of Buddhism, I bolster the view of religion as a form of empiricism, and also demonstrate how knowledge of diverse religious formations can help us expand the content of our "religion and science" discussions. The utility of the idea of religion as empiricism lies in its ability to explain the persistence of religion despite the widespread and long-standing expectation that it should fade away in the face of scientific progress. This essay argues that, ultimately, any characterization of religion and/or science needs to be measured by the particular insights it reveals, rather than the claim to be exhaustive.

Beyond definitions

The attempt to define science and religion in terms of essential characteristics or clear boundaries has failed. So, to counteract the habit of bandying about "science" and "religion" as if they refer to monolithic entities, we now have the corrective assertion that there are many sciences, and many religions. As important and unavoidable as corrective observations are, they sometimes become essentializations of their own in the opposite direction. The observation that there are many sciences, with varying practices and methodological criteria, has given rise to the field of science studies, which pays attention to the social, historical, and institutional contexts that affect the constitution of the sciences (Latour 1986, 1999; Shapin and Schaffer 1989; Shapin 1994). But there is also the extreme thesis that scientific ideas and practices are *entirely* the by-products of social forces within which intellectual commitments play no discernible role (see thesis by Bloor 1991; see critique by Laudan 1996: 183–209). The essentializing view of science as a rational and methodologically distinct enterprise is replaced by the essentializing construct of "society" as the reality behind science.

Likewise, in the study of religion, the thesis that all human beings and societies respond to the divine in various ways has been exposed as a Christian idea that is complicated by the actual study of non-Christian cultures (Fitzgerald 2000; Dubuisson 2003; Masuzawa 2005). If we look at "religious" traditions such as Buddhism, Confucianism, and Shinto, key elements like a creator God and a transcendent notion of salvation are missing, and the term "religion" becomes either misapplied or overly vague. "Religions" can be dissolved into the minutiae of singular histories, undermining any overriding or universal "religion." Not even the entity of "Buddhism" can survive this deconstructive historical gaze: Rather than standing for a "disembodied corpus of scripture, doctrine, mythology, and ethics that can be extracted readily from its specific regional and cultural deployments," it is averred that a "pure or unadulterated Buddhism is little more than an analytic abstraction posited by Buddhist polemicists, apologists, reformers, and now scholars" (Sharf 2002: 13, 16). It seems that we cannot generalize about Buddhism any more than about religion by appealing to any enduring principles, commitments, or objectives. Only its endlessly varying historical instances are deemed to be real.

Our perception of both religion and science, then, has swung from the unified and purposive "one" to the disparate and potentially meaningless "many." But the latter direction is no less essentializing in its tendency to substitute social forces over others as exclusively real. Any act of conceptualization potentially leads to essentialization unless we are mindful of how concepts work. In this essay, I use the category of empiricism, or the reliance on sensory information, as a conceptual "cleaver" to isolate a particular aspect of science and religion that can be compared. Science is many things, but its commitment to empiricism is central and emblematic. Hence "empiricism" picks out an obvious aspect of science without being reductive. Religion, too, can be defined in diverse and even competing ways, but in discourses about "religion and science," religion is typically made to refer to theological beliefs. Hence "empiricism" picks out an underemphasized aspect of religion that expands our sense of religion and provides new insights about its connection to science. Understood as a "conceptual cleaver," the term empiricism abstracts the entities of science and religion, ignoring all of their other aspects for the sake of a particular insight rather than a totalizing characterization.

Scientific and religious empiricism

Empiricism is both a description of how people negotiate the world, and an explicit statement of epistemological principle – the contention that sensory observation and evidence are the most reliable forms of knowledge. Science is uncontroversially empirical in the latter, self-conscious way. This is not to say that empirical procedures are the necessary condition for qualifying as a science – mathematics and computer science, for example, focus on the formal rather than empirical parts of scientific practice. But the rise of modern science itself was clearly and centrally animated by an explicit affirmation of empirical values. The emergence of "Baconian science" in the seventeenth century embraced a new inductive method, most famously outlined by Francis Bacon, which rejected the deductive syllogisms of scholastic natural philosophy in favor of an experimental program. This empirical method carefully observed nature by artificially constraining it with mechanical devices, "exhibiting it under conditions it could never have attained with the forceful intervention of man" (Kuhn 1985: 175). The seventeenth century marks a fundamental shift in criteria of knowledge away from the Aristotelian demand for certain, rational demonstration to the probable certainties afforded by inductive observations (Hacking 1975).

But relying on the evidence of the senses in order to guide and adjust our relationship to our environment, leading to the development of technology and engineering, is not the monopoly of science, and the emergence of modern science was possible only because of the extensive history of this universal human activity. Religious ritual and mythology can be forms of empirical practice, and have created countless marvels of engineering in the ancient world, such as Stonehenge, the Egyptian pyramids and obelisks, Easter Island moai, Nazca geoglyphs, Parthian batteries, and so on. We must acknowledge, of course, that empirical methods reached an unprecedented milestone in seventeenth-century Europe, both qualitatively and in the level of conscious articulation. This led to a systematization of practices that, two centuries later, flowered into the nomenclature of "science" and the grouping of previously separate disciplines such as "biology," "physics," and "chemistry" under the same professional umbrella. In fact, some historians insist that "science" refers only to what emerged in nineteenth-century Europe, being quite distinct from even the "natural philosophy" of the seventeenth century that was entirely bound up with Christian theological investigations (Harrison 2006).

This is a perfectly valid way of demarcating when science began, if the purpose is to pinpoint the appearance of certain institutions and the nomenclature of "science" itself. But it is problematic if the objective is to confine science to the moment it purportedly became independent of Christian inspirations, assumptions, and purposes. The ongoing perception of conflict between religion and science should make us deeply skeptical of this alleged divorce. The fact that current scientific theories about the origins of the universe and of life on our planet are thought to challenge Christian narratives is not evidence that they have gone their separate ways. On the contrary, the prevailing idea that science can undermine belief in God displays the near impossibility of segregating science from Christian religion. This example, however, follows the standard of fixating on their competing narratives about the creation of life and the origins of the universe. Far less attention has been paid to religion and science as continuous as well as competing forms of empirical practice.

The bias towards defining religion as a matter of what people profess about the universe has been identified as a Christian and particularly Protestant habit. Hence many religion scholars now use social science methodologies to look at ritual and social practices, particularly in light of the heavy emphasis they are given in non-Christian traditions. Such practices are the part of religion that enables people to deal with their social and natural environment. Religious rites, for example, are the ceremonial structures and actions that help people manage their day-to-day concerns, including social relationships and passages in personal identity, illness and misfortune, and anxiety about death and the dead. Ritual, social hierarchy, and ethical norms create a religious technology of environmental management.

The idea of a "religious technology" might strike some readers as an over-reaching metaphor. It seems a stretch to liken the techniques of, say, funerary rites to the technology that got us to the moon or cured polio. But scholars have long suggested that religion, along with magic, is a form of "primitive science" that works to ameliorate natural conditions such as illness, and to predict and control natural forces such as the weather. This observation, initially made by James Frazer (*The Golden Bough*, 1890), has been entangled with over-reaching nineteenth-century progressive theories of its own about the march of human knowledge towards perfection, moving from the "primitive" stage of religion and magic to the "real" knowledge of modern science. Absent the grand theory of progress, however, the observation is still useful.

Recent scholarship that interprets religion functionally, as a form of evolutionary adaptation, for example, reads religion as all about its technological prowess. David Sloan Wilson characterizes the early Christian community as a "remarkable piece of social engineering," in which religious and ethical teachings were used to promote higher rates of reproduction, relative to its Roman neighbors, and create a welfare state that took care of its poor and sick within an empire lacking social services. What we really have here, Wilson concludes, is "not a divine miracle but a miracle of psychological and social engineering that Roman society lacked and Christian society provided" (2002: 154). Wilson also considers the Balinese water temple system, in which a religious ritual structure is the mechanism that irrigates and distributes water for thousands of rice farmers over an area of hundreds of square kilometers. A detailed computer simulation "showed that the water temple system was close to optimal at solving the trade-off between water use and pest control" (*ibid.*: 130), and modern technology and bureaucracy have not been able to improve upon it. Clearly one considerable aspect of religious communities and their belief systems is that they are adaptive to their environment, whether it is to solve practical agricultural problems or to provide the aid and comfort required for emotional and physical flourishing.

We should avoid the category confusion, then, of equating religion with its doctrines about creation while touting science for its empirical standards such as "experimentally testable predictions" and "falsifiability" (see e.g. Root-Bernstein 1984). This compares apples with oranges in order to conclude that religion and science are different. Given the immense complexity of what "religion" can signify, however, this view of religion is arbitrary and needs to be defended. A narrow view of religion as centered on metaphysical commitments – usually with the accompanying view that science, on the other hand, is devoid of faith and doctrine – fails to see religion's empirical and practical side. This way of defining religion ensues in large part from the way Christianity tends to see itself. In order to enlarge and balance our perceptions of religion, it is helpful to turn to diverse cases of religion. For the present purposes, the example of Buddhism is particularly useful.

Buddhist empiricism

Buddhism is a religion that explicitly affirms the importance of empirical knowledge, both as the content of its teachings and as a test of its own validity. Its meditative tradition, as the fruit of its empirical practice, is now routinely referred to as a "technology" for the amelioration of mental and personal pain, and Buddhism's interest in the mind finds ready affinities with psychology and cognitive science. "[…] like the training of a physicist," the Dalai Lama states, "the acquisition of mental skills is a matter of volition and focused effort; it is not a special mystical gift given to the few" (2005: 156). Again, my purpose is not to essentialize Buddhism and identify it solely as an empirical practice while ignoring its other more patently "religious" aspects. My reason for turning to Buddhism is that it articulates empirical values in an explicit and thoughtful manner, thereby giving voice to an aspect of *all* religions that does not receive much publicity. The example of Buddhism is highly useful, in other words, for carrying out my analytical endeavor to relate religion and science as empirical practices. Another way of putting it might be that the example of Buddhism helps me to identify the practical wisdom of sensory experience and evidence as a key aspect of religions generally.

All human beings, and even animals, rely on sensory experience and evidence to negotiate their way in the world. Most cultures, however, do not articulate empiricism as an epistemological principle, and argue for its superiority to other forms of knowledge. It is quite interesting, then, that the earliest sources of Buddhism record that the Buddha did just this, elevating empirical knowledge above all other kinds and justifying his teachings by an appeal to its practical fruit – in this case, the alleviation of personal suffering. Buddhism arose in the milieu of brahminical religion, with its authoritative priests and their claims of inerrant knowledge preserved in divine scriptures. The Buddha, however, rebukes the Brahmins who taught the existence of the eternal soul (*atman*) and union with the deity Brahma, on the grounds that they have never seen these things face-to-face. He likens the Brahmins to a string of blind men: "the first one sees nothing, the middle one sees nothing, the last one sees nothing. The talk of these Brahmins learned in the Three Vedas turns out to be laughable, mere words, empty and vain" (*Tevijja Sutta* DN 1.235–53). In Baconian empiricism, "no source of factual information possessed greater reliability or inspired greater confidence than the direct experience of an individual. The legitimate springs of empirical knowledge were located in the individual's sensory confrontation with the world" (Shapin 1994: 202). The Buddha appeals to the same principle of sensory knowledge, elevating it above the revealed knowledge and revered tradition embodied in ancient texts.

In describing the parameters of his own teachings, the Buddha states that he will proclaim upon everything that is within the range of sense perceptions. Those who presume to say anything beyond that, he continues, will be vexed and unable to answer when subjected to questioning. "Why? Because [their theories] would not be within the range of experience" (*Sabba Sutta* SN 4.15–20). In the *Kalama Sutta* (AN 1.188–93), the Buddha instructs the gathered crowd not to accept a teaching based on tradition, hearsay, scripture, logic, its pleasing nature, or regard for the teacher. He invites them to follow his path only upon seeing for themselves that it is wholesome, without blame, and conducive to their benefit and happiness. The Buddha famously proclaims "*ehi passiko*," "come and see," which is a command to test his teachings rather than accept them at his word. His injunction to "know for yourself" is paralleled by the British Royal Society's motto "*Nullius in verba*," "On no man's word."

A central feature of Buddhist empiricism is its desire to stay away from speculative metaphysical theories that cannot be concretely resolved and that generate only argument and conflict. The purpose of privileging the realm of sensory experience is that it is inter-subjective, or collective, and therefore conducive to agreement. The Buddha famously refused to indulge metaphysical questions such as "Is the world eternal?" and "Is the world infinite?". In his analogy of the man struck by the poisoned arrow, the Buddha says that asking such questions is like demanding useless information about the arrow and neglecting the immediate medical procedures needed to save his life (*Culamalunkya Sutta* MN 1.426–32). The Buddha likens his teachings to medical treatment that can heal immediate suffering, as opposed to the argumentative distractions of speculative philosophy. Contrary to our image of religion as steadfast adherence to metaphysical doctrines, the Buddha identifies attachment to ideologies as a poisoned arrow, or a primary source of suffering.

These points testify to the wealth of intellectual rivalry and philosophical movements in the Buddha's time. The Buddha was not the only one who reacted to brahminic religion, but was part of a larger uprising that expressed itself through many competing views, including "secular" ones such as reductive materialism. From the Buddha's perspective, the critics of brahminism were often no more warranted than their target. In the midst of all these rival views, the Buddha posits a second-order standard for what justifies a teaching: His focus goes beyond the content of the teaching *per se* to underscore the standard of practical and moral benefit, so clearly articulated by the idea of healing a mortal wound. This standard is clearly and persistently applied to Buddhist teachings themselves. The teaching of *karma* and rebirth, for example, is justified on the grounds that it encourages moral rectitude in one's present life and brings future benefits if rebirth turns out to be true (*Apannaka Sutta* MN 1.401–13). In order to discourage followers from idolizing his own teachings as inherently sacred, the Buddha compares them with a snake that can turn around and harm those who mishandle it, and a raft that should be abandoned once it has served its purpose (*Alagaddupama Sutta* MN 1.133–34).

The concrete accomplishments of science fuel the claim that science has displaced religion in the function of revealing the ultimate truth of everything. This claim forgets modern science's own ideal of holding all hypotheses quite loosely, willingly abandoning any theory when a more productive one comes along. Because of the conflicts generated by irresolvable philosophical arguments, both the Buddha and seventeenth-century natural philosophers thought it imperative to develop a space where people can agree with each other based on their inter-subjective experience of what works. The empirical attitude is interested in reliable information that leads to practical results, rather than what is "true," because truth claims habitually reach beyond the domain of sensory verification. As the Buddha recognized, however, the human tendency to erect idols is most difficult to break, particularly when something works. At that point, our intelligibility structures, whether the philosophical materialism spawned by science or the mythological narratives of religion, are elevated into metaphysical absolutes. In looking at religion, our cultural fixation on metaphysics suppresses religion's claim to the "because it works" argument, perhaps reversing the actual priority of things.

The persistence of religion

It appears that I am perilously close to sliding into yet another essentializing interpretation of religion as "nothing but" an adaptive mechanism – an impression advanced by my use of Wilson's evolutionary interpretation of religion above. Functionalist interpretations, such as those of Marx, Freud, Durkheim, and now the evolutionists, are not neutral affairs, but the instruments of a "scientific" analysis that is self-consciously opposed to religious ones. Hence it is no wonder that defenders of religion steer clear from the interpretations expressly designed to subvert their own sense of religion. But, to reiterate, conceptual knives do not displace one element in favor of another. Instead, they follow the scientific analytical practice of isolating features that are useful to look at. In the present case, the construct of empiricism demonstrates its utility by helping us to see why science has not succeeded in replacing religion.

In my reference to James Frazer's interpretation of religion as primitive science, I perhaps implied that progressive theories about the march of knowledge from religion to science have been left behind. In point of fact, however, the survival of this social evolutionary world-view persistently surfaces in our ongoing cultural discourses about religion and science. The most prosaic version of this is the common, but sincere, bafflement people express about why religion persists, or as Wilson helpfully paraphrases: "How could anyone be so stupid as to believe in all that hocus-pocus in the face of such contrary evidence?" (Wilson 2002: 228). Richard Dawkins expresses this sentiment most pointedly by calling people who reject evolution based on religious commitments stupid, insane, or wicked (1989). Everywhere in our cultural airwaves and print, we see expressions of incredulity that people still practice religion, and cognitive malfunction of one sort or another is offered as explanation.

Such discourse is myopic as well as flippant. Even the ostensibly sensible call for better science education is misguided because it assumes that if only everyone learns the evidence in favor of evolution, religious opposition will simply melt away. In their recent book, evolutionary biologists Marc Kirschner and John Gerhart (2005) lay out their theory of "facilitated variation" in order to explain the rise of diverse and complex phenotypic traits in organisms. In addressing the weakest part of Darwinian theory – the question of how organisms generate phenotypic variation – they blithely suggest that strengthening evolutionary theory will help *defuse* the battle over evolution in public schools (*ibid.*: 245). Evolution, they believe, will simply win out over religion by dint of compelling facts.

It is more likely, however, that the arsenal of facts in favor of evolution will be matched by counter-facts produced within the paradigm of "creation science," "intelligent design," and future variations thereof. The battle over evolution is not a matter of facts compelling what one ought to believe, but rather of prior commitments determining what is a compelling fact. These commitments, in turn, are not determined by one's level of education, and they do not stratify neatly between the smart and the stupid. People embrace *both* science and religion to the degree that they produce practical benefits and improve their lives. Understanding religion only as metaphysical claims means endless befuddlement about why it will not wither away.

Pointing out that religion produces worldly and pragmatic goods does not undermine the importance of religious beliefs. On the contrary, it underscores their practical value. As the Buddha empirically observed, what one believes is important because it influences one's actions, and those actions in turn determine the kind of community and environment we create. He defined *karma* not as overt actions, which was its prior meaning, but rather as mental states – that is, the intentions and motivations that are determined by one's beliefs and attitudes. Beliefs create intentions; intentions create actions; and actions create our quality of life. It is quite likely the case that religion persists not because of inadequate scientific education, but because people value the kind of life religion engenders. By the same token, opposition to evolution is not driven by obtuse denials of obvious and helpful scientific observations such as the mutation of bacteria. Instead, it is engendered by evolutionary theory's companion narrative that life is nothing but the competition and struggle for existence. It is this belief, and the kinds of motivations and actions it encourages, that spark religious opposition. As the Dalai Lama puts it, "we humans have a dangerous tendency to turn the visions we construct of ourselves into self-fulfilling prophecies" (2005: 115).

The empirical benefits offered by religion and science compete with each other only to the extent that we insist they do. This insistence is prevalent in contemporary Western society because of its tendency to reduce religion to a scientifically untenable belief system. Many theologians active in the religion and science dialogue respond by seeking to integrate scientific narratives such as evolution into biblical ones, often to the chagrin of other Christians. Another response, however, can be to recalibrate our view of religion, as I have attempted to do here. This encourages the kind of scenario manifested by contemporary East Asians, who take advantage of both traditional Chinese and modern scientific medicine because of the observable benefits of each, without much worry about the fact that their respective views of the body are irreconcilably different. It is illogical to abandon the benefits of one system for the sake of strict theoretical consistency. From this perspective, the persistence of religion is highly rational, rather than the conundrum many suppose.

Is it possible that taking seriously this evolutionary view of religion as a form of pragmatic adaptation, as I do here, is to concede that scientific knowledge does indeed surpass religion, at least in its understanding of the real "whither" and "why" of religion itself? Let us be careful here. The concept of adaptive functionality applies equally, if not more, to science itself. Science clearly garners its social prestige from the technological adaptiveness it confers on its beneficiaries. Hence the functionalist "nothing but" interpretation can apply to religion and science equally. The current enthusiasm for evolution as the grand theory of everything, including but not limited to religion, suffers the bind of having to explain why the human cultural practice of evolutionary interpretation should be exempt from its own analysis. To claim that certain scientists have broken free of their hapless bondage to the laws of evolution to see the transcendent "fact" of human bondage to the laws of evolution speaks the kind of revelatory language normally attributed to religion. It is possible to reduce *both* religion and science to nothing but adaptive mechanisms, or, conversely, to elevate them to universal truth. What is sauce for the goose is sauce for the gander. Using characterizations as cleavers rather than absolutes, however, is a much better strategy for keeping the complexity and multiplicity of religion and science intact.

Conclusion

It is necessary to identify a plurality of concepts that are capable of carving out religion and science in different ways. In addition to empiricism, some obvious ones include looking at them as social institutions and as faith-based adherence to belief systems. In addition to discerning which characterizations are useful, the point is to create an adequate number of categories in order to relate religion and science in sensible ways.

So far, the modern discourse on religion and science has taken on the strategy of opposing, segregating, or integrating them. But it has done so without paying explicit attention to which parts of them are comparable. Take, for example, the thesis that religion and science are "non-overlapping magisteria" in which science tells us the facts about the natural world whereas religion deals with ethics and values (Gould 1999). This position ignores the detail that religion and science can deal with the world in very similar ways, as the category of empiricism shows, complicating the idea that they do not overlap. The thesis that religion and science oppose each other along some axis of the irrational versus the rational suffers the same kind of myopia. This is not to aver that religion and science always do the same things. The point is to clarify which aspects of each we are examining in relation to each other, and for what purpose. The question of how religion and science relate, and whether they conflict or harmonize, depends significantly on what we choose to discuss.

References

List of abbreviations for in-text references:

AN: *Anguttara Nikaya*
DN: *Digha Nikaya*
MN: *Majjhima Nikaya*
SN: *Samyutta Nikaya*

References

Anguttara Nikaya, translated by Nyanaponika Thera and Bhikkhu Bodhi (1999) as *Numerical Discourses of the Buddha*, Lanham, MD: AltaMira.

Digha Nikaya, translated by Maurice Walshe (1995) as *The Long Discourses of the Buddha*, Somerville, MA: Wisdom Publications.

Majjhima Nikaya, translated by Bhikkhu Nanamoli and Bhikkhu Bodhi (1995) as *The Middle Length Discourses of the Buddha*, Somerville, MA: Wisdom Publications.

Samyutta Nikaya, translated by Bhikkhu Bodhi (2000) as *The Connected Discourses of the Buddha*, Somerville, MA: Wisdom Publications.

Bloor, David (1991 [1976]) *Knowledge and Social Imagery*, Chicago, IL: University of Chicago Press.

Dalai Lama (2005) *The Universe in a Single Atom: The Convergence of Science and Spirituality*, New York: Morgan Road Books.

Dawkins, Richard (1989) "Book Review of *Blueprints: Solving the Mystery of Evolution*, by Maitland Edey and Donald Johanson," *The New York Times*, section 7, April 9.

Dubuisson, Daniel (2003) *The Western Construction of Religion: Myths, Knowledge, and Ideology*, William Sayres (trans.), Baltimore, MD: Johns Hopkins University Press.

Fitzgerald, Timothy (2000) *The Ideology of Religious Studies*, New York: Oxford University Press.

Gould, Stephen Jay (1999) *Rocks of Ages: Science and Religion in the Fullness of Life*, New York: Ballantine.

Hacking, Ian (1975) *The Emergence of Probability: A Philosophical Study of Early Ideas about Probability, Induction, and Statistical Inference*, London, New York: Cambridge University Press.

Harrison, Peter (2006) "'Science' and 'Religion': Constructing the Boundaries," *Journal of Religion* 86(1): 81–106.

Kirschner, Marc and John Gerhart (2005) *The Plausibility of Life: Resolving Darwin's Dilemma*, New Haven, CT: Yale University Press.

Kuhn, Thomas (1985) "Mathematical versus Experimental Traditions in the Development of Physical Science," in *Post-Analytic Philosophy*, John Rajchman and Cornel West (eds), New York: Columbia University Press, 166–97.

Latour, Bruno (1986) *Laboratory Life: The Construction of Scientific Facts*, Princeton, NJ: Princeton University Press.

——(1999) *Pandora's Hope: Essays on the Reality of Science Studies*, Cambridge, MA: Harvard University Press.

Laudan, Larry (1996) *Beyond Positivism and Relativism: Theory, Method, and Evidence*, Boulder, CO: Westview Press.

Masuzawa, Tomoko (2005) *The Invention of World Religions, or, How European Universalism was Preserved in the Language of Pluralism*, Chicago, IL: University of Chicago Press.

Root-Bernstein, Robert (1984) "On Defining a Scientific Theory: Creationism Considered," in *Science and Creationism*, Ashley Montagu (ed.), New York: Oxford University Press, 64–94.

Shapin, Steven (1994) *A Social History of Truth: Civility and Science in the Seventeenth Century*, Chicago, IL: University of Chicago Press.

Shapin, Steven and Simon Schaffer (1989) *Leviathan and the Air-Pump: Hobbes, Boyle, and the Experimental Life*, Princeton, NJ: Princeton University Press.

Sharf, Robert (2002) *Coming to Terms with Chinese Buddhism: A Reading of the Treasure Store Treatise*, Honolulu: University of Hawai'i Press.

Wilson, David Sloan (2002) *Darwin's Cathedral: Evolution, Religion, and the Nature of Society*, Chicago, IL: University of Chicago Press.

Further Reading

Kulatissa Nanda Jayatilleke's *Early Buddhist Theory of Knowledge* (London: G. Allen & Unwin, 1963) and David Kalupahana's *Buddhist Philosophy: A Historical Analysis* (Honolulu: University of Hawai'i Press, 1976) emphasize the empirical nature of Buddhist thought. Contemporary anthropological studies routinely emphasize the social functions of religion, such as J. Stephen Lansing's *Priests and Programmers: Technologies of Power in the Engineered Landscape of Bali* (Princeton, NJ: Princeton University Press, 1991) – the main source for David Sloan Wilson's discussion of the Balinese water temple system. Sharon Suh's *Being Buddhist in a Christian World: Gender and Community in a Korean American Temple* (Seattle, WA: University of Washington Press, 2004) is a field study of how the activities of a Buddhist temple, along with Buddhist beliefs and rituals, help Korean immigrants in Los Angeles to cope with their economic and cultural displacement. For the study of Christianity, Rodney Stark's *The Victory of Reason: How Christianity Led to Freedom, Capitalism, and Western Success* (London: Random House, 2005) and many of his other titles focus on early Christianity, applying economic rational choice theory to explain religion.

3

SCIENCE AND RELIGION

From the historian's perspective

Geoffrey Cantor

Over the past two or three decades, a number of historians of science have directed their attention to the historical inter-relations of science and religion. Rather than being committed to any strong *a priori* view about how religion and science should – or should not – inter-relate, they have closely and critically interrogated the primary sources in order to ascertain how scientists, theologians, and others of past generations have addressed, and often struggled with, issues at the intersection of science and religion. What has emerged is an exciting new appreciation of the complexity and diversity of science–religion relationships.

Towards a new historiography

The work of this new generation of historians needs to be set against earlier ways of conceiving the historical relations between science and religion. For most historians of earlier generations, two factors – one philosophical, the other cultural – conspired to create a sharp separation between science and religion. The philosophical input came from positivism, which claims that empirical evidence is the only basis for legitimate knowledge claims. Auguste Comte coined the term "positivism" in his *Cours de Philosophie Positive* (1830–42) and portrayed positive knowledge as the highest form of knowledge. To articulate the relation between positive knowledge and earlier types of knowledge, Comte posited a three-stage progression, starting with the theological stage. During that stage, God is conceived as the direct cause of physical phenomena, such as illness or the fall of a heavy body. In the second stage – the metaphysical stage – metaphysical causes are instead evoked. Thus the fall of the heavy body might be attributed to the force acting on it; force being metaphysical (rather than physical) because forces are unobservable. In the final stage, according to Comte, scientists confine themselves only to observables; thus for a positivist the falling body's motion is to be described in terms of the distance travelled and time taken. By contrast, claims about the existence and attributes of God were deemed to be matters not of empirically based knowledge, but of opinion, and were generally dismissed as nonsense. Thus for most positivists, science displaced religion in the onward march of progress. In accordance with this positivist view of history, George

Sarton, one of the leading historians of science of the first half of the twentieth century, considered that during its development science gradually emancipated itself from religion. Likewise, Alexandre Koyré (another major historian of the period) banished religion from his account of the rise of modern science in the seventeenth century (Osler 2009).

To appreciate the other factor that influenced earlier generations of historians, we need to acknowledge that, until about the mid-nineteenth century, science and religion were closely inter-related. Particularly in Britain, the highly popular argument from design offered one means of bonding the two together. This fairly widespread, but by no means total, consensus broke down principally during the third quarter of the nineteenth century. Evidence of this breakdown is provided by the publication of a number of works that were widely perceived as atheistical and caused outrage in religious circles, such as the anonymously authored *Vestiges of the Natural History of Creation* in 1844 and Charles Darwin's *On the Origin of Species* in 1859. Yet, as Frank Turner (1974, 1978, 2009) has argued, we should not see these specific publications as causing the split between science and religion; rather, they are indicators of some profound social changes to both science and religion. For example, science was becoming increasingly professionalized and, in order to raise the status of science, its old alliance with religion – exemplified by the now outdated parson–naturalist – was being repudiated. Also, the old theodicies that attributed religious meaning to the physical world were being subject to increasing criticism and were seen as intellectually bankrupt.

By the 1870s, the members of an *avant garde* within the scientific community were proclaiming themselves to be scientific naturalists – naturalists in the sense of allowing only natural, material causes in their science, not supernatural ones. For these and other reasons there was an increasing sense of tension between science and religion during the later decades of the century, and this tension led in turn to conflict between the two. One highly visible flashpoint was the presidential address delivered by the physicist John Tyndall at the meeting of the British Association for the Advancement of Science held in Belfast in 1874, in which he evoked a materialist philosophy of science that caused a storm of protest. The title of John Draper's book published the following year – *History of the Conflict between Religion and Science* – captured the widely held perception that science and religion were thoroughly opposed to one another. Here the "conflict thesis" was born; a thesis that postulates a necessary conflict between science and religion.

Throughout much of the twentieth century, historians of science were heirs to the dual legacy of positivism and the conflict thesis. Thus, in writing the history of modern science, religion was either ignored or seen as a force opposed to science. The latter position was most apparent in the frequently cited examples of Galileo's conflict with the Catholic Church and the religious opposition to evolution – a theme that was nurtured by the 1925 "Scopes Monkey Trial." Such examples have repeatedly been used to demonstrate that there is a necessary conflict between science and religion.

Both the positivist heritage and the conflict thesis came under scrutiny in the 1950s and 1960s, when the history and philosophy of science emerged as a new discipline. Among philosophers of science there was extensive opposition to positivism, which found its most popular expression in the Wittgenstein-inspired *The Structure of Scientific Revolutions* (1962) by Thomas Kuhn. Rather than seeing the inexorable march of science as more and more empirical evidence was added, Kuhn argued that on (admittedly rare) occasions, one scientific theory (and all that went with it) replaced another. This marked a discontinuous change – a scientific revolution. Thus, to give Kuhn's most carefully worked out example, the Ptolemaic Earth-centred paradigm in astronomy was replaced by the Copernican paradigm over a period of some two centuries. Although positivism was not demolished by Kuhn – indeed, positivism still has many followers within the scientific community – a number of alternative accounts of science now became available, including those founded on the sociology of science. In their researches, historians of science avidly made use of these new insights.

Kuhn's anti-positivist thesis also addressed two other important issues. One was that each paradigm consisted of not only a theory and evidence, but also a bundle of non-empiricist commitments. Although in *Structure* Kuhn did not reflect explicitly on the role of religion, in opposing the positivist account of science he opened the door to allowing religion some role in the development of science, and thereby sanctioned the interaction between religion and science. Second, like many of his generation, Kuhn opposed the Whig agenda for a history of science that requires the historian to chart across time the inexorable accumulation of scientific knowledge, leading to the superior knowledge of our own time. Instead, historians now appreciated the need to understand scientists of the past in their own terms, and as facing problems that may seem alien to our present-day viewpoint. Thus historians of science could re-evaluate the histories of, say, alchemy or the phlogiston theory held by late eighteenth-century chemists. Such topics were no longer to be dismissed as gibberish and their proponents as misguided. Instead, the new contextualist historians sought to understand how Isaac Newton or Joseph Priestley viewed the world. In many cases, including both Newton and Priestley, the historian could no longer sideline their religious views. Contextualism thereby opened the door to addressing issues of science and religion.

A new agenda

Although a few historians of science initially responded to these challenges by addressing issues of science and religion afresh, the publication of John Hedley Brooke's *Science and Religion: Some Historical Perspectives* in 1991 reflects the new wave of interest in the subject. As well as offering a well researched history of science–religion inter-relations, in this and other works Brooke provided a new historiography for the subject, one that has been endorsed and developed by a number of other historians.

Brooke's first move was to challenge the existing assumptions, especially the conflict thesis and other master narratives that have frequently been imposed on the historical record. Using a wealth of historical examples, he showed the inadequacy of such narratives. For example, they fail to address Newton's theological views about God's role in creating and sustaining the physical universe, and also the many subtle arguments between Galileo and his clerical contemporaries, not all of whom condemned the Sun-centred system. History, then, has been used as a laboratory in which the master narratives of science–religion interaction have been tested and found wanting. Moreover, as Brooke and others have argued, these master narratives impose ahistorical and thoroughly inappropriate notions of both "science" and "religion" on past ages; both terms having undergone immense changes of meaning since the seventeenth century. Instead, and in line with the new contextualism, historians need to appreciate just how actors in earlier periods conceived "science", "religion", and the relation between them. Thus, while we may see science and religion as separate and easily separable activities, for writers through to the seventeenth century and perhaps beyond, no such separation existed. Peter Harrison has even argued that "[s]o inextricably connected were the dual concerns of God and nature that it is misleading to attempt to identify various kinds of relationships between science and religion in the seventeenth and eighteenth centuries" (Harrison 2006: 86).

Brooke also brought to the subject a new and welcome conception of the historian's role. In the introduction to his 1991 book, he insisted that the historian should not "pretend to tell a complete or definitive story" of the science–religion relationship (Brooke 1991: 5). Likewise, in another publication, Brooke and his co-author argued that the value of history consists "precisely in the fact that there is multiplicity – both in the stories to be told and in the manner of their telling" (Brooke and Cantor 1998: 35). This commitment to pluralism exposes a value central to the new historiography, and especially the view that historians should avoid trading in stereotypes – of either the scientist or the theologian. Moreover, rather than resigning history to crude master narratives that serve to bolster partisan interests, Brooke considered that the role of history is to provide "critical perspectives" on science–religion interactions. Serious, critical historical scholarship, he wrote, "has revealed [… the] extraordinarily rich and complex […] relation between science and religion in the past. […] The real lesson turns out to be complexity" (Brooke 1991: 5). Many of the historical case studies published over the past twenty years have explored this complexity. Not only have they shed fresh light on such cases as the Galileo affair, but they have opened up new ways of understanding science–religion relations.

Relating science and religion

In arguing for the diversity of science–religion interactions, Brooke cited several of the functions that religious beliefs can perform in respect to science. They have, for example, provided scientists with presuppositions; thus Michael Faraday considered that, as only God can create or annihilate both matter and "force," both these entities must be conserved in the regular operations of nature. This principle of "force" conservation underpinned his own researches, especially in the areas of electromagnetism and electrochemistry (Cantor 1991). Again, religion has frequently provided a sanction for science. This was particularly important in the late seventeenth century, when many doubted whether science was an acceptable activity. Thus, in his *History of the Royal Society* (1667), Thomas Sprat sought to legitimate the activities of the Society's members by arguing that science is an aid to Christianity because it inculcates a sense of piety in its practitioners. Likewise, design arguments have frequently been used not only to direct the reader from nature to God, but also to show that the pursuit of science does not threaten religion, but gives it support (Brooke 1991: 19–33).

It has become fashionable to view design arguments as naïve and as inhibiting the development of science. While design arguments certainly lost much of their credibility in the latter half of the nineteenth century, historians now recognize that during the two previous centuries they performed important functions within science, including (as indicated above) helping to legitimate scientific activity. Moreover, they proved attractive to many scientists and provided a way of appreciating God through the study of nature both in the field and in the laboratory. They also performed important conceptual roles. As Darwin appreciated from reading William Paley's *Natural Theology* (1802), there was design in nature since the structure and function of an organism were intimately related. The perception of design in nature has also often been endowed with aesthetic significance. Thus, when Copernicus argued in favor of the heliostatic system, he pointed out that it was more coherent and beautiful than the Earth-centered system and was therefore the one that manifested God's design. Einstein, likewise, famously quipped that "when judging a physical theory, I ask myself whether I would have made the Universe in that way had I been God" (Brooke and Cantor 1998: 227).

Many other forms of science–religion interaction are to be found in the current literature. Matthew Stanley's recent book on the Quaker astrophysicist Arthur Stanley Eddington provides one particularly informative example. Stanley identifies a number of values that are evident in both Eddington's Quakerism and his science. For example, like other contemporary Quakers, Eddington rejected the quest for absolute truth in religion and instead insisted that the search for spiritual truths was an ongoing process. Eddington applied a similar open-ended principle in his astrophysical theorizing, rejecting the rigid approach dominant among contemporary theoreticians, who based their models on true premises. Eddington's Quaker commitments also included his pacifism. As a conscientious objector during the First World War, he confronted the military tribunal at Cambridge and avoided imprisonment by undertaking the famous eclipse expedition in 1919 in order to test Einstein's general theory of relativity. Stanley thus argues that Eddington's science was firmly based on Quaker values (Stanley 2007).

Not only has religion influenced science, but science has also exerted an immense impact on religion. For example, outside the fundamentalist camp, most Christians have long accepted the great age of the universe and the evolutionary origins of organisms, even of humans, and have had to struggle with such problems as the wastage in nature that seems to clash with the notion of a benevolent deity. Or, to give one more specific example, late nineteenth-century Quakers and other liberal Christians adopted the doctrine of progressive revelation as a religious correlate of biological evolution.

While some scientists have had their religion strengthened through the pursuit of science, science has contributed to others losing their faith in conventional religions.

Scientism – the creation of what the German chemist Wilhelm Ostwald called an "ersatz religion" – provides one extreme but fascinating example. The best known case is Auguste Comte's positivist religion, in which "humanity" was worshipped in place of God. His "religion of humanity" gained a substantial following in late nineteenth- and early twentieth-century Britain and France, and still exists in Brazil (Brooke and Cantor 1998: 47–57).

Historians studying science–religion relations in specific historical contexts have repeatedly emphasized the importance of social and political factors. Thus present-day arguments between evolutionists and creationists in America are not simply about which is the best theory to account for animal species and even humankind. Like many subsequent confrontations, the famous 1925 "Monkey Trial" was over the politics of education – what should be taught in the classrooms of Dayton, Tennessee. One of the key issues was whether education should be controlled locally or whether it should be imposed by outsiders from the northern states. As Adam Shapiro has noted, "The anti-evolution trial came to be seen as an expression of the tensions between urban industrial and rural agricultural cultures in America" (Shapiro 2009). In our own day, evolution remains a highly charged political issue, not only in the United States, where politicians are aware of the power of the fundamentalist Christian lobby, but also in many other countries. In the Muslim world, for example, evolution is often presented as Western and responses to Darwin's theory are therefore often influenced by attitudes towards the West (Numbers 2006).

Science and religion as practices

Although much attention has been paid to the cognitive connections between science and religion, an important recent trend has been to understand both in terms of practice; this develops the increased interest in scientific practice among historians of science. One particularly informative example is provided by John Heilbron (1999), who explored the Catholic Church's immense commitment to addressing a particular astronomical problem. Over several centuries, Catholics have utilized astronomical observations to determine the date of Easter, which falls on the Sunday following the first full moon after the vernal equinox. In order to perform this calculation, Catholic astronomers developed observational instruments, utilized advanced mathematics, and performed numerous accurate observations on the Sun's motion. The Sun's trajectory had to be determined in order to predict the vernal equinox, and thus the date of Easter. A number of churches, such as San Petronio in Bologna, were used as observatories; light admitted through an aperture high on their walls projected an image of the Sun on the church floor, into which a scale was set. Thus astronomers used the actual fabric of churches to make their measurements. This involvement in astronomy may seem surprising, given the Church's opposition to Galileo. Yet, as Heilbron argues, the Catholic Church's commitment to science was not limited to determining the date of Easter. Over an extended period it became a major patron of science and Jesuits in particular have contributed greatly to science and science education. The tradition of Catholic-sponsored science continues today with the Vatican Observatory, which now includes a research group in Arizona as well as its headquarters at Castel Gandolfo near Rome.

Publishing provides another type of practice, and one that historians have recently studied in depth. Rather than focusing solely on the arguments contained in early science and religion texts, such as Paley's *Natural Theology* and the Bridgewater Treatises (first published in the early 1830s), historians have analyzed the entire network of communication involving such texts, including the roles of authors, publishers, reviewers, libraries, and readers.

In *Science and Salvation*, Aileen Fyfe (2004) analyzed the scientific publications of the evangelically oriented Religious Tract Society (RTS), which was founded in 1799. In order to help save souls, the RTS published cheap religious works that were widely distributed. However, by the 1820s a number of publishers had inundated the lower end of the market with cheap books, including secular works of popular science that, according to many Christians, posed a threat to religion. In response, in the 1840s the RTS started to publish books on science and other educational topics, including titles such as *Solar System* and *Plants and Trees of Scripture*. In adopting a "Christian tone," these works sought to show that science was not inimical to Christian faith; instead, Christians should study science – but science with a Christian orientation. Although some of the scientific works published by the RTS were manifestly evangelical, many of their publications adopted a softly edifying style that would be acceptable to a wide spectrum of believers and were intended to encourage non-believers to take the first steps towards conversion.

Like other studies of religious publishing, Fyfe's book moves the focus away from the elite scientific community and to the popularizers of science and their non-expert audiences. Although a few elite scientists wrote popularizations of science during the latter half of the nineteenth century, the authors of works directed to non-expert readerships were often clergymen or women, many of whom portrayed science within a religious framework (Lightman 2007). Moreover, during the second quarter of the century a mass readership was created. Thus many Victorians had their views of science moulded by works issued by religious publishing houses. The RTS, as Fyfe points out, "brought a knowledge of the sciences and novel questions relating to salvation to an ever-expanding audience" (Fyfe 2004: 15). As with the RTS's publications, many of the popular works on science portrayed it within a Christian frame; perhaps emphasizing that the harmonious structure of the physical world was due to its design by the wise and benevolent God. Jonathan Topham, whose research has been directed to book history, especially at the science–religion interface, draws the following conclusion about this book-history approach: "By refocusing their attention on the everyday practices of a far wider range of people than have previously been considered, historians can recover the nuts and bolts of the cultural history of science and religion. The history that can be built from them is not only innovative, but ultimately more satisfactory" (Topham 2009).

As well as the religious book trade, historians have studied the religious periodical press, which by the 1840s was highly differentiated, with most religious denominations and sects possessing and controlling their own periodical publications. Contrary to the view that religious people eschewed science, recent research has shown that most religious periodicals in the Victorian period carried a significant amount of science. Thus, by studying its scientific content, historians have come to appreciate the importance of the religious periodical press in the dissemination of science, and also how attitudes to science differed across the religious spectrum. The classic study is Alvar Ellegård's *Darwin and the General Reader* (1958), which analyzed how key aspects of the theory of evolution were received by over 100 periodicals during the period 1859–72. Ellegård found that Unitarian and Broad Church periodicals were most supportive of evolution, while Methodists were most opposed to it, with the Low Church only slightly less antipathetic. A number of more recent studies of the reception of evolution and other aspects of science have made sophisticated use of religious periodicals. As Topham notes, "the manner in which periodicals served to shape the religious identities of their readers is particularly important for those seeking to understand how religious people came to relate science to their daily religious practice in nineteenth-century Britain" (Topham 2009).

Religion and religions

Much of the historical writing on science and religion has focused on Protestant responses to science, particularly in Britain and increasingly in America. Yet we should not expect a single and distinct Protestant attitude to science, as Protestantism encompasses a great diversity of belief, and a great range of attitudes to science. Moreover, while the Protestant experience raises a number of important general issues concerning science, it should not be taken as typical of all religions. Although some work has been undertaken on other religious traditions, the study of comparative religious responses to science is still in its infancy (Brooke and Numbers 2011).Yet scholars need to appreciate the context-based histories of the different religions, and not try to assimilate them to a single model (Harrison 2006: 91–97).

The history of Roman Catholic responses to science has been overshadowed by the Galileo affair and by such interventions as Pope Pius IX's promulgation of the *Syllabus of Errors* (1864), which sought to repress scientific innovation. However, Heilbron has rightly emphasized the importance of the Church itself, and the Jesuit order in particular, in the development of science (Heilbron 1999). Moreover, as with Protestantism, there was no single Catholic response to science, despite the authority exercised by the Vatican. In general terms, Catholic scientists in France and Italy have been far freer to pursue science than those in Spain and South America. Recent work on Catholic responses to evolution not only has emphasized these national variations, but also has pointed out that, except in the area of human evolution, Catholic opposition to Darwin has been fairly muted (Artigas *et al.* 2006).

Much has been written about such medieval Jewish writers as Maimonides and Gersonides, who avidly encompassed the science of their day, albeit critically. Within Judaism there is a strong tradition of respect for learning and also a tradition of questioning received wisdom; these help explain why there has been relatively little Jewish opposition to evolution (Cantor and Swetlitz 2006). Some have also argued that these pro-science attitudes within traditional Judaism account for the large numbers of Jews who pursued scientific careers in twentieth-century America and Europe. However, as Noah Efron has shown, many of these Jews were attracted to science precisely because it offered a way of distancing themselves from their Jewish background and of entering the secular world (Efron 2007). The study of science and religion needs to encompass not only the positive interactions of the two, but also how science has been used to create non-religious identities.

There is currently much interest in the history of Islamic science, which possessed its own strong scientific tradition from the middle ages to about the sixteenth century, by which time it entered a period of decline. Historians of Islamic science are deeply divided over how to understand modern science in relation to this earlier period, especially as modern science is a Western export to Muslim countries, thus raising significant issues about the politics of colonialism. Some commentators have used history to justify the superiority of Islam, arguing that early Muslim scientists made scientific discoveries that were rediscovered by the West only many centuries later. Other historians have sought to identify a tradition of uniquely Islamic thought running through history. Others still have used the critical historical method. It will be interesting to see how historical scholarship develops in this controversial area over the next few years and in its relation to Islamic engagements with modern science.

Finally, historians of science and religion should not ignore how science has been deployed in the service of atheism and agnosticism. Not only are such uses a significant part of the study of science and religion, but it is often necessary to understand them in order to appreciate responses by religious writers. Thus, for example, Thomas Henry Huxley provoked a flurry of books defending the link between Christianity and science, while in our own day numerous works have been published in response to Richard Dawkins' alignment of science with atheism.

References

Artigas, M., T.F. Glick and R.A. Martinez (2006) *Negotiating Darwin: The Vatican Confronts Evolution, 1877–1902*, Baltimore, MD: Johns Hopkins University Press.

Brooke, John Hedley (1991) *Science and Religion: Some Historical Perspectives*, Cambridge: Cambridge University Press.

Brooke, John Hedley and Geoffrey Cantor (1998) *Reconstructing Nature: The Engagement of Science and Religion. The 1995–1996 Gifford Lectures at Glasgow*, Edinburgh: T&T Clark.

Brooke, John Hedley and Ronald L. Numbers (eds) (2011) *Science and Religion around the World*, New York: Oxford University Press.

Cantor, Geoffrey (1991) *Michael Faraday: Sandemanian and Scientist*, London: Macmillan.

Cantor, Geoffrey and Marc Swetlitz (eds) (2006) *Jewish Tradition and the Challenge of Darwinism*, Chicago, IL: University of Chicago Press.

Dixon, Thomas, Geoffrey Cantor and Stephen Pumfrey (eds) (2009) *Science and Religion: New Historical Perspectives*, Cambridge: Cambridge University Press.

Efron, Noah J. (2007) *Judaism and Science: A Historical Introduction*, Westport, CT: Greenwood Press.

Fyfe, Aileen (2004) *Science and Salvation: Evangelical Popular Science Publishing in Victorian Britain*, Chicago, IL: University of Chicago Press.

Harrison, Peter (2006) "'Science' and 'Religion': Constructing the Boundaries," *Journal of Religion* 86: 81–106.

Heilbron, John L. (1999) *The Sun in the Church: Cathedrals as Solar Observatories*, Cambridge, MA: Harvard University Press.

Lightman, Bernard (2007) *Victorian Popularizers of Science: Designing Nature for New Audiences*, Chicago, IL: University of Chicago Press.

Numbers, Ronald L. (2006) *The Creationists: From Scientific Creationism to Intelligent Design*, 2nd edn, Cambridge, MA: Harvard University Press.

Osler, Margaret J. (2009) "Religion and the Changing Historiography of the Scientific Revolution," in Dixon *et al.*, *Science and Religion*, *op. cit.*

Shapiro, Adam R. (2009) "The Scopes Trial – Beyond Science and Religion," in Dixon *et al.*, *Science and Religion*, *op. cit.*

Stanley, Matthew (2007) *Practical Mystic: Religion, Science, and A.S. Eddington*, Chicago, IL: University of Chicago Press.

Topham, Jonathan R. (2009) "Science, Religion, and the History of the Book," in Dixon *et al.*, *Science and Religion*, *op. cit.*

Turner, Frank M. (1974) *Between Science and Religion: The Reaction to Scientific Naturalism in Late Victorian England*, New Haven, CT: Yale University Press.

——(1978) "The Victorian Conflict between Science and Religion: A Professional Dimension," *Isis* 49: 356–76.

——(2009) "The Late-Victorian Conflict of Science and Religion as an Event in Nineteenth-Century Intellectual and Cultural History" in Dixon *et al.*, *Science and Religion*, *op. cit.*

Further reading

Probably the best introductions to the topic are John Hedley Brooke's *Science and Religion* (cited above) and Thomas Dixon's *Science and Religion: A Very Short Introduction* (Oxford: Oxford University Press, 2008). The mythology surrounding science and religion is tackled in Ronald L. Numbers (ed.), *Galileo Goes to Jail and Other Myths about Science and Religion* (Cambridge, MA: Harvard University Press, 2009). There are several useful collections of historical essays, including John Hedley Brooke, Margaret J. Osler and Jitse van der Meer (eds), *Science in Theistic Contexts: Cognitive Dimensions* (Chicago, IL: University of Chicago Press, 2001); Thomas Dixon, Geoffrey Cantor and Stephen Pumfrey (eds), *Science and Religion* (cited above); David C. Lindberg and Ronald L. Numbers (eds), *God and Nature: Historical Essays on the Encounter between Christianity and Science* (Berkeley, CA: University of California Press, 1986); David C. Lindberg and Ronald L. Numbers (eds), *When Science and Christianity Meet* (Chicago, IL: University of Chicago Press, 2003); and James D. Proctor (ed.), *Science, Religion, and the Human Experience* (New York: Oxford University Press, 2005). For comparative perspectives, see John Hedley Brooke and Ronald L. Numbers (eds), *Science and Religion around the World* (New York: Oxford University Press, 2011) and Toby E. Huff, *The Rise of Early Modern Science: Islam, China, and the West* (Cambridge: Cambridge University Press, 1993). For Islamic perspectives, see Taner Edis, *An Illusion of Harmony: Science and Religion in Islam* (New York: Prometheus Books, 2007); for the role of Jews in science, see Noah J. Efron, *Judaism and Science: A Historical Introduction* (Westport, CT: Greenwood Press, 2007); on Roman Catholicism, see Don O'Leary, *Roman Catholicism and Modern Science: A History* (New York: Continuum, 2006) and Ernan McMullin (ed.), *The Church and Galileo* (Notre Dame, IN: University of Notre Dame Press, 2005).

4
THE PHYSICS OF SPIRIT
The indigenous continuity of science and religion

Brian Yazzie Burkhart

One of the first questions that students of Native American religion ask is, "who are the Native American gods and how many of them are there?". They are often quite surprised to hear that the English term "god" does not really apply to the manner in which Native traditions approach the divine mystery. Although there is great variety in the details of Native Spirituality, many key characteristics seem to be common. One of these is that the agents of creation are not often cast as human-like, but as *diyin* (Navajo) or *wakan* (Lakota), as power, energy, and movement. Lakota medicine man John Fire Lame Deer describes it this way: the Great Spirit "is not like a human being. […] He is a power. That power could be in a cup of coffee" (Fire and Erdoes 1972: 265–66). This power of divinity is inherently creative and not restricted to divine acts, but is continuous with common creative events, even of ordinary human creativity. Tewa philosopher and scholar of Native science Gregory Cajete points out that "[c]reativity in all forms is part of the greater flow of creativity in nature" (Cajete 2000: 15). Human creativity is an expression of the exact process and energy that is expressed in the divine creation. Creativity, power, energy, transformation, and movement are closer approximations of a Native sense of the divine than the ordinary English words: God, holy, sacred, and divine being. These few highlights of Native religion and science underscore the possibility of viewing science and religion as one whole from an indigenous perspective. In Western thought, by contrast, science and religion have often been understood as independent domains of understanding and awareness – many times seen as in intractable conflict.

In this essay, I attempt to take a small step toward clarifying a tiny part of the meaning of the vast complex of Native American religion in the context of this worry about an intractable conflict between science and religion. I attempt to articulate part of the manner in which the practice of religion in Native cultures is continuous with the practice of science. I also try to make clear some of the ways in which Native religion conflicts with aspects of science in a broadly Western sense. In my attempt to forge some ground for a clearer understanding of Native thought in the context of religion and science more broadly, I touch on the following important topics: the relationship between gods and humans, religious and scientific cosmologies, and conflicts between place-centered and history-centered religion and science.

The continuum of gods and humans

Native religion, from the start, seems rather unorthodox to the Western tradition. The uniqueness of these traditions led Western religious scholars for generations to conclude that Native culture had no religion, since there seemed to be no real god or even divinity in the Western sense of these concepts. Even the best modern examples of the academic study of Native religion often fall short of grasping the deeper meanings of Native spiritual traditions, which is not surprising given that the bulk of this research has been conducted by non-adherents, and the categories for the academic study of Native traditions are, as Osage theologian George Tinker (undated) writes, "constructed in a cultural context alien to the traditions themselves." Even traditional adherents of Native religion practices deny, in a way, the label of religion in favor of "a way of life." Part of what motivates many Native Americans to call their religious practices a way of life is that they feel little commonality with the theology that is normally attached to what is generally labeled religion, particularly in the Western world. One such discontinuity arises in the relationship between gods and humans. Western religion emphasizes the being and existence of God, while Native religion emphasizes the power of God or gods. In Native religion, this often results in no concept whatsoever of god as a being. Where there is a more concrete concept of God or gods in a Native context, the more abstract capacity, and the knowledge required to achieve such capacity, is emphasized over any abstract sense of the being of such a god.

A striking way to put this, in contrast, is to say that in a Native American context, questions regarding the existence of God make no sense. To ask such a question would be the same as asking whether the rain, the wind, or even gravity exists. God in this context is simply the open category of the experienced, and yet to be experienced, power and movement in the universe. God is ordinary and mundane as much as divine and holy. The everydayness of Native religion is hard to appreciate from a Western point of view. In the Navajo creation story, the earth-surface people are told the following about the *diyinii* (holy people or gods): "You will see a holy one when you see a white feather (of an eagle), when you see a bluebird, a yellowbird, a big blackbird. […] And when white corn, yellow corn, blue corn, variegated corn, and plants move (grow). […] And too, every day, every night, every dawn, every year your mother (Changing Woman) will be instructing you (in person). Arise, go to sleep, eat, drink, defecate, urinate, by means of all these she will be instructing you!" (Wyman and Haile 1970: 324–25). This mundaneness of divinity makes the Native religious attitude appear more like that of ordinary scientific inquiry.

Even the boundary between humans and gods is itself rather porous. Many of the Navajo ceremony stories (a tradition with a fairly concrete concept of gods) describe how an ordinary youth, after setting himself apart from his family, comes into association with a god for a time, after which he returns to his family to share what he has learned, before permanently leaving them and becoming one of the gods himself (Reichard 1970: 55–56). From this pattern, we can observe that it is not something in the nature of a being that makes him or her a god or a human, but rather something about the knowledge and capacity one has acquired.

Divinity is an acquired rather than genetic or inherent quality in the Navajo view. It is through the acquisition of knowledge that one becomes divine. The capacities that one gains in association with being divine do not exist as an inseparable part of being. These are capacities that one must acquire and continually choose to exercise. Of the divine capacities, perhaps the most significant is creativity, which is why a god is so often referred to as creator. In the Navajo universe, all is created: emotions, natural phenomena, language, birth, death, even gender. This creation is always connected with ritual, which creates an inseparable bond between scientific process and religious ceremony. The gods created through the same process of ritual that occurs in ordinary human ritual today. What separates the two is a greater knowledge and capacity on the part of the divine ritual creation.

The ritual process comes in two parts: the acquisition of knowledge, and empowering of that knowledge into the world through a ritual form. As the Lakota medicine man Black Elk describes it, a vision must be brought into a ritual form for it to have power (Black Elk and Neihardt 1988). In the Navajo creation, even the gods must receive some personal instruction through some kind of personal experience (a vision or otherwise), and they must ritually exercise what they learn in order for it to have power, in order for creation to occur. This process is the same for gods and humans and so, in the end, the capacity or power of divinity is available not only to *diyinii* but also to humans in everyday and ceremonial acts of creation and ritual.

In the Navajo view, the gods are also dependent upon humans, as much as humans are dependent upon the gods. The life energy of the *diyinii*, particularly those associated with the Dawn, the Sun, and the Moon, is reciprocally exchanged with the earth-surface people on a daily basis. This symbiosis is the essence of the relationship between gods and humans. Humans need the gods, as would appear obvious, since they are the source of so much power. It is through them that health and happiness is restored and maintained. However, the gods need human power and ritual as well. It is through human prayer, one might say, that the gods are sustained, that their health and happiness is restored and maintained. John Farella provides a good example in the description of Corn. Corn is a sacred being in many Native traditions, and for the Navajo, it is quite clearly *diyinii*. However, Corn is a domesticated plant. Various *diyinii* (the Sun, the Earth, and Water) help it grow, but without humans to cultivate it, there would be no Corn at all. In return for the cultivation of the Corn, humans are fed. The corn meal and corn pollen are used by humans to feed the *diyinii* through offerings (corn pollen is offered to the Sun each morning at dawn). Humans grow and reproduce as the Corn reproduces. Through this process, the other *diyinii* increase in power or capacity: The Sun, the Earth, and Water increase in the sense that they are now able to create and sustain more, evidenced by the abundance of Corn and the people who live by it (Farella 1984: 30). Humans participate in this circle of sustaining health and happiness through even the most mundane-seeming daily ceremony and ritual.

This sense of the divine and its relationship to the human is not unique to Navajo religion. In the Lakota way of being, *Wakan Tanka*, which is often translated as Great Spirit, can be analyzed with further nuance. "*Wa*" is the word that describes action that is taken in or through something, like something that is accomplished through a vessel. "*Kan*" refers to veins, like those that carry blood through the body, like those arteries through which life's energy flows in human beings. "*Tanka*" means really big or grand. Howard Bad Hand, Lakota singer and writer, describes *Wakan Tanka*, finally, as "action into the pathway of life in its grandest" (Bad Hand 2002: 33). In this way, the Great Spirit is not really a being and *Wakan Tanka* is not the essence of a being. The Great Spirit is the totality of both the vessel, and movement through that vessel that is the energy of life at its grandest. It is the simple blood and blood vessels in a human being, the sacred pipe (bowl and stem) through which the smoke and prayers of the people move, as well as the artery and movement in its totality that makes all these little vessels and actions possible.

The physics of Native religion

It might not be surprising to most readers that the categories of religion and science as generated by Western tradition do not apply neatly to indigenous traditions of knowledge and ceremony, since Western science and religion have generally been taken as more advanced, and so-called "primitive" traditions have been defined by their non-abstract and animistic graspings, which are often seen as early stages of development toward more advanced stages of monotheism in religion and mathematical reasoning in science. Yet the details of the manner in which indigenous people continue to intertwine so-called secular knowledge (astronomy, biology, physics, and so on) with spiritual understanding (ceremony structure and timing, healing and health, and so on) may be surprising to many readers who have long rejected notions of the primitive and advanced in religion and science. It may surprise readers that Native religion and science are not understood best as non-abstract at all – much less as traditions that appear destined to progress from these primitive forms to more abstract Western science and monotheistic religion. Theoretical physics, as one example, has begun to conceptualize the universe in more Native terms (Capra *et al.* 1991). John Briggs and David F. Peat describe creation as a living process in terms very similar to the Native understanding. They tell us that creativity flows from the "implicate order" of the universe to produce material or energetic manifestations that become the "explicate order." This movement of creation is the same for galaxies as it is for quarks and leptons (Briggs and Peat 1999: 28–30).

For many millennia, Native science and religion have operated with a fairly developed understanding of these developments in physics. This advanced understanding of physics is apparent even in the ordinary cosmological narratives. For the Navajo, creation is a process of emergence. Various manifestations of worlds occur, where different sorts of beings literally climb into the sky in order to crawl through holes into subsequent ones, until the present world, called the fifth world, is manifest. In the earliest of worlds, "wind-beings" are already present. Some of these beings are clumsily translated in English as: Female Substance, Male Substance, Darkness, Dawn, Thought, Speech, the Four Directions, and so on. The potential of reproduction and transformation is already present in the most primal of realities. Female Substance, for example, co-mingles with the East to produce First Woman (who is not an actual human being but a *diyinii* or more fundamental power of the universe). This process of transformation, where what is transformed then transforms itself, and so on, happens over and over again even as the seemingly ordinary transformations of human energy in giving birth, the creation of art, or even resourcefully dealing with a car that is stuck in the mud.

This understanding of reality, of what is and how it comes to be, is strikingly similar in Western science. Chaos, complexity, and systems theories view the interplay of transformation and what is transformed as a similar self-organizing process. The classic Western scientific perspective views order as equilibrium, as seen in static structures, for example. The new perception of order is seen in non-equilibrium, as in turbulence, for example. The turbulent flows of air in wind are understood as highly organized patterns of vortices that divide and subdivide again and again on smaller and smaller scales. It is at these points of instability that unpredictable and creative events take place. It is where new order emerges spontaneously. In Navajo creation, it is out of this instability that a new world emerges.

Twentieth-century quantum physics has also shown us that the seemingly stable world of objects dissolves into wave-like patterns of interconnectedness and probability at the subatomic level. Subatomic particles do not appear to be isolated objects that we might call "things," but rather a kind of interconnectedness between things that, in turn, gives rise to interconnectedness between further things, and so on (like the powers that transform into furthers powers in Navajo creation). Physicist David Bohm articulates this according to what he calls the "enfolded order" (Bohm 1995). He suggests that, at its deepest essence, what *is* is not a collection of material things, but rather a process or movement. He calls this the *holomovement*, or movement of the whole. In Lakota, this is something like what we described earlier as *Wakan Tanka* or Great Spirit, understood as the biggest artery of life and energy and the action or movement that flows through that artery. This movement, both in Bohm's physics and in Lakota religion, is responsible for the explicit forms of reality that we recognize as trees, rocks, rivers, and so on.

In addition, for Bohm and the Lakota the vastness of the enfolded order of process and movement significantly outstrips the explicate order of temporary and recognizable things. The symbolism of the traditional teepee as two cones (one inverted on the other) is useful here. The idea is that another teepee begins where the lodge poles spread out at the top of the physical teepee. The explicit teepee is only part of the whole, which spreads out well beyond what is manifest, but is a part of reality of the teepee as much as what is visible.

In Navajo thought, the perhaps recognizable transformation, movement, or ordering that arises from male and female substances is coupled with the mirroring of thought and speech in much the same way that the visible and invisible are mirrored in the two cones of the Lakota teepee. The premise for Navajo physics is that all existence has the dual nature of implicate and explicit order as articulated by Bohm. Thought and speech are implicate and explicate mirrors of each other. Thought is the unmanifested or interconnectedness that is transformed into the manifested or divided and subdivided form of speech. In the Navajo creation story, this world as we know it was actually sung into existence after the careful plans (thoughts) of the *diyinii*. But Thought, as a being and as action, is generated, itself, out of Thought's unmanifested mirror, *ehozhin*, which we might call Awareness. The manifested and unmanifested mirroring of all aspects of reality is the basic pattern that makes up the metaphysical fabric of reality in the Navajo or Lakota universe.

Native religious understanding is not very primitive then after all. It is also a mistake to describe Native thought as "animistic." The view that Native cultures see the world through the lens that is constructed around the Eurocentric labeling of so-called "primitive" traditions as animistic is hardly feasible, given the complexities of these so-called primitive views as articulated above. In large part, the label "animistic" is pejorative, attempting to construct Native traditions as irrational through an extreme oversimplification that serves to demonize these views. The reductive labeling of Native views as animistic paints a picture of simple-minded children seeing the world as filled with beings exactly like themselves, with no capacity to see the complex nuances of the diversity of the phenomena of experience. The reality seems to be quite the opposite: Certain aspects of Native thought seem to show a richer understanding of these nuances than the sometimes oversimplified reifications of classical Western science. In another way, however, the European tradition of referring to Native world-views as forms of animism is quite correct, if understood non-reductively, since the term "animism" can literally be understood as "life-ism." In Navajo thought, the mirroring of the manifested and unmanifested in all existence reveals a notion of being alive that is identical with transformation and movement. Gary Witherspoon, in his work on Navajo language and thought, puts it like this: "[t]he assumption that underlies this dualistic aspect of all being and existence is that the world is in motion, that things are constantly undergoing processes of transformation, deformation, and restoration, and that the essence of life and being is movement" (Witherspoon 1977: 48). Life and movement are so nearly equivalent in the Navajo language and thought that the stem *naal* is combined with various prefixes to express the concepts of being alive, coming to life, enduring, lasting, quick movement, and even ordinary concepts like moving my hand to pick up a stick.

The Navajo language mirrors Bohm's view of the process of the enfolding order as it temporarily becomes explicit in the superficial reality of things. As Harry Hoijer describes the language, Navajo verbs "center very largely around the reporting of […] 'eventings.' These 'eventings' are divided into […] states by the withdrawal of motion" (Hoijer 1974: 145). He concludes that "the Navajo define position as the resultant of the withdrawal of motion" (*ibid.*: 146). The verbal nature of Native languages is one more indication of the deep understanding of the complex nature of life and existence as movement. Taiaiake Alfred, *Kanienkeha* (Mohawk) philosopher, indicates that the emphasis on naming and labeling in European languages that are structured around nouns, rather than verbs which emphasize movement and action, trick colonized people into understanding their own personal identities as things. He says, "[t]ake my own name, for example, Taiaiake, in English is a proper noun that labels me for identification. In *Kanienkeha*, it literally means, 'he is crossing over from the other side.' […] In fighting for our future, we have been misled into thinking that 'Indigenous,' or […] 'Cree' or 'Mohawk' […] is something that is attached to us inherently and not a descriptions of what we actually do with our lives" (Alfred 2005: 33) David Peat, in his book on Blackfoot physics, mentions the manner in which "chance, flux, and process" are "perfectly reflected in many Native languages. […] With its emphasis upon verbs, it perfectly reflects a reality of transformation and change" (Peat 2005: 237). There are nouns in Native languages, but "like the vortex that forms in a fast flowing river, the nouns are not primary in themselves but are temporary aspects of the ever-flowing process" (*ibid.*). David Bohm argued that noun-based languages like English are impoverished and misleading. What was needed, he claimed, was a language based on processes and movement, transformation and change. He called this hypothetical language the "rheomode," a language based on verbs and verbal structures. What he wanted is already in place in any number of Native languages that have been in existence for millennia, something he realized shortly before his death, when he met a number of Algonkian speakers (*ibid.*: 238). What Bohm almost missed, and what Alfred indicates that languages like English hide, is a very powerful and nuanced understanding of movement and life (pejoratively labeled "animism") embedded in Native language and inherent in Native religious thought.

Some unresolved conflicts

One must not assume too much about the compatibility of Western science and religion with Native thought. There is a level of abstraction and process in Western science and a level of abstraction from the sacredness of place in Western religion that has bred a great deal of conflict with Native world-views. Vine Deloria Jr., Dakota philosopher of Native religion, emphasizes the spatial aspects of Native religion. In Native religion, Deloria explains, something is experienced in a particular place by a particular community. This experience gives rise to symbols and narratives of meaning for those places and people (Deloria 1973: 72). In Western religion, the spatiality of religious experience is ignored, since "the manifestation of deity in a particular local situation is mistaken for a truth applicable to all times and places, a truth so powerful that it must be impressed upon peoples who have no connections to the event or cultural complex in which it originally made sense" (*ibid.*: 66). Western religion appears to float free of place, as shown by its ability to move anywhere in the world and carry the same force of conviction. In Western religion, God works through time and history and needs no particular place in which to be revealed. A church can be torn to the ground without diminishing God's capacity to be revealed. In Native thought, the structure of religious tradition "is taken directly from the world around them, from their relationships with all other forms of life" (*ibid.*: 67). Context is then just as important as content of revelation or religious structure. Deloria describes the geographical aspect of Native religion in this way: "[t]he places where revelations were experienced were remembered and set aside as locations where, through rituals and ceremonials, the people could once again communicate with the spirits. Thousands of years of occupancy on their lands taught tribal peoples the sacred landscapes for which they were responsible and gradually the structure of ceremonial reality became clear" (*ibid.*: 67). The sacred geography of Native religion is seen as sacrilege in the context of Western religion, as evidenced by the proclivity of giving Native sacred sites English names associated with the Devil (in Wyoming, *Mato Tipila*, the Lodge of the Bear, is known in English as Devil's Tower). In addition to attempts by Western religion to demonize Native sacred places, the U.S. Supreme Court has interpreted the protection of religious freedom required by the Constitution as not applying to Native religions' sacred geography (Lyng vs. NICPA). The Western religious bias of Western law ignores the fact that destroying or even desecrating a Native sacred place destroys the capacity of divine revelation. In Western religious terms, this would be akin to destroying the Bible, Torah, or Qur'an, which are seen as the vehicles through which God reveals himself.

Western science does have a place for sacred geography of a sort. Western science values the existence of species and the diversity of ecosystems. The existence of sacred place such *Dook'o'oosłííd* (Navajo name for the San Francisco Peaks in Arizona) can then have some value to science. However, it is not the same kind of value as given to these places in Native religion, and can give rise to great conflict with the Native view of sacred geography. The value of species diversity within ecosystems is a value of kinds, and not of particulars – *Mato Tipila* or *Dook'o'oosłííd* have no value as the particular places that they are; they only have value as a thing of its kind. "Sacred" in this sense reduces to "rare." Western science finds no value in Native sacred places unless there is something of scientific value that cannot be just as easily studied elsewhere. Native religion views the particularity of the thing and its relationships as determinative of its sacredness. *Dook'o'oosłííd* is seen by thirteen Arizona tribes as an essential source of continual spiritual revelation and renewal. Recently, the U.S. Ninth District Court of Appeals denied attempts by these tribes to stop a ski resort on land managed by the U.S. Forest Service from using treated wastewater to significantly expand the resort. The District Court found no place in Western law for the protection of Native religion as regards sacred geography. The arguments that have remained powerful, as this case continues on appeal, are those that point to possible environmental damage and negative health effects from the treated wastewater (www.savethepeaks.org). In most attempts to protect Native sacred places, there is no clear damage within the lens of Western science: no endangered animals, no physical health concerns, no ecosystem degradation. Western science's attempts to frame a discussion about the Native sacredness of place have been supremely limited. As should be clear from the discussions of Native religion in this chapter, Native people would claim that, wherever sacred places are under threat of strip-mining, snow-making and the like, the animals, all physical health, and the stability of the ecosystem are under threat. Perhaps the starkness of this disagreement is indicative not of a deeper conflict between Native religion and Western science, but of a lack of integration between achievements in science (deeper understandings of the complex system of life) and the manner in which science is brought forth in policy and legal debates about sacred places. More integration in this regard could provide Native sacred places with a brighter future and perhaps even resolve much of this residual conflict between Western and Native world-views.

References

Alfred, T. (2005) *Wasáse: Indigenous Pathways of Action and Freedom*, Peterborough, Ontario: Broadview Press.

Bad Hand, H.P. (2002) *Native American Healing*, New York: Keats Publishing.

Black Elk and J.G. Neihardt (1988 [1932]) *Black Elk Speaks: Being the Life Story of a Holy Man of the Oglala Sioux*, new edn, Lincoln, NE: University of Nebraska Press.

Bohm, D. (1995 [1980]) *Wholeness and the Implicate Order*, London and New York: Routledge.

Briggs, J. and F.D. Peat (1999) *Seven Life Lessons of Chaos: Timeless Wisdom from the Science of Change*, 1st edn, New York: HarperCollins.

Cajete, G. (2000) *Native Science: Natural Laws of Interdependence*, 1st edn, Santa Fe, NM: Clear Light.

Capra, F., D. Steindl-Rast and T. Matus (1991) *Belonging to the Universe: Explorations on the Frontiers of Science & Spirituality*, San Francisco, CA: HarperCollins.

Deloria, V. (1973) *God is Red*, New York: Grosset & Dunlap.

Farella, J.R. (1984) *The Main Stalk: A Synthesis of Navajo Philosophy*, Tucson, AZ: University of Arizona Press.

Fire, J. and R. Erdoes (1972) *Lame Deer, Seeker of Visions*, New York: Simon & Schuster.

Hoijer, H. (1974) *A Navajo Lexicon*, Berkeley, CA: University of California Press.

Peat, F.D. (2005 [2002]) *Blackfoot Physics: A Journey into the Native American Worldview*, Boston: Weiser Books.

Reichard, G.A. (1970 [1963]) *Navaho Religion, a Study of Symbolism*, 2nd edn, New York: Bollingen Foundation; distributed by Pantheon Books.

Tinker, George (undated) *Encyclopedia of North American Indians* (online). http://web.archive.org/web/20050330085408/http:/college.hmco.com/history/readerscomp/naind/html/na_032600_religion.htm

Witherspoon, G. (1977) *Language and Art in the Navajo Universe*, Ann Arbor, MI: University of Michigan Press.

Wyman, L.C. and B. Haile (1970) *Blessingway*, Tucson, AZ: University of Arizona Press.

Further reading

Conversations on science and religion in the context of Native Studies are often seen as foundational related to the work of Vine Deloria Jr. His book *Custer Died for Your Sins: An Indigenous Manifesto* (New York: Macmillan, 1969) began an indigenous conversation on a multitude of topics in the areas of philosophy, science, and religion. Deloria's *God is Red* (cited above) is a seminal expression from a Native perspective of the deep interconnections of spirit, place, and nature. Deloria's essays, such as "Relativity, Relatedness, and Reality," "Ethnoscience and Indian Realities," and "The Religious Challenge" in *Spirit and Reason: The Vine Deloria Reader* (Golden, CO: Fulcrum, 1999) extend and clarify the discussion. Essays such as "American Indian Metaphysics" and "The Schizophrenic Nature of Western Metaphysics" by Deloria with Daniel R. Wildcat in *Power and Place: Indian Education in America* (Golden, CO: Fulcrum, 2001) show how the metaphysics of indigenous science and religion is based on an understanding of the social and relational fabric of reality. Gregory Cajete's *Native Science: Natural Laws of Interdependence* (cited above) show how Native science is an expression of the "inherent creativity of nature as the foundation for both knowledge and action" (Cajete 2000: 15). Most recently, Thomas M. Norton-Smith shows in *The Dance of Person and Place: One Interpretation of American Indian Philosophy* (Albany, NY: SUNY Press, 2010) that the indigenous concept of "spirit" is better understood using modern scientific concepts rather than more accepted frameworks of religious mysticism.

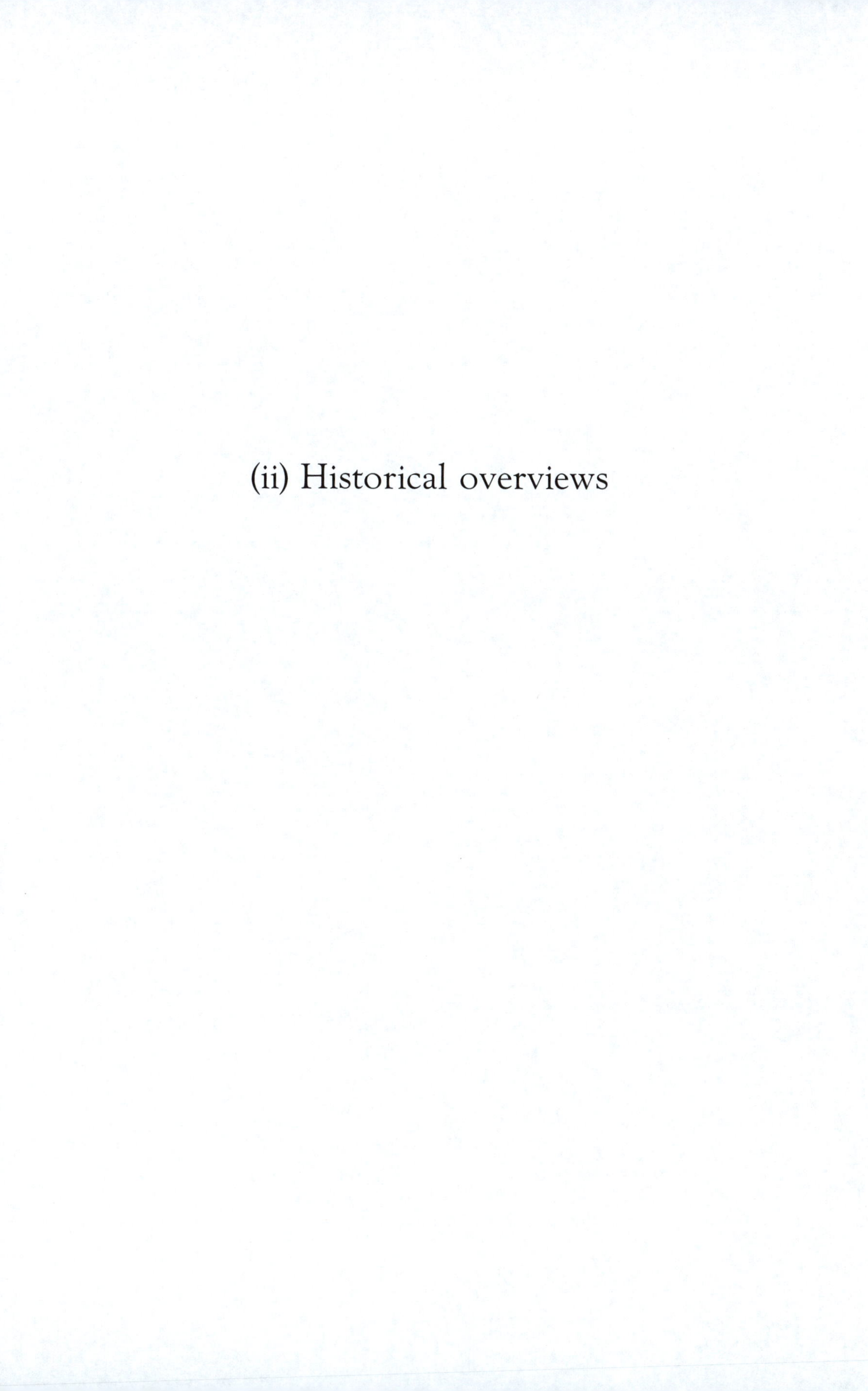

(ii) Historical overviews

5
ISLAM AND SCIENCE

Ahmed Ragab

In studying the relation between science and religion in the greater Middle East and the Islamic World, using the traditional Eurocentric division of science and religion, which was formulated in the European Renaissance and Enlightenment, cannot yield accurate conclusions and often leads to anachronistic or Eurocentric analyses. Here we look at different scientific, philosophical, and religious disciplines, discourses, and paradigms as integral parts of a socio-intellectual environment, where different methods, ideas, theories, and discursive strategies are exchanged, debated, and developed in conjunction, while keeping an eye on debates on sources of knowledge and on epistemic authority of scholars, ideas, and methodologies. Moreover, analysis should pay close attention to political and socio-intellectual debates of legitimacy, which constitute particular dynamic distributions of social and intellectual capital.

Themes of analysis

At the core of the debates between scholars of science, religion, and philosophy, a number of themes are important in order to analyze these debates without essentializing different disciplines or focusing on the most violent or heated episodes of these intellectual exchanges.

Perceptions of science and religion

Here we look at science not only as the product of the laboratory, but rather as a social and intellectual practice, the position, intellectual authority, and boundaries of which are defined organically within the contemporaneous intellectual sphere. Similarly, different social changes affect the perception of religion and its role in society. Although the religious discourse depends on a number of quasi-permanent texts, the understanding, interpretation, and perception of these texts effectively change the meaning and significance of religion.

The analysis of the perception of science and religion involves investigating debates on the meaning of knowledge, its different sources, and their degree of legitimacy.

The scientific and religious processes

As processes of intellectual production, both scientific and religious practices formulate their own rules and methods, which help grant them epistemic authority, social legitimacy, and intellectual influence. However, these rules (such as the scientific method of thinking and the rules of interpretation of religious texts) are not permanent, but rather are organically connected to the social and intellectual scene. As these rules and strategies change, the perception of the discipline, whether scientific or religious, changes, and their place in society and their intellectual interactions change as well.

Epistemic authority and the socio-intellectual space

The socio-intellectual and political space available for different disciplines and agents influences how they develop their discourses, communicate their narratives, and formulate their arguments. In turn, this affects their epistemic authority, leading to organic changes in the entire intellectual scene. This space depends on factors such as patronage, methods of communication, socio-intellectual capital, and political and socio-economic context.

From the "Classical Age" to the early modern period

This period is conventionally considered to have started with the translation movement under the Abbasid Caliphate and ended with the destruction of Baghdad by the Mongols.

Early translation movement

Throughout the eighth century, many scholars took to translating various Greek, Persian, and Indian writings into Arabic, making these works accessible to a larger group of students and scholars. The Academy of Gundeshapur, which was established under the Sassinid rule in the end of the fifth century, flourished under Chosroes, and gave refuge to many Greek Nestorian scholars who fled the Byzantine persecution and played a significant role in leading this early translation movement and scientific debate.

In 813, al-Ma'mun became the Abbasid Caliph following the regicide of his brother al-Amin. Under al-Ma'mun, the House of Wisdom, which was established by his father al-Rashid, expanded rapidly to become a huge library and school, and the center of a rapid and expansive translation movement. This movement was led by people such Hunayn ibn Ishaq, a Nestorian physician, translator, and philosopher, and al-Kindi, a philosopher and mathematician (Rosenthal 1975).

The translations allowed for the rapid circulation of ancient works, aided by a fertile environment of theological and philosophical debates, where Muslim scholars debated with Christian and Jewish scholars, establishing the foundations of a new Muslim theology or Kalam. The Mutazilites, who emerged as a theological school in the eighth century, developed their arguments using logic, Aristotelian, and neoplatonic ideas, and were able to recruit al-Ma'mun himself in becoming the most important school of theology (Hourani 1976).

Mihna

Under various socio-political and intellectual influences, al-Ma'mun proclaimed the Mutazilite theology to be the official theology of the Islamic Caliphate, and instituted a series of trials where scholars of religion and of religious law were examined and required to profess the new theology. This series of trials extended over fifteen years, under two other caliphs after al-Ma'mun's two successors. The main points of debate concerned the Mutazilite belief in absolute monotheism, which necessitated the finiteness of the universe, the argument that the Scripture is created and finite as well, and the rejection of anthropomorphic descriptions of God.

The finiteness of the universe went against Aristotelian cosmology, which was espoused by many philosophers and scientists. Aristotelians believed in the infiniteness of the universe, the permanence of cosmic movements, and the existence of God outside the universe.

The creation of the Scripture caused most of the uproar. The theological counterargument was largely an argument of methodology and of sources of knowledge. While Mutazilites proclaimed the creation of the Scripture based on logical and philosophical theorizations, the opposing theological views, led by scholars of prophetic traditions and headed by Ahmad ibn Hanbal, refused to answer the question and argued that there was no clear answer for it in the Scripture, which was the only legitimate source of knowledge for them. Moreover, Mutazilites sought to interpret the anthropomorphic descriptions of God in the Scripture, arguing that they logically cannot be literal, while traditionists argued for limited or no interpretation of the Scripture, and that the conclusions of intellectual theorization are only secondary to what was mentioned in the Scripture.

On this methodological level, peripatetic philosophers and scientists and Mutazilite theologians were closer in position, as they agreed on the meaning and sources of knowledge and were able to hold more productive debates, which contributed to the maturation of these disciplines. On the other hand, the popular conviction of the traditionist, more orthodox theological position put enormous pressure on Mutazilite theologians and philosophers and contributed to the development of new schools of theology.

The Mihna/trial was terminated in 848 with an apparent victory of the traditionist views, but with dissemination of the debate to the far-reaching corners of the empire. This debate contributed to shaping scientific theories and religious doctrines over the following three centuries.

Maturation of science, philosophy, and theology

The late ninth to early tenth centuries witnessed the rapid weakening of the Abbasid central authority in Baghdad and the establishment of numerous kingdoms and principalities in the east of the empire, which owed only nominal loyalty to the Abbasid Caliph and competed together for more influence. In the west, a Shiite Caliphate was established in 909 in North Africa and consolidated its empire in 969 by occupying Egypt and establishing Cairo as the capital. Soon after, they controlled Arabia and the Levant, threatening nominal Abbasid control over the region of Iraq.

The political decline of the central authority allowed for the existence of multiple centers and metropoles, where sovereigns patronized scientific and philosophical inquiries and where different theological views developed under the protection of sympathetic rulers. Meanwhile, the travel culture, seasonal religious travels, and the Arabic language facilitated the movement of scientific, philosophical, and theological productions across these political borders.

Rapid progress in scientific inquiry and discovery took place in various courts spearheaded by the likes of Rhazes (medicine), Sijzi (astronomy), and Khawarizimi (mathematics), who worked for different courts and rulers in Persia and Iraq. Al-Farabi, a student of al-Kindi, developed Aristotelian and neoplatonic philosophical inquiry.

Brethren of Purity, a secret society of philosophers and scientists, appeared on the intellectual scene during the tenth century and espoused Shiite theology as based on Pythagorean philosophy and cosmology. In their collection of fifty-two treatises, they theorized for the Isma'ili Shiite theology adopted by the Fatimids, whom they supported and to whom they paved the road intellectually. Abu Hayyan al-Tawhidi, who admired the work of the Brethren of Purity, developed neoplatonic philosophy and introduced aesthetics to Islamic theology and science. In 972, al-Azhar mosque was inaugurated in Fatimid Cairo and became the beacon of Isma'ili Shiite theology. The Fatimids established another "House of Wisdom" in Cairo in 1004; a huge library that hosted many scholars in various disciplines, paralleling the Abbasid establishment.

In 912, a new school of theology broke off from the Mutazilite school under the guidance of Al-Ash'ari. The Asharites drew their positions between those of the Mutazilites and those of the traditionists, claiming the supreme authority of the Scripture but allowing for limited interpretations. Asharites were occasionalist theologians, who rejected Aristoltelian physics and cosmology, which are based on inherent movements, infinity, and absolute regularity of the universe, and argued for continuous creation and the role of divine providence in maintaining the universe (Halevi 2002). This theology gave impetus to the work of physicists and astronomers such as al-Biruni (973–1048), who was involved with his famous contemporary Avicenna (980–1073), the spearhead of Aristotelian philosophy and science, in numerous debates, argued for the movement of the Earth, and was sympathetic to heliocentric cosmology. One of Biruni's most significant discoveries was the calculation of the diameter of the Earth, which was 16 kilometers less than modern calculations.

The Asharite theology supported and was inspired by atomist physics, which developed Epicurean views and argued that matter is made of small particles, which moved freely and randomly and coalesced to form different earthly and cosmic bodies. To the Asharites, this view allowed for the continuous creation and divine will holding the universe from disintegration. Al-Ghazali (1058–1111), who was a prominent Asharite theologian, wrote "The Incoherence of Philosophers," attacking peripatetic philosophers such as Avicenna and al-Farabi and arguing for limited interpretation of the Scripture.

Mongolian invasion, Sunni revivalism

Through the twelfth and thirteenth centuries, Crusaders attacked the Levant contributing to the fall of the Fatimid caliphate and the establishment of the Sunni revivalist Ayyubid states in Egypt and the Levant. In Andalusia and Northern Africa, the Almoravids and Almohads, which espoused the Sunni doctrine and Ashari theology, controlled the region and sponsored the exile of many scholars and philosophers, and the persecution and conversion of many non-Muslim scholars, many of whom fled to the East. The wars of the Reconquista forced many Jewish scholars to flee and threatened the intellectual environment of Andalusia. In the East, the Mongolian invasion in the thirteenth century put an end to the Abbasid Caliphate in Baghdad and destroyed the House of Wisdom.

The economic decline, the political instability, and the destruction of many centers of scientific inquiry affected the intellectual environment severely. However, scholars such as Averroes (1126–98) and Maimonides (d. 1204) continued to add to philosophical, scientific, and theological inquiry. Averroes argued against Al-Ghazali's "Incoherence" and theorized for the interdependence of philosophy, science, and theology. Maimonides' "Guide for the Perplexed" was widely read and studied in different scholarly circles throughout the Middle East.

The post-classical period

With the establishment of new, strong empires such as the Mamluk empire in Egypt and the Levant and the Illikhanid empire in Iraq, Persia and central Asia, another era of socio-economic prosperity and relative political stability began. The socio-economic and political development allowed for more codification of the rules governing different scientific practices and legal proceedings in search of more predictability and a more institutionalized intellectual environment. In the Mamluk empire, the appointment of four chief judges representing the four schools of law limited the space for free legal interpretation to serve the rapidly growing commercial and social structures. Also, the establishment of large state- or elite-sponsored madrasas gave certain theological views precedence over others and allowed for more uniformity of jurisprudence and theology. The huge hospitals run by the court physicians; the observatories run by court-appointed astronomers; building projects funded by the state and the elites; and the chairs for teaching medicine, philosophy, mathematics, and logic, sponsored in the different madrasas by the courts and political and military elites, led to more standardization and to the production and propagation of certain ideas at the expense of others (Rapoport 2003). However, none of these institutions acquired an irrevocable legitimacy or an unquestionable authority, and the debates on authority and legitimacy remained active throughout the medieval and early modern period.

The educational institutions and structures were required to produce efficient employees to fill the ranks of the bureaucracy, the judiciary, the hospitals, and the madrasas. Under this pressure, more people were educated, but towards more practical concerns of daily functioning of the empire and the society, and less attention was given to methodological debates or ground-breaking discoveries. The old debates continued, but to a lesser extent, and gave way to a more homogeneous intellectual environment focusing on direct and practical concerns in philosophy, theology, and law, and on application and practice in the sciences (Makdisi 1961).

Epidemics, famines, wars, and economic decline after the discovery of new trade routes changed the intellectual environment. The relation between science and religion changed as well, with scientific disciplines spearheaded by "crafts" such as medicine and astronomy, while more theoretical endeavors fell to the background; and with religious studies centered around the law and jurisprudence, with less interest in the bigger questions that had occupied the intellectual space before.

As the balance of power changed in Europe to the detriment of the Ottoman empire, political and financial elites in the Middle East became interested in sponsoring scholars and scientists from Europe, who traveled across the Ottoman empire in the seventeenth and eighteenth centuries, working as physicians, geographers, botanists, and instructors of the elite's children. Furthermore, the development of expatriate European communities in the Middle East, with their schools and missionaries, allowed for the movement of new European sciences to the Middle East. The new scientific practices, many of which had strong connections to some medieval theories, moved smoothly within the Middle Eastern intellectual environment, and there seemed to be little intellectual friction between the old and new scientific practices on the one hand, and the large religious educational and intellectual institutions on the other.

Debates in pre-modern scientific disciplines

Physics

Aristotelian physics was the most prominent and widely accepted view on matter and the material world. This theory relied on the presence of four main elements, which constituted the entire material universe in the sub-lunar sphere. Outside the sub-lunar sphere, celestial bodies were formed of a different, more superior element, and moved in perfect circles around the Earth. This theory, as espoused and developed by many Islamic philosophers, such as Avicenna and Averroes, implied the eternity of the universe and that the entire cosmological formation has existed since eternity and is infinite in nature (Averroes 2001).

Coming into contact with the religious notions of instantaneous creation, philosophers and scientists were inspired to develop the Aristotelian principles and the theological doctrines in different directions. Averroes, who was a judge, a physician, and a philosopher, argued that instantaneous creation contradicts the main tenets of Islamic creed, as it implies a change in the will of God, who is unchanging and permanent. Some Mutazilite theologians argued that instantaneous creation is necessary to ensure the uniqueness of the Deity and argued, still in line with Aristotelian theory, that this theory does not imply the eternity of the universe by necessity.

Al-Ghazali found the Epicurean atomist theory to provide a more plausible understanding of the world. According to the ancient and medieval atomist theory, all beings are made of infinitely small indivisible particles called atoms, which coalesce to form different beings. Muslim Epicurean physicists believed that these atoms have an inherent continuous random movement, which would not allow them to stay in form save for the will of God, who can keep bodies intact. This view was adopted by schools of occasionalist theology, which also claimed a continuous act of creation by God in the form of preserving bodies from inevitable disintegration. On the other hand, other Epicurean scientists, along with many theologians and religious scholars, such as Imam Fakhr al-Din al-Razi, argued for a single moment of instantaneous creation, where bodies were formed and where a continuous progressive process of disintegration begins, leading to the eventual end of the world.

Medicine

Unlike other fields, where multiple theories competed, medicine remained largely dependent on the humoral theory founded by Hippocrates and Galen, and its development at the hands of Rhazes, Avicenna, Maimonides, Ibn al-Nafis, and others.

The intellectual authority of this theory proposed a considerable challenge to a certain corpus of prophetic traditions, where Muhammad suggested some remedies and behaviors concerning plague, leprosy, and other diseases.

Ibn Qayyim al-Jawziyah, a famous scholar of prophetic traditions and of jurisprudence who believed in "non-interpretation," showed such confidence in the Galenic tradition that he presented compelling interpretations of "medical" prophetic traditions so that they correspond to the rules and conclusions of the humoral theory. He argued that Muhammad's "medical" commandments are not transcendent and are based on his specific experience in the deserts of Arabia. People of the cities, like Cairo and Damascus, should devise their own medicine along Galenic principles.

The religious perception of the purity of the soul inspired Ibn al-Nafis to question Galenic anatomy, which presumed that the right and left halves of the heart are connected through minute perforations. Starting from Galen's assumption that the soul lies in the left half of the heart, Ibn al-Nafis argued that polluted blood cannot be mixed with the soul and that a separate circulation must exist involving the right side of the heart to purify the blood in the lungs before it reaches the left side and mixes with the soul. This theory was the precursor for the discovery of the pulmonary circulation.

Astronomy

In the introduction of his "Incoherence," al-Ghazali addressed a certain disagreement around the phenomena of lunar and solar eclipses, which were explained by the regular movement of the Moon and the Sun around the Earth. In one of his famous traditions, Muhammad advised his followers to pray to God at the moment of eclipse. This tradition was seen as a sign of direct divine intervention leading to eclipses, which require or recommend prayers. Al-Ghazali accepted the astronomical explanation and warned against rejecting these findings. He refuted the conclusions based on Muhammad's tradition and considered the command for prayer unrelated to the nature of the event, arguing that Islam ordered people to pray at noon and at dusk; none of which is out of the ordinary or cannot be explained by astronomy.

The circular movement of the planets described by astronomers inspired a number of mystic and Sufi practices and doctrines, such as the Mavlavi Sufism, which viewed the eternal circular movement as a sign of perfection and full devotion to the Lord. Religious stories about prophets, who were chosen by God to travel to the heavens, such as Idris/Enoch, were reconsidered in view of the astronomical findings, and some religious scholars located the different sites of heaven in relation to the planetary positions. Also, planets, their movements and sizes inspired other similes, which compared particular planets with the most prominent angels.

On the other hand, the rejection of astrology by some religious scholars gave impetus to some astronomers' rejection of astrology. In fact, the religious and legal debate around the legitimacy and permissibility of astrology fueled and reflected a scientific debate in astronomy and physics, where some Aristotelian astronomers rejected astrology based on the different nature of bodies in the celestial and sub-lunar spheres, which renders any interactions between them illogical. Brethren of Purity, who espoused Pythagorean theological views, rejected Aristotelian physics relying on the validity of astrology, which implies that all bodies are made of the same elements.

As shown previously, the relations between different scientific and religious disciplines in the medieval and early modern period cannot be described along a strict division of science and religion. Instead, different religious and scientific practices engaged in common debates and inquiries, and provided mutual inspiration leading to changes in the entire intellectual sphere, reformulating their own identities, authorities, and roles in society.

From the nineteenth-century Nahda to the contemporary period[1]

The arrival of the French expedition on Egyptian shores represented one of the first and most violent assaults on the heart of the Ottoman Middle East, and was considered by many scholars to be a turning point in the modern history of the Middle East, signaling the beginning of a new era in the region. Peter Gran, among others, argued that the Ottoman Middle East witnessed a vibrant intellectual life during the eighteenth century, which preceded the changes happening in the aftermath of the French expedition. At the intellectual level, the French expedition led to two main effects, which cannot be fully understood through the prism of East–West encounters.

In a trial to legitimize the presence of French troops and to lessen public disdain, Bonaparte assembled a council of the most prominent sheikhs of the country to aid the French authorities in running the affairs of the region. This change in social and political role gave al-Azhar, the most prominent religious university in the region, a leading place and allowed its scholars to attain higher positions in the state apparatus, and to claim the respect and the deference of the political power due to their religious authority.

The second important effect of the French expedition was the attempt of the colonial power to impress the local population through a public display of technology, which had a major impact on the intellectual environment in the region, and would play a significant role in the perception of science in the Middle East.

The interactions between science and religion in the Middle East in the modern and contemporary periods can be traced through the following main stages.

The Nahda/awakening period (nineteenth century)

The Nahda signifies the period of rapid state-sponsored modernization in the Middle East, which took place variably throughout the nineteenth century. In Istanbul, long-standing imperial bureaucratic and technical elites were responsible for the introduction of European science, technology, and educational system without much contact with the standing religious elites, which were not an influential part of the imperial administration and played an increasingly marginalized role throughout the nineteenth century. In Cairo, on the other hand, the religious scholarly elite was the only educated elite to be trusted by the modernizing authorities. Aided by European residents of the region, these scholars, who graduated in al-Azhar, were responsible for founding the new educational system, and for the introduction of modern science and technology. Here the interactions between modern scientific and religious discourses were far more pronounced at the socio-political level (Findley 1980).

Rifa'ah Rafi' al-Tahtawi, who was a graduate of al-Azhar and appointed by Muhammad Ali to accompany the first mission of young cadets training in Paris, represents an interesting and pivotal position in this debate. Al-Tahtawi learned principles of mathematics, astronomy, and natural philosophy from a number of French professors and tutors, and engaged in translating a large number of books while in Paris. On his return, he led the translation of dozens more books, established a school of translators under the auspices of the ruler, and became the spearhead of an educational reform.

Al-Tahtawi insisted on linking modern science to the Islamic Middle Ages, highlighting the role played by Muslim scientists in the European Renaissance. In this manner, al-Tahtawi was presenting a genealogical identity for modern science, which enhances its connections to the Islamic heritage not from an intellectual point of view but from an identity perspective. In this sense, introducing modern sciences from Europe at the hands of European technicians and scientists was integrated in a historical tradition and was, in fact, a return to what is originally Islamic. Similarly, the translated text books of the new Egyptian technical schools, such as the schools of medicine and engineering, presented the process of modernization as a revival of Islamic sciences at the hands of enlightened rulers (Livingston 1996).

On the other hand, al-Tahtawi and his colleagues perceived/presented science not as an *episteme* but as a *techne* through highlighting the significance of technological achievements and improvements in daily life, regardless of the theoretical and paradigmatic traditions underlying these technological achievements. Science was perceived as a neutral technical practice, which was coincidentally attached to certain intellectual and social practices in Europe. While these practices contradicted contemporaneous religious views, technical knowledge was instrumental to a powerful nation and was viewed as perfectly separable from its ideological and theoretical underpinnings.

Early twentieth century and the popularization of science

During this period, the intellectual elite changed radically in its identity, training, and aptitude. The new elite was formed of graduates of European-style schools, missionary schools, as well as universities in the main European intellectual centers. This allowed for the appearance of many journals, magazines, and newspapers, which engaged in the popularization of sciences. Many of these publications addressed direct technical needs of their readerships, such as methods to manufacture glue, or to treat acne. Other magazines specialized in a particular kind of technical knowledge, such as the famous "mamlakat al-Nahal/The Kingdom of Bees," which presented the reader with scientific methods in apiculture (Elshakry 2008).

At the same time, *al-Azhar Magazine* (1929), along with other publications, featured the writings of a number of religious scholars and scientists of religious background, who insisted on the genealogical connection of modern science to the Islamic middle ages. Writings on the scientific interpretation of sacred texts gained popularity, where religious scholars argued that the Quran should be viewed as a book of nature as well as of religion, and that it contains, albeit in hidden and cryptic language, references to modern scientific facts, which prove the divine nature of the text.

The religious intellectual elites of the period encountered evolution, which constituted a scientific theory and a socio-political discourse, as Darwin and Huxley's writings were translated to Arabic. Religious authors argued that Darwinism was not based on scientific facts and that it was refuted by most scientists in Europe, and evolution was portrayed as a political ideology that was forced on science. In that sense, evolution was rejected by many religious scholars through emphasizing a particular perception of science and technology, only enhancing and solidifying the authority and legitimacy of science in society. Science and its technical products became an essential part of intellectual life, and debates on the origin of science and the compatibility of Western sciences with Islam gave place to questions about what is scientific and what is political (Atighetchi 2007).

The 1950s and 1960s and the nationalist projects

The middle decades of the twentieth century witnessed the rise of nationalist and pan-Arabist projects. With an agenda of national independence, nationalist projects espoused a second renaissance whereby the Arab center of the Middle East would use modern science to overcome the setbacks suffered during the Ottoman period. This approach led to massive increases in the number of college graduates and massive propaganda about the importance of modern science and technology in achieving the main national projects. At the same time, the rapidly decreasing margin of free press and the nationalization of many print houses dramatically reduced the number of journals and publications, which had formerly contributed to the popularization of science (Aishima and Salvatore 2009).

In 1961, Nasser added new scientific faculties to al-Azhar, where curricula of religious sciences were added to the curricula taught in similar faculties in other universities. This project emphasized the view of science as a technology, which is completely devoid of any ideological meaning or intellectual attachment, and is totally compatible with religious belief. Curricula of medicine, biology, and physics were stripped from evolution, taxonomy, and the Big Bang theory, which were deemed either non-scientific or unnecessary for the development of science as technical knowledge.

Throughout the 1950s, Sayyid Qutb, who would become an inspiration for many Islamist movements, argued in his exegesis, entitled "In the Shades of the Qur'an," for the necessity of perfecting the use of modern technology for the benefit of the nation, and assured that the Islamic spiritual life as described in the Qur'an is the guarantee for a balanced society, where science would truly blossom without the destructive influences of materialist politics, morality, and ideology. Qutb argued strongly against the scientific interpretation of the Qur'an, then not in vogue, because it strips the sacred text from its true meaning and puts it in danger by comparing it with ever-changing scientific production (Nettler 1994).

The 1980s and the rise of contemporary Islamist projects

The rise of Islamism in the 1980s and 1990s has been analyzed by many scholars, who present different theories explaining its reasons, mechanisms, and development. In the matter of science, this period did not present new ideas or conceptions as to the interactions of science and religion. Instead, it accentuated the previously described phenomena.

At the socio-intellectual level, this period allowed for a larger sphere of communication for different religious scholars and intellectuals, which benefited from a tolerant/supportive state policy, and led to the further spread of particular interpretations of religion and perceptions of science.

The technical dimension of science was emphasized along with stressing the importance of the identity of the practitioner, who was increasingly classified according to his/her religion and religiosity. The literature on scientific interpretation and on prophetic medicine spread widely and became a staple of popular culture, taking the form of prime-time TV shows and extensive publications. Medicine occupied the center of the science–religion interactions, owing to its direct and plausible utility and its engagement with the personal choice of the patient, where religiosity plays a significant role (Salvatore 2000, Ragab 2012).

At the same time, the importance of religious law, even if not applied by the state, but rather at individual level, increased dramatically. Religious authorities were sought to legalize and agree on different new technologies such as *in vitro* fertilization (IVF), organ transplantation, blood transfusion, cloning, stem-cell research, etc. This led to a further increase in the importance of medicine and biology in this debate, as most of these fatwas or legal opinions were related to medical and biological technology (Atighetchi 2007).

The new discourse relied mainly on two main notions: the benefit of the nation, and the preservation of religious morality. The benefit/*manfa'ah* of a particular technology was the main reason for its legality and acceptance, while its connection with, or facilitation of, the spread of "Western moral decadence" was the main reason for its refusal. In this context, organ transplantation was accepted by most scholars on the basis of its benefit for Muslims, while IVF was heavily criticized and viewed as a possible threat to tracing ancestry, before it was finally believed that its benefits outweighed its risks.

As above, the perception of science as a technical practice, unconnected to any intellectual structure, helped its rapid introduction and acceptance and shaped the debates around science and religion from the early nineteenth century. With this perception, intellectual society was able to produce a new scientific discourse, which is stripped of any controversy, and can even acquire an Islamic identity based on the religion of the practitioner. This perception gave science an uncontested legitimacy and promoted re-reading the religious texts in quest of interpretations that will accommodate modern technologies. With a rapidly developing communication space, this new sciento-religious discourse gained popularity and played a role in shaping the intellectual make-up of new scientists and practitioners of science, who became more dependent on the opinions of religious scholars, and played a role in enhancing the position of religious legal opinion in legitimizing modern technology.

Note

1 This section covers the Ottoman Middle East and its development to the contemporary period.

References

Aishima, H. and A. Salvatore (2009) "Doubt, Faith and Knowledge: The Reconfiguration of the Intellectual Field in Post-Nasserist Cairo," *Journal of the Royal Anthropological Institute* 15(1): 41–56.

Atighetchi, D. (2007) *Islamic Bioethics: Problems and Perspectives*, Dordrecht, the Netherlands: Springer.

Averroes (2001) *The Book of the Decisive Treatise Determining the Connection between the Law and Wisdom & Epistle Dedicatory*, Provo, UT: Brigham Young University Press.

Elshakry, M.S. (2008) "Knowledge in Motion: The Cultural Politics of Modern Science Translations in Arabic," *Isis* 99: 701–30.

Findley, C.V. (1980) *Bureaucratic Reform in the Ottoman Empire: The Sublime Porte, 1789–1922*, Princeton, NJ: Princeton University Press.

Halevi, L. (2002) "The Theologian's Doubt: Natural Philosophy and the Skeptical Games of Ghazali," *Journal of the History of Ideas* 63(1): 19–39.

Hourani, G.F. (1976) "Islamic and Non-Islamic Origins of Mu'tazilite Ethical Rationalism," *International Journal of Middle East Studies* 7(1): 59–87.

Livingston, J.W. (1996) "Western Science and Educational Reform in the Thought of Shaykh Rifaa al-Tahtawi," *International Journal of Middle East Studies* 28(4): 543–64.

Makdisi, G. (1961) "Muslim Institutions of Learning in Eleventh Century Baghdad," *Bulletin of the School of Oriental and African Studies* 24(1): 1–56.

Nettler, R. (1994) "A Modern Islamic Confession of Faith and Conception of Religion: Sayyid Qutb's Introduction to the Tafsir, fi zilal al-Quran," *British Journal of Middle Eastern Studies* 21(1): 102–14.

Ragab, A. (2012) "Resurrection, Reinterpretation and Reconstructions: Prophetic traditions and modern medicine in the Middle East," *Journal of the American Oriental Society*, 132 [forthcoming].

Rapoport, Y. (2003) "Legal Diversity in the Age of Taqlid: The Four Cheif Qadis under the Mamluks," *Islamic Law and Society* 10(2): 210–28.

Rosenthal, F. (1975) *The Classical Heritage in Islam*, Berkeley, CA: University of California Press.

Salvatore, A. (2000) "Social Differentiation, Moral Authority and Public Islam in Egypt: The Path of Mustafa Mahmud," *Anthropology Today* 16(2): 12–15.

Further reading

F. Rosenthal, *The Classical Heritage in Islam* (cited above) presents a collection of primary texts discussing the place of classical Greek heritage in medieval Islamic culture. The birth and development of the new theology and how it was affected by Greek philosophy and sciences was studied by George Hourani in several publications such as "Islamic and Non-Islamic Origins of Mu'tazilite Ethical Rationalism" (cited above).

Cosmological doctrines represented the most important interface between science and religion in the medieval period. Nasr's introduction to Islamic cosmology is a useful survey of the different schools: S.H. Nasr, *An Introduction to Islamic Cosmological Doctrine* (Albany, NY: SUNY Press, 1993).

The works of Elshakry and Livingston on the Nahda period are very useful: M.S. Elshakry, "Knowledge in Motion" and J.W. Livingston, "Western Science and Educational Reform in the thought of Shaykh Rifaa al-Tahtawi" (both cited above).

Finally, the changing relations between science and religion throughout the 1960s and 1970s are studied in H. Aishima and A. Salvatore, "Doubt, Faith and Knowledge" (cited above). The rise of Islamism in the 1980s and its effect on the relation between science and religion is studied in A. Salvatore, "Social Differentiation, Moral Authority and Public Islam in Egypt" and D. Atighetchi, *Islamic Bioethics* (both cited above).

6
CHRISTIANITY AND SCIENCE

Gary B. Ferngren

Introduction

For more than a century, the perceived relationship of Christianity to science has largely been informed by the thesis, expressed by John William Draper and Andrew Dickson White, that Christianity was hostile to science and had a long history of opposing scientific progress. The Draper–White thesis had its origins in the Enlightenment, with its view that the history of science was a series of conflicts between science and Christianity. This was believed especially true of the Roman Catholic Church, which was rooted in the church's alleged intolerance of new ideas that challenged religious orthodoxy. White's *A History of the Warfare of Science with Theology in Christendom* (1896) exercised much influence and has been repeatedly cited by both scientists and historians in support of the assertion that Christianity has throughout history hindered scientific progress. This view was always improbable, given the fact that many of the most distinguished scientific investigators, from the Scientific Revolution to the end of the nineteenth century, were practicing Christians. But by skillful manipulation of sources, White so convincingly argued his case that he is still regarded as an authority in spite of the fact that his work is replete with errors and misinterpretation. While the Draper–White thesis has frequently been challenged, it was only in the last three decades of the twentieth century that it was systematically examined by David Lindberg, Ronald Numbers, John Brooke, and other historians of science, who argued that the situation was much more complex. Indeed, John Brooke has suggested that the "conflict thesis" be replaced by a "complexity thesis" that takes into account the historical context of disputes between science and Christianity, which were characterized by a variety of attitudes and circumstances. "What we find," writes David Lindberg, "is an interaction exhibiting all of the variety and complexity with which we are familiar in other realms of human endeavor: conflict, compromise, understanding, misunderstanding, accommodation, dialogue, alienation, the making of common cause, and the going of separate ways" (Ferngren 2000: 266).

Before we examine the historical relations between Christianity and science, we must define terms. What we call *science* today did not exist in the ancient and medieval worlds; indeed, the term did not come into widespread use until the late nineteenth century. The study of nature was termed *natural philosophy*. It was one of three branches of philosophy (the other two were moral and metaphysical) that dealt with the physical sciences. To speak of "science" in the ancient and medieval worlds is to employ an anachronism. The term *Christianity* must also be defined properly. The Christian church has never been monolithic. Even in its earliest centuries, it experienced divisions and a wide variety of points of view. There has never been a general Christian attitude towards science. Neither theologians nor natural philosophers can be said to have had uniform views any more than Christians and scientists have today. In general, one can say that educated Christians of all periods, like educated persons of every faith, tended to accept the prevailing scientific views of their time. In this regard they did not usually differ from, say, educated pagans, Jews, or Muslims.

Early Christianity

Christianity began with its founder, Jesus of Nazareth (c. 4 BC–c. AD 30). It spread slowly at first throughout the eastern Mediterranean, then more rapidly in successive centuries, in spite of the fact that Christians were persecuted by the Roman authorities, until AD 313, when Christianity become a legal religion. It was in the second century AD that Christian intellectuals, such as Tertullian and Origen, whom we term Apologists, began the process of trying to harmonize Christian revelation with Graeco-Roman thought. Before their conversion, the Apologists had been educated in classical pagan (that is, non-Christian) schools in which the curriculum was philosophy. Classical philosophy held an ambiguous appeal for Christian intellectuals. On the one hand, they themselves had received their education in Greek and Roman culture and they were deeply influenced by it. On the other hand, classical philosophy was thoroughly pagan, and many of its beliefs seemed antithetical to those of Christianity. The assimilation of Greek science by early Christians was aided by their belief, taken over from Judaism, that God had revealed himself to human beings in two "books": in special revelation through the Bible and in general revelation through nature. The theme is found throughout the Old Testament, for example in Psalm 19, where the first half of the Psalm (vv. 1–6) describes how God reveals himself through nature, while in the second half (vv. 7–11) the writer describes God's revelation of himself in the written word of his law. The metaphor of God's two books encouraged Christians to value nature as reflecting God's glory and majesty.

The Apologists struggled to interpret Greek philosophy through the lens of Christian theology and to appropriate as much of it as they found compatible with their own faith. These church Fathers, as we call them, "hellenized" Christianity by incorporating Greek science and medicine into a coherent Christian world-view. In so doing, they created a pattern for the subsequent Christian assimilation of non-Christian learning in philosophy and science. It was a pattern that Western European Christians would follow again in the thirteenth century, when the writings of the philosopher Aristotle were translated into Latin and introduced into European universities. Medieval Christians asked whether Aristotle could be studied profitably and without danger to their faith. After some initial doubts, they decided that he could. The pattern has continued to the present time.

Augustine (354–430), the greatest Latin Father of the church, believed that the study of natural philosophy was legitimated when it served a higher purpose, such as helping to understand scripture or lending support to Christian theology. Augustine created a new role for natural philosophy, which assured it a place in the emerging Christian culture that was formulated in late classical antiquity. We call this approach the *handmaiden* role of natural philosophy. It was one that would endure throughout the Middle Ages and well into the modern period, and it created for natural philosophy an important niche in Christian studies.

The Middle Ages

With the collapse of the Western Roman Empire at the end of the fifth century, educational institutions were destroyed in the general collapse that accompanied the Germanic conquest of the West. Manuscripts and the learning that accompanied them were preserved only in monasteries. As literacy disappeared, only monks remained literate. Far from opposing the natural philosophy of antiquity, the monks treasured it. Little in the way of new scientific knowledge was accumulated; it was all that monasteries could do, in the deteriorating conditions of the time, to preserve what came down to them and to transmit it to future generations. It was the institutions of the church that kept alive any semblance of natural philosophy during the early Middle Ages (*c*. 500–*c*. 1000).

With the resumption of trade in the eleventh century, cities grew quickly in Western Europe, and along with them a revival of Roman civilization. Cathedral schools replaced monastic schools, and universities were founded in some sixty cities. At the same time, the works of Greek authors – especially of Aristotle, which had been preserved by the Arabs and the Byzantine Greeks in Constantinople – were translated into Latin and formed the curriculum of the new universities. Among the newly translated texts were Aristotle's treatises on natural philosophy. His works were recognized for their unique authority and importance in natural philosophy, and they immediately gained recognition at the University of Paris. But they raised problems because many of Aristotle's views were contrary to Christian belief. Aristotle taught, for example, that the soul is mortal; that the world was not created and is therefore eternal; and that God is an "unmoved mover," who does not even know that the world exists. His unacceptable theology led to controversies over his works, which were banned in 1210 and 1215, but which gained official recognition as required texts at Paris in 1255. Aristotle's scientific ideas were eventually harmonized with Christian theology by brilliant synthesizers such as Albert the Great and his pupil Thomas Aquinas, and he came to dominate European science and theology within a Christian context for some 400 years. The controversy over his works was partly an academic one, not merely an attempt by the church to restrict free thought. Medieval universities, which were supported by the church, were relatively tolerant in permitting philosophical speculation in cosmology and other areas of natural philosophy.

The Scientific Revolution

The Scientific Revolution can be said to have begun with the posthumous publication in 1543 of Nicolaus Copernicus' *On the Revolutions of the Heavenly Spheres* (*De revolutionibus orbium coelestium*), in which Copernicus espoused a heliocentric or Sun-centered model of the solar system. Since Ptolemy of Alexandria had refined the geocentric or Earth-centered model in the second century AD, it had been universally accepted in the West and was considered fully compatible with the biblical picture of the universe. Like most of those who made leading discoveries in astronomy and mechanics, Copernicus was a Christian. His theory was not widely accepted for several reasons. It contradicted biblical statements that seemed to imply a geocentric cosmology; and it offered no better explanation of the orbits of the planets than did the geocentric system, although mathematicians found the new theory more convenient. By 1600 there were probably no more than ten people in Europe who accepted the new theory, many of them rejecting it on scientific, rather than theological, grounds.

One man who did accept it was Galileo Galilei (1564–1642), a mathematician rather than a natural philosopher. As early as 1597, Galileo had come to accept the Copernican theory, but he did not publicly announce his views until 1613 owing to his fear of the Inquisition, which had been introduced into Italy to root out those of Protestant sympathies. His publication in 1615 of the *Letter to the Grand Duchess Christina* led to his appearance before the Inquisition. The issue was not so much the acceptance of a new theory of the universe as it was Galileo's attempts at biblical interpretation, which he, as a Catholic layman, had no right to engage in. In a series of meetings with the eminent Cardinal Bellarmine, Galileo was informed that the Church would accept the Copernican theory if it could be proven, but if it could not, scripture should be interpreted to teach that the Earth was the center of the universe. In 1616, Copernicus' *De revolutionibus* was ordered to be suppressed until it was corrected, and Galileo was prohibited from teaching or defending Copernicus' views until they could be demonstrated to be more than a hypothesis. Galileo maintained his silence until 1632, when he published a debate between imaginary proponents of the geocentric and heliocentric views in his *Dialogue on the Great World Systems*. Galileo was summoned to Rome, subjected to trial in 1633, and forced to recant his belief. He spent the remainder of his life living comfortably under house arrest until he died in 1642. While his trial and condemnation have often been cited as an example of the Catholic Church's hostility to science, the issues were much more complex. Fear of the Protestant Reformation, the subsequent rise of the Roman Inquisition to stamp out heresy, academic disputes between mathematicians and natural philosophers (the former thinking that they understood astronomy better than the latter), and papal politics provided the backdrop for Galileo's celebrated trial, and the ensuing controversy cannot be understood apart from its immediate historical context.

Galileo's championing of Copernicanism led to the widespread acceptance of heliocentrism by 1650, especially in Protestant (northern) Europe, where his books could be published without restriction, and over time in Catholic countries. Aristotelian mechanics had been closely intertwined with geocentrism, and the abandonment of the latter led to the search for an alternative model to replace Aristotelianism.

Philosophers found one in the theory of corpuscular materialism, which they borrowed from classical Epicureanism. It was a mechanical model, in which natural phenomena could be explained solely in terms of matter, and motion by the interaction of atoms. It seemed to fit an emerging picture of the both terrestrial and celestial mechanics as operating by physical laws that could be described mathematically. Several leading philosophers, such as René Descartes and Pierre Gassendi, devised mechanical philosophies in the seventeenth century, but they were careful to separate them from theology. The greatest synthesizer of the discoveries of the Scientific Revolution was Sir Isaac Newton (1642–1727). By his discovery of gravity, Newton brought into a single, coherent model the discoveries that had been made in both terrestrial and celestial mechanics by such astronomers and mathematicians as Galileo, Johannes Kepler, and Tycho Brahe. Contrary to Aristotle, who taught that the heavenly bodies behaved according to different laws than terrestrial objects, Newton found in gravity a universal principle that bound them together and allowed the whole of nature to be explained by uniform laws that could be described in mathematical terms. He described these laws in *The Mathematical Principles of Natural Philosophy* (*Principia Mathematica Philosophiae Naturalis* [1687]). It became the definitive synthesis of the discoveries that emerged from the Scientific Revolution and provided the foundation for classical mechanics.

The growing acceptance of the mechanical philosophy in the latter half of the seventeenth century led to the creation of *natural theology*, whose proponents argued that the existence and attributes of God could be derived from natural reason rather than special revelation. It became popular in the eighteenth century with both deists and rationalistically inclined Christians. The influence of Newton's mechanical picture of the world was taken to support the belief that the universe was an amazingly crafted machine that had been intricately designed by God. That belief was supported by the scientific discoveries that had been made possible by the invention of both telescope and microscope. With the microscope, one could see beautifully designed snowflakes, no two of which were alike. Exquisite butterflies' wings and spiders' webs provided an argument for the perfection of God's creation at the microcosmic level. Seeing the design of God in nature became a popular foundation for ideas of providence that were drawn not from the Bible but from nature by those who rejected or underplayed special revelation. The teleological argument, or argument from design, became the cornerstone of natural theology. It states that the universe as a whole reveals an adaptation to ends that is evidence of a conscious purpose or a creative intelligence: the idea that such an impressive universe points to the God who created it. God came to be described by deists as the divine craftsman, geometer, or architect. Deists advocated what they called *natural religion*, a religion that they argued was common to all humanity. They defined it as teaching the Fatherhood of God and the brotherhood of all men. God had placed the light of nature in every human heart, and no additional special revelation (as in the Bible) was necessary. God could be known through nature alone. Not all proponents of natural theology were deists; some were theists who reacted against the influence of Puritanism in England in the seventeenth century. These theists emphasized the rationality of the Christian faith rather than personal spirituality. The influence of natural theology supported a widespread belief that religion (both Christian and deist) and natural philosophy were in harmony. This belief lasted till the mid-nineteenth century.

Earth science

In the seventeenth and eighteenth centuries, natural philosophers tried to weave together geology and theology in what became known as *physico-theology*. They developed what were called *theories of the Earth* that harmonized biblical chronologies with physical science. Fossils were the most obvious physical evidence, and they were generally attributed to the biblical flood, or the Great Deluge, in what became known as diluvialism. The age of the Earth, which was computed by biblical genealogies, was thought to be no more than about 6000 years. By the late eighteenth century, some naturalists were coming to doubt that all or most of the fossil-bearing strata could be attributed to the Flood of Noah. They found that geological formations were too complex and some of the sedimentary strata too thick to have been the result of a single flood. The most influential geologist who proposed a non-diluvial theory of geologic history was Charles Lyell (1797–1875). Lyell did considerable field work on the European continent, examining extinct volcanoes in central France as well as Mount Etna, which was (and still is) an active volcano on the island of Sicily. He became convinced that changes in the Earth's surface had taken place over a long period and had preceded humankind. Lyell set forth his theory in a work entitled *Principles of Geology*, which he published in three volumes (1830–33). In it, he rejected diluvialism for what became known as *uniformitarianism*. He argued that geological processes took place slowly, by small-scale changes rather than great catastrophes, and over long periods of time. They did so according to uniform laws of nature that were the same in the ancient world as in the modern world. The implication was that the Earth was very old, much older than was suggested by biblical chronology. Lyell's view did not produce strong opposition from Christians. Although he was a deist, he refused to draw any theological implications from his theory, arguing that it was purely scientific. The result was that there was little active hostility to uniformitarianism in Britain, and the newly emerging breed of professional geologists, who took over the field after Lyell, abandoned the biblical Flood as an organizing idea in accounting for changes in the Earth's geologic history. It came to be widely interpreted as a world-wide event that left no permanent marks; later, many biblical scholars came to interpret it as a non-universal, local flood that had been confined to the Mesopotamian valley or the Middle East. Lyell's theory of uniformitarianism completely separated the geologic history of the Earth from biblical history. Christians could now take what used to be biblical chronology as applying only to human beings – specifically to the story of the redemption of the human race – and not to the age of the Earth.

Evolution

Aristotle's influence on *natural history*, the discipline that dealt with the study of living animals and plants, lasted until 1850. The idea that all species were fixed, that they didn't change, was basic to Aristotle's views of natural history. Charles Darwin (1809–82) had, like all naturalists, accepted the Aristotelian view as a young man. What changed his views were the personal observations he made as a member of a scientific expedition to South America aboard the *HMS Beagle* from 1831 to 1836. The ship made stops along the coast of South America, where Darwin collected specimens of plants and animals and made extensive notes on flora and fauna. He was especially impressed by the variety of species on the Galapagos Islands. He found striking differences not only between species on the islands and those on the mainland, but also among those on each island. Darwin's findings led him to reject the idea that species were specifically adapted to a particular locale. He came to the conclusion that environmental factors regulated the size of the population of all living things, and that only individuals most fitted to their environment would survive and pass on their characteristics to their offspring.

Theories of evolution, which sought to eliminate all forms of divine intervention in the development of animal or human life, had preceded Darwin. They originated in the Enlightenment and had come to be widely accepted by the mid-nineteenth century as part of the divine plan for creating life by non-supernatural means. The major contributions of Darwin to evolutionary theory were the ideas of *random variation* and *natural selection*. Darwin argued that there exists great variation among even closely related individuals. In any environment, some members of a species have combinations of traits that help them in the struggle for life. In the intense competition for existence, a slight variation may give an advantage to some individuals. Darwin argued that, over a long period, a reduction and eventual elimination of the less favorable variations will bring about a gradual transformation of a species. A species that adapts to its environment avoids extinction. Herbert Spencer called this process "the survival of the fittest." Darwin developed his ideas in his book *On the Origin of Species* (1859).

The reception of Darwin's ideas was mixed, and did not necessarily create a divide along religious and non-religious lines. Some leading scientists (such as Louis Agassiz and William Dawson) rejected his theory on scientific grounds, while some Christian clergymen (such as Charles Kingsley and Henry Drummond) enthusiastically accepted it, seeing no theological issues. Several leading Christians who were practicing scientists (such as Asa Gray and James McCosh) publicly accepted evolution. Within a decade after the publication of *Origins*, some form of evolutionary theory had gained the support of many scientists, though natural selection remained controversial. The publication of *The Descent of Man* (1871), in which Darwin provided a naturalistic explanation of morals by accounting for them by natural selection, proved far less acceptable to Christians and to many others who could not accept the philosophical materialism that his views implied.

Debate over the extent and implications of naturalistic evolution continued throughout the twentieth century. Social Darwinists adapted Darwin's theory to social and economic matters and argued that the principle of the survival of the fittest was suited, for example, to capitalism. Critics such as William Jennings Bryan believed that the materialistic implications of Darwin's theory had undercut the moral basis for society and had led to European imperialism and militarism, which were amply demonstrated in the First World War. The moral implications of a theory that had no place for spiritual values caused the Scopes Trial, which was held in Dayton, Tennessee in 1925, to attract much public interest. The trial polarized American opinion, but in spite of the legal victory of the anti-evolutionist side, the press portrayed the trial as a reactionary attempt by fundamentalists to hinder scientific progress. The moral issues that Bryan attempted to highlight were overwhelmed by the perception that he represented a nativist anti-intellectualism. Christian anti-evolutionism (which generally took the form of biblical catastrophism or flood geology) remained an intellectual backwater until the 1960s, when it emerged as a popular movement in conservative Christian circles under the name "scientific creationism," with the publication of *The Genesis Flood* by John C. Whitcomb and Henry M. Morris (1961). It was not until the 1940s that the modern synthesis of genetics and natural selection provided a theory that accounted for biological evolution by random variation and genetic mutation.

Physics and cosmology

The Newtonian synthesis that was created by the publication of Newton's *Principia* remained essentially unchanged for more than two centuries. Beginning in about 1895, changes came quickly that transformed physics. The first were Albert Einstein's theories of special (1905) and general (1915) relativity. Perhaps even more challenging to the dominant mechanical view of classical physics was the Heisenberg uncertainty principle, according to which both the position and momentum of a sub-atomic particle could not be perfectly known. According to this principle, which is basic to quantum mechanics, motion is not deterministic, as in classical mechanics, but probabilistic. Albert Einstein never accepted it, asserting that "God doesn't play dice with the universe." Others argued that it was no longer possible to hold to traditional deterministic views of matter.

If discoveries in physics (and the debates they engendered) seemed difficult for laypersons to understand, those in cosmology seemed more straightforward and had greater theological implications. One such theory in cosmology was Georges Lemaître's Big Bang theory. Lemaître was a Belgian abbot and physicist who, in the 1930s, proposed the theory that the universe had begun as a "primeval atom" of extremely dense matter that had exploded in the long distant past. George Gamow and other researchers worked out the implications of the theory between 1946 and 1953. The British astronomer Fred Hoyle proposed an alternative, the steady state theory, that the universe is eternal and that matter is continuously being created in space. By the mid-1970s, subsequent research had confirmed the Big Bang theory and largely eliminated the steady state theory, although it and several alternatives continued to be maintained by a minority of cosmologists. Unlike biology, in which undirected evolution was often claimed to support philosophical materialism, Big Bang cosmology was said by several writers (such as Paul Davies and Frank Tipler) to argue for the existence of a transcendent creator, since the universe had a definite beginning and therefore must have a creator.

Another theory of cosmology that evoked much debate was the anthropic principle, which asserted that the universe seems so finely tuned that it is unlikely that human beings were merely an accident of undirected cosmic evolution. The theory holds that if several physical features of the universe had been very slightly different at its earliest moments, no human life could have arisen. A universe that was designed to produce intelligent life requires a designer. Hence cosmic evolution is teleological and the inhabited universe is anthropocentric. It is not surprising that the religious implications of the anthropic principle (which not all its exponents accept) have been controversial, since it resurrects themes that were thought to have been laid to rest long ago, such as design in nature and a divine creation. It is not surprising that recent theories of cosmology have been much discussed for their seeming to lend credence to Christian claims that the universe was created by God.

Conclusion

The "conflict of science and Christianity" has been a familiar theme in the literature since the publication in 1896 of Andrew Dickson White's *History of the Warfare of Science with Theology in Christendom*. Much ink has been spilled in citing familiar examples of alleged conflict, from the condemnation of Galileo to the Scopes Trial. Yet a dispassionate survey of the evidence suggests that a more nuanced understanding is required. Christianity has drawn heavily on biblical texts that made it receptive to the study of nature. The Old Testament theme of nature pointing to its creator by inspiring awe and wonder at his works led to the Christian view of God's two books: general revelation, in which God revealed himself to all humankind; and special revelation, which was found in the Jewish and Christian scriptures. The pursuit of natural science has traditionally been justified in Christian thought because it was believed to lead to a greater appreciation of God's handiwork and therefore to point humans to consider his ways. At the same time, there have been those Christians, some of them anti-intellectual, but many of them sincere and learned scholars, who have maintained that certain discoveries in science undermined revealed theology. The issue has rarely been whether science is dangerous to Christian belief; rather it has been focused on how one should relate science to scripture or, to put it in theological terms, how one should harmonize general and special revelation. The rejection of new discoveries in science that seemed to pose a threat to Christian belief – as in the reception of Aristotelean natural philosophy, or heliocentric cosmology, or Darwinian evolution – generally resulted, after a period of intense controversy, in Christian acceptance of the new ideas and the theological accommodation that was necessary to ingest the new discoveries. In a sense, the process resembled that of the scientific establishment. New scientific theories are not accepted by the scientific community without intense debate or even initial rejection. In part, the shift that required Christians to adapt to new thinking after every "scientific revolution" was the result of their having tied theology so closely to an established scientific model that Christians had come to think of it as an essential component of their theology, as was the case in the geocentric model of the universe.

But, in history, Christian theology and science have probably more often been in relative harmony or in mutual coexistence than they have been in conflict. This was certainly the case after the church made its peace with Aristotle's works after 1255, and during the eighteenth and early nineteenth centuries, when natural philosophy was intellectually fashionable. While the scientific enterprise today is generally conducted on naturalistic assumptions (either methodological or metaphysical), beginning in the last decade of the twentieth century there emerged a growing interest in the relationship of science to religion, which suggests the belief that, in a complementary way, both contribute to our understanding of the universe and our lives within it.

References

Brooke, John Hedley (1991) *Science and Religion: Some Historical Perspectives*, Cambridge: Cambridge University Press.

Copernicus, Nicolaus (1939 [1543]) *On the Revolutions of the Heavenly Spheres*, Charles Glenn Wallis (trans.), Great Books of the Western World Vol. 16, Chicago, IL: Encyclopedia Britannica, 499–838.

Darwin, Charles (1952 [1859, 1871]) *On the Origin of Species by Means of Natural Selection* and *The Descent of Man and Selection in Relation to Sex*, Great Books of the Western World Vol. 49, Chicago, IL: Encyclopedia Britannica.

Draper, John William (1928 [1874]) *History of the Conflict Between Religion and Science*, New York: Appleton.

Ferngren, Gary B. (ed.) (2000) *The History of Science and Religion in the Western Tradition: An Encyclopedia* (New York: Garland).

Galilei, Galileo (1989 [1615]) "Galileo's Letter to the Grand Duchess Christina," in *The Galileo Affair: A Documentary History*, Maurice A. Finocchiaro (ed. and trans.), Berkeley, CA: University of California Press, 87–118.

——(1953 [1632]) *Dialogue on the Great World Systems*, Thomas Salusbury (trans.), revised, annotated, and with an introduction by Giorgio de Santillana, Chicago, IL: University of Chicago Press.

Lindberg, David C. and Numbers, Ronald L. (eds) (1986) *God and Nature: Historical Essays on the Encounter Between Christianity and Science*, Berkeley, CA, University of California Press.

Lyell, Charles (1990–91 [1830–33]) *Principles of Geology*, three volumes, Chicago, IL: University of Chicago Press.

Newton, Isaac (1934 [1726]) *Mathematical Principles of Natural Philosophy*, 3rd edn, Andrew Motte (trans.), Great Books of the Western World Vol. 49, Chicago, IL: Encyclopedia Britannica, 1–372.

Whitcomb, John C., Jr., and Henry M. Morris (1961) *The Genesis Flood: The Biblical Flood and its Scientific Implications*, Philadelphia, PA: Presbyterian and Reformed Publishing Co.

White, Andrew Dickson (1896) *A History of the Warfare of Science with Theology in Christendom*, New York: Appleton.

Further reading

The History of Science and Religion in the Western Tradition, edited by Gary B. Ferngren (cited above), provides a comprehensive survey of the historical relationship of science with the Western religious traditions (most prominently Christianity) in 103 articles written by experts in their field. Ian G. Barbour introduces major themes in his *Religion and Science:*

Historical and Contemporary Issues (San Francisco, CA: HarperSanFrancisco, 1997). David C. Lindberg and Ronald L. Numbers (eds.), *When Science and Christianity Meet* (Chicago and London: University of Chicago Press, 2003), focus on twelve "encounters" at the intersection of science and Christian theology. In *Science and Religion: Some Historical Perspectives* (cited above), John Hedley Brooke argues for a more nuanced "complexity thesis" in place of the familiar conflict thesis in issues of science and religion. See also John Brooke and Geoffrey Cantor, *Reconstructing Nature: The Engagement of Science and Religion* (Edinburgh: T& T Clark, 1998). On the early Christians' appropriation of secular medicine, see Gary B. Ferngren, *Medicine and Health Care in Early Christianity* (Baltimore, MD: Johns Hopkins University Press, 2009).

On Galileo, see Annibale Fantoli, *Galileo: For Copernicanism and for the Church*, George V. Coyne, S.J. (trans.) (Vatican City: Vatican Observatory, 1994); and an important study by Mario Biagioli, *Galileo Courtier: The Practice of Science in the Culture of Absolutism* (Chicago, IL: University of Chicago Press, 1993). Peter Harrison explores Protestant influences on science during the Scientific Revolution in *The Bible, Protestantism, and the Rise of Natural Science* (Cambridge and New York: Cambridge University Press, 1998). The theological implications of Darwin's ideas are explored in John Durant (ed.), *Darwinism and Divinity: Essays on Evolution and Religious Belief* (Oxford and New York: Blackwell, 1985). A pathbreaking study of the Protestant reception of Darwinism is James R. Moore, *The Post Darwinian Controversies: A Study of the Protestant Struggle to Come to Terms with Darwin in Great Britain and America, 1870–1900* (Cambridge: Cambridge University Press, 1979). A revisionist study of the Scopes Trial is Edward J. Larson's *Summer for the Gods: The Scopes Trial and America's Continuing Debate Over Science and Religion* (Cambridge, MA: Harvard University Press, 1997). See also Ronald L. Numbers, *The Creationists: The Evolution of Scientific Creationism* (New York: Knopf, 1992) and *Darwinism Comes to America* (Cambridge: Harvard University Press, 1998). On modern physics and theological issues, see R. J. Russell, W. Stoeger, and George Coyne (eds), *Physics, Philosophy, and Theology: A Common Quest for Understanding* (Vatican City: Vatican Observatory, 1988). For a comprehensive summary of cosmologies and their philosophical and theological underpinnings, see Stanley L. Jaki, *Science and Creation: From Eternal Cycles to an Oscillating Universe* (Edinburgh: Scottish Academic Press, 1974). On the much debated anthropic principle, see John D. Barrow and Frank J. Tipler, *The Anthropic Cosmological Principle* (Oxford and New York: Clarendon Press, 1986).

7
FEMINISM, RELIGION, AND SCIENCE

J. Jeanine Thweatt-Bates

In addressing, even briefly, the intersection of three such contested terms, attention to definitions is a necessity. For this essay, I write from my specific location in the religion and science dialogue within Christian theology, asking the question, how has feminism in its various forms intersected with and contributed to this ongoing dialogue? By the phrase "the religion and science dialogue" I refer to the ongoing discussion within Christian theology specifically, which focuses on the question of how theology and the sciences are, and should be, related as forms of human knowledge.

While keeping in mind that feminism, as a movement, is no more singular than "religion" or "science," I will take pastoral theologian Pamela Cooper-White's general definition as a starting point: "Feminism means taking seriously the call for social, economic and political parity, and equal rights and responsibilities, of women with men, and looking unflinchingly at the painful realities and the negative impact on both men and women, of *patriarchalism* (literally, rule of the fathers), both historically (especially in Christian theology as it pertains to the history of the church) and in contemporary societies" (Cooper-White 2008: 365).

This attention to the need for equality and the injustices of both past and present inequalities takes many forms, leading Cooper-White to inventory the various forms of feminism: radical feminism, grounded in Marxist–feminist ideals and essentially revolutionary; liberal feminism, grounded in Enlightenment values and emphasizing the goal of equal access to existing structures of social power; essentialist feminism, grounded in an ontology of essential difference between the genders and valorizing the feminine; the multiplicity of feminisms emerging in the 1980s and beyond, such as Womanist, *mujerista*, and "two-thirds world" feminisms, emphasizing the need for recognition of multiple perspectives and contexts within feminism; and more recently, postmodern and postcolonial feminisms, which share a concern to critique and deconstruct universal truth claims and dominant theoretical and historical discourses (Cooper-White 2008: 19–22). The multiplicity of feminist critiques and concerns, as outlined here, serves as a reminder that not all forms of feminism will be concerned with the religion and science dialogue or contribute to it in a univocal fashion.

In general, the religion and science dialogue within Christian theology has intersected with feminism in two major areas, one methodological and one topical: philosophy of science and epistemology, and feminist ecotheology. Many religion and science scholars rely on a philosophy of knowledge that insists upon contextualization, situatedness, and the importance of hermeneutics in order to engage in interdisciplinary dialogue with the sciences on equal epistemological footing; thus, even when explicitly feminist concerns are absent from the religion and science discussion, feminist contributions to epistemology and philosophy of science have enabled and framed the religion and science dialogue. In ecotheology, feminist theologians' alternative models of God and doctrines of creation intersect with environmental ethics, and therefore religion and science.

However, generally speaking, and despite these two areas of contribution and overlap, the religion and science dialogue within Christian theology often overlooks topics of explicit feminist concern, with ecotheology being the major exception. One reason for this lack of direct engagement may be the broad theoretical focus of much of the religion and science dialogue to date, for example, a thematic focus on "the human" within which the category of gender largely disappears. This suggests a need for further and more explicit engagement of feminism(s) within the religion and science dialogue, from both a philosophical and a theological perspective.

Background

There can be little debate that, historically, women have been largely excluded from the institutional power structures of both the Christian religion and the sciences; to begin, it is worth briefly exploring the reasons for this parallel historical marginalization of women. These are not particularly difficult to trace; Greek philosophical views of women typically held them to be naturally inferior to men, and the influence of Greek philosophy on both Christianity and natural philosophy in the West cannot be overestimated. In particular, the synthesis of Aristotelianism and Christian theology by Thomas Aquinas solidified the view of women as naturally inferior as not only a conviction of natural philosophy, but of Christian doctrine as well (Miles and Henry 2002).

The association of rationality with masculinity and of passion with femininity is the obvious point from which the exclusion of women arises in the spheres of both science and religion. Seen as inherently incapable of rationality, women were the entry point for sin into the world through Eve's inability to resist passion and temptation; seen as incapable of rationality, women were, by definition, uneducable. These gender associations (masculine/rational, feminine/passion) persisted, in various permutations, throughout the seventeenth, eighteenth, and nineteenth centuries, articulated in religious, philosophical, and scientific explanations of male and female character. Sara Miles and John Henry comment, "In spite of various changes in intellectual outlook from the Greeks, to the scientific revolution, through the Enlightenment, and on to the establishment of evolutionary biology and the major scientific achievements of the twentieth century, the alleged incapacity of women for public life and high achievement remained so persistent as to be scarcely credible" (Miles and Henry 2002: 367).

Even while philosophers such as Immanuel Kant began to seek ways to articulate religion and morality in strictly rational terms, at the same time other Enlightenment thinkers increasingly came to view religious faith as non-rational belief, leading to the "feminization" of religion (*ibid.*: 365). The feminization of religion led to a shift from earlier characterizations of women as inherently morally deficient (as an extension of being rationally deficient) to an alternative view of women as naturally morally superior; however, this superiority was seen as an extension of maternal passions; female leadership, while effective in parachurch organizations, still functioned within a system of ultimate institutional (male) religious authority (*ibid.*). This "feminization" of religion as non-rational belief subsequently prompted various responses in defense of religion: While some continued to argue apologetically on behalf of the rationality of religion, others accepted the private, individual nature of religious belief and sentiment.

Epistemology and philosophy of science

This association of masculinity, rationality, and science, and the corresponding "feminization" of religious belief, impinges directly on current religion and science dialogue. One of the initial burdens of interdisciplinary engagement between religion and science is the necessity of critiquing this particular strand of Enlightenment philosophy: If religious belief is by definition irrational (that is, "feminized"), then dialogue between religion and science is pointless – indeed, impossible. Thus one obvious point of contact between feminism, religion, and science lies in the contestation of the meaning of "rationality," and its historically exclusive association with masculinity and science.

Taking up the defense of religious belief and practice as a rational, rather than irrational, endeavor has therefore been one of the primary preoccupations of religion and science dialogue within Christian theology. Discussions of philosophy of science in the religion and science context often begin with a critique of Enlightenment foundationalism, and sketch a trajectory through the epistemological proposals of Karl Popper and Thomas Kuhn into recent social epistemological proposals that define scientific knowledge as the collaborative product of specific communities and contexts (Popper 1956; Kuhn 1970; Barbour 1990: 106–36). Contextualizing scientific knowledge in this way dismantles, to a large degree, the inherited "scientism" of the Enlightenment, which privileges scientific, empirical knowledge as the sole paradigmatic form of human rationality.

J. Wentzel van Huyssteen's postfoundationalism, for example, reframes human rationality as operative in all the domains of human living, as an evolutionarily adaptive mechanism for coping with the world, and therefore inclusive of specific reasoning strategies and disciplinary domains while not being limited to any one of them (van Huyssteen 1999). By redefining human rationality in this way, van Huyssteen validates the rationality of the sciences while simultaneously arguing that scientific reasoning is but one of many reasoning strategies. This, of course, counters the Enlightenment presumption of the irrationality of religious faith, re-opening the possibility of viewing religious belief and theological discourse as rational.

Specifically, this means negotiating the twin epistemological dangers of objectivism and relativism (in van Huyssteen's terminology entailed by foundationalism and non-foundationalism, respectively). Van Huyssteen's postfoundationalism splits the difference between these undesirable alternatives by recognizing the plurality and specificity of epistemic communities and forms of rationality, while positing an inclusive notion of "shared resources of rationality," which enables communication across different academic disciplines and specific epistemic communities.

This general reframing of rationality for the purposes of allowing dialogue between theology and the sciences does, as Ian Barbour notes in the landmark *Religion in an Age of Science*, incorporate, or at least echo, feminist critiques as part of the epistemological reconsideration of scientific objectivity (Barbour 1990: 77–79). In a section entitled "Objectivity and Relativism," Barbour treats feminist critiques as a particular form of epistemological social constructivism, focused on gender. By articulating the persistent but often tacit association of masculinity, rationality, and the sciences, feminist philosophers of science also arrive at the necessity of reframing objectivity and redefining human rationality beyond the narrow confines of the Enlightenment.

Evelyn Fox Keller's (1978) article "Gender and Science" opened the door to consideration of gender within scientific practices and institutions, an area of critique that has subsequently focused on three major topics: the scientific study of women, the role of women within the sciences, and the gendered nature of scientific epistemology. Historical studies seek not simply to demonstrate the historical exclusion of women from the sciences, but also to unearth the previously unacknowledged contributions of women within the sciences, as well as charting the ways in which femininity and female bodies have been defined scientifically. Philosophical critiques seek to articulate the connection between masculinity, notions of objectivity, and scientific practices, identified first by Keller, and construct alternative epistemological proposals for scientific practice.

The epistemological critique that science itself has been historically gendered masculine has taken multiple forms within feminism, and goes beyond simply noting the historical exclusion of female practitioners. Carolyn Merchant argues in *The Death of Nature* that Francis Bacon, the "father of modern science," extensively employed gendered metaphors, viewing nature not simply as female but as a wild and uncontrolled female to be subdued and controlled. In the fragment known as "The Masculine Birth of Time," Bacon writes, "I am come in very truth leading to you Nature with all her children to bind her to your service and make her your slave […] to stretch the deplorably narrow limits of man's dominion over the universe to their promised bounds" (Bacon 1964 [1653]: 62). These gendered metaphors, embedded within the initial articulation of scientific method and philosophy, continue to shape assumptions regarding appropriate methods and purposes of scientific inquiry.

In addition to critiquing the gendering of science at this deep conceptual level, feminists critique the role that gender biases play in the selection of problems for research, the formulation of scientific theories, and the interpretation of data. Both Donna Haraway and Sarah Blaffer Hrdy have argued that research practices within the field of primatology, for example, have been formulated in ways that reflect gender bias on multiple levels, in over-emphasizing male aggression and dominance and overlooking female social roles within primate groups, as well as privileging particular methods of study over others (Haraway 1989; Jackelén 2003: 218). Without explicit attention to the ways in which scientific knowledge is gendered, scientific objectivity becomes identical with masculinity. Thus redefining scientific objectivity means not only acknowledging the historical gendering of notions of scientific objectivity, but also constructing alternatives that avoid perpetuating this mistake. Here, proposals such as Sandra Harding's "strong objectivity," Helen Longino's "contextual empiricism," and Donna Haraway's "situated knowledges" attempt to retain a modified form of objectivity while acknowledging the historical, social, contextual, and constructed nature of human knowledge.

Thus one epistemological challenge for feminists, parallel to the problem for theologians seeking dialogue with the sciences, is how to reframe notions of objectivity without lapsing into incommensurability and relativism. For theologians, the issue at stake is the rational character of religious belief; for feminists, the issue is the normativity of the feminist critique itself. Donna Haraway writes, "we would like to think our appeals to real worlds are more than a desperate lurch away from cynicism and an act of faith like any other cult's," concluding, "the further I get with the description of the radical social constructionist programme and a particular version of postmodernism, coupled to the acid tools of critical discourse in the human sciences, the more nervous I get"(Haraway 1991). The usefulness of these feminist critiques and proposals for alternative scientific epistemologies for religion and science dialogue lies in their negotiation of this simultaneously epistemological and ethical problem; as Christian theologians seek to address this same issue, feminist epistemologies of science serve as models and conversation partners (Pederson 1995).

Ecotheology

Just as feminist philosophers of science wrestle with the question of whether science is inherently masculine, in a somewhat parallel development within Christian theology, feminist theologians have wrestled with the question of whether the Christian religion is inherently patriarchal. While some have concluded that this is so, making it impossible to be both feminist and Christian, others have argued that patriarchalism is a historical distortion which can be corrected through a critical appropriation of Christian tradition. Working from within the Christian theological tradition, Rosemary Radford Ruether, Sallie McFague, and others have identified one important distortion in the way that models of God and corresponding notions of creation and stewardship have been articulated. Feminist ecotheology, then, is a topical rather than methodological overlap between feminism and the religion and science dialogue, and it enters the dialogue by way of theology rather than philosophy.

This is not to say, however, that ecofeminist concerns are unconnected to the feminist epistemological critique of the sciences outlined above; on the contrary, ecofeminism is rooted in the critique of the coding of scientific reasoning as masculine, and nature, its epistemological object, as feminine. The explicit articulation of control and domination as the goals of scientific inquiry, coupled with the gendering of nature as feminine, leads to "the domination of nature in both the metaphors of scientific theory and in candidates for scientific research, with devastating implications for nature" (Clifford 1992: 74). This becomes not simply an epistemological critique, but an ethical one as well.

This critique, which sees science not simply as gendered masculine, but as actually misogynistic, resulting in views of a feminine-gendered nature as passive resource to be exploited or unruly object to be dominated, overlaps with the concerns of feminist theologians within the Christian tradition regarding the doctrine of creation, the construction of models of God as Creator, and resulting interpretations of the proper relationship between human beings and creation. Re-examination of the Genesis narratives of creation critique the assumption of humanity's divinely sanctioned status as rulers and exploiters of nature, often focusing on competing interpretations of the *imago dei* and the ontological separation of humanity from the rest of God's creation. Models of God that emphasize immanence over transcendence lead to doctrines of theological anthropology that emphasize kinship and embeddedness within God's cosmic creation, which in turn lead away from exploitative attitudes toward nature to an ethic of care of God's creation.

These themes are prominent within the religion and science context, as they explicate the theological and ethical dimensions of the notion of humanity's embeddedness within the natural world. Insofar as "ecological considerations are an aspect of the world that science describes, [they] form an important part of the data for a critical-realist theology which takes science seriously"(Southgate *et al.* 1999: 204). For theologians within the religion and science dialogue, the notion of human embeddedness within the natural world is a lesson of evolutionary biology and its related disciplines that must be taken seriously, in all of its hermeneutical, theological, and ethical implications. These implications reach further than, but include, the ecotheological, and thus overlap with and incorporate the work of feminist theologians such as Ruether and McFague. Peacocke, Southgate *et al.*, and Barbour all interact with and constructively critique Sallie McFague's theological proposal of the world as God's body (Barbour 1990: 123–24, 320–21; Peacocke 1993: 167–68; Southgate *et al.* 1999: 214–16).

Opportunities for further engagement

In deconstructing Enlightenment notions of objectivism while seeking to retain a modified objectivity, and in challenging and expanding narrow definitions of human rationality that privilege scientific over other forms of knowledge, feminist philosophers of science, even when not explicitly invoked, have framed and contributed to this necessary epistemological prolegomenon in the religion and science dialogue. Even so, while the social dimensions of scientific epistemology have been integrated into the religion and science dialogue, the feminist critique of the gendered nature of scientific knowledge, practices, and institutions has not necessarily been fully appreciated. Antje Jackelén identifies feminism(s) as one of three challenges for the current dialogue between Christian theology and the sciences, indicating that, despite the specific contributions of feminist philosophy of science and feminist ecotheology to the dialogue, attention to explicitly feminist concerns within it have been lacking. Specifically, Jackelén names three areas in need of further attention: issues of ethics and politics involving women, men, and children; issues of exclusion and inclusion of women and minorities; and epistemological issues regarding how gender categories and biases inform research agendas and interpretation of data (Jackelén 2003). Interestingly, the items on Jackelén's list all hit upon themes within feminist critiques of science and epistemology, suggesting that while feminist philosophies of science have not been entirely absent from the religion and science dialogue, they have not been fully present either.

Gender categories and biases exist within the Christian theological tradition as well as within the sciences, of course, and so Jackelén's third item may be taken to apply not simply to the sciences, but to the religion and science dialogue within Christian theology itself. Much of the current religion and science dialogue has been focused on broad existential concerns and philosophical questions, such as questions of cosmological origin and teleology, or questions of human origin and purpose (Ward 2008). With this broad focus, the operative category becomes "the human," in a universal categorical sense within which gender disappears, even when the explicit project is to integrate into our theological constructs the empirical knowledge of human bodies and minds that the various sciences make available. Arthur Peacocke, for instance, writes, "we are chiefly concerned with what the sciences can tell us about human *being*, about what human beings *are*, what the theological textbooks have traditionally called 'the doctrine of man' – the distinctive nature of humanity, the *humanum*" (Peacocke 1993: 213). Similarly, Ian Barbour's quest to construct a scientifically informed theological anthropology aims at a definition of universal human nature that, despite its careful consideration of embodiment, proceeds without reference to gender (Barbour 2002: 71–100). Here, the traditional theological focus on "the human" and the sciences' historical exclusion of gender as an interesting and meaningful topic or category collude in the disappearance of gender from the religion and science discussion of "the human."

Thus one obvious locus for further engagement of feminism within religion and science dialogue is that of specifically gendered and multiple human embodiments. Moving beyond a notion of a presumed normative human embodiment, often *de facto* male, which has heretofore framed philosophical, ethical, and theological considerations of "the human," Donna Haraway's work on "cyborg" hybridity emphasizes the need for close empirical attention to the way in which human embodiments often defy our pre-prepared ontological categories. In a similar vein, recent critiques of feminist theology, articulated in disability theologies (as in Nancy Eiesland) and queer theologies (as in Marcella Althaus-Reid), underscore the significance of specific embodiments in the practice of theology. Here, gender becomes one of several ways in which human embodiments may differ; gender therefore does not disappear into a universalized category of the human, nor does it appear as an abstract category in the strictly dichotomous opposition of masculine and feminine. The strategy for subverting this problematic dichotomy is not simply constructing an ever-elusive *via media*, but pluralizing the options of normative human embodiments such that the dichotomy itself disappears within that plurality.

The challenge this offers to the religion and science dialogue is to take these multiplicities of the human into account within the syntheses of religious and scientific thought on theological anthropology, rather than working at a level of abstraction that presumes a universality that may indeed simply cover over important differences, including gender. The notion of the "posthuman," as articulated within Haraway's work on cyborgs and companion species, is one means introducing the notion of multiplicity of human embodiments within the religion and science discussion. Discussions of the posthuman intersect with other, already active topics within religion and science, such as ecotheology (in considering the ontological and ethical relationship of humans and other animals); bioethics and technology (in exploring the theological and ethical implications of specific technologies); and neuroscience and psychology (in considering the implications of notions of the multiple self), and thus the posthuman offers a promising strategy for encouraging a greater specificity across many diverse religion and science conversations in Christian theology.

Such specificity is important, not simply as a corrective to theoretical or systematic theological formulations within religion and science, but in order to attend faithfully to the ethical and political dimensions of the religion and science dialogue as well. As Ann Pederson notes, the way in which feminists such as Haraway and Harding have connected epistemology and ethics constitutes one concrete contribution to the religion and science dialogue; the issue is not simply knowledge as such, but whose knowledge counts, and how that knowledge is put to use (Pederson 1995). Here, Jackelén's contention that "raising issues of ethics and politics" constitutes the first challenge that feminism offers the religion and science dialogue comes into play; not only as a challenge simply to consider specific political and ethical issues, but to consider them in ways that take into account the political, economic and social dimensions of scientific knowledge and practice, and the multiple perspectives and locations of the men, women, and children potentially affected by such issues.

Finally, articulating the painful realities of the exclusion of women from both religious and scientific structures of social power, both historical and current, is an ongoing and indeed double challenge to the religion and science dialogue within Christian theology. As I come from a tradition that stubbornly refuses not only to ordain women, but to welcome female voices in public worship, the intersection of religion and science on the exclusion of women from structures of institutional authority and power is a personal one. It is obvious, from this vantage point, that particular theologies intersect with particular forms of social knowledge in a way that reinforces the *status quo*; yet it is equally obvious, from this vantage point, that one of the best ways of challenging these unjust practices is therefore to pay close attention to the ways in which our increasing and shifting scientific knowledge of our multiply formed, gendered bodies and selves unravels theologically sanctioned essentialism and sexism. The religion and science dialogue has produced many constructive reformulations of theological anthropology, focusing on the implications of multiple sciences (evolutionary biology, psychology, the neurosciences, paleoanthropology, etc.) for this locus of Christian theology, but these scientifically informed theological anthropologies often do not specifically address gender. Consideration of gender, within both the scientific and theological discourses under consideration, is a first step toward identifying how the religion and science dialogue might contribute to necessary reformulation of theological notions and reformation of ecclesial practices regarding gender.

References

Bacon, F. ([1653] 1964) "The Masculine Birth of Time Or the Great Instauration of the Dominion of Man Over the Universe," in *The Philosophy of Francis Bacon: An Essay on its Development from 1603 to 1609 with New Translations of Fundamental Texts*, B. Farrington (ed.), Liverpool, UK: Liverpool University Press, 59–72.

Barbour, I. (1990) *Religion in an Age of Science (Gifford Lectures 1989–1991, Volume 1)*, San Francisco, CA: HarperOne.

——(2002) *Nature, Human Nature, and God*, Minneapolis, MN: Fortress Press.

Clifford, A. M. (1992) "Feminist Perspectives on Science: Implications for an Ecological Theology of Creation," *Journal of Feminist Studies in Religion* 8(2): 65–90.

Cooper-White, P. (2008) "Feminism(s), Gender and Power: Reflections from a Feminist Pastoral Theologian," *Journal of Pastoral Theology* 18(2): 18–46.

Haraway, D. J. (1989) *Primate Visions: Gender, Race and Nature in the World of Modern Science*, New York: Routledge.

——(1991) "Situated Knowledges: The Science Question in Feminism and the Privilege of Partial Perspective," in *Simians, Cyborgs and Women: The Reinvention of Nature*, D. J. Haraway (ed.), New York: Routledge, 183–201.

van Huyssteen, J. W. (1999) *The Shaping of Rationality: Toward Interdisciplinarity in Theology and Science*, Grand Rapids, MI: William B. Eerdmans.

Jackelén, A. (2003) "Science and Religion: Getting Ready for the Future," *Zygon* 38(2): 209–28.

Keller, Evelyn Fox (1978) "Gender and Science," *Psychoanalysis and Contemporary Thought* 1: 409–33.

Kuhn, T. (1970) *The Structure of Scientific Revolutions*, Chicago, IL: University of Chicago Press.

Merchant, C. (1980) *The Death of Nature: Women, Ecology, and the Scientific Revolution*, San Francisco, CA: Harper & Row.

Miles, S. and J. Henry (2002) "Gender," in *Science and Religion: A Historical Introduction*, G. B. Ferngren (ed.), Baltimore, MD: Johns Hopkins University Press, 359–73.

Peacocke, A. (1993) *Theology for a Scientific Age: Being and Becoming – Natural, Divine, and Human*, Minneapolis, MN: Fortress Press.

Pederson, A. M. (1995) "Instability and Dissonance: Provocations from Sandra Harding," *Zygon* 30(3): 369–82.

Popper, K. R. (1956) *The Logic of Scientific Discovery*, London: Hutchinson's University Library.

Southgate, C., C. Deane-Drummond, P. D. Murray, M. R. Negus, L. Osborn, M. Poole, J. Stewart and F. Watts (1999) *God, Humanity and the Cosmos: A Textbook in Science and Religion*, Harrisburg, PA: Trinity Press International.

Ward, K. (2008) *The Big Questions in Science and Religion*, West Conshohocken, PA: Templeton Press.

Further reading

Evelyn Fox Keller's "Gender and Science" essay is anthologized in *Reflections on Gender and Science* (New Haven, CT: Yale University Press, 1985). For further reading in feminist philosophy of science, *The Gender and Science Reader*, edited by Ingrid Bartsch and Muriel

Lederman (New York: Routledge, 2001), contains essays by key scholars covering all major aspects of feminist critique of scientific epistemology and practice; see also Helen Longino, *Science as Social Knowledge: Values and Objectivity in Scientific Inquiry* (Princeton, NJ: Princeton University Press, 1990); Sandra Harding, *Whose Science? Whose Knowledge?* (Ithaca, NY: Cornell University Press, 1991); and Donna Haraway, *Modest_Witness@Second_Millennium. FemaleMan©_Meets_OncoMouse™: Feminism and Technoscience* (New York: Routledge, 1997). Carolyn Merchant's *The Death of Nature* (cited above) investigates the gendered metaphors at work within the sciences; Nancy Tuana's *The Less Noble Sex: Scientific, Religious and Philosophical Conceptions of Woman's Nature* (Bloomington, IN: Indiana University Press, 1993) offers an analysis of the ways in which religious and scientific views on women's nature have influenced each other; Anne Fausto-Sterling's *Myths of Gender* (New York: Basic Books, 1992) examines scientific studies that claim to uphold some biological basis for innate gender and sexual differences.

8
JEWS AND THE STUDY OF NATURE

Noah Efron

"Mankind and we ourselves have been much concerned as to the direction in which our particular abilities during these past two hundred years have been exerted," Cyrus Adler told New York Jewish society, who had squeezed into the ballroom of the Hotel Astor on March 4, 1931 to honor Albert Einstein. Adler, the President of the Jewish Theological Seminary, insisted that Einstein's accomplishments were simply the latest example of Jewish scientific genius. Einstein is, Adler said, "the flowering of many centuries of endeavor." Jews had always done their part for science, he told his rapt audience, and science had always been a part of Judaism (Adler 1933: 346).

This way of looking at things, which remains popular, oversimplifies a complex state of affairs. There was no single, enduring *Jewish* attitude toward nature and its study. In every time and place, a blend of theological, social, and practical concerns determined the place of natural wisdom (as science was sometimes called in earlier times) in Jewish intellectual life. Jews have sometimes been apathetic about natural wisdom, sometimes opposed to its pursuit, and sometimes at its vanguard. This is no surprise. When looked at over the span of millennia, Judaism has few constants. Jews have lived around the globe, spoken dozens of languages and dialects, made their living and built their communities in countless ways, eaten different foods, worn different clothes, worshipped differently. All that was common to different Jewish communities in different epochs was an agreement that an ever-growing bookshelf is canonical. What's more, over the past two centuries, the authority of traditional texts and traditional ways has waned for many Jews, and today most Jews are unfamiliar with the books by which their ancestors lived. So it is no surprise that there is no such thing as *a* Jewish attitude towards science.

To make matters more complicated, what we think of as science today has also been different in different times and places. Greek philosophers saw nature differently from church fathers, who held different views from Muslim intellectuals. So the first thing to understand when trying to grasp the relationships between Judaism and science is that, strictly speaking, there is no such thing as "Judaism" (not, at least, a unified thing that has been the same in different times and places) and there is no such thing as "science" (not, at least, a unified thing that has been the same in different times and places). What there is instead is a long history of how various Jews regarded and absorbed the various sciences of their day and place. The only way to understand Jewish attitudes towards the sciences is in their historical contexts. Such consideration reveals certain themes that recur sporadically, amidst a great deal of variation.

Early Judaism

Ancient Hebrews and natural wisdom

The Hebrew Bible records little of the nature of the cosmos; what appears is partial, enigmatic, and inconsistent. The Bible's heavens are nowhere modeled or described in numbers, in the way the heavens were, say, in the detailed, cuneiform astronomical tables of Babylonian priests. Until the Hebrew calendar was formalized in the fourth century, each new month was declared only after two witnesses testified to seeing the new moon. In contrast to other great ancient cultures, Israelites were reticent to *calculate* their calendar in advance. The heavens – their shape, structure, and workings – seemingly interested ancient Israelites less than some of their neighbors.

The Earth was a different story. Ancient Israelites sought to divine the pattern behind the animals and plants. Understanding earthly ontology – the categories by which nature is organized – mattered more to them than understanding the heavens, a fact best illustrated by the rules of *kashrut* – of what is prescribed to eat, and what is proscribed. With these rules, all the animals on Earth are organized and categorized, with the "pure" separated from the "impure."

Just how much the Israelites could and should *control* nature was a matter of ambivalence. The Bible includes uneasy pronouncements about medicine, astrology, and magic, three disciplines that involved manipulating nature, sometimes waylaying its course, sometimes controlling it to serve human ends. The Bible usually portrays such undertakings as effective, but frequently as also dangerous and illicit, granting humans power that ought to rest in God's hands.

The order of nature in the Bible is sometimes fixed and sometimes fluid. Manipulating and controlling nature is sometimes admired and sometimes detested. It was this feature of the Bible's treatment of nature that left it fertile ground for all sorts of later opinions about nature. Jews through the generations justified a great variety of opinions about nature, natural philosophy, and science by reference to the Bible. Insofar as nature is concerned, the Bible was evocative, powerful, and opinionated, yet it remained an open book.

The sages of the Talmud and natural wisdom

Jewish tradition holds that the Bible is written Torah, and the Talmud is oral Torah. Together they are the most important of Jewish books, and by most measures, the Talmud is the more important of the two. Its role in determining the nature of a millennium and a half of Jewish life has been enormous.

The Talmud gathers texts produced over hundreds of years and across thousands of miles. It brims with information, customs, ideas, and attitudes, including many assimilated from Babylonian, Greek, Roman, Assyrian, Egyptian, and other cultures. The Talmud displays complicated reactions to these influences, at times anxious, at times accepting, at times registering a blend of feelings of cultural superiority and of cultural inferiority.

The Talmudic view of nature includes all these reactions. One canonical Talmudic consideration of the size and structure of the universe, for instance, compares Jewish views with those of the "sages of the nations" and reaches the nonplussed conclusion that "their view is preferable to ours" because it fits better with observation and reason (BT Pesahim, 94b). The admission that the "sages of the nations" were right and the "sages of Israel" were wrong comes with startling ease, perhaps because the rabbis did not think knowledge about nature – which they tellingly called "Greek wisdom" or "foreign wisdom" – was very important.

But indifference is not the only attitude towards philosophy of nature on display in the Talmud. One renowned rabbi boasted that "there were a thousand pupils in my father's house; five hundred studied Torah and five hundred studied Greek wisdom." But in the same passage, one also finds: "Cursed be a man who rears pigs and cursed be a man who teaches his son Greek wisdom!" (BT Sotah, 49b). In a single paragraph, "Greek wisdom" engenders enthusiasm and scorn.

However they regarded natural wisdoms in the *abstract*, the rabbis of the Talmud were eager to use them, when practical need arose. Many discussions in the Talmud settled on mathematics when it served some practical end. Astronomy earned vigorous inquiry, perhaps because of its relevance to determining precisely when religious feasts and the Sabbath began. Rabbis were careful in their anatomies of various worms, ants, hornets, eels, etc., as they indicated whether these animals are kosher.

Still, the Rabbis were often conflicted about when and how nature should be managed or manipulated. The Talmud reports bans on magic, not because magic does not work, but because it *does* work, healing the sick, circumventing or visiting disaster, and so on. Medicine, astrology, and other practical arts were at once revered and reviled.

Thus, concerning both the sciences and their applications, the Talmud canonized a plural attitude. It also canonized the notion that Jews do not have unique insight about nature. For later generations eager to understand and harness nature, the Talmud provided support for their enthusiasm and warrant to seek wisdom from the scholars of the pagans, Muslims, and Christians.

Middle Ages

In the centuries after the Talmud was finalized, Jewish settlement spread, often far from the Middle East, into North Africa and Europe. It was in Muslim lands that natural philosophy received the most careful and creative attention from the seventh to twelfth centuries. During those centuries, Islamic civilization spread over vast territories in which other cultures had laid deep roots. By virtue of geography alone, Islam absorbed Greek, Egyptian, Indian, and Persian traditions of thought. This was an asset of incalculable value. It allowed practical know-how of each culture to diffuse throughout Islamic civilization, and bridged with a single scholarly tongue – Arabic – vast geographical and cultural divides, linking people and traditions that otherwise might not find common language.

Amidst all this diversity, Jews found a place in Arabic mathematics, natural philosophy, and medicine. They first embraced Arabic natural philosophy and medicine, beginning in the ninth century in cosmopolitan centers of Islam such as Baghdad. In the ninth to eleventh centuries, especially in Muslim Spain, this engagement reached its most brilliant expression. Toward the end of that period, as Christians fitfully recaptured portions of the Iberian peninsula, Jewish intellectual culture inevitably changed. Arabic ceased to be the sole language in which the Jews of Spain, North Africa, and the Middle East wrote about astronomy, astrology, and mathematics. Hebrew was pressed into service, and a rich technical vocabulary was devised in Hebrew where none had existed earlier. Soon, fewer Jewish intellectuals were fully at home with Arabic or Latin as a philosophical vernacular. Language would, from this point on, remain a barrier – never insurmountable, but an obstacle nonetheless – between Jewish and non-Jewish intellectuals until the start of modern times.

Political instability in Spain led Jews to travel, some southward to North Africa and the Middle East, but most northward into Christian Europe. Many of the great Jewish natural philosophers of medieval times were less the product of a Muslim or a Christian ambience than of moving from one to the other. Even those Jews who stayed in one place often found a mixture of Muslim and Christian influences. This allowed Jews to mediate between these cultures (often literally translating from one to the next).

All of these trends were evident in the work of the outstanding Jewish natural philosophers of the period, towering figures such as Abraham Bar Hiyya (d. c. 1145), Abraham ibn Ezra (1089–1167), and, above all, Moses ben Maimon (1135–1204), the towering figure of Jewish medieval thought who was known in Latin as Maimonides, and among Jews by his Hebrew acronym, Rambam.

Maimonides grew up in Cordoba, settled in Fez, Morocco when he was twenty-five, and five years later moved to Egypt, where he lived out the rest of his life. There he became a court physician, and a rabbi of tremendous international reputation. He wrote a treatise on logic, and many medical treatises, but most of his work was philosophical and religious in character. Maimonides insisted that humans are incapable of achieving positive knowledge of God's essence, asserting that only negative attributes of God – what God is *not* – can be known with certainty. Still, Maimonides believed, it is possible for scholars to come to know God's *activity*. This view provided powerful motivation to study the physical world, and it had enduring appeal for Jewish intellectuals, remaining influential in some circles to this day.

By Maimonides' day, Provence, a region in the south-east of France, was on its way to becoming a center of unique and influential Jewish scholarship. When Spain was invaded by the Almohads, waves of Spanish Jews escaped to Provence, and what had been a center of *Ashkenazi* rabbinic culture (which originated in central Europe) absorbed a great number of *Sephardi* scholars (drawing on traditions originating in Spain and the Levant) who brought with them different sensibilities and different libraries. This meeting of cultures produced extraordinary results, sparking a bright flash of interest among Jewish scholars in philosophy and natural philosophy, and led to the creation of a remarkable library of Hebrew natural philosophy. It was in Provence that a great number of important books of metaphysics, logic, mathematics, astronomy, physics, medicine – classics by Aristotle, Euclid, Hippocrates, Menelaus of Alexandria, Galen, Ptolemy, Porphyry, Avicenna (Ibn Sina), Averroes (Ibn Rushd), al-Farabi, al-Kindi, Thabit ibn Qurra, al-Razi, and many others, forming a pantheon of great ancient and medieval philosophers of nature – were translated into Hebrew from originals in Arabic and Latin.

The greatest Jewish natural philosopher of medieval times was a Provençal Jew named Levi ben Gershom (1288–1344), or Gersonides. Gersonides wrote brilliantly on astronomy, logic, mathematics, geometry, biology, and philosophy. He drew up astronomical charts, he reported, "at the request of many great and noble Christians." Bishops consulted Gersonides on questions of mathematics. He dedicated a Latin work on trigonometry to Pope Clement VI, and drew astrological charts at the request of at least two Popes. Gersonides was a Jewish natural philosopher integrated, in a small but significant way, into the broader woof and warp of European natural philosophy.

The success of Gersonides as natural philosopher meant less than it at first seems, and more. Natural learning was a rarified interest, shared by a small number of scholars. Its social impact was limited. But it had symbolic impact that affected how Jews viewed natural learning itself. Some Jews came to see natural learning as linked to other nations and other religions. It continued to be referred to as "external," "Greek," or "foreign" wisdom. It was the sole area, in medieval times, in which books written by others – by pagans, Muslims, and Christians – were eagerly translated into Hebrew and scrutinized by Jews. It was a matter about which Hebrew texts were sought by non-Jewish scholars. It had not escaped Jews that the meeting of different cultures seemed to spur interest in natural knowledge, just as, in its limited way, the pursuit of natural knowledge seemed to spur the meeting of cultures.

Early modern times

Jews in the early modern period frequently lamented that the scientific traditions of their medieval forebears had shriveled. It was a mean time. The fifteenth and sixteenth centuries saw great upheavals for the established Jewish communities of Europe, Africa, and Asia. In 1492, every last Jew in Spain was forced either to convert or to leave. Five years later, the same happened in Portugal. Throughout the fifteenth and sixteenth centuries, small-scale expulsions, city by city or region by region, were common throughout Europe. These jarred and jolted the Jewish communities of Europe. Jews found themselves increasingly in ghettos, sometimes because they were forced into them, sometimes because they preferred them, and often for both reasons at once. In such an atmosphere, Jews had less scholarly exchange with their neighbors, including about matters of natural philosophy.

Still, there were small numbers of Jews who embraced natural philosophy, sometimes because they saw it as a way of sparking exchange with their neighbors. One such Jew was David Gans (1541–1613). Gans – who met and admired the towering astronomers of his day, Tycho Brahe and Johannes Kepler – spent his life describing, teaching, and promoting liberal disciplines among Jews. In Gans' day, a small group of Jewish devotees of natural philosophy found an unexpected foothold at the Court of Holy Roman Emperor Rudolf II, which hosted Jewish alchemists, metallurgists, doctors, and engineers (Efron 1997).

Jews studied natural philosophy and, especially, medicine elsewhere as well, nowhere more than in Italy. By the sixteenth century, the University of Padua was recognized as the site of the best medical school in Europe, and it became a forge for a particular sort of early modern Jewish intellectual. Joseph Solomon Delmedigo (1591–1655), for example, began medical studies in Padua when he was fifteen, encountering Galileo there. Delmedigo eventually traveled to Cairo, then Constantinople, through Vilnius, Lublin, Krakow, Hamburg, and Amsterdam. He treated princes and top-flight Christian scholars, and wrote books advocating Copernican astronomy, complementing Kepler, and praising scientific wonders from logarithms to telescopes to thermometers (Ruderman 1995, 118–52).

Delmedigo's career – like that of the many others who studied medicine at Padua – demonstrates that, among Jews seeking discourse with Christian intellectuals of the day, natural philosophy held special interest. One reason for this was their hunch that these were subjects Jews and Christians could agree about, whereas they would never see eye to eye about God.

Over the ensuing centuries, Jews continued to find links between the study of nature and the social relations between Jews and Christians. Baruch Spinoza (1632–77), for instance, abandoned his Jewish studies in Amsterdam at seventeen in favor of Latin, natural philosophy, and philosophy. Before reaching thirty, he wrote that "God is, in relation to his effects or creatures, no other than an immanent cause," by which he meant that God comprises everything found in nature, and has no existence outside nature. As one historian put it, "Spinoza imparted order, cohesion, and formal logic to what in effect was a fundamentally new view of man, God, and the universe rooted in philosophy, nurtured by scientific thought, and capable of producing a revolutionary ideology" (Israel 2001: 159–60). Scholars have tried for years to figure out what, if anything, was *Jewish* about Spinoza's views. Spinoza was a Jew, but even more than this, he was a European intellectual. The philosopher David Hume concluded that Spinoza's "doctrine of the simplicity of the universe, and the unity of that substance" did away with the notion of an active God, whether Jewish or Christian. Indeed, Spinoza's philosophy eliminated by caveat the notion that there are innate differences between races and peoples.

And if this is true, then Spinoza was perhaps the first Jew for whom science was not just a vehicle to bridge between Jews and other believers, but a vehicle by which to discredit the world-view that took religious identity to be fundamental and binding. Spinoza may have been the first Jew for whom science was at the heart of a philosophy that called for Jews, Christians, Muslims, and atheists to be considered, first and foremost, as citizens.

Modern times

Europe after the "Enlightenment"

In the eighteenth century, when what historians call "the Age of Enlightenment" began, few Jews were active in European science. This is no surprise. Jews remained mostly excluded from universities. Two-thirds of Europe's million and a half Jews in 1800 were in any case concentrated in Russia, Poland, and Galicia, far from the main centers of scientific activity in England, France, and Germany. Science itself was a gentleman's pursuit, not one by which one could make a living. Jews, then, were four times excluded from science. They were hard-pressed to get the education science demanded. They mostly lived far from where science was practiced. They found little encouragement from Christian "gentlemen of science." And few Jews at the start of the nineteenth century were wealthy enough to devote themselves to an unpaid avocation.

These circumstances changed in the nineteenth century. Jews began to find a place in western science at this time because the natures of the West, of science, and of Jews all changed in these years. Europe in the nineteenth century saw the advent of the "isms": "liberalism," "radicalism," "socialism," "individualism," "constitutionalism," "humanitarianism," "nationalism," and "communism." Behind these new words lay new notions of what government meant, and what it meant to be a citizen. The influence of churches and aristocracies waned. The conviction became commonplace that citizens ought not be privileged or stigmatized by their backgrounds or beliefs.

In this atmosphere, what it meant to be a Jew in the West changed. "The Jewish question" forced itself onto the agenda of Europe, for Christians and Jews alike. And while Jews continued to be stigmatized for generations to come, it became difficult for rulers, legislatures, and courts to justify (in principle, at least) assigning Jews a status inferior to other citizens. As a result, in the nineteenth century Jews gained greater access to the institutions of European society.

Among these were scientific institutions, which were themselves emerging in new forms in nineteenth-century Europe. Universities returned to being principal sites for the generation of scientific knowledge, laboratories sprang up, and the sciences "professionalized," establishing disciplinary professional associations. Indeed, science as we know it today was forged in the nineteenth century.

The changes in Europe's politics, its science, and the status of its Jews were intertwined. Liberal politics and science, each championing the ideal of *progress*, were seen to support one another. Liberal politics would bring government increasingly into the humane service of the citizen, just as science would bring the natural world increasingly into the humane service of the liberal state and its citizens. Liberal and republican politics promised to sweep away the self-serving influence of traditional elites. Science promised to sweep away ill-founded traditional beliefs about nature and the world. Both were seen as forces of liberation and emancipation. This vision of science and politics appealed to many of Europe's Jews, who flocked to campuses during the second half of the nineteenth century, especially in Germany. Soon, growing numbers of Jews began to enter into science. They went from being invisible to ubiquitous everywhere science was pursued – universities, industry, and private research laboratories. Twelve per cent of Nobel Prizes won by Germans in the first years of the awards went to Jews. During that period, science came to seem like a heroic pursuit in the eyes of many German Jews, who saw it as a road to liberation, to truth, and to fellowship with other Germans. This persuasion remained strong until the rise of Nazism in the 1920s and 1930s, and the forced removal of Jews from laboratories, universities, and hospitals.

The twentieth century

By the end of the nineteenth century, there was barely a place on Earth without Jews. The push and pull of an emerging new world order spread Jews as if by centrifugal force. Most ultimately settled in one of three places: America, Revolutionary Russia, or Palestine. It was in these three destinations that Jews made their greatest mark in science, and that science left its greatest mark on the lives of Jews (Slezkine 2004: 207).

This was especially true in the United States. Over the course of the twentieth century, 38 per cent of American Nobel laureates in physics, 42 per cent in physiology and medicine, and 28 per cent in chemistry shared a Jewish heritage. By the century's end, the number of Jewish science professors at America's best universities was eight times what one would expect based on their population. Through most of the century, the popular face of science in America was usually a Jewish one: Einstein, above all, but also men such as Robert Oppenheimer, Richard Feynman, Carl Sagan, and Stephen Jay Gould, who were best-selling authors and scientific celebrities lionized for their eccentric genius (Efron 2007: 164–67).

As Jews found purchase at the forefront of science, science found purchase at the forefront of American Jewish culture. Immigrants dreamed their children would become professors of physics and physiology, or find success as physicians. Science was praised from the pulpit, and rabbis boasted of their acceptance of new scientific theories, especially the Darwinism that so disturbed some of their Protestant and Catholic colleagues. Books extolled the grandeur of the Jewish contribution to science. Scientists served on boards of Jewish organizations. Prosperous Jews donated big sums to promote science, endowing university chairs and departments, funding research centers, and building science museums, planetariums, and aquariums.

Jews in America encountered few barriers to entering science. In this, science differed from corporate business, law, and other professions that promised social status and economic security. To many, this fact signaled that science was more *meritocratic* than other professions. Indeed, many Jews concluded that science was worth promoting because science itself could promote meritocracy, and hence democracy, in America. The Jewish sociologist of science Robert K. Merton wrote in 1938 that the hallmarks of science are "intellectual honesty, integrity, organized skepticism, disinterestedness, and impersonality." Science appeals, in part, because it could never "become the handmaiden of theology or economy or state." The New York biologist and writer Benjamin Gruenberg insisted that "science is a means of broadening the sympathies and cultivating tolerance toward other groups, races, nationalities, tastes and philosophies." This view of science was embraced by Jewish philanthropists, philosophers, politicians, journalists, novelists, businessmen, and rabbis, all of whom believed that the scientific world-view would make America into a place where merit, not ancestry or religion, would determine whether one succeeded.

Something similar was at work in the Soviet Union. The rush of Jews into Russian science was as remarkable as the rush of Jews into American science. When the twentieth century began, more than five million Jews lived in the Russian Empire. They were banned from large cities, and forced to live in an area called the Pale of

Settlement (what is today Latvia, Lithuania, Ukraine, and Belorussia). Within the Pale, half lived in small Jewish *shtetls* (or the outlying country) and half lived in towns and cities, where they spoke Yiddish and dressed differently from their peasant and laborer neighbors.

In the decades before the Russian Revolution, discriminatory laws were partially reversed, and more than a million Jews moved to Russia's largest cities. Jews attended secular secondary schools and universities. After the revolution, the status of Jews changed dramatically. Officially, Soviet society allowed no religious discrimination and, in reality, Jews found few obstacles to schools and jobs in the USSR. The revolution had crushed the old elites of Czarist Russia. This meant opportunities for previously oppressed minorities, opportunities enthusiastically exploited by Jews. By 1939, a Soviet Jew was more than three times more likely to finish secondary school than other Soviet citizens, and ten times as likely to complete university.

Most of these Jews went into science, medicine, or engineering. By the 1950s, though Jews were one-seventieth of the population, they accounted for over one in ten Soviet scientists. Over 30 per cent of Soviet Nobel Laureates up to 1975 were Jews. In this, the success of Jews in Soviet science resembled that of American Jews.

There were many reasons why this was so. The revolution had sparked both great growth in science and a great migration of Jews from the former Pale to the largest cities in the USSR. Hundreds of thousands of jobs in science came into being at just the moment when many Jews were entering the urban labor force. The crushing need for suitable applicants matched well the swelling ranks of Jews with fresh university degrees. Science in the Soviet Union, as elsewhere, was strongly associated with progress, improvement, and modernity. Soviet prophets and leaders – Marx, Engels, Plekhanov, Lenin, Trotsky, and Stalin – had each described their outlook as "scientific," and saw in science a tool for reconstructing society. In the first years of the Soviet Union, driven by a lingering sense of cultural inferiority and sincere passion for the values of the revolution, Jews embraced science both as a means for achieving progress, and as a token that they themselves were *progressive*.

Further, some Jews embraced science because science itself was so valuable to the revolution. To be a scientist was to demonstrate commitment to the Soviet ideal. And when the corruptions and oppression of the Soviet regime became too blatant to ignore, science remained a profession through which one could remain a contributing Soviet citizen without being overly involved with the degrading ideological casuistry of Soviet life.

In short, science provided for Jews of the Soviet Union a profession that was modern, progressive, praiseworthy, and at once universalist and patriotic. In this, it offered opportunities like those that many American Jews sought in science, as some nineteenth-century German Jews sought before them. When the great emigration of Soviet Jews to Israel began in the 1970s, waves of these Jews brought with them scientific training and skills, and expectations that these would smooth their assimilation into their new home. These were, after all, the same expectations that had drawn many of these Russian Jews, and their parents and grandparents, to science in the first place.

In Israel, too, science thrived for both practical and ideological reasons. Per capita, Israel today has more engineers than anywhere else (135 per 10,000 citizens, compared with eighty-five in the USA), and many more physicians (450 per 10,000 compared with twenty-three in the USA). Israeli scientists publish more scientific papers than those of any other nationality (110 papers per year per 10,000 citizens). The country has the world's third largest concentration of high-tech companies. Israel's armed forces owe their success to advanced technology and the science behind it.

Indeed, science has been at the core of Israel's self-image since before it declared its independence. Theodor Herzl, the founder of modern Zionism, described the Jewish state in his utopian novel *Altneuland* (*Old–New Land*) as a technological wonderland administered by modern scientific principles. Once the state came into being, Israel's first President was Chaim Weizmann, an indefatigable Zionist politician, but also a renowned chemist who was the director of the British admiralty laboratories in the First World War. When he retired, Albert Einstein was asked to replace him. Israel's fourth President, Ephraim Katzir, was a biophysicist of world reputation. It seemed, for a time, that the road to the presidential residence in Jerusalem ran through the laboratory.

This was so because science and technology fitted snugly with many of the aims and ideals of Zionism. They were used to establish Jewish title to the land, sometimes explicitly, as by archeologists who documented ancient Israelite sovereignty over it, and sometimes through a more complicated chain of reasoning. Science and technology made plain the notion that Jewish settlement of Palestine was, in the end, a Western project imbued with Western ideals and committed to advancing those ideals in the East, and in this sense it reflected colonial sensibilities of Zionism. By embracing science, some Zionists deliberately associated the Zionist project with the progressive West and with the great achievements of Jewish scientists abroad. In this way, science meshed well with the *ideology* of Zionism, just as it served the practical needs of a country without natural resources laboring to establish a modern economy. Writing in *The New York Times* on the tenth anniversary of Israel's independence, Prime Minister David Ben-Gurion described the young country as "a bastion of democracy, liberty and universal cultural values based on the teaching of Israel's prophets and the achievements of modern science." This view of science was one shared at the time by many Jews, in the many places where they found themselves around the world.

Conclusion

Having now surveyed Jewish attitudes towards science, and natural philosophy before it, it is easy to see that there never was a "Jewish" science, nor could there ever have been one. Jewish views of the study of nature through the centuries have been so diverse that they are irreducible; they have no common denominator. Sometimes, in some places, Jews worried about the implications of this or that theory for Hebrew piety. But such concerns were rare. Science–religion clashes that occasionally engaged Catholics and Protestants never materialized much among Jews, for several reasons. In contrast to the Catholic Church, Jews never developed institutions with the reach and power to declare a book, a theory, or an idea to be anathema. To be inquisitorial, you need an inquisition. Jews had no inquisition, and lacked the centralized political power to convene one. Further, Jews lacked an *ideal* of consensus. Accepting multiple interpretations – what one scholar called "the Rabbis' apparent lack of interest in making a theologically coherent whole out of their disparate beliefs" – remained a foundational principle of Jewish intellectual life. And if one does not seek compatibility and harmony, one is unlikely to experience conflict.

Still, lack of conflict is not the same as active interest, and Jews have shown the latter only episodically – in ninth-century Baghdad, twelfth-century Fostat, fourteenth-century Perpignan, sixteenth-century Prague, seventeenth-century Amsterdam, eighteenth-century Berlin, and so forth – at least until modern times. Through most of Jewish history, in most places, Jews viewed natural knowledge as somehow "foreign" or "external" to Judaism itself. This is perhaps the only belief about natural knowledge shared consistently by eighty generations of Jews. This belief meant different things to Jews in different times and places. To some, it meant that the statements of the natural philosophers might be true, but were of only limited interest. To others, it demonstrated that some of God's secrets had been deciphered by "the wise men of the nations," whose labors should be appreciated by Jews. To many Jews, it meant that attitudes towards nature and its study could never be teased apart from attitudes towards other people and, more to the point, other *peoples*. The natural, for Jews, became inextricable from the social.

It is clear that, for some Jews, the social implications, the social *possibilities*, of natural philosophy or science were part of the appeal. This was true for rare individuals in medieval and early modern times. But it was in the late nineteenth and especially in the twentieth century that this view reached its zenith. During these years, Jews devoted themselves with unparalleled vigor to science. Some, at least, did so because they believed that the sciences would make religion and ethnicity irrelevant. Jean Paul Sartre captured the logic of this view when he observed that "there is not a Jewish way of mathematics; the Jewish mathematician becomes a universal man when he reasons." For most of the modern era, Jewish scientists and science-enthusiasts who embraced science and sought to advance it did so not as Jews, but rather as "universal" human beings. Indeed, most of these Jews embraced science with nothing less than religious fervor precisely because, as they understood it, science left no place for religion on campus, in the lab, and beyond. In Germany, the United States, the Soviet Union, Israel and, indeed, everywhere else where Jews excelled in modern science, they engaged in the study of nature, pointedly, as human beings rather than as Jews.

References

Adler, Cyrus (1933) "Albert Einstein – The Flowering of Many Centuries of Jewish Endeavor," in *Lectures, Selected Papers, Addresses*, Philadelphia, PA: privately printed, 346–49.

Efron, Noah (1997) "Irenism and Natural Philosophy in Rudolfine Prague," *Science in Context* 10(4): 627–49.

——(2007) *Judaism and Science: A Historical Introduction*, Westport, CT and London: Greenwood Press.

Israel, Jonathan (2001) *Radical Enlightenment: Philosophy and the Making of Modernity, 1650–1750*, Oxford and New York: Oxford University Press.
Pines, Shlomo (1970) "Maimonides, Rabbi Moses Ben Maimon" in *Dictionary of Scientific Biography* 9, New York: Scribner, 27–32.
Ruderman, David B. (1995) *Jewish Thought and Scientific Discovery in Early Modern Europe*, New Haven, CT: Yale University Press.
Slezkine, Yuri (2004) *The Jewish Century*, Princeton, NJ: Princeton University Press.

Further reading

Much been written about Jews and the study of nature through the ages. For an expanded account, see my own *Judaism and Science: A Historical Introduction* (cited above). For an anthology of ancient Jewish texts concerning medicine and biology, see Fred Rosner's translation and adaptation of Julius Preuss' monumental classic, *Biblical and Talmudic Medicine* (Northvale, NJ: J. Aronson, 1993). For a fascinating philosophical interpretation of the attitudes of the savants of the Talmud towards what would later be called science, see Menachem Fisch's *Rational Rabbis: Science and Talmudic Culture* (Bloomington, IN: Indiana University Press, 1997). You will find meticulously researched essays about various aspects of Jewish engagement with natural knowledge in Y. Tzvi Langermann's *The Jews and the Sciences in the Middle Ages* (Aldershot, UK: Brookfield Ashgate/Variorum, 1999). For an account of Jews and medicine during this period, see Joseph Shatzmiller, *Jews, Medicine, and Medieval Society* (Berkeley, CA: University of California Press, 1994). The *nonpareil* scholar of early modern Jewish involvements with natural knowledge is David B. Ruderman. Of his many valuable works, see especially *Jewish Thought and Scientific Discovery in Early Modern Europe* (cited above). On twentieth-century Jews and science, see David Hollinger's remarkable essays in *Science, Jews, and Secular Culture: Studies in Mid-Twentieth-Century American Intellectual History* (Princeton, NJ: Princeton University Press, 1996) and Yuri Slezkine's more impressionistic, but equally remarkable *The Jewish Century* (cited above). For a very different, more philosophical account of Judaism and science, see Norbert Samuelson's essay "Judaism and Science," in Philip Clayton's and Zachary Simpson's *Oxford Handbook of Religion and Science* (Oxford: Oxford University Press, 2006, 41–56) and his recent book *Jewish Faith and Modern Science: On the Death and Rebirth of Jewish Philosophy* (Lanham, MD: Rowman & Littlefield, 2008).

Part II

SCIENTIFIC AND RELIGIOUS MODELS OF THE WORLD

(i) Cosmologies and cosmogonies

9
COSMOLOGY

Joel R. Primack and Nancy Ellen Abrams

Scientific cosmology is the study of the entire universe, its history, structure, and composition. Long considered highly speculative, cosmology has in recent years become a precise science in which detailed theoretical predictions are routinely confirmed by increasingly powerful observations. Nevertheless, fundamental questions still remain to be answered. Cosmologies existed long before science – they were the stories every culture told, and still tells, about the origin of the world and the place of humans in the big picture. All religions include origin stories, which are generally based on the understanding of nature at the time when the religion was founded. This has led both to interesting conversations and to some of the deepest conflicts between science and religion. In this essay we discuss the history of changing cultural cosmologies in the West, the radically different cosmology that is emerging today from modern astrophysics, and some of the religious implications of this new scientific picture.

Development of cosmology in the West

In the ancient Middle East, the universe was pictured as consisting of a flat earth under a domed sky, and the whole creation was surrounded by primeval water. In ancient Egypt, the earth, air, and sky were pictured as gods. In ancient Babylon, there was a similar picture, with the world created by a struggle between gods. The origin stories in the Hebrew Bible are based on a similar flat earth picture, but with the parts no longer considered to be gods.

There have only been two great cosmological shifts before; the third one is happening now. The first great shift in cosmology was the realization by the ancient Greek scientists that the Earth is not flat, but spherical. Eratosthenes, who coined the term "geography" and wrote the first book on the subject, was the third director of the great royal library and research center in Alexandria. By observation of the angle of the Sun at two different latitudes and measurement of the distance between them, he accurately determined the circumference of the spherical Earth without ever leaving Egypt. Hipparchus was the greatest of the ancient Greek astronomers. His careful observations and sophisticated trigonometry allowed him to discover that the direction of the Earth's rotation axis moves in a circle on the sky, and thus what we call the North Star was not due north in the past, and will not be in the future.

In Alexandria in the first century AD, Claudius Ptolemy created a detailed geometrical theory that accounted for the observed motion of the planets. The spherical universe became the standard cosmic picture for a millennium and a half, from the late Roman Empire through the medieval Christian and Muslim centuries. The Moon, Sun, and planets were carried by circles or nested spheres, with the entire structure revolving around the Earth every day, and with heaven on the outside. This was described by Dante in his *Divine Comedy* (1321). Its structure reflected the hierarchical medieval world picture, in which everything from God to the lowly worms formed a great chain of being, with various ranks of humans in the middle.

The second great change in cosmology was initiated when Nicholas Copernicus proposed a different cosmic picture in his *On the Revolutions of the Heavenly Spheres* (1543), with the Sun at the center, the Moon going around the Earth, and the Earth and other planets going around the Sun. This heliocentric system avoided several peculiarities of planetary motion in the geocentric system. Galileo Galilei made the first detailed observations of the sky with the newly invented telescope, and in *Starry Messenger* (1610) he reported that the Milky Way consists of countless stars and that the Moon has mountains. His discovery that four moons revolve around the planet Jupiter supported Copernicus's theory, since it was analogous to the motion of the planets around the Sun. With the telescope, Galileo could finally observe the phases of Venus, and in 1611 he discovered that Venus goes from crescent to round, which means it is sometimes on the far side of the Sun – which contradicts the Ptolemaic system. However, in a vain effort to preserve the traditional geocentric picture, the Catholic Church in 1633 forced Galileo to recant his advocacy of the heliocentric picture, and imprisoned him for the rest of his life.

The Copernican Revolution, as this second shift in cosmology is called, was a process that took place over two centuries, and those responsible became the founders of modern science. Based on careful astronomical observations by Tycho Brahe, Johannes Kepler showed that the planets move around the Sun in elliptical orbits with the Sun at one focus. Kepler also determined the speeds with which they move around their various orbits. Isaac Newton's *Mathematical Principles of Natural Philosophy* (1687) showed that all of these aspects of planetary motion were naturally explained if the planets are held in their orbits by a gravitational force that falls off as the square of their distances from the Sun. Newton's theory also accounted for the tides on the Earth, and correctly predicted the return of comets. Newton thought that God must have put the planets in their orbits and that God would occasionally adjust the system. Based on Newton's physics, the philosopher Immanuel Kant created the first scientific cosmological theory in his book *Cosmogony* (1754). Kant proposed that the Solar System formed by physical processes from a rotating gas cloud that was cooling and contracting. The physicist Pierre-Simon Laplace developed this theory without any reference to a creator. This was the beginning of a scientific origin story based on physics.

But it was only about the origin of the Solar System. As to the larger universe, Newton speculated that it must be infinite in order that everything not fall to the center. Yet Kepler, Heinrich Wilhelm Matthäus Olbers (1758–1840), and others pointed out that if the universe were also infinitely old, then there would be a star in every direction so the night sky should be brightly lit, which it obviously is not. So the nature of the large-scale universe remained a mystery.

Modern cosmology

For millennia it was assumed, as Genesis implies, that human beings like us have been on the Earth for its entire several thousand-year existence, except for the first five days. Then, in the nineteenth century, scientists tried to understand how mountains and river deltas formed, and they discovered that some of these processes must have taken hundreds of millions of years. This was the beginning of the discovery of "deep time." Throughout the nineteenth century, as excavations for canals and railroads occurred across Britain and the United States, dinosaur bones and other fossils were uncovered, and the realization dawned on people that countless entire species had become extinct long ago. By the mid-twentieth century, scientists using radioactivity determined that Earth and the Solar System itself are far older still – 4.6 billion years old. Compared with this vast age, we humans just evolved yesterday.

At the beginning of the twentieth century, most astronomers thought that our galaxy, the Milky Way, was the entire universe. Astronomers observed blurry objects called nebulae, which were thought to be gas clouds. But in 1924, the astronomer Edwin Hubble showed that some of the nebulae were actually galaxies far outside the Milky Way. Then, in 1929, Hubble made the even more stunning discovery that distant galaxies are receding from our galaxy with a velocity proportional to their distance, which means that the universe is expanding. This discovery had actually been predicted by Alexander Friedmann and Georges Lemaître, using Albert Einstein's general theory of relativity, which is our modern theory of space, time, and gravity. Interestingly, Einstein himself resisted this implication of his theory. Lemaître argued that if the universe is expanding, there must have been a time in the past when everything was close together – now called the Big Bang. But there was no direct evidence for that yet.

In the mid-twentieth century, there was lively debate in astronomy between the steady state theory and the Big Bang. The steady state proponents argued that the universe is basically unchanging, with matter constantly appearing to form new galaxies as the old ones expanded apart. The steady state theory was seriously undermined by the discovery in 1965 that heat radiation from the Big Bang fills the universe. It was further undermined by the discovery that very distant galaxies are not like nearby ones. When we look out into space, we are looking back in time, so this discovery showed that the universe has been changing since the Big Bang.

Cosmology is a historical science, like geology and evolutionary biology. These sciences attempt not only to understand the way the universe, the Earth, and living systems work, but also the historical paths that led to the present. It is sometimes claimed that, because the actual past was unique, the historical sciences provide a lower grade of knowledge than laboratory sciences such as physics and chemistry, in which the effects of changing conditions can be explored through experiments. This claim that the historical sciences are inferior is especially popular with people who prefer biblical or other traditional accounts of our origins. It is also popular with postmodern thinkers. But this is a serious misunderstanding. In both the laboratory sciences and the historical sciences, as theories improve, they not only explain what is known, but predict what will be discovered. In the historical sciences, though, predictions concern what will be discovered about what happened in the past.

In cosmology, the application to the expanding universe of general relativity, thermodynamics, and statistical and nuclear physics led to key predictions that were later confirmed. One was the prediction that the light elements produced by the Big Bang were almost entirely hydrogen and helium, in the ratio by mass of three to one, with just the predicted slight trace of heavy hydrogen (deuterium). Another was that the universe is filled with the heat radiation of the Big Bang, known as the cosmic background radiation. This radiation was discovered in 1965, but it is the details of how it looks that have revealed much about how the universe began. In order for structures such as galaxies to have grown gravitationally since the Big Bang, there had to have been slight differences in the density of the universe from place to place, right from the beginning. These differences would have to be observable as slight differences in the temperature of the cosmic background radiation in different directions. By 1980, though, improving measurements of the cosmic background radiation had nevertheless failed to detect such differences.

Meanwhile, evidence had been accumulating that most of the mass of galaxies and galaxy clusters was not contained in the stars of those galaxies, or in any other visible form. In the 1930s, galaxies in a nearby galaxy cluster were shown by the astronomer Fritz Zwicky to be moving much too fast, according to what was known at the time. He concluded that there had to be large amounts of unseen mass holding the cluster together. He called the implied unseen mass "dark matter" ("dark" in this context meaning "non-luminous"). Stars and gas were subsequently also found to be moving much too fast around galaxies. It was initially proposed that neutrinos, the one form of invisible matter then known, might be the dark matter gravitationally binding these cosmic structures together, but neutrinos were soon shown to be incapable of producing the observed galaxy distribution. This is because neutrinos (known as "hot dark matter") have much less mass than electrons, which implies that they must have been moving very rapidly in the early universe – so they could not hold the forming galaxies together. More massive invisible particles, known as "cold dark matter," were predicted by theories in particle physics, such as supersymmetry, to possibly be very abundant in the universe. They would have been moving very sluggishly in the early universe. This has turned out to be the unseen mass whose existence Zwicky had inferred.

The theory of cold dark matter is now considered the standard theory of structure formation in the universe. According to the theory, cold dark matter is the main form of matter in the universe. It cannot be atoms of any kind, or any of the components of atoms: protons, neutrons, and electrons. The theory as detailed in 1984 predicted key details in the cosmic background radiation – the level of fluctuations – that were actually discovered by the Cosmic Background Explorer (COBE) satellite in 1992.

However, other observations posed problems for the still-developing science of cosmology. One major paradox was that the ages of the oldest stars in the Milky

Way appeared to be substantially greater than the time since the Big Bang. These age estimations were based on extrapolating backward using the measured expansion rate of the universe. But in 1997–98 a recalibration of the distances to the stars in the Milky Way, based on crucial data from the Hipparcos satellite, lowered the ages of the oldest stars, and the discovery that the expansion of the universe has been speeding up increased the calculated time since the Big Bang. These observations determined that about 95 per cent of the cosmic density consists of mysterious invisible things: about 25 per cent cold dark matter and about 70 per cent dark energy. Atoms make up about 5 per cent, but most of those atoms are between the galaxies and are invisible. All the atoms that we see in the entire universe, in the form of stars, gas, dust, planets (including our own), and the galaxies, total only about half of one per cent of the cosmic density.

Thus we live in a double dark universe, dominated by dark matter and dark energy. This theory has led to predictions of the properties of the cosmic background radiation and the distribution of the galaxies that have turned out to be in spectacularly good agreement with observations. It is the first cosmological theory to be supported by an enormous amount of high-quality data, and it is now generally accepted by working astronomers.

In the double dark cosmology, dark matter is our friend. Dark matter has grown into concentrations called halos, within which clouds of hydrogen and helium atoms can cool and form stars, and this process created the galaxies. Over the evolution of the universe, dark matter halos have bound together the galaxies gravitationally, as well as binding groups and clusters of galaxies. Outside dark matter's gravitational hold, the dark energy is tearing apart unbound structures and accelerating the expansion of space, carrying away all distant galaxies. Thus we owe our existence and future to dark matter.

There are still three big challenges to this modern cosmological theory. The first is determining the physical nature of the dark matter and dark energy. Most physicists expect that dark matter will be found to be some sort of elementary particle, and it might be produced at the Large Hadron Collider in Geneva, or discovered by increasingly sensitive laboratory experiments. Popular theories predict that dark matter particles annihilate with each other, which could be confirmed by observing the cosmic rays produced. As to dark energy, the best way to determine its nature is by sensitive measurements of how distances have increased and structures have grown in the expanding universe. All measurements to date are consistent with the dark energy being Einstein's "cosmological constant" – that is, a property of space itself – but theoretical cosmologists are exploring many alternative possibilities. Years ago, people thought the universe might eventually stop expanding and collapse, possibly in a Big Crunch that would lead to a new Big Bang. But now we know that dark energy is actually making the universe expand faster and faster. There is no evidence to suggest that the universe will ever stop expanding and collapse, but until the nature of the dark energy is better understood, it will be impossible to predict how the universe will evolve into the distant future.

The second challenge is determining how galaxies form in the double dark universe. Progress is occurring through the interplay of increasingly powerful observations and steadily improving supercomputer simulations.

The third challenge is determining what set up the initial conditions for the Big Bang. Our best modern account of what set up those initial conditions is the theory of cosmic inflation, according to which, in the earliest fraction of a second, the universe underwent an exponential expansion. Inflation theory holds that the entire visible universe grew from a size smaller than an elementary particle to the size of a newborn baby. During this inflation process, quantum fluctuations produced exactly the slight differences in the density of the universe from place to place, which grew during the subsequent 13.7 billion years into the galaxies and clusters of galaxies that astronomers observe today.

The theory of cosmic inflation is consonant with modern particle physics, and it is the only known theory that properly sets up the Big Bang. Its predictions have been tested and found to be consistent with observations. But what happened before cosmic inflation remains a mystery. When we extrapolate the equations back to find the origin of cosmic inflation, the most likely possibility is that inflation is still going on almost everywhere outside the universe that was created by our Big Bang – since, once this sort of inflation exists, it goes on eternally. But tiny pockets or bubbles form in it, which become big bangs that evolve into universes. Our universe would then be a bubble of space–time in eternal inflation. But there would be no possibility of communication between different bubble universes – which might even have different laws of physics. The hypothetical realm of eternal inflation is sometimes called the "multiverse." Keep in mind, however, that the theory of eternal inflation is untested, and a theory without supporting data has not yet crossed the border from metaphysics into physics, although it might some day.

Anthropic cosmology?

Our human existence requires that the universe must be very old and very large, since it took billions of years for galaxies to form; for enough stars within them to live and die to create the heavy elements of which rocky planets like ours are made; and for life to evolve to our level of complexity. During all that time, the universe has been expanding. The modern standard models of cosmology and particle physics make it possible to calculate what would happen if the cosmological parameters – such as the strengths of the forces of nature, or the masses of the elementary particles – were different from their measured values, and it turns out that a universe like ours, with creatures like us, could not exist if any one of these properties was significantly different. However, it has been found that if two or more of the physical constants were changed, interesting universes quite different from ours might be possible, in which creatures like us could nevertheless exist.

Still, this does not answer the question of what determined the fundamental constants of nature to be such that we humans could exist, and there have been multiple speculations about this "anthropic" question. One possibility is that there is only one set of mathematically consistent values, which might be explained by a more fundamental theory that is yet to be discovered. Another is that countless kinds of universe exist in the multiverse, and ours by chance is one of the rare ones with the right physical laws for our sort of life. Yet another is that God set up the universe just right for us. But, of course, this raises questions such as where this God came from, and what its nature could possibly be.

Cosmology and religion

There have long been connections between cosmology and religion, and other aspects of culture. Since at least the time of ancient Egypt, rituals carried out by rulers and priests have been thought to be essential to preserving the orderly functioning of the cosmos. The cycle of the seasons and the motions of the stars and planets have been interpreted as connected to the gods, and thus relevant for predicting the fates of individuals or nations.

Traditional creation stories around the world have mainly fallen into three categories, depending on their view of time: (1) the world is *cyclical* (it continually changes in the short term, but in the long term the cycle itself is unchanging); (2) time is *linear* (the world is always changing, and time goes in one direction); or (3) the world is *unchanging* (although, if created, it went through changes in a distant, irretrievable past). It turns out that all three of these modes of storytelling may be part of the new cosmology, because each applies on a different size scale. On the scale of the Earth, for which humans have intuition, the seasons are cyclical, and so are the births and deaths of generations of living beings and the movements of the planets and comets. On the size scale of the Big Bang and cosmic evolution, the universe is changing in one direction. It is now expanding faster and faster, and we know of no evidence that it will ever contract. But if the theory of eternal inflation is right, then on the grandest of size scales the multiverse is unchanging, because universes burst forth endlessly, yet *on the whole* nothing changes.

Science grew in the West from the Hebrew and Greek presumption of a lawful universe. The Greek pre-Socratic philosophers Thales and Anaximander made science possible within a universe of gods. They did this not by denying the supernatural, but by inventing that very concept, because in doing so they also invented its opposite, the natural. Natural phenomena, they could then claim, are those phenomena that are not the products of willful divine influences, but are regular and governed by cause and effect.

The religious affiliations of the greatest cosmologists – including Aristotle, Ptolemy, Copernicus, Galileo, Kepler, Newton, and Einstein – were within the religious mainstream of their times. However, their discoveries sometimes challenged religious presuppositions. Although Galileo was persecuted by his own branch of Christianity, his work was quickly accepted in Protestant Europe. But the English poet John Donne, responding to Galileo's *Starry Messenger*, wrote

> 'Tis all in pieces, all coherence gone,
> All just supply, and all relation;
> Prince, subject, father, son, are things forgot […]

Donne appreciated that, in overthrowing the hierarchical medieval cosmos, Galileo's discoveries would undermine the hierarchical organization of medieval society.

Sometimes religious preferences proved consonant with cosmological discoveries. Well before the conflict between the steady state and Big Bang theories was resolved by new evidence, Pope Pius XII in 1952 expressed a strong preference for the Big Bang because of its harmony with the religious idea of the creation of the universe. On the other hand, the relatively recent adoption of a literal interpretation of the Genesis origin stories and of "scientific creationism" by some conservative Protestant churches in the United States has led to a continuing confrontation with science, especially regarding whether the historical sciences will be taught in the public schools. This politicization of science education is perhaps the main reason that only about half of US citizens – a much smaller fraction of the population than in any other industrialized country – realize that the Earth and the universe are more than a few thousand years old.

Traditional creation stories start with "In the beginning … " But it may never be possible to discover the "beginning." A practical alternative is to perceive time outward from the present, as science discovers it. A tiny consciousness of history is mirrored in a tiny consciousness of the future. Many people who think of the Earth as only a few thousand years old have no compunction about ending it shortly. For some messianic believers, this symmetric sort of closure gives the whole thing meaning. But our Solar System will continue to exist for billions of years until the Sun becomes a red giant star and, ultimately, a fading white dwarf, and after our Milky Way galaxy merges with the great galaxy in Andromeda in a few billion years it will grow brighter for a trillion years. It may become completely isolated as galaxies not gravitationally bound to it disappear over the cosmic horizon due to the accelerating expansion of the universe. Our view of the distant future, like that of the distant past, grows increasingly fuzzy, but without doubt both must be thought of in many billions of years, not thousands.

One thing that has become clear from the highly counter-intuitive nature of the scientific universe is that most of the imagery and concepts familiar from biblical and other origin stories cannot describe it. And yet there are concepts from such ancient traditions that resonate with certain aspects of our scientific picture. For example, in the ancient Egyptian and biblical cosmologies, primeval waters pre-dated the creation; the world was created in their midst and they continued to surround the world. Dark matter is indeed primeval – it came out of the Big Bang – and it surrounds and permeates our galaxy; on a larger scale, if the theory of eternal inflation is right, eternal inflation is even more primeval and surrounds our entire universe. In the creation story at the beginning of Genesis, God created light on the first day, separated the waters and created dry land on the second day, created vegetation on the third day, and created the Sun, Moon, and stars on the fourth day. It is true that the light of the Big Bang long preceded the creation of the first stars – but the Earth and its vegetation could not come into existence until generations of stars produced the heavy elements of which the Earth, and all living creatures, are made.

In both the ancient and the medieval cosmologies, a spiritual reality surrounded the ordinary world. When the Newtonian picture overthrew the medieval, the universe became physical all the way out, possibly to infinity. But now that we have a well supported theory that explains the origin of structure throughout the visible universe, we can understand phenomena on size scales that no earlier culture even imagined, let alone understood, from the tiniest to the greatest – from elementary particles to superclusters of galaxies. These, however, are not physical objects in the common-sense meaning of solid, visible, and unquestionably here, since elementary particles are not particles like marbles, but really probabilities that something is happening; and superclusters are not bound together gravitationally, but are flying apart as the expansion of the universe accelerates. The phenomena of everyday life, for which humans have developed intuition over millennia, occur from about the size of a gnat to that of the Sun, and things happening in this range of size scales are what most people think of as physical reality; but beyond them in the directions of both the large and small lies a new kind of reality that can neither be seen nor experienced directly, yet has been discovered by science to permeate and surround our everyday world.

With increasingly powerful instruments, we humans observe radiation from cosmological objects and construct our universe by interpreting what we see. Just as the ancients thought that their rituals and other actions upheld the universe, we now understand that our own theoretical interpretations are the foundation of our mental picture of the amazing universe in which we live, and thus, in some deep sense, we too uphold our universe.

References

Adams, Fred and Greg Laughlin (1999) *The Five Ages of the Universe: Inside the Physics of Eternity*, New York: Simon & Schuster.

Barbour, Ian G. (1990) *Religion in an Age of Science*, San Francisco, CA: Harper & Row.

——(2000) *When Science Meets Religion*, San Francisco, CA: HarperSanFrancisco.

Barrow, John D. and Tipler, Frank J. (1986) *The Anthropic Cosmological Principle*, Oxford: Clarendon Press.

Clayton, Philip (1997) *God and Contemporary Science*, Grand Rapids, MI: Eerdmans.

Campbell, Joseph (1986) *The Inner Reaches of Outer Space*, New York: Harper & Row.

Cornford, Francis M. (1991[1912]) *From Religion to Philosophy: A Study in the Origins of Western Speculation*, Princeton, NJ: Princeton University Press.

Davies, Paul (1988) *The Cosmic Blueprint: New Discoveries in Nature's Creative Ability to Order the Universe*, New York: Simon & Schuster.

——(1992) *The Mind of God: The Scientific Basis for a Rational World*, New York: Simon & Schuster.

——(2007) *The Cosmic Jackpot: Why our Universe is Just Right for Life*, Boston: Houghton Mifflin.

Drees, Willem B. (1990) *Beyond the Big Bang: Quantum Cosmology and God*, La Salle, IL: Open Court.

Ferris, Timothy (1988) *Coming of Age in the Milky Way*, New York: William Morrow.

Frankfort, Henri, H. A. Frankfort, J. A. Wilson, T. Jacobsen and W. A. Irwin (1946) *The Intellectual Adventure of Ancient Man: An Essay on Speculative Thought in the Ancient Near East*, Chicago, IL: University of Chicago Press.

Gingerich, Owen (2006) *God's Universe*, Cambridge, MA: Belknap Press of Harvard University Press.

Greene, Brian (2003) *The Elegant Universe: Superstrings, Hidden Dimensions, and the Quest for the Ultimate Theory*, New York: W.W. Norton.

Guth, Alan (1997) *The Inflationary Universe: The Quest for a New Theory of Cosmic Origins*, Reading, MA: Addison-Wesley.

Harrison, Edward R. (1985) *Masks of the Universe*, New York: Macmillan.

——(1987) *Darkness at Night: A Riddle of the Universe*, Cambridge, MA: Harvard University Press.

——(2000) *Cosmology: The Science of the Universe*, Cambridge: Cambridge University Press.

Hetherington, Norriss S. (1993) *Cosmology: Historical, Literary, Philosophical, Religious, and Scientific Perspectives*, New York: Garland.

Kuhn, Thomas S. (1957) *The Copernican Revolution*, Cambridge, MA: Harvard University Press.

Lewis, C.S. (1994) *The Discarded Image: An Introduction to Medieval and Renaissance Literature*, Cambridge: Cambridge University Press.

Lindberg, David C. and Numbers, Ronald L. (eds) (1986) *God and Nature: Historical Essays on the Encounter between Christianity and Science*, Berkeley, CA: University of California Press.

Mathews, Clifford N. and Varghese, Roy Abraham (eds) (1995) *Cosmic Beginnings and Human Ends: Where Science and Religion Meet*, La Salle, IL: Open Court.

Matt, Daniel (1996) *God and the Big Bang: Discovering Harmony Between Science and Spirituality*, Woodstock, VT: Jewish Lights.

Numbers, Ronald L. (1977) *Creation by Natural Law: Laplace's Nebular Hypothesis in American Thought*, Seattle, WA: University of Washington Press.

Primack, Joel R. and Abrams, Nancy Ellen (2006) *The View from the Center of the Universe: Discovering Our Extraordinary Place in the Cosmos*, New York: Riverhead.

Rees, Martin (1997) *Before the Beginning: Our Universe and Others*, Reading, MA: Addison-Wesley.

——(1999) *Just Six Numbers: The Deep Forces that Shape the Universe*, New York: Basic Books.

Toulmin, Stephen and June Goodfield (1965) *The Discovery of Time*, New York: Harper & Row.

Further reading

The topics in this essay are discussed in greater detail in the authors' book *The View from the Center of the Universe* (cited above), which includes references. The books by Cornford, Ferris, Kuhn, Lewis, and Toulmin and Goodfield contain relevant historical material; those by Adams and Laughlin, Barrow and Tipler, Davies, Guth, and Rees concern modern cosmology; and those by Barbour, Clayton, Gingerich, and Matt are introductions to the interactions between religion and cosmology. Harrison's *Cosmology* is an especially accessible introduction to scientific cosmology with historical and philosophical reflections, although it is now somewhat dated.

10
ASTRONOMY
From star gazing to astrobiology

Grace Wolf-Chase

Astronomy is the scientific study of the material universe. It contains many branches today. Two areas of particularly intense focus are cosmology and astrobiology. Cosmology is the scientific study of the universe as a whole – its history, evolution, and future. In contrast, astrobiology concerns itself with life in the universe – its origins, evolution, and future. Astrobiology is a highly inter- and multi-disciplinary endeavor, which incorporates both the physical and biological sciences. The essay by Primack & Abrams in this volume (Chapter 9) summarizes modern scientific cosmology and its impact on traditional origins stories found in religions. Just as all religions include origins stories, all religions are concerned with human beings and their relationship to other life and to the universe as a whole. In this essay, I examine how scientists have come to understand the evolving conditions that have made possible the emergence of life in the universe, and how this impacts on how we humans view ourselves and our place in the universe. I present a broad overview of how technological advancements have enabled the successive inclusion of physics, chemistry, and biology into astronomy, and have changed the culture of science. It is impossible to discuss all of the ways in which technological advancements have led to new discoveries in astronomy, or to include the many thousands of scientists who have contributed to these discoveries through the ages, but I explore a few of the astronomical highlights over the past 400 years.

The co-evolution of astronomy and its tools

As I write this article, we have just finished celebrating the International Year of Astronomy 2009 (IYA2009), a global effort initiated by the International Astronomical Union (IAU) and UNESCO to mark the 400th anniversary of the first use of a telescope for astronomical observations by Galileo Galilei in 1609 (IAU 2009). One of the major goals of IYA2009 was to increase scientific awareness and curiosity worldwide under the central theme, "The universe, yours to discover." Over 130 countries committed to IYA2009 in various ways, forming local groups to coordinate a range of scientific activities. As in all scientific fields, the progress of astronomy over the past 400 years has been intimately connected to the development of increasingly sophisticated tools, which enable ever more precise and detailed observations. These observations give rise to a progressively deeper understanding of the universe and our place in it.

Tools, observations, hypotheses and theories

The invention of new tools in astronomy has rapidly led to the discovery of previously unknown objects or phenomena. At the same time, astronomy has been a "theory-driven" science in that many astronomical predictions have been made, based on known scientific principles or extrapolated from observations and experiments performed on Earth. Many of these predictions subsequently have been borne out by observations, sometimes long after the predictions were made. In this section, we briefly examine some examples that are particularly relevant to our later discussion of life in the universe.

The planets Mercury, Venus, Mars, Jupiter, and Saturn can be seen with the unaided eye, and have been known as distinct from the stars since antiquity. In this sense, these planets were never "discovered." The word "planet" comes from the Greek word for "wanderer," and indeed, the movements of the planets in the sky are different from the so-called "fixed" stars (see e.g. Harper 2001). Galileo's telescopic observations, including his discovery of satellites of Jupiter, craters on the Moon, sunspots, and the phases of Venus, were pivotal to our modern understanding of the heavenly bodies as other worlds, and to the acceptance of the heliocentric theory, which places the Sun at the center of our Solar System. The planet Uranus was the first planet discovered through telescopic observations by William Herschel and his sister, Caroline, in 1781. On the other hand, John Couch Adams and Urbain Le Verrier predicted Neptune's existence and location by applying Isaac Newton's universal law of gravitation to observed anomalies in the orbit of Uranus. Neptune was subsequently observed telescopically, at its predicted position, by Johann Gottfried Galle and Heinrich d'Arrest in 1846. The discovery of many other Solar System objects, including the discovery of Pluto by Clyde Tombaugh in 1930, was enabled through the development of astrophotography using photographic plates, and later by more sophisticated digital imaging techniques (Smithsonian National Air and Space Museum 2002).

Many phenomena in astronomy have been hypothesized well before observational tools could test the hypotheses. A striking example of this is the nebular hypothesis of the origin of the Solar System, which was put forth independently by Immanuel Kant and Pierre-Simon Laplace in the eighteenth century. Kant and Laplace proposed that the Sun and its planets formed from a spinning cloud (nebula) in space, that was pulled together by gravity, flattened out into the shape of a disk as the slower-moving material accumulated at the center, eventually becoming the Sun, and the faster-spinning material accumulated further out, eventually becoming the planets (Smith 2004: 6). The nebular hypothesis was based on Newton's universal law of gravitation and two pieces of observational evidence: (1) all the planets lie more or less in a plane; and (2) all the planets orbit the Sun in the same direction. It remained a hypothesis well into the twentieth century, because there was no way to test it.

Today, we speak of "protoplanetary theory" because we can test hypotheses of our Solar System's origin by conducting observations or *in situ* experiments within our Solar System, and, as we will see, by studying other star and planetary systems that are currently forming.

The development of astrophysics, astrochemistry, and astrobiology

Angelo Secchi, S.J., a former director of the Vatican Observatory, has been dubbed the "Father of Astrophysics" for his pioneering work in applying spectroscopy to astronomical observations and classifying stars according to their spectral types during the nineteenth century (Maffeo 1991: 13). His observations laid the groundwork for connecting the spectral types of stars to their chemical compositions in the twentieth century, when quantum mechanics provided an understanding of how light interacts with matter. As tools continued to be developed enabling the applications of twentieth-century science to astronomical discoveries, astronomy evolved from a science almost exclusively constrained to studying the positions and motions of objects in space, to a science concerned with the composition and history of the universe and its constituents. The dissertation of Cecilia Payne-Gaposchkin, the first person to be awarded a PhD in astronomy by either Radcliffe (1925) or Harvard, is considered one of the finest in twentieth-century astronomy (Gingerich 2008). Payne-Gaposchkin correctly posited that hydrogen, which is now understood to be the most abundant element in the universe, is far more abundant in the Sun than on Earth, a result that initially encountered much ridicule in the astronomical community.

The development of instruments that detect light across the electromagnetic spectrum has enabled astronomers to view the non-visible universe at wavelengths from radio waves to gamma rays. Radio and infrared detectors, built from the middle of the twentieth century, revealed huge clouds of gas and dust in interstellar space that are too cold to emit visible light. The discovery of these molecular clouds helped make possible a branch of astronomy known as astrochemistry, and facilitated direct observations of what are now understood to be the birthplaces of stars and planetary systems. Although the formation of stars and planets is a process that spans tens of millions of years, large surveys of these star-forming regions reveal many objects in different stages of evolution, so it is possible to describe the relevant processes and their timescales statistically. Theoretical models include physics and chemistry to predict how systems will evolve. These models are then compared with observations and refined as new observations become available.

The term "exobiology" has been used since the early 1970s to denote the search for life beyond Earth. The term "astrobiology" has been used more recently, with a broader focus that includes the origin and evolution of life on Earth, but the two terms are otherwise synonymous. With mounting evidence of other planetary systems beyond our Solar System, as well as the discovery of life in extreme environments on Earth, NASA's Astrobiology Institute was established in 1996 to address three fundamental questions: How does life begin and evolve? Is there life beyond Earth, and, if so, how can we detect it? What is the future of life on Earth and in the universe? These questions are scientifically reframed versions of questions that have been asked in one form or another since the dawn of civilization: Where did we come from? Are we alone? Where are we going? (NASA 2009).

The scale of the universe

In addition to increasingly detailed studies of the cosmos from Earth, during the past several decades it has become possible to study our world from space. The stunning photograph of the Earth from lunar orbit during the *Apollo* 8 mission in December 1968 provided humanity with an unprecedented view of our planet from a distance of about a quarter of a million miles (NASA 2008a). The emotional impact of this view is highlighted at the entrance to the "Shoot for the Moon" exhibition at the Adler Planetarium in Chicago, where a larger-than-life statue portrays astronaut James A. Lovell as he covers the Earth with his thumb held at arm's length (Rotblatt-Amrany and Amrany 2005). Many robotic spacecraft have sent back images of the Earth from interplanetary distances, such as the surface of Mars (*Opportunity* rover), and the orbits of Mars (*Mars Global Surveyor*), Saturn (*Cassini*), and beyond Neptune (*Voyager 1*). Astronomer and science popularizer Carl Sagan described the appearance of Earth from *Voyager 1*, at a distance of 3.7 billion miles, as "a mote of dust suspended in a sunbeam" (Sagan 1994: 6).

The diameter of our Solar System at the orbit of Pluto is roughly 6 billion miles; however, the distance between our Sun and the next nearest star is about 24 trillion miles. Our Sun is one among more than 200 billion stars that form a large group known as the Milky Way Galaxy. The Milky Way Galaxy has the shape of a flattened disk with spiral arms, nearly 600 quadrillion miles in diameter. On scales of interstellar distances and larger, one of the units commonly used as a measure of distance is the light year, which is the distance light travels in a year, just under 6 trillion miles. The nearest star (aside from the Sun) is therefore slightly over four light years distant, and the diameter of our Galaxy is roughly 100,000 light years. Our Galaxy is one among hundreds of billions of galaxies in the part of the universe we can observe. Galaxies themselves are arranged in groups or clusters. Our Galaxy is part of the Local Group, which is roughly 5 million light years in diameter. The furthest observable galaxies lie at a distance of about 13 billion light years, although the universe itself may be incomprehensibly larger even than this (see e.g. the essay by Primack and Abrams, Chapter 9 in this volume).

What these enormous distances mean is that, as we look further out into the universe, we probe increasingly earlier times in the history of the universe. This is because of the time it takes light to travel these enormous distances. We see an object that is 1 billion light years away not as it looks today, but as it appeared 1 billion years ago. This means that astronomers have a "fossil record" of the history of the universe, much as geologists and biologists have a fossil record of the history of the Earth in rock layers. Indeed, what we see as we look further and further out into space indicates that the universe has changed dramatically over the eons. These observations have enabled us to construct a timeline of the universe from its birth about 13.7 billion years ago, through the formation of the first stars and galaxies, through the ongoing formation and evolution of stars and planets.

The origins of stars and planets

With the exception of hydrogen, helium, and lithium, which were produced when the universe was only a few minutes old, essentially all the other elements have been produced by nucleosynthesis in the deep interiors of stars, or in explosions of massive stars known as supernovae. These massive stellar explosions are particularly important because they seed the interstellar medium with heavy elements that can be incorporated into subsequent generations of stars and planetary systems. These elements are critical to life – the elements on our world and in our bodies were produced billions of years ago, in the interiors of stars that "lived" and "died" before our Sun and Solar System were born.

While observations of other galaxies across cosmic distances enable us to study how galaxies have evolved over time, observations of objects within our own Galaxy allow us to reconstruct a picture of how stars and planetary systems form and evolve today. This is so because many of these objects lie at distances of "mere" hundreds and thousands of light years, so they probe very recent history in terms of the 13.7 billion year history of the universe.

Star formation as an ongoing process did not become accepted by the scientific community until the middle of the twentieth century, in part through the observations of Viktor Ambartsumian, who noted that loose aggregates of stars known as associations should be unstable against galactic tidal forces and disperse over time (Smith 2004: 208–9). Meanwhile, during the 1930s, Hans Bethe's work on nuclear reactions led him to the discovery of the reactions that supply the energy in stars, and earned him the Nobel Prize in Physics in 1967 (Nobel Lectures 1972). Fusion reactions in the cores of stars like our Sun can power these stars for about 10 billion years, but the predicted lifetime of stars much more massive than our Sun is only several million years. These and other pieces of independent evidence pointed toward star formation as an ongoing process, but studying the various stages posed enormous challenges, since the spatial and time scales involved are vast, and the early stages are enshrouded in dust and could not be observed prior to the development of telescopes that record non-visible light.

At a distance of about 1600 light years, the Orion Nebula is the nearest region that is currently forming massive as well as low-mass stars. Here, "low-mass stars" refers to stars similar to, or less massive than, our Sun. In 1994, disk-shaped structures surrounding sun-like stars were observed in silhouette against the bright gas in the Orion Nebula by the Hubble Space Telescope (Hubblesite 1994). Since the mid-1990s, many of these protoplanetary disks, or proplyds, have been observed in other nebulae containing very young stars. These proplyds are also observed with infrared telescopes and radio interferometers, which enable us to determine important physical properties such as temperature, mass, and composition, and indicate these objects are the long-sought-after planetary systems in formation. The existence and ubiquity of these objects suggests that the formation of planets generally accompanies the formation of stars.

What was known over 200 years ago as the nebular hypothesis has finally reached the status of "protoplanetary theory". Observations have been made of the initial stages of dense interstellar clouds collapsing under gravity as well as the protoplanetary disk stage of evolution. One surprising discovery that was not anticipated by theory was that the early stages of star formation are accompanied by energetic outflows of material as well as collapse. Microwave observations revealed these energetic outflows before the discovery of proplyds, because they span much larger distances in space (Snell *et al.* 1980: L17–L22). These outflows are generally bipolar; that is, they emanate from the infant star in two opposite directions, and are generally aligned perpendicular to the protoplanetary disks. A typical protoplanetary disk is approximately the size of our Solar System, but a bipolar outflow from a young star can span more than ten light-years of space. Outflows may play an important role in clearing away nascent cloud material and may also compress nearby dense clouds, triggering the formation of new stars.

Among its many contributions to astronomy, the Spitzer Space Telescope has provided an unprecedented infrared view of the plane of our Galaxy (University of Wisconsin-Madison 2008). Infrared light penetrates the dusty clouds in our Galaxy and reveals many more stars and nebulae than optical imaging. Infrared (and microwave) observations indicate that interstellar space contains many complex organic molecules that are also found on Earth. In fact, large hydrocarbon molecules permeate the clouds imaged by Spitzer, indicating that organic material is ubiquitous. These interstellar clouds are sculpted into arcs and circular features that show how winds and radiation from stars sculpt their environments and sometimes trigger the birth of new stars.

Our current picture of star formation has changed in many significant details, but the overall picture that has emerged closely resembles the hypothesis put forth centuries ago for the formation of our own Solar System. Observations over the past few decades strongly suggest that most, if not all, stars form with planets. We also now know that most stars form in clusters – with "siblings", so to speak. There is strong evidence that even our Sun, now an isolated star, formed in an environment similar to the Orion Nebula (Hester *et al.* 2004: 1116–17). Star formation even appears to be a self-sustaining process. Outflows from supernova explosions can compress nearby molecular clouds and trigger the gravitational collapse of new stars, and so can outflows and radiation from very young stars. In a sense, there is a parallel here with the biological world – just as life can recreate itself, so can stars. Given the sheer number of stars in our Galaxy (over 200 billion), and hundreds of billions of galaxies beyond, these discoveries have profound implications for the possibility of discovering life beyond the Earth.

Life in the universe

The NASA Astrobiology Roadmap defines a planet or planetary satellite to be habitable if it can sustain life that originates there, or if it sustains life that is carried to the object. Habitable environments must provide extended regions of liquid water, conditions favorable for the assembly of complex organic molecules, and energy sources to sustain metabolism (NASA 2008b: 716). The requirement for liquid water has motivated both remote and *in situ* searches for traces of past or present water in our Solar System; however, the search for life beyond Earth is no longer confined to exploring the Solar System. Planetary systems like our Solar System may be very common in the universe. The protoplanetary disks described earlier have the dimensions of our Solar System, billions of miles across; however, once individual planets have formed from such disks, they are merely thousands of miles in diameter. Finding dim planets orbiting stars that are trillions or quadrillions of miles away has indeed been a challenge, but several methods are used, which reinforce each other and yield similar or complementary results (e.g. NASA Jet Propulsion Laboratory 2009; Schneider 2009).

In 1995, sixty-five years after the discovery of Pluto, the Swiss team Didier Queloz and Michel Mayor announced the discovery of the first planet orbiting another star similar to our Sun. In the same year, Geoff Marcy and Paul Butler announced the discovery of two other exoplanets, or extrasolar planets, as these objects are called. These exoplanets were discovered indirectly, via the Doppler method, which essentially measures "wobbles" of stars produced by the gravitational pull of an orbiting planet. The physical mechanism is the same, which, for example, causes Neptune's orbit to be affected by Uranus' orbit, but the discovery of exoplanets required advances in spectrometer technology and observational techniques during the 1980s and 1990s. The current tally of exoplanets is well over 400, and typically increases on the scale of weeks or even days (Schneider 2009). In fact, equipment owned by amateur astronomers is now capable of reproducing some of these discoveries (e.g. Gary 2007). The earliest exoplanets that were detected are giant planets that orbit very close to their stars, because these planets were initially the easiest to detect via the Doppler method. This result was surprising because, in our Solar System, giant planets like Jupiter have larger orbits around the Sun than the terrestrial planets. Today, a variety of techniques that are sensitive to different planet sizes and orbits are used to identify exoplanets. As subsequent observations have been made with increasingly sensitive instruments, a great variety of planetary systems have been discovered, and some of these systems may more closely resemble our Solar System.

The detection of Earth-sized exoplanets has become possible recently through observatories such as NASA's Kepler mission, named for Johannes Kepler, who published his first two laws of planetary motion in 1609 in his book *Astronomia Nova*, and the third in 1619 in *Harmonices Mundi* (Kepler Mission 2009). Kepler's empirical laws can be derived from Newton's laws of motion and universal law of gravitation. From an Earth-trailing orbit, the Kepler observatory is monitoring more than 100,000 stars continuously over a 3.5-year period. The Kepler mission utilizes an instrument known as a photometer that records the light output from astronomical objects. The orbits of some exoplanets cross in front of, or transit, their stars as viewed from Earth. Kepler's photometer records changes in the brightness of stars when this occurs. Shortly after its launch in March 2009, Kepler obtained data on a giant transiting planet that had been detected previously from Earth. Kepler detected not only the transit of the planet known as HAT-P-7b, but the occultation as it passed behind its star, and the small changes in brightness due to the phases of the planet as it orbited. It seems fitting that, 400 years after Galileo's discovery of the phases of Venus, humans should detect the phases of a planet 1000 light years away, approximately 100 million times more distant than Venus.

By the end of its mission, the data acquired by Kepler will allow a meaningful estimate of the frequency of terrestrial planets in our Galaxy that are potentially like

Earth. Transit detections can provide a wealth of information about the physical characteristics of planets, such as mass, size, density, and even atmospheric composition. Plans for future observatories include technology and methods to search for signs of life (biosignatures or biosigns) in the atmospheres of extrasolar planets (Astrobiology Web 2006: 785). These searches will be complemented by SETI (Search for ExtraTerrestrial Intelligence) Institute programs, which conduct surveys for artificial radio signals (signals produced by technology) indicative of sentient life (SETI Institute 2011). For the first time in history, humanity has the capability of finding evidence that life exists on other planets, perhaps life that, like us, is capable of exploring the universe, and pondering questions relating to both its existence and its meaning. If biosigns are detected on planets orbiting nearby stars, this would suggest that life has evolved in a great many places in the universe; however, a null result may simply indicate that life beyond Earth is rare, but not absent. If only a single sentient species evolved in each galaxy, there could still be an uncountable number of them, but because of the distances involved, we might never learn of their existence.

Astrobiology and religion

Science today shows us that humans are a part of, rather than apart from, the universe. Recent advances in molecular biology have unveiled a remarkably diverse biological community on Earth, which nonetheless shares common ancestry. Modern molecular methods that compare conserved DNA sequences common to all life indicate that Earth's entire biota can be represented by a single family tree (Astrobiology Web 2006: 793). Furthermore, new studies have expanded the list of animal species considered to be self-aware; that is, animals that are able to distinguish themselves as individuals separate from other members of their species. For example, pigs have recently joined these ranks, along with elephants, dolphins, magpies, gray parrots, and some primates (Holden 2009: 919). The incredible diversity of both microscopic and macroscopic life on the Earth suggests that, if anything, science fiction has erred conservatively with respect to conceiving the characteristics of life that may have evolved elsewhere.

A critical emphasis of many religions is on relationships – the relationship between humans and God, humans and other forms of life, and the relationship of humans to the cosmos. How we view life beyond Earth is an extension of how we view non-human life on Earth. For monotheistic religions that regard God as the ultimate source of the universe (or mulitiverse, for that matter), this may require rethinking presuppositions about what it means to bear the "image of God." Although science can, and arguably should, inform ethics, science cannot dictate ethics. The increasingly likely possibility of life beyond Earth requires careful consideration of how human beings should regard this life. Notice that in the latter two sentences I've crossed over from "can" to "should" terminology, the latter being traditionally addressed within religious frameworks. With these considerations in mind, the American Association for the Advancement of Science (AAAS) maintains an ongoing Dialogue on Science, Ethics, and Religion that facilitates communication between scientific and religious communities (AAAS 2010).

From renaissance scholars to citizen scientists

Since I started this essay with a discussion of Galileo and how technology has shaped our understanding of the universe, it seems appropriate to end with a discussion of how the culture of science has changed over the past 400 years. Since the days of Galileo, astronomy has become increasingly a community effort. The days of the individual "renaissance scholar," educated and fluent in multiple disciplines, have given way to the era of the specialist, working with many team members, each bringing their expertise and training to bear on addressing new scientific questions. In the twenty-first century, it is no longer even possible for scientists and their students to mine the vast astronomical databases acquired by contemporary instruments. This fact has led to the development of "citizen science" programs that utilize new web tools and infrastructure to enable the general public to participate in active scientific research through tasks such as inspecting and characterizing features in large high-resolution images (Zooniverse 2011). These tasks help scientists create new catalogues, discover new types of objects, and identify further scientific questions. Citizen science benefits both science and society through inviting the public to gain a better understanding of how science works by becoming part of the discovery process. Science, like religion, has become an intensely communal endeavor.

References

AAAS (2010) "AAAS Dialogue on Science, Ethics, and Religion," Washington, DC: American Association for the Advancement of Science, www.aaas.org/spp/dser.

Astrobiology Web (2006) "The Astrobiology Primer: An Outline of General Knowledge – Version 1," *Astrobiology* 6(5): 735–813, www.astrobiology.com.

Gary, Bruce L. (2007) *Exoplanet Observing for Amateurs*, brucegary.net/book_EOA/x.htm.

Gingerich, Owen (2008) "Cecilia Payne-Gaposchkin: Astronomer and Astrophysicist," www.harvardsquarelibrary.org/unitarians/payne2.html.

Harper, Douglas (2001) "Online Etymology Dictionary," www.etymonline.com.

Hester, J. Jeff, Steven J. Desch, Kevin R. Healy and Laurie A. Leshin (2004) "The Cradle of the Solar System," *Science* 304(5674): 1116–17.

Holden, Constance (ed.) (2009) "Who's that Swine?" *Science* 326: 919.

Hubblesite (1994) "Hubble Confirms Abundance of Protoplanetary Disks around Newborn Stars," hubblesite.org/newscenter/archive/releases/1994/24/image/b/.

IAU (2009) "The International Year of Astronomy 2009," International Astronomical Union and UNESCO, www.astronomy2009.org.

Kepler Mission (2009) "Kepler Mission: A Search for Habitable Planets," NASA Ames Research Center, kepler.nasa.gov.

Maffeo, Sabino, S.J. (1991) *In the Service of Nine Popes: 100 years of the Vatican Observatory*, George V. Coyne S.J. (trans.), Vatican Observatory Foundation: 13–15.

NASA (2008a) "Earthrise at Christmas," www.nasa.gov/multimedia/imagegallery/image_feature_102.html.

——(2008b) "NASA Astrobiology Roadmap 2008," *Astrobiology* 8(4): 715–30, astrobiology.nasa.gov/roadmap.

——(2009) "Astrobiology: Life in the universe," astrobiology.nasa.gov.

NASA Jet Propulsion Laboratory (2009) "PlanetQuest Exoplanet Exploration," planetquest.jpl.nasa.gov.
Nobel Lectures (1972) *Physics 1963–1970*, Amsterdam: Elsevier.
Rotblatt-Amrany, Julie and Omri Amrany (2005) "Quest for Exploration" statue at the Adler Planetarium.
Sagan, Carl (1994) *Pale Blue Dot: A Vision of the Human Future in Space*, New York: Random House, Inc.
Schneider, Jean (2009) "The Extrasolar Planets Encyclopaedia," exoplanet.eu.
SETI Institute (2011), www.seti.org
Smith, Michael D. (2004) *The Origin of Stars*, London: Imperial College Press.
Smithsonian National Air and Space Museum (2002) "Discovering New Planets," www.nasm.si.edu/etp/discovery/disc_planets.html.
Snell, R.L., R.B. Loren and R.L. Plambeck (1980) "Observations of CO in L1551 – Evidence for Stellar Wind Driven Shocks," *Astrophysical Journal Letters* 239: L17–22.
University of Wisconsin-Madison (2008) "GLIMPSE: The Galactic Legacy Infrared Mid-Plane Survey Extraordinaire," www.astro.wisc.edu/glimpse.
Zooniverse (2011) "Real Science Online," www.zooniverse.org

Further reading

Most of the references cited in this essay are websites due to the breadth of the material covered and the rapid timescale over which astronomical content is updated. Many of these sites contain links to excellent references for further exploration of the subject matter. Nevertheless, I recommend several books for those looking for a general overview of these topics. Appealing to a lay audience, Govert Schilling and Lars Lindberg Christensen, *Eyes on the Skies: 400 Years of Telescopic Discovery* (Berlin: Wiley-VCH, 2008) is a special publication launched for the International Year of Astronomy 2009. For astrobiology, Iain Gilmour and Mark A. Sephton (eds) *An Introduction to Astrobiology* (Cambridge: Cambridge University Press, 2004) is an introductory undergraduate textbook compiled by experts in the field. "The Astrobiology Primer: An Outline of General Knowledge" (cited above) presents an overview of the discipline, with sections written by experts in the individual scientific fields. I also recommend *Exploring the Origin, Extent, and Future of Life: Philosophical, Ethical and Theological Perspectives*, ed. Constance M. Bertka (Cambridge: Cambridge University Press, 2009), a book that grew out of a series of astrobiology meetings held by the AAAS in 2003–04. As the future of life in the universe is beyond the scope of my essay, I suggest Fred C. Adams and Greg Laughlin, *The Five Ages of the Universe: Inside the Physics of Eternity* (New York: Simon & Schuster, 1999) for a discussion of how the evolution of the universe may affect life in the distant future.

11
HINDU COSMOGONY/ COSMOLOGY

Gerald James Larson

Introduction

Unlike discussions regarding the origin of the world (cosmogony) [Sanskrit = *jagad-utpatti*] or the metaphysical nature of the world (cosmology) [Sanskrit = *bhuvana-jnana*] in Jewish, Christian, and Islamic traditions that focus on God as a creator *ex nihilo*, Hindu discussions are interestingly different. God is never a creator *ex nihilo* in South Asian thought (whether Hindu, Buddhist, or Jaina), but nevertheless God (Ishvara) or the Absolute (Brahman) – or, if one prefers, any of the proper conventional names such as Brahma, Vishnu, Shiva, Krishna, and so forth – plays a crucial role in what might be called "enabling" the world to unfold and take shape. This is the case in terms of the various conceptualizations of space, time, and deity in Hindu thought. The term "various," however, is important here. From the earliest periods for which we have textual or archaeological evidence, for example the Vedic and Upanishadic period, the epic period, and so forth, there is no single cosmogony or cosmology accepted by all developing Hindu traditions. There is, rather, a rich pluralism of tales, myths, legends, and speculations, most of which involve God (Ishvara) or the gods in one form or another, but none of which is normative for Hindu religious traditions as a whole.

Nevertheless, during the early and mid-centuries of the Common Era, in a class of texts known as *Puranas* (literally "old" or "ancient" tales about the origins and structures of the world), in certain law books such as the well known *Manu-smriti* (the "Laws of Manu"), and in some early philosophical texts such as the *Yogasutra* and its commentaries, a certain convergence of ideas emerges regarding the origins and structure of the world. At first glance, these imaginative stories about the origins of the world appear to be little more than what Hegel once characterized as "the fanciful polytheism of the Hindus" (Hegel 1988: 289). Upon closer examination, however, the convergence of ideas appears to provide an intriguing rationale for a unique understanding of the nature of the universe (*jagat*, *bhuvana*, *loka*), the nature of human behavior and becoming (*karman* and *samsara*), and the nature of divinity or God (Ishvara).

Among the many sources that might be used to describe the various Hindu accounts of the world, I make use of two principal textual sources: (1) the discussion of world-periods (*yuga*) and world geography (*dvipa, loka*) as set forth in the *Vishnu-purana*, Book I, Chapter III (Wilson 1972:19–24) and Book II, Chapter II (Wilson 1972: 134–41); and (2) the "knowledge about the world" (*bhuvana-jnana*) as set forth in the commentary, attributed to a certain Vyasa, on *Yogasutra* III.26 (Larson and Bhattacharya 2008: 91–99). The account in the *Vishnu-purana* is largely a popular mythological characterization, whereas the account in the *Yogasutra* represents a somewhat more philosophical/theological interpretation. Both accounts are typical of, although not identical to, the sorts of discussion one finds in most of the other *Puranas*, the great epics, *Mahabharata* and *Ramayana*, the Hindu law books, and in most Buddhist and Jaina accounts as well (Jacobi 1961a: 200–202, 1961b: 155–61; La Vallée-Poussin 1961a: 187–90, 1961b: 129–38). In what follows, the details of the cosmology and the many technical names employed need not be delineated in full, since these are for the most part archaic discussions having little more than archival interest. The overall general outlines of these cosmological reflections must be discussed, however, for the sake of understanding the unique world-view of the Hindus.

Hindu world-periods (*yuga*) – cosmological time

According to the typical account as set forth in the *Vishnu-purana*, Vishnu sleeps in the great cosmic ocean, reclining on the cosmic serpent Shesha. A lotus plant grows out of the navel of Vishnu, and on one of the petals of the lotus flower, a drop of fluid appears from which emerges the god Brahma, the creative force. Brahma fashions a great world-egg (Anda), which contains the entirety of the phenomenal, empirical world "from Brahma down to a blade of grass." The universe at the outset is perfect and complete, and is known as the *Krita Yuga*, the "Well Constructed" or Perfect Period, that unfolds for 1,728,000 human years, during which time everything functions in keeping with its inherent nature. Towards the end of the period, however, a decay begins to set in that leads to a second period known as the *Treta Yuga*, the "Three-Quarters Period," or the period in which only three-quarters of the world-egg maintains its original excellence, the remaining quarter becoming increasingly decadent. This second world-period unfolds for 1,296,000 human years, and again, towards the end of the period, a further decay sets in that leads to the third period known as the *Dvapara Yuga*, the "Two Quarters Period" or the "One-Half Period," in which half of the world maintains its original excellence, the other half becoming increasingly decadent. This third period unfolds for 864,000 human years and leads to a final, fourth period, the *Kali Yuga*, the "One-Quarter Period," in which the one quarter of excellence is completely overshadowed by three quarters of decadence, unfolding for 432,000 human years, or, in other words, only one-tenth of the perfection that was the case at the outset. The sequence 4, 3, 2, 1 is derived from the four-numbered "die" (plural: "dice") in Indian gaming, with 4 having the perfect value and 1 the least.

Altogether, the four *yugas* make a total of 4,320,000 years, referred to as a "Great Yuga" (*mahayuga*) leading to a general dissolution (*pralaya*) after which Brahma reconstitutes the world-egg for the next set of four periods. 1000 of these Great Yugas taken together are known as a *Kalpa* and are equivalent to one day in the life of Brahma, or, in other words, 4,320,000,000 human years. Brahma rests for one night of equal length, bringing one to a total of 8,640,000,000 human years. Brahma lives for 360 such days and for 100 years, thereby abiding for 311,040,000,000,000 (8,640,000,000 × 360 × 100) years. At this point, Brahma has exhausted himself and withdraws back into the lotus plant, leading to a Great Dissolution (*maha-pralaya*), after which there is a period of quiescence equal in length to everything that has unfolded. At the end of the period of quiescence, a new lotus plant emerges from the navel of sleeping Vishnu, and a new Brahma emerges to fashion another world-egg (Anda) for a replay of the preceding process, and, of course, the process repeats itself endlessly. There is, finally, neither an absolute beginning nor an absolute ending, only the pulsating episodes of recursive becoming.

It should also be mentioned for the sake of sketching in our particular place in this vast schematic that each *Kalpa* in this vast recursive process is further divided into fourteen *Manvantaras* ("Human-Intervals"), each of which contains approximately seventy-two "Great Yugas" (or *mahayugas*). Our current *Manvantara* is known as *Manu Vaivasvata*, and our current Kalpa is *Varaha Kalpa*. Furthermore, we are now in the *Kali Yuga* of our world-period, which commenced on February 17, 3102 BCE (Jacobi 1961a: 201).

Hindu world geography (*dvipa, loka*) – cosmological space

The scope of the spatial cosmology is as vast as the temporal unfolding, and, as is the case with the description of the world-periods, the details of the geographical cosmology are set forth in numerous passages in the law books, the great epics, and the *Puranas*. I prefer the *Yogasutra* account (under III.26), however, since it relates the geographical cosmology to the intuitive insights of the accomplished Yogin, thereby providing greater insight into how the cosmology functions in the overall Hindu world-view. Section III of the *Yogasutra* deals with the "extraordinary cognitive capacities" (*vibhutis, siddhis*) attained by Yogins when they have achieved advanced levels of Yogic awareness through the practice of "comprehensive reflection" (*samyama*). The sutra or verse itself, namely III. 26, simply states, "When the sun [or perhaps better, the '*surya-dvara*,' the 'solar-entrance' in the region of the navel or heart] becomes the focus for comprehensive reflection (*samyama*), knowledge of (various) worlds (*bhuvana-jnana*) becomes possible." According to the sutra, in other words, references to the Sun, Moon, Pole Star, and so forth, refer to places in the body of the Yogin (the microcosm of the biological body) as well as phenomena in the external world (the macrocosm of the manifest universe) (Larson and Bhattacharya 2008: 92).

The commentary on this *Yogasutra* verse (attributed to Vyasa) then provides a summary description of these worlds (*bhuvanas*). If the preceding cosmology of world-periods provided the temporal unfolding of the cosmic egg (*brahmanda*), fashioned by Brahma, we are now informed about the spatial content of the cosmic egg or, in other words, the content of the universe. Altogether, there are seven worlds enclosed within the cosmic egg (*brahmanda*). From the top down, they are as follows:

Satya-loka – the "world of truth" – the highest or seventh level
Tapo-loka – the "world of discipline or asceticism" – the sixth level
Jana-loka – the "world of living beings" – the fifth level.

These first three, taken together, make up the *Brahma-loka*, populated by the high gods and extraordinary beings of the world, belonging to Brahma.

Mahar-loka – the "world of Prajapati" (the "lord of creatures") – the fourth level
Mahendra-loka – the "world of Indra" – the third level.

The third and fourth levels, together with the fifth, sixth and seventh, all make up the realms of "heaven" (*svar*).

Antariksha-loka – the "world of the intermediate regions" from the Pole Star (Dhruva) through the stars and planets up to the summit of Meru, the sacred mountain at the center of the earth – the second level
Bhur-loka – the "world of earth" – the first level, which in turn is divided into three segments:

(1) *Vasumati* (our "Earth") with its seven continents (*dvipa*), including Jambudvipa (the "rose-apple" subcontinent or India), six additional continents in concentric circles (Shaka, Kusha, Krauncha, Shalmala, Gomedha, and Pushkara), each surrounded by oceans, respectively, of salt water, sugar-cane juice, wine, clarified butter, curds, milk, and fresh water (the names refer to different trees, plants, and so forth)
(2) *Patalas* – the "nether" regions – seven in all, in descending order from Patala, to Talatala, Vitala, Sutala, Atala, Rasatala, and ending with Mahatala
(3) *Narakas* – the "hells" – again, seven in all, in descending order from Andhatamisra (darkness) through Kalasutra (air), Maharaurava (wind), Raurava (fire), Ambarisa (water), Mahakala (earth), and ending with the lowest "hell," *Avici*.

Throughout these various worlds are all sorts of deities and creatures working out their Karmic trajectories through ongoing cycles of manifestation, or coming forth and withdrawal (*pralaya* and *maha-pralaya*). This is the case with Brahma and the world-egg (*brahmanda*) or universe as well. That is, the so-called "creative-force," Brahma, sometimes identified with Hiranyagarbha, the "golden germ or womb," and the world-egg undergoes periodic manifestation and withdrawal as well. Put somewhat differently, the worlds, whether in manifestation or in withdrawal, are subject to a beginningless (*an-adi*) process (*parinama*) of time or becoming (*bhava*), as we have already described earlier. Precisely how the cycles unfold is determined by the trajectories of the various species of beings that have been self-constructed by the afflictions (*kleshas*), actions (*karma*), ripenings (*vipaka*), and resulting residues (*vasanas, ashayas, samskaras*) of their own behavior or functioning.

The text concludes by pointing out that two sorts of beings are outside of the world-egg: the "disincarnate" (or disembodied) ones (*videhas*) and the "dissolved in nature" ones (*prakriti-layas*). The former, the "disincarnate" ones, are those beings (primarily certain *devas* as well as Yogins) who have attained a temporary reprieve from ordinary becoming (*bhava*) because of having conquered attachment to gross objects (*bhutas*) and sense longings. They have attained at least a temporary spiritual liberation (*kaivalya*). The latter, the "dissolved in nature" ones, are those beings or Yogins who have attained an even longer, but still temporary, reprieve from ordinary becoming (*bhava*) because of having conquered attachment to the mind and ego. They have become dissolved (*laya*) in unmanifest nature, which also brings with it a temporary spiritual liberation (*kaivalya*). Both sorts, however, are still predisposed towards one or another yearning for becoming (*bhava*). In other words, both sorts are still predisposed to the vicissitudes of time. Both sorts of beings, therefore, whether gods or Yogins, because of the inclination (*adhikara*) towards becoming, will fall back eventually into the temporal realm of the world-egg.

Altogether, then, the sorts of beings that make up the beginningless world of becoming (*bhava*, *samsara*) include the myriad of living beings within the world-egg (*brahmanda*) of Brahma, "from Brahma down to a blade of grass," as well as those caught up in the nether worlds and hells. There are the seven higher worlds, ranging from the highest "world of truth" (*satya-loka*) down to the "world of earth" (*bhur-loka*). Then there are the seven "nether" worlds below the level of the earth, and the seven "hells" down to the lowest hell of Avici, together making twenty-one levels of becoming (three levels of seven each) from the top of the world-egg down to its base. Also, there are the "disincarnate" ones (*videhas*) and the "dissolved in nature" ones (*prakriti-layas*), temporarily in reprieve from becoming, but destined to re-enter the realm of becoming when their own predispositions ripen. Likewise, of course, there are the fully successful Yogins who, through comprehensive reflection, have attained "spiritual release" (*kaivalya*) and will never again be subject to the process of becoming and, hence, will never again have a place within the world-egg or universe. In other words, although these Yogins were initially within the beginningless process of becoming, they have been able to extricate themselves with certainty and finality from the subsequent ongoing process.

What is distinctive about God (Ishvara) in this Yoga account of Hindu cosmology is that God is none of these. God is neither any of the conventional "gods," for example, Brahma, Vishnu, Shiva, *et al.*, nor is God involved in the spatio-temporal content or functioning of the manifest universe. God is described, rather, as a particular pure (that is, contentless) consciousness, an "eternal excellence" untouched by afflictions, actions, or the consequences of actions or long-term Karmic predispositions of any kind. God can only be denoted by a vibrating non-sense sound, the sacred syllable, "Om"! Thus, according to this account of cosmology in the *Yogasutra*, if God is not touched by afflictions, actions, the consequences of actions, and the resulting traces and/or predispositions, then obviously God cannot be a "creator" in any meaningful sense, nor can God be "personal" in any intelligible sense. "What" or "who," then, is God? God as consciousness cannot be a thing or entity, and because consciousness is contentless or object-less, it can only appear or be described in terms of what it is not, an apophatic or negative theology with a vengeance, or, if you will, a negative theology that borders on an "a-theistic" "theism," that is, the presence of a God, neither creator nor person, but, rather, a transcendent consciousness the witnessing presence of which "enables" all things to be, a divine, beginning-less cosmic constant that exhibits the recursive pulsations of manifest being.

The tripartite significance of Hindu cosmology

Having set forth in general outline the overall temporal and spatial characterization of Hindu cosmology together with at least a few comments about the accompanying theology, let me now proceed to focus on three salient axioms of Hindu cosmological thinking: (1) synchronic phylogeny; (2) diachronic ontogeny; and (3) precessional cosmology. By the term "phylogeny" I mean the Hindu account of the development of the material world and its sentient species. By "ontogeny" I mean the Hindu account of the development of the individual organism (whether human, animal, divine, and so forth). By "precessional" I mean the manner in which Hindu cosmology unfolds in keeping with the notion of the "precession of the equinox," namely, that the universe is, overall, running down or declining, just as the equinox falls backward through the zodiac or ecliptic (Larson, 1980: 303–16, 1983: 161–67, 1993: 373–88; Larson and Bhattacharya 2008: 91–100). I am using the term "axiom" in the general sense of an established principle accepted commonly among Hindu practitioners.

The Hindu axiom of synchronic phylogeny

Our modern notions of history and conventional historical thinking are, for the most part, absent in Hindu thought. There is, of course, a notion of history for Hindus. It is just not our modern notion. What, then, is the Hindu notion? What is striking about the temporal and spatial conceptualization as set forth above in terms of Hindu world-periods and Hindu world geography is that everything is perfect, properly formed, and excellent at the outset of the world. Nothing new can emerge that is not already presupposed and fully formed at the outset, and that which is fully formed was or is, as it were, without beginning (*an-adi*)! In an interesting essay, "History, Change and Permanence: A Classical Indian Perspective," M. Deshpande (1979: 9–10) points out that there is a deep conservatism or "preservationism" in classical Hindu thought. He comments,

> Thus there was no history in a real sense. All forms existed, and it is a matter of pure accident that certain forms are or are not found in a particular text, a particular time or a particular region. Thus, the problem of "existence" was separated from the problem of "attestation." Non-attestation did not imply non-existence. While eternal existence was the fact, the attestation and non-attestation of forms was a matter of historical accident.

Whatever changes occur, either in language or in society, are never dealt with historically, but are treated rather as "options." Hence, language, society, and cosmos were dealt with largely in a deductive fashion. The human community is not to be viewed as developing over time diachronically. It is to be viewed, rather, in terms of "synchronic phylogeny."

> While western science and civilization seem to be based on a continuously self-improving process of experimentation and induction of new general principles, classical Indian tradition "claims" to be authoritative by being a purely deductive tradition whose first principles have been unalterably established.[…]
>
> History as viewed from this deductive perspective is not a matter of new creation of events or new inventions, but simply an unfolding of implicit aspects and values of the eternally self-existing reality.
>
> (*ibid.*: 18–19)

It almost appears as if there were a deliberate embracing of "unhistoric history" by classical Indian thought, the embracing of a "synchronic phylogeny" whereby we are continuously looking back and remembering the eternal first principles that are truly authoritative and make possible the options with which we must continually live.

The Hindu axiom of diachronic ontogeny

Yet, in a completely paradoxical manner, the synchronic phylogeny wherein everything is fully formed at the outset carries with it a second axiom, which, in a puzzling way, appears to undercut the first. The second axiom can be expressed in the following manner. If it is the case that everything is fully formed at the outset, beginninglessly, then so, likewise, are all sentient creatures throughout the extended universe. There never was a time, in other words, when I or any other sentient creature was not, since all were there at the outset. Hence, through all the unfolding periods of becoming, I, along with all other sentient creatures, must also have been becoming, or, in other words, the axiom of Karma and rebirth, or *samsara*. My identity in this particular lifetime is shaped by a diachronic series of preceding lifetimes stretching back to a beginning-less beginning! In any particular lifetime of a sentient being, the creature is part of an unfolding synchronic whole, but the particular identity of a given lifetime has been shaped by an incredibly complex series of diachronic actions (*karman*), which have determined my synchronic place in this particular rebirth. Moreover, if it is the case that the process is beginningless and, hence, infinitely so, then my actions as a sentient being have undoubtedly brought me into almost every possible life-form that has been formed from the outset, beginninglessly. There appear to be, therefore, two continually intersecting processes. On the one hand, there is the synchronic phylogeny of everything having been fully and perfectly formed at the outset. On the other hand, there is a continuously operating diachronic ontogeny of individual sentient beings, whose trajectories in lifetime after lifetime are determined by the synchronic presuppositions coming from the past being projected into the future by my continuing actions as an individual sentient being. From one point of view, the system is completely determined (synchronically). From another point of view, the system is completely open and free, in the sense that at any given point-instant I, and all sentient beings, must engage in action that will shape my future becoming (ontogenetically).

The Hindu axiom of precessional cosmology

Oddly enough, however, there is still another axiom in Hindu cosmological thinking that always accompanies the intersecting processes of synchronic phylogeny and diachronic ontogeny. Not only is everything present in its perfect and well formed nature at the outset (synchronic phylogeny; Krita Yuga, recursively replicated), and not only are all sentient beings nevertheless undergoing recurring diachronic identities based upon their Karma in lifetime after lifetime (diachronic ontogeny among and between the various worlds from the *satya-loka* at the zenith to the lowest Avici hell at the nadir), but the entire cosmic drama is continually in decline. The world is continually running down, falling backwards or regressing from its original excellence. Hindu cosmological thinking, of course, is not unique in this regard. The notion of the world running down is frequently accepted in the ancient world. It is widely accepted in the ancient Near East, in ancient Greece, and to some degree in ancient China as well. The reasons for decline are not always clear. To refer again to Deshpande's "History, Change and Permanence,"

> It is not very clear why such a doctrine of decline developed in ancient India. It is conceivable that the invasion of the Greeks and the emergence and dominant political and social position of the non-Vedic religions like Buddhism and Jainism were viewed to be "darker times" in comparison with previous ages, and this might have led to the theory of four ages.
>
> (*ibid*.: 6)

More likely, however, in my view, is that the notion of declining ages has very little to do with modern, Western-style historical conditions, but rather has a great deal to do with ancient traditions of "astronomy"/astrology that were widespread throughout the ancient world. Because the plane of the Earth's equator is at a slight angle (twenty-three and one-half degrees) to the ecliptic, the vernal equinox of the beginning of spring "precesses" or moves backward through the ecliptic or the zodiac one degree of arc about every seventy-two years. It takes approximately 26,000 years (or, more precisely, just under 26,000 years) for this precession or falling backwards to make a full circle so that the vernal equinox can occur again at its starting point. According to one calculation, the oldest zodiacs were constructed by using the fixed star Aldebaran in the exact middle of Taurus, thereby making the vernal equinox at one degree of Aries around 4139 BCE (Gleadow 1969: 55ff). Other calculations have also been used, and various "Ages" of the world can be constructed depending upon how one calculates the various sequences. Quite apart from the precision of such "Ages" and the raging polemics among astrologers, the basic notion of precession or falling backwards along the ecliptic or zodiac in a time frame of roughly 26,000 years was widely recognized in the ancient world. It is known as the "Great Year", and I would argue has its analogue in the Yuga theory of the Hindus. All of the numbers mentioned in the Yuga theory discussed earlier – 1,728,000; 1,296,000; 864,000; and 432,000 years – together with some seventy-two "Human-Intervals" (*manvantaras*), appear to reflect a comparable understanding of the "Great Year." The basic number 432,000 is a multiple of both 60 (= 72) or 360 (= 12), the latter providing a characterization of the year, and the former

(72 × 360 "days" in the life of Brahma, or 25,920 "years") the "Great Year" or "Cosmic Year."

The large numbers used by the Hindus are probably due to their desire to express mathematical ratios and relations in term of whole numbers. Since so much ancient knowledge relating to astronomy/astrology is traceable to the ancient Near Eastern cultures of Babylonia and Sumeria, it could well be the case that the Hindu numbers also reflect the influence of the sexagesimal system of numbering (based on the number sixty, in contrast to the later decimal system based on the number ten) from the ancient Near East. Clearly, ancient India learned a great deal from the ancient Near Eastern cultures and the Greeks. A. L. Basham comments,

> Western astronomy brought to India the signs of the zodiac, the seven-day week, the hour, and several other ideas. […] Like all ancient astronomy, that of India was restricted owing to ignorance of the telescope. […] With the naked eye as their sole means of observation the Indians knew only the seven planets of the ancients [Sun, Moon, Mercury, Venus, Mars, Jupiter, and Saturn]; to these […] two more were added, Rahu and Ketu, the ascending and descending nodes of the moon. […]
>
> For purposes of calculation the planetary system was taken as geocentric, though Aryabhata in the 5th century suggested that the earth revolved round the sun and rotated on its axis. […] The precession of the equinoxes was known […] as were the lengths of the year, the lunar month, and other astronomical constants. These calculations were reliable for most practical purposes, and in many cases more exact than those of the Greco-Roman world. Eclipses were forecast with accuracy and their cause understood.
>
> (Basham 1981: 492–93)

In using the expression "precessional cosmology," however, it is not my intention to enter into the problem of origin or diffusion or scientific explanation – I leave all of that to the appropriate experts in the history of ancient science and mathematics – but, rather, to point to a dominant mind-set regarding the unfolding of time. The mind-set is one of falling backwards, of precessing, and hence, at least in the classic Hindu formulation, of the present and future always becoming the past (or, in other words, Karma and rebirth). The present is the past, and the future will be the past. Even the beginning, since it is beginning-less, is only a modality of the past. What is and what will be has already been, and my "historical" task is to understand what I was, to lift the amnesia or remove the cobwebs so that I can remember and be mindful about what I am. The Hindu view is akin to Faulkner's (1951: 92) famous comment, "The past is never dead. It's not even past." Like the modern astronomer or cosmologist, who recognizes that when one looks into the night sky, one is looking into the past, so the ancient Hindu recognizes that when one acts in the present for the future, one is reliving and re-enacting what has already been. It is not only the light from the night sky that comes to us from the distant past. Most of our emotions, our basic drives, and our physical bodies come to us from the past. To be sure, we are free to act in what appears to be the "present" moment, but we are not changing the present. We are only rearranging the past, or, put somewhat differently, the notion of a linear past, present, and future becomes suddenly problematic. This conundrum or paradox about the direction of time is what led Nietzsche (1882: 107) to his great "What if".

> What if some day or night a demon were to steal after you into your loneliest loneliness and say to you: "This life as you now live it and have lived it, you will have to live once more and innumerable times more; and there will be nothing new in it, but every pain and every joy and every thought and sigh and everything unutterably small or great in your life will have to return to you, all in the same succession and sequence […]?"

Given such a mind-set of precessional cosmology, there are only two possible options: either acquiescing or adjusting to or harmonizing with what is (was); or somehow renouncing precessional cosmology (in terms of the quest for *moksha* or *nirvana* or some other renunciatory technique). From one point of view, one can describe precessional cosmology as cyclical, so long as one remembers the crucial intuition that it is a cycling neither into the present nor into the future, but rather a continual precessing or falling backwards into the past.

References

Basham, A. L. (1981) *The Wonder That Was India*, Calcutta: Rupa and Co. (reprint).

Deshpande, Madhav (1979) "History, Change and Permanence: A Classical Indian Perspective," in *Contributions to South Asian Studies*, Volume 1, Gopal Krishna (ed.), Delhi: Oxford University Press.

Faulkner, William (1951) *Requiem for a Nun*, New York: Random House.

Gleadow, Rupert (1969) *The Origin of the Zodiac*, New York: Atheneum.

Hegel, G. W. F. (1988 [1827]) *Lectures on the Philosophy of Religion, The Lectures of 1827*, Peter C. Hodgson (ed.), Berkeley, CA: University of California Press.

Jacobi, Herman (1961a) "Ages of the World (Indian)," in *Encyclopedia of Religion and Ethics*, Volume 1, James Hastings (ed.), New York: Charles Scribner's Sons.

——(1961b) "Cosmogony and Cosmology (Indian)" in *Encyclopedia of Religion and Ethics*, Volume 4, James Hastings (ed.), New York: Charles Scribner's Sons.

Larson, Gerald James (1980) "Karma as a 'Sociology of Knowledge' or 'Social Psychology' of Process/Praxis," in *Karma and Rebirth in Classical Indian Traditions*, Wendy Doniger O'Flaherty (ed.), Berkeley, CA: University of California Press.

——(1983) "The Structure of Ancient Wisdom, Part II," *Journal of Social and Biological Structures* 6: 161–67.

——(1993) "The Trimurti of Smrti in Classical Indian Thought," *Philosophy East and West* 43 (3): 373–88.

Larson, Gerald James and Ram Shankar Bhattacharya (eds) (2008) *Yoga: India's Philosophy of Meditation*, Volume XII, *Encyclopedia of Indian Philosophies*, Karl H. Potter (General Editor), Delhi: Motilal Banarsidas.

La Vallée-Poussin, Louis de (1961a) "Ages of the World (Buddhist)" in *Encyclopedia of Religion and Ethics*, Volume 1, James Hastings (ed.), New York: Charles Scribner's Sons.

——(1961b) "Cosmogony and Cosmology (Buddhist)," in *Encyclopedia of Religion and Ethics*, Volume 4, James Hastings (ed.), New York: Charles Scribner's Sons.

Nietzsche, Friedrich (1882) *The Gay Science*, W. Kaufman (trans.), cited in *Continental Philosophy*, R. C. Solomon and D. Sherman (eds), Oxford: Blackwell, 2003.

Wilson, Horace Hayman (ed./trans.) (1972) *The Vishnu Purana*, Calcutta: Punthi Pustak.

Further reading

For detailed accounts of the Hindu gods and goddesses, the best books continue to be Sukumari Bhattacharji's *The Indian Theogony* (London: Cambridge University Press, 1970) and David R. Kinsley's *Hindu Goddesses: Visions of the Divine Feminine in Hindu Religious Traditions* (Berkeley, CA: University of California Press, 1986). For useful introductory discussions of cosmogony and cosmology in the study of religion, see Mircea Eliade (ed.), *Encyclopedia of Religion*, Volume 4, articles "Cosmogony," 94–100 (Charles H. Long) and "Cosmology," 100–119, in three separate entries: "An Overview" (Kees W. Bolle); "Hindu and Jain Cosmologies" (W. R. Kloetzli); "Buddhist Cosmology" (W. R. Kloetzli) (New York: Macmillan, 1987). Although now quite old, the essays by Herman Jacobi and Louis de La Vallée-Poussin in the Hastings *Encyclopedia of Religion and Ethics* (cited above) are still essential reading for the study of cosmogony and cosmology in South Asian thought.

12
MODERN COSMOLOGY AND RELIGIOUS NATURALISM

Donald M. Braxton

Religious naturalism

Religious naturalism (hereafter RN) is not so much a religion as it is a philosophical proposal for the recreation and redefinition of what counts as religion in light of the ascendency and productivity of science. As Primack and Abrams note in Chapter 9 in this volume:

> One thing that has become clear from the highly counter-intuitive nature of the scientific universe is that most of the imagery and concepts familiar from biblical and other origin stories cannot describe it.
>
> (p. 100)

While the concept of religion is notoriously difficult to define, it is certainly the case that, from an empirical point of view, religion has been characterized universally by beliefs and behaviors that follow from the postulation of supernatural agents (McCauley and Lawson 2002). Given this historical reality, it often strikes scholars of religion as oxymoronic therefore to speak of "religious naturalism." Nevertheless, a serious effort is under way to reframe the most basic assumptions of what might constitute a religion. The motivation for such a reframing is to embrace modern cosmology and retain some of the emotional states associated with religious awe.

In contrast to other potential religious responses to modern cosmology, the task of RN is strikingly different. Existing religious traditions will have the primary responsibility of seeking to reconcile their pre-scientific cultural inheritances with modern cosmology. They will have to sift their treasure trove of received wisdom and measure it against what is scientifically possible, probable, and credible. Some features may be retooled. Others may simply be abandoned. And others still may be revivified. As Primack and Abrams suggest, they will have to seek out those aspects of their religious traditions that "resonate with certain aspects of our scientific picture." Of course, to resonate is not the same as to concur, as so many hasty so-called "new age" proposals would have us believe, so the identification of resonance is at best only the beginning of any such effort. To be successful, such efforts would need to progress beyond mere poetic analogy. In sharp contrast to retooling ancient religions, RN is audacious enough to want to start from scratch. More precisely, it claims the freedom to trawl through all the received wisdom of the religious traditions of the world in an effort to find some essential feature or features of the religious experience, and then to attempt to reconcile these traits with current cosmology. Its inspiration comes from the scientific description of the natural world itself. Its task is to evolve a set of practices, concepts, metaphors, music, financial systems, institutional designs, and the whole panoply of religious paraphernalia that can be erected on what science says about the world and human placement with it.

But can such a task be accomplished? There are at least three issues that must be surmounted, and it seems to the current author that these issues can serve as developmental milestones to a successful RN. The first issue is simply why the potential advocates of RN do not abandon the religious impulse altogether, advocating rather for a form of naturalism? This certainly seems to be the advice of Richard Dawkins in *The God Delusion* (2006), or Dan Dennett in at least some incarnations (*Breaking the Spell*, 2007). Moreover, it is likely to be a response common to naturalists the world over who have no particularly religious sentiments. Presumably, for RN, the designation "religious" adds value to naturalism. That conceptual move needs to be justified. If a satisfactory answer can be offered to that question, then the second obvious and pressing question is just what RN might look like as a fully fledged religious option given that all identifiable religious behavior seems to depend on a bedrock assumption, namely that the task of religion is to influence supernatural agents? What, for example, might motivate the performance of rituals, ascetic practices, or prayer? That is in essence the second question. Finally, even if the first two issues have been addressed adequately, a third question is whether RN actually has the capacity to attract participants on a large scale. At the moment, RN is largely a debate between various elites, usually scientists, philosophers, and, more ambiguously, some theologians. It is not clear to this point, however, that it can disseminate itself to the point where it might actually possess a laity beyond a few small idiosyncratic enclaves. These three issues stand between RN and any motivated reader of this essay who is not already committed to RN's proposed paradigm shift.

The first question: Why not simply be naturalists?

It is clear from even a brief perusal of RN documents that scientific understandings of the natural world drive the sensibilities of the group (Goodenough 1994; Abram 1997; Crosby 2007; Raymo 2008). Religious naturalism begins with the best available scientifically assembled hypotheses about the universe as it is currently understood, and then it seeks to extend characteristic religious emotions to these claims. It is, in effect, science with an acknowledgement of a sense of wonder and awe at the dimensions and complexity of the natural world. To be privy to the workings of the universe in a way that no prior age of our species has been is, from the vantage point of RN, to be filled with amazement at the fact that we are here at all, and to perceive the stirrings of a sense of gratitude given the sheer improbability of that fact (Goodenough 1998). Religious naturalism embraces and builds upon the tradition of religious devotion encouraged by the early modern scientists of the sixteenth and seventeenth centuries in their theistic ruminations on the "two books of God," but jettisons as irrelevant their theistic cosmology (Bacon 1605: VI, 16). With Darwin, RN admits that, from the evolutionary perspective, "there is grandeur in this view of life, with its several powers […] from so simple a beginning endless forms most beautiful and most wonderful" (Darwin 1859: ch. XV), but it eliminates as uninformative any reference to a Creator breathing life into these forms. With Einstein, RN contends that "he who knows Nature knows God, but not because Nature is God but because the pursuit of science in studying Nature leads to religion" (Jammer 1999: 148–49). This long history of religious inspiration derived from the scientific investigation of nature is where RN locates its heritage.

But what of those scientists who have "no ear" for religious inspiration? Steven Weinberg, for example, is notorious for his claim that the more we know about the universe, the more it appears to be pointless (Weinberg 1977), something quite far from those scientists who experience powerful emotions of blessing, gratitude, reverence, and awe. (Compare, for example, the dialogue between Weinberg and the theologian/astronomer Polkinghorne at www.counterbalance.org/cq-jpsw/index-frame.html.) My suspicion is that, as occurs in so many cases, the disagreement originates in unexplored assumptions. In a word, the issue is definitional. Religious naturalism defines religion as an evolved cultural system designed over thousands of years to facilitate the fitness of the organisms that play host to it (Jablonka and Lamb 2005; Richerson and Boyd 2005; Rue 2005). Or, to rephrase, religion is a natural by-product of how human beings have evolved, how they structure their societies, and how they direct their emotions toward constructive (and sometimes destructive) ends. To date, these cultural systems have trafficked in supernatural agencies because such concepts worked well with the kinds of minds we possess and they produced often very desirable outcomes, perhaps the most important of which is achieving group cohesion, coordination, and cooperation (Sober and Wilson 1998; Wilson 2002; Pyysianinen and Hauser 2009). To be sure, received religious traditions are far from optimal at any of these tasks. For example, the tribalism of much religion worked well for Neolithic villagers, but it is likely the most common source of religious violence in today's highly mobile world. Likewise, moral suasion was often achieved through religious indoctrination, but the cost of such indoctrination has been terror in the face of an angry god for any and all transgressions (Avalos 2005). Scientists who are naturalists but not religious surely can agree minimally that religion often serves such pro-social purposes and, other things being equal, has managed a serviceable job of it. So, at the least, scientists who lack a religious ear nevertheless ought to be capable of appreciating the potential role of religion in the promotion of human flourishing, even if they lack the interest in religion themselves (Wilson, 2007).

Critics of religion, such as Richard Dawkins, point to many of the failings and superstitions of religions past and present, but typically fail to appreciate the constructive role religion has played in human history. Religious naturalism advocates are surely with Dawkins in his criticism of the absurd assumptions of pre-scientific religious claims and the sometimes offensive behaviors religion can underwrite, but they underscore also the constructive and pro-social side. The question they raise is whether we can retain the constructive and pro-social aspects of religion while stripping religion of its supernaturalism. If this step can be made, then perhaps the pro-social benefits of religion may be utilized to promote human flourishing, but not at the expense of an adequate scientific understanding. At least this opportunity is the most basic motivation of RN.

The second question: Can RN evolve from a proposal to a religion?

And so the second issue arises: What might religion look like if it is stripped of its supernaturalism? Loyal Rue is an astute philosopher of religion who provides us with guidance at this point. He suggests that, beyond a basic narrative world-view, religions require various supporting systems if they are to survive and flourish over time. It is not enough that religions offer a coherent cosmology, or that they can claim a few followers here or there. Religions require what Rue calls "ancillary strategies," the self-reinforcing structures requisite for any cultural system to replicate itself successfully over time. His list of such structures is as follows:

(1) a set of institutions that house the organization of the religion
(2) a set of ritualized behaviors that dramatize and reinforce the basic religious narrative
(3) a distinctive aesthetic that trains the senses of those socialized in the religion
(4) an intellectual system that engages and directs the cognition of the religious body
(5) an experiential system that is designed to regularly provoke extraordinary experiences.

(Rue 2005)

In reading RN literature, one gathers relatively quickly that, of the five demands listed above, RN is strongest in the domain of aesthetics and experience, impoverished on its institutional level, and utterly flummoxed by the prospects of ritualized behaviors. For our purposes here, we assume that the intellectual system is simply the current state of scientific investigations into the natural world. Its cosmology is the cosmology of Primack and Abrams. Let us consider the four demands.

The arguments for RN are strongly aesthetic in nature. Consider Ursula Goodenough's *The Sacred Depths of Nature* (1998). The book is set up as a series of chapters organized along lines of increasing biological complexity. Each chapter consists of a clinical, scientific description of its subject, followed by a set of "reflections" characterized by memories, poetry, and philosophical speculations. The final chapter is on speciation, explaining the process as understood by evolutionary biology. Reminiscent of Darwin's riverbank reflections, Goodenough now calls for a celebration of the distinctiveness of species and the tremendous variety that biologists study. From this consideration, she suggests various emergent religious principles under the heading "taking on ultimacy." Chief among these principles is something she calls "a covenant with mystery." This covenant precipitates quite naturally to Goodenough, it seems, in a sense, gratitude. She writes: "Hosannah! Not in the highest, but right here, right now, this" (*ibid.*: 169). Note that the transition is loose philosophically. How compelling one finds an argument that moves from scientific explanation to prescribed religious reaction depends largely upon an assumed aesthetic appreciation. The reflections are really suggested resonances between scientific understanding and human emotional states. They are not necessary deductions in any sense. Can a scientist grasp, for example, the full complexity of speciation processes and the diversity of life, yet not undergo the conversion to gratitude? It would come as a shock to many practicing biologists if they could not. Thus Goodenough seems to necessitate a leap here no less fideistic than other religious traditions.

As one might expect, it appears that RN also has a fairly well articulated experiential foundation. I would characterize the typical experiential matrix of RN as a hybrid of the active environmentalism and workbench science supplemented by various kinds of peaking and meditative opportunities in the natural world. Donald Crosby (2002) begins with an aesthetic experience of nature – "The pervasive beauty of nature appeals to our better instincts and inspires reverence, awe, and respect." – but again quickly transmutes this subjective state into prescriptive and exhortatory recommendations for achieving peaking religious experiences.

> A walk in the woods or along the beach brings refreshment and rest to the soul. The crisp coolness of the morning air with the song of birds in the background makes one glad to be alive. A person in the final hours of life earnestly requests to be taken outside to experience for one last time the precious glories of the natural world […] All of this is magic, miracle, wonder. I am a part of it, and it is a part of me. Here are rightness, fitness, and goodness.
>
> (*ibid.*: 123)

In a way that is clearly analogical to traditional religious discourse, Crosby's arguments rest largely on testimonials to the transformative experiences nature affords. In the absence of such peaking experiences, it is not clear that his more philosophical formal arguments will convince, since they seek merely to intellectually unfold the sensations presupposed in the peaking behavior. But religions have always built their epistemological edifices upon appeals to revelation. Religious naturalism differs only in the sense that its visions seem to be granted at the hands of the natural, and not at the hand of supernatural interventions.

On the institutional level, RN is currently impoverished, subsisting primarily in enclaves where naturalist sensibilities are tolerated and in various intellectual circles. In recent years, the Institute for Religion in an Age of Science (IRAS) has become the most popular forum for the discussion of RN. Indeed, if there is a home institution for RN, IRAS is probably it. The Institute is an organization founded more than fifty years ago. Its principal activity is hosting an annual summer retreat. The format is largely academic, although there are ritual dimensions to the conference, with a chaplain on-call, and noon and evening services. In large measure, these services are quite hospitable to RN themes, but the liturgy, sermons, prayers, and music are largely derived from more traditional and theistic religious practices. Beyond the annual IRAS conference, the Unitarian Universalists play host seemingly to RN advocates, but these advocates appear to be widely scattered and perhaps far between. A virtual community of Unitarians who advocate for RN exists and seeks to advance RN interests within the Unitarian Universalists (www.uurn.org). Finally, several discussion boards and listservs exist where RN advocates debate a wide variety of issues in threaded conversations. As the reader can see, rarely does RN graduate to the level of a free-standing institution, with the one possible exception being a free-standing Jewish community in the reformed tradition called Beth Or in the suburbs of Chicago (www.bethor.com). Interestingly, there is no indication of organization's status as a religious naturalist body; rather, the community seems to self-label as a form of religious humanism. In sum, RN is largely a proposal for a religious network than it is an actual existing one. At least based on the current status, RN manifests in more traditional religious enclaves where it appears most often in "adult education classes" as a topic of conversation.

The previous observation points to the additional fact that RN is ritually challenged. In all the locations where RN is discussed or advocated, when ritualized behaviors are displayed, they are almost all parasitic on traditional forms of theism. Yet, if RN has a *raison d'être* beyond naturalism, it is to awaken the religious emotions in response to nature. The primary mechanism for manipulation of the human emotions in religious settings is ritualized behavior through song, dance, and other group activities. Here we encounter a behavioral paradox in the movement that unfolds thus. First, RN is a philosophical movement. Second, RN is a philosophical movement that wants to elicit emotional connection. Third, doctrine and philosophy are notoriously unappealing to the religious sentiments and are rather late and elite products in the evolution of religious forms. Fourth, the paradox results that, from the point of view of the anthropology of religion, a ritually challenged religion has little chance of having an impact on its members.

So what are the difficulties here? I believe there are several. First, to the extent that the inspirational moments of RN derive from the scientific workbench, where reason, controlled experimental conditions, and the spirit of experimentation itself rule, it is hard to derive ritualized behaviors. Such emotions are evoked when critical reasoning skills and experiment are suspended. Ritual is governed by canons of orthopraxy, not innovation. Many rituals have no inherent logic other than rather transparent *ad hoc* explanations. The sensibilities of the practicing scientist are often offended by such irrationality and public emotional display. Second, advocates of RN often seem to have been raised in more traditional religious venues and carry with them a sense of the importance of the ritual life of the community. In this regard, they have come to appreciate the role such behaviors play in the synchronization of the social group, the stirring of the emotions, and, in particular, the inspiration of moral commitment. Ideally, RN advocates want to utilize these evolved features of religion because they are so deeply wired into human beings, but to refocus them toward more scientifically viable world-views. While an interesting proposition in theory, this aspiration has proven exceedingly difficult in practice.

Professional anthropologists – rather than the philosophers, scientists, and theologians who make up the majority of public RN advocates – will immediately see difficulties in making this transition. First, ritual behaviors are not prone to intentional reform. The mistake of rationalistic intellectuals who study religion philosophically is often to assume that it is mostly about commitments to a systematic world-view, or the cultivation of a set of pro-social activist policies for improving the world. Empirical studies of religion suggest, however, that this is very far from the case. Anthropologists view ritual behavior as continuous with widespread ritual activities of non-human animals. Indeed, it is quite impossible to understand ritual in humans without also understanding the social workings of ritualized and pre-rational primate behavior more generally. Dominant males demand displays of submission from subordinates, just as gods demand submissive displays from disciples, to note one significant example. The role of eye contact in primate social life is closely connected with the role of eyes in religious iconography, prayer postures, and other rituals, to name another. It is unlikely that these behaviors are intellectually corrigible. Second, empirical studies of religious beliefs and behaviors indicate that rationalized doctrines rarely steer religious choices, and that religions the world over often violate the theologically correct teachings of the elites. Catholics worship Mary despite years of theological prohibitions. Gods are localized in particular places, such as churches, statues, and pilgrimage sites, despite strict insistences on the omnipresence of supernatural powers. Likewise, petitions to the gods must be articulated and are answered through discrete acts of communication, despite the doctrines of omniscience. Finally, magical practices such as faith healing, incantations, potions, astrology, and the evil eye abound in all the religions of the world, even among the most educated societies. Thus, to start out with a scientific world-view and then to seek intentionally to invent novel ritualized behaviors is probably naïve.

In the end, ritualized behaviors are about efficacy, where efficacy is the result of the ability of the practitioners to influence supernatural agents and powers as believers understand them. For the RN advocate, no such assumption is possible. The result is unfortunately that, despite the pious desire to wed ritual to scientific, informed world-views, it is difficult to see how an intentional reform of ritual can be successful. In fact, it seems that quite the reverse will occur: The more ritual is subjected to scientific scrutiny, the less likely it will be to survive. Of course, this does not mean that scientists cannot be ritual beings. They most certainly are. What it does imply is that scientists and scientifically informed religious practitioners tend to be ritual practitioners only despite science, or to the extent that they bracket their science commitment when they enter what they think of as the religious sphere.

The third question: Can it attract a mass following?

Now we come to the most pressing question of all. Assuming that RN can surmount the issues raised by the first two hurdles, can RN hope to achieve a widespread following? Can it graduate from a salon discussion, subservient to a traditional religious body, to become an independent religious body with a committed laity? Will RN transcend its origins as an intellectual exercise to become an institutional reality?

Here the evidence is thinnest of all. Religious naturalism advocates are surely convinced that it has to attract a mass following in the face of widespread environmental degradation, a core impulse behind RN loyalties (Rue 2005). Human overshooting of the carrying capacities of the world signals the inaccuracy of the assumptions of traditional religions about the true place of human life on the planet; and, for many, only religious commitments have the motivational power to encourage large swathes of humans to make the necessary sacrifices to attain sustainability (Peters 2002). In the absence of radical reform of the religions, many RN advocates believe our species is on the road to eco-collapse and perhaps even extinction. Moreover, many RN practitioners have achieved a naturalist world-view only with the most serious investment in time and resources. Their scientific understandings of the world are hard-fought and hard-won accomplishments. As with all such costly conversions in any religious tradition, a strong evangelical zeal is a consequence, because it helps to solidify and legitimate the price the convert has paid, and continues to pay, for being at odds with the received wisdom of the religious community. Is the desire for evangelizing on behalf of RN simply a pious yearning? The answer may be yes. Here's why.

The scientific study of religion suggests some very serious impediments to achieving the goals of RN. First, an extensive body of research in the cognitive science of religion suggests that supernaturalism is inherent in religion, and not simply accidental. Religion is about gods, demons, angels, vampires, ancestors, and otherworldly realms, because these types of concept are well adapted to the kinds of minds human have (Boyer 2001; Barrett 2004). In a word, supernaturalism is natural to human cognition (Boyer 1994). By contrast, scientific understandings of the world are quite difficult to achieve, and downright impossible to sustain, even among the most trained minds. Take, for example, evolutionary thinking. Margaret Evans has studied the impact of scientific education on children for the past twenty-five years (Evans 2000, 2001, 2008; Poling and Evans 2004). In study after study, she has discovered that children are default creationists, even when they are subject to extensive social training in scientific world-views in their families of origin. Her findings do not imply that evolution cannot be learned, or that creationist impulses cannot be worked around or situationally turned off. Yet evolutionary cognition requires a variety of mental tricks that are very difficult to sustain. To name but a few: (1) human beings need to shut off their tendency to project teleological reasoning onto the natural world; (2) human beings come wired with a hair-trigger for agency detection that over-reports or, in other words, generates a plethora of false positives; (3) human beings are biased toward essentialist thinking about natural kinds such that the probabilistic thinking required by modern understandings about species, consciousness, and modern physics is very difficult to sustain; (4) supernatural concepts are a highly refined subset of conceptual products that enjoy a competitive advantage for retention in memory and for further cultural transmission; and (5) supernatural concepts are not subject to normal canons of falsification and, as a result, can be sustained fideistically even when shown to be highly improbable by scientists. These five considerations are merely the tip of the iceberg when it comes to what the cognitive science of religion has taught us about how religion operates. But already they raise very serious reasons to doubt the likely success of an intellectual movement like RN.

But that is not to say that RN's task is impossible. A distinctive feature of human beings is that, via culture, they have the ability to alter their environment radically

(Henrich and McElreath 2007). In such an altered environment, it is conceivable that humans can change the selection criteria by which culture is transmitted, and even how brains/minds are wired. For example, Europe is remarkable as a social experiment in that it displays widespread disinterest in religion and acceptance of scientific understandings of the world (Zuckerman 2009). As a result, naturalism and atheism are far more culturally salient than in any other place on the planet. It is possible to make the argument that, with adequate social security measures, higher standards of living, and more readily available science training, such attitudes might be possible elsewhere. The greatest hope for RN is that such experiments in finding "cultural work-arounds" for our current set of cognitive biases might proliferate. It is on that thin hope that RN rests.

Conclusion

This essay suggests that RN is largely an intellectual movement to revise what religion is and how it can be pursued. It is a religious option that seeks to derive from the findings of contemporary science and cosmology a religiously inspirational world-view and evolve a set of practices that can harness the emotional impact of religious devotion. Thus its task in response to the current products of science is quite different from other pre-scientific religious traditions. This is both its strength and its weakness. Its strength is that it has the ability to start from scratch. It seeks not to save its core teachings from an onslaught by modern science's ubiquity, but to found its religious experiences on that very same ubiquity. At the same time, this is also its greatest weakness, since science is a very difficult cultural pursuit requiring a great deal of dedication and rigor. Supernatural thinking, by contrast, seems to enjoy a competitive advantage over science simply because it costs us much less cognitively. Moreover, religion is notoriously recalcitrant to change, in particular because evolution designed it that way. It is able to resist tremendous amounts of counter-evidence. The best hope for a successful RN, therefore, is a radical alteration in the cultural matrix wherein supernatural and natural explanations compete. Only such an alteration would make supernaturalism too costly to maintain and shift the competitive advantage to naturalism. And under such conditions, it is conceivable that RN might flourish.

References

Abram, David (1997) *The Spell of the Sensuous: Perception and Language in a More-Than-Human World*, New York: Vintage.

Atran, Scott (2002) *In Gods We Trust: The Evolutionary Landscape of Religion*, Oxford: Oxford University Press.

Avalos, Hector (2005) *Fighting Words: The Origins of Religious Violence*, Amherst, NY: Prometheus Books.

Bacon, Francis (1970 [1605]) *The Advancement of Learning*, Freeport, NY: Books for Libraries Press.

Barrett, Justin (2004) *Why Would Anyone Believe in God?*, New York: AltaMira Press.

Boyer, Pascal (1994) *The Naturalnesss of Religious Ideas*, Berkeley, CA: University of California Press.

——(2001) *Religion Explained*, New York: Basic Books.

Crosby, Donald A. (2002) *A Religion of Nature*, Albany, NY: SUNY Press.

——(2007) "Religious Naturalism," in Paul Copan and Chad V. Meister (eds) *The Routledge Companion to the Philosophy of Religion*, London: Routledge, 1145–62.

Darwin, Charles (1859 [2006]) *From So Simple a Beginning: The Four Great Books of Charles Darwin*, New York: W.W. Norton.

Dawkins, Richard (2006) *The God Delusion*, New York: Houghton Mifflin Harcourt.

Dennett, Daniel (2007) *Breaking the Spell*, New York: Viking Adult.

Evans, E. M. (2000) "Beyond Scopes: Why Creationism Is Here to Stay," in *Imagining the Impossible: Magical, Scientific and Religious Thinking in Children*, K. Rosengren, C. Johnson and P. Harris (eds), Cambridge: Cambridge University Press, 305–31.

——(2001) "Cognitive and Contextual Factors in the Emergence of Diverse Belief Systems: Creation Versus Evolution," *Cognitive Psychology* 42: 217–66.

——(2008) "Conceptual Change and Evolutionary Biology: A Developmental Analysis," in *International Handbook of Research on Conceptual Change*, S. Vosniadou (ed.), New York: Routledge, 263–94.

Goodenough, Ursula (1994) "The Religious Dimensions of the Biological Narrative," *Zygon: Journal of Religion and Science* 29: 603–18.

——(1998) *The Sacred Depths of Nature*, New York: Oxford University Press.

Guthrie, Stewart (1993) *Faces in the Clouds*, New York: Oxford University Press.

Henrich, Joseph and Richard McElreath (2007) "Dual-inheritance Theory: The Evolution of Human Cultural Capacities," in *The Handbook of Evolutionary Psychology*, R. I. M. Dunbar and Louise Barrett (eds), Oxford: Oxford University Press, 555–70.

Jablonka, Eva and Marion J. Lamb (2005) *Evolution in Four Dimensions*, Cambridge, MA: MIT Press.

Jammer, Max (1999) *Einstein and Religion*, Princeton, NJ: Princeton University Press.

Levitin, Daniel J. (2006) *This Is Your Brain on Music*, New York: Dutton.

McCauley, Robert N. and E. Thomas Lawson (2002) *Bringing Rituals to Mind: Psychological Foundations of Cultural Forms*, Cambridge: Cambridge University Press.

Peters, Karl (2002) *Dancing with the Sacred: Evolution, Ecology, God*, Philadelphia, PA: Trinity Press International.

Poling, D. A. and E. M. Evans (2004) "Religious Belief, Scientific Expertise, and Folk Ecology," *Journal of Cognition and Culture: Studies in the Cognitive Anthropology of Science* 4: 485–524.

Pyysianinen, Ilkka (2004) *Magic, Miracles, and Religion*, New York: AltaMira Press.

Pyysianinen, Ilkka and Marc Hauser (2009) "The Origins of Religion: Evolved Adaptation or By-Product?," *Trends in Cognitive Science* 14(3): 104–9.

Raymo, Chet (2008) *When God is Gone, Everything is Sacred: The Making of a Religious Naturalist*, South Bend, IN: Sorin Books.

Richerson, Peter J. and Robert Boyd (2005) *Not By Genes Alone: How Culture Transformed Human Culture*, Chicago, IL: University of Chicago Press.

Rue, Loyal (2005) *Religion Is Not About God*, New Brunswick, NJ: Rutgers University Press.

Sober, Elliot and David Sloan Wilson (1998) *Unto Others: The Evolution and Psychology of Unselfish Behavior*, Cambridge, MA: Harvard University Press.

Soerensen, Jesper (2007) *A Cognitive Theory of Magic*, New York: AltaMira Press.

Tremlin, Todd (2006) *Minds and Gods: The Cognitive Foundations of Religion*, Oxford: Oxford University Press.

Weinberg, Steven (1977) *The First Three Minutes*, New York: Basic Books.

Whitehouse, Harvey (2000) *Arguments and Icons*, Oxford: Oxford University Press.

Wilson, David Sloan (2002) *Darwin's Cathedral: Evolution, Religion, and the Nature of Society*, Chicago, IL: University of Chicago Press.

Wilson, Edward O. (2007) *The Creation: An Appeal to Save Life on Earth*, New York: W.W. Norton.

Zuckerman, Phil (2009) "Atheism, Secularity, and Well-Being," *Sociology Compass* 3(6): 949–71.

Useful websites

www.religiousnaturalism.org/index.html – the official website of RN.

www.librarything.com/catalog.php?view=ReligiousNaturalism – an eclectic list of resources from which RN claims to take inspiration.

www.uurn.org – the RN discussion site for the Unitarian Universalists.

www.bethor.com – the only institution of which the author is aware that claims to be a religious naturalist community.

www.counterbalance.org/cq-jpsw/index-frame.html – the Polkinghorne–Weinberg dialogues.

Further reading

Review articles are always snapshots of a conversation in progress. Nowhere is this observation more relevant than in science, as theory revision is constantly under way in light of new data. In addition to the literature already cited in the text, I suggest that the interested reader pursue the following journals and books. The journal *Zygon* (Wiley) is an important outlet for RN publications. A topically organized text on the study of religion these days is *The Routledge Companion to the Study of Religion*, edited by John R. Hinnells (Routledge, 2005). Two rigorous philosophical investigations of RN are by David Ray Griffin – *Religion and Scientific Naturalism* (SUNY Press, 2000) and *Reenchantment without Supernaturalism* (Cornell University Press, 2001). As a process philosopher, Griffin makes constructive claims for a process theism that few religious naturalists share, but his history and philosophical analysis is acute. Finally, a fine book by Loyal Rue entitled *Everybody's Story: Wising Up to the Epic of Evolution* (SUNY Press, 1999) is a standard in the repertoire of most religious naturalists.

13
COSMOLOGY AND THEOLOGY

Antje Jackelén

A history of interaction

The history of the relationship between theology and the natural sciences in the Western world is not unlike the dynamics of a growing family. In medieval times, theology was the queen of sciences. In the thirteenth century, Thomas Aquinas created a powerful synthesis of the best knowledge about religion, philosophy, and nature. His principal resource was the philosophy of Aristotle, which had come to Christian Western Europe thanks to the high standards of Muslim scholarship. Christian theology in and of itself also inspired scientific inquiry. Where God is understood as the creator who has endowed the cosmos with order and humans with creative rationality, inquiry into how the cosmos works can indeed become a way of worship. Reading and understanding both "the book of scripture" and "the book of nature" can be noble and necessary enterprises. In that sense, early modern science was very much a child of theology. Quite a number of the pioneers of modern science were close to theology or the church (Brooke 1991). When Johannes Kepler formulated what has become known as his third law of planetary motion, he felt "carried away and possessed by an unutterable rapture over the divine spectacle of the heavenly harmony" (Caspar 1959: 267).

Nevertheless, just as children have to struggle their way through adolescence, the natural sciences had to strive for their emancipation and autonomy. Commonly, Galileo's conflict with the Catholic Church and Darwin's theory of evolution are presented as the classical clashes between science and theology. Cosmology and evolution both presuppose the concept of "deep time", whose counter-intuitiveness – given the limitations of a perspective that is intellectually and emotionally informed by the length of a human lifespan – complicated the acceptance of this new knowledge.

The impression that there was a univocal Christian outcry against progress in science that was only gradually modified into more friendly relationships is a false one, however. Dissent often expressed a critique of institutions, rather than of ideas. In reality, in response to the so-called Copernican revolution, as well as in response to the theory of evolution, Christian scholars adopted from the beginning a wide variety of strategies.

Deep time, Genesis and geology

The so-called Genesis and geology debate between 1790 and 1850 demonstrates something of the flexibility of relationships between science and religion. It resulted from the discovery of deep time, mediated through the fact that geology operated with a significantly larger time scale than was usually assumed in biblical exegesis in those days. The debate was a matter of religion within science, rather than religion versus science. Leading Christian theologians and scientists together strove to keep the book of nature and the book of scripture in consonance by introducing various attempts at harmonization. A new genre of literature developed that dealt with the harmony of the Bible and science. Catholics as well as Protestants, of various denominational shades, were involved in the effort to devise reconciliation outlines.

How was the biblical *hexaemeron*, the six days of Genesis 1, to be reconciled with the fossil record of an immense geological and cosmological past? Some argued that each day of creation signified a period that could accommodate millions of years. Others chose to insert a time gap between the first two verses in Genesis 1. The first verse is then read as a retrospective summary of a primordial creation of matter and the cosmic system, whereas the second verse, "the earth was a formless void," was interpreted as a vast slot of time preceding the creation of humans and their world. In the early nineteenth century, this model seemed almost perfect – theologically sound and scientifically credible. Yet its glory was soon to fade as increased understanding of the reality of deep time turned quasi-literal understandings of biblical chronology obsolete. Yet others opted, therefore, for a timeless understanding of the biblical *hexaemeron*: The six days do not represent periods of whatever length, but six ideas that are constitutive of God's creation (cf. Brooke 1991: 192–225; Brooke and Cantor 1998).

These models provided science with freedom to pursue its investigations of the physical world. At the same time, biblical literalism was also weakened from "inside," as historical-critical methods started to be used in the study of scripture. Furthermore, the field of comparative religion gave a wider understanding of the role of creation myths and their cultural interdependence. With growing hermeneutical sensitivity, the genre of myths was revisited. Since myths convey that which is hard to express in the language of facts, their truth claims exceed literal readings.

As this shows, the attempt to yoke new scientific knowledge with theological knowledge about cosmos and creation can look back on centuries of history. However, rather than being a history of competition between "pure ideas," it is a history of interacting contexts, where the local institutional, socio-political, cultural, or economic capital often trumps the intellectual capital (Livingstone 2003).

Understanding the relationship between science and religion requires awareness of patterns of development within theology itself. Occasionally, science and theology appear to be totally different in their methods of research. While scientists build hypotheses, collect data, and interpret them in order objectively to prove or disprove their hypotheses, theologians remain always stuck with the same old truth they are repeating over and over. If theologians disagree, it is not because of data, but mere subjectivity. Or so some people think. Yet in reality, this is not how theological scholarship works. Theologians have looked at data all along, data about the physical and social world as well as data about the texts they deal with; they interpret these data and draw their conclusions. In the light of these data, older hypotheses are thrown away or modified, new ones embraced ... until another circle of data and interpretation causes further revisions. Methods and processes in science and in theology are different, but not *all that* different (see e.g. Murphy 1990; Peacocke 1993).

The cosmic Christ and cosmology

Theology has always depended on non-theological models of thought in order to frame its discourse about God and the cosmos. For centuries, Christian theologians have drawn on philosophers, especially Plato and Aristotle. When philosophy of nature turned into science, it was science that contributed to the shaping of theological thought about nature. Generally, the assumption was not that science would lend objective truth to theological statements. More often, scientific theories would provide inspiring metaphors for the articulation of a theological language that matches contemporary contexts.

In regard to cosmology, it was in fact a very early development in theology that prepared the ground for theological thought models that would be required more than a millennium later. This was achieved by linking emerging theological thought with the best knowledge of the time.

Theologians of the early church faced the task of finding adequate ways of communicating how to understand this Jesus Christ who came to be the center of Christian faith. One of their major achievements in the struggle for a language that would successfully convey that message was the concept of the cosmic Christ. The means of getting there was the combination of the Greek concept of Logos with the ensuing understanding of Jesus Christ as the incarnate Logos. In his *Jesus Through the Centuries*, Jaroslav Pelikan states that "By the fourth century it had become evident that of all the various 'titles of majesty for Christ' adapted and adopted during the first generations after Jesus, none was to have more momentous consequences than the title Logos, consequences as momentous for the history of thought as were those of the title King for the history of politics." (Pelikan 1999: 58). Why? The word *logos* has multiple meanings, such as word, mind, reason, structure, and purpose. The identification of Jesus as Logos had tremendous intellectual, philosophical, and scientific implications. "For by applying this title to Jesus," Pelikan points out, "the Christian philosophers of the fourth and fifth centuries [...] were enabled to interpret him as the divine clue to the structure of reality (metaphysics) and, within metaphysics, to the riddle of being (ontology) – in a word, as the Cosmic Christ." (Pelikan 1999: 58). The identification of Jesus and Logos provided the potential of a Christian world-view that would be able to relate to a cosmology of then unknown dimensions. Logos came to be understood as the word of God that made the world possible, and also as the structure that makes the world intelligible. The history of science, as well as the history of theology, exemplifies how this understanding of Christ the Logos could work as a stimulus to explore both nature and ideas. The belief in partnership between divine revelation and human reason has fostered an understanding of creation as nature and cosmos, and of nature and cosmos as creation.

Pelikan praises the dialectic inherent in the concept of Christ as Logos. On the one hand, "the divine Reason disclosed in Christ had endowed human reason with a capacity for penetrating the workings of created nature" (Pelikan 1999: 64), thus calling for an exploration of the cosmos and for a scientific story of creation. On the other hand, the Logos is and remains the Logos *of God*, so that the very structure of the universe is not easily accessible for the human mind. In this sense, the concept of logos preserves an awareness of the limitations humans experience in their capacity of understanding ultimate reality. Due to this dialectic, "the cosmos was reliably knowable and at the same time it remained mysterious, both of these because the Logos was the Mind and Reason of God" (Pelikan 1999: 65).

Cosmology and a cosmovision

Creation stories and motifs in the Bible are not primarily about how the cosmos got started. Rather, they offer an answer to the question: *What does it mean?* What does it mean that there are stars and planets, water and land, flora and fauna? What does it mean to live in a world shaped by the interplay of nature and culture? What does it mean to be human, made of thermodynamic waste or stardust, less than a speck in the universe, and yet interfering with the future of this planet (cf. Psalm 8)? A theological perspective on cosmology is more about present and future than about origins and beginnings. Rather than exhausting its interest in the proper understanding of the history of the cosmos, it raises the question of a cosmovision – a vision of what it means to inhabit a world vast in space and vast in time, and what the ultimate end of this cosmos might be.

In formulating such a vision, scientific cosmology continues to challenge Christian theology on some of its limitations. Deep time and ongoing expansion of the universe rightly question geocentrism and anthropocentrism in theology. "Maker of Heaven and Earth" resonates differently with a Ptolemaic universe than with Big Bang cosmology. "Christ the Light of the World" may mean one thing in a flat-earth perspective and something quite different in a double dark universe. The advocacy and power of the Holy Spirit is likely to be understood in different ways, depending on whether we see the cosmos as a great chain of being, or whether we live in what may or may not be a universe of eternal inflation. If we owe our existence and future to dark matter, how then do we find appropriate language for the great promises of Christian eschatology? How is it that God acts in the cosmos?

Divine action

In its simplest form, the problem of divine action boils down to the question: Who is acting – God or nature? Is the cosmos a system that can be explained in its own terms, that is, in terms of natural processes and causes, or is God acting in it? Put this way, the problem reads: either God or nature.

However, there has not always been an apparent either–or of nature and God. In the late fourth century, the church father Basil of Caesarea delivered a series of nine sermons on Genesis 1: 1–25. These sermons are quite amazing because Basil includes a lot of information about botany, zoology, geography, and astronomy, most of which reflects very well the level of scientific knowledge of that time. Even more amazing is the ease with which Basil moves between "God" and "nature" as actors. Nature has an active causal role. It is nature that "encloses the costly pearl in the most insignificant animal, the oyster;" nature has placed the grain of the wheat "in a sheath so as not to be easily snatched by grain-picking birds;" nature has placed such powerful organs of voice in the lion "that frequently many animals that surpass him in swiftness are overcome by his mere roaring." Animals follow "the law of nature strongly established and showing what must be done," and so do humans: We have got "natural reason which teaches us an attraction for the good and an aversion for the harmful […] implanted in us," and we have "natural virtues toward which there is an attraction […] from nature itself."

Basil goes so far as to say that teachings about social order are merely a continuation of natural order. When Paul gives directions regarding human relationships, he just "binds more tightly the bonds of nature." Nevertheless, in spite of the active causal role Basil attributes to nature and the law of nature, he has no problem whatsoever in seeing God in the same things. Basil praises the sea urchin for its capacity of forecasting calm or rough waters by its behavior. By this, he concludes, "the Lord of the Sea and the winds placed in the small animal a clear sign of His [God's] own wisdom." Hence: "There is nothing unpremeditated, nothing neglected by God. His unsleeping eye beholds all things. He is present to all, providing means of preservation for each." For Basil, God apparently acts "in, with and through" nature, and there is no contradiction in that. So where does the problem come from?

Divine action became a problem in the light of the success of physics. The stronger modern (classical) physics became, the more the universe appeared to be a closed physical system, where interactions are regular and law-like, where processes can be accounted for in terms of their causal histories, and where all irregularities eventually will have perfectly natural explanations. The cosmos appears to be self-explicative. There is no causal space left for any God.

Before we turn to possible solutions of the problem, we must be clear about the philosophical framework that has shaped the way we usually talk about causes. The scheme of cause and effect that has had a strong influence on Western tradition originated from Aristotle, who distinguished between four types of cause: material causes that describe the effect that matter has on a thing (the properties something has in consequence of the matter it is made of, e.g. a flammable material will burn); formal causes that work through the form that is inherent to an organism (e.g. what transforms a caterpillar into a butterfly); efficient causes – probably the most familiar to us – that operate between objects in order to move or change them; and final causes, that explain changes in terms of the final purpose of something (that which moves an organism toward that for which it was designed, its *telos*). These definitions were adopted and modified by Thomas Aquinas. In the shape Thomas gave them, they continue to influence theological and philosophical thought in our days. He retained the first three kinds of cause and reinterpreted the fourth one. Final cause, according to Thomas, means the overall purpose of God. He insisted that all four causes are represented in every event. This means that, apart from the three "natural" causes (material, formal, efficient), there is a divine cause involved in every event. These two categories of cause are often referred to as primary (God) and secondary (nature) causes. Neo-Thomists have applied Thomas' thought in the theory of "double agency." It holds that God is the primary cause of all that is. Yet God works consistently through secondary causes, represented by the laws of nature and the activities of conscious agents.

The interpretation of cause and of the existence of causal gaps that would allow a connection between natural and divine causation (often called the "causal joint") is crucial to the question of divine action. Is there an opening in the causal structure of the natural world that allows for divine input? Is such an input compatible with a scientific world-view? Is the plausibility of divine action the most we can hope for, or can we go so far as to claim that accounting for divine action represents an increase in knowledge about the natural world that should be taken into account by everybody?

In spite of his powerful synthesis of earthly and celestial mechanics, Isaac Newton could not account for certain planetary movements. He saw remaining irregularities in some planetary orbits that might increase "till this system wants a reformation," as he expressed it (Newton 2003: 403). This reformation, of course, was supposed to be God's job. Thus was born the unfortunate concept of the God of the gaps. It means a God filling in the gaps of current knowledge and consequently, as the level of knowledge advances, a God who is pushed more and more to the margins and into irrelevance. No wonder that Pierre-Simon Laplace, when asked where God was in his cosmological system, was able to reply, "I had no use for this hypothesis," because in his days, the problem of the apparently irregular orbits had been solved. God, in Newton's understanding, was an omnipotent being whose role was to manage a world that was understood more and more in analogy with a clockwork mechanism. Newton could not foresee that his clockmaker God would very soon be condemned to inactivity due to the excellent functionality of the clockwork. Newton's God ended up both homeless and jobless. The location of divine action at the edges of current knowledge is a bad one. It illustrates all too well the saying that the theology that marries the science of today may well find itself widowed tomorrow.

Models of interventionist divine action, implying a God who intervenes and tinkers with efficient causes to the point of violating the laws of nature, do not honor the best of theological and scientific knowledge. Alternative models come, broadly speaking, in three types.

Limited divine action – proposals in this model suggest that God is the origin of all things, the initiator of creation; the rest is up to natural order. This is the solution adopted by deism. It is reconcilable with the doctrine of creation out of nothing (*creatio ex nihilo*), but not with the concept of continuous creation (*creatio continua*). It is a minimalist and thin concept. God acted once, and that's it. It leaves many of the most salient features of the Christian story unaccounted for, since it cannot explain how God can act in history; how God can become incarnated and redeem the world in Jesus Christ; how God can empower men, women, and children with the Holy Spirit; and how God can lead the world toward its consummation in the *eschaton*.

Parallel divine action suggests that God acts at a level different from the level of scientific observation. This model builds on the distinctions between causes according to Aristotle and Aquinas. The distinction between primary and secondary causation allows the assumption that God acts in every event, yet at a different level, a level that per definition would not be susceptible to physical description. It is a strength that such a model does away with a Humean understanding of miracles as events that violate the laws of nature. Instead, it suggests that we think of miracles in terms of entanglement of two or more causal chains creating enormously special coincidences, although all the elements that lead to such coincidences appear to be in perfect consonance with the laws of nature.

However, parallel models also come with flaws: they support a two-world thinking. There are no compelling reasons for scientists to take the level of divine causation seriously; it seems irrelevant to understanding and interpreting the natural world. On the other hand, scientists cannot repudiate it either, because it is per definition outside the competence of scientific observation.

A third group of proposals, that I choose to call models of *entangled divine action*, try to solve some of these problems. These models assume that, in one way or another, divine action takes place within the framework of natural processes such that we can describe them with scientific methods. This effort is supported by developments in science, ranging from evolutionary biology to quantum physics, that move us beyond a deterministic paradigm toward an indeterministic view of nature. While some models explore mainly the question of causal gaps in terms of top-down, whole–part, and bottom-up relationships, others focus on the concept of cause itself. Using emergence as a key concept, Philip Clayton has argued that we need a new theory of causation (Clayton 2004). Since emergence is a result of observation, not the imposition of a metaphysical principle, it qualifies well to broaden our concept of causality and thus help us to develop a more adequate notion of divine action. Clayton turns his attention toward psychic entanglement: The task is to demonstrate that mental phenomena can have causal effects on the body and the world. If such mental causation is a viable notion, then, Clayton concludes, it is scientifically acceptable to speak of divine causality "as a form of causal influence that prepares and persuades" (*ibid*.: 628). Even this approach, indebted to process philosophy, results in an ambiguous openness: The eye of faith may see final causality, that is, ultimate purposes that pull the cosmos toward its final *telos*, and science can neither confirm nor deny such claims.

The question of God's action is closely linked to the question "What kind of God are you talking about?" Newton understood God primarily in terms of omnipotence and omnipresence. Newton's God is the holder of ultimate power, the one who determined the initial conditions from which the universe could develop its lawlike behavior. This God started the clock and watched over the proper performance of its mechanism, intervening and correcting it, if necessary.

It did not take long, however, before this concept of divine action was fiercely critiqued. The philosopher Gottfried Wilhelm Leibniz argued in the early eighteenth century that Newton's God must be an awfully poor clockmaker, since this God constantly needs to intervene and correct nature. Wouldn't a perfect God create nature in a way that makes frequent interventions unnecessary? Indeed, it seems that Newton's focus on God's omnipotence is a theological trap. Leibniz focuses on wisdom instead as God's foremost attribute. In infinite wisdom, God, from the beginning, put into motion the interplay of the natural forces, according to a most beautiful pre-established order, so that any interventions by God are not mandated by a nature needing correction, but rather need to be understood solely as acts of God's free mercy. The counter-argument is, of course, that it is not a diminution, but the true glory of divine workmanship, that nothing is done without God's continual government and inspection.

It stands clear, however, that the difference between divine action as necessary and as an act of grace is linked to different understandings of who and how God is. A God who is first and foremost the omnipotent ruler seems in need of showing greatness by necessary intervention. A God whose first and foremost attribute is wisdom is known by the beauty of pre-established harmony that leaves room for God's action as an outflow of the free exuberance of divine grace.

The benefit of dialogue

A positive appreciation of the natural world is part of Christian tradition. The natural world is a gift. In fact, according to Christian anthropology, we should regard as a gift not only nature as such, but also our knowledge about nature (science) and the technology we have developed (cf. Wisdom of Solomon 7: 15–30; Job 12: 7–10; Romans 1: 20) – although in a critical manner, not naïvely, since it all works within the framework of sin and salvation.

Christian tradition is gifted with a high appreciation of intellectual capabilities while maintaining a strong sense of mystery. This is a very good basis for seeking literacy, both in faith matters and in science matters. The following stanza from a hymn by Frederick Pratt Green (1970) summarizes this attitude well.

> For the harvests of the Spirit,
> thanks be to God;
> for the good we all inherit,
> thanks be to God;
> for the wonders that astound us,
> for the truths that still confound us,
> most of all, that love has found us,
> thanks be to God.

Through the eyes of faith, God is known to us not primarily in terms of divine action, but in terms of trust. Our relation to God is built not upon understanding how divine action works in the cosmos, but on the answer to the question: In whom do you trust the most? This, of course, does not rule out our desire to understand how God acts, but the focus is a love-relationship with God. That is the difference between faith understood as *fides*, belief, and as *fiducia*, as trust. In other words, it is about God for us, not about an abstract theism. It is about God who calls you, me, and the cosmos toward fulfillment.

One of the Christian formulae that try to describe the presence of Christ in the Eucharist applies quite well also to the notion of divine action. As we can think of Christ being present "in, with, and under" bread and wine, so we can imagine God acting in, with, and under, or through, the natural order of our world. The "in, with, and through" provides an open answer, in the light of which we can live with confidence, facing unresolved issues as well as diligently and daringly exploring those "wonders that astound us" and "the truths that still confound us."

Cosmology forms an important part in the dialogue between science and theology. The cosmos not only *has* history; it *is* history. Looking out in space is looking back in time. The dialectics of knowledge and ignorance, the link to metaphysics and speculation, all instill a sense of humility, wonder, awe, poetry, and contemplation that connects the universal with the existential.

Science cannot heal the eternal wound of existence, as Friedrich Nietzsche observed in the nineteenth century. "Our whole attitude toward nature, the way we violate her with the aid of machines and the heedless inventiveness of our technicians and engineers, is *hubris*;" he complained. "We violate ourselves nowadays, [...] we nutcrackers of the soul, [...] as if life were nothing but cracking nuts" (Nietzsche 1989: 113). Even theology can lend itself to hubris and nut-cracking. Engagement with cosmology can be mutually beneficial in preventing science from the excesses of positivism or scientism, and religion from the decline into speculation or moralism.

Maybe the Norwegian writer Jostein Gaarder (2000) has got something right (the idea rather than the number!) when he has one of his characters remark "The applause for the Big Bang was heard only fifteen billion years after the explosion." Aren't we in the middle of that applause?

The task of interpreting our knowledge remains. The time-honored theological task of *fides quaerens intellectum* – faith seeking understanding – is a task as arduous and rewarding as ever, also when it comes to cosmology.

References

Alexander, H.G. (ed.) (1956) *The Leibniz–Clarke Correspondence*, Manchester, UK: Manchester University Press.

Aquinas, Thomas (1956) *On the Truth of the Catholic Faith:* Summa Contra Gentiles, *Book III: Providence*, V. J. Bourke (trans.), Garden City, NY: Doubleday, 226–35.

——(1975) *Summa Theologiae, Volume 14: Divine Government* (Ia.105.5), T. C. O'Brien (trans.), London: Eyre & Spottiswoode, 75–79.

Brooke, John Hedley (1991) *Science and Religion: Some Historical Perspectives*, Cambridge: Cambridge University Press.

Brooke, John and Geoffrey Cantor (1998) *Reconstructing Nature*, Edinburgh: T& T Clark.

Caspar, Max (1959) *Kepler*, C. Doris Hellman (trans.), London: Abelard-Schuman.

Clayton, Philip (2004) "Natural Law and Divine Action: The Search for an Expanded Theory of Causation," *Zygon* 39: 615–36.

Gaarder, Jostein (2000 [1999]) *Maya*, James Anderson (trans.), London: Phoenix House.

Gillespie, Charles C. (1959) *Genesis and Geology: A Study in the Relation of Scientific Thought, Natural Theology, and Social Opinion in Great Britain, 1790–1850*, New York: Evanston/ London: Harper & Row.

Green, Fred Pratt (1970) "For the Fruit of All Creation," in *Evangelical Lutheran Worship*, Minneapolis, MN: Augsburg Fortress, hymn 679.

Livingstone, David (2003) *Putting Science in its Place: Geographies of Scientific Knowledge*, Chicago, IL: Chicago University Press.

Murphy, Nancey (1990) *Theology in the Age of Scientific Reasoning*, Ithaca and London: Cornell University Press.

Newton, Isaac (2003 [1704]) *Opticks*, Amherst NY: Prometheus.

Nietzsche, Friedrich (1989) *On the Genealogy of Morals and Ecce Homo*, Walter Kaufmann (ed.), New York: Vintage Books.

Peacocke, Arthur (1993) *Theology for a Scientific Age* (enlarged edn), London: SCM Press.

Pelikan, Jaroslav (1999) *Jesus through the Centuries: His Place in the History of Culture*, New Haven, CT and London: Yale University Press.

Russell, Robert J. and Kirk Wegter-McNelly (2003) "Natural Law and Divine Action," in *Bridging Science and Religion*, T. Peters and G. Bennett (eds), Minneapolis, MN: Fortress Press, 49–68.

Saint Basil (1963) *Exegetic Homilies*, Sister Agnes Clare Way, C.D.P. (trans.), Washington, DC: Catholic University of America Press.

Thomas, Owen C. (ed.) (1983) *God's Activity in the World: The Contemporary Problem*, Chico, CA: Scholars Press.

Further reading

Although somewhat dated, Ted Peters' edited volume *Cosmos as Creation: Theology and Science in Consonance* (Abingdon Press, 1989) offers an accessible discussion of issues related to cosmology and theology. Philip Clayton and Arthur Peacocke present a variety of perspectives on the God–world relationship in *In Whom We Live and Move and Have our Being: Panentheistic Reflection on God's Presence in a Scientific World* (Eerdmans, 2004). Hermeneutical challenges to the dialogue between science and theology are further discussed in my *The Dialogue Between Science and Religion: Challenges and Future Directions* (with Carl S. Helrich, Pandora Press, 2004); for the relationship between eschatology and science see my "A Relativistic Eschatology: Time, Eternity, and Eschatology in Light of the Physics of Relativity," *Zygon* 41 (2006): 955–73.

(ii) Quantum theoretical approaches and causality

14
QUANTUM THEORETICAL APPROACHES AND CAUSALITY

Gregg Jaeger

Quantum mechanics is a revolutionary theory of the motion of physical objects in space and time. It was built up through the accumulation of new ideas after the turn of the twentieth century, and reached mathematical maturity roughly a quarter of a century later. Since this early beginning, physicists and philosophers have grappled with its broad and deep philosophical meaning. A number of different interpretations of the theory, which have differing philosophical emphases, have been offered. The world picture that quantum mechanics provides differs dramatically from that of all previous theories of physics, in several respects. This is so regardless of which of the several available interpretations of its formalism one considers.

The quantum world picture differs from its predecessors most significantly in the following respects: the way that objects can be described individually; how definite such individual descriptions can be; the way that the parts of objects are related to the larger wholes they make up. Important questions regarding this quantum world picture remain incompletely resolved. These include how the behavior of physical objects can be explained using the principle of causation. This question must also be reconciled with the theory of space and time, that is, relativity. Although the world picture provided by quantum mechanics can be highly counter-intuitive, it is the most successful theory in the history of physics and remains essentially unrivaled.

One thing that made quantum mechanics a revolutionary physical theory relative to its predecessors is that the descriptions it provides of physical objects and processes are limited in specific ways. The descriptions given by those previous widely accepted physical theories are not. In particular, its descriptions differ from those of its immediate and very intuitively understandable predecessor, classical mechanics. Classical mechanics is the description of motion and behavior of objects in the tradition established by Isaac Newton. Classical theory puts no fundamental limitation on the description of objects. In quantum mechanics, both the simultaneous specification of the properties of objects and one's ability to make precise simultaneous measurements of these properties are limited in a way that can be mathematically specified.

The famous uncertainty principle provides the mathematical relation governing the imprecision of the description of certain pairings of properties. For example, the position and momentum of a material particle can neither be specified nor measured with perfect precision at the same moment. One and/or the other of these properties will have a degree of uncertainty not arising from experimental error. Specifically, they can be specified and measured only with uncertainties which, when multiplied together, exceed a specific minimum value. An important broad principle that was introduced to explain this and similar limitations of the quantum mechanical description of the world is that of complementarity, introduced by the founder of the Copenhagen school of interpreting quantum theory, Niels Bohr. This and related theoretical constraints were understood by Bohr and others, most importantly Albert Einstein, as potentially limiting the application of previously accepted physical and philosophical concepts and, therefore, the physical world picture.

Quantum theory thus suggests the presence of an objective sort of indefiniteness of physical quantities that is not found in classical physics. Due to the uncertainty principle, in general, whenever a subset of physical properties is precisely specified, another corresponding subset of others cannot be. Bohr held that complementarity is the deeper and more general principle operating in the quantum world, which is responsible for these limitations. He argued not only that there are comprehensive theoretical limitations on specifying pairs of physical properties such as position and momentum, but there is also a general limitation on providing both a continuous space–time description of quantum objects and a causal description of their behavior. As Bohr put it, when considering quantum-physical phenomena one is forced

> to adopt a new mode of description designated as complementary in the sense that any given application of classical concepts precludes the simultaneous use of other classical concepts which in a different connection are equally necessary for the elucidation of the phenomena.
>
> (Bohr 1934: 10)

By contrast, in the older, classical mechanical theory, the mathematical quantities identified with the properties of objects *can* all be simultaneously specified, in principle. In this sense, classical objects can be thought of as being in entirely definite physical states. These states are essentially the same as the precise description of the material objects of ordinary experience. The set of such possible simultaneous values are taken there to constitute "state space."

Mathematically, classical state space is a construction in which the descriptions of individual objects are representable as points. As time passes, these points move along precisely specifiable paths. The paths are such that every physical property, including position in physical space, is at every time uniquely determined by the object's properties at any earlier time so long as it is not influenced by a number of other objects: The paths are clear tracks leading from the past into the future with an inescapable certainty. This evolution is given mathematically by differential equations in which properties are directly represented by functions. Thus a strict form of causality was understood to apply to all physical objects, whether or not they are known or measured by human beings, in classical theory.

In quantum mechanics, by contrast, physical states are given as vectors in an abstract mathematical space, and physical properties are provided only indirectly and statistically, by average values on that space, rather than exactly. Because a direct and precise description of the properties of objects is impossible in quantum mechanics, the principle of causality appears inapplicable in any strict form. Furthermore, the descriptive restrictions of quantum mechanics have been understood by many to threaten the previously widely held philosophical realism regarding physical objects. Under a basic realist world-view, the description of material objects mathematically given by physics is understood to be a direct reflection of an objective state of affairs that is independent of the knowledge of the minds of humans or other beings. Such a world-view accords well with the preceding classical theory of the motion of matter in the universe, but not obviously in the case of quantum mechanics.

The speed of propagation of causal influences in space–time, such as those carried by physical objects, is understood in modern physics to be restricted by some universal numerical value. Relativity, with which quantum mechanics should be compatible, identifies this universal value with the speed of light. Individual objects are traditionally physically identified by their unique histories, paths in space–time constrained by this speed limit to lie within cone-shaped regions of space–time, known as "light cones." This is connected with the concepts of localization in space and the independence of individual objects: Individuals are typically independent, occasionally interacting and doing so only with other objects with which they come into direct local contact. By restricting causal influences to finite speeds, their locality enables individuals to be identified without confusion. However, without this restriction, objects can be in interaction without having to be in the same location in order to interact; in particular, they could be in continual interaction with other objects and almost entirely fail to be independent. In quantum mechanics, the incompatibility between the local causal description and the space–time description of objects and their interactions directly prevents this means of providing physical identity from being applied.

These novel characteristics of quantum mechanics led Einstein to conclude that it is unsatisfactory as a fundamental theory of physics. He identified the problem by clearly specifying criteria the satisfaction of which is essential to a proper physical description of the world. For Einstein, these criteria ought to be satisfied by quantum mechanics or any other physical theory. He hoped thereby to retain the sort of coherent realist physical world picture that had previously been provided by classical mechanics. In particular, together with his colleagues Boris Podolsky and Nathaniel Rosen, forming the trio later known as "EPR," Einstein argued that, without these essential elements, any physical theory is incomplete. EPR proposed three clear criteria, the conjunction of which they argued to be in conflict with existing quantum theory. These were: a reality criterion, a locality criterion, and a completeness criterion. Given that the logical conjunction of the three criteria contradicts quantum theory, because the reality and locality criteria could not be given up, it must be the completeness criterion with which quantum mechanics conflicts. By implication, quantum mechanics in its current form would be surpassed by some later complete physical theory.

EPR presented a forceful argument against the adequacy of quantum theory by stressing the importance of locality as an essential characteristic of objective physical objects. They provided a physical scenario showing that the lack of local causality under quantum mechanics is problematic under the assumption that the theory is a complete fundamental theory, if it is also to accord with the traditional realist world-view of physics. They envisioned two elementary particles in a joint physical state that is irreducible to the individual states of these components alone. The two particles were also taken to be separate from each other, in the sense of relativity. The important characteristic of this state is that it predicts strict correlations between the properties of the two objects, no matter which property is measured. That is, given the value of the variable for one particle, that of the other can be only *one* other value, regardless of any measurements made on them.

Einstein described his concerns regarding the quantum physical description of objects in such a situation as follows.

> I just want to explain what I mean when I say that we should try to hold on to physical reality. We all of us have some idea of what the basic axioms of physics will turn out to be […] whatever we regard as existing (real) should somehow be localized in time and space. That is, the real in part of space A should (in theory) somehow "exist" independently of what is thought of as real in space B. When a system in physics extends over the parts of space A and B, then that which exists in B should somehow exist independently of that which exists in A. That which really exists in B should therefore not depend on what kind of measurement is carried out in part of space A; it should also be independent of whether or not any measurement at all is carried out in space A. If one adheres to this programme, one can hardly consider the quantum-theoretical description as a complete representation of the physically real.
>
> (Born 1971: 164)

Thus, Einstein argued, quantum mechanics cannot be a fundamental theory. However, the conception of what constitutes completeness according to EPR in 1935 was then, and still remains, far from having been universally accepted.

The specific argument of EPR was similarly questioned because of the contrary-to-fact nature of the measurements required by the reality criterion, namely,

> If, without in any way disturbing a system, we can predict with certainty (i.e., with probability equal to unity) the value of a physical quantity, then there exists an element of physical reality corresponding to this physical quantity.
>
> (Einstein *et al.* 1935)

In particular, their argument depends on the performance of two measurements that *cannot* be made jointly in quantum mechanics. Followers of the Copenhagen school of interpreting quantum mechanics, for example, certainly would not view the corresponding properties as both real (cf. Greenberger *et al.* 1990). Einstein and so-called naïve or literal realists, however, do not accept such restrictions on the simultaneous reality of physical properties, rejecting complementarity as a fundamental principle. Einstein also rejected the fundamentally probabilistic description of phenomena that it requires.

Einstein said that Bohr's complementarity interpretation was "furnishing to the true believer a soft pillow" and declared that "God does not play dice with the universe." To this extent, the understanding of the completeness and domain of quantum mechanics depends on the interpretation of the theory. Ultimately, one's choice of interpretation of quantum theory depends on a combination of considerations that are both philosophical and physical in character. Very broadly speaking, the more subjectivist, that is, dependent on human perspective an interpretation is, the less it requires of the theoretical description of objects and processes of quantum mechanics.

It is significant that the argument of EPR was made in the context of a pair of objects as opposed, say, to the context of an individual object such as a single subatomic particle. Indeed, Einstein had, early on, made a related argument involving only a single particle that was more clearly unconvincing than the EPR argument for that reason. As mentioned above, quantum mechanics describes a counter-intuitive relationship between individual objects (such as electrons and nuclear particles) and the compound objects they are capable of forming (such as atoms and ions). In classical theory, a compound system can be fully and intuitively described using only the states of its components: it is reductionist. The specification of the quantities, such as positions and momenta, of components is sufficient for the description of the whole system, in that theory. The classical description is thus one akin to the description of any collection of objects as a clockwork whose components are well specified and build on each other in an obvious way. By contrast, the best quantum mechanical description of a compound system as a whole, in many instances, is that in which the states of the component systems are extremely ill specified, while at the same time the relationships between the parts can be precisely specified, for all of their possible values, although these values remain indefinite: it is generally holist.

One can speak of the construction of objects out of parts in quantum mechanics, for example, the building of an atomic nucleus out of protons and neutrons, or the building of that sort of particle, the nucleon, out of specific combinations of the three more basic particles known as quarks. However, the quarks themselves appear incapable of independent existence: They are confined within the nucleons and other related particles and are never found alone – this phenomenon is known as "quark confinement." Even in the case of electrons, which are particles that can be found alone, one finds surprising behavior when these are in "bound" states within atoms. For example, electrons that are bound within atoms or within ions are found to combine together in ways that are extremely limited by comparison with what is allowed on a classical picture for a similar combination of objects (that is, objects attributed the same basic physical properties of mass, angular momentum, and electrical charge). In the case of bound electrons, the Pauli exclusion principle restricts the number of electrons capable of possessing the same orbital angular momentum components. In fact, this principle provides a basis for chemistry by explaining the so-called Aufbau process.

More generally, in a quantum system made of smaller components, the constituents may lose their individuality and do so in specific ways. In more complex systems of atoms in metals, behavior is found that is not directly reducible to that of the component atoms – so-called "collective behavior" is exhibited which has no classical analogue. The individuality of components is, in general, found to re-emerge when the components are singled out by specific measurements on them made one at a time, separating them from the larger whole. Again, however, the standard quantum mechanical description is the only one that provides a correct prediction of what is observed in the world for a broad range of phenomena.

Under the assumption that there is local causality similar to that captured by the criteria of EPR, John S. Bell derived a number of fairly simple mathematical inequalities. These were later followed by a number of similar relations, which have all come to be known as Bell-type inequalities. These have been shown to be incompatible with the results of experimental tests based on the observation of joint events occurring at a distance. It has been demonstrated experimentally that local causality is incompatible with the behavior of entire classes of composite microscopic objects. Tests measuring correlations of properties using interferometer apparatus show that composite quantum systems exhibit holistic behavior; correlations are indeed observed that cannot be explained as arising from a common cause.

In relation to such interference phenomena, Paul A.M. Dirac famously noted that light particles, or photons, are capable of interfering with themselves and only with themselves, "each photon interferes only with itself. Interference between two different photons never occurs" (Dirac 1958). This provides a natural and easily generalized quantum mechanical indicator of identity: The existence of an individual is manifested through the ability of manifest quantum interference (Jaeger 1995). A general quantum complementarity relation has also been found between the visibility – roughly speaking, the size of the interferometric "fringes," that is, the up-and-down modulation of detections of particles such as exhibited on a photographic plate – for component particles on the one hand, and on the other hand, the compound system they make up.

The component interference visibility and two-particle interference visibility have been shown both theoretically and experimentally to be mathematically complementary: As one becomes larger, the other becomes smaller, and *vice versa*, regardless of whether these particles are light particles or material particles (Jaeger *et al.* 1995). Together, Dirac's dictum and these interference results support the view that holism is characteristic of composite quantum objects: the individuality of components is reduced, observable through the decrease of interference in a subsystem at the same time as an *increase* of the interference in the whole composite system. The interference visibilities show that, as the larger whole comes together, the individual parts give up their individuality to that of the whole. In particular, there is a more unified whole as the whole formed of the two components becomes more "entangled"; the two-particle interference visibility has been called the "visibility of entanglement," for just this reason (Gühne et al. 2002). Because the whole formed by two particles is not precisely localized, it is not unnatural for the correlations between properties of the parts to be extremely strong.

Another aspect of quantum mechanical experiments is the possible role of conscious observers in the manifestation of properties of quantum objects. At a minimum, this would regard the observer's ability to choose the properties to measure. The related question of the relationship between physical causality and the free will of human observers is one with a long history. If there is strict physical causality and human beings could be described in essentially physical terms, free will would appear to be impossible. In quantum physics, however, limitations on physical causality weaken restrictions on free will. This is so even in a world picture wherein all properties of human beings would be reducible to physical properties. Moreover, in the interpretation of quantum theory, both by those of the Copenhagen school and of the more conservative Princeton school – which includes Dirac and John von Neumann, who provided the definitive mathematical formulations of the theory – the freedom of human beings to choose at will measurements to be made on physical objects is assumed.

Wolfgang Pauli, an advocate of the Copenhagen interpretation, saw free will as fundamental to quantum mechanics. He writes, "The non-deterministic character of the natural laws postulated by quantum mechanics rests precisely upon [the] possibilities of a free choice of experimental procedures complementary one with the other" (Pauli 1954). For his part, Bohr, the originator of the Copenhagen school, argued that quantum mechanics allows for the possibility of free will through its mathematical structure:

> The freedom of experimentation, presupposed in classical physics, is of course retained and corresponds to the free choice of experimental arrangement for which the mathematical structure of the quantum mechanical formalism offers the appropriate latitude.
>
> (Bohr 1934: 73)

How unique this is to quantum mechanical indeterminism remains the subject of debate, however. Determinism had already come into question in classical mechanics by the time of the introduction of quantum theory. In particular, it had already been shown that mechanical systems could behave in ways that are extremely sensitive to initial situations, so that in practice future behavior is not always determinable on the basis of experimental results, even in classical theory.

The physicist of classical mechanics Pierre-Simon Laplace believed that the universe, for him the contents of space – an elaborate physical system described by classical mechanics – is subject to strict determinism. He portrayed its strict causal nature as follows.

> We ought then to regard the present state of the universe as the effect of its anterior state and as the cause of the one which is to follow. Given for one instant an intelligence which could comprehend all the forces by which nature is animated and the respective situation of the beings who compose it – an intelligence sufficiently vast to submit these data to analysis – it would embrace in the same formula the movements of the greatest bodies of the universe and those of the lightest atom; for it, nothing would be uncertain, and the future, as well as the past, would be present to its eyes.
>
> (Laplace 1814)

Even in classical mechanics, several conditions must be met for the description of a physical system of objects at scales smaller than the universe to be deterministic. For example, the system in question must be a truly closed one. That is, it must not be influenced by entities outside of its own boundaries. The complete universe, assuming it to have finite contents, is a closed system by definition. However, any subset of its objects over the scale of seconds of time is almost certainly *not* closed, but is influenced from outside; external influences introduce randomness into its description. Thus Emile Borel commented that the classical description of gas "composed of molecules with positions and velocities which are rigorously determined at a given instant is […] a pure abstract fiction" (Borel 1914).

Randomness that is irreducible to human ignorance of an objective physical situation was increasingly accepted after the introduction of formalized quantum mechanics. However, great physicists such as Einstein and Erwin Schrödinger remained concerned about losing strict causality within physics. Indeed, Einstein commented to Schrödinger that

> [The] business about causality causes me a great deal of trouble. Can the quantum absorption and emission of light ever be understood in the sense of the complete causality requirement, or would a statistical residue remain? […] I would be very unhappy to renounce complete causality.
>
> (Born 1971: 23)

Rather than entirely objecting to probabilistic laws, as already mentioned, Einstein objected primarily to there being irreducible probabilistic laws in a fundamental theory. Nonetheless, Einstein saw philosophical realism as a more important characteristic of the world than strict causality. However, it was the non-local nature of the quantum mechanical world picture that concerned him most.

The objective indefiniteness of properties of quantum objects, also noted above, was presented by Werner Heisenberg as a novel rendering of the concept of natural potentiality. This new sort of potentiality is related to, but different from, that discussed by Aristotle, which was of a more teleological, that is, goal-directed character. On Heisenberg's conception, future physical situations are not strictly determined; instead, a number of specific possibilities exist with various probabilities of becoming actual events in the future. Thus quantum mechanics seems naturally to suggest the possibility of a probabilistic causality.

Probabilistic causality is a weak sort of causality, wherein effects need only be probabilistically related to their causes so that causes do not necessarily give rise to effects. In particular, on this conception of cause, causes are primarily required most importantly to increase only the probability of their effects, among other things; further qualifications to this requirement would include background information. Providing causal background descriptions would help avoid difficulties associated with exceptional events that might go against the general tendency of effects to occur, given causes; one must be sure to keep the background fixed. However, the EPR scenario, which involves entangled quantum particles, presents significant challenges even for such a loosened notion of causality to apply in the quantum mechanical context (Eells 1991). Thus local causality continues to appear incompatible with the quantum theoretical description of the physical world.

References

Bohr, N. (1934) *Atomic Theory and the Description of Nature*, Cambridge: Cambridge University Press.

Borel, É. (1914) *Le Hasard*, Paris: F. Alcan.

Born, M. (1971) *The Born–Einstein Letters*, M. Born (trans.), London: Walker and Co.

Dirac, P. A. M. (1958) *The Principles of Quantum Mechanics*, 4th edn, Oxford: Clarendon Press.

Eells, E. (1991) *Probabilistic Causality*, Cambridge: Cambridge University Press.

Einstein, A., B. Podolsky and N. Rosen (1935) "Can Quantum-Mechanical Description of Physical Reality be Considered Complete?," *Physical Review* 47: 777.

Greenberger, D.M., M. A. Horne, A. Shimony and A. Zeilinger (1990) "Bell's Theorem without Inequalities," *American Journal of Physics* 58: 1131.

Gühne, O., P. Hyllus, D. Bruss, A. Ekert, M. Lewenstein, C. Macchiavello and A. Sanpera (2002) "Detection of Entanglement with Few Local Measurements," *Physical Review* A66: 062305.

Jaeger, G. (1995) *New Quantum Mechanical Results in Interferometry*, Ann Arbor, MI: UMI.

Jaeger, G., A. Shimony and L. Vaidman (1995) "Two Interferometric Complementarities," *Physical Review* A51: 54.

Laplace, P.-S. (1951 [1814]) *A Philosophical Essay on Probabilities*, E. W. Truscott and F. L. Emory (trans.), New York: Dover, 3–4 (original: *Essai philosophique sur les probabilitiés*, Paris: Courcier).

Pauli, W. (1954) "Wahrscheinlichkeit und Physik," *Dialectica* 8: 112.

Further reading

The following are valuable sources of information regarding the key philosophical issues in the foundations of quantum theory that address the topics discussed here. P. A. Schilpp's edited volume, *Albert Einstein: Philosopher–Scientist*, 3rd edn, Vols I and II (Open Court, 1970) contains the autobiography of Albert Einstein, twenty-five critical essays on his work, Einstein's reply to his critics, and a bibliography of his works, many of which relate to these issues, particularly locality and realism in modern physics. Dugald Murdoch's *Niels Bohr's Philosophy of Physics* (Cambridge University Press, 1989) is a valuable source of information on Bohr's complementarity interpretation of quantum mechanics and its implications, as is J. Honner's *The Description of Nature* (Clarendon Press, 1987). Finally, Abner Shimony's *Search for a Naturalistic World View*, Vol. 2 (Cambridge University Press, 1993) treats most of the above issues in detail and from a contemporary perspective, in particular, Bell-type inequalities and their relation to locality.

15
QUANTUM MECHANICS AND SOME HINDU PERSPECTIVES

Varadaraja V. Raman

Introduction

Quantum mechanics is a creation of twentieth-century physics. It is also a culmination of more than three centuries of modern science, based on a methodology and framework that differs from ancient efforts at grasping the complexity of the phenomenal world. Its findings are therefore quite different from those of earlier sciences. Given this, one may wonder how one can talk about quantum mechanics from any traditional religious perspective. Indeed, one cannot, and perhaps one ought not to, if one is dealing with the formulas and findings of atomic and subatomic physics. Attempts to show that theories of the wave–particle duality, the electron-spin, or the quark model are implicit in ancient writings are likely to be plain wrong, and simply cannot be taken seriously by anyone practicing technical physics.

But there is another side to quantum mechanics: The world-view it engenders, the notions it leads to regarding causality and determinism, and the picture it paints of the nature of ultimate reality. Quite unexpectedly, quantum mechanics has wrought drastic changes in these basic elements of the classical physicist's appraisal of the physical world. On these fundamental issues, the rise of quantum mechanics generated controversies and disagreements even among the creators of the field. Some of these have not died out. What is remarkable is that, on some of these matters, there seem to be uncanny parallels between quantum mechanics and the insights articulated by certain classical Hindu thinkers. However, it is important to remember that identifying similes can be poetically meaningful, but they don't always reflect ontological equivalence between modern scientific findings and ancient metaphysical visions.

The bases for my remarks will be philosophical, not religious or theological. The ideas to be discussed emerged primarily in the context of epistemological inquires, rather than from religious and scriptural authorities, although in the Hindu context religion and philosophy formed a seamless whole. But there was also the explicit understanding that knowledge of reality was of two categories: one relating to the physical and temporal world of everyday experience, which may be acquired by the intellect through logic and empiricism; the other relating to the transcendent, which may be achieved only through an altogether different mode: the spiritual.

It is important to bear in mind the following in this discussion: Not all authors from the Hindu world hold the same views on these questions. After all, we are talking more philosophy than physics here, more about interpretations than experimental data. Secondly, the ideas explored will all be of a qualitative nature, for there are no ancient equivalents to the mathematical formulas of quantum mechanics. Finally, these ideas are to be taken for their intrinsic interest, and not as apologetic arguments for Hindu world-views. Unlike some writers on these matters, my goal is not to convince the reader that the ancient Hindus knew all about quantum mechanics. It is to be noted that many of the points I discuss have arisen from quantum physicists themselves, not from Hindu theologians.

To cite but one example, the centrality of consciousness stressed by classical Hindu thinkers in their interpretation of the world was emphasized by Eugene Wigner: "When the province of physical theory was extended to encompass microscopic phenomena through the creation of quantum mechanics, the concept of consciousness came to the fore again. It was not possible to formulate the laws of quantum mechanics in a fully consistent way without reference to consciousness" (Wigner 1970). One of the most eloquent spokespersons for insisting that the primacy of consciousness is revealed by quantum mechanics is the Hindu physicist Amit Goswami (1995, 2001). Roger Penrose is among the many physicists who have tried to connect consciousness with quantum mechanics (Penrose 1994). Some other serious physicists are also beginning to reconsider the human-marginalization aftermath of the Copernican discovery (Primack and Abrams 2006).

The sources of Hindu visions

The literature on Hindu philosophies is vast. Also, as noted above, there are a great many differing schools of thought within the Hindu world. After all, the system has a history spanning more than three millennia, and it has never had a pontificating authority to dictate what is right thinking (orthodoxy), and what is not, although the schools of thought have themselves been classified as orthodox and heterodox by modern commentators.[1] So, not all Hindu thinkers see eye to eye on the nature of ultimate reality, on cause and effect, or on the intricacies of the human mind and consciousness. What this means is that, as in other dynamic philosophical, and cultural systems, there are, as there have always been, many creative thinkers on fundamental questions. Interestingly, interspersed in all the rich and variegated writings are nuggets of world-views that, when interpreted appropriately, sound very much like some of the things that quantum physics has uncovered about matter and motion; observer and observed. We are not talking here about an ancient religion that one tries to drag into the modern scientific world-view; rather, it is the modern scientific (quantum-mechanical) world picture that is catapulted back into some of the Hindu/Buddhist theses. Thus, for example, Schrödinger tried to adduce support for the basic Vedantic vision. In a widely read book he stated explicitly: "the plurality that we perceive is only an appearance; it is not real. Vedantic philosophy, in which this is a fundamental dogma, has sought to clarify it by a number of analogies, one of the most attractive being the many-faceted crystal which, while showing hundreds of little pictures of what is in reality a single existent object, does not really multiply that object" (Schrödinger 1964: 18–19).[2]

Determinism, uncertainty, and the karma doctrine

Perhaps the grandest success of classical (Galilean/Newtonian) physics was its recognition that the laws governing the mechanical evolution of the physical universe could be formulated as (linear second-order) differential equations. One property of such equations is that, for any set of boundary (initial) conditions, the solutions are uniquely determined. What this implies is that, if one knows the status of a mechanical system at any instant of time, one can, in principle, calculate its status at any future instant. This is the core idea in strict (Laplacian) determinism, which underlies all of classical physics (Laplace 1951: 4ff).

This view does not take into account the complex changes that arise in biological and social systems (mutations, history, for example) and that become even more problematic in psychological systems. Moreover, for any reckoning of the state of a system, we need to observe it. Observation implies interaction with what is observed, often, though not necessarily, via reflected light. At the classical (macrocospic) level, such observations don't affect the observed system in any tangible or significant way.

However, as was first shown by Werner Heisenberg, this is not the case with quantum systems (Wheeler and Zurek 1983: 62–84). In the microcosm, entities are susceptible to perturbation even by a photon. This means that a single photon that is used to locate an electron automatically affects the state (position and momentum) of the electron. This is the source of the uncertainty that is intrinsic in the measurement of quantum systems. From the traditional Hindu perspective, as from any other religious perspective, there is really nothing corresponding to the physical state of microcosmic entities, because in the ancient world there was no empirical awareness of atoms and sub-atoms, let alone any parametric description of them. These are largely nineteenth- and twentieth-century ideas.

But the notions of determinism and indeterminism do become relevant in the human context. Here, it is not the state of the electron or molecule that is relevant, but the state of the individual in the course of one's life. That state is determined not by the physical forces acting on the individual, but by the consequential actions (*karma*) done earlier in one's life, or even in a previous life. On the other hand, the future state of an individual is undetermined in that it will depend on the consequential actions that are performed right now. This is the so-called law of *karma* (Pappu 1987). Clearly, these have little to do with the quantitatively defined terms (position, momentum, etc.) that physics is concerned with. But we may draw an analogy here: Action may be taken here as equivalent to observation in quantum physics, since it is action that affects the course of one's life. Corresponding to the Heisenberg principle, one might say that it is impossible to predict a person's future state with 100 per cent precision because that state will be determined not so much by the past, as by what he or she does now. It is important to point out that karmic determinism (a qualitative action reaction principle in the human context) is not the same as Laplacian determinism in the physical world. Rather, there is only an interesting parallel.

This is in marked contrast with the doctrine of fatalism conveyed through the famous lines of Omar Khayyam (Fitzgerald 1989: LXXIII), which shows more of the determinism of classical physics,

> And the first Morning of Creation wrote
> What the Last Dawn of Reckoning shall read.

Subject–object

A matter of central importance in any epistemological reflection on scientific knowledge is whether and to what extent our experiences, understandings, and interpretations of the physical world are independent of our own human framework. On this hinges the crucial claim of objectivity that is the hallmark of modern science. Quantum mechanics has revealed that, at the microcosmic level, there is no clear-cut separation between the observer and the observed, meaning that the demarcation between mute matter and measuring mind dissolves into an undifferentiated totality at the core of physical reality.

Volumes have been written in the classical Hindu world on the question of subject–object identity and distinction. One school of thought maintained, for example, that, "both the soul (or the knower) and all that it knows as subjective ideas or as external objects existing outside of us are but transformations of pure intelligence" (Dasgupta 1928: 38). One may interpret this by saying that there can be no knowledge of any kind unless whatever it is out there is mapped on human intelligence, awareness, and understanding, that is, on the brain. This perspective calls into question the classical and naïve realist view to the effect that the world is exactly as it appears to us through our senses. Indeed, at least a semi-idealistic view is forced upon us when we try to grapple with the foundations of quantum mechanics. Here, knowledge itself (certainly in the microcosmic domain) arises or can arise only from the merger of the observer with the observed. In this irreducible merger of the subject and the object, we are torn away, as it were, from the classical world picture. The Samkhya system of Hindu thought "posits an infinite plurality of pusrushas" (experiencing principles); it also leads to the insight that "[a]ll acts are caused by instruments. Knowledge is an act and therefore caused by an instrument which must be the senses" (Radhakrishnan 1967: 255). In other words, the role of the observer is inevitable, and it is active. Thus the Samkhya worldview becomes very relevant in the observer–observed context.

Another tenet of the Vedantic view is that reality itself is one undifferentiated whole. In other words, "The world, which we perceive and believe to be rational and intelligible, as well as the ego of which it is the object, must both be referred to the same source, i.e. Pure Consciousness" (Iyer 1965: 136). It may well be that by some process, not unlike the splitting of the single unified field into the fundamental forces at the initial Planck-seconds of cosmic birth, at some point in cosmic evolution, the primordial ontological One-ness split into a knowing mind (*purusha*) and a known objective world (*prakriti*). The experiencing *purusha* is eternal, and the individual consciousness embedded in each of us is only a fragment of the cosmic consciousness. The term *prakriti* is often translated as "nature," but it also denotes "that which evolves and produced everything" (Williams 2001: 98). This does not imply that the unity no longer exists, but that the unity now appears as multiplicity. Just as it is only in the highest energy regimes that the force-fields unify, it is only in higher states of human consciousness that the underlying unity behind the diversity is recognized. In other words, from a Vedantic perspective, one may consider variety in the force-fields and in the world as real at only one level of consciousness.

Entanglement

An associated idea, which is also crucial in quantum epistemology, is that ultimately all systems are mutually intertwined. Classical views hold that objects and entities in the world are distinct and independent, except insofar as they interact mutually through force fields. But, in the quantum world, there is a built-in connectedness among micro-entities binding them together inextricably. Thus, if a photon splits into two, and the latter move apart, each one is linked inexorably to the other through this entanglement. Their states are linked in their non-observed phase. By this one means, for example, that the spin state of photons resulting from a single photon can be one of several possibilities rather than a specific one. However, when an observation is made on a photon, its spin is determined. Instantaneously, the spin of the other photon will also be completely specified, no matter how far away it is. In other words, the actualization (wave-function collapse) of the state of one photon simultaneously causes a corresponding actualization in the other photon. This (highly technical) interconnection at a distance follows from the mathematical formalism, but it is difficult to visualize it in the world such as we know it. In fact, some have argued that it is equivalent to extrasensory perception (ESP) (Radin 2006). Nevertheless, this theoretical result enjoys experimental confirmation. It leads to the notion that, at its core, the universe is a web of tangled entities. This aspect of the phenomenal world is referred to as quantum entanglement (Fraser 2006).

What this implies is that, even though superficially we observe and seem to recognize the world as made up of so many discrete entities, it is in fact not so. There is also a notion of metaphysical entanglement in Hindu thought, where it says that every individual soul (*purusha*), in its material-body manifestation, is entangled with *prakriti* (material dimension of the universe). In particular, the *Advaita* (Non-dual) Vedantic school stresses the one-ness of the world, the ultimate essential unity behind all the multiplicity. The eighth-century thinker Gaudapâda affirmed, "When we look at all things in a connected manner they seem to be dependent, but when we look at them from the point of view of reality or truth the reasons cease to be reasons" (Dasgupta 1963: 427).[3] In other words, there is behind the veil of the delusion of separateness a cosmic entanglement which is hidden from our ordinary perception. This veil of misperception is called *māyā*.[4]

In other words, not unlike quantum systems that are entangled with other quantum systems, the various *purushas* are also mutually entangled. From a human perspective, according to Vedanta, it is this entanglement that is the ultimate cause of human suffering. This is the reason for stressing the principle of detachment (disentanglement) in the Hindu–Buddhist world for ending all suffering. Recognition and internalization of this entanglement is also regarded as spiritual enlightenment in that it reveals the ultimate one-ness behind the diversity. In fact, one of the primary doctrines that is expounded in the Upanishads is the identity of individual and the Cosmic spirit: *tat tvam asi*, Thou art that. Schrödinger referred to its relevance when he wrote: "but inconceivable as it seems to ordinary reason, you – and all other conscious beings as such – are all in all. Hence this life of yours which you are living is not merely a piece of the entire existence, but it is in a sense the *whole*; only this whole is not so constituted that it can be surveyed in one single glance. [… This] is what the Brahmins express in that sacred, mystic formula: *Tat tvam asi*, this is you" (Schrödinger 1964: 21–22).

The entanglement idea of quantum physics thus hints at a world-view in which everything in the universe is inseparably linked to every other thing: a cosmic interconnectedness that makes ours a seamless whole rather than a composite quilt. However, the Vedantic vision is more than interconnectedness: It is the identification of every apparently composite element with the Whole. The Advaita Vedantic thesis is that the distinctions that seem to be there in the experienced world, and our own isolation from other things and people, are but blurred visions of the truth about ultimate reality, which is one inconceivable totality (Mahadevan 2006). In this context, we may consider the Bohm interpretation of quantum mechanics. Here, what seem to be autonomous and stable structures are products "in the whole flowing movement," and they "will ultimately dissolve back into this movement" (Bohm 1980: 14). This again reads very much like an echo of the Vedantic view. One scholar put it this way: "There is one and only one reality, the imperishable and inexpressible Brahman. The world of our senses and intellect is merely a world of names and forms having no reality apart from Brahman" (Puligandla 2002: 1314).

The question as to how one integral reality became or seems to be a complex multiplicity is a profound philosophical puzzle. The Hindu explanation for this is that the multifaceted nature of the physical world arises from a built-in constraint (perhaps within the brain) that causes the appearance of separateness when in fact there isn't any. As mentioned above, this splitting of unity into complex diversity is attributed to *māyā*: the illusion-generating principle that operates on the human mind. A central affirmation of Vedanta is that it is possible to penetrate the opaque wall of *māyā* and see the underlying unity behind it. However, this can be achieved only through mystic merger (Pande 1991).

Many worlds interpretation

In the late 1950s, Hugh Everett proposed an interpretation of wave-function collapse by which every time a measurement is made and one of the possible eigenvalues of the probabilistic distribution of eigenstates is determined, one dimension of reality is actualized while, simultaneously, the other eigenvalues are actualized in other worlds (Everett 1973). In other words, there is a continuous multiple-reality-generating process in place, such that the experienced world is only one of many (an almost infinite number of) worlds that are constantly emerging. The idea may seem fantastic at first blush, but is quite consistent with the mathematical formalism of quantum mechanics (Deutsch 2000).

There is really no comparable picture in any traditional world-view. The idea of space–time-wise totally separate parallel universes (the many worlds interpretation) is an entirely modern concept, based on the interpretation of the wave-function collapse. It is an interesting, speculative hypothesis that is not inconsistent with the formalism of quantum mechanics. However, in the Hindu Puranic lore, there are several worlds beyond the terrestrial–physical (Mani 1975). Known as *lokas*, these are worlds between which communication and migration cannot occur through physical channels. Not unlike the Aristotelian view of a celestial world and a sub-lunar (terrestrial) world, in the Hindu metaphysical vision there are other transcendental *lokas* where beings and laws are altogether different. It is by no means the kind of multiverse that follows from the Everett interpretation of quantum mechanics. However, there is a superficial similarity in that here, too, other worlds are imagined between which and our own there can be no communication via the normal spatio-temporal channels.

We may also look upon this from another perspective. Recall that "M-theory allows for 100^{500} sets of apparent laws" (Hawking and Mlodinow 2010: 119). Since, in the Hindu world-view, the tangible universe is taken as a creation of *māyā*, we may imagine a cosmic operator M (Māyā) of which U is an eigenfunction. In fact, it has several eigenfunctions, so that $MU_k = L_kU_k$, where each U_k represents a universe, and each eigenvalue L_k represents the totality of the laws obtaining in Universe U_k. It is important here, as elsewhere, to resist the temptation of equating interesting conceptual parallels with ontological or epistemological equivalence.

Causality

Causality is a fundamental concept in physics and philosophy. It is at once obvious and elusive. That every occurrence has a cause is patent even to the most casual observer. A sudden happening without rhyme or reason is seldom accepted by normal-thinking people. One may look upon the dynamic aspect of the world as no more than the evolution of phenomena due to the action of various causes. Science tries to uncover the basic causes that generate the world of experience, and formulates these as the laws of nature. But the philosophical analysis of the notion of cause leads to some quite difficult technical problems.

For the present discussion, suffice it to say that quantum mechanics has brought about basic changes in our common-sense notions of cause. The discovery and study of the phenomenon of radioactivity was a death knell for the classical notion of causality, certainly insofar as it operates in the microcosm. Classical physics was followed by the Bohr model of the hydrogen atom, where again the transitions of the excited electrons were not governed by any strict causal law. In the framework of quantum mechanics, we can determine very precisely what fraction in a sample of radioactive nuclei will decay in a given time, but it is impossible, in principle, to know which particular nuclei will disintegrate.[5] Soon after the enunciation of the uncertainty principle, Heisenberg famously wrote: "Quantum mechanics definitely establishes the non-validity of the law of causality" (Heisenberg 1963: 62). Briefly put, in microcosmic processes, there are situations where the ordinarily recognized instigator of an event (cause) is not apparent at all. That is why one says the causality does not hold there. Hempel went so far as to say that causality plays no role at all in scientific explanation (Hempel 1965: 2.2).

One possible perspective, if not explanation, for the apparent breakdown of causality in these events may be found in a classical Hindu idea. Normally, one speaks of only cause and effect. But in the Hindu world-view, one should consider three distinct factors. These are referred to as *kriyâ*, action or that which occurs (the effect); *kâranâ*, cause or that which leads to the action; and *kartâ*, the agent that is responsible for initiating the action. In the framework of physics, one considers only the first two of these. Thus, for example, if we take the parabolic orbit of a projectile, the orbit traced is the effect (*kriyâ*) here. Gravity and the laws of motion are the cause (*kâranâ*) for this. And the person who projected the ball was the agent (*kartâ*). However, in many instances, the *kartâ* is by no means obvious. Thus the elliptic orbit of the planets is due to whatever caused them to be projected in a particular way initially. We can never know what that initial *kartâ* was. In such cases, one does not even inquire into it, and assumes that the initial planetary projections happened by pure chance.

One could envisage *kartâs* in the quantum world that act according to strict probabilistic laws, but their existence cannot be (and has not been) perceived, directly or indirectly. In a way, perhaps this would correspond to the hidden variable idea of the De Broglie-Bohm school (Hiley and Bohm 1993). In other words, the incompleteness of quantum theory, as stated by Einstein, may be looked upon as arising from our lack of knowledge of the *kartâs* that operate in microcosmic processes. Indeed, this would correspond in quantum mechanics to the Divine Action idea of the Vashishtâdvaita school and of some Christian theologies.

Another view of causality expressed by Hindu thinkers is that the phenomenal world is no more than an incessant series of metamorphoses that a single ultimate principle is undergoing. There is but one primordial cause for the universe, and the rest are mere transformations. Thus, it says in the *Chândogya Upanishad* (VI.1.4) "Just as by the clod of clay all that is made of clay becomes known, the modification being only a name arising from speech while the truth is that it is just clay." In one mainstream Hindu view, that ultimate causative principle is known as *Brahman*. This may strike the modern reader as pure metaphysical speculation. However, if we consider the framework of modern science, we find a very similar proposition. Ultimately, all the manifestations in the phenomenal world may be viewed essentially as ephemeral transformations of matter–energy. Likewise, in the view of quantum mechanics, there are only wave-functions in which are latent all the attributes and potential of the physical world. The collapse of wave-functions is what leads to the actualization of physical reality.

Scholars such as David Bohm have thought deeply about the metaphysics of mind and reality, and found some ways out of the conceptual paradoxes of quantum physics (Bohm 1980). The point is that much of the confusion arises from our understanding (or lack of understanding) of the brain–mind relationship. A deeper grasp of this might reveal that the traditional two-value logic with the excluded middle need not necessarily be a requirement for the functioning of the world (Comfort 1984: 4.1).[6]

We may note in passing that, according to the Sāmkhya school of thought, what we reckon as effects are the actualization of what was already present in what we regard as the causes. Thus the *satkārya* thesis of the Sāmkhya school considers cause–effect through the analogy of oil in the sesame seed: the former (oil: effect) is already implicit in the latter (seed: cause). This is not unlike the notion of emergence in the modern context (Clayton 2005).

Subnatural and supernatural

The theoretical framework of science does not permit any factor that involves supernatural agencies of realities. In the religious context, the term "supernatural" brings to mind beings and forces that have magical properties, that can violate the laws of nature, that communicate with humans from a mysterious somewhere, etc. In this matter, as in many other pre-modern scientific world-views, the traditional Hindu vision diverges from the scientific. In the religious context, one assumes the existence of principles undergirding the physical universe, and that are supernatural in the religious–mythic sense.

However, it is important to be clear about the term. One generally means by "supernatural" something that is beyond space and time, has no matter–energy component to it, and thereby defies all attempts to detect or locate it. In other words, the main attributes of the supernatural are invisibility, intangibility, insubstantiality, and non-localizability. But the framework of science rests on basic laws, and these laws are invisible, intangible, insubstantial, and non-localizable. From this standpoint, it may not be appropriate to describe the laws of nature as supernatural, because they do have all these features of the supernatural, except that they are not personalized as in the religious framework.

In the Hindu view, too, there is an invisible, intangible, insubstantial, and non-localization principle governing the functioning of the universe. Aside from *Brahman* (cosmic consciousness), there is also the idea of *Rta* (*Rita*), which refers to cosmic order, both physical and moral, that sustains the universe. There is a verse in the Rig Veda (VI.39.4) which speaks of Divinity thus:

> He, shining, caused to shine what shone not,
> By Law (*Rta*) he lighted up the dawn.
> He moves with steeds yoked by Eternal Order (*Rta*)
> Making Man happy by the chariot-nave that finds the Light.

It has therefore been pointed out that it is "*Rta* that holds together the cosmos through natural law, is the discipline of life through moral law; and it is also the discipline of form that makes Beauty" (Bose 1988: 45).

On the other hand, science (physics) traces the ultimate origin of the universe to subnature: the insubstantial realm of entities that arise from vacuum fluctuations. The *Brahman* of the Hindu world-view, envisioned as the insubstantial immaterial palpitation that is presumed to be at the foundation of the world, may also be considered as subnature.

String theories and Hindu views

As is well known, string theories are efforts to account for the variety in the physical world in terms of ultimate entities, which have come to be called strings. In this picture, every tangible aspect of the world is traced to vibrations of unimaginably minute fundamental entities called strings. This notion that what undergirds the universe are fundamental vibrations would have seemed strange to nineteenth-century atomists, even though they recognized the all-pervasiveness of electromagnetic waves. It is interesting to recall in this context that, in the Upanishadic framework, the substratum of the universe is the subtle *aum*: a serene vibration whose audible manifestation is the sacred chant with which every Hindu prayer begins. It says in the Mandukya Upanishad that "All that is the past, the present, and the future, all that is, is only the syllable *aum*. And whatever there is beyond the threefold time, that too is only the syllable *aum*." (Radhakrishnan 1995: 695). In other words, cosmic vibrations link both the perceived and the unperceived (transcendent) worlds.

Then again, in its expanded version, M-theory is a body of five different string theories, and has countless different solutions. Current physics prompts us to realize that a pluralist perspective is the only way we can grasp the nature of ultimate reality. This reminds one of the assertion of a Rig-Vedic sage poet to the effect that whatever the single ultimate reality may be, it is described differently by different people.[7]

Concluding thoughts

Some metaphysical notions are more than speculative fantasy. They could well be insights into deeper aspects of reality. Passages in ancient Hindu texts seem to suggest that certain ideas that the ancient thinkers propounded on the nature of ultimate reality go beyond the naïve realism of classical physics. While one must keep in mind the fundamental distinctions between the kinds of truths revealed by modern physics and the insights provided by ancient world-views, it is also true that the philosophical quagmire into which quantum physics has been sliding during the past few decades has turned topsy-turvy our common-sense pictures of a solid, substantial world of cause and law, of rigid particles and conserved quantities, of smoothly flowing time and three-dimensional space. As we delve more deeply into the remote recesses of atoms and nuclei, funny things begin to happen: Mathematical clouds of probability take over, electrons seem to know, information seems to get transmitted instantaneously, everything seems to be interconnected, and a good many more strange things are taking place in the microcosm. In the depths of black holes and in the singularities of quarks, space and time and physical laws themselves become warped and dissolved. So one begins to wonder if those visionaries, metaphysicians, and philosophers of ancient India may have stumbled upon some profound truths about the perceived world that, because of their very nature, cannot be adequately expressed in words. They were perhaps not far from the mark in insisting that in the stark, denuded aspect, stripped of matter and mind, there is a level of reality that only pure consciousness can experience, and pure consciousness can only experience, not convey through words. Recall Wittgenstein's famous observation: "Whereof one cannot speak, thereof one must be silent." Could it be that now, at long last, after countless tortuous turns of reason and experimentation, of mathematics and microscopes, quantum physics is slowly beginning to get a glimmer of what those sage-poets were speaking about? (Raman 1989: 212). Could it be that, as some Hindu thinkers said, there are two kinds of truth – *parâ* and *aparâ* – transcendental truths that, like the wave-function before collapse, exist in a different realm; and empirical truths that, like the wave-function after observation, can be grasped though logic and reason, measured and manipulated? (*Mundaka Upanishad*, I.4).

Notes

1 In the textbooks one speaks of six orthodox schools: The Nyâya, the Vaiseshika, the Samkhya, the Yoga, the Purva Mimamsa, and Vedanta; and the heterodox: The Buddhist and the Carvaka (materialist) schools. The former accept the sanctity of the Vedas, the latter do not.

2 Although the book *Mein Leben, Meine Weltansicht* was published only in 1961, it consists of two essays, the first of which was written in 1925, right when Schrödinger was steeped in quantum mechanics. His famous equation was published in December 1926. For more on the history of the Schrödinger equation, see Paul Foreman and V. V. Raman, "Why was it Schrödinger who Developed de Broglie's Ideas?," *Historical Studies in the Physical Sciences* 1 (1969) 291–314.

3 It should be pointed out that these ideas are also part of the framework of Mahayana Buddhism. Indeed, some have maintained that Gaudapâda himself was probably a Buddhist thinker (Dasgupta 1963: 423).

4 The notion of mâyâ is central to Vedantic philosophy: It says essentially that the world (reality) is not what it appears to be, and true knowledge/awakening arises when the delusion of multiplicity dissolves and the unity behind it all is experienced.

5 This is equally true of predicted traffic fatalities for a given holiday season: One can say with confidence (roughly) how many deaths will occur, but one simply cannot say who will be the victims. This is because human events occur on the hypercomplex plane (Raman 2009: 72–75).

6 This idea has also been elaborated by Basarab Nicolescu in his elaboration of the notion of transdisciplinarity (Nicolescu 2002).

7 Rig Veda (I.164.46): *Ekam sad vipra bahudha vadanti* (Truth is one, the learned call it variously).

References

Bohm, David (1980) *Wholeness and the Implicate Order*, London: Routledge.

Bose, Abinash Chandra (1988) *The Call of the Vedas*, Bombay: Bharatiya Vidya Bhavan.

Clayton, Philip (2005) *Mind and Emergence: From Quantum to Consciousness*, Oxford: Oxford University Press.

Comfort, Alex (1984) *Reality & Empathy: Physics, Mind, and Science in the 21st Century*, Albany, NY: SUNY Press.

Dasgupta, Surendranath (1928) "Philosophy of Vasubandhu in Vimsatika and Trimsika," *Indian Historical Quarterly* 4(1).

——(1963) *A History of Indian Philosophy*, Cambridge: Cambridge University Press.

Deutsch, D. (2000) *The Fabric of Reality*, London: Penguin.

Everett, H. (1973) *Many-Worlds Interpretation of Quantum Mechanics*, Princeton, NJ: Princeton University Press.

Fitzgerald, Edward (trans.) (1989) *Rubaiyat of Omar Khayyam*, reprint, London: Penguin.

Fraser, Gordon (2006) *The New Physics for the Twenty-First Century*, Cambridge: Cambridge University Press.

Goswami, Amit (1995) *The Self-Aware Universe*, New York: Tarcher/Putnam.

——(2001) *The Physicists' View of Nature: The Quantum Revolution*, New York: Springer.

Hawking, Stephen and Leonrad Mlodinow (2010) *The Grand Design*, New York: Bantam Books.

Heisenberg, W. (1963) *Quantum Theory of Measurement*, J. Wheeler and W. Zusec (eds), Princeton, NJ: Princeton University Press.

Hempel, Carl G. (1965) *Aspects of Scientific Explanation and Other Essays in the Philosophy of Science*, New York: The Free Press.

Hiley, B. J. and D. Bohm (1993) *The Undivided Universe*, New York: Routledge.

Iyer, K. A. Krishnaswamy (1965) *Vedanta or The Science of Reality*, Holenarsipur: Adhyatma Prakasha Karyalaya.

Laplace, Pierre-Simon (1951) *A Philosophical Essay on Probabilities*, Frederick Wilson Truscott and Frederick Lincoln Emory (trans.), New York: Dover Publications.

Mani, Vettam (1975) *Puranic Encyclopedia*, New Delhi: Motilal Banarsidass.

Penrose, Roger (1994) *Shadows of the Mind: An Approach to the Missing Science of Consciousness*, Oxford: Oxford University Press.

Primack, Joel R. and Nancy Ellen Abrams (2006) *The View from the Center of the Universe: Discovering Our Extraordinary Place in the Cosmos*, New York: Penguin.

Mahadevan, T. M. P. (2006) *The Philosophy of the Advaita*, reprint, Delhi: Bharatiya Kala Prakashan.

Pande, Narasimhacara (1991) *Māyā in physics*, Delhi: Motilal Banarsidass.

Pappu, S. S. Rama Rao (ed.) (1987) *The Dimensions of Karma*, Delhi: Chanakya Publications.

Puligandla, R. (2002) *That Thou Art: Wisdom of the Upanishads*, Fremont, CA: Asian Humanities Press.

Radhakrishnan, Sarvepalli (ed.) (1967) *History of Philosophy Eastern and Western*, Vol. 1, London: George Allen & Unwin.

——(1995) *The Principal Upanishads*, Delhi: Oxford University Press.

Radin, Dean I. (2006) *Entangled Minds*, New York: Paraview (Simon & Schuster).

Raman, Varadaraja V. (1989) *Glimpses of Indian Heritage*, Bombay: Popular Prakashan.

——(2009) *Truth and Tension in Science and Religion*, Ossipee, NH: Beech River Books.

Schrödinger, Erwin (1964) *My View of the World*, Cecily Hastings (trans.), Cambridge: Cambridge University Press.

Wheeler, J. A. and H. Zurek (1983) *Quantum Theory and Measurement*, Princeton, NJ: Princeton University Press.

Wigner, Eugene (1970) *Symmetries and Reflections: Scientific Essays*, Cambridge, MA: MIT Press.

Williams, Monier (2001) *Indian Wisdom or Examples of the Religious, Philosophical and Ethical Doctrines of the Hindus*, Delhi: Rupa & Co.

Further reading

Since the 1930s, science-inclined philosophers have been reflecting on the similarities, if not conceptual relationships, between quantum mechanics and metaphysical truths. Thus we had books on Vedanta and science from Hindu thinkers (K. A. Krishnaswamy Iyer, *Vedanta or the Science of Reality*, cited above), and also from Western scientists who had gained acquaintance with Indian thought (E. Schrödinger, *What is Life?*, London: Macmillan, 1946). In the last decades of the twentieth century, the number of books on the subject grew: *Physics and Eastern Mysticism*, Shambala, 1975; Gary Zukav, *The Dancing Wu Li Masters: An Overview of the New Physics*, New York: William Morrow and Company, 1979; Swami Jitatmananda, *Modern Physics and Vedanta*, Mumbai: Bhavan's Book University, 1986. From the last decade of the twentieth century onwards, books on the subject began to appear from more technical perspectives: Amit Goswami, *The Self-Aware Universe* (cited above); Richard L. Thompson, *Maya: The World as Virtual Reality*, Alachua, FL: Govardhan Hill, 2003.) There is no question but that the deep insights of ancient Hindu spiritually inspired thinkers embody remarkably profound views on consciousness, human knowledge, and reality. For some modern writers, it is difficult to distinguish empirically and mathematically acquired understandings of physical reality from perspectives gained through entirely different modes. As a result, not all such books are necessarily serious science, while in internet postings some exaggerated and questionable claims on the subject appear periodically.

16
QUANTUM THEORY, PHILOSOPHY, AND THEOLOGY
Is there a distinct Roman Catholic perspective?

William R. Stoeger, S.J.

Quantum mechanics, along with the special and general theories of relativity, ushered in a contemporary physics that has been amazingly fruitful and has completely changed the way we view reality. The other prong of this thoroughgoing scientific revolution has been biological evolution in tandem with genetics and molecular biology. But quantum mechanics and the much richer quantum field theory it eventually spawned have been distinctive in revealing a fundamental realm – the sub-microscopic realm – of reality, which behaves in a very different way from the everyday reality we experience, and yet enables everyday reality to be what it is. The standard results of quantum theory are very reliable – and precisely model the behavior of particles, fields, and detectors as they interact. Despite that overwhelming success, there are deep and unresolved controversies about the philosophical interpretation of quantum theory – about what it is really telling us about reality. Is there ontological indeterminacy – and even insufficiency – at the quantum level? Does quantum theory really reflect reality as it is at that level, or is it merely providing us with phenomena that veil its true nature?

Over the years – especially recently – the various philosophical interpretations of quantum theory have generated theological questions and speculations, ranging from the meaning of God's providence in a universe dominated at its most fundamental by statistics and uncertainty – albeit within definite limits – to conceiving quantum indeterminacy as a "window of opportunity" for God to act "directly" in nature without contravening the laws of nature. How are we to evaluate quantum theory, and particularly the philosophical and theological opportunities and challenges that flow from it, from a Roman Catholic point of view? Is there a distinctive Catholic perspective?

Our concluding answer to these questions is that Catholic theology and teaching has nothing specific to say about quantum theory as such – since it is a legitimate and highly successful branch of natural science, Catholic religious perspectives are not able to exercise any relevant critique of its findings or scientific interpretations. Further, Catholic views strongly affirm that there can be no inherent conflict or contradiction between the results of the sciences, such as quantum mechanics and quantum theory, and Catholic teaching – or more generally between the conclusions of reason and those of faith – if each is properly understood. The Catholic position goes on to encourage openness to, acceptance of, and respect for whatever the sciences discover – however strange and counter-intuitive – as a fruit of our rationality and as an indirect reflection of the Creator in nature. Creation is God's work, and as such our deeper understanding and contemplation of it reveals the divine.

As we have already indicated, closely associated with the results and scientific interpretations of quantum theory are its philosophical interpretations. It is with some of these that Catholic theology and teaching could conceivably take issue – if they are found to be in direct conflict with a clear philosophical position following from, or essential to, Catholicism. It is very unlikely that a philosophical interpretation of quantum theory would be strongly supported by scientific findings and understanding and at the same time be in clear conflict with Catholic theological principles and tenets properly understood. In fact, there has been to my knowledge no example of this so far. There have been, and are, philosophical positions that are at variance with Catholic philosophy and theology and appeal to quantum theory for support. But none of them is in any way compellingly required by quantum theory and our elaborated understanding of it.

In this discussion, I substantiate these general conclusions, first of all by giving a brief overview of some of the key features of the quantum world, secondly summarizing the standard scientific/philosophical interpretation (the Copenhagen interpretation) with a brief mention of other competing interpretations, and thirdly indicating several of the key puzzles regarding the quantum world. After that, I present some of the philosophical and theological ideas that quantum theory has generated. Finally, I discuss several of these in light of the best understandings coming from the Catholic theology and teaching.

The quantum world

The idea of the wave-function – or quantum state – is central to quantum theory. It represents all the features of a physical system (Shimony 2001: 3–16). This completeness can be interpreted in various ways – as all aspects of "the reality," or more often simply as "all those that can be systematically measured" (Stoeger 2001: 83). This is already an example of the differing scientific and philosophical interpretations that quickly emerge in this field. The square of the wave-function gives the probability of any possible outcome of any measurement that can be made of, and any operation that can be performed on, a given system. However, as is well known, there are properties of an electron, such as position and momentum, for instance, which cannot be precisely determined simultaneously. An exact measurement of position would mean we know absolutely nothing about the value of the momentum; and an exact measurement of momentum would mean we would know nothing about the electron's location. This is the well known Heisenberg indeterminacy – or uncertainty – principle. According to some standard interpretations, the electron possesses neither a position nor a momentum until it is measured – until it interacts with the detector. Furthermore, this uncertainty or indeterminacy is objective – it is not a result of our lack of knowledge, but is an ontological characteristic of reality at the quantum level. These *are* already interpretations! But they are interpretations that flow directly from the observationally substantiated physics.

Very closely connected with the wave-function and the Heisenberg indeterminacy principle are two other central ideas. The first is "complementarity" – the strange property that a quantum system will manifest one realization of itself in one type of measurement or observation, and a very different realization in a second type of experiment. The experiments are incompatible – and the two different manifestations are not simultaneously real, according to the usual interpretation (Stoeger 2001: 89). By far the most commonly known complementarity is the wave–particle duality of all material systems. Under some experimental conditions, a system will manifest particle characteristics – under others, wave characteristics.

The second idea is that, in any measurement, the measuring apparatus and observer interact with the system being measured or observed. Therefore the result is revelatory not simply of that system, but rather of that system in interaction with the detector and the observer. Thus any measurement or observation inevitably affects it. Furthermore, any macroscopic measurement or observation results in only one of the many possible outcomes that measurement or observation could have generated under identical circumstances. Many identical observations will yield a variety of different outcomes. The frequency of each outcome divided by the total number of outcomes represents the probability of that outcome, as given by the square of the wave-function.

Two other important, but somewhat strange, properties of quantum systems are non-separability and entanglement. Non-separability refers to the fact that the fundamental integrity of the system is given by the wave-function, and not by the particles that may be partial manifestations of it. The wave-function is not localizable, though the particles may be. Because of the ontological priority of the wave-function, we often observe "correlated actualization of potentialities over space-like intervals" (Shimony 1989: 373–95) – that is, intervals that cannot be causally connected except by signals traveling faster than the speed of light. This means that, no matter how far apart the particles of a given wave-function travel, they continue to be closely related – that is, their properties remain correlated. Thus a measurement of one of them automatically and instantaneously induces a realization of specific system-compatible properties in the others. So, if we measure one electron in a zero-spin system to have a positive spin (spin-up), the other electron will automatically be measured spin-down – even if there is no time to communicate the result of the first measurement to the second electron. Entanglement refers to the property whereby the sum – or superposition – of two or more states is effected, even though none of the component states is. So we might well find in a system that a state 1 + 2 is present, even though neither state 1 nor state 2 is. Often, the clearest demonstrations of non-separability involve the measurement of entangled states.

The "trademark" property of the quantum world is that the energy, angular moment, spin, charge, etc. of these systems come only in quanta – in "packets" of a specific size – and not in a continuous spectrum of sizes. Finally, there is the important principle of correspondence, which connects the quantum world with the classical macroscopic world with which we are more familiar. This principle is that the quantum description of reality must mesh seamlessly with the classical description in a very specific limit – as Planck's constant effectively goes to zero, or equivalently for very large quantum numbers. All of reality is embraced by the quantum world, but its peculiar characteristics are only manifest at sub-microscopic scales and in very special macroscopic situations. As we go to larger scales, the quantum description is indistinguishable from the classical description.

The Copenhagen interpretation and its critics

The standard Copenhagen interpretation of quantum theory is strongly, but not definitively or uniquely, indicated by the physics. Before briefly presenting it, it is essential to recognize that, at the level of physics itself, quantum theory does not need any further interpretation than is already present in it (Stoeger 2001: 91). The Copenhagen interpretation moves one step beyond this to assert the following conclusions (Shimony 1989: 393–95; Stoeger 2001: 92): (1) the interaction between the object measured and the detector is never negligible; (2) the properties of a quantum system that are measured by incompatible experiments are *not* simultaneously real (complementarity); (3) the wave-function describes all there is to the quantum system (completeness); (4) particles or other objects emanating from a quantum interaction cannot be cleanly separated or individuated; and (5) the measurement – or interaction – with a macroscopic system is the only process that gives a quantum system unambiguous properties and meaning. These elements of the Copenhagen interpretation stress the basic and objective character of the uncertainty, indeterminacy, the probability, and the complementarity of the quantum world (Stoeger 2001: 91–92) – and effectively rule out the role of "hidden variables" that could operate behind the scenes, so to speak, thus rendering those hallmark features of the quantum world merely subjective or epistemic, and not objective.

There are other interpretations of quantum theory that are taken seriously these days. One in particular is the consistent histories interpretation. Some versions of it are very close to the Copenhagen interpretation – and, according to some experts, an improvement on it. However, the details are rather technical and beyond the scope of this discussion.

A well known competitor to the Copenhagen interpretation, which rests on an alternative quantum theory pioneered by David Bohm and developed over the years by many other physicists and philosophers, relies on non-local hidden variables, which, as indicated, would eliminate the fundamentally ontological and indeterministic character of quantum phenomena (Cushing 2001: 99–110). This interpretation is still consistent with the physics (local hidden variables are not). However, Bohm's theory does not appear to be anywhere near as elegant, as fruitful, or as compelling from the point of view of the physics and its applications. Therefore it has not received the serious attention the standard Copenhagen and related interpretations have. It has not – at least so far – been ruled out, though.

Thus there is a strong, but not absolute, support (nothing in the natural sciences is absolute or final) for affirming that the quantum characteristics we have been discussing are features of reality at that level – and not just the result of our incomplete knowledge of that quantum world itself. There is a sense in which the quantum world *is* veiled – in that we only know it by interacting with it, not independently of our interactions with it. But it is only *partially* veiled (Stoeger 2001: 93–96) – our interactions with it, and our increasing understanding of the results of those interactions, *do* tell us something about that world.

Key enigmas of the quantum world

One of the key puzzles that quantum mechanics presents to us scientifically and philosophically is how all the allowed possible outcomes of a given experiment given by the wave-function are in effect instantaneously "replaced" or collapsed into just one of them by a measurement or observation. This is often referred to as "the measurement problem." There is very strong evidence that the allowed possibilities really exist in a definite sense in the quantum system as a superposition – a combination of "almost activated potentialities" – but that, upon interaction with a macroscopic detector, just one of them is selected for realization in the classical realm. And there is no explanation in the theory for which possibility is selected! Furthermore, it is clear that, before the measurement, the system was not just in the state indicated by the measurement. This means that the uncertainty and probability that is a central feature of the quantum world is indeed ontological, and not simply the result of our ignorance – that is, not simply epistemological.

There is some strong emerging evidence that this "collapse of the wave-function" to just one of its possible outcomes in a measurement is at least partially due to its complex interaction with the macroscopic environment represented by the detector, or whatever the wave-function encounters in its interactions. But that cannot fully explain or account for which one of those possibilities is realized. At its most basic, quantum physics reveals an important irreducibly statistical aspect to reality. There is an intrinsic, fundamental uncertainty and indeterminacy that characterizes the quantum world which underlies the world and universe, and everything that emerges from it. It is crucial, however, to stress two other points. First of all, this uncertainty or indeterminacy is narrowly and rigorously constrained – not anything can happen – and the allowed outcomes still respect causality and must fall within a certain well defined range of parameter values given by the theory. Thus it would be – and I think it definitely is – an unwarranted stretch to conclude that important philosophical principles, such as the principle of sufficient reason, are violated by quantum phenomena. Secondly, these quantum phenomena reveal the radically relational character of reality, even at its most basic levels, and, of course, the active role of the observer or measurer in determining what is actually observed. The observer – or more generally anything with which a wave-function interacts – effects the phenomena observed, precisely by interacting with the wave-function.

Some philosophical and theological reflections on the quantum world

Among the many religious and theological responses to the revelations about the sub-microscopic world provided by quantum physics are two that are central.

The first sees quantum phenomena as a severe challenge to the order and definiteness of nature, and to God's effective governance of it. The uncertainty and indeterminacy that reign at the quantum level are theologically unsettling, and seem to some to contradict God's continuing creative and providential roles in reality – and even a critical realist hold on a well behaved and intelligible causal fabric upon which those roles seem to rely. The most notable example of a Catholic intellectual who objects to the Copenhagen interpretation of quantum theory for philosophical reasons is Stanley Jaki (1978: 165–213, 1986: 1–21). However, his particular negative assessment has found little acceptance among leading Catholic and Protestant philosophers and theologians.

The second theological response sees in quantum indeterminacy a window of opportunity for God to interact directly in nature to guide and determine the course of events, without disturbing or intervening in nature in a detectable way. In recent years, this idea has been extensively developed by Robert John Russell and his collaborators Nancey Murphy and Thomas Tracy. They refer to their proposal as "non-interventionist objective divine action" (NIODA) (Russell 2001: 293–328; Tracy 2001: 235–58; and references therein). According to this suggestion, since at the quantum level nature specifies only the probability of measurement or observation of a collection of different outcomes – not one definite outcome – God can act directly to insure a specific, allowed outcome that is more in keeping with God's intentions and plans, without disrupting the laws of quantum theory. We shall discuss this possibility more fully in the next section.

What about the challenge that some have seen in the standard, prevailing interpretations of quantum theory to notions of a well behaved, intelligible causal underpinning of reality, and therefore the challenge to God's creative and providential action within it? This is actually the essence of Albert Einstein's own philosophical unease about quantum phenomena. There are a number of points that can be made. With regard to our growing knowledge of the quantum world itself, Ernan McMullin's reflections are particularly relevant. He insists that what is eliminated through quantum theory according to the Copenhagen interpretation is not the reality and intelligibility of the world, but rather the conception of its behavior at the sub-microscopic level as classical – as similar to what we experience on the macroscopic level (McMullin 1984: 8–40; Allen 2006: 65, 108–9).

This is correct. The quantum world is just very different from the classical macroscopic world with which we are familiar – even though the quantum world provides the necessary foundations for the classical world. In our controlled interactions with the quantum level through our use of macroscopic detectors and recording apparatus, we essentially project some aspects of that quantum world (such as one particular realization of a wave-function) into our classical world. Other aspects are left behind. We know that they are left behind because repeated measurements under identical conditions yield different results! Or measuring the same wave-function by a very different procedure yields an interference pattern indicative of a wave, rather than of particle.

Secondly, as McMullin has stressed elsewhere (McMullin 1998: 389–414), God as Creator can work through chance and statistical causal chains just as effectively as through classical laws of nature. One of the philosophical implications behind this is simply that physical causality continues to operate at the quantum level – but that it manifests itself in our macroscopic interactions with that level by projections onto unique classical quantities, such as a specific time, velocity, or momentum, which are not proper characteristics of the quantum world itself. Thirdly, more adequate understanding of divine creation would see it, along with God's providence, as perfectly consistent with the standard Copenhagen-like interpretations of quantum mechanics and quantum field theory. We shall have more to say about this in the next section. Fundamentally, it involves seeing God's sustaining nature as it is both in its existence and in its function. The creative relationship enables and empowers nature to be what it is at every level (Stoeger 2008: 225–47 and references therein) – but does not involve God micromanaging it or substituting for its deficiencies.

Catholic theology's engagement with the sciences and with quantum theory

Though, as I indicated at the beginning of this essay, Catholic teaching and theology have not engaged quantum theory and its interpretations explicitly, we can – even from this silence and from the general tenor of its engagement with the natural sciences as a whole – discern a definite stance. First of all, the Catholic position has been clearly that both the natural sciences and philosophy are disciplines oriented towards knowledge and understanding, each with its own autonomy and methods. Therefore they demand respect for, and serious consideration of, their conclusions insofar as they are well supported by the evidence and arguments proper to each. Secondly, the Catholic Church has always strongly encouraged scientific research and philosophical reflection (Pope John Paul II 1998: paras 49, 51–53, 63, 106). Thirdly, relationship between faith and reason – and therefore between faith and the natural sciences and philosophy – is based on the principle that "there can never be any real discrepancy between faith and reason," since "the things of the world and the things of faith derive from the same God" (*Catechism of the Catholic Church* 1994: 43; Pope John Paul II 1998: para. 53). This principle is clearly reflected in many of the Church's and the Pope's statements on the relationships between science and theology, and in much of Catholic theological work in this area.

Thus it is not surprising that there is no explicit Catholic position on quantum theory, or even directly on philosophical interpretations of quantum theory. Catholic theologians and philosophers have studied and reflected on them in various ways, primarily using them as resources for deepening and updating their engagement with our contemporary understanding of nature. But their work does not constitute an official position. These facts are indications that the basic principle just discussed is at work, and that there is a pervasively perceived independence and compatibility between Catholic theology and teaching on the one hand, and the findings and standard interpretations of quantum theory on the other. Nothing present in the science is in obvious conflict with faith or the Catholic understanding of it.

In fact, with regard to strictly scientific issues, findings, and conclusions, theology possesses no professional interest or competency. If there appears to be a conflict between what science discovers or concludes and what Catholic teaching holds, then the Catholic position is that there is some misunderstanding or misinterpretation on one side or the other, or on both sides. So far, however, this has not occurred in any noticeable way with regard to our scientific understanding of the quantum levels of reality.

When it comes to philosophical interpretations of quantum theory – and certainly their extension to theological proposals for divine action – we are at least one step removed from the natural sciences themselves, and somewhat different considerations are in play. To the extent that a given philosophical interpretation (such as the Copenhagen interpretation) is compellingly supported by experimental and theoretical results, including its long-term success and fruitfulness for the understanding and coherence of quantum physics itself, it enjoys the same acceptance as the scientific conclusions themselves. As we have already mentioned, except for a few notable exceptions – such as Stanley Jaki – Catholic thinkers have not found standard interpretations of quantum theory objectionable. More often than not, they have found them stimulating and deeply consonant with Catholic philosophy and theology. More importantly, there has not been any official statement directly critiquing or commenting on them.

However, philosophical interpretations, conclusions, and speculations that are not directly indicated by scientific findings must be judged on other grounds, such as the strength of the support they receive from philosophical, scientific, and broader interdisciplinary considerations. These have more potential for finding themselves in tension, or even conflict, with Catholic theology and teaching – especially to the extent that they maintain positions that go beyond the competencies of quantum physics, and beyond the direct philosophical interpretation of its results. Though, as I have already mentioned, Catholic teaching and theology consider philosophy distinct from theology and independent in its quest for truth, it is possible for certain philosophical conclusions and positions to be in conflict with faith and with theology. For instance, positivistic, anti-realist, or anti-metaphysical positions would fall into this category (Pope John Paul II 1998: paras 46–47, 53, 55).

The clearest recent statement of this critical stance towards philosophical positions can be found in Pope John Paul II's encyclical *Fides et Ratio*, where he says that "It is the Church's duty to indicate the elements in a philosophical system which are incompatible with her own faith. In fact, many philosophical opinions concerning God, the human being, human freedom and ethical behaviour engage the Church directly, because they touch on the revealed truth of which she is the guardian" (*ibid.*: para. 50). At the same time, the writings of Pope John Paul II strongly promote and encourage bold, ground-breaking, and imaginative philosophical inquiry as essential in our quest for truth and understanding (*ibid.*: paras 51, 56, 103–4). As a matter of fact, however, none of the philosophical speculations stemming from interpreting quantum theory have received direct negative critique in official statements from the Catholic Church.

If we turn to the openings and opportunities that quantum theory provides to philosophy and to theology, what position does Catholicism take towards these? Again, in these cases there has not been any explicit or official response negatively or positively. However, Catholic intellectuals and theologians have certainly engaged these opportunities. Many have referred to quantum theory as providing clear evidence – relying on the standard Copenhagen-like interpretations – that reality is not basically deterministic. At the same time, a few have generalized key quantum concepts and applied them to Christian and Catholic theology and spirituality (O'Murchu 1997). More recently, a number of Catholic philosophers and theologians have explicitly engaged Russell's NIODA proposal (Russell 2001: 293–328) in a detailed way (Carroll 2008: 582–602; Jacobs 2008: 542–81). It is not possible to go deeply into their assessment of the proposal here. Some of their principal reservations cluster around what we might call the incompatibility of NIODA with some of the principal insights of the best of traditional Catholic theology of creation – based on precise understandings (Carroll 2008: 582–602; Stoeger 2008: 225–47; and references therein) of *creatio ex nihil/creatio continua* and the distinction between primary causality and secondary causality. Needing some "window of opportunity," as provided by quantum uncertainty, for God to act in a special way in the world really seems to undercut the causal adequacy of the quantum processes themselves at their own level, and to require that God act directly in nature as a secondary cause, instead of immanently through God's ongoing creative empowering relationship with secondary causes. Furthermore, as Jacobs points out (Jacobs 2008: 542–81), the philosophical and theological points of reference, motivations, and rhetoric of NIODA are very different from those operative in a Roman Catholic theological context. Certainly, this in itself does not equate to Catholic disapproval of NIODA, but it entails some severe, unresolved issues, and falls outside central Catholic theological and philosophical instincts, intuitions, and preferences.

Conclusions

Though Catholic teaching and theology have not explicitly and officially reacted to quantum theory and its standard interpretations, there is every indication that Catholic views and the science are compatible, and that the Catholic position strongly encourages both continued scientific and theological research in these areas. However, it is possible that some unwarranted philosophical extrapolations from our scientific understanding of the quantum world would be in conflict with Catholic theology and philosophy – which is the case also for other areas of the natural sciences, such as biological evolution. Catholic thinkers have eagerly engaged the opportunities provided by quantum physics, though Catholic theologians by and large have found some key theological proposals based on quantum theory (such as NIODA) somewhat contradictory with Catholic theology's approach to creation and to divine action.

References

Allen, Paul L. (2006) *Ernan McMullin and Critical Realism in the Science–Theology Dialogue*, Aldershot, UK: Ashgate.

Carroll, William E. (2008) "Divine Agency, Contemporary Physics, and the Autonomy of Nature," *The Heythrop Journal* 49: 582–602.

Cushing, James T. (2001) "Determinism versus Indeterminism in Quantum Mechanics: A 'Free' Choice," in *Quantum Mechanics: Scientific Perspectives on Divine Action*, Robert John Russell, Philip Clayton, Kirk Wegter-McNelly and John Polkinghorne (eds), Vatican City State and Berkeley, CA: Vatican Observatory Publications and Center for Theology and the Natural Sciences [this volume is hereafter abbreviated *QMSP*], 99–110.

Catechism of the Catholic Church (1994), Rome and New Hope, KY: Urbi et Orbi Communications.

Jacobs, Philip J. (2008) "An Argument over 'Methodological Naturalism' at the Vatican Observatory," *The Heythrop Journal* 49: 542–81.

Jaki, Stanley (1978) *The Road of Science and the Ways to God*, Chicago, IL: University of Chicago Press.

——(1986) "Chance or Reality: Interaction in Nature versus Measurement in Physics," in his *Chance or Reality and Other Essays*, Lanham, MD: University Press of America.

McMullin, Ernan (1984) "A Case for Scientific Realism," in *Scientific Realism*, J. Leplin (ed.), Berkeley, CA: University of California Press, 8–40.

——(1998) "Cosmic Purpose and the Contingency of Human Evolution," *Theology Today* 55(3): 389–414.

O'Murchu, Diarmuid (1997) *Quantum Theology: Spiritual Implications of the New Physics*, New York: Crossroad Classic.

Pope John Paul II (1998) *Fides et Ratio*, Washington, DC: USCCB Publishing.

Russell, Robert John (2001) "Divine Action and Quantum Mechanics: A Fresh Assessment," in *QMSP*, 293–328.

Shimony, Abner (1989) "Conceptual Foundations of Quantum Mechanics," in *The New Physics*, Paul Davies (ed.), Cambridge: Cambridge University Press, 373–95.

——(2001) "The Reality of the Quantum World," in *QMSP*, 3–16.

Stoeger, William R. (2001) "Epistemological and Ontological Issues Arising from Quantum Theory," in *QMSP*, 81–98.

——(2008) "Conceiving Divine Action in a Dynamic Universe," in *Scientific Perspectives on Divine Action: Twenty Years of Challenge and Progress*, Robert John Russell, Nancey Murphy and William R. Stoeger, S. J. (eds), Vatican City State and Berkeley, CA: Vatican Observatory Publications and Center for Theology and the Natural Sciences, 225–247.

Tracy, Thomas F. (2001) "Creation, Providence, and Quantum Chance," in *QMSP*, 235–58.

Further reading

Abner Shimony's two short articles "Conceptual Foundations of Quantum Mechanics" and "The Reality of the Quantum World" give a very accessible and reliable summary of quantum theory and the Copenhagen interpretation (all these suggestions are cited above). My essay "Epistemological and Ontological Issues Arising from Quantum Theory" goes somewhat more deeply into the philosophical and theological implications of quantum mechanics. Robert Russell's contribution on "Divine Action and Quantum Mechanics" summarizes the NIODA proposal and the arguments for it. Pope John Paul II's Encyclical *Fides et Ratio* provides a relatively recent and complete official statement of the Catholic Church's stance regarding the relationship of philosophy and the natural sciences with faith and theology. William E. Carroll's article "Divine Agency, Contemporary Physics, and the Autonomy of Nature" provides a clear exposition of the usual Catholic theological stance that is compatible with quantum theory and critical of invoking it to provide an opening for divine action.

17
QUANTUM THEORY, CAUSALITY, AND ISLAMIC THOUGHT

Mehdi Golshani

Introduction

Classical physics started with the works of Galileo, Newton, etc., and developed rapidly in the eighteenth and nineteenth centuries. But by the end of the nineteenth century, physicists encountered some major problems that classical physics could not handle. Two new theories were proposed to handle these problems: the special theory of relativity and the quantum theory. It was quantum theory that shattered the philosophical foundations of classical mechanics.

Among the philosophical innovations of quantum theory, it was the renunciation of determinism and the principle of causality by quantum theorists that attracted the attention of Muslim scholars. Whereas most Muslim physicists have followed the standard Copenhagen interpretation of quantum physics, some eminent philosophers have strongly opposed the Copenhagen interpretation of quantum mechanics, especially with regard to causality. On the other hand, some Muslim theologians have embraced Copenhagen's attitude towards the principle of causality.

Philosophical foundations of quantum theory

Classical physicists believed in an objective reality independent of us; in the general validity of the causality principle; and in our ability to get a true picture of physical reality.

Quantum physics, which was developed by Bohr, Born, Heisenberg, Pauli, Schrödinger, Dirac, etc. and interpreted by Born, Heisenberg, and others, shook the philosophical foundations of classical physics and established a new framework for the description and interpretation of micro-phenomena. This interpretation is known as the standard or the Copenhagen interpretation. Among the important innovations of quantum theory was its rejection of causality.

Classical physicists believed in determinism – in the predictability of the future of an isolated system from its present state. Probability was used in some cases like the kinetic theory of gases. But the general belief was that the state of gas particles can be precisely determined from the laws of motion.

It was Max Born who formally brought in the notion of probability in quantum mechanics and rejected determinism in micro-physics. In his study of the scattering problem, he reached the conclusion that the result of an atomic collision cannot be uniquely determined. His solution was the denial of determinism in micro-physics. But he admitted that this was a philosophical decision, rather than a merely physical one: "I myself am inclined to give up determinism in the world of atoms, but that is a philosophical question for which physical arguments alone are not decisive" (Wheeler 1983: 54).

But the most obvious way in which quantum mechanics refuted determinism was through Heisenberg's uncertainty principle, introduced in 1927. Heisenberg obtained the so-called uncertainty relations:

$$(\Delta x)\ \text{æ}\ (\Delta p) \geq h/4\pi$$

where (Δx) and(Δp) represent, respectively, the uncertainty in the measurement of coordinate x and its conjugate momentum p, and h is Planck's constant (Wheeler 1983: 62–84).

Heisenberg's initial interpretation of this relation was that one cannot determine an electron's coordinate and momentum precisely at the same time. Therefore it is not generally possible to determine the future of physical systems from their present state. But Heisenberg jumped from this epistemological position to an ontological one, denying the principle of causality. Thus, in his 1927 paper on the uncertainty relations, he said:

> As the statistical character of quantum theory is so closely linked to the inexactness of all perceptions, one might be led to the presumption that behind the perceived statistical world there still hides a "real" world in which causality holds. But such speculations seem to us, to say it explicitly, fruitless and senseless. Physics ought to describe only the correlation of observations. One can express the state of affairs better this way: Because all experiments are subject to the laws of quantum mechanics, and therefore to equation (1) [i.e. the uncertainty relations], it follows that quantum mechanics establishes the final failure of causality.
>
> (Wheeler 1983: 83)

Since then, physicists have predominantly refuted the validity of causality in the atomic world, and have taken this uncertainty to mean the ruling of chance in this domain.

Some eminent physicists and philosophers welcomed Heisenberg's interpretation of uncertainty relations. They thought that the indeterminism of the atomic world solved the problem of human free will. Their argument was in the following form: Since psychological processes depend on physical processes, which are indeterminate, so they too must be indeterminate. In Eddington's words:

> If the atom has indeterminacy, surely the human mind will have an equal indeterminacy; for we can scarcely accept a theory which makes out the mind to be more mechanistic than the atom.
>
> (Jammer 1973: 589)

Some physicists, including Albert Einstein, did not accept the renunciation of causality. He considered the statistical character of quantum theory to be due to its incompleteness, and he expected physics to return to determinism. Furthermore, Einstein and some notable physicists and philosophers did not see any inconsistency between the rule of causality and human freedom (Benagem 1993: 306). In their view, an appeal to indeterminacy for the explanation of human free will is not right. Because, even if we base our decision making on physical processes, it is the result of the behavior of a macroscopic ensemble of particles, not a single particle, where even according to the standard view causality holds. Furthermore, although causality does not prove human freedom, it is not inconsistent with it, and even supports it. Because, without the applicability of causality, how can one attribute any action to an agent?

There have been three main criticisms, by physicists and philosophers, concerning quantum physicists' rejection of causality in the atomic domain.

(1) Heisenberg's uncertainty principle deals with measurements, rather than the underlying realities. What the arguments of Heisenberg implied was, at most, the denial of exact predictability. But Heisenberg jumped from an epistemological position, referring to our ignorance, to an ontological position, implying the refutation of the principle of causality. This jump, from an epistemological claim to an ontological one, is based on the philosophical assertion that what cannot be measured does not exist. As Feyerabend remarked:

> It is to be admitted, however, that most derivations of the uncertainties, and especially those based upon Heisenberg's famous thought-experiments, do make use of philosophical theories of meaning. Usually these arguments […] only establish that inside a certain interval measurements cannot be carried out, or that the products of the mean deviations of certain magnitudes cannot be ascertained below Planck's constant *h*. The transition from this stage of the argument to the assertion that it would be meaningless to ascribe definite values to the magnitudes in this interval is then achieved on the basis of the principle that what cannot be ascertained by measurement cannot be meaningfully asserted to exist.
>
> (Feyerabend 1962: 258)

The uncertainty in the prediction of measurable quantities is an empirical one, not requiring the denial of causality. Because, from our inability to measure exactly, we can't conclude that there is a fundamental indeterminism in microphysics. In the words of Stanley Jaki:

> The Copenhagen interpretation implies the fallacious inference from a purely operational to a strictly ontological proposition, namely that an interaction that cannot be measured exactly cannot take place exactly.
>
> (Jaki 1989: 151)

(2) We should note that our failure in the discovery of a cause does not mean its non-existence, and we have no ground for saying that modern science has discovered all the relevant factors. This has been elegantly described by Henry Stapp:

> And contemporary quantum theory treats these events as random variables, in the sense that only their statistical weights are specified by the theory: the specific actual choice of whether this event or that event occurs is not fixed by contemporary theory.
>
> The fact that contemporary physical theory says nothing more than this does not mean that science will always be so reticent. Many physicists of today claim to believe that it is perfectly possible, and also satisfactory, for there to be choices that simply come out of nowhere at all. I believe such a possibility to be acceptable as an expression of our present state of scientific knowledge, but that science should not rest complacently in that state: it should strive to do better. And in this striving all branches of scientific knowledge ought to be brought into play […] In this broader context the claim that choice comes out of nowhere at all should be regarded as an admission of contemporary ignorance, not as a satisfactory final word.
>
> (Stapp 1993: 216)

(3) The standard interpretation of quantum mechanics is not the only avenue for the explanation of observations in the atomic realm. In fact, there are causal versions of quantum formalism, such as Bohmian mechanics, which account for the experimental results equally well.

Some of the opponents of the orthodox interpretation of the uncertainty relations believed that the uncertainty observed at quantum level is due to our ignorance about variables which are not presently accessible to us. In 1932, von Neumann argued that one cannot construct hidden variable theories which reproduce all predictions of quantum mechanics (von Neumann 1955: 305–24). But David Bohm constructed such a theory in 1952 (Bohm 1952: 160, 180). This indicated that there were some loopholes in von Neumann's argument. In 1964, Bell demonstrated that one of von Neumann's assumptions was not compelling (Bell 1966: 447). In constructing his causal theory, Bohm had implicitly relaxed this assumption. In Bohm's view, there is no convincing argument for the denial of a sub-quantum level at which strict causality holds.

The reception of the uncertainty relations in the Islamic world

In the Islamic philosophy, the principle of causality is defined in the following way: Every event requires a cause. From this principle, two corollaries follow (al-Sadr 1980: 305; Mutahharti 1998 [1419]: 651–54).

- Causal necessity – every event has a sufficient cause, and with the presence of that cause, the event is present.

- Congruence between cause and effect – a certain cause can produce a certain effect, that is, similar causes entail similar effects.

All eminent Muslim philosophers have accepted the principle of causality and its corollaries (causal necessity and congruence between cause and effect) and have believed that these corollaries are inseparable from the principle of causality, and that any violation of them leads to the violation of the causality principle (Ibn Sina 1960: 39, 167). But Muslim theologians have differed as far as accepting the principle of causality or its corollaries is concerned (Mutahharti 1998 [1419]: 544).

The validity of the principle of causality can be inferred from the Qur'an. Thus, for example, the Qur'an talks frequently about the unchangeable patterns of God in the universe:

> [Such has been] the course of God with respect to these who have gone before; and you shall not find any change in the course of God.
>
> (Qur'an 33: 62)

Furthermore, the existence of patterns in nature means the existence of natural laws, and this, in turn, means that the principle of causality is valid.

In the Qur'anic view, the course of events in nature follows a certain measure, and every natural being has a definite and precise life span:

> And there is not a thing but with Us are the treasures of it, and We do not send it down but in a definite measure.
>
> (Qur'an 15: 21)

In the Qur'an, one finds many cases in which the role of certain intermediary causes in the occurrence of some events is mentioned:

> And God has sent down water from the cloud and therewith given life to the earth after its death.
>
> (Qur'an 16: 55)

> And We sent down the winds fertilizing […]
>
> (Qur'an 15: 22)

Some well known Muslim theologians (*Mutakalimun*), particularly those belonging to the Asharite School, used some verses of the Qur'an of the type:

> The commandment is wholly God's […]
>
> (Qur'an 7: 54)

plus some verses that indicate the occurrence of miracles, to refute the rule of causality in the physical world, and they attributed the occurrence of every event to God's will. These theologians believed in the doctrine of occasionalism, according to which there is no causal connection between creatures, God is the only immediate cause of all events, and objects have no intrinsic properties. In their view, the connection between what is usually believed to be a cause and what is believed to be an effect is not a necessary connection. Furthermore, observation can indicate only a conjunction between two events, rather than a causal relation. The assumption of causal nexus is a habit of our mind, being a result of the observation of the conjunction of certain events. Thus, for example, it is not fire that causes the cotton to burn, rather, it is God who makes the cotton burn, and if God does not want it the fire would not burn the cotton. Al-Ghazali (1058–1111), a chief representative of Asharism, challenged the necessity of causal connection, as he did not see the relation of cause and effect as being one of logical entailment, that is, there is no logical contradiction in assuming that fire may not burn a piece of cotton. The relation between fire and burning is one of possibility, not necessity, and the burning may happen if God wills so. It is God who is responsible for making the cotton burn when it is brought into the presence of fire. But God could prevent the cotton from being burned upon meeting a fire, as it happened in the case of the prophet Abraham, when he was thrown into the fire. In Al-Ghazali's words:

> The connection between what is habitually believed to be a cause and what is habitually believed to be an effect, is not necessary according to us […] Their connection is due to the prior decree of God, who creates them side by side, not to its being necessary in itself, incapable of separation. On the contrary, it is within [divine] power to create satiety without eating […] The philosopher denied the possibility of [this] and claimed it to be impossible.
>
> Let us then take a specific example – namely, the burning of cotton, for instance, when in contact with fire. For we allow the possibility of the occurrence of the contact without the burning, and we allow as possible the occurrence of the cotton's transformation into burnt ashes without contact with the fire. [The philosophers], however, deny the possibility of this.
>
> The discussion of this question involves three positions.
>
> The first position is for the opponent to claim that the agent of the burning is the fire alone, it being an agent by nature [and] not by choice – hence incapable of refraining from [acting according to] what is in its nature after contacting substratum receptive of it. And this is one of the things we deny. On the contrary, we say:
>
> The one who enacts the burning by creating blackness in the cotton, [causing] separation in its parts, and making it cinder or ashes, is God, either through the mediation of His angels or without mediation. As for fire, which is inanimate, it has no action. For what proof is there that it is the agent? They have no proof other than observing the occurrence of the burning at the [juncture of] only contact with the fire. Observation, however, [only] shows the occurrence [of burning] at [the time of the contact with the fire], but does not show the occurrence [of burning] by [the fire] and that there is no other cause for it.
>
> (Al-Ghazali 1997: 170–71)

The Asharite theologians thought that the admittance of secondary causes would result in denying God's power. The observed regularities in the world are not due to causal nexus, but are constant conjunctions between certain events, which can be attributed to God's habit of making certain events succeed certain other events. God acts in the universe without using intermediary causes, but He normally follows His habit, though He is not obliged to do so, as He is Omnipotent. In his commentary on Iji's *al-Mawaqef*, Jurjani (d. 1437) said:

> There is no relation between successive events except that some are created, out of [God's] habit, after some other ones, like burning which follows the touching of fire.
>
> (Jurjani 1992: 241)

As far as human free will (*al-ikhtiyar*) is concerned, Asharites first took the position of strict occasionalism. Then some of them softened their position and embraced the doctrine of acquisition (*kasb*), according to which all human acts are God's creation. The so-called voluntary acts are created with will and power, but both human choice and human power for realizing the choice are created by God (Al-Ghazali 1957 [1377]: I, 110). In short, humans do not create their own acts; rather, they acquire them.

Now, although the most prevalent position attributed to Asharite theologians, and specifically to Al-Ghazali, concerning causality is that of occasionalism, some of their writings indicate that they do not deny the existence of causal connections; rather, they deny causal necessity or the congruence between cause and effect. For example, a certain effect could arise from a cause not known to us, or expected by us:

> The second [view] consists of our saying that this is due to causes, but it is not a condition that the cause [here] would be one which we have experienced. Rather, in the treasury of things [enactable by divine] power there are unknown wondrous and strange things, denied by someone who thinks that nothing exists but what he experiences.
>
> (Al-Ghazali 1997: 226)

In this view, the main issue between Al-Ghazali and philosophers such as Ibn Sina is that while Al-Ghazali admits causality, he denies the necessary connection that Muslim philosophers assumed between creaturely causes and their effects. Muslim philosophers, however, believed that the denial of causal necessity leads to the denial of the causality principle itself (Mutahharti 1998 [1419]: 651–52).

Now, whereas there are some indications that Al-Ghazali remained undecided between his two positions concerning causality (Al-Ghazali 1985: 68–69), some scholars believe that he remained strictly Asharite and never deviated from occasionalism (Marmura 1995: section VI, 2002: 108). He used Ibn Sina's ideas, but reinterpreted and molded them in Asharites' occasionalist terms. There are also scholars who believe that he did not have a consistent position on this matter (Dunya n.d.: 254). In any case, it is Al-Ghazali's occasionalist reading of causality that makes the comparison with standard interpretations of quantum physics relevant, and this is what some scholars have done.

After the advent of quantum theory in physics, and the acceptance of Heisenberg's uncertainty principle as signifying the rule of chance in the micro-world, some scholars have revived the forsaken theory of the Asharites, and they have appealed to quantum theory to support their claim (al-Faruqi 1983: 92–93; Hardy 1993: 1165–77, Yoksuloglu Devji 2003). They have welcomed the negation of causal laws and also the strict predictability of natural events. In their view, this confirms the unlimited power of God and opens the door for the occurrence of miracles. The Copenhagen interpretation, too, admits the existence of regularities in the physical world, but attributes them to the fact that some events have higher probabilities of occurrence than others. These higher probabilities resemble Asharites' concept of "God's Habit." The miracles are examples of the cases where God does not follow His Habit.

Unlike Asharite theologians, Muslim philosophers did not welcome Heisenberg's interpretation of uncertainty relations. Their objections to this interpretation have been on the following grounds (which resemble those of Einstein, Louis de Broglie, Bohm, etc.).

(1) The denial of the causality principle means the negation of any real connection between parts of the world (Mutahharti 1998 [1419]: 651), that is, a world of disconnected parts.

(2) The impossibility of prediction in atomic domain results from our ignorance about the deterministic laws governing the micro-world, rather than the ineffectiveness of the principle of causality and its corollaries in the atomic world (Mutahharti 1998 [1419]: 686). This could be due to our lack of necessary experimental tools (al-Sadr 1980: 314) or due to the immeasurability of the effects of the observer on the experiment.

(3) The generalization of the results of a limited number of experiments in the form of general laws and scientific theories becomes meaningful if the principle of causality holds (Mutahharti 1998 [1419]: 685), because in accepting something as a law, we also accept that:

- every effect has a cause,
- the relation between cause and effect is indispensable,
- similar causes entail similar effects.

Thus the principle of causality provides an *a priori* basis for science – it is a metaphysical principle which science can neither prove nor disprove, and without which no scientific law can be established (Mutahharti 1998 [1419]: 334–47, 683–85). According to M. B. al-Sadr (1972: 110–11), rationalists have to embrace the causality principle as an *a priori* principle.

(4) Causal necessity confirms human free will, rather than negating it (Mutahharti 1998 [1419]: 613, 689), because human actions are the result of human instincts, tastes and distastes, sentiments, reasoning, and human will. All of these lead to one's decision making. When one wants to do something, one would look for preferences and then would weigh them and finally make the decision. But the external factors do not make an efficient cause, and one could go against them. It is the totality of all factors, including one's will, that constitutes a sufficient cause for one's actions.

Some eminent contemporary Muslim scholars (Jafari 1968 [1388]: 25, 129; al-Sadr 1984 [1405]: 34) have questioned the rule of causality – specifically the necessity of causal nexus – in the domain of human free will. They believe that the relation of a voluntary act and its prerequisites is not a necessary and determined one, that is, a human soul has authority upon its voluntary acts. This view, however, is not shared by the majority of Muslim philosophers, who do believe in the strict rule of causality.

(5) The denial of the principle of causality amounts to the denial of reasoning, because a proof is the cause of our accepting the desired result, and if the tie between the proof and the result were non-essential, the proof could not lead to the result. Then, nothing would be the result of a proof and any proof might lead to any result. This was, in fact, the argument presented by the Muslim philosopher Ibn Rushd in his refutation of Al-Ghazali's denial of causality. According to Ibn Rushd (1126–98), the denial of causality is tantamount to the denial of knowledge:

> Denial of cause implies the denial of knowledge, and denial of knowledge implies that nothing can be really known, and that what is supposed to be known is nothing but opinion, that neither proof nor definition exist, and that the essential attributes which compose definitions are void. The man who denies the necessity of any item of knowledge must admit that even this, his own affirmation, is not necessary knowledge.
>
> (Ibn Rushd 1978: 319)

(6) The occurrence of miracles does not prove the violation of the principle of causality; rather, it indicates that there are other causes present, beyond the ones known. Tabatabaei (1902–81), an eminent contemporary philosopher, concurs: "Any natural effect has a natural cause. But we can't confine natural causes to the ones known to us" (Tabatabaei 1382/1962: 298). Furthermore, the occurrence of miracles does not imply the cancellation of the laws of nature. As Mutahharti (1920–79), another noted contemporary philosopher, pointed out:

> Miracle is the dominance of one law over another law, rather than the cancellation of a law or the replacement of a law by another one. No law in the world is ever cancelled.
>
> (Mutahharti 1995 [1416]: 447)

(7) What is usually called cause in physical sciences is not an efficient cause; rather, it is an intermediary cause which prepares the ground for God's bounty. So, one can say that God is the cause for everything, but He makes everything under certain terms and through certain means; and, of course, all of these means are creations of God Himself. As Sadr al-Din Shirizi (1571/72–1640), well known as Mulla-Sadra, puts it:

> Another group of philosophers and some elite among our Imamiyyah scholars say that objects vary in their acceptance of existence from the Origin. Some do not yield to existence unless another being precedes them, in the same way that accident should follow substance. Thus the Creator, whose power is unlimited, grants the existence according to the

> possibilities through a particular order and in consideration of its various capabilities. Some come directly from Him, some through an intermediary or intermediaries. In the last case, nothing can come into existence unless its means and pre-requisites come into reality. God Himself is the Cause without a cause. Requirements for existence are not the result of deficiency in the Almighty's power, but due to weakness in the receiver of emanation.
> (Sadr al-Din Shirazi 1981: 371–72)

Conclusion

The principle of causality was a postulate of Islamic philosophy, and Muslim philosophers found it in concordance with their interpretation of the Qur'anic verses. Theologians belonging to the Asharite school, however, denied the principle of causality or its corollaries such as causal necessity. The development of quantum theory, in the first quarter of the twentieth century, revived the old controversy concerning causality in the Islamic world. Most of the Muslim physicists have embraced the Copenhagen interpretation of quantum theory. But many Muslim philosophers have resisted the denial of causality on essentially the same grounds as physicists such as Einstein.

The following is a summary of Muslim scholars' encounters with the standard interpretation of quantum theory, mentioning the similarities (Hardy 1993: 173–76).

(1) According to the standard interpretation of quantum mechanics, an electron has no inherent properties until a measurement is made. Similarly, in the Asharites' occasionalist view, the attributes associated with objects are the result of God's actions. God is the immediate cause of every effect. The similarity between the two schools is that both deny any necessary connection between cause and effect.

(2) Similarly, the Copenhagen interpretation attributes the regularities seen in nature to the fact that some events have higher probabilities of occurrence than others, whereas in the Asharites' occasionalist view, regularities are attributed to God's Habit. In short, in both the Asharites' occasionalist view and the Copenhagen interpretation of quantum theory, objects have no inherent attributes and no independent existence, and the events are not exactly predictable.

(3) The position of Muslim philosophers regarding causality is the same as that of the proponents of the causal interpretation of quantum theory, and their objections to the Copenhagen acausality are very similar to those of Einstein, Bohm, etc.

References

Al-Ghazali, A. M. (1957 [1377]), *Ihya Uulum al-Din*, four volumes, Cairo.

——(1985) *Iljam al-'awamm an ilm al-kalam*, M. M. al-Baghadi (ed.), Beirut: Dar al-Kitab al-Arabi, 68–69.

——(1997) *Tahafut al-Falasifah/The Incoherence of the Philosophers*, Michael E. Marmura (trans.), Provo, UT: Brigham Young University.

Bell, J. S. (1966) "On the Problem of Hidden Variables in Quantum Mechanics," *Reviews of Modern Physics* 38(3): 447–52.

Benagem, T. (1993) "Struggle with Causality," *Science in Context* 6(1):306.

Bohm, D. (1952) "A Suggested Interpretation of Quantum Theory in Terms of Hidden Variables, I and II," *Physical Review* 85: 166–93.

Dunya, Suleiman (n.d.), *al-Haqiqah fi Nazr Al-Ghazali*, Cairo: Dar al-Maarif bi-Misr, 254.

al-Faruqi, Ismail R. (1983) "The Causal and Tellic Nature of the Universe," in *Islamic Scientific Thought and Muslim Achievements in Science*, Vol. 1, papers presented at the International Conference on Science in Islamic Polity, Islamabad: Pan Graphics.

Feyerabend, P. (1962) "Problems in Microphysics," in *Frontiers of Science and Philosophy*, R. Colodny (ed.), Pittsburg, PA: Pittsburg University Press.

Hardy, Karen (1993) "Causality Then and Now: Al Ghazali and Quantum Theory," *American Journal of Islamic Social Sciences* 10(2): 165–77.

Ibn Rushd (Averroes) (1978) *Tahafut al-Tahafut/The Incoherence of the Incoherence*, Vols I and II, Simon van den Bergh (trans.), Cambridge, UK: Cambridge University Press.

Ibn Sina (1960) *al-Shifa: Ilahiyyat*, G. C. Anwati (ed.), Cairo: Organisme General des Imprimeries Gouvernementales.

Jafari, M. T. (1968 [1388]) *Jabr wa Ikhtiar/Fatalism and Free Will*, Tehran: Shirkat-e Sahami Inteshar.

Jaki, Stanley L. (1989) *God and the Cosmologists*, Edinburgh: Scottish Academic Press.

Jammer, M. (1973) "Indeterminacy in Physics," in *Dictionary of the History of Ideas*, Vol. 2, P. P. Winer (ed.), New York: Charles Scribner's Sons.

Jurjani, M. S. S. (1992) *al-Sharhul li'l Mawaqif*, Vol. 8, Qum: Intesharat Sharif Razi.

Marmura, M. E. (1995) "Ghazalian Causes and Intermediaries," *Journal of the American Oriental Society* 115: 89–100.

——(2002) "Ghazali and Asharism," *Arabic Sciences and Philosophy* 12: 91–110.

Mutahhari, M. (1995 [1416]) *Majmue Athar/Collected Works*, Vol. 4, Tehran: Sadra Publications (in Persian).

——(1998 [1419]) *Majmue Athar/Collected Works*, Vol. 6, Tehran: Sadra Publications (in Persian).

von Neumann, J. (1955) *Mathematical Foundations of Quantum Mechanics/Mathematische Grundlagen der Quantenmechanik*, R. T. Beyer (trans.), Princeton, NJ: Princeton University Press.

al-Sadr, M. B. (1972) *al-Usus al-Mantiqiyyah li'l Istiqra/The Logical Foundations of Induction* (in Arabic), Beirut: Dar al-Taaruf.

——(1980) *Falsafatuna/Our Philosophy*, Beirut: Dar al-Taaruf li'l Matbuat (in Arabic).

——(1984 [1405]) *Buhuth fi Ilm al-Usul/Studies in the Foundations of Jurisprudence*, M. Hashemi (ed.), Qum: al-Majmaal-Ilmi (in Arabic).

Sadr al-Din Shirazi (1981) *al-Hikmah al-Motaaliyah fi al-Asfar al-Aqliyyah al-Arbaah/The Transcendent Wisdom in the Four Intellectual Journeys*, Vol. 6, Beirut: Dar Ihya al-Turath al-Arabi (in Arabic).

Stapp, H. P. (1993) *Mind, Matter, and Quantum Mechanics*, New York: Springer-Verlag.

Tabatabaei, S. M. H. (1992 [1413]) *Majmue Maqalat, Soalat and Pasokhha/Collected Articles, Questions and Answers*, Vol. 1, S.H. Khosrowshahi (ed.), Tehran: Daftar Nashr Farhang Islami (in Persian).

Yoksuloglu Devji, Umit (2003) "Al-Ghazali and Quantum Physics: A Comparative Analysis of the Seventeenth Discussion of '*Tahafut al-Falasifah*' and Quantum Theory", MA thesis, Canada: McGill University.

Further reading

Mario Bunge's *Causality and Modern Science* (New York: Dover, 1979) examines various formulations of the causality principle and its place in classical and modern science (especially in quantum theory). David Bohm's *Causality and Chance in Modern Physics* (London: Routledge & Kegan Paul, 1984) deals with the concepts of cause and chance and their applications in physics. He goes over the history of "mechanical philosophy" and those aspects of it that were maintained throughout the developments of physics. Then, by introducing different levels of explanation, he offers his own causal interpretation of quantum mechanics. Finally, the book *Mulla Sadra and Comparative Philosophy on Causation* (London: Salman-Azadeh, 2003), edited by Seyed G. Safavi, gives a good perspective on the views of Muslim philosophers on the causality principle over the past 400 years.

(iii) Complexity, emergence, and eliminativism

18
ELIMINATIVISM, COMPLEXITY, AND EMERGENCE

Terrence Deacon and Tyrone Cashman

The emergence paradox

The evolutionary perspective turned the classic worldview on its head. Since Roman times, the world was understood to be hierarchic in structure, explained by a transcendent mind at the top. From there, the great chain of being cascaded down through angels, humans, frogs, protozoa, and finally stones. Inverting the chain of being switched mind from being the ultimate explanation of things, to being the mystery to be explained. As an early critic of Darwin protested, this theory assumes that "Absolute Ignorance" is the ultimate artificer, even of life and mind (MacKenzie 1868).

However, the notion that the distinctive properties of life and mind were produced by a blind mechanism from inanimate matter runs counter to a fundamental assumption of Western thought. It is expressed in the oft-quoted dictum of the Roman poet–scientist Lucretius: "*ex nihilo nihil fit*," from nothing, nothing [can be] produced (1994 [n.d.]). Later, the principle was expressed another way by the medieval philosopher–theologians who borrowed a maxim derived from Roman secular law: "*Nemo dat quod non habet*," no-one gives what he does not have. For the scholastic theologians, this maxim articulated their conviction that no creation can have more perfect characteristics than the cause that gave rise to it.

To imagine that modern science and philosophy have now fully abandoned this principle would be mistaken. The first law of thermodynamics states that neither matter nor energy can be created nor destroyed, and the second law tells us that, ultimately, orderliness always gives way to disorder. Physical change always and only involves a rearrangement of material and energetic properties that are already there. No chemical transformation will turn lead into gold, and perpetual motion machines, constantly recycling the same capacity to do work, are impossible. Because the capacity to do work depends on the second law – the spontaneous breakdown of ordered states – in the absence of outside interference, a more ordered consequence cannot arise spontaneously from a less ordered antecedent. This precludes the possibility of future orderliness bringing itself into being – a limitation that must be true of every physical process, including your reading and understanding these words.

Yet this familiar mental activity of reading exhibits characteristics that appear, at least on the surface, to violate this stricture. Presumably, your reading this text was initiated by considerations about what information it *might* provide you, though this was only a possibility. Moreover, the content conveyed by these words is neither the ink on the paper, the sounds they could refer to, or the neural patterns they have invoked. These are "intentional" phenomena in both senses of that word: (1) actions organized with respect to achieving certain consequences, and (2) relationships of reference in which something present is linked to something absent and abstract.

The evolutionary world-view assumes that the functional organization of living processes and the intentional and experiential nature of mental processes arose spontaneously, out of blindly mechanistic chemical reactions. And yet it also assumes that living functions are organized with respect to arrangements that are not immediately present, something merely possible, and perhaps not even that. For these end-organized features of life and mind to be genuine, and yet to have arisen from physical phenomena lacking any hint of these most fundamental attributes, the *ex nihilo* principle would have to have been violated.

Efforts to resolve this paradox have often led to simple denials of one or the other horns of this dilemma. One can either argue that functional and intentional properties are ultimately just mischaracterized complex mechanical properties – eliminativism; or that they were always already present even in the simplest mechanical interactions – panpsychism. However, if we wish to accept both assumptions, and thus argue that the resulting paradox is only apparent, we must demonstrate the coherence of a third causal paradigm – emergentism.

Pre-scientific delusions?

The evolutionary paradigm is assumed by many to represent the final victory of strict materialism over some version of purposive or end-directed causality in the world. Even where exquisitely adapted organisms are concerned, all are explained as complicated forms of efficient cause – just the pushes and pulls of blind mechanism. In the second half of the twentieth century, compelling new discoveries in diverse fields of science led many, such as the philosopher Paul Feyerabend, to claim that even our knowledge of our own minds might be deeply flawed. Our conviction that we are agents with ideas, feelings, and purposes is not an empirical fact, derived from simple direct experience, but is instead a theory-based conception, and could be false. As the original substances posited to explain fire and heat – phlogiston and caloric – were later abandoned by science, commonsense mental constructs such as "beliefs" and "desires" might be dispensed with when the causal details of neuroscience became understood. These, he argued, were part of a pre-scientific theory of mind that a mature science of brain function will replace with more fundamental, mechanistic accounts: an enterprise he called "eliminative materialism."

The claim is that such representational and teleological concepts are entirely unnecessary for a scientific account of mind. These presumed higher-order properties are simply the residue of a "folk psychology" that science will eventually replace. Like phlogiston, there is ultimately no such thing as a belief, a desire, or an intention, other than a specific arrangement of synaptic weights in a human brain. Correspondingly, this implicitly suggests that teleological concepts such as "function" and "adaptation" in biology are also mere heuristics that can be replaced by explicit descriptions of the component chemical and physical mechanisms.

Always already there

Eliminative materialism can be contrasted with panpsychism, in its various forms. Rather than arguing that mentalistic and teleological phenomena are merely incompletely analyzed and falsely characterized mechanistic processes, panpsychism argues just the opposite: the phenomena of intentionality, representation, and awareness are real and distinct from mere mechanical relationships, but they are present in attenuated form in every physical event in the universe. If the *ex nihilo* maxim is necessarily true, and these features of life and mind are undeniable, then a trace of these properties must be present in some form in all material processes.

Panpsychism doesn't necessarily imply an idealist metaphysics, however. William James, for example, argued that all physical events have a dual aspect – mental and material – a view he called neutral monism; and Alfred North Whitehead argued that each physical (even quantum) occasion involves a minimal precursor to experience and agency. By assuming that an active and outwardly directed aspect is basic to any causal interaction (a dynamic he termed "prehension"), more complex forms of awareness and agency can be explained as compositional variants of basic causality.

Critics argue that assuming that mind-like attributes are primitive merely postulates them into existence, and sidesteps the hard problem of accounting for their atypical properties. To this explanatory weakness is added the theory's inability to account for why there is no evidence of the unique properties of mind at levels of chemical or nuclear interactions, and why the distinctively teleological and intentional behaviors of mind, when they do occur, do so only in animals with nervous systems.

Emergence: seeking the middle ground

To many, these two extremes are both untenable. Beginning in the nineteenth century, a number of philosophers and scientists sought to unify our theoretical understanding of what we are, and our place in the physical universe, without denying either the validity of the facts and theories of the natural sciences, or our immediate experience of being living beings with beliefs, desires, agency, and so forth. The initial steps were taken by John Stuart Mill (1843). Mill was struck by the fact that two toxic and dangerous substances, chlorine gas and sodium metal, when combined together produce common table salt, an essential nutrient for animals and humans. Mill viewed this radical change in properties to be analogous to some special combinatorial logic that must have produced life from mere chemistry. He argues that although "organised bodies are composed of parts, similar to those composing inorganic nature [...] it is certain that no mere summing up of the separate actions of those elements will ever amount to the action of the living body itself" (*ibid.*: Book III, ch. 6, §1).

Mill reaffirms here the ancient claim that "the whole is greater than the sum of the parts." Influenced by Mill's arguments, the British essayist George Henry Lewes coined the term "emergence" in his five-volume work *Problems of Life and Mind* (1874–79) to characterize the way novel higher-order properties arise from such special compositional relationships. Efforts to define the metaphysical foundations for the concept were undertaken by three British scholars of the early twentieth century, the philosophers C. D. Broad (1925) and Samuel Alexander (1920), and the comparative psychologist Conwy Lloyd Morgan (1923). Each provided slightly variant accounts of what emergence entailed. Broad's conception was close to that of Mill in arguing that the properties that emerged via compositionality could exhibit fundamentally discontinuous causal laws from those that characterized the components in isolation, and that distinct "bridging laws" are required to link levels of incommensurate causal organization. Alexander argued that there were indeed distinctive higher-order forms of causality associated with minds, compared with simple physical processes, and that the link between them was in some way fundamentally unpredictable from lower-order processes, though not a case of absolute discontinuity. This has two implications: emergence is a function of unpredictability, not ontological novelty; and emergent properties of mind must in some form permeate the world. Morgan argued that evolution exemplified emergent processes. As organisms reproduce and interact with the world, they spontaneously produce higher-order variant features that may exhibit unprecedented discontinuities of causal agency, such as occurred with the advent of human culture.

The emergence debate

Despite these efforts, the fundamental dilemma posed by the *ex nihilo* maxim would not go away. As early as 1926, a serious criticism of emergentism was leveled by the American philosopher Stephen Pepper. He argued that the British emergentists' theories can't avoid two implicit dilemmas: Since emergence must be understood as a physical change or shift, either there is a causal regularity that links the emergent state to the previous state, or else the properties ascribed to the emergent state are nothing more than the totality of the lower-level properties. And if the emergent state is absolutely unpredictable from the prior state, then it is pure chance and no physical principle is required to account for it, otherwise it must be predictable.

Slight variations on the emergence concept were subsequently developed to work around these criticisms. For example, the Nobel laureate psychologist Roger Sperry (see e.g. Sperry 1980) suggested that the emergence of consciousness from neural processes was due to configurational effects that imposed "top-down" causal influences on lower-level neural processes, in much the same way that being combined into a wheel alters the movement capabilities of its constituent parts. And a related variant on the emergentist theme, known as "functionalism," became popular in cognitive theory in the 1970s (see e.g. Putnam 1975). It is often characterized using a computer analogy, arguing that higher-order (such as software) functions might be seen as indifferent to any specific substrate (such as hardware). In this case, their functional (causal) powers would arise from their organization, and not from any specific material substrate properties. In the terminology of this paradigm, functional consequences are "multiply realizable."

These modern variants of the "more than the sum of its parts" view were dealt a devastating blow by the contemporary philosopher Jaegwon Kim. In a series of articles and monographs in the 1980s and 1990s, Kim (e.g. 1993, 1999) argued that if all causal interactions must ultimately be embodied by interactions of material and energetic constituents that can neither be created nor destroyed, then assigning causal power to various higher-order configurations of these constituents is to do double book-keeping. So-called higher-level properties are all realized by their lower-level constituents and their relationships to one another. There isn't any extra causal power over and above that which is provided by this physical embodiment (such as the operations of the hardware). Everything else is a gloss or descriptive simplification of what goes on at that level.

Kim's criticism is almost certainly right, given the assumptions of this part/whole conception of causality, but rather than undermining the concept of emergence, it suggests that certain assumptions must be wrong. A number of contemporary emergence theorists have answered this criticism by arguing either that the notion of compositionality is not as simple as Kim and most eliminativists have assumed, or that the assignment of causal power to the lowest possible level of compositionality is a mistake. Determining simple decomposition into proper parts is, for example, a problem when it comes to the analysis of organisms. The vast majority of molecules constituting an organism are enmeshed in a continual process of reciprocal synthesis, in which each is the product of the interactions among many others in the system. They exist, and their specific properties are created by one another, as a result of this higher-order systemic synergy. With cessation of the life of the organism – that is, catastrophic dissolution of these critical reciprocal interrelationships – the components rapidly degrade as well. So their properties are in part derived from this synergistically organized higher-order dynamic.

Paul Humphreys (e.g. 1997a, 1997b) has argued that the most basic quantum components of the universe suffer a related problem, one that he calls "fusion," in which component properties are not just recombined at higher levels. Because of the intrinsically probabilistic dynamics of quantum interactions, the lower-level properties effectively disappear or get dissolved as the higher-order properties emerge. Nobel laureate physicist Robert Laughlin similarly argues that higher-order material processes are in effect "protected" from certain details of these lower-order quantum processes, and thus enjoy a level of causal autonomy. Both approaches can be seen as modern augmentations of Mill's original molecular argument, but taking quantum effects into account. They suggest that what constitutes a part may depend on its involvement in the larger dynamical configuration. But if so, then Kim's eliminativist causal power assumption is called into question.

Notice that these criticisms of the part/whole assumption make dynamics an essential factor. If the compositionality of physical phenomena is a consequence of dynamical relationships, then there are no ultimate entities that possess all the causal power. Mark Bickhard thus responds to Kim's assumptions about physical compositionality by pointing out that "particles participate in organization, but do not themselves have organization." Indeed, he argues, point particles without organization do not exist (and in any case would lead to other absurd consequences). The particles of contemporary quantum physics are the somewhat indeterminate loci of inherently oscillatory quantum fields. Oscillatory phenomena are irreducibly processual, and thus are intrinsically dynamic and organized. So if *process organization* is the irreducible source of the causal properties at the quantum level, then, according to Bickhard, it "cannot be delegitimated as a potential locus of causal power without eliminating causality from the world" (Bickhard 2003).

It follows that, if the organization of a process is the fundamental source of its causal power, then fundamental reorganizations of process at whatever level they occur can be associated with the emergence of novel forms of causal power as well.

Dynamical systems: one leap forward, one step back

In the second half of the twentieth century, questions about emergence began to be asked in a new way, with a focus on dynamics. New terms of art became common: fractals, strange attractors, butterfly effects, order out of chaos, non-linear dynamics, and especially self-organizing processes. These effects were studied in both the non-living world and the living world, in processes as diverse as snow crystal growth and the foraging of ant colonies. New computing tools played a critical role in this research by simulating these processes through the repetition of simple algorithmic operations enormous numbers of times at very high speeds. A pioneer of this field, John Holland, summarizes the thrust of this work as attempting to answer the question "how can the interactions of agents produce an aggregate entity that is more flexible and adaptive than its component agents?" (Holland 1998).

One of the major contributors to the understanding of self-organization was Nobel laureate Ilya Prigogine (see e.g. Prigogine and Stengers 1984), who demonstrated that the spontaneous generation of order from non-order in physical systems can occur in persistently far-from-equilibrium thermodynamic processes. This little-understood thermodynamic process, by which higher-order regularity spontaneously arises from lower-order unorganized interactions, showed clear parallels with processes demonstrated in groups of organisms and computer models, even though the mechanisms of interaction might be radically different. Recognizing the universality of these effects offered a new paradigm within which to conceive of emergent transitions, and made empirical investigation of emergent phenomena a scientifically attractive new area of research. An additional benefit was that it began to offer a new way of understanding concepts of *order* and *disorder*, which are often claimed to exist either merely in the eye of the beholder, imposed by interpreting something in terms of an abstract model of form; or as shaped entirely by extrinsic forcing. The realization that non-linear and far-from-equilibrium systems can regularize spontaneously, and can recover regularity after extrinsic disturbance – as does a whirlpool in a stream – exposed a non-equilibrium loophole in the second law.

As a result of these discoveries, emergence was no longer considered merely a philosophical issue, and gained scientific credibility. The thrust of this approach was not, however, to explain the purposive, representational, experiential, and normative features of life and mind. The goal was instead to explain complexity. If the iteration of simple, non-linear interactions could produce complex and even chaotic structures and dynamics, then it might be possible to understand the complexities of living organisms and brain functions as products of these sorts of interactions.

In the realm of the cognitive sciences, the shift to non-linear dynamical systems theory was seen by its proponents to be the definitive antithesis of the eliminative account suggested by the dominant computational theory of mind. Whereas computation is based on the assumption that mental processes are direct mechanistic embodiments of "symbolic" inference (such as rule-governed token manipulation where the tokens represent features of the world), dynamical systems researchers argue that there are no representations *per se*, just holistic effects of non-linear dynamical processes. The neuroscientist Walter Freeman, who pioneered one of the most sophisticated dynamical systems models of perception (of odor), makes the implicit representational eliminativism of this approach unambiguous when he says that "The concept of 'representation' […] is unnecessary as a keystone for explaining the brain and behavior" (Skarda and Freeman 1987: 184).

So, despite the emergence framing, and the instructive empirical examples it provides, the concept of emergence developed in dynamical systems approaches includes a decidedly eliminativist attitude toward semiotic and normative phenomena. The implication is still that intentional and teleological concepts can be eliminated once tools for handling complex dynamics are made available.

There are, however, reasons to doubt that non-linear complexity alone accounts for the counter-intuitive nature of these phenomena, because even quite simple systems must be able to exhibit intrinsic, end-directed, and normative properties. These properties characterize living processes, and the first spontaneously arising precursors to life must have been simple.

Emergence, configuration, and constraint

So the dynamical systems approach to emergence can be seen as a critical contribution and a partial retreat. It helps address issues of the origins of synergy and organization, while at the same time avoiding confronting issues of function, intentionality, teleology, and value. Another tacit assumption implicit in all these approaches may be responsible for their failure adequately to address these original challenges: the assumption that the (emergent) whole is greater than the sum of its parts (and their relationships). In contrast, Deacon (2006) argues just the opposite. His contention is that the key to understanding emergent phenomena is to understand organization in terms of what is not included, not realized, not present – a property he describes as "constitutive absence." In other words, the configuration, form, or order of something is constituted both by what is present and what is absent. Focusing only on what is present is what leads to the apparent paradox of emergence. The emergent attributes we need to explain are all, in one way or another, defined by something absent.

For example, a dynamical regularity, like a whirlpool, forms as possible trajectories of movement become progressively restricted due to the interaction of the components. The term for this restriction of features is "constraint:" That which reduces the possible degrees of freedom of a process. From the dynamical systems perspective, a limitation on the degrees of freedom to change is merely something less than random or chaotic, and thus conversely determines some degree of regularity and correlation. This conception of organization recognizes that it exists irrespective of any comparison with an extrinsic or ideal model. From this perspective, self-organization is merely an intrinsically arising asymmetric change from more to fewer dynamical tendencies, which results when a system is continually perturbed, or pushed away from thermodynamic equilibrium.

The second law is not a necessary law. It is a ubiquitous tendency, but a tendency can have exceptions. The ubiquity of the second law tendency is due to the fact that in any real system there are a great many opportunities for trajectories of change and dimensions of interaction. Random (unconstrained) interactions will, statistically over time, explore all corners of this "opportunity space." The net result is a breakdown of constraints, an increase in disorder, and a reduction of regularity. A system that is far from equilibrium is one that is characterized by certain constraints not being dissipated; either the prevention of certain dynamical interactions (e.g. by barriers) or persistently redistributing features in an asymmetric way (e.g. by introducing a temperature gradient). When interactions can proceed unimpeded (e.g. when extrinsic constraints are removed), intrinsic constraints on the distribution of component attributes will tend to break down. But partially impeding this spontaneous process – for example, by allowing it to proceed only in limited ways, such as confining the expansion of hot gases within a cylinder to only one direction – is a constraint on possible dimensions of change that can be tapped to do work, and thus to impose constraints on some other system (such as propelling a vehicle against the drag of friction or the pull of gravity).

As the second law's spontaneous dissipation of constraints results in a reduction of the capacity to do work, so, too, the creation of new kinds of constraints offers the potential to do new kinds of work. This complements Bickhard's view that process organization is the ultimate source of causal power. If novel constraints can be intrinsically generated under certain special (e.g. far-from-equilibrium) conditions, then novel forms of causal power can emerge. Emergence results from the spontaneous exploitation of this capacity of constraints to engender further constraints.

From constraint to self-organization to organism

In his insightful 1968 Nobel presentation, Michael Polanyi pointed out that a machine is a mechanism defined by "boundary conditions" imposed by the designer through the choice of materials and the way they are allowed to interact. This is as true of a computer as of an internal combustion engine. So its function is defined not so much by the dynamical laws that it realizes, but by the possibilities of dynamics that are not expressed – its constraints. Thus a machine breaks down when these constraints are violated in some significant way. The loss of function is due to an increase in the degrees of freedom. Polanyi made a similar argument about living organisms. There are no new laws of chemistry involved in life, but rather highly specific and complex constraints on the allowed chemistry that constitutes an organism. Thus the loss of life results from a significant increase in the degrees of freedom of component processes. This insight still overlooks a critical difference between organisms and machines, however: Organisms generate their own critical constraints, intrinsically.

The importance of this extrinsic/intrinsic distinction was made explicit almost two centuries earlier by the philosopher Immanuel Kant. He distinguishes organism from machines with respect to two attributes: "An organized being is, therefore, not a mere machine. For a machine has solely motive power, whereas an organized being possesses inherent formative power, and such, moreover, as it can impart to material devoid of it – material which it organizes. This, therefore, is a self-propagating formative power, which cannot he explained by the capacity of movement alone, that is to say, by mechanism. The definition of an organic body is that it is a body, every part of which is there for the sake of the other (reciprocally as end, and at the same time, means)" (Kant 1952 [1790]). The parts or elements of an organism are constrained to interact in such a way that they produce one another, reciprocally. In this way, unlike a mere machine, the form of the interactions generates the components that interact, and the form of the components constrains the interactions they engage in. A vast many critical constraints are generated intrinsically by virtue of this reciprocity.

The "formative power" that Kant refers to is not, then, merely constraint on motion or change, but constraint on the production of constraints. This is where the loophole in the second law becomes important – where native constraints of molecular form and patterns of energy flow translate into constraints of dynamic form such that more orderly processes derive from less orderly ones – where self-organizing processes play the critical role. But, while self-organizing dynamics do not in themselves provide an account of the intentional and teleological features of life and mind, they may provide an essential bridge from simple thermodynamics to this realm of consequence-organized processes. The tendency of far-from-equilibrium processes to develop intrinsic regularities (constraints) in response to persistent perturbation away from equilibrium is the key to the "formative power" invoked in Kant's characterization.

Most self-organizing processes in the non-living world are fragile and transient. They are entirely dependent on a steady flow of energy, and sometimes of matter. They quickly dissipate if these boundary conditions change in any significant way. Self-organizing systems thus succumb easily to the dissipative tendencies of the second law unless they are supported and held in place within a larger, self-maintaining, non-equilibrium system. What allows an organism to maintain its component self-organizing subsystems in existence, and to use them as vital subsystems of its own general dynamic, is that its various self-organizing processes are arranged in precise reciprocity with respect to one another, so that they are (as Kant surmised) alternately and collectively both product and producer. Their synergy is in this way maintained by this very reciprocity. It is a higher-order self-organizing dynamic composed of lower-order self-organizing chemical processes. Moreover, the capacity to synthesize all essential components and their interrelationships reciprocally also constitutes the capacity to *reproduce* this whole individuated dynamics using entirely new components. With this capacity, the possibility of evolution is born.

Adaptation, representation, and normativity

This convoluted means by which intrinsic constraint-generation processes come to support their own propagation is what separates intentionality from mere dynamics. Correspondence is a necessary condition for both adaptation and intentionality, but not a sufficient one. There are innumerable correspondences in the world that have no functional value and are not representations. The preservation and reproduction of constraints by a lineage of organisms is the basis of the memory that enables trial-and-error testing of the correspondence between the requirements of this process and available environmental resources. Without this, natural selection could not increasingly converge toward functional correspondence.

For an organism to survive and reproduce, the raw materials and energy required for its far-from-equilibrium form-generating (constraint-producing) processes must correspond to what its environment allows. Thus the sleek lines of fish are fitted to their need to move through water, and the long tongues of certain insects and birds are fitted to the deep necks of their favorite nectar-producing flowers. This correspondence is like a mirror image or photo negative of these environmental features. But notice that the way correspondence arises in biological evolution is different from the way it arises as a river cuts its way through a variable terrain so that its deviations correspond to this topography. Though both are consequences of a recurrent process, in organisms it is not merely due to mechanical interaction, but is a necessary consequence of its incessant form-generating nature. An organism's forms and behavioral tendencies in this way come to re-present certain configurational features of its environment because this correspondence promotes the perpetuation of these same synergistic processes. In Darwinian terms, this results from the generation of numerous variants of a given process in different individuals, and the elimination of those with variants that don't sufficiently correspond to the environment. In this way, configurational features of the environment relevant to the perpetuation of the whole synergistic complex become reflected in its component dynamics. It is the intrinsic generation of constraints that embody (or re-present) some aspect of the environmental constraints that contribute to the process that makes this re-presenting possible, that is, survival.

Interpretation processes more generally also involve a generate-test-cull logic to bring the generation of semiotic forms into correspondence with one another and with relevant environmental features. Although this comparison does not directly address the subjective features of conscious experience, it is a first step toward demonstrating how any process or artifact can come to be *about* something else, that is not present. We can thus understand the generation of semiotic forms in brains as self-organized attractors in neural circuits, as have some dynamical systems theorists. But now we can additionally understand these as representations of non-present features, by virtue of the way that many must synergistically complement one another in order to persist stably and be tested against supportive or non-supportive extrinsic phenomena as their generation becomes action and actions produce consequences. So, by analogy, mental representation can be seen as a higher-order internalization of this general attribute of life, though in terms of a neurological virtual ecology. In this virtual ecology, the forms generated are purely dynamical and fleeting, the adequacy or inadequacy of a given adaptive process leads only to preservation or extinction of a mental habit, and the capacity to assimilate new forms into the formative process builds skills (dynamics) and memories (constraints), not bodies.

With the rise of life, there is one more attribute that is a defining characteristic of intentional and teleological process: normativity. In the parts of the universe that are completely describable in terms of basic physics and chemistry, there is no useful or un-useful, no right or wrong, no good or bad. But because organisms are far-from-equilibrium systems, maintained only by their intrinsically self-organizing composition, they are continually being undermined and, as a result, their persistence is far from guaranteed. If, in the process of generating forms that might correspond with relevant attributes of the world, the correspondence is not sufficiently close, they will likely perish along with the form-generative characteristics that distinguish them. Similarly, for the internalized form-generating processes that constitute the discriminative and behavioral adaptations of a nervous system, those that are insufficiently correspondent to the world with respect to achieving some supportive consequence will either be forgotten, become inhibited, or lead to further adaptive efforts to converge toward sufficient correspondence. This suggests that the self-supportive synergy of life is paralleled by a coherence-promoting tendency among interdependent mental processes. Thus representations, like biological adaptations, can be more or less accurate with respect to some semiotic synergy, and can fail in their correspondence in a way that undermines the higher-order system of form-generating (sign-generating) processes for the sake of which they were produced. In this respect, the normative character of an adaptation or representation is a function of the self-realizing tendency implicit in the self-organizing processes that constitute the "self-propagating formative power" from which both life and mind emerge.

Emergence *ex nihilo*

Ironically, this approach to emergence agrees with the great medieval theologians who inform us that no-one gives what he does not have, as well as with Lucretius' "no free lunch rule" – the proscription against getting something from nothing. Although this approach to the emergence problem provides a process by which the novel properties associated with life and mind can have emerged – for example, function, information, representation, normativity, and eventually sentience and consciousness – this explanation requires no addition (or subtraction) to the matter, energy, or fundamental physical laws of nature.

Everything that has emerged is the result of a hierarchy of constraints – specific forms of absence that give rise to further, even more complex forms of absence. What is novel is the new forms of constrained dynamical process, from simple, self-organizing processes to the formative synergy of organisms. Each emergent step upwards from thermodynamic processes creates a platform for yet further levels of constrained dynamics, and thus the possibility of novel forms of work. The higher-order reciprocity of self-organizing processes, which provides organisms with the ability to acquire, preserve, and reproduce constraints in correspondence with the world, is the basis of both the informational and normative features of life.

The physical efficacy of these conserved constraints that constitute the content of representations and the functions of adaptation neither cheats the first law nor violates the second law. No new material or energetic properties are added, and no form or direction toward an end is imposed from without. As new forms of constraint emerge from prior constraints, they merely bring new capacities to perform work into being. This is why information and representation are always relationships between something present and something that is *not*, and why function, purpose, and sentience are always dynamical processes organized with respect to something they are *not*.

Amazing new properties have been, and are being, emerged, and there is nothing new being added. There is no *thing* new. No new laws. What *is* "new" and "more" are new modes of *not being*, new forms of constraint. So indeed, nothing *does* give what it doesn't have.

This conclusion may seem counter-intuitive because of our conviction that the emergence of life and mind has increased, not decreased, our degrees of freedom (free will). Increasing levels and forms of constraint do not immediately sound like contributors to freedom. In fact, however, they are essential. What we are concerned with is instead *freedom of agency*, not lack of restriction on all causal possibility. And by agency we mean the capacity to change things in ways that, in some respects, run counter to how things would have proceeded spontaneously without this intervention. So what we are concerned with is not some abstract conception of causality, but rather with the capacity to do work, to resist or counter the spontaneous tendencies of things. But as we have seen, this capacity depends on the creation of the appropriate constraints. The evolution of our higher-order capacities to create and propagate ever more complex and indirect forms of constraint, from the self-organizing processes that build our bodies to the production of scientific theories that guide our technologies, has in this way been the progressive emergence of an ability to restrict sequences of causal processes to only very precise options. It's the ability to produce highly diverse and yet precise constraints – absences – that provides us with our nearly unlimited capacity to intervene in the goings on of the natural world. It is in this strange, convoluted sense that our freedom emerges from nothing.

References

Alexander, Samuel (1920) *Space, Time, and Deity*, two volumes, London: Macmillan.

Bickhard, Mark H. (2003) "Process and Emergence: Normative Function and Representation," in *Process Theories: Crossdisciplinary Studies in Dynamic Categories*, J. Seibt (ed.), Dordrecht, the Netherlands: Kluwer Academic, 121–55.

Broad, C. D. (1925) *The Mind and Its Place in Nature*, 1st edn, London: Routledge & Kegan Paul.

Deacon, Terrence W. (2006) "Emergence: The Hole at the Wheel's Hub," in *The Re-Emergence of Emergence*, P. Clayton and P. Davies (eds), Boston: MIT Press, 111–50.

Holland, John (1998) *Emergence: From Chaos to Order*, Reading, MA: Helix Books.

Humphreys, Paul (1997a) "How Properties Emerge," *Philosophy of Science* 64: 1–17.

——(1997b) "Emergence, Not Supervenience," *Philosophy of Science* 64: S337–45.

Kant, Immanuel (1952 [1790]) *The Critique of Judgement: II. Teleological Judgment*, James Creed Meredith (trans.), Chicago, IL: University of Chicago Press, 42: 550–613.

Kim, Jaegwon (1993) *Supervenience and Mind*, Cambridge: Cambridge University Press.

——(1999) "Making Sense of Emergence," *Philosophical Studies* 95: 3–36.

Lewes, George Henry (1874–79) *Problems of Life and Mind*, five volumes, New York: Houghton Mifflin.

Lucretius (1994 [1951; n.d.]) *On the Nature of Things/De Rerum Natura*, R. E. Latham (trans.), introduction and notes by John Godwin, revised edn, London: Penguin.

MacKenzie, Robert Beverley (1868) *The Darwinian Theory of the Transmutation of Species Examined* (published anonymously "By a Graduate of the University of Cambridge"), London: Nisbet & Co., quoted in a review, *Athenaeum* 2102, February 8: 217.

Mill, John Stuart (1843) *System of Logic*, London: Longmans, Green, Reader, and Dyer.

Morgan, Conwy Lloyd (1923) *Emergent Evolution*, London: Williams and Norgate.

Polanyi, Michael (1968) "Life's Irreducible Structure," *Science* 160 (3834): 1308–12.

Prigogine, Ilya and Isabelle Stengers (1984) *Order out of Chaos*, New York: Bantam Books.

Putnam, Hillary (1975) *Mind, Language, and Reality*, Cambridge: Cambridge University Press.

Skarda, C. A. and Walter J. Freeman (1987) "How Brains Make Chaos in Order to Make Sense of the World," *Behavioral and Brain Sciences* 10: 161–95.

Sperry, Roger (1980) "Mind–Brain Interaction: Mentalism, Yes; Dualism, No," *Neuroscience* 5: 195–206.

19
PHILOSOPHICAL IMPLICATIONS OF EMERGENCE

Timothy O'Connor

Is there nothing new under the Sun? Consider the great variety of complex structures and patterns of activity that have appeared over time within the 13.7-billion-year-old universe – physical, chemical, and (much later) biological and psychological. Is there reason to say that all such systems are, at bottom, nothing more than atoms in motion? This question has been with us, unresolved, ever since the seventeenth century, when the strongly anti-reductionist philosophy of nature handed down from the ancient Greek Aristotle was displaced by the successes of the new mechanical philosophy. Aristotle theorized that plants and animals are irreducible wholes whose behavior is governed in part by organizing principles wholly separate from those governing inanimate matter. By contrast, according to the mechanical philosophy, *all* physical processes (whether in or out of living systems) are describable and predictable, in principle, in terms of laws of motion governing their basic parts.

Obstacles to simple versions of the mechanical philosophy soon became apparent, but the basic "reductionist" vision of the natural world as fully describable and explainable solely by reference to the properties and forces that govern the world's most elementary constituents was embraced (and continues to be embraced) by many thinkers. Physics Nobel laureate Steven Weinberg (1993) is the most prominent contemporary scientific advocate of reductionism. In contemporary philosophy, advocates of a generally reductionist conception are David Armstrong (1997) and David Lewis (1986: Introduction). Alexander Rosenberg (2006) and Jaegwon Kim (1998) defend reductionist views with respect to biology and the mind, respectively. Opposition to this vision was generally rooted in its perceived inability to explain the human mind. The proposed alternatives to austere reductionism were often equally extreme. In the mind–body dualism of Descartes and his followers, minds are wholly distinct substances from bodies, possessed of their own causal powers, which include the power to affect and be affected by bodies (more specifically, the brains that inhabit the bodies that "belong to" individual minds in a happy but theoretically strange "monogamy"). Others, unsatisfied with the bifurcation of the world into two radically distinct kinds of substance, which have seemingly inexplicable tendencies to interact in such monogamous pairings, ran the reduction in the opposite direction: It is the category of *body* that is reducible in the end to that of mind (more exactly, to collections of "ideas" or particular perceptual states, such as your present visual state as you read this text). Such was the famous proposal of the eighteenth-century "idealist" philosopher George Berkeley and then, in more radical guise still, David Hume.

As the "special" sciences of chemistry, and later biology and psychology, began to develop and mature, it became clear that the structures and processes that are the focus of these domains could be rigorously studied in terms having nothing to do with those of basic physics. Purely biological concepts and laws could powerfully describe biological processes completely independently of any appeal to physics. Beginning with John Stuart Mill, the sensible middle-ground position came to be occupied by those adopting the general philosophy of "emergence," according to which "new" properties and laws "arise out of" certain types of physical arrangement, something that could not have been predicted in advance on the basis of the more fundamental physical principles, but instead must be accepted "with the natural piety of the investigator." Important philosophical emergentists in this mostly British tradition up through the first third of the twentieth century were Samuel Alexander, C. Lloyd-Morgan, and C. D. Broad.

Two factors were central to the demise of this robust scientific–philosophical tradition: First, there was no shared precise concept of emergence. Instead, different thinkers gave their own gloss to it, in ways that weren't obviously mutually consistent. As a result, it seemed to be a rather vague philosophical viewpoint rather than a concept that could be made rigorous and potentially tested in relation to quantified theories. (It didn't help that the notion of emergence these thinkers were attempting to articulate was a species of a more general stance of "holism" that was developed in an anti-scientific direction in the philosophy of Hegel and the Absolute Idealists of the late nineteenth century.) Second, and even more importantly, a couple of spectacular scientific successes of the twentieth century seemed to provide direct evidence against emergence as these thinkers conceived it. Common to all the emergentist views of this era was a neatly "layered" understanding of nature: There are discrete and isolated strata or levels within the most complex systems found in the natural world; each level features a unified system with its own same-level properties and special laws governing their co-evolution over time. The first major blow to this picture came in the 1920s with the advent of quantum mechanics, which was able to explain the basic properties of hydrogen, the simplest chemical atom, in terms of the arrangement and properties of its sub-atomic constituents. And in the 1950s, Watson and Crick uncovered the double-helix structure of DNA, a key part of a successful program of analyzing the phenomena of life in more fundamental electro-chemical terms. In each case, properties of a special science were seen to encompass complex phenomena involving "lower-level" entities, thereby puncturing the hermetically sealed "layers of nature" postulated by the British emergentists.

Does this kind of evidence from twentieth-century science – the two mentioned are merely prominent instances of a whole raft of confirmed data pointing in the same general direction – decisively or strongly confirm the reductionist view? Many suppose so, but this judgment rests on a conflation of the general concept of emergence with the particular account of emergence proposed by the British emergentists, an account that appears unnecessarily crude in hindsight. They thought in terms of relatively insulated layers in nature, whereas we now know that "lower-level" processes often directly impinge upon, and partly regulate, those at higher levels. (One need think only of the subtle chemical influences on mood and cognition that the work of recent decades has revealed.) But emergence need not be yoked to the simple picture of earlier theorists: It is quite possible that higher-level features of a system have a "downward" causal influence on the evolving microstructure that sustains them, even as the lower-level processes play a vital dynamical role in the way emergent processes themselves unfold. In other words, we should replace the picture of mostly horizontal, or same-level, causal patterns within each level with one in which there is a complex web of myriad upward and downward causal influences that jointly determine the system's evolution through time (for a defense of this view, cf. O'Connor and Wong 2005 and Murphy *et al.* 2009). Nothing in the successes of the more fundamental sciences in illuminating some higher-level phenomena precludes the applicability of this more subtle sort of emergentist framework.

There is a tendency, especially for scientists, to conflate what we have reason to believe is the case with what we have *methodological* reason to take as the most fruitful starting hypothesis. Even if the mental is emergent from the physical, if you wish to understand the details of just how mental features emerge, and the difference they make to the overall functioning of the organism, you must have a thorough understanding of the purely physical processes from which they emerge. Thus, in practice, you should push a reductionist approach as far as you can, thereby isolating any emergent features there may be, allowing for highly specific descriptions of their character and function. But your typical scientist, unlike the philosopher, does not spend much time thinking about what will turn out to be true at the end of scientific inquiry. (Terrence Deacon, co-author of Chapter 18 in this volume, is one of several exceptions to this broad generalization.) Rather, she is thinking about what working hypotheses are most useful in advancing current understanding of a specific domain.

Furthermore, it seems to many of us that emergence is no mere theoretical possibility: The nature of animal consciousness and, perhaps, mentality more generally appear to be spectacular counter-instances to the program of reductive analysis. Despite the enormous strides in neuroscience since its infancy in the 1950s, no-one has a clue when it comes to understanding these mental phenomena in reductive physical terms. It remains a mystery how our highly structured neural architecture gives rise to subjective experiences, thoughts, and feelings. The situation seems unlike that facing biologists in the early twentieth century. Lacking a good understanding of the biochemical mechanisms that sustain life, some scientists of that time were willing to countenance the idea that some or all biological properties are not reducible to anything more fundamental. At the present time, there is a great deal of information concerning basic neural mechanisms underlying the complex operations of the human brain. And the obstacle to reduction of psychological phenomena is not our relatively impoverished understanding of how low-level mechanisms together give rise to more complex functions directly tied to subjective experience. It is that (ignoring the eliminativist's radical suggestion that we lack direct acquaintance with our own experiences) the development of increasingly sophisticated models of more complex functions doesn't seem to take us any closer to the goal. Conscious experiences continue to appear to be altogether different kinds of phenomena, intrinsically, from those of electrochemistry. I join some other philosophers in suggesting that it's time to abandon that reductionist dream in favor of an emergentist understanding, on which the appearance of new basic properties within certain neurally complex physical systems must be accepted, as Samuel Alexander put it, "with the natural piety of the investigator." It is a fundamental fact, which may nevertheless be fruitfully studied and eventually explained in detail in non-reductive fashion – by spelling out the basic inventory of emergent properties, detailing the precise conditions under which physical systems give rise to them, and isolating the precise behavioral impact their presence has on the system.

As noted, there are a variety of ways in which people have sought to characterize emergence (see O'Connor and Wong 2006 for a survey.) Philosophically, the most significant understandings are those that challenge the claim that the micro-physical realm is "causally closed" or "complete," with no high-level properties directly affecting micro-physical phenomena. On closure-denying emergentism, emergent properties are basic properties no less than are negative charge or mass (if current physics holds up). As such, they make a non-redundant causal difference to how the world unfolds. Only this strong conception of emergence can underwrite certain metaphysical claims about the reality of (at least some) composite systems and the explanatory significance of the laws that appear to regulate them, including especially the complex systems that are human persons. (For discussion see O'Connor and Wong 2005; O'Connor and Churchill 2010.) This understanding of emergence is different from that of Deacon and Cashman, who propose that we think of emergence not in terms of the *addition* of basic laws or propensities, but rather in terms of specific forms of *absence* – increasing systemic constraints that preclude many forms of physical possibility present in unorganized matter, possibilities that would lead to systemic dissolution. There can be no question that this alternative perspective captures something important, even revolutionary, to our modern understanding of complex systems. But one may well question whether the reality of "increased constraints" emergence in nature will suffice for addressing every sort of philosophical concern.

For example, a basic metaphysical question that philosophers ask concerns the relationship of parts and wholes. Do wholes *really* (fundamentally) exist at all, or is our reference to them a mere convenience, a useful fiction for referring to what is but a swarm of particles obeying completely general laws of physics that have led them to collate in a stable bonding relationship? Look down at this book. Is there really a composite object *in addition to* all the sub-atomic particles "arranged bookwise"? Why should we say that if *everything* concerning the trajectory those particles trace through space and time can be fully accounted for without mentioning any composite object that is [allegedly] the book? Of course, looking at the world in a less fine-grained way – those of chemistry, biology, and psychology and other social sciences – is useful, indeed necessary, to beings like us and discloses interesting patterns that one can't see when peering at the behavior of fundamental particles and fields. Not seeing the forest for the trees, and all that. It's just that, strictly speaking, it appears to be *dispensable*. Another way to get at what's behind the question is this: when God (a being not subject to our rather severe limits of perspective and computation) counts up all the physical objects in the universe, does he have to count the book in addition to all the particles that at any time have constituted the book? If you say yes, why should he not also count the book-plus-your-right-ear? That sounds absurd, of course, but wherein lies the difference, exactly? Some simple answers may occur to you, but careful reflection shows that it is very hard to draw a relevant distinction between the book and such arbitrary "scattered" objects as the book-and-right-ear – *unless* there is reason to suppose that the book, unlike the other candidate object, does fundamental causal work, that is, unless the book "earns its keep." I don't see that this condition is satisfied by Deacon and Cashman's increasing-constraints analysis of complexity generally. That may well be a *necessary* condition on a complex system's earning its keep, but it does not suffice.

The need for a stronger variety of emergence is even clearer when we move from the general case of parts and wholes to the particular case of human beings and the ever-changing parts that compose us. We see human beings as having a special dignity in nature as autonomous (self-directed) agents; as being properly subject to moral appraisal; and as having moral worth, such that imposing harm or death on human beings is, in most circumstances, a grave moral wrong. Again, it is very hard to see, from a clear-eyed metaphysical point of view, why these things should be true if human persons do not, in the final analysis, make any fundamental difference to how the world unfolds. Our authors contrast freedom of agency with unrestricted causal possibility. But this is a false choice: freedom of choice does indeed require the ability to harness physical forces in specific directions, but it also requires the openness of the future to real alternatives. We need the right kind of causal indeterminacy *and* the ability to exploit the opportunities it presents in a goal-directed way (cf. O'Connor 2000 for my own views on the subject).

A third way in which emergent properties are relevant to the concerns of philosophy is one we noted at the outset: Emergence provides a satisfying way to underwrite the fundamental unity of the universe, avoiding the extremes of reductionism and mind–body dualism. Both extremes have long seemed philosophically unsatisfactory: reductionism, because it appears to be inconsistent with the distinctive character of our mental life – the qualities of mental experience seem quite unlike physical qualities as disclosed by science, and there is an irreducible subjectivity, or point of view, associated with being a subject of experience – and the special significance we attach to humans and other conscious animals; mind–body dualism, because it seems incongruent with facts about the deeply embodied nature of animal mentality, as reflected, for example, in the way that psychological maturation is tied to the process of gradual biological development. On closure-denying emergentism, as on increasing-constraints emergentism, there is no distinct *entity* which is the human or animal mind. Instead, we are complex biological systems that undergo processes that are partly distinct from, though causally sustained by, the biological, and specifically neurobiological, processes of the living organism.

Finally, I note that an emergentist vision of human beings has relevance to the philosophical–religious question of the possibility of survival of death. If reductionism were true, survival of death is hard to envision: When I die, my body will decay and my constituting particles will scatter throughout the biosphere, possibly entering other human beings. Emergence (like mind–body dualism) opens up some possibilities concerning survival of death, though it takes a bit of imagination (cf. O'Connor and Jacobs 2010).

At the same time, adopting an emergentist perspective (as opposed to a stronger sort of mind–body dualism) further enables a conciliatory attitude between science and religion. On the one hand, it avoids positing a this-far-and-no-further attitude to the attempt to attain a thorough scientific understanding of the fundamental processes that make up the ongoing lives of the remarkable animals that are human beings. On the other hand, it also serves to remind one of the very partial and ongoing nature of scientific inquiry, encouraging the humility and open-mindedness characterizing the scientific spirit at its noblest. There remain wide-open, religion-friendly possibilities concerning the nature of the human mind, and any conclusive scientific pronouncements on them are likely a long way off.

References

Armstrong, David (1997) *A World of States of Affairs*, Cambridge: Cambridge University Press.

Kim, Jaegwon (1998) *Mind in a Physical World*, Cambridge, MA: MIT Press.

Lewis, David (1986) *Philosophical Papers*, Vol. II, New York: Oxford University Press.

Murphy, Nancey, George F. R. Ellis and Timothy O'Connor (eds) (2009) *Downward Causation and the Neurobiology of Free Will*, New York: Springer.

O'Connor, Timothy (2000) *Persons and Causes: The Metaphysics of Free Will*, New York: Oxford University Press.

O'Connor, Timothy and John Churchill (2010) "Is Nonreductive Physicalism Viable Within a Causal Powers Metaphysic?," in *Emergence in Mind*, Graham and Cynthia Macdonald (eds), Oxford: Oxford University Press, 43–60.

O'Connor, Timothy and Jonathan D. Jacobs (2010) "Emergent Individuals and the Resurrection," *European Journal for Philosophy of Religion* 2: 69–88.

O'Connor, Timothy and Hong Yu Wong (2005) "The Metaphysics of Emergence," *Noûs* 39: 659–79.

——(2006 [rev.]) "Emergent Properties," *Stanford Encyclopedia of Philosophy*, http://plato.stanford.edu/entries/properties-emergent/.

Rosenberg, Alexander (2006) *Darwinian Reductionism: Or, How to Stop Worrying and Love Molecular Biology*, Chicago, IL: University of Chicago Press.

Weinberg, Steven (1993) *Dreams of a Final Theory*, New York: Pantheon Books.

Further reading

Jordi Cat gives a masterful, detailed overview of issues and perspectives concerning the relationship among the sciences in "The Unity of Science," *Stanford Encyclopedia of Philosophy*, 2007, http://plato.stanford.edu/entries/scientific-unity/. There are three excellent collections of contemporary essays on philosophy of mind that explicitly treat reductionist and emergentist themes: Carl Gillett and Barry Loewer, *Physicalism and Its Discontents* (Cambridge University Press, 2001); George Bealer and Robert Koons (eds), *The Waning of Materialism:*

New Essays (Oxford University Press, 2010); and Graham and Cynthia Macdonald (eds), *Emergence in Mind* (Oxford University Press, 2010). For a representative collection of essays on the general topic of emergence over the past three decades, see Mark Bedau and Paul Humphreys (eds), *Emergence: Contemporary Readings in Philosophy and Science* (MIT Press, 2007). A good collection of new essays reflecting current debates is Antonella Corradini and Timothy O'Connor (eds), *Emergence in Science and Philosophy* (Routledge, 2010). For a wide-ranging mix of essays by scientists and philosophers addressing the theme of emergence in thinking about human action and moral responsibility, and doing so in the concrete terms of contemporary research in neuroscience and social psychology, see Nancey Murphy *et al.* (eds) *Downward Causation and the Neurobiology of Free Will* (cited above).

20
EMERGENCE AND CHRISTIAN THEOLOGY

James W. Haag

A significant portion of the interaction between religion and science, especially between Christian theology and science, can be described as a trial-and-error balancing act. Both scientists and theologians have tended to tread lightly in the realm of potential conversation (e.g. Haught 1995) or consonance (e.g. Peters 1999) or integration (e.g. Barbour 1997). The impetus for this hesitation resides in the fear that one may be relinquishing too much. That is, uncertainty of too much compromise looms large with both scientists and theologians. This defensive background has resulted in a sizeable variety of foreground solutions to the religion and science dialogue. In a way, this entire volume is a testament to that diversity. This is why the subject of this chapter is so interesting. For some, emergence is not merely an overnight fad with short-lived solutions to relating science and religion. Rather, it represents a shift that could potentially provide a viable bridge between these two disciplines.

What is emergence?

Deacon and Cashman's introductory chapter (18) offers a useful and concise assessment of emergence. As a way of focusing the discussion, I will briefly and as clearly as possible explain why emergence is such an important and promising topic.

About two millennia ago, Aristotle unwittingly came up with the slogan now oftentimes associated with emergence: "The whole is something over and above its parts and not just the sum of them" (Aristotle 1998: Book VIII, Part 6). What does this mean? Consider an automobile. There are many parts that make up a car (spark plugs, doors, wheels), but we cannot simply dump all of these parts on the floor and claim we have a car. There must be some type of special organization of the parts in order for the final product to qualify as a car. This is a very generic example of the logic Aristotle was employing in his parts/whole statement – you cannot simply add parts together and get the whole. Now, apply this logic to the natural world and the complexity and possibilities explode. With the car, the organization needed to fit the parts together is imposed from the outside by a factory worker or mechanic. In nature, the organization arises (emerges) spontaneously; it self-organizes. One might say our current problem is that we are attempting to apply mechanical explanations (how a car gets put together) to organism explanations (how a cell develops). Deacon poignantly states: "Organisms are not built or assembled" (Deacon 2006). Emergence is slowly shifting how we think about these issues.

To follow this out, consider the ideas running through your head right now. Our ideas are probably the most intimate aspects of who each of us is; they help make up our personal identity. Where do the ideas come from? We might describe features of our childhood, moments in a college classroom, or deep discussions with colleagues. While this may appear to be the case from our perspective, modern science and philosophy counter these commonsensical explanations. Why? Built into the Western conception of science is a very old and powerful assumption: Reality is to be found in the simplest parts. In other words, look to the most basic level – both spatially (the smallest bits) and temporally (the original cause) – and you will find the "really real" of the world. Philosopher Owen Flanagan refers to this approach as "smallism" (Flanagan 2002: 216–17). So, where do the ideas in your mind come from? It depends on where you find the smallest and significant parts – options on the table include neurons (see Churchland 1999); genes (Dawkins 1976); and quantum information (Walker 2000). If this assumption shades our interpretations, then it will be easy to abandon the phenomena of wholes because the parts will be viewed as more fundamental and thus more important. The prime difficulty with this position is that it eliminates many of the world's features that most consider to be valuable and important, but also genuinely real (consciousness, religion, ethics, etc.).

Emergence is a direct challenge to the eliminative reductive view prominent today. It is certainly not the first, but it comes with powerful explanatory tools (systems theory, complexity theory, non-equilibrium thermodynamics, etc.). The challenge is steep because the very connection between parts and wholes must be explained, not simply assumed.

Why emergence?

Why is emergence something theologians might take seriously? Simply, it appears to offer the best of both worlds. As Deacon and Cashman usefully articulate, early in the twentieth century, several schools of philosophical thought grappled with understanding the system of life on a grand scale. Many were *biological mechanists*, maintaining that the terms most fitting and appropriate for explaining life were ones dealing with the arrangement and interaction of an organism's parts. At the opposite end of the metaphysical spectrum lie *substantial vitalists*, who held that mechanical descriptions of life were insufficient because they ignored the need for some non-physical explanation. Emergentists developed a position somewhere in the middle of these two extremes by emphasizing mechanism's physical basis, but also acknowledged vitalism's sense that there was more to life than just physics. The task for emergentists was to maintain this delicate balance between physical processes and the irreducible properties of life.

By splitting the difference between extreme versions of reductionism and inflationism, emergence offers the science-minded theologian intellectual traction. Issues so important to theology (personhood, free will, creativity, etc.) are given status as legitimate phenomena needing assessment. If emergence theory continues to provide viable and accurate descriptions of reality, theologians will likely consider its effects in broad theological terms. For instance, does the part–whole relationship prominent in emergence give us insight into how differing religions might relate? Perhaps, in Christianity, it sheds light on possible denominational relations? Theological loci such as christology and eschatology will certainly also have interesting implications resulting from the relation of theology and emergence. However, for the purposes of this chapter, I focus on the doctrine of God. There are two reasons for this: (1) for monotheistic religions (taken here to include Judaism, Christianity, and Islam), theologians are going to tie all other theological concepts to symbols of God; and (2) the vast majority of contemporary efforts to relate theology and emergence give foremost consideration to the question of God.

Theological dualism

A central tenet of emergence is that complex wholes are not somehow pre-formed in evolutionary history. As Deacon and Cashman write in Chapter 18 of this volume: "The evolutionary world-view assumes that the functional organization of living processes and the intentional and experiential nature of mental processes arose spontaneously, out of blindly mechanistic chemical reactions" (p. 194). Theology, however, has a vested interest in there being at least one pre-formation: God. If God is not somehow at the genesis of everything, then God becomes another emergent feature of the world. For Christians, the Creator cannot be the result of the created, be it the evolutionary process or the human mind. Said differently, theologians have a considerable interest in keeping an ontological distinction between God and the world. Some have countered this idea and located God squarely within the developmental processes of the world. With emergence, this option is most famously proposed in Samuel Alexander's idea of "Deity." Alexander explains: "As actual, God does not possess the quality of deity but is the universe as tending to that quality […] Thus there is no actual infinite being with the quality of deity; but there is actual infinite, the whole universe, with a nisus to deity; and this is the God of the religious consciousness" (Alexander 1920: 361–62). A severe difficulty with Alexander's position is that God is never fully God – God is always emerging. It violates the notion that God is *a se* (completely independent of all else). Niels Henrik Gregersen is right that Alexander's view "places God in the position of the predicate, that is, as the secondary one, while the material universe would take the logical place of the subject" (Gregersen 2006: 315). Most Christian theologians are going to be unwilling to accept such a position.

One of the reasons Alexander's position is unsurprising is because it is rooted in emergence's reliance on naturalism. Naturalism is an abstract term that has been understood in many ways, typically preceded by a modifying term identifying one's interests. Some have included: reductive and liberal (Strawson, 1985), bald and acceptable (McDowell 1998), metaphysical and epistemological (Kornblith 1994), conceptual and methodological (Shatz 1993), religious (Stone 1992), and ontological

(Raley 2005). One might say that the constant through all of these versions of naturalism – and the feature I want to keep in focus – is the claim that, as far as we know, reality is "exhausted by the natural world" (McDowell 1998: 173). If the natural sciences explain nature, and nature is all there is, one can see where impending discord could arise for the theologian. That is, some might fear that emergence may simply be a disguised version of the reductive approach that is abhorrent in theology.

The challenge, then, is for theologians to account for God in such a way that the emergence description of the world is still maintained, and yet minimal theological compromise is needed. Philip Clayton – the foremost contemporary theologian dealing with emergence – endeavors to remain within a naturalistic explanatory system, but theological considerations prevent him from applying emergence *carte blanche*. Certain theological themes (i.e. God) draw him away from emergence and its naturalistic account of the world to non-naturalistic explanations. Clayton's move is one that will certainly be embraced by many other theologians precisely because emergence appears to be closed off to notions of transcendence. Clayton believes, "If one has to countenance some measure of dualism, the relation between an infinite God and a finite world is the right place to locate it" (Clayton 2004: 187). To be clear, he is not willing apathetically to adopt dualism as a portrayal of the world (a move he believes is impossible, considering scientific descriptions of reality), but God is beyond reality and cannot be encapsulated by scientific descriptions, even emergence versions. *Contra* Alexander, God is not another emergent feature of the world alongside others; not even a special emergent feature.

This issue of theological dualism is one all theologians will face when considering science and theology, but with emergence the stakes are even higher. Considering this, we can recognize two general options available for the theologian. Either she follows emergence until theological commitments disallow further acceptance; or he attempts to rethink theological symbols in a way consistent with emergence.

Consider a broad example: one might note juxtaposition between Deacon and Cashman's use of "*ex nihilo nihil fit*" (from nothing, nothing [can be] produced) and the theological commitment to "*creatio ex nihilo*" (creation out of nothing). The theological dualist may decide that, on the question of God's creation, emergence is to be left behind. Someone unwilling to abandon emergence might find ways to rethink our interpretation of creation myths (see, for example, process theology). This is not to insinuate that these are the only options, only to note that the possibilities available for the theologian will require concession – either theologically or scientifically. Clayton has set the challenge, and there are two prominent theologians who take it up, each following a different path. Arthur Peacocke develops a tactic he calls "emergent monism" whereby he argues panentheistically that Clayton's dualistic split is necessary. Gordon Kaufman argues for "serendipitous creativity" as an alternative symbol for God and shifts theological language in such a way, making a dualistic move unnecessary.

Arthur Peacocke: emergent monism

Theological dualism appears to show potential – it allows the theologian to embrace emergence in its totality, but it also allows for a supplementary clarifying trait (i.e. God). At the very least, it appears to prevent the theologian from compromising too much. The primary motivating factor for theologian Arthur Peacocke's approach to science and theology is this claim: "[N]atural realities, although basically physical, evidence various levels of complexity with distinctive internal interrelationships among their components such that new properties, and also new realities, emerge in those complexes – in biology in an evolutionary sequence" (Peacocke 2007: 270). Basically, he believes that the picture of reality set forth through emergence is monistic and hierarchical – the result is what Peacocke terms "emergent monism." The result is that, for Peacocke, emergence is not simply about the basic parts resulting in unique and novel wholes; additionally, the complex whole is capable of affecting the basic parts. This concept is very prominent in emergence discussions and typically goes by the name downward or top-down causation – Peacocke refers to it as "whole–part influence."

Deacon and Cashman reference Roger Sperry's use of top-down causation, I find Clayton's definition more straightforward: "[T]he process whereby some whole has an active non-additive causal influence on its parts" (Clayton 2004: 49). It is the phrase "causal influence" that is the crux of this definition – what is "causal influence?" There is no direct efficient causal relation between higher- and lower-level phenomena. Instead, the higher-level phenomena are said to constrain the lower. While numerous scholars take the "constraint" route, Alicia Juarrero provides one of the more interesting positions. Her approach is a combination of system theory, information theory, and emergence. One important aspect of constraint that Juarrero highlights is that far-from-equilibrium dissipative systems – like those suggested by Ilya Prigogine (see Prigogine and Stengers 1984) – do not require substance-to-substance causation. She writes, "Self-organizing structures are not concrete things. Dissipative structures and autocatalytic webs are meta-stable networks of transformations, nested, hierarchical arrangements of *organizational* patterns: 'structures of process'" (Juarrero 1999: 124). This perspective means that "top-down causation" does not "cause" in some collision-like interaction, that is, through efficient causation.

So, how do constraints downwardly cause? Juarrero expands her analysis by identifying "context-sensitive constraints," which are important because of their ability to limit "randomness without eliminating disorder altogether" (*ibid.*: 136). When previously unrelated parts become interrelated into a distributive whole, one sees the effect of context-sensitive constraints. Juarrero uses Bénard cells as an example. In this phenomenon, liquid molecules, when heated to a certain temperature, form hexagonal cells because this pattern, on a plane, happens to be the most even distribution of heat release. What causes the water molecules to form these symmetric cells? It certainly was not the water molecules themselves. It was not the heating source *per se* – heat the liquid too quickly and the cells will not form. Instead, it was the need to give off heat as efficiently as possible. This obviously is not a cause in any basic sense. As Juarrero notes, "A complex dynamical system emerges when the behavior of each molecule suddenly depends both on what the neighboring molecules are doing and what went before. When components, in other words, suddenly become context-dependent" (*ibid.*: 139). Context-sensitive constraints are unique because they allow the whole to influence the parts in a way other than efficient, billiard ball causation. Juarrero states her position plainly: "Top-down causes cause by changing the prior probability of the components' behavior" (*ibid.*: 146).

Peacocke wants to take this model of top-down causation and apply it to the entire cosmos. He argues that there is a hierarchy in nature of different levels – each level contains its own regularities, depending on what that level is composed of. Any higher level can affect a lower level by just changing (or constraining) the context of the regularities. Theologically, this becomes interesting because Peacocke contends that God acts in the world via the same logic. That is, the application of emergent monism to theological concerns, for Peacocke, is a logical move: "[T]heological language refers to what one might call the apex in human experience of the hierarchy of complexity" (Peacocke 2007: 277).

Peacocke writes: "[M]ediated by such whole–part influences on the world-as-a-whole (as a *System*-of-systems) and thereby on its constituents, God could bring about the occurrence of particular events and patterns of events – those which express God's intentions."(*ibid*.: 274) This is a panentheistic approach whereby God is related to the world in totality, and yet God is both transcendent to, and immanent in, the world. Since there is a continuance between the whole and the parts, Peacocke believes he can avoid claims of a miracle-acting God who violates the laws of nature. If God is the ultimate whole to the world's parts, then God can act through top-down causation (i.e. whole to part) analogously to the dynamical system that emerges in Bénard cells.

A bit ironically, emergent monism comes with a healthy dose of theological dualism. Even though the panentheistic vision attempts to "formulate a single ontological vision rather than sharply separating the becoming of the world from the timelessness and aseity of the divine being" (Clayton 2006: 319), there also remains the "'ontological gaps(s)' between the world and God" (Peacocke 2007: 278). While Peacocke's is a theology that takes seriously the emergentist world-view, the inclusion of an ontological distinction between God and the world will make it difficult, if not impossible, to find ultimate reconciliation between emergence and theology – it may be the closest a robust theism can come to consonance.

Gordon Kaufman: serendipitous creativity

Of course, theological models that note a dualistic separation between the world and God are not the only potential Christian responses to emergence. Theologian Gordon Kaufman has developed a model for God that is potentially more compatible with emergence precisely because it does not require the jump that Clayton describes.

For Kaufman, scientific explanations of the cosmos make it difficult, if not impossible, to maintain traditional, personal metaphors for God. Emergentists tell us that personal-type beings appear only after billions of years of processes, and did not somehow exist at the beginning. This is exactly why Clayton espouses theological dualism. Nancy Frankenberry articulates this idea when she states, "'No doer before the deed' is needed to account for ontological identity or agency, for the doer is produced precisely in and through the becoming of the deed, as the effect and not the cause of its own conditions" (Frankenberry 2006: 338). It is the theologian's job to rethink God-talk in light of her present-day situation, and Kaufman contends that this demands a shift in focus from an agent-type God (that does demand

Clayton's split) to a process-type God. More specifically, he proposes that we think of God not as *the creator*, but as *creativity* itself.

What does it mean to say that God is creativity? Initially, one might see Kaufman resurrecting a form of vitalism – one of the poles emergence tries to balance – where God is portrayed as some inherent force or power working within or behind the evolutionary processes. However, Kaufman wants to avoid this position since, "To regard creativity as a kind of 'force' is to suggest that we have a sort of (vague) knowledge of an existing something-or-other when in fact we do not" (Kaufman 2004: 56). Instead, Kaufman insists that God (creativity) is that process that leads to genuine novelty in the world, from the Big Bang to the present day. This evolutionary picture of the cosmos emphasizes ongoing change over fixed permanency. The massive expansion of the universe after the Big Bang brought with it the emergence of stars, cellular life, and human beings. Kaufman sees these moments in time – along with billions of others – as occurring within distinct "*trajectories* or *directional movements*" (*ibid.*: 42). Human beings just so happen to be on the trajectory that has been the source for imagination, inquiry, and illumination. He writes, "Construing the universe in this way, as constituted by cosmic serendipitous creativity that manifests itself in trajectories of various sorts, is important because it helps us see that our proper place in the world, our home in the universe, is the evolutionary–ecological trajectory on which we have emerged" (*ibid.*: 47). Thus, when we look to the world around us, we witness a remarkable creative process in which all aspects of the cosmos have arisen. These trajectories are the result of what Kaufman calls "serendipitous creativity."

It is a serendipitous process because of the appearance of a sort of fortuitous nature to the evolution of the cosmos: "More happens than one would have expected, given previously prevailing circumstances, indeed, more than might have seemed possible" (*ibid.*: 56). All the results of evolutionary processes, including human beings, could just as easily have not emerged. However, the fact that humans are here, and able to reflect on the processes out of which they arose, produces awe-inspiring reflection. For this reason, Kaufman claims that creativity is a suitable way to talk about God because creativity is inherently mysterious, though creativity is not mystery itself. He notes that creativity "differs from 'mystery' in that it directs attention to the coming into being of the new, whereas 'mystery' (when used in a theological context) refers to fundamental limits of all human knowledge and carries no such further meaning" (*ibid.*: 55). Relating to the apophatic tradition, Kaufman continually emphasizes that God is beyond immediate or direct human contact. However, to avoid confusion, he notes: "God is *creativity*, not one of the creatures" (Kaufman 2007: 926). It is not a type of theological dualism, since Kaufman's phrasing avoid strict ontological claims; rather:

> Creativity, in this view, is not a quasi-scientific explanation of why and how new realities come into being; it is rather the word we use to identify and call attention to one of the profound mysteries of life: the mystery of new realities continuously being created, the mystery of complex things emerging from less complex, the mystery of the coming into being of the universe and ourselves in that universe, the mystery of an open and unknown future into which we all are moving.
>
> (*ibid.*: 927)

Clearly, Kaufman's alternative rethinks a number of theological themes. Without belaboring any theological shortcomings, we can notice that God as creativity can mesh more soundly with emergence; at least more than Peacocke's dualistic move. This is not to say that Kaufman's God as creativity completely fits with emergence: "Although we can describe this model of emergence with some precision, this in no way overcomes the profound mystery at the root of this amazing creativity" (*ibid*.: 919). After all, theologians recognize that, if we have full explanatory power over God, this very prospect would raise doubts.

The future

Theologian Philip Hefner contends that emergence is a topic drawing considerable attention from a variety of thinkers – from theologians to computer scientists, from biologists to sociologists – because it is embedded in a common experience we all share (see Hefner 2008). These experiences are typically routine, but, when reflected upon, can provoke in us a sense of wonder and bewilderment. This is certainly why theologians like Peacocke and Kaufman have given attention to this explanatory schema. While chemical reactions, organism organization, human social behaviors, and even divine action are clearly different, there appears to be a potential for common logic inherent to each. We would not want this loose analogy to be exploited, but at a basic stage each exhibits a special relationship between parts and a whole. Examples that take these unique parts-to-whole relationships are all around us, whether we identify them or not. Perhaps the most important reason theologians should consider emergence is because it is "emerging" as a robust and seemingly accurate description of reality. As an additional perk, emergence aligns well with our human experiences and, as articulated throughout, is not immediately closed off to theological considerations. The interaction between emergence and theology is still in its beginning stages – likely because emergence itself is only now slowly finding traction in the sciences, but there is also the strong possibility that theologians are fearful of adopting a theory that may well fade away into intellectual history. Deacon and Cashman's introductory article should convince us that this disappearance is a very unlikely scenario. The explanatory power of emergence is growing and theologians would be well served to explore its implications for the whole of theological loci. While concessions are probable, it may be the case that the interaction between emergence and theology is the most salient method available. And, after all, moving toward truth claims is a goal shared by all in this effort.

References

Alexander, Samuel (1920) *Space, Time, and Deity*, Vol. 2, London: Macmillan.

Aristotle (1998) *The Metaphysics* in *The Complete Works of Aristotle*, two volumes, Jonathan Barnes (ed.), Princeton, NJ: Princeton University Press.

Barbour, Ian G. (1997) *Religion and Science: Historical and Contemporary Issues*, San Francisco, CA: HarperCollins.

Clayton, Philip (2004) *Mind & Emergence: From Quantum to Consciousness*, New York: Oxford University Press.
——(2006) "Emergence from Quantum Physics to Religion: A Critical Appraisal," in *The Re-Emergence of Emergence: The Emergentist Hypothesis from Science to Religion*, Philip Clayton and Paul Davies (eds), New York: Oxford University Press, 303–22.
Churchland, Paul M. (1999) *The Engine of Reason, the Seat of the Soul*, Cambridge, MA: MIT Press.
Dawkins, Richard (1976) *The Selfish Gene*, Oxford: Oxford University Press.
Deacon, Terrence (2006) "Emergence: The Hole at the Wheel's Hub," in *The Re-Emergence of Emergence: The Emergentist Hypothesis from Science to Religion*, Philip Clayton and Paul Davies (eds), New York: Oxford University Press, 111–50.
Flanagan, Owen (2002) *The Problem of the Soul: Two Visions of Mind and How to Reconcile Them*, New York: Basic Books.
Frankenberry, Nancy (2006) "Religious Empiricism and Naturalism," in *A Companion to Pragmatism*, John R. Shook and Joseph Margolis (eds), Malden, MA: Blackwell, 336–51.
Gregersen, Niels Henrik (2006) "Emergence in Theological Perspective: A Corollary to Professor Clayton's *Boyle Lecture*," *Theology and Science* 4(3): 309–20.
Haught, John (1995) *Science & Religion: From Conflict to Conversation*, New York: Paulist Press.
Hefner, Philip (2008) *Religion-and-Science as Spiritual Quest for Meaning*, Proceedings of the Sixth Annual Goshen Conference on Religion and Science, Kitchener, Ontario: Pandora Press.
Juarrero, Alicia (1999) *Dynamics in Action: Intentional Behavior as a Complex System*, Cambridge, MA: MIT Press.
Kaufman, Gordon (2004) *In the Beginning … Creativity*, Minneapolis, MN: Fortress Press.
——(2007) "A Religious Interpretation of Emergence: Creativity as God," *Zygon: Journal of Religion & Science* 42(4): 915–28.
Kornblith, Hilary (1994) "Naturalism: Metaphysical and Epistemological," in *Midwest Studies in Philosophy*, Vol. XIX, Peter A. French, Theodore E. Uehling, Jr. and Howard K. Wettstein (eds), Notre Dame, IN: University of Notre Dame Press, 39–52.
McDowell, John (1998) *Mind, Value and Reality*, Cambridge, MA: Harvard University Press.
Peacocke, Arthur (2007) "Emergent Realities with Causal Efficacy: Some Philosophical and Theological Applications," in *Evolution & Emergence: Systems, Organisms, Persons*, Nancey Murphy and William R. Stoeger, S.J. (eds), New York: Oxford University Press, 267–83.
Peters, Ted (1998) *Science and Theology: The New Consonance*, Boulder, CO: Westview Press.
Prigogine, Ilya and Isabelle Stengers (1984) *Order Out of Chaos*, New York: Bantam Books.
Raley, Yvonne (2005) "Ontological Naturalism," *Pacific Philosophical Quarterly* 86: 284–94.
Shatz, David (1993) "Skepticism and Naturalized Epistemology," in *Naturalism: A Critical Appraisal*, Steven J. Wagner and Richard Warner (eds), Notre Dame, IN: University of Notre Dame Press, 117–45.
Stone, Jerome A. (1992) *The Minimalist Vision of Transcendence: A Naturalist Philosophy of Religion*, Albany, NY: SUNY Press.
Strawson, P.F. (1985) *Skepticism and Naturalism: Some Varieties*, New York: Columbia University Press.
Walker, Evan Harris (2000) *The Physics of Consciousness: Quantum Minds and the Meaning of Life*, New York: Perseus Books.

Further reading

As mentioned in this chapter, the newness of emergence in science is also felt in theological responses. However, there are a few resources that are useful and important if one is going to engage this field of work. Two of them are edited volumes. One is Nancey Murphy and William R. Stoeger, S.J.'s *Evolution & Emergence: Systems, Organisms, Persons* (Oxford University Press, 2007). The other is Philip Clayton and Paul Davies' *The Re-Emergence of Emergence: The Emergentist Hypothesis from Science to Religion* (Oxford University Press, 2006). There is some overlap in these volumes, but the overall content provides some of the best and only work available in emergence and theology. Perhaps the greatest resource for the Christian theologian is Philip Clayton's book *Mind & Emergence: From Quantum to Consciousness* (cited above). To date, it is the most thorough and accessible approach to emergence written by a theologian. One final resource is a collection of articles that have appeared in *Zygon: Journal of Religion and Science*. The first group can be found in Volume 41, Number 3 of 2006. Another assortment can be found in Volume 42, Number 4 of 2007.

21 BUDDHISM, EMERGENCE, AND ANTI-SUBSTANTIALISM

Charles Goodman

In Chapter 18 in this volume, "Eliminativism, complexity, and emergence," Terrence Deacon and Tyrone Cashman present a series of provocative interpretations of recent scientific theories that have important resonances with Asian philosophy and especially with Buddhist thought. Members of many Buddhist traditions would especially be inclined to agree with Deacon and Cashman's denial that the forms of complexity that emerge at higher levels include real substances, and could provide additional arguments to support it. Indeed, Buddhists would take this denial to have major implications for ethics and for spiritual practice. Some of the other issues Deacon and Cashman discuss were investigated in various ways by different philosophical schools in Asia, leading in some cases to conclusions similar to theirs. Although these pre-modern traditions of thought did not have access to the scientific findings that inform contemporary discussions, some subsets of their teachings may actually be well supported by certain of these recent discoveries.

The great Buddhist philosophers of India and Tibet never heard about Darwinian evolution, but they might have found that theory helpful if they had. These Buddhists explicitly denied the existence of a creator God. Hindu and other theist opponents used the argument from design against them, and they lacked the empirically grounded and emotionally compelling response that Darwin's theory could have given them if it had been possible for them to know about it. But Buddhists were not entirely without a response to the argument from design, a response that allowed them to endorse their own version of the maxim *ex nihilo nihil fit*.

Buddhist philosophers did not accept the idea that effects must already be present, in some form, in their causes. They knew this view as the *satkaryavada*, or Doctrine of a Real Pre-existent Effect, defended by the Samkhya and Advaita Vedanta schools of Hindu philosophy. Indeed, this thesis is quite central to Advaita Vedanta, which used it to construct the following inference: God is the cause of the world. The true substance of the effect must already be present in the cause. Therefore, everything in the world has God as its true substance; everything is merely a manifestation of

God. The resulting non-dualistic pantheism was not acceptable to Buddhists, although some felt that it came closer to their views than many other forms of Hindu thought; Shantaraksita, the syncretic Buddhist idealist whose missionary work helped begin the Tibetan Buddhist tradition, described Advaita as having "only a small fault" (Krishnamacharya 1984: 123; translation by the author).

In place of the view that the effect is already present in the cause, Buddhist scholastic philosophers, especially in Tibet, accepted the view that each phenomenon that arises has a substantial cause (Tib. *nyer len gyi rgyu*) that is similar to its effect. In this respect, they could have agreed with the Latin medievals: no-one gives what he does not have. Yet they rejected the idea of an initial creation of the universe.

While denying the doctrine of creation by a God, the historical Buddha refused to endorse any view about the temporal or spatial extent of the universe. All mature Indian Buddhist schools, though, affirmed that cyclic existence is beginningless. Whatever we observe today is the result of a chain of causation that stretches backward through limitless time. The complexity of sentient beings as they exist today, and the good or bad fortune they currently enjoy, depends on the moral quality of the actions of those beings in previous lives. Living creatures are well adapted to their environments because their *karma* has caused them to arise in environments, and with characteristics, that allow them to survive – or, on a more radical interpretation, because the existence and nature of the physical world is itself the result of *karma*, so that the world comes into existence as an appropriate background for the karmic drama that continues to unfold. No divine creator is needed, and none would be possible, since a permanent, unchanging entity cannot exert causal efficacy.

These teachings are the basis for the most important rational argument for reincarnation to be found in the Buddhist tradition, as offered by the great epistemologist Dharmakirti. He starts with the assumption, stated above, that whatever arises needs a substantial cause that is similar to it. He also assumes that no mental phenomenon can be similar, in the relevant sense, to any physical phenomenon. Dharmakirti supports these two assumptions with criticisms of the Carvaka, the primitive form of skeptical materialism that had already been developed in India. He then applies these two premises to the first moment of consciousness in any given individual's life. This moment of consciousness must have had a substantial cause, which cannot have been a physical phenomenon and cannot have been a previous moment of consciousness in that very life. Therefore, that person must have had a previous life, such that the last moment of consciousness in that former rebirth can serve as the substantial cause for the first moment of consciousness in this rebirth. Tibetan Buddhist apologists today frequently rely on this argument.

The set of issues discussed by Deacon and Cashman are considered in various other places in South Asian Buddhist literature, notably in the genre of Buddhist thought known as the Abhidharma (or in Pali, Abhidhamma.) Abhidharma texts attempt to systematize the scattered philosophical teachings of the Buddhist scriptures into a single, coherent system. There are several such systems, corresponding to different schools of Buddhist thought in India. Historically, the most significant of these systems are the Pali Abhidhamma, which forms the principal philosophical basis for the Theravada Buddhist religion which is now so important in Southeast Asia; and the systems of the Vaibhashikas and Sautrantikas, whose views are discussed at length in a major text, the *Abhidharma-kosha* of Vasubandhu. This treatise, probably written in the fifth century CE, plays a major role in the education of Tibetan Buddhist monks and has also been widely read in East Asia.

As Deacon and Cashman note, Jaegwon Kim has recently argued that the assignment of causal efficacy to higher-order entities faces a serious problem about overdetermination. Though developed for entirely different purposes and in a completely different intellectual context, this argument resembles, in some respects, ideas that are quite central to the Abhidharma tradition. Philosophers writing in that tradition, the Abhidharmikas, accept what is known as the causal efficacy test: only those entities capable of exerting causal efficacy can be considered as ultimately real. Entities that do not have causal efficacy must be regarded as mere conceptual constructions overlaid by the mind on a more fundamental reality. These Abhidharmikas, moreover, argued that where what we would regard as a whole consists of many parts, only the absolutely simplest parts have any genuine causal efficacy. We might ordinarily treat composite things as having causal efficacy, but as they inherit their causal powers entirely from their parts, all the genuine causal efficacy resides at the lowest level, the level of parts that are utterly simple.

This relentlessly reductionist view stands opposed, then, to the claim that a whole can be greater than the sum of its parts. In fact, in no sense is the whole something over and above its parts; discourse about the whole is just an ontologically misleading way of discussing the parts. Nor is it the case that, according to this account, there is an entity called "the sum of the parts." We can consider the parts together in our minds, and come to believe or talk as if there were a sum of the parts, but these mental operations do not bring into existence a real entity; there are still just the parts. (An interesting discussion of the slogan "the whole is the sum of its parts" can be found in van Inwagen 1990: 30, in which van Inwagen denies that this slogan can naturally be used to express any interesting or controversial metaphysical thesis.) And if these Buddhists had heard someone speak about the set of the parts, they would also have denied any real, mind-independent existence to an abstract object of this kind; at the time of the composition of the *Abhidharmakosha*, the Buddhist tradition was already taking a stand against abstract objects, a trend that would lead to the development of worked-out conceptualist theories in the lineage of Dignaga and Dharmakirti.

On the other hand, the philosophers of the Abhidharma did not think that their view would lead to an eliminative materialism, a conclusion they would have seen as deeply unattractive and threatening to their spiritual commitments. Instead, they took momentary mental phenomena to be among the simple parts of sentient beings. And they held an interactionist view on which causal influence could flow between mental and physical phenomena. So this tradition of Buddhist thought did not consider either eliminative materialism or emergentism, views whose primary motivation is based on science of which the Abhidharmikas knew nothing.

It is interesting to note, however, that there is one particular aspect of the Abhidharma that does seem to require something like emergence: the concept of derived form. In several Abhidharma systems, there are two major categories of "form" (Skt. *rupa*): basic physical entities and sensible qualities. The members of both categories are simple, momentary entities, and from the Abhidharma perspective, the members of both categories are objectively real. The basic physical entities are tropes, instances of four fundamental kinds of local qualitative character: cohesion, expansion, movement, and solidity. These four kinds of trope can be referred to, somewhat misleadingly, as water, fire, air, and earth. The key point for present purposes is the relation between these basic physical entities, which are regarded as too small to be individually perceptible by our senses, and the sensible qualities, or derived form, that we actually perceive. Here the Abhidharmikas do not want to restrict causal efficacy to the lower level; colors, sounds, and so on can be genuinely causally efficacious, on their view. Unlike composite things, which are to be understood through a reductionist strategy, tiny, momentary patches of color and shape are seen in this tradition as simple, and as not reducible to basic physical entities. Therefore, to get from the lower level to the higher, a process at least analogous to emergence will be needed.

Why didn't the Abhidharma tradition regard mental phenomena as analogous to derived form? That is, why didn't they embrace the fundamentally materialist approach of regarding mental phenomena as emerging from, and dependent on, physical phenomena? To justify their views would require a deep and difficult exploration; perhaps it could not be done. But it is relatively easy to explain their views. Accepting such a materialist account would have required them to give up too many of the religious aspects of the Buddhist tradition. The Abhidharma developed a powerful way of reconciling reincarnation with no-self: they saw rebirth as the continuation of a process, like the spread of a fire, and not as the transmigration of a substantial entity. It would have been more difficult to reconcile reincarnation with materialism. If mental phenomena emerge from, and are dependent on, the physical processes within the brain, then it seems overwhelmingly likely that the destruction of a particular brain would cause the corresponding series of mental phenomena to stop. Abandoning reincarnation, in turn, would have required a radical reinterpretation of the Buddhist path to Awakening. In the absence of a flourishing tradition of natural science, there was no intellectual pressure for materialism in ancient India powerful enough to motivate anyone in the Abhidharma schools to explore what such a reinterpretation would look like.

Members of the Abhidharma schools were not the only Buddhists who considered the issues we are discussing; indeed, we can identify similarities between the conclusions offered by Deacon and Cashman and philosophical views found in several forms of the Buddhist tradition. Deacon and Cashman assert that when higher-order processes and forms of structure and complexity emerge, "There is no *thing* new." It follows from this claim that an individual person, who after all must be a result of emergence, does not exist as a thing. This claim is more or less exactly aligned with the fundamental Buddhist doctrine of no self; "does not exist as a thing" would be a possible literal translation of Sanskrit *na dravyasat*, one way in that language of expressing the view of almost all Buddhist philosophers about the ontological status of persons and other composite entities.

In particular, one Buddhist philosophical school, the Middle Way School or Madhyamaka, understands the way things are to be emptiness. Negatively, emptiness is closely connected with not being a thing. To understand the world in terms of emptiness involves rejecting any view of things as real, independent substances. But another aspect of the teaching of emptiness is the broad and central importance of reciprocity and interdependence. Phenomena do not exist on their own, and cannot be understood or characterized on their own, but only in relation to each other. This is what Deacon and Cashman assert about the parts of a living thing. Philosophers of the Middle Way School would generalize such claims quite widely.

For any attempt to develop a contemporary articulation of the views of the Middle Way School, quantum mechanics will be crucial. Many traditions of Indian thought, both Buddhist and non-Buddhist, maintained that matter could be analyzed into fundamental, indivisible particles or atoms (sometimes called in Sanskrit *paramanu*.) The Madhyamikas, those belonging to the Middle Way School, did not deny that the concept of elementary particles could be useful for certain purposes. They did reject the ultimate, real, or independent existence of these particles. At certain earlier phases in the development of physical science – say, in the late nineteenth century – such a denial of the fundamental ontological status of particles would have been regarded as implausible. Those wishing to sustain this kind of denial might have had to resort to dubious empirical claims, such as asserting without evidence that every material particle must necessarily have proper parts, so that the hierarchy of particles goes infinitely far down. The best science of today, however, as Deacon and Cashman point out, is naturally interpreted as positing particles that exist only in relation to fields, and not as the ultimate constituents of reality. In quantum field theory, particle number is not a relativistic invariant, so that in a certain sense, how many particles exist in a given region of space depends on your point of view. A field, in turn, is unlikely to be seen as an enduring, independently existing substance; so that, at the basic physical level, substance has completely vanished, leaving us with a collection of interdependent processes. Of course, these results might conceivably be overthrown by future generations of scientific progress. Moreover, the interpretation of quantum mechanics is one of the most controversial issues in the philosophy of science, and there are writers with much greater expertise than I possess who might reject the preceding account. So the remarks I have offered should be taken in a tentative, but hopeful, spirit. Large numbers of ill-informed and conceptually sloppy writers have claimed that modern physics lends support to Asian religions. The intellectual limitations of these authors notwithstanding, their main thesis may be true.

According to Deacon and Cashman, as new and more complex forms of organization appear at higher and higher levels, nothing that emerges should be considered a substance. This claim accords with the well known discussion in VI.150–65 of Candrakirti's *Introduction to the Middle Way School* (*Madhyamaka-avatara*) (Huntington 1989: 175–77). Here, Candrakirti compares a human being to a chariot. This is a very important Buddhist simile, probably over 800 years old in Candrakirti's time. In analyzing the chariot, Candrakirti rejects a total of seven accounts that might be given of the way in which the chariot relates to its parts, offering explicit arguments against some and simply dismissing others. In the same way, the corresponding seven accounts will also fail to capture the relation between a person and the parts of that person. This complex set of arguments leads up to the main Madhyamaka conclusion on this issue: "the basis of clinging to an 'I' is not an entity" (Huntington 1989: 175).

So, for example, Candrakirti asserts that the chariot is not identical to its parts. After all, how can many things be identical to one thing? A more defensible version of this kind of claim might be that the chariot is identical to the composite of its parts, or, as we might say today, the mereological sum of its parts. About this alternative, Candrakirti says: "If the carriage were simply the composite [of its parts], then it would exist even when [the parts] were disassembled" (Huntington 1989: 176). Against both views, he could also have presented the argument that, from the point of view of common sense, the replacement of a single part leaves us with numerically the same chariot; but if the chariot is identical with the parts themselves, or with the composite of the parts, it's hard to see how such a statement would be true. On those views, mereological essentialism should be true of the chariot.

On the other hand, a chariot is not a separate entity distinct from its parts. We do not see, or otherwise observe, an extra entity distinct from the parts, so we have no evidence for its existence. As noted above, all the causal efficacy of the chariot derives from its parts, so we could not possibly have any evidence for the existence of a distinct, additional entity. In fact, all the properties we ascribe to the chariot derive from the parts, so the chariot, conceived of as a substance distinct from its parts, becomes an entity we cannot characterize, think about, or understand.

Candrakirti also considers the possibility that the chariot might be shape. But this must either be the shape of the individual parts, or the shape of the composite of the parts. Suppose we grant that the chariot does not exist while it is disassembled. When the chariot is assembled, the shape of the individual parts does not change, so the chariot, which comes into existence in the process of assembly, cannot be the shape of the individual parts. Now Candrakirti takes it that the opponent who proposes that the chariot is shape does not accept the composite of the parts as itself a real entity. So how can a real substance exist as the shape of something that does not exist?

Having rejected these and other alternatives, Candrakirti concludes: "The image of an effect, with an unreal quality of intrinsic being, [arises] in dependence on an unreal cause. One must realize that all things are produced in this way" (Huntington 1989: 176). This teaching is profoundly counter-intuitive – which is exactly what Madhyamikas such as Candrakirti would expect the truth to be. On their view, sentient beings are born with innate ignorance, a powerful mental process that continuously reifies the self. (For a discussion of the distinction between innate and acquired ignorance, see Tsong kha pa 2002: 196.) Each of us has a nearly irresistible tendency to think "I am a real thing," and to relate to all of our experience on the basis of holding this belief both consciously and subconsciously. According to Buddhists, this belief is the real source of selfishness, fear, hatred, craving, and aggression. Philosophical argument may be able to convince us, at an intellectual level, that there is no really existing self; if our engagement remains at this level, we will continue to have nagging doubts: "Mustn't I really exist in some way or another?" Those doubts can be pacified by an authentic direct experience of no-self brought on by spiritual practice. But after the immediate effects of such an experience have subsided, the practitioner's actual relation to the lived world will continue to be conditioned by the subconscious process that constructs a sense of self. Only through awakening to what is at the very deepest level can this subconscious process be completely overcome.

There is one other Buddhist teaching that should be mentioned here, since it seems to have strong affinities at least with the general spirit of Deacon and

Cashman's views. This is the exclusion theory of meaning (Skt. *apoha*) developed by the lineage of Buddhist epistemologists founded by Dignaga and Dharmakirti. These Buddhist epistemologists wished to oppose the philosophy of language of the Nyaya school of Hindu philosophy, which postulated real, permanent universals as the meanings of words. They sought to uphold the conventional status of language against another Hindu philosophical school, the Mimamsa, which regarded the Vedas as eternal and without any author, and therefore held that Sanskrit is the only truly natural language and is in some sense embedded in the fabric of the universe. And they wished to avoid a complete and unqualified nominalism, like that of the materialist Carvakas, which they feared would make thought, and in particular inference, impossible.

For Dignaga and Dharmakirti, we give meaning to words through a process of conceptual construction, in which we group together things we take to have similar causal efficacy. In taking the word "cow" to refer to, among other things, a particular cow, Bossie, we perform an operation of exclusion: a mind regards Bossie as excluded from the class of all non-cows. Buddhist epistemologists thought that this account would allow them to explain the ability of words to express general meanings without postulating real universals. The exclusion theory thus fits with and reinforces the anti-substantialist message that Buddhists share with Deacon and Cashman. By attributing meaning to a process of exclusion, centrally based on a process of double negation, it also harmonizes with the two authors' emphasis on constraint and negation as sources of new kinds of order and significance. It would be interesting to explore further whether there are deep affinities, or merely shallow similarities, between these views, which after all pertain to rather different areas of philosophy.

I have tried to show that there are large areas of agreement between the teachings of Buddhism, and especially of the Middle Way School, and the theses of Deacon and Cashman. To the extent that Deacon and Cashman's views are potentially controversial interpretations of scientific findings, Buddhists would have reason to endorse these interpretations; to the extent that these views are actual findings of science, Buddhists can claim new scientific support for some of their own doctrines. But they would also go on to point out that the anti-substantialist view of emergence proposed by Deacon and Cashman may have far-ranging and radical implications not noted by those authors. What are the implications for ethics if a human being is not a substance? The existence of constraints may well make it possible for work to be done, but if a person is not a thing, who does that work? If there is no unitary and autonomous entity to do the work, then have we really established space for autonomy? What would it actually be like to live your life and relate to your experience without thinking of yourself as a thing, or even without any sense of self at all? Deacon and Cashman's explorations of emergence and complexity have led them to the mouth of a rabbit-hole that may go far deeper than they realize.

References

Huntington, C.W. (trans.) (1989) *The Emptiness of Emptiness: An Introduction to Early Indian Madhyamika*, Honolulu: University of Hawai'i Press.

van Inwagen, Peter (1990) *Material Beings*, Ithaca, NY: Cornell University Press.

Krishnamacharya, Embar (ed.) (1984 [1926]) *Tattvasamgraha of Shantaraksita with the Commentary of Kamalashila*, Baroda: Oriental Institute.

Tsong kha pa (2002) *The Great Treatise on the Stages of the Path to Enlightenment*, Vol. 3, Lamrim Chenmo Translation Committee (trans.), Ithaca: Snow Lion.

Further reading

For arguments in favor of the claim that an unchanging and permanent entity could not exert causal efficacy, as applied to an alleged permanent soul, see chapters 26 and 28 of William Edelglass and Jay Garfield's *Buddhist Philosophy: Essential Readings* (Oxford University Press, 2009.) For more on Dharmakirti, see John Dunne's *Foundations of Dharmakirti's Philosophy* (Wisdom Publications, 2004.) A very helpful discussion of *apoha*, to which I am indebted, can be found in Part III, and especially chapters 11–12, of Georges Dreyfus's *Recognizing Reality: Dharmakirti's Philosophy and its Tibetan Interpretations* (SUNY Press, 1997.) I investigate the issue of derived form and its place in the Abhidharma world-view in Charles Goodman, "The *Treasury of Metaphysics* and the Physical World," *Philosophical Quarterly* 54 (216) (2004): 389–401. A well informed exploration of the ontological status of particles in relativistic quantum mechanics, including the implications of the claim that particle number is not a relativistic invariant, can be found in Paul Teller's *An Interpretive Introduction to Quantum Field Theory* (Princeton University Press, 1995). I explore the possible ethical implications of the doctrine of no self in Charles Goodman, *Consequences of Compassion: An Interpretation and Defense of Buddhist Ethics* (Oxford University Press, 2009.) Chapter 8 of this book discusses free will. For a very different perspective on free will in Buddhist philosophy, see Mark Siderits' "Beyond Compatibilism: A Buddhist Approach to Freedom and Determinism," *American Philosophical Quarterly* 24(2) (1987): 149–59.

(iv) Evolutionary biology and suffering

22
THE BIOLOGICAL ANTECEDENTS OF HUMAN SUFFERING

Ursula Goodenough

Where does suffering come from? Why do we suffer? If deities are all-powerful and loving, why do they condone the suffering of the innocent? Responses to such questions have been reached using philosophical and religious insights, but recent scientific inquiry offers up helpful understandings as well, understandings that are important to include in any full consideration of the suffering phenomenon.

This chapter lifts up some of these science-based understandings. It is organized into six sections. The first presents a primer on the scientific concepts that are drawn upon in considering suffering from a biological perspective. The second offers a scenario for the origins of suffering in the context of the origins and evolution of life, and proposes a minimalist concept – *biological suffering* – that applies to all of life. The third considers which organisms also undergo *experienced suffering*, with attention to the uncertainties that attend the project of defining experience. The remaining three sections offer naturalistic perspectives on the relationship between suffering and physical, social, and psychological pain, topics that are given more humanistic/religious perspectives in other chapters of this volume.

Core concepts in biology and emergence theory

Basic properties of life

All present-day organisms and their viruses share core features. All possess genomes, usually comprised of long macromolecules called DNA. Each genome carries instructions for making a particular kind of organism or virus. The instructions are encoded in units called genes and in the regulatory elements that determine whether or not, and to what extent, a given gene is expressed in a particular cell under particular circumstances.

When a particular gene is expressed, a particular protein is produced. When, as is usually the case, many of the genes in a genome are expressed in a given cell, the cell comes to contain many different kinds of protein, all of which are relevant to carrying out the cell's ongoing activities. Once a protein is synthesized, it folds into a specific shape that defines both its activities and its ability to interact with the shapes of partner proteins, the result being the formation of multi-protein complexes. Some protein complexes are structural, serving as cellular bricks-and-mortar. Others, called enzymes, serve as catalysts (assistants) for biochemical reactions.

Biochemistry proceeds in accordance with the laws of thermodynamics, taking energy from external sources, usually in the form of photons or the chemical bonds in foodstuffs (substrates), and using it to synthesize molecules such as DNA and proteins. Biosynthesis in present-day organisms entails elaborate chemical reactions that are unlikely to occur on their own, but readily take place in the presence of the appropriate enzymes. Since enzymes are proteins, and protein biosynthesis is catalyzed by enzymes, the overall process is said to be autocatalytic – cells are literally enabling themselves to make themselves, all in consultation with their regulated genomes.

Returning to gene expression, we can refine our concept by saying that an organism expresses particular sets of genes under particular sets of circumstances so that the appropriate structures are assembled and the appropriate biochemistry is catalyzed. The proximate goal is self-maintenance – each cell is configured, via elaborate feedback loops between its gene-expression system and its biochemistry, to acquire substrates and convert them into cellular components.

While the proximate goal of organisms is self-maintenance, the distal (ultimate) goal is to reproduce – to make copies of the genome and transmit them to the next generation. Present-day organisms boast a dazzling array of strategies for carrying out reproduction, from the simple act of dividing-in-two to the elaborate sexual strategies of animals, but the end result is the same: New organisms, endowed with the same kinds of genetic instructions as their parents, are brought forth into the world.

Common ancestry

All modern organisms carry out their business in much the same way: DNA-based genomes encode regulated instructions for engaging in appropriate self-assembly and self-maintenance; energetic substrates are converted biochemically into DNA, proteins, and other cellular components; and genome copies are transmitted to future generations. Scientific inquiry has established that the genes responsible for dictating these basal "housekeeping" activities, be it in humans, or flies, or maples, or amoebae, or bacteria, are very similar (homologous) to one another, as are the proteins they encode. This discovery has led to a core understanding: All modern organisms share a common ancestor that also had this same set of housekeeping genes and proteins. The common ancestor, denoted with an arrow in Figure 22.1, is estimated to have lived more than 3 billion years ago, and to have given rise to the three major radiations illustrated in Figure 22.1: the Archaea, the Bacteria, and the Eukaryotes.

Bacteria and Archaea are all small unicells and until recently were thought to be the same kind of organism, but they are now recognized as distinctive lineages.

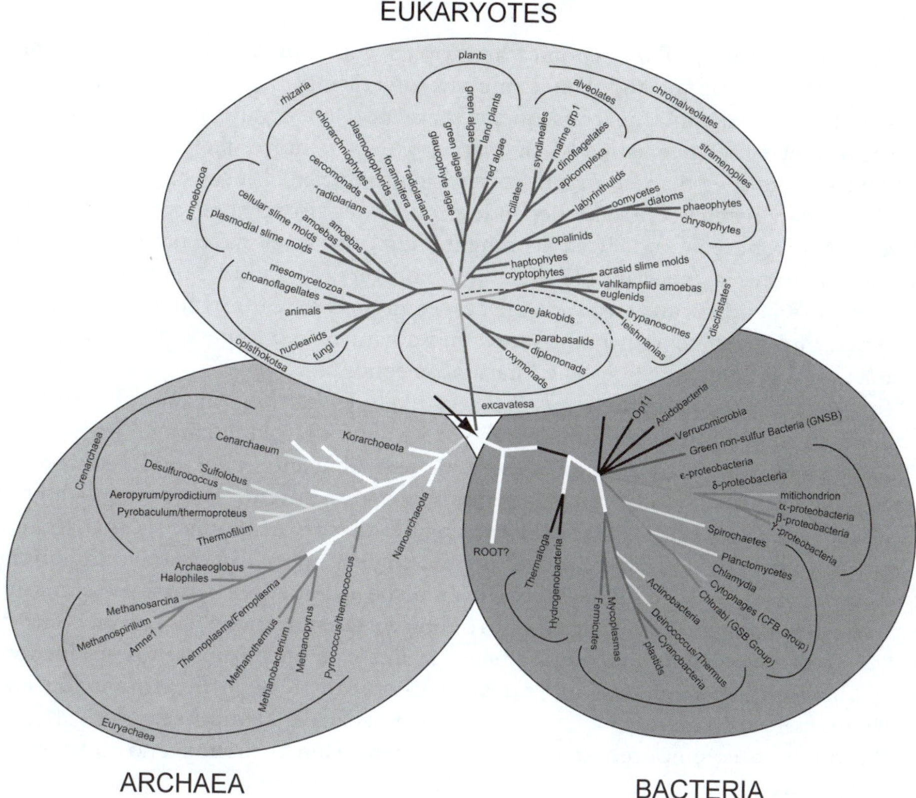

Figure 22.1 Three major domains of life (Archaea, Bacteria, and Eukaryotes) and their relationship to the common ancestor of all life (arrow)
Courtesy of Sandra Baldauf

Archaea are found in restricted environments (niches) such as hot springs, while bacteria are by far the most abundant organisms on the planet and inhabit countless niches. Eukaryotes, perhaps originating as a fusion between an archaeal and a bacterial cell, are often unicellular as well; but in several lineages, notably those found in the plant and opisthokont radiations (Figure 22.1), each organism is multicellular, with different cell types performing different functions that collectively assure the self-maintenance of the organism writ large. The two familiar multicellular lineages within the opisthokonts are the fungi and the animals, with humans being very recent members of the animal lineage.

The heart of the matter, then, is that all modern organisms trace back to the same common ancestor, and all carry out cellular activities using a homologous set of housekeeping genes/proteins; yet each lineage and each species is also distinctive, uniquely adapted to carrying out its life-perpetuating project in a particular niche. The process that simultaneously generated this conservation and this diversity is called biological evolution.

Biological evolution

During reproduction, DNA genomes are copied with impressive fidelity, but mistakes (mutations) occur and hence mutant organisms arise. The mutations are apparently random, but the consequences are not: an organism carrying mutant instructions is either not as likely, or just as likely, or more likely to self-maintain and hence reproduce than an organism carrying the original instructions, where the likelihood parameter is critically dependent on the environmental context in which those instructions play out. If environmental circumstances were uniform – if this were a homogenous, invariant planet – then biodiversity would be minimal. But that is not the case, and because it is not the case, a mutant set of instructions might be a non-starter in one environmental context and a winner in another. The process that generates this judgment call is called natural selection.

Mutations in housekeeping genes are very likely to be non-starters. The proteins specified by these genes are running the store, working with partner proteins to replicate DNA, or metabolize substrates, or assemble into structural cell components. Changing them is like randomly modifying a carburetor or a timing belt after it's already in synch with the rest of the engine: the usual outcome is that the car fails to run properly and often, as we say, the engine "dies." By contrast, mutations affecting more specialized traits involved in niche negotiation – such as taking up iron, resisting drought, finding a mate, avoiding a predator – may, in a given context, lead to a more successful outcome and hence facilitate an organism's self-reproduction, in which case these new ideas are expected to spread through the population and eventually perhaps play a role in defining a new species. Natural selection, that is, acts both to conserve housekeeping traits (selecting against variants) and to promote diversity in traits that relate to ecological adaptation (selecting for variants).

Origins of life

The common ancestor to all of modern life (Figure 22.1, arrow) had a regulated DNA-based genome and carried out a complex metabolism; therefore it could not have arisen from non-life in one fell swoop (save by miraculous intervention, an explanation not germane to naturalistic accounts). Instead, simpler forms of life must have arisen first, subsequently evolving into the common ancestral form. In considering what an early form of proto-life might look like, we can review our minimal list of features that characterize all present-day organisms:

(1) ability to capture and utilize energy from the environment
(2) self-maintenance
(3) reproduction
(4) capacity to evolve.

Sherman and Deacon (2007) offer a model (Figure 22.2) for a simple form of proto-life that displays these four features. As in all such models, it is assumed that the planet was already provisioned with molecules, like simple sugars, created via early Earth chemistry, perhaps in deep-sea vents. Sherman and Deacon propose that these

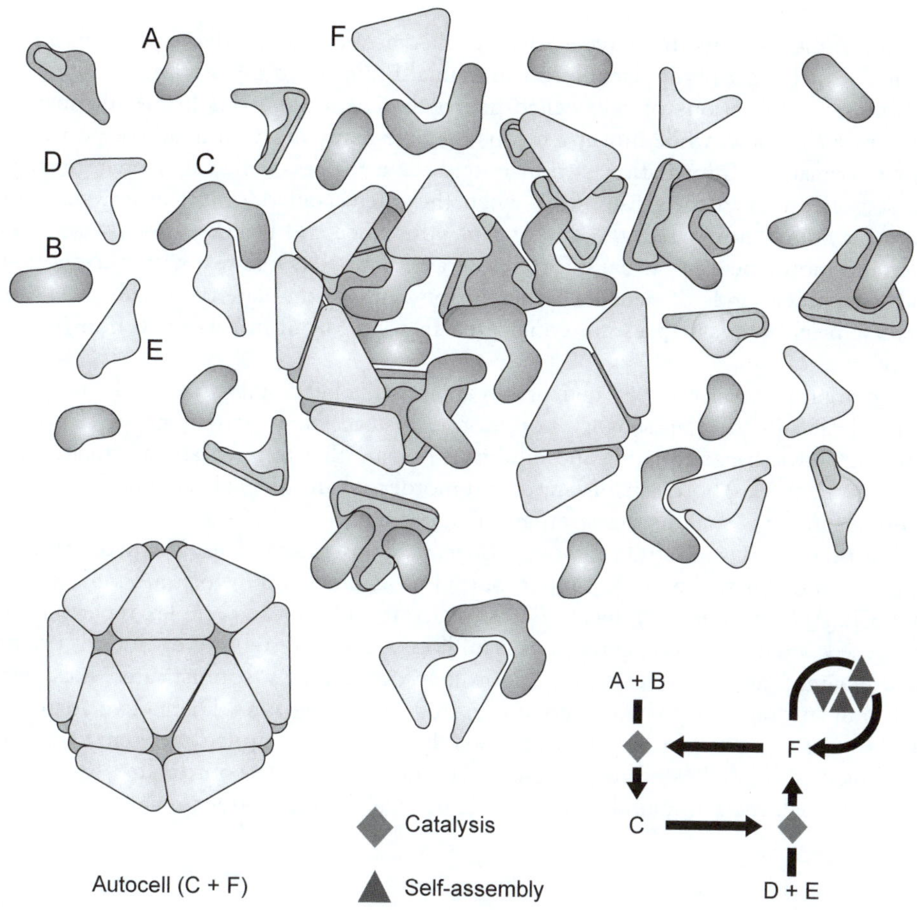

Figure 22.2 Autocell model. Substrates from primal soup (A + B) combine to form C, while substrates D + E combine to form F. F and C serve as catalysts for these two reactions; with each traverse of the cycle, more catalysts are made (hence an autocatalytic cycle). F also self-assembles to form a container around the catalytic set. This container occasionally disrupts, allowing fresh substrate to enter
Courtesy of Terrence Deacon

"primal soup" molecules came to serve as substrates for an autocatalytic biochemistry (feature 1 above), with one of the catalysts also serving as a self-assembling container that maintains the integrity of the catalytic set while allowing occasional substrate entry (2). They go on to suggest how such an entity, which they call an "autocell," might reproduce by breaking up and reconstituting itself (3), and how it might evolve when encountering novel substrates or circumstances (4), all in the absence of an independent informational system such as DNA. The autocell model, while fully hypothetical, lifts up for us the bare-bone necessities of being a life-form without being distracted by the complex traits that have evolved to service the well-being of present-day organisms.

Brains

Of the countless traits that have evolved to mediate ecological adaptation, we can be forgiven for having particular interest in animal brain-based perception.

Brains are collections of cells called neurons. Sensory neurons bring information in from the outside, while motor neurons mediate many of the animal's responses to that information. Information is transmitted via a process called neuronal "firing:" Sensory neurons in the nose "fire" when they detect an odorant; motor neurons from the spine "fire" when the doctor taps your knee and it jerks in response. Sensory and motor neurons usually form close associations (synapses) with one another and with other kinds of neurons, wherein they either stimulate or inhibit the firing of their neighbors (synapses are considered in more detail in a later section of this chapter).

The brain is a collection of neurons in an animal's head, and most of the neurons in the brain are neither sensory nor motor. Instead, they participate in elaborate synaptic networks, stimulating and inhibiting one another to integrate, modulate, and store (as memories) both sensory input and motor output. They also regulate complex internal functions such as digestion and respiration.

The brain of a well studied worm, *Caenorhabditis elegans*, has 312 neurons that suffice to coordinate the modest input–output modalities of the worm. A well studied mollusk, *Aplysia californica*, has c. 20,000 neurons and a more complex repertoire of integrated behaviors. During the c. 500 million years of vertebrate evolution, brains have enlarged and complexified to coordinate increasingly sophisticated lifestyles, with human brains estimated to contain c. 100 billion neurons. Distinctive anatomical domains of vertebrate brains (thalamus, hippocampus, optic lobes, etc.) contain neurons that are dedicated to particular activities, but all are coordinated to serve a common goal: the self-maintenance, and hence well-being, of the animal.

Emergence

We are now in a position to step back and consider our description of life from a perspective known as emergence. More detailed versions of the emergence paradigm are presented elsewhere (Goodenough and Deacon 2006; Sherman and Deacon 2007).

The core idea of emergence is summarized in the phrase "Something else from nothing but." A trait, such as the motility of a worm, entails numerous nothing-buts – the biochemistry mediated by housekeeping proteins in the muscle and nerve cells, the synthesis and self-assembly of the proteins involved in neuronal firing and muscle contraction, the correct positioning of the nerves and muscles during worm embryonic development. Motility does not proceed normally unless all of these underlying features are in place. Yet worm motility is something else than a collection of its constituent nothing-buts – it emerges as a consequence of their relationships to one another.

Key to our focus here is the fact that natural selection acts on emergent properties. Natural selection doesn't "see" the thermodynamics, or the genes, or the proteins; it only "sees" how the worm moves. If a worm's motility repertoire enables it to maintain itself and reproduce in its environmental context, then that form of motility, with all its underlying nothing-but features, is the form likely to be found in the next generation. If it functions less adequately than another form of worm motility, then it is less likely to be encountered in future generations.

Emergent properties arise in numerous non-living contexts as a consequence of thermodynamics and relationships between molecular shapes (morphodynamics); the surface tension of liquids and the patterns of snowflakes are familiar examples. The emergent properties that collectively constitute an organism – its biological traits – are also driven by thermodynamics and morphodynamics (recall how proteins fold into shapes that define their productive activities and their interactions). But biological traits have an additional feature: they are about something, for something. They have a purpose. They participate in an overall goal, an organism's well-being: worm motility is about finding food, and hydration, and mates. The advent of life introduced to the planet a novel parameter, driven by natural selection, that Deacon calls "teleodynamics" (*telos*: purpose). Living beings engage in regulated thermodynamics and morphodynamics *so that* teleodynamic outcomes emerge that perform functions of importance to the organism, functions that are then fodder for natural selection.

With this much background, we are in a position to develop a biological perspective on suffering and its manifestations in various kinds of beings, including humans.

Suffering from a biological perspective

To deflect a possible misunderstanding, it is important at the outset to address the matter of word choice. In the sections that follow, I will be attributing states such as awareness, and attention, and suffering to the likes of amoebae and plants. In doing this, I am not suggesting that such organisms are aware, and attentive, and suffer in the same fashion as the reader. Rather, I am lifting up biological commonalities in these states that extend across all life-forms. Once these commonalities are identified, we will give due consideration to their distinctive manifestations in particular kinds of organisms.

To develop a naturalistic account of suffering, we can begin with our minimalist autocell (Figure 22.2), and ask how it might evolve such that it is more likely to reproduce itself. An obvious innovation would be the acquisition of systems that take the measure of, and respond to, features of the environment. Thus, for example, if the container subunits of the autocell came to display binding sites for a substrate present in the primal soup, the substrate molecules would concentrate in the vicinity of the autocell and be more likely to enter when the container opens. Such binding sites, that is, would enable energy utilization (1 on our list above) and self-maintenance (2), the prerequisites for reproduction.

Such an environment-interactive system represents a prototype of what we can call awareness, a feature of all modern organisms (including viruses), and hence a feature of the common ancestor and presumably earlier forms of proto-life. The autocell, we would say, is aware of the useful substrate (via its binding sites) in the same way that a plant is aware of a light source (via its pigments), an animal is aware of a food source (via visual or odorant cues), and a virus is aware of a cell surface with which it can productively interact (via binding sites on its capsid). The autocell system is simpler than these modern systems, to be sure, but the basic idea is the same throughout.

We will have more to say about how awareness works in the next section; for present purposes it suffices to say that awareness systems monitor features of the environment that influence the self-maintenance of a particular kind organism. Some of these features are said to be hedonic (food source, mate source) and some noxious (toxins, predators). In multicellular organisms, distinct awareness systems are instantiated in distinct cell types – leaf cells deploy light-absorption systems while root cells deploy mineral uptake systems – and these are integrated to generate a flourishing outcome for the organism as a whole.

Importantly, awareness is restricted to relevant features of the environment: Plants selectively absorb wavelengths of light that they can use to drive photosynthesis (hedonic) and shield themselves from damaging wavelengths (noxious), while the remaining wavelengths are ignored. A given type of insect seeks particular kinds of food source and ignores most of what's out there. Another way of expressing this is to say that awareness systems focus an organism's attention on a subset of environmental features relevant to its well-being.

Organisms with awareness systems – that is, all organisms – also possess the capacity to ascertain whether or not all is well. If all is not well – if available light is too weak, or of the wrong wavelength – then organisms deploy what we can call, generically, amelioration systems (Latin, *meliorare*, to make better) that are intimately coupled with awareness. A hungry animal seeks food while a well fed animal rests; a poorly illuminated plant turns to grow towards favorable light while shielding itself from toxic light. Injured or infected plants and animals sense the insult and recruit molecules to the sites of injury or infection that repair the wounds and combat the pathogens. An organism is capable of self-maintenance, and hence reproduction, to the extent that it is aware of hedonic deficits and/or noxious excesses and can ameliorate these circumstances.

A well studied example of an amelioration system, found from bacteria to humans, is known as the heat-shock response. When organisms are subjected to higher-than-optimal temperatures, many of their proteins start to denature, losing their critical folded shapes, which threatens all housekeeping functions. The response is an up-regulated expression of a number of genes encoding "chaperones" that bind to the compromised proteins and keep them from degenerating further until temperatures return to normal.

Organisms whose amelioration systems fail to cope with an adversity like heat shock are organisms that die. Organisms experiencing no adverse circumstances, either because none has arisen or because pre-existing difficulties have been resolved, are organisms in a state of well-being. This leaves us with organisms that are actively dealing with difficult circumstances.

I suggest that these organisms are in a state of biological suffering. The Latin etymology of suffer is to bear up (*ferre*, to bear; *sub*, up), where a close synonym is to endure (*durare*; to harden). Amelioration entails expending effort; attention is actively focused on resolving the situation. During this process, the organism is struggling, is under stress, is suffering.

Such a perspective on suffering allows us to speak of degrees of biological suffering. A plant in low light suffers less than a plant in long-term darkness. A plant in darkness that is also responding to heat shock is suffering to a yet greater extent, and if it is also drying out, its suffering may cross the life–death border. Biological suffering has both qualitative (which amelioration systems are operating) and quantitative (how many in total) dimensions, whether manifested in a bacterium or a human being.

Biological suffering versus experienced suffering

From a naturalistic perspective, amelioration systems are adaptive – indeed, they are essential – and the suffering endured during the deployment of these systems can therefore be considered as "the price paid" to avoid death and achieve well-being. Left to be addressed is how suffering is experienced by a suffering organism, a question that quickly moves to the question of how a given organism experiences its experience in general.

To approach this question, it is helpful to consider the awareness trait from an emergence perspective.

We began our consideration of awareness with the simplest case: an autocell carrying a binding site for a needed substrate on the outer surface of its container. Molecules that detect specific features of the environment, or detect products produced by other cells in a multicellular organism, are called receptors. In present-day cells, receptors are usually proteins associated with the lipid membrane that surrounds each cell. When modern receptors are activated by external stimuli, they change their shape, a shape-change that is detected by a second protein inside that cell, which in turn changes its shape, stimulating a shape change in a third molecule, and so on, a sequence called a signal-transduction cascade. Activation of the cascade informs the cell of the stimulus, and the cell initiates an appropriate response, such as moving towards (hedonic) or away from (noxious) the stimulus, or altering its biochemistry and/or gene expression in some way.

The full circuit – receptor-based awareness, signal transduction, and appropriate response – can be called sentience. The nothing-buts of sentience are the receptors and the transduction-cascade and response components; the emergent property can be called cellular sentience, a feature of all cells, be they single-celled organisms or members of a multicellular organism. Your fat cells, for example, carry receptors for the hormone insulin; when the pancreas secretes insulin in response to high blood glucose, insulin binds to the fat-cell receptors, eliciting a signal-transduction cascade, the outcome being that the fat cells take up glucose from the blood and convert it into storage lipid. The fat cell is made aware of the glucose situation via the hormonal signal, and responds in an adaptive fashion. Your fat cells have blood-glucose sentience, whereas most of your other cell types lack this trait.

Animals, as we have said, came up with specialized cells called neurons that mediate much of their sentience. Neuronal nothing-buts are simple variants on the nothing-buts of cellular sentience. Sensory neurons carry receptors for the external stimuli they are specialized to detect, such as light by the eye and odorants by the nose, and their shape changes elicit the signal-transduction cascade we call neuronal firing. When a firing cascade reaches a synapse, the excited neuron secretes small hormones called neurotransmitters, and the neuron at the other side of the synapse carries receptors for these neurotransmitters. Neurotransmitter/receptor binding causes the second neuron to fire, which in turn releases neurotransmitters to excite, or perhaps inhibit, the third neuron down the line, and so on. We can call this modality neuronal sentience, and when, as is the case for most animals, some or most of the neurons reside in brains, we can speak of brain-based sentience.

Human brains have evolved the apparently unique capacity to manipulate the symbolic systems we call language, generating the emergent modality we can call symbolic sentience (Deacon 1998). Apparently emergent from symbolic sentience is our sense of an "I-self," the narrative being that wakes up in the morning and falls asleep at night and dominates what we often call our consciousness. Hence we can also speak of "I-self sentience," which is experienced as being immaterial and even ethereal. While we can offer precise accounts of how neuronal sentience emerges from its nothing-buts, and we understand some features of how brain-based sentience arises, a scientific understanding of the emergence of symbolic and I-self sentience in human brains is not yet on offer.

This brief consideration of awareness and sentience systems positions us to consider our question: How is experience – in this case the experience of sentience – experienced? Does a fat cell experience its sentience of the insulin response? Most would say no, perhaps arguing that it is only organisms that have experiences, and the fat cell is but part of an organism. But that doesn't get us very far. Does a single-celled organism such as an amoeba experience its food-source sentience? Does a worm experience its sentience of a potential mate? How might we think about these things?

We humans, of course, carry a strong bias here because we each hold an I-self account of what it's like to experience our version of experience, and hence what it's like to experience suffering, and we assume that all humans experience experience, and hence suffering, in familiar ways. But we quickly move onto soft sand as we extend these inferences to non-humans. Granted that all organisms suffer in the biological sense, does a bacterium experience suffering? Or does it just undergo biological suffering? How about a plant? A caterpillar? A dog? As this list moves "up" the ladder to organisms with increasingly complex nervous systems, our tendency to attribute shared experience, and hence shared suffering experience, tends to increase, but when challenged, we realize that we don't *really* know what it's like to be any other organism except ourselves (an experience that is often pretty mystifying as well).

So when is suffering biological suffering alone, and when is it also experienced suffering? If we set the bar at having a nervous system, this means that most of the suffering that has occurred, and is now occurring, on the planet is non-experienced, since most organisms lack nervous systems. The food-deprived amoeba or bacterium, the plant plunged in darkness or subject to a wound, pays the suffering price, but does not feel the price.

But even nervous systems don't provide a clear cut-off. When we watch a fly thrashing about in a spider's web, it looks like it's experiencing suffering: we have no difficulty mapping its frantic chaotic movements onto our feeling states were we in such circumstances. But are the neuronal signals simply telling the fly to pay attention to the need to ameliorate the situation, or is the fly experiencing anything in the way of anguish or frustration? Does the fly have an "I," a non-language-based self-knowledge, that suffers? We can hold opinions on this axis – and some religious traditions offer tenets on this point – but no-one knows for sure.

Suffering and physical pain

Our naturalistic proposition holds that an organism is aware of hedonic and noxious features of its environment that are relevant to its well-being, and is in a state of suffering while its amelioration systems are acting to correct a dearth of the hedonic or an excess of the noxious. That said, the term "suffering" is commonly associated with an excess of adversity rather than with a dearth of the good. Moreover, the occurrence of pain is usually included in this perspective, as in the common locution "pain and suffering." Hence the remainder of the chapter focuses on adversity and pain.

The term "nociception" is used to describe the ability to detect and respond to aversive/noxious environmental stimuli. Sophisticated nociception systems are found in bacteria and single-celled eukaryotes (Rogers *et al.* 2007), mediated by elaborate receptors and signal-transduction cascades; hence nervous systems are clearly not required for nociception.

With invertebrate animals, we come to an interesting juncture. Whereas invertebrates are richly endowed with sensory neurons that mediate nociception (Tobin and Bargmann 2004; Hwang *et al.* 2007; Barr *et al.* 2008), they apparently lack the kind of sensory neuron, called the nociceptor, that mediates the sensation of vertebrate pain. To quote from Somme (2005):

> Several examples are known in which insects continue with normal activities even after severe injury. An insect walking with a crushed foot will apply it to the substrate with undiminished force. Locusts have been seen to continue feeding whilst being eaten themselves by preying mantis, and aphids continue to feed when eaten by coccinelid beetles. A male mantis continues to mate although eaten by his partner, and a tsetse fly will try to suck blood although half dissected during an experiment.

Hence the sensation of pain as we humans would describe it is apparently a vertebrate invention: nociceptors are restricted to fish (Ashley *et al.* 2007) and the land vertebrates. That fly caught in a web is clearly suffering, and it may or may not be experiencing its suffering, but it is apparently not experiencing pain.

The firing of nociceptors can be thought of as an adaptive add-on to nociception systems: It stimulates, via synaptic interactions with other systems, withdrawal behaviors and attention to an injury (such as "favoring" an injured limb); it also stimulates learning/memory to avoid dangerous activities in the future. Rare humans with a congenital absence of pain perception are highly compromised, subject to severe burns and self-inflicted bites of the tongue and lips.

Figure 22.3 summarizes some of the genes involved in establishing the human pain response in the brain, spinal cord, and peripheral tissues; the full complexity of the pain system is covered in several excellent reviews (Diatchenko *et al.* 2007; Foulkes and Wood 2008). While many domains of the brain are involved in pain processing (the "pain matrix" in Figure 22.3), a key region is the anterior cingulate cortex/gyrus, which is in turn differentiated into at least four sub-regions. In addition to pain, this region is also involved in processing both positive (happy) and negative (sad) emotions (Vogt 2005; Fujiwara *et al.* 2009).

To the extent that the pain response operates to reinforce nociception, and hence the amelioration process, it can be considered a useful trait. Moreover, analgesics and meditative/acupuncture practices are available that mitigate or abolish the acute pain resulting from injury or medical procedures, and these have greatly abated the pain component of human and domesticated animal suffering. Indeed, persons

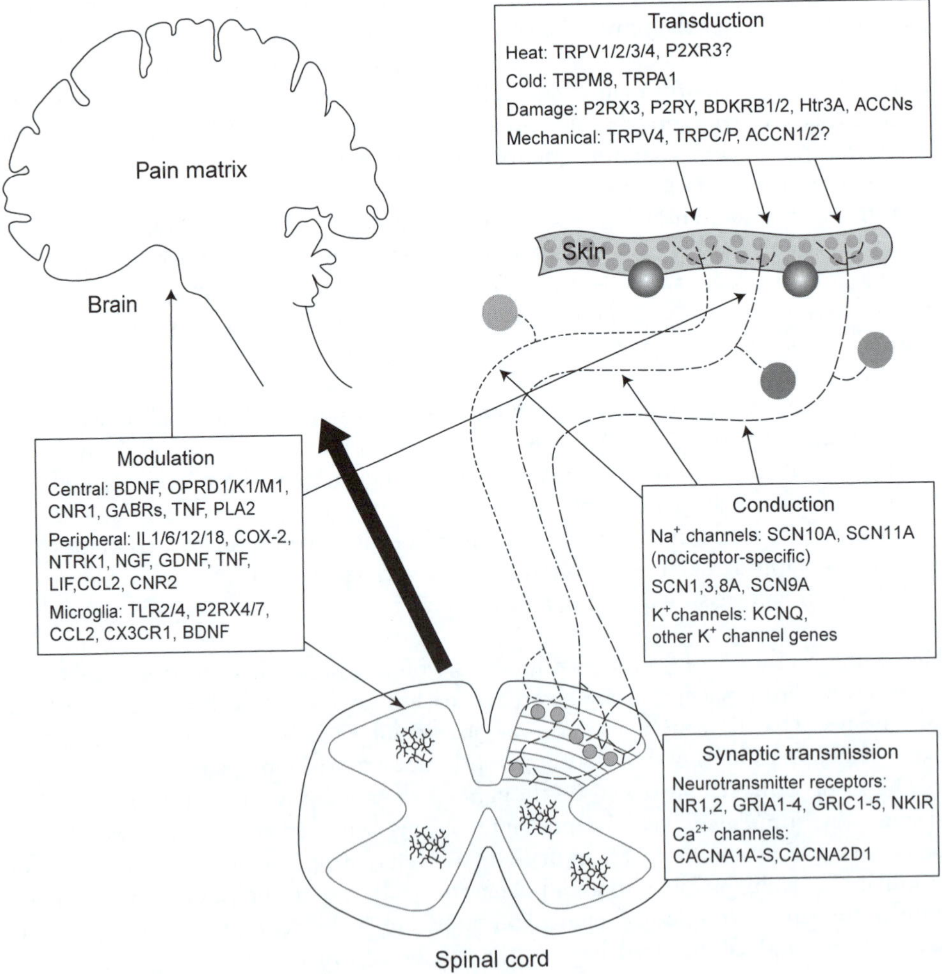

Figure 22.3 Genes associated with the human pain response (Foulkes and Wood 2008)

medicated for pain may report that they are not suffering, even while their bodily amelioration systems are frantically attempting to remedy the situation.

That said, it is estimated that 15–20 per cent of human adults live with some form of chronic physical pain that is not obviously in the service of amelioration systems and is unresponsive to analgesics or other practices (Diatchenko *et al.* 2007). Here we encounter an example of things gone awry: Acute pain may be adaptive, but chronic pain is clearly not: it is a "dysfunctional sensation" (Foulkes and Wood 2007) wherein suffering is not moving towards a corrective outcome. Suffering has become uncoupled from resolution.

Suffering and social pain

Many animals, including humans, are social, and a key factor in the well-being of any social organism involves functional, coherent relationships with group members and an understanding of one's place in the group. Many cognitive and emotional systems are involved in human sociality (Behrens *et al.* 2009), and suffering results when these are in deficit, much as when physical needs are in deficit.

For humans, at least, dysfunctional social integration – being excluded from a group, for example, or feeling envy towards another – is painful; we speak of the agony of shame and the anguish of loneliness. Interestingly, regions of the brain's anterior cingulated cortex, noted above as involved in physical pain, have been implicated in such experiences of "social pain" (Eisenberger *et al.* 2003; Takahashi *et al.* 2009), suggesting evolutionary overlaps in the development of the two pain systems. In addition, the anterior cingulate cortex has been shown to be active when persons are witnessing, and experiencing empathy with, the pain of others (Singer *et al.* 2004), a feature also attributed to so-called "mirror neurons" in the inferior frontal gyrus (Kilner *et al.* 2009).

As is the case with physical pain, the acute pain of a social rejection or a struggle with envy can be considered adaptive, calling attention to the need to repair relationships, whereas the chronic pain of a social disability, or the pain induced by a malevolent social context, is invariably debilitating, and often loops back to manifest itself in bodily disorders. Here again, suffering can become uncoupled from resolution.

Suffering and psychological pain

Given that our I-selves are deeply socially constructed (Taylor 1989), social and psychological pain often overlap. That said, we can become steeped in private anguish, be it from acute distress (e.g. loss of job), or chronic distress, as with mood disorders (e.g. depression) or challenged reality perception (e.g. psychosis). As with physical and social pain, psychological pain can trigger the search for remediation, often undertaken in psychotherapeutic or religious contexts. Pharmaceutical intervention is increasingly able to blunt the suffering wrought by mood disorders, but many chronic "mental disorders" remain as stubbornly untreatable as chronic physical or social pain.

The long view of suffering

The long evolutionary view of suffering is that it is an inherent feature of life. All creatures, and likely even the first forms of proto-life, are endowed with sentience systems that pay attention to relevant parameters, and activate amelioration systems when those parameters are found wanting, such that well-being is restored. Suffering is part of the package, the price paid for the gift of being alive at all. And, no matter where one places the bar that distinguishes organisms that "feel" their suffering from those that do not, the fact that suffering is part of the overall package offers, I would suggest, a kind of solace. As long as one is suffering/enduring, then one is still alive, and the hope for a return to well-being – as contrasted with death – is still on offer.

That said, we have also lifted up conditions in which suffering becomes decoupled from resolution and takes on a life of its own, as with chronic physical, social, or psychological pain that derives from unidentifiable sources or from sources that fail to respond to applied amelioration systems. A possible form of solace for persons in these situations is the understanding that this suffering is not their "fault," that a system designed to be adaptive has, in their case, gone awry through no agency of their own. It's difficult enough to suffer helplessly; feeling guilty about it only makes things worse.

While suffering is a biological trait, the concept can be extended, metaphorically, to social systems. Social systems can also be said to suffer as they seek to resolve impasses, such as injustice or poverty, that threaten their well-being. Again, the long view insists that such suffering is worth the effort, and human history records that, over the long haul, we are making halting progress in societal amelioration.

References

Ashley, P. J., L. U. Sneddon and C. R. McCrohan (2007) "Nociception in Fish: Stimulus–Response Properties of Receptors on the Head of Trout *Oncorhnchus mykiss*," *Brain Research* 1166: 47–54.

Barr, S., P. R. Laming, J. T. A. Dick and R. W. Elwood (2008) "Nociception or Pain in a Decapod Crustacean?," *Animal Behavior* 75: 745–51.

Behrens, T. E. J., L. T. Hunt and M. F. S. Rushworth (2009) "The Computation of Social Behavior," *Science* 324: 1160–64.

Deacon, T. W. (1998) *The Symbolic Species: The Co-Evolution of Language and the Brain*, New York: Norton.

Diatchenko, L., A. G. Nackley, I. E. Tchivileva, S. A. Shabalina and W. Maixner (2007) "Genetic Architecture of Human Pain Perception," *Trends in Genetics* 23: 605–13.

Eisenberger, N. I., M. D. Lieberman and K. D. Williams (2003) "Does Rejection Hurt? An fMRI Study of Social Exclusion," *Science* 302: 290–92.

Foulkes, T. and J. N. Wood (2008) "Pain Genes," *PLoS Genetics* 4: 1–9.

Fujiwara, J., P. N. Tobler, M. Taira, T. Iijima, and K.-I. Tsutsui (2009) "Segregated and Integrated Coding of Reward and Punishment in the Cingulated Cortex," *Journal of Neurophysiology* 101: 3284–93.

Goodenough, U. and T. W. Deacon (2006) "The Sacred Emergence of Nature," in *The Oxford Handbook of Religion and Science*, P. Clayton and Z. Simpson (eds), New York: Oxford University Press, 854–71.

Hwang, R. Y., L. Zhong, Y. Xu, T. Johnson, F. Zhang, K. Delsseroth and W. D. Tracey (2007) "Nociceptive Neurons Protect *Drosophila* Larvae from Parasitoid Wasps," *Current Biology* 17: 2105–16.

Julius, D. and A. I. Basbaum (2001) "Molecular Mechanisms of Nociception," *Nature* 413: 203–10.

Kilner, J. M., A. Neal, N. Weiskopf, K. J. Friston and C. D. Frith (2009) "Evidence of Mirror Neurons in the Human Inferior Frontal Gyrus," *Journal of Neuroscience* 29: 10153–59.

Rogers, L. F., K. L. Markle and T. M. Hennessey (2007) "Responses of the Ciliates *Tetrahymena* and *Paramecium* to Vertebrate Odorants and Tastants," *Journal of Eukaryotic Microbiology* 55: 27–33.

Sherman, J. and T. W. Deacon (2007) "Teleology for the Perplexed: How Matter Began to Matter," *Zygon* 42: 873–901.

Singer, T., B. Seymour, J. O'Doherty, H. Kaube, R. J. Dolan and C. D. Frith (2004) "Empathy for Pain Involves the Affective but not Sensory Components of Pain," *Science* 303: 1157–62.

Somme, L. S. (2005) "Sentience and Pain in Invertebrates. Report to Norwegian Scientific Committee for Food Safety," http://jillium.nfshost.com/library/pain.htm.

Takahashi, H., M. Kato, M. Matsuura, D. Miobbs, T. Suhara and Y. Okubo (2009) "When Your Gain is My Pain and Your Pain is My Gain: Neural Correlates of Envy and *Schadenfreude*," *Science* 323: 937–39.

Taylor, C. (1989) *Sources of the Self: The Making of Modern Identity*, Cambridge MA: Harvard University Press.

Tobin, D. M. and C. I. Bargmann (2004) "Invertebrate Nociception: Behaviors, Neurons, and Molecules," *Journal of Neurobiology* 61: 161–74.

Vogt, B. A. (2005) "Pain and Emotion Interactions in Subregions of the Cingulated Gyrus," *Nature Reviews Neuroscience* 6: 533–44.

23
SUFFERING THROUGH TO SOMETHING HIGHER

Holmes Rolston, III

The Darwinian world is often said to be "red in tooth and claw," recalling Tennyson's phrase (1850). Some biologists continue to speak of "survival of the fittest," though most prefer to characterize the process as "survival of the better adapted" – recognizing that various skills, not just bloodshed, contribute to survival. The central determinant is the struggle for life. Such struggle is not present in all causal relations; there is none in astronomy or geology. It appears in biology, where over evolutionary time the fight for life deepens into sentience, and sentience into suffering.

Darwinians were not the first to realize that struggles drive life. That is an ancient truth, found, for instance, in the first noble truth of Buddhism. Theodicy has been a perennial task in theology. But struggle for survival has come to be seen as the paradigm truth in biology, where nothing makes sense without it. This forces philosophers and theologians to see what sense they can make of it.

Stress versus suffering

Ursula Goodenough chooses to use the term "suffer" to describe any organism under stress. In her use, plants suffer, as do microbes. She appeals to the Latin etymology, to bear up (*ferre*, to bear; *sub*, up). "Endure" is a close synonym, from the root *durare*, to harden. All organisms have "awareness" – she says – through which they focus "attention;" and, facing threat, they have coping "amelioration systems" which can make things better. Plants detect and act upon environmental signals. A protozoan moves up a gradient toward light or away from a toxic substance. In simpler organisms, an aversive action is "just" suffering, not "experienced" suffering.

She can, of course, stipulate such meanings; she must also realize that she is stretching more common meanings of these terms. In the usage of most English speakers, "unexperienced suffering" is a contradiction in terms. If a physician reported: "The patient is suffering but doesn't feel anything," we would hardly know what to think. Biologists do commonly say that plants are "irritable," may be under "stress," "healthy," or "sick."

The terms above are found in ordinary English, but Goodenough has a more technical term: "nociception," which describes "the ability to detect and respond to aversive/noxious environmental stimuli." This is present in organisms without neurons, such as plants. Other organisms (perhaps insects) have the kinds of neurons that detect such threats, but lack the kinds of neurons that register pain. Pain seems to arise in vertebrates. These pain-generating neurons are called nociceptors, although she also tells us that there is nociception without neurons. There she is atypical; most define "nocioception" as "the neural process of encoding and processing noxious stimuli."

While I generally agree with what she is trying to say, I would phrase it differently. Plants clearly defend their own lives. Plants make themselves; they repair injuries; they move water, nutrients, and photosynthate from cell to cell; they store sugars; they make tannin and other toxins and regulate their levels in defense against grazers; they make nectars and emit pheromones to influence the behavior of pollinating insects; they emit allelopathic agents to suppress invaders. They can reject genetically incompatible grafts. As much as animals, they are tested for adapted fit, for their capacity, in Goodenough's term, to "endure." Their stress, by my account, stops short of suffering.

Felt experience, neural suffering

As most biologists would use these terms, "pain" comes only with neurons, when there appears, in Goodenough's terms, "experienced suffering." In evolutionary natural history, there are two singularities. The first, from the origin of life onward, is the evolution of the genetic capacity to store and process information, genotypes producing functional, adapted phenotypes. But with neuronal nets of increasing complexity, life crosses another singularity: the threshold of felt experience.

As with everything else in evolutionary development, this crossing and its subsequent development will have taken place gradually, but that ought not to obscure the fact that there is momentous emergent novelty. Both scientists and philosophers seek to have precise concepts, clear definitions, daylight or dark, but discover a world with increments across twilight zones. With increasing neuronal complexity, there appears *inwardness*, felt experiences. With still more, there appear what philosophers call *qualia*, consciously entertained experiential mental states such as sensations, feelings, perceptions, desires. Increasingly, there is "somebody there." There appears phenomenology of experience, as when a person (or a rat?) smells strong cheese. Across the spectrum, there is agency, awareness, in the sense that action is provoked by felt stimuli, but only with increasing neuronal sophistication is there self-awareness, reflective inwardness. (Compare the difficulty of analysis here with reflecting on a person's own coming into existential being – fetus, newborn, infant, child, adult.)

Goodenough here portrays simple neurology as little different from other cellular reactive responses. "Neuronal nothing-buts are simple variants on the nothing-buts of cellular sentience." A neuron in an eye registers light; a root cell in a plant registers water. She can easily do this, given the way she uses "awareness." She can then move to "brain-based awareness." She may be right about whatever were the simplest neurons in earliest evolutionary history, perhaps right about some today (such as the simplest neurons in an ant). Next, Goodenough moves to human brains with their "emergent modality we can call symbolic sentience," and emerging from that "our sense of an 'I-self,' the narrative being that wakes up in the morning […] and dominates what we often call our consciousness." There is, as she well knows, several billion years of evolutionary emergence telescoped here, with radical transformations.

Just when and how there appeared what might be a precursor to neurons is not known; with some evidence this was about 700 million years ago. The diversity of existing nervous systems is enormous. Some scientists have wondered if nerves evolved independently more than once, although recent opinion, based on genetic and molecular analysis, indicates a single (monophyletic) origin (Hirth and Reichart 2007). The most primitive organisms to possess a nervous system are cnidarians, a phylum of mostly marine animals. In their diffuse nervous systems (as found in jellyfish, sea anemones, corals), nerve cells are distributed throughout the organism, often organized into nerve nets with synapse-like connections, perhaps with ganglia, local concentrations of neurons that are more highly connected. Sensory neurons connect with effector neurons without central integration. Presumably there is present some diffuse experience of feeling; it is difficult to know.

Central nervous systems evolve later. It is not known when they first appeared nor what their earliest function was. The presumed earliest ancestors are identified as "urbilateria," of which there are fossil traces (Arendt *et al.* 2008). Flatworms exhibit bilateral symmetry, breaking previously radial symmetry. This more is different. The nervous system evolves to consist of longitudinal nerve cords, with peripheral nerves connecting to sensory cells, and at one end a "brain," as for instance in the two joined cephalic ganglia in *Planaria*. There does appear to be present felt experience, though such mental states are simple (Tye 1997). There are endorphins (natural opiates) in earthworms, which indicates both that they suffer and that they are naturally provided with pain buffers (Alumets *et al.* 1979). So nerve cells appear and radically elaborate capacities across evolutionary history.

There is a sense, however, in which tracing this as incremental elaboration obscures the radical, startling innovation of organisms with felt experience (subjects) in what were before living organisms devoid of such felt experience (objects). The evolutionary account can seem to deliver felt experience bit by bit, rather than swiftly, but it is also true that felt experience appears where absolutely none was before. Incremental qualities joined and rejoined are also re-formed and transformed into novel qualities. One gets, at length, pleasure and pain by organizing millions of unfeeling atoms.

Slowing things down and putting together molecular parts does not really alleviate the lack of theory explaining how inwardness comes out of outwardness. It only spreads the inexplicable element thinly, rather than asking us to swallow it in one lump. No doubt there was an evolutionary genesis of neurally based mind, capable of conscious pleasures and pains. But we have no logic by which one derives biological conclusions out of physical premises, and, taking these as premises in turn, one then derives psychological conclusions.

The molecular accounts of ionic currents and chemistries in neurons describe the technical conditions necessary for the production of subjective experience, with no account of the necessary or intelligible derivation of what emerges. "Nobody has the slightest idea how anything material could be conscious. Nobody even knows what it would be like to have the slightest idea about how anything material could be conscious" (Fodor 1992: 5).

Goodenough is agnostic about whether non-neural organisms can be said to "experience" suffering, though fairly confident that they "suffer," since they have her "awareness." She is not willing to "set the bar at having a nervous system" since the wounded plant "pays the suffering price, but does not feel the price," leaving us back at her puzzle of unfelt suffering. Perhaps her main point is that we hardly know what to think, and, put that way, she does have a point. It is difficult to extrapolate to animal levels and make judgments about the extent of their suffering.

A safe generalization is that pain becomes less intense as we go down the phylogenetic spectrum, and is often not as acute in the non-human as in the human worlds (Eisemann *et al.* 1984). The main evidence for this is their simpler neurology and absence of pain-like behavior – as in the case that Goodenough cites of insects continuing to eat while they are themselves being eaten.

Pain in evolutionary and cultural history

Each seeming advance – from plants to animals, from instinct to learning, from sentience to self-awareness, from nature to culture – steps up the pain. Earthen natural history might almost be called the evolution of suffering. But it would be equally plausible to call it the evolution of caring. Pain is both experientially and logically in counterpoint to pleasure, but Goodenough tends to let the evolution of pleasure lie in the background of her account.

Another generalization from both evolutionary and cultural history is that all advances come in contexts of problem solving, with a central problem in sentient life the prospect of hurt. In the evolution of caring, the organism is quickened to its needs. The body can better defend itself by evolving a neural alarm system. There are logical and empirical connections between the heroic and the harsh elements in life.

An organism can have needs, which is not possible in inert physical nature, a feature simultaneously of its pro-life program and of the requirement that it overtake materials and energy. If the environment can be a good to it, that brings also the possibility of deprivation as a harm. To be alive is to have problems. Things can go wrong just because they can also go right. In an open, developmental ecological system, no other way is possible. All this first takes place at insentient levels, where there is bodily duress, as when a plant needs water.

Sentience, arriving with neuronal perception, brings the capacity to move about deliberately in the world, and also to get hurt by it. Some insects might have sense organs – sight or hearing – without any capacity to be pained by them. But sentience is not invented to permit mere observation of the world. It rather evolves to awaken some concern for it. In developing animal life, sentience with its counterpart, suffering, is an incipient form of love and freedom – to risk again stretching some terms. A neural animal can love something in its world and is free to seek this, a capacity greatly advanced over anything known in immobile, insentient plants. It has the power to move through, and experientially to evaluate, the environment. The appearance of sentience is the appearance of caring. The earthen story is not merely of goings on, but of "going concerns."

Pain is an energizing force, as much as it is disequilibrating. Suffering not only goes back-to-back with caring sentience, it drives life toward pleasurable fulfillment. Not only does the good presuppose concomitant evil, but the evil is enlisted in the service of the good. We come up in the world against suffering, but we could not come up in the world any other way. This truth is both paradoxical and partial, but nevertheless it penetrates into the essence of pain. Individually, one wants to be rid of pain, and yet pain's threat is self-organizing. It forces alarm, action, rest, withdrawal. It immobilizes for healing.

Early and provident fear moves half the world. Suffering, far more than theory, principle, or faith, moves us to action. We should not posit the half-truth for the whole; we are drawn by affections quite as much as pushed by fears. These work in tandem reinforcement; one passes over into the other and is often its obverse. In this sense, pain is a pro-life force. Not all suffering is thrust upon us from without; much of it comes from internal collapse, as with the pains of failing life in age or cancer. Even here, the body typically does things that make sense in fighting the collapse, postponing the end, although death is inevitable. The death of individuals is superseded by what this makes possible, new exploratory forms, mutant beings, which will be selected for their better adaptedness to the problems that beset their progenitors. Where pain fits into evolutionary theory, it must have, on statistical average, high survival value, with this selected for.

There is "social suffering" (in Goodenough's term) as when one is ostracized, or loses a job. This, like physical suffering, can be adaptive. The ostracized may reform and become more cooperative; those who seek and find work support both themselves and their societies. A frequent distinction here distinguishes between pain and affliction. Animals can endure pain, but not affliction, since the latter requires reflective capacities about being wronged, mistreated, unlucky, pensive about "nature, red in tooth and claw," and so on. In humans the relationship between bodily wounding or deprivation and pain is quite complex, involving cognitive factors such as cultural conditioning and psychological evaluation of the situation. In psychological experience, there can be no will without a testing of will. There can be no compassion without pain.

Such benefits are the biological and psychological purpose of pain, even though there is an overshooting of this in cases where pain is of no benefit to, and even crazes, particular sufferers. Such dysfunctional pain Goodenough calls "chronic pain." Here suffering has "gone awry" and is not correcting anything gone wrong. All that she has to say about counterproductive suffering is that those in such chronic suffering, physical or social, may take some solace in that their suffering is not "their fault." Of course, only humans have such reflective capacities. It should be possible here to inquire further whether selection for adapted fit might trim such counterproductive pain back toward productive levels. If the pain is not serving any adaptive function on average, it will not be selected for. If it results in reduced reproduction, it will be selected against.

This increase of suffering can be put bleakly. Each organism is doomed to eat or be eaten, to stake out what living it can, competing with others. Perhaps there is more efficiency than waste, more fecundity than indifference, but each organism is ringed about with competitors and limits, forced to do or die. Each is set as much against the world as supported within it. But, seen more systemically, the context of creativity logically and empirically requires this context of conflict and resolution. The system, from the perspective of the individual, is built on competition and premature death. The generating and testing of selves by conflict and resolution is prolific, filling up habitats with better adapted fits. Organisms occupy niches providing life support, in an ecology of inter-dependent, mutually supporting species.

Suffering and creativity

The result of such struggle is cybernetic creativity. In what he calls a "twenty-first century view of evolution," James A. Shapiro concludes: "Thus, just as the genome has come to be seen as a highly sophisticated information storage system, its evolution has become a matter of highly sophisticated information processing" (Shapiro 1998: 10, 2005). The genome, a reservoir of previously discovered genetic know-how, is both conserving this and constantly generating further variations (new alleles), tested in the life of the organism (the phenotype). The better adapted (better informed) variants produce more descendants. What is novel on Earth is this explosive power to generate vital information. In this sense, biology radically transcends physics and chemistry.

The emergence of neural networks deepens the cybernetic dimensions of life. A neuron is functionally "for" information detection and transfer. Advancing neural development makes possible acquired learning, discovering information and storing it for future use in the lifetime of the individual. Behavior is more labile, less stereotyped. Increased capacities to suffer are concomitant with, and perhaps inseparable from, increased powers of cognition – broadly speaking. This means humans can suffer more than birds, and birds more than ants, made possible by increasing neuronal capacities. Within species, however, this need not mean that Einstein suffers more than the village idiot.

Although, realizing this, the cybernetic dimension of life helps to correct an over-emphasis on the accidental, the wandering in evolutionary development, this account can be misleading if it leads to an over-emphasis on the computational. An organism is not hardware, not software, but "wetware," struggling to survive and to maintain its kind. No computers reproduce themselves by passing a single set of minute coding sequences from one generation of computers to the next, like sperm and egg, with the next generation of computers self-organizing from this single transferred information set. Storing, retrieving, and using information are certainly important. But cognitive processors as such do not suffer; they do not grow hungry, fear pain, risk their lives caring for a next generation of young, or seek to avoid death. This is an agentive, emotive, affective cybernetics of historically developing, storied life.

An environment entirely hostile would slay life; life could never have appeared within it. An environment entirely irenic would stagnate life; advanced life, including human life, could never have appeared there either. Oppositional nature is the first half of the truth; the second is that none of life's explosive advance is possible without this dialectical stress. Muscles, teeth, eyes, ears, noses, fins, legs, wings, scales, hair, hands, brains – all these, and almost everything else, come out of the need to make a way through a world that mixes environmental resistance with environmental conductance.

Mobility is inseparably related to predation. We admire the muscle and power, the sentience and skills that could only have evolved in predation. Autotrophs synthesize their own food; heterotrophs eat something else. Could we have had a world with only flora, no fauna? Possibly not, since in a world in which things are assembled, something has to disassemble them for recycling. A photosynthetic world would be a largely immobile world. Some species must sit around and soak up sunlight; other species will capture this value to fuel mobility. Still other species will rise higher on the trophic pyramid, funded by capturing resources from below for greater achievements in sentience, cognition, and mobility.

No-one thinks that a merely floral world would be of more value than a world with fauna also. In a floral world, there would be no-one to think. Heterotrophs must be built on autotrophs, and no autotrophs are sentient or cerebral. Could there have been only plant-eating fauna, only grazers, no predators? Possibly, though probably there never was such a world, since predation preceded photosynthesis. Even grazers are predators of a kind, though what they eat does not suffer. Again, an Earth with only herbivores and no omnivores or carnivores would be impoverished. The animal skills demanded would be only a fraction of those that have resulted in actual zoology – no horns, no fleet-footed predators or prey, no fine-tuned eyesight and hearing, no quick neural capacity, no advanced brains.

Nor are all benefits to the predators. The individual prey, eaten, loses all; but the species may gain as the population is regulated, as selection for better skills at avoiding predation takes place, and the prey not less than the predator will gain in sentience, mobility, cognitive and perceptual powers. Being eaten is not always a bad thing, even from the perspective of the prey species. The predator depends on a continuing prey population; they have entwined destinies.

Goodenough concludes: "Suffering is part of the package, the price paid for the gift of being alive at all." I agree. A world without blood would be poorer, but a world without bloodshed would be poorer too. There would be no lions. "The young lions roar for their prey, seeking their food from God" (Psalm 104: 18–24). Also, it would be a world without humans – not that humans cannot now be vegetarians, but that the evolution of humans would never have taken place. The experiences of need, want, calamity, and fulfillment have driven the natural and cultural evolution of the ability to think.

Culture is a foil to the hostility of nature, though it is also a product of evolutionary inventiveness and requires ecological support. Within culture, the creative advances come when humans, facing difficulty, are roused to some unprecedented effort. Arnold Toynbee expressed this in the "challenge-and-response" formula, finding it characterizing the emergence of every great world culture (Toynbee 1935: 271ff). In the Hegelian dialectic, this is thesis, antithesis, synthesis. The major advances in civilization are processes that have often wrecked the societies in which they occurred. In cultures, only those that can respond when challenged, re-emerging from disasters, continue to shape the course of world history.

Cruciform nature

There was naïveté in the divine-blueprint model that was so upset by Darwin's discovery of nature red in tooth and claw. At the start-up creation, the Big Bang, fine-tuning does seem appropriate, as claimed by those cosmologists advocating the anthropic principle. But for genesis on Earth, this was a bad religious model, really, as well as a non-scientific one. In the Genesis stories, God brings forth Earth from a formless void, separates waters and land, and then says: "Let the earth bring forth living creatures according to their kinds" (Genesis 1: 24). God watches this happen and, as swarms of creatures come forth, sees that it is good. "The earth produces of itself (Greek: *automatically*)" (Luke 4: 28). There is spontaneous self-creation. Earth speciates.

The blueprint model knew nothing of the constructive uses of suffering in such speciation. It knew nothing of the wisdom of conflict. There are sorts of creation that cannot occur without death, and these include the highest created goods. Death can be meaningfully put into the biological processes as a necessary counterpart to the advancing of life. Life needs death, if there is to be more life. Anything that would give the individual organism immortality would destroy the evolution of species. The evolutionary process seems to thrive on the struggles for fitness that slay all the successive individuals.

In the biblical model in either testament, to be chosen by God is not to be protected from suffering. It is a call to suffer and to be delivered as one passes through it. The election is for *struggling* with and for God, seen in the very etymology of the name Israel, "a limping people" (Genesis 32: 22–32). Jacob limps physically, and this is taken up symbolically in his struggles with God. The divine son takes up and is broken on a cross, "a man of sorrows and acquainted with grief" (Isaiah 53: 3).

Biblical writers rejoice in nature; they also speak of nature laboring in travail. Paul speaks of how "the whole creation has been groaning in travail together until now" (Romans 8: 22). The root metaphor is "birthing," seen also in the Latin root for "nature:" *natans*, going back to the Greek. "Groaning in travail" is in the nature of things from time immemorial. Such travail is the Creator's will, productive as it is of glory.

The individual organism, self-actualizing as it is, is a player in a bigger drama that is going on, so to speak, "over its head," or that is "bigger than itself." The uniqueness of any particular genetic make-up is a one-off event, temporary, instantiated in an organism, tested for its fitness, and thereby it has a role in a recombinatorial process by which the species survives, making possible the myriad other lives that ensue in that species lineage. Every species has to reproduce itself from generation to generation; it absolutely must regenerate or else go extinct.

The conservation of life is through the reproduction of life. Something is always dying, and something is always living on. True, the co-actors are not so much cooperators as they are enmeshed in a series of checks and balances, controls, feed loops, and feedback loops; but, equally true, just this system is the vital context of all life. Individuals are "emptied into," given over to, "devoted" to, or "sacrificed" for these others in their community. Fitness is dying to self, sending newness of life to a generation to come (Rolston 2001).

But, it will be objected, there is little or nothing voluntary in these animal and plant behaviors. The creatures can only acquiesce in this order of evolutionary generation in which they are embedded; they cannot do otherwise. So there is nothing to commend them for, and this is a radical difference with a voluntary self-limiting on behalf of others, as found in the life of Jesus or the lives of the saints. True, but! Anyone who thinks much about freedom soon finds complex contexts in which freedom blends with determinism, with destiny.

Even those actors that might seem to be most free can equally sense an inescapable calling to roles in which they must acquiesce. "Thy will, not mine, be done." "Here I stand, I cannot do otherwise." Freedom is within a historical and environmental necessity. Persons, like other creatures, find themselves amidst their particulars in time and space, a setting within which they must work. Any blending of option, openness, indeterminacy, contingency, with inevitability, determinism, controls, givenness is elusive and permits no simple resolution.

There is autonomy in the creatures, in botanical and zoological senses. Plants are on their own in the world, defending their own forms of life, and reproducing this generation after generation. There are external controls, but these defenses are innate in their genes (as they are also in ours). Animals do what they spontaneously desire, and they are so made as to desire instinctively reproduction and distributing their form of life as widely as is in their power. All organisms, in reproduction, also spontaneously generate variations, novelties vital to their searching for better adapted modes of life.

No organism voluntarily chooses its form of life; no wild organism has the power reflectively to consider voluntary self-limitation on behalf of others as one of its options. Biologists find, at most, only glimmerings of sympathy in primates (de Waal 1996: 40–88). That level of choice appears only with humans, whatever the precursors out of which it emerged. Even humans do not choose to be *Homo sapiens*, though, as members of the species *Homo sapiens*, they have optional lifestyles unprecedented in the fauna and flora. Neither do humans choose this life-and-death–birth-and-rebirth order of being in which they too are caught up; they can only acquiesce in it. Neither do humans choose whether life must persist midst its perpetual perishing.

So far from making the world absurd, suffering is a key to the whole, not intrinsically, not as an end in itself, but as a transformative principle, transvalued into its opposite. The capacity to suffer through to joy is a supreme emergent and an essence of Christianity. Yet the whole evolutionary upslope is a lesser calling of this kind, in which renewed life comes by blasting the old. Life is gathered up in the midst of its throes, a blessed tragedy, lived in grace through a besetting storm.

The enigmatic symbol of this is the cross. One needs also the sign of the Logos, of intelligibility and order. In nature, there is first simply formation, and afterward information. Only still later does nature become cruciform. But the story does develop so, at least on this Earth. The cross here is not nature's only sign, but it is a pivotal one. It would also be a mistake to say that life is nothing but a cross, for life is gift and good news too. Still, all its joys have been bought with a price. The drama is Logos and Story, Cross and Glory. The way of history, too, like that of nature, only more so, is a *via dolorosa*. In the cruciform model, the evils both in spontaneous nature and in history, symbolized as death, are transformed and reinforce a larger pattern, symbolized under the themes of resurrected life. "Unless a grain of wheat falls into the earth and dies, it remains alone; but if it dies, it bears much fruit" (John 12: 24). In that sense, the aura of the cross is cast backward across the whole global story, and it forever outlines the future (Rolston 2006: 286–93).

"I believe in Christ in every man who dies to contribute to a life beyond his life," confessed Loren Eiseley (1962: 46). But that theme, willingly or unwillingly, is everywhere in the plot; it is the alpha and omega, prefigured in nature and essential to history. All the creatures are forever being sacrificed to contribute to lives beyond their own, like the lamb slain from the foundation of the world. Blessedness is success on the far side of sorrow. Every life is chastened and christened, straitened and baptized in struggle. Everywhere there is vicarious suffering. The global Earth is a land of promise, and yet one that has to be died for. All world progress and developing history is ultimately brought under the shadow of a cross. The story is a passion play long before it reaches the Christ. Since the beginning, the myriad creatures have been giving up their lives as a ransom for many. In that sense, Jesus is not the exception to the natural order, but a chief exemplification of it.

Life is suffering, but life is suffering through to something higher. Life is unsatisfactory, as it is also satisfying, for the dissatisfactions drive the creative process, discovering new satisfactions. The grass, the flower of the field, is clothed with beauty today and gone tomorrow, cast into the fire. The sparrow is busy about her nest, sings, and falls. Jesus knew these things, and noticed in the same breath that trouble enough comes with each new day (Matthew 6: 25–34). Tribulations come as surely as does the Kingdom. The hard, straitened way leads to life. But day by day we press forward in trials, in the will that this pageant continue. We believe that we could not have come this far and would not have the strength to struggle on were it not for some power greater than ourselves at work in nature and history. Earth is a providing ground. Some providential power (and can it be merely a naturalistic one?) guarantees that the story continues across all its actors. In this perspective, regenerative suffering makes history. Tragic beauty is the law of the narrative.

References

Alumets, J., R. Hakanson, F. Sundler and J. Thorell (1979) "Neuronal Localisation of Immunoreactive Enkephalin and ß-endorphin in the Earthworm," *Nature* 279: 805–06.

Arendt, Detlev, Alexandru S. Denes, Gáspár Jékely and Kristin Tessmar-Raible (2008) "The Evolution of Nervous System Centralization," *Philosophical Transactions of the Royal Society B* 363: 1523–28.

Eiseley, Loren (1962) "Our Path Leads Upward," *Reader's Digest* March: 43–46.

Eisemann, C. H., W. K. Jorgensen, D. J. Meritt, M. J. Rice, B. W. Cribb, P. D. Webb and M. P. Zalucki (1984) "Do Insects Feel Pain? – A Biological View," *Experientia* 40: 164–67.

Fodor, J. (1992) "The Big Idea: Can There Be a Science of Mind?," *The Times Literary Supplement* July 3: 5–7.

Hirth, F. and H. Reichart (2007) "Basic Nervous System Types: One or Many?" in *Evolution of Nervous Systems*, Vol. 1, Jon H. Kaas (ed.), San Diego, CA: Academic Press, 55–72.

Shapiro, James A. (1998) "Genome System Architecture and Natural Genetic Engineering," in *Evolution as Computation*, Laura F. Landweber and Erik Winfree (eds), New York: Springer-Verlag, 1–14.

——(2005) "A 21st Century View of Evolution: Genome System Architecture, Repetitive DNA, and Natural Genetic Engineering," *Gene* 345: 91–100.

Rolston, Holmes, III (2001) "Kenosis and Nature," in *The Work of Love: Creation as Kenosis*, John Polkinghorne (ed.), London: SPCK and Grand Rapids, MI: Eerdmans, 43–65.

——(2006) *Science and Religion: A Critical Survey*, new edn, Philadelphia, PA: Templeton Foundation Press.

Tennyson, Alfred Lord (1850) *In Memoriam*, Part LVI, Stanza 4.

Toynbee, Arnold J. (1935) *A Study of History*, Vol. 1, 2nd edn, London: Oxford University Press.

Tye, Michael (1997) "The Problem of Simple Minds: Is There Anything It Is Like to be a Honey-Bee?" *Philosophical Studies* 88: 289–317.

de Waal, Franz B. M. (1996) *Good Natured: The Origins of Right and Wrong in Humans and Other Animals*, Cambridge, MA: Harvard University Press.

Further reading

Willem B. Drees, *Is Nature Ever Evil? Religion, Science, and Value* (Routledge, 2003): three dozen contributors use both science and religion to examine the value structure of the natural world, its order, goodness, beauty, life, and its harshness, disorder, death, and indifference. Austin Farrer, in *Love Almighty and Ills Unlimited* (Doubleday, 1961) concludes: "The more we love, the more we feel the evils besetting or corrupting the object of our love. But the more we feel the force of the besetting harms, the more certain we are of the value residing in what they attack; and in resisting them are identified with the action of God, whose mercy is over all flesh" (pp. 164–65). Arthur R. Peacocke, "The Challenge and Stimulus of the Epic of Evolution to Theology," in *Many Worlds*, Steven Dick (ed.) (Templeton Foundation Press, 2000) describes a structural logic about creatures inevitably dying and preying on each other. We cannot conceive of any other way by which the immense variety of biodiverse organisms might have appeared. But the appearance of humans and their distinctive search for meaning raises questions the biological sciences cannot answer (pp. 89–117). For Peacocke, "The Cost of New Life," in *The Work of Love: Creation as Kenosis*, John Polkinghorne (ed.) (Eerdmans, 2001), the insight that God's relation to the world is self-offering and self-limiting can be illuminated by evolutionary history. There is continuous emergence of new and more complex life, and this inevitably involves an increase in capacities to suffer. My "Does Nature Need to be Redeemed?" *Zygon: Journal of Religion and Science* 29 (1994): 205–29 answers "no," although theologians have traditionally been confused about this, thinking nature as well as humans to be "fallen." See also Rolston (2006) *Science and Religion: A Critical Survey* (cited above), especially xxxix–xliii, 133–46, 286–93 on suffering and cruciform naturalism. Gloria L. Schaab's *The Creative Suffering of the Triune God: An Evolutionary Theology* (Oxford University Press, 2007) considers the positions of prominent theologians, but focuses on Arthur R. Peacocke. The freedom, autonomy, and self-creativity of evolving life can be integrated with their constant pain, suffering, and death. The triune God can be seen to suffer in, with, and under the creative processes of natural history. For Christopher Southgate, *The Groaning of Creation: God, Evolution, and the Problem of Evil* (Westminster John Knox, 2008), pain, suffering, death, and extinction are intrinsic to the evolutionary process. The world is "very good" and also "groaning in travail;" the living creatures subjected by God to that travail are seen as essential to their creation.

24

MAGIC, MONOTHEISM AND NATURAL EVIL

Classical and modern Jewish responses to suffering

Lawrence Troster

Introduction

There is a long and varied history of Jewish responses to the problem of suffering. The pre-modern explanations for suffering existed on a sliding scale that ranged between the poles of a magical/theurgic and a strict monotheistic world-view. The magical/theurgic world-view assumed the existence of demons and angels that are semi-independent of divine control. In this world-view, human beings have the ability to tap into magic power that enables them to control the forces of evil and suffering and allows them to perform "operations intended to influence the Divinity, mostly in its own inner state or dynamics, but sometimes also in its relationship to man" (Idel 1988: 157). These operations usually consisted of the traditional rituals and practices, but also included magical rites and objects. While it may be objected that this world-view is pagan or polytheistic, and thus outside of a normative Judaism, a broad definition of monotheism as it is actually practiced can include such a perspective (Sommer 2009: 145–47).

At the other extreme, the strictly monotheistic world-view denied the reality of magic and demons. It therefore held that all human suffering must come either from some divine purpose, such as punishment for sin, or for testing the sufferer; or from the fact of material existence – since humans are composed of earthly matter, it is inevitable that they will eventually sicken and die. It was not unusual that Jews often held views somewhere along this scale and not at one extreme or another. Rarely were there attempts to reconcile these apparently conflicting world-views in any logical or systematic way. This contradiction existed because the magical/theurgic world-view was existentially satisfying to the individual, while the strictly monotheistic world-view allowed for a system of meaning for national Jewish suffering set within a meaningful eschatology.

Magic not only provided an explanation for suffering, but also held out the hope of appropriate therapy. It allowed for the possibility that humans could exercise power and control over the capricious and hostile forces that beset life. However, such a world-view compromised divine omnipotence. An adherence to a stricter monotheism eliminated the theological problems of the existence of demons and magic, but resulted in the distancing of God from Creation, made human beings feel powerless before the vagaries of life, and introduced the unsettling moral problems of the suffering of the innocent. The monotheistic explanation for suffering asserted that it came from human sin or disobedience to God's will, but this theology did not often conform to the real facts of human existence. It is not surprising, therefore, that strict monotheism has not been followed in actual religious practice for most of the history of Judaism. Instead, a kind of qualified monotheism characterized the day-to-day lives of most Jews. As a result, Jewish philosophy, as an expression of strict monotheism, never came to be as widespread or popular as the more magical and theurgic theology of Kabbalah, which integrated both world-views into one system. In fact, it is possible to say that before the modern period, the strictly monotheistic world-view was practiced only in the Middle Ages by a small elite group of philosophically inclined adherents (Sommer 2009: 146).

With the rise of modern science in the seventeenth, eighteenth and especially nineteenth centuries, there was a decline in the belief in the demonic/theurgic world-view in the Jewish communities of Western Europe and North America. The new scientific perspective excluded the invisible demonic realm, and modern medicine was able to supply natural reasons for most human illness and suffering. But the new scientific world-view also undermined strict monotheism's explanations for human suffering: Pain, disease and natural catastrophes were also given natural explanations, and the traditional role assigned to God in the day-to-day governance of the world became a theological problem.

This problem of divine providence became especially acute for Jews after the Holocaust of the Second World War. As a result, most post-Holocaust theology usually rejected traditional theodicies and instead focused on human free will as the real source of evil and suffering. While few modern Jewish theologians or philosophers have directly confronted the scientific challenges to the traditional explanations of pain and suffering, nonetheless the concept of "natural evil" has been mostly eliminated, and the biological necessity for pain and suffering (similar to the perspective in Chapter 22 of this volume) is now accepted theologically, even if, existentially, the realm of the demonic still holds sway in the imagination (Troster 1986).

Israelite and biblical responses to evil and suffering

The Bible is not a single book, but a library containing many volumes and many different voices within those volumes. The Bible also represents various minority and dissenting perspectives that probably do not reflect the actual religious views or practices of the majority of Israelites. Many biblical texts are critiques of, or attempts to reform, the beliefs and rituals of the majority (Geller 2004).

From biblical sources and archaeology, it is possible to reconstruct some of the characteristics of Israelite religion. The God of the Israelites, *YHVH*, lived in the heavens surrounded by a celestial host which included the Sun, Moon, planets and stars (Psalm 148). God occasionally came down to Earth in the form of a warrior riding a chariot or a cherub and whose power was manifest in the storm (Psalm 48). In order to create the universe, *YHVH* had to defeat the opposing forces of evil/chaos, which included demons, and which could nonetheless still potentially arise in the future to thwart His purposes (Levenson 1988). *YHVH* was worshipped in shrines and temples, where the primary mode of worship was animal sacrifice. Divination was widely practiced, and prophets were consulted either at the shrines or in wandering bands. Other magical practices included the use of amulets, fertility fetishes, ordeals, healing rituals, and necromancy. *YHVH* was the most powerful god, and the forces of evil could be fought with His help, and/or with magical practices that were virtually identical to those of the surrounding pagan cultures.

Israelite religion thus supplied ready explanations for evil and suffering along with ready cures: magical practices along with appeals through sacrifice and prayer to *YHVH* for help. National sin, such as worshipping another god, could also bring down the anger of *YHVH*, and the subjugation of the Israelite to foreign powers was the punishment for disloyalty.

Against the majority beliefs and practices of Israelite religion, the Bible preserves four dissenting traditions: the Deuteronomic–covenantal, the Priestly–cultic, the Prophetic, and the Wisdom (Geller 2004). These traditions expressed a much stricter form of monotheism, which rejected many of the basic premises of Israelite religion. As Jacob Milgrom has written of the Priestly–cultic tradition:

> It posits the existence of one supreme God who contends neither with a higher realm nor with competing peers. The world of demons is abolished; there is no struggle with autonomous foes because there are none. With the demise of the demons, only one creature remains with "demonic" power – the human being.
>
> (Milgrom 1991: 42)

The Priestly–cultic and the Deuteronomic traditions tried to reform Israelite theology and its expression in the cult into a stricter monotheistic structure. This introduced, however, what became the classic problem of theodicy: If there is only one God and there are no demons or other forces of chaos/evil, then all suffering, including the suffering of the righteous, must come from God. This strict monotheism is expressed by one of the late Isaianic prophets:

> I am the Lord and there is none else; beside Me there are no other gods;
> I gird you with strength, though you have not known Me,
> so that all may acknowledge, from the rising of the sun to its setting,
> there is none apart from me. I am the Lord, there is no other.
> I form light and create darkness, make well-being and create evil; I the Lord do all these things.
>
> (Isaiah 45: 5–7)

As Mary Douglas (2000: 9–11) has noted, removing the demons created an existential gap between the elite's theology and the actual lives of the average Israelite. Thus the Priestly–cultic tradition, as chiefly represented in the book of Leviticus, had to find a new source of explanation for suffering, and did so in the theology of impurity and with reformed rituals centered on that new theology.

The biblical views on suffering that arose from these new theologies came in two stages. The first stage, from pre-exilic times (before 586 BCE), centered on a strong corporate identity: Suffering from sin came upon the family, clan and nation rather than on individuals through a cause-and-effect process built into the order of Creation. Punishment did not necessarily come immediately – it could happen cross-generationally. The main source of sin is disloyalty and disobedience to God. Since Creation began as good and harmonious, it was only through human misuse of free will that evil was introduced into the world. Therefore all suffering is defensible as punishment from a good and just God. God is constantly active in the world, and uses the forces of the natural world as well as human agents to carry out His punishments. And, while there may be suffering that seems arbitrary, it is in fact all part of God's plan (Simundson 1992: 220–21).

The next stage took place in post-exilic times (post-586 BCE): there was some lessening of the corporate identity and the meaning of an individual's suffering gained greater attention. So Ezekiel and Jeremiah (Ezekiel 18; Jeremiah 31: 29–30) asserted that there is no cross-generational retribution – the suffering of an individual must be from their own sin. Other explanations for suffering also emerged: Suffering can have a redeeming value for both the nation and the individual. There are also biblical sources from this period, such as the books of Ecclesiastes, which challenged the theology of divine justice by protesting against the suffering of the innocent. Eschatological explanations also begin to come to the fore: If someone (or indeed the whole nation of the Jews) seems to be suffering unjust suffering or oppression, they will nonetheless be redeemed at some time in the future and perfect justice will ultimately prevail (Simundson 1992: 223–24).

Because the biblical texts became part of a sacred canon, biblical responses to evil and suffering became the templates for later Jewish responses to the problem of suffering. And, although strict monotheism was the primary source of these responses, the world of the demons remained (Propp 1999: 437).

Second Temple and rabbinic responses

In the Second Temple period (500 BCE–70 CE), the two world-views for the most part were accepted by most Jews without question. As Seth Schwartz has noted, the strict monotheistic and the magical/theurgic view (what Schwartz calls "The Myth") can be found sometimes in the same document without any apparent awareness of how they contradict each other (Schwartz 2001: 74–87). In fact, the magical/theurgic world-view generated apocalyptic works that often approach a dualist theology: God is not really in control of this world; it is in the hands of the demons and rebellious angels. Human beings are their victims, but eventually God will restore order and justice. Many of the texts written in this period reflect this dichotomy and arise out of the need to explain evil in the face of the apparent failure of the strict monotheistic theology canonized in the Torah to explain the oppression of the Jews by foreign powers. In the few texts that do not have such a dualistic theology, and arise out of the Wisdom tradition such as the books of Job, Ecclesiastes, and Ben Sira, this failure became an acute theological problem. One of the answers that gained great prominence at this time was the evolution of a belief in an afterlife: resurrection of the body at some future time and/or the survival of the soul. Both concepts were eventually accepted and combined among some Jews into a single eschatology that provided the main consolation for human suffering until the modern age (Cohen 2006: 83–88)

The one exception to these explanations appeared in one work of the Hellenistic Jewish philosopher Philo of Alexandria (20 BCE–50 CE). In his book *On Providence*, Philo explains that the suffering of the righteous lies not in their actions, but in being part of the natural cycles of the world that affect all human beings without distinction. Therefore suffering is not a problem of God's justice, but the ordinary course of natural law (Kraemer 1995: 49–50). Philo also rejected the magic/theurgic world-view. Indeed, for Philo, "magic" is the true knowledge of Creation, while what most people call magic he considers to be trickery, fraud, and the use of poisons (Philo 1937: 539–41).

In the period that saw the development of rabbinic Judaism (70–500 CE), all of the previous explanations for suffering continued. In rabbinic documents, the primary explanation for human suffering was just punishment from God. But some of the rabbinic material also shows the alternative biblical explanations: Suffering may be sometimes arbitrary, it can also be a sign of divine love, and suffering in this world will be corrected by reward in the next (Kraemer 1995). But the rabbis also accepted the magical/theurgic world-view. Later rabbinic literature especially is filled with references to demons as sources of human suffering and with magical ways to counteract them (Bohak 2007: 351–425). Because many of the rabbinic ideas about magic and demons became incorporated in normative Jewish belief and practice, the magic/theurgic world-view was rarely challenged before the modern period. Since they believed in demons as a real threat to human life and health, the issue for them was to understand which magical practices fell under the prohibitions found in Leviticus and Deuteronomy, and which were permitted. Indeed, one could say that for most Jews at this time, demons constituted their version of "natural evil."

Medieval and early modern responses

While traditional rabbinical authorities in the Middle Ages (500–1500 CE) continued to accept the two-world-view explanations on human suffering without attempting to reconcile the contradictions, two new perspectives came into existence: the philosophic tradition and the Kabbalistic stream of Jewish mysticism. Among most Jews, the existence of demons and the practice of magic continued to be a normative part of their existence and allowed them both an explanation for suffering and methods to counteract it (Trachtenberg 1939).

While not all Jewish philosophers completely rejected the two world-views, some of the most important figures, such as Saadiah Gaon, Abraham Ibn Ezra, and Moses Maimonides, broke with rabbinic tradition on the belief in magic and demons and advocated a very strict monotheism. Theodicy then became a major issue for Jewish medieval philosophy as its adherents needed to explain how an omnipotent, good God could allow for evil and human suffering. The tendency in Jewish medieval philosophy was to deny the existence of "natural" evil and to locate real evil within the moral choices of human beings.

The most important figure in this tradition was Moses Maimonides (1135–1204). While Maimonides made no explicit statement about the existence of demons, he did not include them in his cosmology (Maimonides 1983: 9–12). Although he believed in angels and other celestial intermediaries between humanity and God, he constantly prohibited any magical practice (except on a few rare occasions when it might soothe the mental distress of a sick person) and he derided any such practice as the province of fools and mental deficients. When Maimonides quoted any of the rabbinic material that, in its original sources, explained a practice as anti-demonological, he either omitted the practice or gave it a naturalistic explanation. This strict monotheistic perspective was attacked by many other rabbinical authorities as heretical since it contradicted the rabbinic sources which had achieved near canonical status amongst medieval Jewry (Shapiro 2000).

In the theology of Maimonides, evil had no independent substance, but was the absence of good as darkness is the absence of light. Therefore no evil comes directly from God. Any independent source of evil, such as demons, would have for him compromised God's omnipotence. Natural evils such as illness, landslides, or floods occur because of the circumstances of corporeal existence and the nature of matter. In the sub-lunar world, change comes about through the destruction and regeneration of physical matter. We experience such things as evil, but in principle they are not. Maimonides felt that such evil is actually rare, and that the greatest amount of evil and suffering in the world comes from the actions of humans. Human evils are of two kinds: those we do to other human beings and those we do to ourselves. These evils can be eliminated through acquisition of the proper opinions, which will lead to proper actions. Maimonides also rejected the rabbinic concept of suffering as a sign of divine love (Maimonides 1963: 2: 430–48).

For Maimonides, it was necessary to restrict the sources of evil and suffering to human free will because of his conception of divine action or providence. Medieval philosophers classified providence into two kinds: general providence (God's care for the world in general or for species in general) and special providence (God's care for each individual human being). Maimonides limited providence in the non-human world to general providence, which meant the establishment and maintenance of the laws of the order of Creation. He also limited special providence to those human beings who were intellectually advanced (Maimonides 1963: 2: 461–85).

The Kabbalistic stream of Jewish mysticism, which began in the eleventh century in southern France and spread to northern Spain, integrated both the magical/theurgic world-view and the strict monotheistic world-view into one systematic theology. In the Kabbalah, all phenomena must reside in, and be a part of, God. Therefore in most forms of Kabbalistic theology evil must, in some sense, come from God. Kabbalah created a concept of evil that operated on two levels: the human world and the events within the divine personality. The early Kabbalists found in the structure of Creation, separate from humanity, a metaphysical basis for evil. This basis for evil, however, is only the *potential* for evil and not the real *existence* of evil within God. This potential for evil only becomes *actualized* evil through human sin. The original harmony in the divine realm, which humanity broke at the time of Adam and Eve, has since then been the locus of the development of a kind of anti-divine realm identified with the Satan of the Bible. The Kabbalists referred to this realm as the *Sitra Achra*, Aramaic for the "Other Side." It is from the Other Side that the demonic power is generated. And while different Kabbalists had various views on magical practice, Kabbalistic interpretations of traditional Jewish practices allow for theurgic power in the sense that humans can, through ritual, prayer, and meditation on divine names, alter the nature of God and repair the evil in the physical world (Idel 1988). In this powerful theology, *everything* that happens in the world, whether natural occurrence or human-caused, is simultaneously an act of God but also the result of human action.

By the end of the Middle Ages, Kabbalah had become the dominant form of Jewish spirituality while the influence of Jewish philosophy declined. The influence of the magical/theurgic world-view continued into the early modern period, where Kabbalah was interpreted as a Jewish way of integrating hermetic philosophy with the new scientific world-view (Idel 1983; Ruderman 1988). But as more Jews were learning and being influenced by modern science in the eighteenth century, especially in medicine, they begin to question the efficacy of traditional rabbinic knowledge and the truth of Kabbalah (Ruderman 1995).

Modern responses

The political and social emancipation of European Jewry in the eighteenth and nineteenth centuries brought knowledge of the western view of science that was able to explain natural phenomena without recourse to either demons or God. Thus Jews (especially those of Central and Western Europe) who assimilated this world-view began to reject the magic/theurgic world-view. Paradoxically, concepts of divine providence also had to change and, as Jewish philosophy was revived in Western Jewry, the Enlightenment view of an abstract God began to gain prominence amongst theologians even as the traditional perspectives remained active in Eastern European Jewry.

As Arthur Green has observed, even as the study of Jewish philosophy was confined to rabbinical seminaries and the study of Kabbalah was discredited as being outside of mainstream Judaism, most Jews' contact with Jewish theology, even in the liberal denominations, came through the prayer book (whether traditional or revised), which retained all the old rabbinic ideas about divine action and the nexus of sin and punishment. It was not surprising, then, that many Western Jews, now trained in the new scientific world-view, thought of Judaism as childish and simplistic. It no longer spoke to the world they lived in, and contributed to Western Jewry becoming highly secularized (Green 2010: 71).

The influence of science in this process may be seen in two examples. Before the advent of anesthesia in the nineteenth century, pain was accepted as a normal part of life even as people attempted to avoid or alleviate it. With the creation of anesthesia, pain is now considered to be abnormal and is not part of the conditions of a healthy life. Thus the traditional connection between suffering and piety is not part of most modern theology. Instead, suffering is a theological problem (Samuelson 2009: 72–73). Secondly, following modern science's materialistic perspective, most modern Jewish theology since the nineteenth century has rejected traditional notions of the afterlife, especially the idea of the resurrection of the dead in the Messianic era. Therefore most Jews believe that this life is the only life they will live. When the catastrophe of the Holocaust struck, many Jews were thus left without any explanation for evil and suffering in this life and no consolation of an afterlife (Kraemer 2000: 142–49).

Thus post-Holocaust theology is left without any traditional solutions for the theodicy problem. There are no real demons, only human ones, and the science that slew the demons was perverted into use for the mass killing. Those who confronted the Holocaust (which only seriously began almost twenty years after the end of the Second World War) opted for a variety of approaches. Aside from those very few among the most traditional Orthodox who still looked to the sin-and-punishment nexus, most choose to preserve the goodness of God at the expense of divine power: The Holocaust occurred because of the exercise of human free will. Various versions of divine self-limitation were expressed, but often still avoid issue of God's involvement: What was God doing during the Holocaust? Some theologians, such as Eliezer Berkovits and Emil Fackenheim, created a kind of an anti-theodicy that refused to accept traditional theodicy as a mode of explanation, and instead posited a kind of theological ambiguity rather than philosophical coherency (Braiterman 1998).

What is interesting is that many of the post-Holocaust theologies used the rhetoric of the demonic to describe what was happening because of the feeling of the concreteness of evil. It was existentially satisfying to use the language of the demonic, even if the demons do not exist except as human beings (Troster 1986). In all of these theologies, there are virtually no attempts to integrate the new scientific knowledge of the natural world into an overall theology of evil and suffering.

The one Jewish philosopher who did create a post-Holocaust theology that tried to encompass evolution and the biology of suffering was Hans Jonas. Jonas tried to respond to what he saw as the nihilism that modern philosophy and science had produced. Jonas did this by showing that every living creature, from the smallest microbe to humankind, shows concern for its own being. They do this by connecting to the world around them in order to stave off death and non-being through metabolism, the exchange of matter with the environment which all organisms must exhibit in order to survive: it is the most basic expression of that organism's struggle for life. With each new level of complexity in evolution, there is an increase of mind which brings a new level of freedom as well as peril and a greater potential for pain and suffering. With the advent of humanity in evolution, being now becomes reflective and must try to understand its place in the whole of which it is part (Troster 2003).

In order to give a metaphysical grounding to his philosophy, Jonas created an idea of God that took into account the Holocaust. He believed that nothing in previous ideas of theodicy was of any use in dealing with the Holocaust. At Auschwitz, "Not fidelity or infidelity, belief or unbelief, not guilt or punishment, not trial, witness and messianic hope, nay, not even strength or weakness, heroism or cowardice, defiance or submission had a place there" (Jonas 1996: 133). And so Jonas asked, "What God could let it happen?".

In response, Jonas created a "myth" of creation in which God displays three critical characteristics. First of all, while God is still a Creator, God is a *suffering* God. The divine suffering is the pain that God feels alongside the pain of God's creations, as well as the disappointments with humanity that God experiences. Secondly, God is a *becoming* God. The becoming God is affected and altered by the events occurring in the universe. Lastly, God is a *caring* God. This does not mean that God intervenes in history in the traditional sense. Instead, God has taken the risk of leaving His human creations with the responsibility of acting for the sake of the universe. For Jonas, not only is divine omnipotence philosophically illogical with creation, but, more importantly, omnipotence can exist in God only at the expense of absolute goodness and complete divine inscrutability. Instead, Jonas chose a conception of God who is good and intelligible, but not omnipotent. Therefore God was silent at Auschwitz not because God chose not to intervene, but because God could not intervene. Jonas locates evil today in the deliberate acts of human beings.

Thus God's limitation is a self-limitation done at the very moment of Creation. Here Jonas connected his idea of divinity with the Kabbalistic doctrine of *tzimtzum*, the contraction of the divine for the purpose of creation. What is then left of the relation of Creation to its Creator? Jonas believed that, "Having given himself whole to the becoming world, God has no more to give: it is man's now to give to him" (Jonas 1996: 142). God can relate to the universe not through direct supernatural actions that contradict the laws of the natural world, but only through the inspiration of certain individuals. Just as our freedom to act in the world is scientifically compatible with causality, then we can accept a kind of divine causality that comes into our inner self, that does not conflict with human free will (Jonas 1996: 156f).

It is the view of this writer that the work of Hans Jonas provides the foundation of a modern Jewish theology of evil and suffering that takes into account the biological background of human suffering and the theological honesty to confront the problems of traditional theodicy (Troster 2006). While a theurgic/magical view of the world may remain existentially, few Jews today resort to magical practices for the alleviation of pain or cure of illness, and most refuse to accept that God is responsible either for natural "evil" events, or for the Holocaust.

References

Bohak, Gideon (2007) *Ancient Jewish Magic: A History*, Cambridge: Cambridge University Press.

Braiterman, Zachary (1998) *(God) After Auschwitz: Tradition and Change in Post-Holocaust Jewish Thought*, Princeton, NJ: Princeton University Press.

Cantor, Geoffrey and Marc Swetlitz (eds) (2006) *Jewish Tradition and the Challenge of Darwinism*, Chicago, IL: University of Chicago Press.

Cohen, Shaye J. D. (2006) *From the Maccabees to the Mishnah* (2nd edn), Louisville, KY: Westminster John Knox.

Douglas, Mary (2000) *Leviticus as Literature*, Oxford: Oxford University Press.

Geller, Stephen A. (2004) "The Religion of the Bible," in *The Jewish Study Bible*, Adele Berlin and Marc Zvi Brettler (eds), Oxford: Oxford University Press, 2021–40.

Green, Arthur (2010) *Radical Judaism: Rethinking God and Tradition*, New Haven, CT: Yale University Press.

Idel, Moshe (1983) "The Magical and Neoplatonic Interpretations of the Kabbalah in the Renaissance," in *Jewish Thought in the Sixteenth Century*, Bernard Dov Cooperman (ed.), Cambridge, MA: Harvard University Press.

——(1988) *Kabbalah: New Perspectives*, New Haven, CT: Yale University Press.

Jonas, Hans (1996) *Morality and Mortality: A Search for the Good after Auschwitz*, Lawrence Vogel (ed.), Evanston, IL: Northwestern University Press.

Kraemer, David (1995) *Responses to Suffering in Classic Rabbinic Literature*, Oxford: Oxford University Press.

——(2000) *The Meanings of Death in Rabbinic Judaism*, London: Routledge.

Levenson, Jon D. (1988) *Creation and the Persistence of Evil: The Jewish Drama of Divine Omnipotence*, San Francisco, CA: Harper & Row.

Maimonides, Moses (1963) *The Guide of the Perplexed* (two volumes), Shlomo Pines (trans.), Chicago, IL: University of Chicago Press.

——(1983) *The Book of Knowledge from the Mishneh Torah of Maimonides*, H. M. Russell and J. Weinberg (trans.), New York: Ktav Press.

Milgrom, Jacob (1991) *The Anchor Bible: Leviticus 1–16*, New York: Doubleday.

Philo (1937) *Volume 7*, F. H. Colson (trans.), Loeb Classical Library, Cambridge, MA: Harvard University Press.

Propp, William C. (1999) *The Anchor Bible: Exodus 1–18*, New York: Doubleday.

Ruderman, David B. (1988) *Kabbalah, Magic and Science: The Cultural Universe of a Sixteenth Century Jewish Physician*, Cambridge, MA: Harvard University Press.

——(1995) *Jewish Thought and Scientific Discovery in Early Modern Europe*, New Haven, CT: Yale University Press.

Samuelson, Norbert M. (2009) *Jewish Faith and Modern Science: On the Death and Rebirth of Jewish Philosophy*, Lanham, MD: Rowman & Littlefield.

Schwartz, Seth (2001) *Imperialism and Jewish Society, 200 B.C.E. to 640 C.E.*, Princeton, NJ: Princeton University Press.

Shapiro, Marc B. (2000) "Maimonidean Halakhah and Superstition," in *Maimonidean Studies 2*, Arthur Hyman (ed.), New York: Ktav Publishing, 61–108.

Simundson, Daniel J. (1992) "Suffering," in *The Anchor Bible Dictionary Volume 6, Si–Z*, David Noel Freedman (ed.), New York: Doubleday, 219–25.

Sommer, Benjamin D. (2009) *The Bodies of God and the World of Ancient Israel*, Cambridge: Cambridge University Press.

Trachtenberg, Joshua (1939) *Jewish Magic and Superstition: A Study in Folk Religion*, New York: Behrman House.

Troster, Lawrence (1986) "The Definition of Evil in Post-Holocaust Theology," *Conservative Judaism* 39(1): 87–98.

——(2003) "Hans Jonas and the Concept of God after the Holocaust," *Conservative Judaism* 55 (4): 16–25.

——(2006) "The Order of Creation and the Emerging God: Evolution and Divine Action in the Natural World," in *Jewish Tradition and the Challenge of Darwinism*, Geoffrey Cantor and Marc Swetlitz (eds), Chicago, IL: University of Chicago Press, 225–46.

Further reading

As mentioned at the beginning of this chapter, the classical and modern Jewish sources on evil and suffering are extremely large and varied. A good review of classical sources is to be found in Louis Jacobs, *A Jewish Theology* (Behrman House, 1973). For modern Jewish thought, see the numerous references in Arthur A. Cohen and Paul Mendes-Flohr (eds),

Contemporary Jewish Religious Thought (The Free Press, 1987). Post-Holocaust theology is also well covered in Elliot Dorff and Louis E. Newman (eds), *Contemporary Jewish Theology: A Reader* (Oxford University Press, 1999). One of the best recent references on the Hebrew Bible, with many useful essays, is Adele Berlin and Marc Zvi Brettler (eds), *The Jewish Study Bible* (Oxford University Press, 2004). See also the work of Jacob Milgrom and Mary Douglas (cited above). Summaries of Second Temple and rabbinic views can be found in the work of Shaye D. Cohen and David Kraemer (also cited above). Kabbalistic ideas about evil and suffering can be found in Gershom Scholem, *Kabbalah* (Quadrangle/The New York Times Book Co., 1974). For a good overview of Jewish philosophy on evil and suffering, see Oliver Leaman, *Evil and Suffering in Jewish Philosophy* (Cambridge University Press, 1995). The impact of modern science is best found in the works of David Ruderman and Norbert Samuelson (cited above). The relationship of Judaism to evolutionary theory can be found in Geoffrey Cantor & Marc Swetlitz (eds), *Jewish Tradition and the Challenge of Darwinism* (cited above). For a complete examination of the work of Hans Jonas, see Hava Tirosh-Samuelson and Christian Wiese (eds), *The Legacy of Hans Jonas: Judaism and the Phenomenon of Life* (Brill, 2008).

25
THE PROBLEM OF SUFFERING IN THEISTIC EVOLUTION

Ted Peters

We are entering a phase of the controversy over Charles Darwin's model of evolution which calls for creative and constructive work on the part of our theistic evolutionists. This call is urgent. Urgently needed is an intellectually credible schema, or even world-view, that places the evolution of life over deep time within a more comprehensive narrative about God's gracious love for the creation.

What makes this call urgent is that the contenders who have dominated the controversy in recent decades have virtually lost their intellectual credibility. Both creationists and intelligent design advocates have lost repeatedly in court cases, restricting promulgation of their views in the public school system. Their views do not pass the test of rigorous science; and theological leaders dismiss these schools of thought because of their recalcitrance at welcoming good science. What is missing here is a respectable theology of nature, that is, a theological picture which incorporates what we know as good science within a vision of God's creative and redemptive plan for this world.

Another major contender in the controversy is atheistic materialism. A new breed of aggressive atheists – evangelical atheists, if you will – are taking advantage of the religious retreat of the creationists and intelligent design forces. The materialists ground their position on Darwin's *On the Origin of Species* much as Muslims ground their position on the Qur'an. However, a close look will reveal that Darwin's model of evolution does not in itself warrant an ideology of materialism, let alone atheism. This position is a religious position – even if anti-religious – that claims a scientific support which is non-existent. Despite their doubtful credibility, the materialists are gaining enormous public visibility and rightly consider themselves as winning in the culture war against religious superstition.

Promoters of the selfish gene theory – the theory that DNA replication drives the evolutionary process – among sociobiologists, evolutionary psychologists, behavior ecologists, and others are generating increasing interest. References to the selfish gene, along with our brain capacity allegedly enhanced during a period of evolutionary adaptedness, are made to explain nearly every subtlety and nuance of psychology and culture. This includes religion. Religion can be explained reductively as a cultural form that promotes reproductive adaptedness. This variant of the Darwinian model apparently explains human religion better than the theologian can explain it. Perhaps by the time you read this, we theologians will be out of a job, replaced by sociobiologists and their children.

The phase of the controversy we currently find ourselves in can be characterized as one of near-theological vacuum being filled by non-theologians who claim scientific authority. The situation is ripe for some bold moves forward.

Our time is calling for those who consider themselves theistic evolutionists to get to work. A minimalist definition of a theistic evolutionist would be one who affirms the fertility of the Darwinian and neo-Darwinian model of evolution and who seeks to reconcile this model with a theological understanding of God as creator and redeemer. This minimalist understanding could apply to a strictly defensive apologist. Perhaps our situation is calling for something more robust, a filled-out picture with a positive understanding of the roles variation in inheritance and natural selection play in God's larger creative and providential work in the natural world. This kind of constructive work I encourage among our present generation of Christian, Jewish, and Muslim scholars.

In what follows, I do not provide a blueprint for this construction to follow. That belongs somewhere else (cf. Peters and Hewlett 2003, 2006). Rather, I would like to identify one of the major difficulties that a theistic evolutionist must confront, namely, suffering in nature. The highest hurdle to jump is not answering how Darwin's concepts of deep time and speciation can be reconciled with the Genesis account. Nor is the highest hurdle the question of divine action, of reconciling God's providential action with natural processes. Rather, the highest hurdle to jump is one that theologians have found daunting for millennia: the theodicy problem. If the Christian theologian claims that this creation is the gift of a loving and gracious God, then why should we expect to find, over nearly 4 billion years, the bloodthirsty history of predator–prey violence and the extinction of species, what Darwin himself called "waste"?

"The long evolutionary view of suffering is that it is an inherent feature of life," writes Ursula Goodenough (Chapter 22 in this volume). If the theistic evolutionist grants that suffering and its concomitant evils are rooted in our biological substrate, then what is the most adequate answer to the question: Where does a God of grace, or love, or care fit into an evolutionary world? In contemporary discussion, at least three potential answers present themselves: (1) the naturalistic argument for grounding human morality in pre-human nature; (2) the free-will defense of God, which values freedom more highly than non-suffering while positing divine kenosis; (3) the application to nature of the Theology of the Cross combined with the theology of new creation. In what follows, I outline the key features of each model. The one I believe is the most adequate is the third, combining the Theology of the Cross with the divine promise for a new creation. In itself, this would not suffice to construct a theistic evolution, but it would provide some founding pillars on which to build a superstructure.

The naturalistic argument for grounding human morality in pre-human nature

The first of the three live candidates for giving an account of suffering while developing a theistic evolution is naturalism. Now, naturalism can come in both an atheistic and a theological form. Richard Dawkins provides us with an example of atheistic naturalism, while Holmes Rolston III proffers a theological variant.

Richard Dawkins provides a naturalistic account that supports his vigorously missionary brand of atheism. According to Dawkins, nature is without purpose, without meaning, and without care. It is pitiless. Darwin's theory of natural selection demonstrates this point. No divine designer, or director, or provider is on the scene to add something nature herself does not provide. All that we have is what nature gives us. To ask for anything more would be unreasonable. We should grow up, become reasonable, and simply accept this fact. This need not be reconciled with a God of grace, because no such God exists.

Dawkins tries to provide a naturalistic ethic, despite the fact that he believes evolutionary history has been driven by the selfish gene, that is, driven by DNA's drive to replicate itself. If nature is without purpose, and if the nature we inherit is dominated by the gene's selfish desire to replicate, then what kind of ethic would be implied? One would expect an ethic of *laissez faire* capitalism, a social ethic that applauds the fittest who defeat their competitors to survive. We would expect racism and genocide. If no God exists, and if nature is our only source for moral guidance, then we should expect a Nietzschean ethic that dispenses with the weak and celebrates the "will to power." Yet this is not the route Dawkins takes us. Rather, Dawkins embraces all the values of the modern Enlightenment: human equality, the pursuit of justice, and even care for the victims of discrimination. Dawkins says that our evolutionary history programmed us not just for survival, but also for "the urge to kindness – to altruism, to generosity, to empathy, to pity" (Dawkins 2006: 221). And, if that is not enough, Dawkins further says that we can overcome our genetic determinism and achieve an ethical standard that transcends our biological inheritance. The problem of suffering is solved by the promise of high-minded human morality. Now, we might ask, how did we get to this kind of ethic from this kind of natural inheritance?

Evidently, a sociobiologist can distinguish between the selfish gene and the less-than-selfish organism. Just because genes are selfish, organisms need not be. Selfishness in the Dawkinsian sense is understood simply as the desire to replicate. "A gene is a replicator with high copying-fidelity" (Dawkins 1989 [1979]: 30). Gene replication is the driving force of natural selection. Those genes that get copied and passed on win in the game of survival-of-the-fittest. The genes that survive are those that get copied and repeated. Yet the organism which the genes have created to carry them from one generation to another need not be selfish in the same way. "We have the power to defy the selfish genes," says Dawkins. We can behave in altruistic ways. We can deliberately cultivate "pure, disinterested altruism – something that has no place in nature" (*ibid.*: 215). Even though suffering is everywhere present in nature, we can defy our biological propensity and decry suffering and work assiduously to minimize or eliminate suffering.

Selfishness at the genetic level makes altruism possible at the organism level, Dawkins is saying. The selfishness of the gene does not automatically transfer to the selfishness of the individual organism. "The whole idea of the selfish gene […] is that the unit of natural selection (i.e., the unit of self-interest) is not the selfish organism, nor the selfish group or selfish species or selfish ecosystem, but the selfish *gene*" (Dawkins 2006: 215). Then he proceeds to list four ways in which organisms may function altruistically. Even though driven by selfish genes, the social habits of individuals or groups may not in themselves be selfish: (1) kin altruism is a form of self-sacrifice on the part of some individuals for other individuals who carry the same DNA, with the result that the shared DNA sequences get passed on; (2) reciprocal altruism applies to one group of organisms that cooperate for the benefit of another group which does not share the same DNA, with the result that both groups survive; (3) enhancing social power through conspicuous generosity, resulting in a reputation for dominance or superiority, thereby attracting mates and passing on genes; and (4) employing this reputation for buying advertising within the group, and increasing the opportunity for mating and gene continuance (*ibid.*: 219–20; see also Dunbar 1992: 145–47). These final two look a lot alike; both operate at the level of the organism in its respective society, where the chances of its genes' survival are enhanced through the attractiveness of generosity to potential mates.

Dawkins celebrates how nature gifts us with the potential for altruism. We human beings can get beyond the limitations of simply serving the selfish need of the gene. We can cultivate the "urge to kindness – to altruism, to generosity, to empathy, to pity. In ancestral times, we had the opportunity to be altruistic only towards close kin and potential reciprocators. Nowadays, that restriction is no longer there." From a strictly Dawkinsian point of view, was altruism a necessary step in evolutionary development? No. It was a misfire or a mistake, something like an unnecessary mutation. Yet we can be thankful for such leaps beyond genetic selfishness. Disinterested care for others belongs in the category of "misfirings, Darwinian mistakes: blessed, precious mistakes" (Dawkins 2006: 221).

Could a theistic evolutionist incorporate Dawkins' selfish gene theory? Perhaps, as long as Jesus' teachings on love – radical self-giving love or *agape* – are said to mark an evolutionary advance in the organism's development of altruism. Something like this is going on in the thought of Holmes Rolston III, who similarly embraces a naturalist approach. He would agree that the roots of our modern ethics lie in our genetic inheritance. But, more than Dawkins, Rolston believes human culture transcends our genetic history. "There are precursor animal roots [to ethics], but few will claim that morality is 'nothing but' genetically determined animal behavior" (Rolston 1999: 228). Cultural epigenesis rides on top of biological genesis.

Should Christians accept a diminished grade of love – a reciprocal altruism – something less than *agape*? No, says Rolston. If one wants to embrace Christian *agape* in its fullest sense, then no evolutionary precedent can account for it. "A genuinely altruistic sense […] a person acts, on the moral account, intending to benefit others at cost to himself or herself, and on the genetic account, increasing the likelihood of the aided person's having offspring over one's having them" (*ibid.*: 248). Kin altruism and reciprocal altruism are poor substitutes for genuine altruism – *agape* love – because they are secretly forms of the selfish gene in action. "All that natural selection permits is forms of quasi altruism that are actually self-interest" (*ibid*.: 251). Sociobiologists such as Dawkins and E. O. Wilson have "the problem of generating generosity. Selfish genes are never generous beyond expedience; that is the core of sociobiological theory" (*ibid*.: 267).

What Rolston, like Dawkins, wants to do is root or ground our highest ethical aspirations in our evolutionary history. Both are naturalists, although Dawkins is the only atheist. Yet their positions are similar. For Rolston, to move from the drive to survive to self-sacrificial dimensions of a moral ideal is to move from what "is" to what "ought" to be. More than genesis, we need epigenesis. "We inherit these selfish genes, but from somewhere too we inherit genes that prompt us to sympathy, to mutual care, and to cooperation, and from somewhere we […] get enough mental power to reflect over our evolutionary genes and to generate an ethic about what *ought* to be in the light of this *is*" (*ibid*.: 269).

In summary, what we find in this first live option is a two-step argument. First, nature does not have any values built in from its point of origin. Nature is amoral. It may appear cruel to us, but that is because we look at nature through moral lenses. Second, the history of nature has led to the development of a moral consciousness and conscience. We are it. We are the result of an evolutionary process which brought moral judgment to natural history. Through evolution, we have risen above our beginnings. Rolston says, "Morality is not intrinsic to natural systems. In fact, there are no moral agents in wild nature. Nature is amoral, but that is not to disparage it. […] Amoral nature is fundamentally and radically the ground, the root out of which arise all the particular values manifest in organisms. This includes all human values, even though, when they come, human values rise higher than their precedents in spontaneous nature" (*ibid*.: 286–87).

When theistic evolutionists try to integrate New Testament commitments with such examples of evolutionary naturalism, Jesus ends up playing the role of the one who introduces an evolutionary advance in altruism. Jesus' ethic of love for the other without expectation of reciprocity is judged to be an advance, yet still on the single evolutionary path. This position offers nothing toward a theodicy, toward justifying a powerful and loving God who, for billions of years before the development of human altruism, allegedly let countless sentient beings suffer as prey and let species go extinct. The nihilism of a purposeless, extra-human universe better accounts for this.

The free-will defense in neo-kenotic theology

We just took a look at a naturalistic argument, which some theologians deem viable for theological appropriation. We now turn to a second alternative, a classical and well worn argument for reconciling a gracious God with creation's suffering, namely the free-will defense. Some contemporary theistic evolutionists have modified the more classic free-will defense by adding an element – by adding divine kenosis to their theodicy. Let us identify this position as an appeal to *divine kenosis combined with valuing freedom higher than relief from suffering*. In contrast to naturalism combined with altruism, this answer is theistic from the outset. It affirms God as creator.

It affirms that God, not nature, is the source and ground of the good. Yet it affirms that nature, not God, is responsible for suffering.

In its classic form, this theodicy relied upon the concept of evil as the *privatio boni* – that is, the privation of the good. In this theological tradition, what is good is identified with being. The highest good is the fullest being. Subordinate goods can be pressed into the service of higher goods. It was Augustine who most fully articulated the principle of evil as the privation of the good, *privatio boni*. "For what is that which we call evil but the absence of the good?" (1961: 11). Suffering is an evil slung in the metaxic tension between being and non-being. Even if we suffer, we are good by virtue of our existence. This applies to all living things. Even in the face of corruption, or suffering, or dissolution, what we deem evil is redeemed, so to speak, when taken up into the comprehensive ensemble which constitutes the universe in its entirety. Individual suffering is a part of a much larger whole, which is good. "Taken as a whole, however, they are very good, because their *ensemble* constitutes the universe in all its wonderful order and beauty" (*ibid*.: 11). The beauty of the whole redeems the corruption of the part. The evil of suffering is mitigated when taken up into a larger whole, the achievement of freedom.

The *privatio boni* provides the classical background. Now, let's move to the foreground. As theistic evolutionists wrestle with the theodicy question in light of evolutionary theory, many add the kenosis hypothesis. Our word "kenosis" comes from Philippians 2: 5–8 (New Revised Standard Bible, NRS): "Let the same mind be in you that was in Christ Jesus, who, though he was in the form of God, did not regard equality with God as something to be exploited, but emptied himself, taking the form of a slave, being born in human likeness. And being found in human form, he humbled himself and became obedient to the point of death – even death on a cross." To empty oneself, or to deny to oneself divinity, is that to which the word "kenosis" refers. Note that the kenotic figure here is the second person of the Trinity, the Son, who empties himself of the Father's divinity in order to become incarnate, to suffer, and to die (cf. Murphy and Ellis 1996). Jesus Christ de-divinizes himself, so to speak, in order to become Emmanuel, God with us.

The interpretation of this passage proffered by our neo-kenotic theologians goes like this: the Creator God withdraws divine power from the creation so that creatures can exert their own power and act freely. The pay-off is this: if God kenotically withdraws from the creation, then the creation is free to act on its own. Creatures can create their own world, so to speak; the world engages in self-organization, or autopoises. Biological evolution is the form of self-organization this world has taken. If, via evolution, the creation has freely organized itself to include suffering and death, then so be it. Suffering and death are the price God pays to create free creatures.

Here is the central thesis: earthly freedom is the product of heavenly absence. By withdrawing divine power, God opens up space for creatures to exert power. Even if God is omnipotent, through kenosis God becomes non-coercive. By withdrawing divine power, God opens up space for creaturely freedom. The absence of God is what makes our free activities possible. What accounts for the specific path that evolution has taken is the contingency and freedom God has provided to the created order. Suffering along the way is a means to a higher good, namely, a community of free individuals. Arthur Peacocke puts it this way: "This self-limitation is the precondition for the coming into existence of free self-conscious human beings […] The cost to God, if we may dare so to speak, was in that act of self-limitation, of *kenosis*, which constitutes God's creative action – a self-inflicted vulnerability to the very processes God had himself created in order to achieve an overriding purpose, the emergence of free persons" (Peacocke 1993: 123–24).

In my judgment, the neo-kenotic theodicy is inadequate. I have three basic criticisms. First, the new kenotic theologians have yet to articulate a way to make their emphasis on freedom compatible with the idea that we have inherited in our genes – selfish genes? – the propensity for violence, evil, and suffering. This evolutionary inheritance appears to be a form of genetic determinism, not freedom. If freedom is the alleged divine goal of God's kenotic activity and of nature's self-organizing capacity, then why are we in moral bondage to our genetic past?

My second critical observation is that the scriptural basis for applying kenosis to the first person of the Trinity and to the doctrine of creation is exegetically problematic. The very passage on which the concept is derived, Philippians 2: 5–8, describes the second person divesting himself of the divinity belonging to the first person. No mention of the first person engaging in self-limitation or de-divinizing appears. So no scriptural warrant exists to apply kenosis to God the Father.

If it is not biblical, might we rescue the neo-kenotic position by appeal to systematic theology? Could we use the term "God" to mean the Godhead, or the Trinity, not just the Father? Well, yes, to be sure. The actions of the Son apply to the actions of God in Godself. If this is what is being said by the neo-kenotic theologians, then they might get by with it.

Even if we rescue this neo-kenotic treatment of the Godhead, we confront a third problem. It has to do with power. It appears that the neo-kenotic theologians make a false assumption about the nature of God's power. They assume that, for creatures to have power and hence freedom, God needs to withdraw. If God is omnipotent and possessing all power, then, they assume, we creatures have none. God's omnipotence is a form of tyranny. So if God withdraws through self-limitation, then we can take advantage of the power vacuum. Only if God lacks power in the world can we have the power to exercise our freedom. For us to be free, God must be absent.

The neo-kenotic theologians seem to presume that there exists a fixed amount of power in the universe, like there is a fixed number of ounces of milk in a gallon. If God gets more, we get less. If we get more, God gets less. Only if we have enough of what God does not have, can we get our daily nourishment. Perhaps this applies to human milk drinkers, where one person has greater thirst than another. But I do not believe it applies to God.

According to the biblical picture of God, God's power empowers us. It does not compete with our power. Rather, our power is a gift from a powerful deity. In the case of the Exodus, for example, God heard the cries of the oppressed slaves in Egypt. God then exerted divine power in order to liberate them from the chains of their taskmasters. Deuteronomy 5: 15 (NRS): "Remember that you were a slave in the land of Egypt, and the LORD your God brought you out from there with a mighty hand and an outstretched arm." Had God decided to be kenotic and withdraw, the Hebrews would have remained helpless in their slavery. Only by exerting power with "a mighty hand and an outstretched arm" could liberation be achieved. Therefore it is a mistake, in my judgment, to rewrite the doctrine of creation in such a way that God's absence replaces God's presence in the creative process.

Divine power is compatible with creation's contingency and with human power. If the neo-kenotic theologians presume all power is of a single type, and that God and creatures compete for it, then this makes them incompatibilists – that is, they cannot accept the idea that God's actions could be co-present to our creaturely free actions. Christopher Southgate argues: "It is now my contention that the language of kenosis in creation tends to arise out of commitment to a questionable spatial metaphor for the God–world relation – the alleged need for God to 'make space' within Godself for the created world and/or an also questionable commitment to incompatibilism – the notion that the free actions of creatures are incompatible with the involvement of God in every event" (Southgate 2008: 53–85).

In summary, I do not recommend that the theistic evolutionist follow completely the strategy proposed by the neo-kenotic variant of the free-will theodicy. I applaud the neo-kenotic attempt to account for God's power combined with God's self-sacrificial love in the service of nature's contingency and human freedom. Yet I fear that this position stands on flimsy exegetical and systematic grounds. Christopher Southgate, however, may offer just the adjustments necessary to render this position effective.

Applying the cross and resurrection to the natural world

With the inadequacy of the first two alternatives in mind, I would like to construct an approach that speaks more adequately to the problem of suffering. Where does a God of grace, or love, or care fit into an evolutionary world? The role of divine suffering is important in the biblical revelation, so perhaps it can be applied to evolution. It may be worth our while to turn to the theology of the cross. In the Reformation theology of Martin Luther and its subsequent development in Jürgen Moltmann, the theology of the cross stresses two messages. First, it is a theory of revelation, revelation hidden behind masks. It insists that God's presence and action in the world are not immediately visible. On the contrary, what God actually does might differ from what we expect. God is hidden. God's majesty and power are hidden behind the masks of humility and weakness. God's eternal life is hidden behind the mask of death; healing behind a mask of suffering. "The manifest and visible things of God are placed in opposition to the invisible, namely, his human nature, weakness, foolishness […] in the humility and shame of the cross" (*Luther's Works* 31: 53). To understand God, says Luther, we must look at the cross and recognize that we do not understand God.

The theology of the cross teaches a second message: God's life shares in the suffering of the world. In the person of Jesus, the triune God suffers. "When the crucified Jesus is called the 'image of the invisible God'," writes Jürgen Moltmann, "the meaning is that *this* is God, and God is like *this*. […] The Christ event on the cross is a God event" (Moltmann 1974: 2005). Can we say that all the suffering of this world is taken up in this representative person, Jesus Christ? Yes. As the universal Logos, the principle by which all things hold together, the actual history of the creation complete with all of its suffering is taken up into the life of the second person of the Trinity, the Son. Jesus Christ is both the embodiment of the physical world and the image of God. God experiences what we experience, both suffering and estrangement.

The next move is crucial. The theologian needs to make a move from history to nature, actually to the history of nature. When we speak of the crucifixion of Jesus, we ordinarily think of it as a historical event. It is a human event, a political event. But in dealing with evolutionary theodicy, we might ask: Could the cross be a natural event as well? Could we apply what we learn about God from the cross to how we understand the natural world, and even how we understand human nature?

George L. Murphy says, "yes." Murphy applies the cross to the natural world. "The crosslike pattern of creation means that Christ crucified has cosmic significance" (Murphy 2003: 33). Murphy goes on: "God suffers *with* the world from whatever evil takes place. […] We begin with the fact that God suffered on the cross, but we do not have to stop with that. God's voluntary self-limitation that enables the world to have its own existence and integrity keeps God from simply preventing all evil in miraculous ways. Evil is then the 'dark side' of an aspect of the goodness of creation, its functional integrity" (*ibid*.: 87).

Application of the theology of the cross to nature gets us only half-way home. What it does is make clear that, if we begin with what we know about God based upon revelation in the cross of Jesus Christ, God is likely to identify as much with the victims of predation and natural selection as with the victors. If this provides a clue to the meaning of creation, we cannot allow inclusive fitness or triumphal progress to define in any exclusive fashion God's providence in the evolution of life. Yet, there must be more. There must be a vision of what the "good" in creation is (Genesis 1: 1–2, 4), which we may apply. This vision is found in the symbol of the new creation.

We appeal now to a natural symbol, the *new creation*, along with its historical anticipation, the Easter resurrection of Jesus. I call new creation a natural symbol, because we associate creation with nature. More frequently, the Bible uses historical or political symbols such as the "kingdom of God" or "the new Jerusalem" when identifying God's redemptive plan. Yet the natural symbols and political symbols are interchangeable. Both point to God's eschatological promise of a new order, a renewed creation which will also be salvation.

Isaiah's prophecy of what we have nicknamed the "Peaceable Kingdom" stands right up and demands notice. Isaiah 11: 6–8 (NRS): "The wolf shall live with the lamb, the leopard shall lie down with the kid, the calf and the lion and the fatling together, and a little child shall lead them. The cow and the bear shall graze, their young shall lie down together; and the lion shall eat straw like the ox. The nursing child shall play over the hole of the asp, and the weaned child shall put its hand on the adder's den." When the Messiah comes to establish God's kingdom, all of nature will participate in a cosmic healing. There will be peace among the animals. No longer will they devour one another to assuage their hunger. Might the theologian say: this is the creation God intended to call "good" back in Genesis 1: 1–2:4a? By the time we finish the Bible with the Apocalypse or Revelation, the creation is in fact good. Healing will have taken place. Disease will have disappeared. So will other forms of suffering. Revelation 21: 1–4 (NRS): "Then I saw a new heaven and a new earth; for the first heaven and the first earth had passed away, and the sea was no more. And I saw the holy city, the new Jerusalem, coming down out of heaven from God, prepared as a bride adorned for her husband. And I heard a loud voice from the throne saying, 'See, the home of God is among mortals. He will dwell with them; they will be his peoples, and God himself will be with them; he will wipe every tear from their eyes. Death will be no more; mourning and crying and pain will be no more, for the first things have passed away.'" When confronting the theodicy question, I find these two prophetic passages to provide the key to the answer, because they indicate how wholeness and healing belong to the heart of the divine plan.

Now, let us turn around and apply the future to the past. Let us apply these eschatological symbols to the doctrine of creation. May we think of the present creation as on the way, so to speak, to a new creation that will deserve the unambiguous title, "very good"?

Ontologically, the new creation takes priority over the present creation. The future of the universe will retroactively determine the meaning of its past and present. From our point of view in the present, we are looking forward toward transformation and fulfillment. "Cosmic and biological evolution instruct us as never before that we live in a universe that is in great measure not yet created," writes John Haught. "In an evolving cosmos, created being as such has *not yet* achieved the state of integrity" (Haught 2003: 168, italics original). Or, elsewhere, "The notion of an unfinished universe still coming into being […] opens up the horizon of a new or unprecedented future. […] *Esse est adventire.* In its depths, nature is promise" (*ibid.*: 170).

For a theistic evolutionist to deal adequately with the Darwinian model of evolution complete with predator–prey violence and the massive history of extinction, the doctrine of redemption must be brought to bear on the doctrine of creation. Robert John Russell recommends this with considerable force. "We need to relocate the problem of natural evil from the doctrine of creation to the doctrine of redemption, where we can find appropriate forms of response shaped by the millennia of theology's grappling with the problem of moral evil. In short, we need to extend the Theology of the Cross and the Resurrection of Jesus to embrace all of life on earth – and in the universe" (Russell 2007: 204).

Constructing the house of theistic evolution

Is all of this only a defensive maneuver on the part of theistic evolution to move out of the neighborhood where creationism and intelligent design live? No. More than a minimal attempt to conflate Darwinian theory with the Christian doctrine of creation, the theistic evolutionist needs to construct a comprehensive vision of God's creative and redemptive plan for the natural world, a vision inclusive of deep time and the suffering associated with natural selection. Borrowing from the theology of the cross and the biblical promise of a new creation, we can apply to the conundra arising out of natural suffering an authentic theology of nature.

My suggested logic has been this: when a disciple with faith looks upon the cross of Jesus Christ, something about God is revealed. One quality revealed is that God in Godself is present to us under the conditions of rejection, suffering, and death. If we insist on believing that a God of power sides only with victory, then God's presence under the conditions of the cross will elude us. Yet if we can confess that in the man from Nazareth we perceive the universal Logos incarnate, and if we perceive that he sums up in himself all the sufferings of the created order, then the sufferings of this world become internal to the divine life. By joining with others willing to admit they adhere to theistic evolution, I have turned to the cross and resurrection of Jesus Christ. Rather than keep all speculative theology within the doctrine of creation, I have asked whether the doctrine of redemption could be equally illuminating on the difficult question of evil and suffering. I have answered in the affirmative.

References

Augustine (1961) *The Enchiridion on Faith, Hope, and Love*, Washington, DC: Regnery Gateway.

Dawkins, Richard (1989 [1979]) *The Selfish Gene*, Oxford and New York: Oxford University Press.

——(2006) *The God Delusion*, New York: Houghton Mifflin.

Dunbar, Robin (1992) "Social Behaviour and Evolutionary Theory," in *The Cambridge Encyclopedia of Human Evolution*, Steve Jones, Robert Martin and David Pilbeam (eds), Cambridge: Cambridge University Press, 1992, 145–49.

Haught, John (2003) *Deeper than Darwin*, Boulder, CO: Westview.

Moltmann, Jürgen (1974) *The Crucified God*, San Francisco, CA: Harper.

Murphy, George L. (2003) *The Cosmos in Light of the Cross*, Harrisburg, PA: Trinity Press International.

Murphy, Nancey and George F. R. Ellis (1996) *On the Moral Nature of the Universe*, Minneapolis, MN: Fortress Press.

Peacocke, Arthur (1993) *Theology for a Scientific Age*, Minneapolis, MN: Fortress Press.

Peters, Ted and Martinez J. Hewlett (2003) *Evolution from Creation to New Creation: Conflict, Conversation, and Convergence*, Nashville, TN: Abingdon Press.

——(2006) *Can You Believe in God and Evolution?: A Guide for the Perplexed*. Nashville, TN: Abingdon Press.

Rolston, Holmes, III (1999) *Genes, Genesis, and God: Values and their Origins in Natural and Human History*, Cambridge: Cambridge University Press.

Russell, Robert John (2007) "Five Key Topics on the Frontier of Theology and Science Today," *Dialog* 46(3): 199–207.

Southgate, Christopher (2008) *The Groaning of Creation: God, Evolution, and the Problem of Evil*, Louisville, KY: Westminster John Knox.

——(2008) "Creation as *Very Good* and *Groaning in Travail*: An Exploration in Evolutionary Theodicy," in *The Evolution of Evil*, Gaymon Bennett, Martinez Hewlett, Ted Peters and Robert John Russell (eds), Göttingen: Vandenhoeck & Ruprecht, 53–85.

Further reading

A fine starting point for exploring evolution and suffering is *The Evolution of Evil*, edited by Gaymon Bennett, Martinez Hewlett, Ted Peters and Robert John Russell (Vandenhoeck &

Ruprecht, 2008). Another useful text in this area, especially for theologians, is my *Sin: Radical Evil in Soul and Society* (Grand Rapids, MI: William B. Eerdmans, 1994). Christopher Southgate's *The Groaning of Creation: God, Evolution, and the Problem of Evil* (cited above) provides an important contemporary reflection on evolution and suffering, as does Celia Deane-Drummond's *Christ and Evolution: Wonder and Wisdom* (Fortress Press, 2009). A useful collection of essays, critical and otherwise, of the doctrine of kenosis as it relates to the biological sciences, including evolution, can be found in John Polkinghorne's (ed.) *The Work of Love: Creation as Kenosis* (William B. Eerdmans, 2001). For a wider perspective on evil and the scientific perspectives, see Nancey Murphy, Robert John Russell and William R. Stoeger (eds) *Physics and Cosmology: Scientific Perspectives on the Problem of Evil* (University of Notre Dame Press, 2007). For more on the perspective of Holmes Rolston III, see his "Does Nature Need to be Redeemed?," *Zygon: Journal of Religion and Science* 29: 205–29 (1994).

(v) The cognitive sciences and religious experience

26
THE COGNITIVE SCIENCES
A brief introduction for science and religion

Michael L. Spezio

Cognitive science for science and religion: a way in

The core focus of cognitive science is to relate the activities of mind, which are never directly observable from a third-person perspective, to those measures that are directly observable, measurable, and sometimes quantifiable from the crucial third-person perspective. Because the activities of mind either exist for us only as traditional language needing replacement (Churchland and Churchland 1998) or as influential, albeit invisible, perhaps emergent, transformations of information (O'Connor 2000; Clayton 2004), cognitive science begins by acknowledging the inferential nature of its work.

Cognitive science, comprised of psychology, neuroscience, computer science, linguistics, anthropology, and philosophy (Miller 2003), is thus central to future interdisciplinary scholarship and decision-making around science and religion, for two primary reasons. First, any perspectives from within religious communities, religious studies, and philosophy that would turn toward public or private decision-making about moral action, education, the environment, the law, and medicine must have a conception of human nature and/or human agency, which necessarily includes the mind. Second, cognitive science is *the* science that seeks to relate the psychological functions of information processing (in thought, emotion, intention, volition, valuation, agency) to the physically measurable signals from the human body (measures from the brain, heart, skin, eyes, breath, bodily posture, bodily movements). Without implying any reduction of psychology to biology or to computer science, cognitive science is *the* science concerned with testing hypotheses about the invisible processes of mind using the visible measures of the body, whether that body is organic and alive, or manufactured and computerized. Indeed, cognitive science is itself an interdisciplinary science because it is not only concerned with associating measurable internal processes in a carbon or silicon body with behavior, but it is centrally concerned with how the mind links these two. This concern with the mind is why experimental psychology is a core part of cognitive science. It is not true, as many students and even some psychologists say, that psychology is the science of behavior. As Noam Chomsky stated at the beginning of the cognitive turn in psychology, saying that psychology is the science of behavior is like saying that "physics is the science of meter reading" (quoted in Miller 2003). Cognitive science is impossible to do in any complete fashion without models of mental processes, since without such models, the measurables (such as brain activity and behavior) have no meaning.

What follows takes up the views of cognition in cognitive science and the methods of cognitive science, prior to turning toward a brief introduction of major loci in cognitive science. Throughout, there is a heavy influence of experimental fields, particularly cognitive psychology, social psychology, information-processing models of mind, and experimental cognitive, affective, and social neuroscience. Less attention will be given to cognitive linguistics, anthropology, and phenomenology (see especially Zahavi 2001; Thompson 2007; Gallagher and Zahavi 2008), not because they are less important, but because of space limitations.

Cognition and cognitive science

The information-processing topics actively engaged by cognitive science are: sensation, perception, attention, memory, language, emotion, intuition, problem-solving, expertise, reasoning, decision-making, and social judgment and interaction. Cognition in these areas, according to current frameworks in experimental cognitive science, is best described as the functions, or processes, or systems of the mind (Anderson 2010: 1–3). Thus cognition includes both explicit (conscious, aware) processing, and implicit (subconscious, subliminal) processing, and all mental aspects of emotion, feeling, etc. To say that a process is a "cognitive" process does not mean, then, that one is aware of, or conscious of, the thoughts involved in that process. Cognitive processes can be, and most of the time are, implicit and unconscious, and the term "cognitive" can apply to emotions just as well as to language, since both involve information processing.

Until recently, however, emotion was often spoken of *as opposed to* cognition. This is no longer recommended practice, since cognitive science has recognized the critical information content in emotional processing (Davidson 2003; Adolphs and Spezio 2007; Goldstein 2011: 300: 13–15). While it may be true that not all cognition involves emotion, it is also true that not all cognition involves, say, language. Thus it makes as little sense to speak in terms of cognition versus emotion as it does to speak in terms of cognition versus language. Emotion, as understood in cognitive science, is a cognitive process because it involves mental processes, functions, and transformations. These mental processes include activation of organized conceptual schemas in the mind. "Feelings" are different from emotions, since they are the conscious awareness of emotions. "Affect" refers to bodily responses that are part of emotion. When the phrase "cognition and emotion" is used in cognitive science, it can mean both a cognitive scientific approach to emotion and a joining of cognition and affect (Oatley 1999: xvii–xviii). These understandings fall under an embodied or "grounded" cognition framework, most recently championed by Barsalou and co-workers (Barsalou 2008). In this way, cognitive science seeks to avoid conflict between "head and heart," and increasingly recognizes two characteristics of information processing in mind: (1) information processing that is ostensibly non-emotional may in fact have implicit emotional attributes, and carry implicit representations of goals and motivations; and (2) information processing is often strongly influenced by the embodied, enacted experiences by which the information was first learned, in each specific modality (vision, hearing, touch, taste, language, etc.) (*ibid.*: 618–19).

Another area of potential confusion relates to the terms "top-down" and "bottom-up" processes in mind. Top-down processes are those that formed during evolution or learning and that link stimulus processing to context, whereas bottom-up processes are those that depend primarily or wholly on basic stimulus properties, ignoring context (Anderson 2010: 56–57; Goldstein 2011: 300: 61–64). Consider the paradigmatic example of Pavlov's dogs (Pavlov 1927). When the dogs salivate upon smelling or seeing the food, it is a bottom-up response. However, when, after the dogs learn that the sound of a bell accompanies the presentation of their food, they salivate to the sound of the bell alone, it is a top-down response. Top-down processing is either explicit (conscious) or implicit (unconscious), controlled or automatic. Bottom-up processing is generally unconscious and automatic. Top-down processing, understood as linking stimulus processing to context, occurs in the cerebral cortex of the brain, but it also occurs in the amygdala, the hippocampus, and other subcortical regions of the brain. There are other uses of the terms bottom-up and top-down in the literature, such as when top-down is identified with conscious processing, and bottom-up is identified with unconscious processing; or when top-down is identified with processing in the cerebral cortex of the brain, and bottom-up is identified with processing in "lower," subcortical regions; or when top-down is identified with controlled processing, and bottom-up is identified with automatic processing. However, when considered in light of how the terms are used in relation to their original meanings for mental processing, these additional uses tend to create confusion.

It is critically important for the interdisciplinary scholar to keep in mind that implicit top-down processing and explicit, conscious top-down processing are known to interact, albeit in complex ways not yet understood. Implicit top-down processing is highly influential in a wide range of human behavior thought to be under strong conscious control (Hassin *et al.* 2005), from stereotyping others (Olsson *et al.* 2005), to deciding who to vote for (Todorov *et al.* 2005; Spezio *et al.* 2008), to judging what is or is not moral (Greene 2007; Murphy and Brown 2007; Woodward and Allman 2007). Similarly, conscious control processes can act as gates for implicit processes (Ochsner and Gross 2005; Wager *et al.* 2008) and can integrate them for adaptive behaviors (Coan *et al.* 2006; Slagter *et al.* 2007; Lutz *et al.* 2009b).

Cognitive science, admittedly, has specialized uses of "cognition" and "cognitive" that often differ from the way these terms are used in philosophy (e.g. cognitive versus non-cognitive theories of morality), theology, and religious studies. Several of those uses and their meanings have been explored in this section. Another aspect of the specialized use of cognition in cognitive science is that any claim regarding cognition should be testable via experimentation or observation. The next section reviews several methods used in such testing.

Method in cognitive science

To test the claims made by theories and models in cognitive science, complex concepts, such as memory, attention, reasoning, emotion, etc., require "operationalization." To operationalize generally means to define a concept in a way that can be quantified. So cognitive scientists proceed from a given model of mental processing to predictions about behavior that follow from the model, to an experimental test to determine if the predictions are in fact observed. Most cognitive scientific approaches use (1) measures of behavior, including performance accuracy, reaction time, and self-report questionnaires; (2) measures of physiological responses, such as heart rate or skin conductance; and (3) measures of brain response. In addition to these measures, cognitive scientists also combine behavioral measures with interventions into neural or physiological systems. One example is the use of transcranial magnetic stimulation (TMS) to temporarily impair the processing in a given brain area, followed by measuring the behavioral changes, if any, that result (for detailed introductions to these methods see Huettel *et al.* 2008; Purves *et al.* 2008).

A brief introduction to functional magnetic resonance imaging (fMRI) is helpful for the interdisciplinary scholar, since so much of what is claimed in the popular literature is based on fMRI data or related techniques. The physiological signal measured by fMRI has complex relationship with the neural information-processing signals in the brain. The physiological measure yielded by fMRI is the blood oxygenation level-dependent (BOLD) signal, which varies with the amount of deoxygenated blood in a brain region. Yet information processing in the brain, according to prevailing theories in cognitive science, occurs in terms of electrical signals from cells called neurons, and assemblies of neurons, not in terms of blood flow.

Until very recently, neuroscience lacked a good understanding of which neural signals most closely corresponded to the BOLD signal. Recently, Nikos Logothetis (2003; see also Logothetis and Wandell 2004) and Martin Lauritzen (Lauritzen 2001; Caesar *et al.* 2003) showed that the BOLD signal is caused not by action potentials of neurons, but by smaller electrical potentials at the junctures, called synapses, between neurons in the brain. This means that the BOLD signal can differ depending only on differences in circuit organization, even for circuits in the same general area of the brain and under circumstances that yield identical numbers of action potentials.

Another aspect of brain-activity measurement by fMRI is that measured BOLD signal changes due to cognitive processing are of the order of 0.1 to 1 per cent of the total measured signal (Raichle 2003). Thus one must always keep in mind that the BOLD signal is generally a contrast in signal between two or more measurements, each conducted under some set of defined conditions. What this means is that reported fMRI activations, or areas where the brain looks to be "lit up" by bright spots, are not the result of the neural circuitry in those areas going from an "off" state to an "on" state. Rather, activations are typically the result of a brain area going from giving a signal of, say, 10 to a signal of 10.05, in a statistically significant manner. BOLD activations are almost always *differential* activations between conditions. This means that the given region may have been activated in all conditions, but more so in some than in others.

When inferring the information processing that associates with a given brain area's activation, it is important to keep in mind that whether or not a brain area is activated during a given information-processing condition does not by itself establish that the brain area is, or is not, required for the information processing function under investigation (Cacioppo *et al.* 2003). Observed brain activation could be (1) due to a failure to control for all key contextual variables in contrasting task conditions; or (2) the result of activity in another circuit in another area entirely, which actually carries out the information-processing function. Conversely, failure to observe brain activation could arise even in the presence of differences in neural activity, if the differences are in different neural circuits that differ substantially in synaptic organization (Logothetis and Wandell 2004). Activation maps resulting from fMRI experiments reported in any one paper are best interpreted as hypothetical associations between information processing and brain activity. These hypotheses require corroboration using other methods.

Finally, one should avoid *reverse inference* when interpreting neuroimaging results. Reverse inference is bad logic, and it is practiced when one assigns a cognitive role to a given brain activation in experiment A based wholly on evidence from experiment B, where experiments A and B are unrelated and used unrelated behavioral tasks. For example, if a number of experiments with fear-related stimuli (such as pictures of snakes or spiders) show activation in the amygdala in response to those stimuli, and in my experiment I see activation in the amygdala to images of puppy dogs, I would be using reverse inference if I inferred from this that puppy dogs caused my participants to be afraid. It would be like saying: fear stimuli activate the amygdala; puppy dog images activate the amygdala; therefore puppy dog images are frightening. It may be that my participants find puppies frightening, but I would need more data to support it, such as participant self-report of puppy fear, or puppy-induced fear-potentiated startle (Davis *et al.* 1993), for example.

It should be emphasized that this account of fMRI methodology in no way undermines its usefulness, when handled appropriately, as a central method in formulating models in cognitive science. The fact is that fMRI allows what was once thought to be impossible: a non-invasive view into brain processing during complex behavior in human participants. Its limitations do not call into question the fMRI neuroimaging literature in general. Indeed, it should be obvious that any scientific methodology will have limits, and that such limits should be acknowledged. Similar issues exist for other methods in cognitive science (electroencephalography, TMS, the lesion/deficit method, computational modeling, etc.).

Cognitive science and religious experience

Having an introduction to the theoretical and methodological considerations of cognitive science allows a more careful assessment of how cognitive science may illuminate understandings of religious experience. For a more in-depth introduction to the context and careful thought required for relating religious concepts and cognitive science, see Peterson (2003).

Research into the experimental cognitive science of meditation and contemplative practice, mystical experience, and religiosity has been increasing. This area can be divided into studies that investigate (1) mystical, or peak, experiences; (2) the effects of meditation in typical participants; (3) the effects of long-term contemplative practice and extreme expertise in meditation (Barinaga 2003); and (4) the sources of religious belief and religiosity. This latter category currently has a limited number of peer-reviewed publications relating to experimental cognitive science (Harris *et al.* 2009; Kapogiannis *et al.* 2009), and tends to downplay the importance of established methodology and conceptual frameworks in the psychology of religion (Emmons and Paloutzian 2003), and the rich field studies by scholars in religious studies.

Two of the major laboratories conducting studies of mystical, peak experiences are led by Andrew Newberg at the University of Pennsylvania and Mario Beauregard at the University of Montreal. Newberg was among the first researchers to use neuroimaging methods to investigate peak experiences, or what he and Eugene d'Aquili termed "absolute unitary being" (d'Aquili and Newberg 1999). Newberg and his group have published several papers about this unique religious experience, implicating the functional disconnection between the superior parietal cortex and those cortical areas involved in perception and spatial orienting (Newberg *et al.* 2001, 2003). Due to the lack of spatial and temporal resolution, and to the caveats regarding the interpretation of blood flow measures already described, this interpretation requires caution (see the extended discussion in Runehov 2007: 137–200). What is beyond doubt is that those who report engaging in meditative practices and experiencing peak moments show differential activation of specific brain regions, when compared with rest.

More recently, Beauregard's group reported results with a rare group of cloistered Carmelite nuns, who nonetheless visited the laboratory for an MRI scanning study. The most prominent finding from this work is that Beauregard observed differentially higher activation in brain regions associated with social and emotional processing, and significantly different patterns of activation in these areas, when comparing recall of intense spiritual intimacy with God ("mystical union" according to the reports) with recall of intense personal intimacy with a friend or family member (Beauregard and Paquette 2006). This finding should put to rest any notion that the spiritual union reported by the nuns is reported out of social conformity or a desire to appear more spiritual than one actually is. More importantly, the findings suggest that the nuns' experience was not simply an increase in social intimacy, or simply a more intense recruitment of networks for social intimacy. The differential patterns of activation suggest non-overlapping neural networks involved in spiritual union and personal intimacy in this group of cloistered nuns.

This may differ from the pattern observed in everyday religious practitioners, as suggested by the work of Schjoedt and co-workers (Schjoedt *et al.* 2009). They claimed, using data from an fMRI experiment, that when a group of young lay Christians engaged in free, personal prayer (compared with when they silently expressed wishes to Santa Claus), prayer simply activated networks comparable with a "normal" (their term) interpersonal interaction. However, the authors' interpretation relies in part on reverse inference. In Schjoedt *et al.* (2009), personal, free prayer elicited greater activation in areas such as the temporoparietal junction, that have in past experiments been associated with tasks requiring active thought about another person's mind (Saxe and Kanwisher 2003; Bedny *et al.* 2009). However, there is no way to be sure that the activations seen in Schjoedt *et al.* (2009) were the result of information processing about another person's mind, because that experiment did not directly test whether the participants did this.

In another investigation comparing neural activations during ritualized prayer (e.g. the Lord's Prayer) with those occurring while expressing wishes to Santa Claus, Schjoedt *et al.* (2008) found activation of the caudate head, a major subcortical brain area strongly associated with learning, specifically with prediction errors relating to reward. That is, the caudate head generally shows increased activation when the actual reward delivered is higher than the expected reward (Bray and O'Doherty 2007; O'Doherty *et al.* 2007; Valentin and O'Doherty 2009). Yet, while Schjoedt *et al.* (2008) concluded that prayers are rewarding, based on the activation they saw in the caudate, the authors did not explicitly test whether the prayers were rewarding to their participants. Further, they did not suggest an explanation of exactly what kind of prediction error elicited the activation. The key question is, what kind of reward could the participants have been receiving, throughout their prayers, that constantly differed from what they expected? Additionally, the caudate is known to show some sensitivity to the type of reward (Valentin and O'Doherty 2009), which was not addressed at all by the authors. So the brain activations seen when contrasting prayer and wishes to Santa Claus might have arisen for other reasons, including reasons pertaining to whether the participants actually believed they were engaged with the presence of another person, or not. This interpretation would indicate an effect of belief, not reward.

In another study by Schjoedt *et al.* (2010), in which they focus on the sources of religious belief and religiosity, charismatic Christian and secular participants were asked to listen to short intercessory prayers for healing, spoken by persons described to the participants as "non-Christian," "Christian," or "Christian known for healing powers." In fact, all the prayers were spoken by non-charismatic Christians. The main reported finding involved brain activations from the Christian group that resulted from a contrast between listening to the non-Christian speaker versus the Christian known for healing powers. There was a widespread increase in brain activation when listening to the non-Christian, relative to listening to the Christian with healing powers, including in areas that other, unrelated experiments have associated with "executive control," or a system involved in managing cognitive conflict and critical thinking. Again, there was no direct test of critical thinking among participants in the experiment. Yet the authors interpreted these activations as arising due to the "power of charisma" to reduce processing involved in critical thinking among charismatic Christians who believe they are listening to a charismatic healer. An equally parsimonious interpretation is that charismatic Christian participants engaged in increased critical thinking when trying to understand why a person described as non-Christian would give an impassioned intercessory prayer in exactly the same fashion as the "Christian with healing powers." That is, the "control" condition in this experiment actually involved a significant contextual conflict to which Christian participants may have been especially sensitive.

In sum, these studies report brain regions being activated during a religiously relevant task, and quickly conclude that the task involves exactly the same cognitive processing that unrelated experiments associate with that brain region, under very different cognitive conditions (also see Harris *et al.* 2009 on "the" neural correlates of religious beliefs). These interpretations depend in part on reverse inference, which is problematic, although the data are quite interesting.

By far the most peer-reviewed work applying cognitive science to the study of meditation and contemplative practice has focused on the efficacy of such practice on health outcomes (Kabat-Zinn *et al.* 1992; Kabat-Zinn *et al.* 1998; Davidson *et al.* 2003), mental processing ability (Lutz *et al.* 2009b; Slagter *et al.* 2009), and compassion (Lutz *et al.* 2009a), both in relatively inexperienced and in expert meditators. In this sustained research effort, consistent findings show that meditation enhances attentional performance through what is thought to be an increased ability to disengage attention from task-irrelevant stimuli, memories, emotions, and processes (Lutz *et al.* 2008; Slagter *et al.* 2009). Importantly, the effort here is motivated primarily not by the discovery of ultimate states or mystical experiences, but by a focus on (1) discovering practices that facilitate mental and physical well-being; and (2) working using the expertise of contemplative adepts to discover new properties of consciousness. This latter project rests on claims from extremely experienced contemplative practitioners, generally those with Eastern practices, that Western notions of consciousness as fleeting or unstable are wrong, and that, within meditation, conscious states, including qualia, can be held for minutes or hours. If such claims are replicable in the laboratory, it would enable a new way to study the neural contributions to consciousness.

References

Adolphs, R. and Spezio, M.L. (2007) "The Neural Basis of Affective and Social Behavior," in Cacciopo, J. T., Tassinary, L. G. and Berntson, G. G. (eds), *Handbook of Psychophysiology*, Cambridge: Cambridge University Press.

Anderson, J. R. (2010) *Cognitive Psychology and its Implications*, New York: Worth.

d'Aquili, E. and Newberg, A.B. (1999) *The Mystical Mind*, Minneapolis, MN: Fortress Press.

Barinaga, M. (2003) "Studying the Well-Trained Mind," *Science* 302: 44–46.

Barsalou, L.W. (2008) "Grounded Cognition," *Annu Rev Psychol*, 59: 617–45.

Beauregard, M. and Paquette, V. (2006) "Neural correlates of a mystical experience in Carmelite nuns," *Neurosci Lett*, 405: 186–90.

Bedny, M., Pascual-Leone, A. and Saxe, R.R. (2009) "Growing up blind does not change the neural bases of Theory of Mind," *Proc Natl Acad Sci USA*, 106: 11312–17.

Bray, S. and O'Doherty, J. (2007) "Neural coding of reward-prediction error signals during classical conditioning with attractive faces," *J Neurophysiol*, 97: 3036–45.

Cacioppo, J.T., Berntson, G.G., Lorig, T.S., Norris, C.J., Rickett, E. and Nusbaum, H. (2003) "Just because you're imaging the brain doesn't mean you can stop using your head: a primer and set of first principles," *Journal of Personality and Social Psychology* 85: 650–61.

Caesar, K., Thomsen, K. and Lauritzen, M. (2003) "Dissociation of spikes, synaptic activity, and activity-dependent increments in rat cerebellar blood flow by tonic synaptic inhibition," *Proc Natl Acad Sci USA* 100: 16000–6005.

Churchland, P.M. and Churchland, P. S. (1998) *On the Contrary: Critical Essays 1987–1997*, Cambridge, MA: MIT Press.

Clayton, P. (2004) *Mind and Emergence: From Quantum to Consciousness*, New York: Oxford University Press.

Coan, J.A., Schaefer, H.S. and Davidson, R.J. (2006) "Lending a Hand: Social Regulation of the Neural Response to Threat," *Psychological Science* 17: 1032–39.

Davidson, R.J. (2003) "Seven sins in the study of emotion: correctives from affective neuroscience," *Brain and Cognition* 52: 129–32.

Davidson, R.J., Kabat-Zinn, J., Schumacher, J., Rosenkranz, M., Muller, D., Santorelli, S.F., Urbanowski, F., Harrington, A., Bonus, K. and Sheridan, J.F. (2003) "Alterations in brain and immune function produced by mindfulness meditation," *Psychosom Med* 65: 564–70.

Davis, M., Falls, W.A., Campeau, S. and Kim, M. (1993) "Fear-potentiated startle: a neural and pharmacological analysis," *Behav Brain Res* 58: 175–98.

Emmons, R.A. and Paloutzian, R.F. (2003) "The Psychology of Religion," *Annual Review of Psychology* 54: 377–402.

Gallagher, S. and Zahavi, D. (2008) *The Phenomenological Mind: An Introduction to Philosophy of Mind and Cognitive Science*, New York: Routledge.

Goldstein, E.B. (2011) *Cognitive Psychology: Connecting Mind, Research, and Everyday Experience*, 3rd edn, Belmont, CA: Thomson Wadsworth.

Greene, J.D. (2007) "Why are VMPFC patients more utilitarian? A dual-process theory of moral judgment explains," *Trends in Cognitive Sciences* 11: 322–23.

Harris, S., Kaplan, J.T., Curie, A., Bookheimer, S.Y., Iacoboni, M. and Cohen, M.S. (2009) "The neural correlates of religious and nonreligious belief," *PLoS ONE* 4: e0007272.

Hassin, R.R., Uleman, J.S. and Bargh, J.A. (eds) (2005) *The New Unconscious*, New York: Oxford University Press.

Huettel, S., Song, A.W. and McCarthy, G. (2008) *Functional Magnetic Resonance Imaging*, Sunderland, MA: Sinauer Associates.

Kabat-Zinn, J., Massion, A.O., Kristeller, J., Peterson, L.G., Fletcher, K.E., Pbert, L., Lenderking, W.R. and Santorelli, S.F. (1992) "Effectiveness of a meditation-based stress reduction program in the treatment of anxiety disorders," *Am J Psychiatry* 149: 936–43.

Kabat-Zinn, J., Wheeler, E., Light, T., Skillings, A., Scharf, M.J., Cropley, T.G., Hosmer, D. and Bernhard, J.D. (1998) "Influence of a mindfulness meditation-based stress reduction intervention on rates of skin clearing in patients with moderate to severe psoriasis undergoing phototherapy (UVB) and photochemotherapy (PUVA)," *Psychosom Med* 60: 625–32.

Kapogiannis, D., Barbey, A.K., Su, M., Krueger, F. and Grafman, J. (2009) "Neuroanatomical variability of religiosity," *PLoS ONE* 4: e7180.

Lauritzen, M. (2001) "Relationship of spikes, synaptic activity, and local changes of cerebral blood flow," *J Cereb Blood Flow Metab* 21: 1367–83.

Logothetis, N.K. (2003) "The underpinnings of the BOLD functional magnetic resonance imaging signal," *J Neurosci* 23: 3963–71.

Logothetis, N.K. and Wandell, B.A. (2004) "Interpreting the BOLD signal," *Annu Rev Physiol* 66: 735–69.

Lutz, A., Greischar, L.L., Perlman, D.M. and Davidson, R.J. (2009a) "BOLD signal *in insula* is differentially related to cardiac function during compassion meditation in experts vs. novices," *NeuroImage*, 47: 1038–46.

Lutz, A., Slagter, H.A., Dunne, J.D. and Davidson, R.J. (2008) "Attention regulation and monitoring in meditation," *Trends in Cognitive Sciences* 12: 163–69.

Lutz, A., Slagter, H.A., Rawlings, N.B., Francis, A.D., Greischar, L.L. and Davidson, R.J. (2009b) "Mental training enhances attentional stability: neural and behavioral evidence," *J Neurosci* 29: 13418–27.

Miller, G.A. (2003) "The cognitive revolution: a historical perspective," *Trends in Cognitive Sciences* 7: 141–44.

Murphy, N. and Brown, W.S. (2007) *Did My Neurons Make Me Do It?: Philosophical and Neurobiological Perspectives on Moral Responsibility and Free Will*, Oxford: Oxford University Press.

Newberg, A., Alavi, A., Baime, M., Pourdehnad, M., Santanna, J. and d'Aquili, E. (2001) "The measurement of regional cerebral blood flow during the complex cognitive task of meditation: a preliminary SPECT study," *Psychiatry Res* 106: 113–22.

Newberg, A., Pourdehnad, M., Alavi, A. and d'Aquili, E.G. (2003) "Cerebral blood flow during meditative prayer: preliminary findings and methodological issues," *Percept Mot Skills* 97: 625–30.

O'Connor, T. (2000) *Persons and Causes: The Metaphysics of Free Will*, New York: Oxford University Press.

O'Doherty, J.P., Hampton, A. and Kim, H. (2007) "Model-based fMRI and its application to reward learning and decision-making," *Ann N Y Acad Sci* 1104: 35–53.

Oatley, K. (1999) "Foreword," in Dalgleish, T. and Power, M.J. (eds), *Handbook of Cognition and Emotion*, West Sussex, UK: John Wiley & Sons.

Ochsner, K.N. and Gross, J.J. (2005) "The cognitive control of emotion," *Trends in Cognitive Sciences* 9: 242–49.

Olsson, A., Ebert, J.P., Banaji, M.R. and Phelps, E.A. (2005) "The role of social groups in the persistence of learned fear," *Science* 309: 785–87.

Pavlov, I.P. (1927) *Conditioned Reflexes: An Investigation of the Physiological Activity of the Cerebral Cortex*, London: Oxford University Press.

Peterson, G. (2003) *Minding God: Theology and the Cognitive Sciences*, Minneapolis, MN: Fortress Press.

Purves, D., Brannon, E.M., Cabeza, R., Huettel, S., Labar, K.S., Platt, M.L. and Woldorff, M.G. (2008) *Principles of Cognitive Neuroscience*, Sunderland, MA: Sinauer Associates.

Raichle, M.E. (2003) "Social neuroscience: a role for brain imaging," *Political Psychology* 24: 759–64.

Runehov, A.L.C. (2007) *Sacred or Neural?: The Potential of Neuroscience to Explain Religious Experience*, Göttingen, Germany: Vandenhoeck & Ruprecht.

Saxe, R. and Kanwisher, N. (2003) "People thinking about thinking people. The role of the temporo-parietal junction in 'theory of mind,'" *NeuroImage* 19: 1835–42.

Schjoedt, U., Stodkilde-Jorgensen, H., Geertz, A.W. and Roepstorff, A. (2008) "Rewarding prayers," *Neurosci Lett* 443: 165–68.

——(2009) "Highly religious participants recruit areas of social cognition in personal prayer," *Soc Cogn Affect Neurosci* 4: 199–207.

Schjoedt, U., Stodkilde-Jorgensen, H., Geertz, A.W., Lund, T.E. and Roepstorff, A. (2010) "The power of charisma – perceived charisma inhibits the frontal executive network of believers in intercessory prayer," *Social Cognitive and Affective Neuroscience*, in press.

Slagter, H.A., Lutz, A., Greischar, L.L., Francis, A.D., Nieuwenhuis, S., Davis, J.M. and Davidson, R.J. (2007) "Mental training affects distribution of limited brain resources," *PLoS Biol* 5: e138.

Slagter, H.A., Lutz, A., Greischar, L.L., Nieuwenhuis, S. and Davidson, R.J. (2009) "Theta phase synchrony and conscious target perception: impact of intensive mental training," *J Cogn Neurosci* 21: 1536–49.

Spezio, M.L., Rangel, A., Alvarez, R.M., O'Doherty, J.P., Mattes, K., Todorov, A., Kim, H. and Adolphs, R. (2008) "A neural basis for the effect of candidate appearance on election outcomes," *Social Cognitive and Affective Neuroscience* 3: 344–52.

Thompson, E. (2007) *Mind in Life: Biology, Phenomenology & the Sciences of Mind*, Cambridge, MA: Belknap Press of Harvard University Press.

Todorov, A., Mandisodza, A.N., Goren, A. and Hall, C.C. (2005) "Inferences of competence from faces predict election outcomes," *Science* 308: 1623–26.

Valentin, V.V. and O'Doherty, J.P. (2009) "Overlapping prediction errors in dorsal striatum during instrumental learning with juice and money reward in the human brain," *J Neurophysiol* 102: 3384–91.

Wager, T.D., Davidson, M.L., Hughes, B.L., Lindquist, M.A. and Ochsner, K.N. (2008) "Prefrontal–subcortical pathways mediating successful emotion regulation," *Neuron* 59: 1037–50.

Woodward, J.F. and Allman, J. (2007) "Moral intuition: its neural substrates and normative significance," *Journal of Physiology – Paris* 101: 179–202.

Zahavi, D. (2001) *Husserl and Transcendental Subjectivity*, Athens, OH: Ohio University Press.

Further reading

The volumes by Anderson (2010) and Goldstein (2011) and the short paper by Miller (2003) (cited above) provide outstanding introductions to experimental cognitive psychology and cognitive science. The volume by Peterson (2003) is perhaps the most comprehensive publication relating theology to the cognitive sciences. The review by Adolphs and Spezio (2007) is useful for readers wanting a better understanding of how neuroscience approaches cognition and affect in understanding social behavior. The review by Emmons and Paloutzian (2003) is required reading for a greater understanding of how scientific psychology approaches the study of religion in general. The best primer in how to interpret MRI and fMRI findings remains the excellent paper by Cacioppo *et al.* (2003), and it is written at a level that does not require technical expertise. Readers who want to pursue their interest in this area are strongly encouraged to move beyond books written for general audiences and to engage with the primary scientific literature.

27
COGNITIVE SCIENCE AND CLASSICAL BUDDHIST PHILOSOPHY OF MIND

Richard K. Payne

Intersection of three discourses

What we are actually looking at are three different, though overlapping, discourses: Western philosophy of mind, Buddhist philosophy of mind, and cognitive science. The question being asked here is: Does anything important exist in the intersection of these three discourses? The interactions between Western philosophy of mind and cognitive science have been dialectic, and both are structured against a shared intellectual background. At present, this shared grounding makes many of the questions, concerns, issues appear "natural," but only because they necessarily follow from the grounding assumptions. In other words, because the underlying assumptions – the terms of the discourse and their implications – are shared, it is assumed that certain things are naturally problematic, and that there are limited ways of attempting to resolve them. The point is not that these assumptions are wrong and need to be replaced by better ones, but rather simply that they *are* assumptions, and that a different set would produce a different constellation of what appear to be "natural" problems in the philosophy of mind.

Limits of Spezio

Spezio's discussion of cognitive science and religion is limited to neurophysiological studies of "religious experience." Commonly, Buddhism is reductively identified with meditation, a representation that fits neatly with modernist definitions of religion as centrally concerned with experience. It is this preconception regarding the nature of religion that is reflected in Spezio's essay opening this section (Chapter 26), which gives almost exclusive attention to neurological studies of religious practitioners. This constriction is based on two interlocking presumptions, and excludes many areas of concern for Buddhist philosophy of mind.

The limitations of Spezio's treatment result from a pair of assumptions: the primacy of experience as definitive of religion, and the primacy of neurophysiology as definitive of experience. In other words, that religion is defined by particular kinds of experiences, experiences that are somehow uniquely religious in character – the circularity of which is evident when expressed this sparely. Further, that experience may be understood in terms of neural activity, thus the particularity of religious experience should be reflected in a particularity of neural activity. This notion that religion is about uniquely religious experiences derives from late-nineteenth-century strategy to defend religion as *sui generis*. However, despite having become implicitly accepted, it distorts our understanding of religion by privileging such activities as contemplation, meditation, and prayer (Groopman 2001).

Buddhist thought, however, never demarcated any special category of experience as somehow uniquely religious, and, except in modernist interpretations, never attributed the power of liberation to experience. Rather than some salvific experience, such as mystical union with God, Buddhism emphasizes the transformative character of insight into the most mundane workings of the world. One of the most important areas of inquiry for classical Indian Buddhist thought was the ordinary working of the mind, which some theorists have argued is exactly the central topic for cognitive science (von Eckardt 1995).

Range of Buddhist concerns in the intersection

The specific issues that will be discussed *infra* include, but are not limited to, issues regarding the effects of meditation on the plastic brain, the sense of a unitary self, the "binding" problem, the continuity of consciousness, and the self-referentiality of consciousness.

Classical Buddhist thought

Abhidharma: *phenomenology, analysis, and speculation*

Rendered literally, *abhidharma* (*abhidhamma*) means the "higher *dharma*," in the sense that it is an abstraction from the teachings of the Buddha as found in the teaching narratives (*sutra*, *sutta*). (For the meaning of the compound *abhidharma*, see Cox 1995: 4). The *abhidharma* literature is usually considered the third of the "three baskets" (*tripitaka*) along with *sutra* and *vinaya* (rules of the orders of monks and nuns). Although frequently treated as if it constituted a specific school of thought, *abhidharma* is more appropriately considered a bibliographic category. There are seven *abhidharma* texts extant in Pali, and an entirely different set of seven extant in Chinese, translated from the Sanskrit. Many commentaries and subcommentaries on these were written by Indic, Tibetan, Chinese, and Japanese Buddhist thinkers. As a body of literature, these do share a common emphasis on speculative psycho-spiritual philosophy. The earliest kind of *abhidharma* literature appears to have been lists of topics (*matrika*), providing mnemonic tools for learning and recalling the teachings. Arranged numerically, this mnemonic function is found even today when Buddhism is presented in terms of such categories as "the four noble truths," "the eightfold path," or "the three marks." The elements in these lists of topics are referred to as *dharmas*, one of the most polyvalent terms in the Buddhist lexicon.

While it is frequently used in the sense of "teaching," as in the term *buddhadharma*, the teachings of the Buddha, it is also used to refer to the analytically ultimate constituents of existence. In the East Asian Buddhist context, its translation term "*ho*" (法) is frequently used to mean ritual or practice, that is, those actions that put the teachings into effect. All of these usages point toward an underlying meaning of that which is ontologically actual (*bhutatatha*). Therefore speech that accords with what is ontologically actual is true, as are the teachings of the Buddha. In the context of *abhidharma* and Yogacara, however, it is appropriate to render "*dharma*" as "existential factor." As they could not be reduced any further by analysis, *dharmas* were considered to be ultimate, or atomic. This is the main conceptual tool not only of *abhidharma*, but of later Buddhist thought as well.

The terms "actual" and "existence" are specifically used here to avoid the term "reality," which comes too heavily laden with Platonic conceptions of the real as the permanent, unchanging, eternal, or absolute essence that defines a particular entity. As an intellectual tradition of over 2.5 millenia in duration, and spread across several different religious, intellectual, and linguistic cultures, Buddhist thought is neither unitary nor consistent on doctrinal matters. However, almost all forms of Buddhism have rejected any concept that implies the existence of a permanent essence. Indeed, much intra-Buddhist debate consists of critical analyses of an opponent's position as entailing belief in such an essence.

One of the central projects of *abhidharma* was the analysis of a person's experience into its constituents, both mental and physical. It is this analysis of experience that makes the *abhidharma* a kind of phenomenology (Lusthaus 2002: 4). By this analytic meditation on one's own experience, one learned to discriminate between those experiential factors that are conducive to liberation (*moksha*) from infatuating craving (*trishna*), and those that further entangle a person in the round of self-recreating dissatisfaction (*samsara*). Once one is able to distinguish liberating from entangling factors, those practices that are effective in moving one along the path to liberation (*marga*) would be clear. In analyzing the nature of existence, the *abhidharma* typically groups *dharmas* into different categories. Distinctions between different forms of *abhidharma* systematization is reflected in debates over the number of *dharmas* and their categorization. Within the literature of the different schools, such lists of factors range from seventy-five (Sarvastivada), to eighty-one and even 100 discrete categories of factors. *Dharma* theory developed in such a fashion that they were considered to exist momentarily, thus requiring explanations for the experience of temporal continuity.

Two systems of organizing the experiential factors are found in the *abhidharma* literature, each reflecting a significant aspect of *abhidharma* thought. The first organizes experiential factors into a series of descriptive categories, and the second organizes them so as to reflect the structures and processes of consciousness. Most generally, the first organizing principle groups the experiential factors into two fundamental categories – conditioned (*samskrita*) and unconditioned (*asamskrita*). The characteristic of being "conditioned" is foundational to Buddhist thought, referring to the concept that all existing things are causally produced. Being causally produced, they are impermanent, and being impermanent, they are integral to the round of self-recreating dissatisfaction. (Though frequently conflated, conditioned and unconditioned are not identical with the familiar categories absolute and relative as found in Western thought.)

The conditioned *dharmas* are themselves further subdivided into three broad categories: those that are conducive to liberation, or beneficial (*kushala*); those that are unconducive, or detrimental (*akushala*); and those that are neutral. More specific groups are then detailed within these broad categories. For example, in one of the *abhidharma* schools, the Sarvastivada, there are eleven *dharmas* of material form (*rupa*), one *dharma* of mind (*citta*), forty-six mental factors (*caitta*), fourteen factors associated with neither form nor mind (*cittaviprayuktasamskara*), and then another three kinds of unconditioned *dharmas*. A particular moment of conscious awareness could be analyzed into an interacting selection of these different kinds of *dharma*. Most importantly, such an analytic meditation on one's own conscious experience would be complete, and not in any way dependent upon, nor revealing, the existence of a permanent, eternal, absolute, or unchanging "self." In other words, as a form of analytic meditative practice, *abhidharma* provided direct experience of the truth that there is no permanent essence, or "self" (*anatman*).

Important to understanding Buddhist philosophy of mind is the group of *dharmas* called "ever present" (*mahabhumika*, lit. "of great extent"), which are constitutive of every moment of conscious awareness. While other factors may or may not be present, these ten *dharmas* are the fundamental structuring basis for all conscious awareness. These ten ever-present *dharmas* are feeling (*vedana*), conception (*samjna*), volition (*cetana*), contact (*sparsha*), attention (*manaskara*), desire (*chanda*), intention (*adhimoksha*), recollection (*smriti*), concentration (*samadhi*), and comprehension (*mati*, *prajna*). This category demonstrates the kind of analysis of consciousness that the *abhidharma* thinkers developed.

A different way of understanding the dynamics of conscious awareness is found in the second organizational system mentioned above. There are three different versions of these groupings of factors, known as the five aggregates (*skandha*), twelve realms of the senses (*ayatana*), and eighteen fields (*dhatu*). The five aggregates are form (*rupa*), feeling (*vedana*), conception (*samjna*), habitual patterns (*samskara*), and consciousness (*vijnana*), which are revealed as all that actually exists when one analyzes what one considers to be one's self. The other two systems describe the process of cognition more explicitly. The twelve *ayatana* are the six sense organs (eye, ear, nose, tongue, body, and mind), and the corresponding six sensory objects (colors/forms, sounds, smells, tastes, tactile sensations, and thoughts). The system of eighteen *dhatus* adds a conscious awareness for each of the six pairs in the system of twelve *ayatanas*.

Yogacara: cognitive processes

Yogacara constitutes a development of, rather than a sharp rupture with, *abhidharma* conceptions of the mind. Most importantly, the concept of *dharmas*, although subject to redefinition, was retained as a fundamental building block of the conceptions of how the mind works.

The key doctrinal claim of the Yogacara is that everything that is known is known through an act of constructive cognition. This is referred to in Sanskrit as *vijnaptimatra* and *cittamatra*, both often rendered rather literally as "consciousness only," which has, however, been misleading. Yogacara theorists generally meant that though the world is not created or projected by consciousness (classic idealism), the mind does play a formative role in the construction of conscious awareness.

Yogacara describes a cognitive system of eight dynamically interrelated parts, or functions (*vijnana*, often translated as "consciousnesses"). Because some of these are the same as those found in Western conceptions of the mind, it is important that we carefully note how the others differ. First, there are the sensory functions of mind, which include the five familiar to us from at least the time of Aristotle's writings on the subject – taste, touch, sight, hearing, and smell – but with the addition of a mental sensory function as well. This sixth function, *manovijnana*, distinguishes Indian Buddhist conceptions of the sensorium from the familiar Aristotelian system of five senses. *Manovijnana* serves to "direct the attention of sense organs toward their objects to produce clear perceptions of these objects. *Manovijnana* also has a cogitative or deliberative function, but such a function is crude and unstable and it might be interrupted in certain states" (Jiang 2006: 58).

The seventh cognitive function is *manas*, mind in the sense of the center of consciousness, where the six perceptual cognitions are brought together. When *manas* views the eighth cognitive function, *manas* mistakenly conceives of it as a self, producing the concepts I, me, and mine.

The eighth cognitive function, the comprehensive ground of cognition (*alayavijnana*), is described as unconscious traces of past experiences that contribute to later conscious experiences. The metaphoric language is used to describe this process. Cognitions "perfume" the *alayavijnana*, becoming "seeds," which mature over the course of time. While this unconscious function has been compared with the Freudian unconscious and the Jungian collective unconscious, it is actually closer to the unconscious as propounded by Helmholtz, that is, cognitive processes of which one is not consciously aware.

Tathagatagarbha/*buddha-nature*

Given the Buddhist analysis of cognition as an ongoing, self-maintaining process (similar to William James' attempted conversion of "self" to a verb: "selving"), a persistent question for Buddhist thought was: How is awakening possible? One answer was that all humans and other sentient beings have an inherent capacity for awakening. *Tathagata* is an epithet of awakened ones, that is, buddhas; *garbha* is, ambiguously, womb or embryo. Thus the compound refers to the potential for awakening. In East Asia, *tathagatagarbha* and *alayavijnana* were identified, leading to the idea rendered in English as buddha-nature.

Although offered as the solution to one problem, these ideas became the subject of debates which continue into the present (King 1997; Matsumoto 1997). Such ideas can easily be interpreted as referring to a permanent, eternal, unchanging, absolute self, though their proponents generally insisted that no such understanding was intended.

Madhyamaka

The Madhyamaka teachings are often summarized under the term "emptiness" (*sunyata*), which has sometimes been misunderstood as a version of nihilism. As has been suggested above, when any existing thing is said to be empty, what it is empty of is any permanent, eternal, absolute, or unchanging essence. It does exist as a consequence of causes and conditions, a further consequence of which is that it is impermanent.

Not only does emptiness function as a corrective to the reification of concepts, such as mind or consciousness, but it is also self-corrective. In other words, emptiness is itself empty (*shunya-shunyata*) – emptiness is not to be reified as an essence of any kind, but is merely a conventional label for the absence of any essence. This reflects a distinction common to all Indian logic between two kinds of negation, that which implies the existence of some alternative, known as an affirming negation (*paryudasapratishedha*), and that which does not, known as a non-affirming negation (*prasajyapratishedha*) (Staal 1962; Hopkins 1996: 723). Emptiness is an instance of a non-affirming negation, that is, it does not imply the existence of any alternative, including itself.

Concerns as such

Neuroplasticity and meditation

Much attention to neuroplasticity as an important aspect of the relation between Buddhism and cognitive science, particularly regarding the efficacy of meditation (Schwartz and Begley 2003; Begley 2007). The received tradition of the adult brain as immutable is, by now, thoroughly discredited. That brain structures continually change over time has definitively replaced the view that the localization of neural functions is immutable (Doidge 2007).

That meditation has structural effects on the brain is therefore in keeping with neuroplasticity (cf. Austin 2006: 141, 2009: 247). And further, that some of these effects may be judged positive – increased happiness and well-being, for example – is not unreasonable. Where this dialogue frequently goes astray, however, is by maintaining the mind–body or spirit–matter dualism, and then interpreting neuroplasticity as evidence for that dualism, a *petitio principii* fallacy.

Presuming both mind–body dualism, and that meditation or thought is somehow "purely" mental, precludes the possibility of seeing what should be the equally obvious alternative conclusion – that neuroplasticity demonstrates that all thought, including meditation, is embodied. It is because thought is an embodied activity that it coincides with the creation of new neural connections, or the reinforcement of existing ones. The neuroplastic effects of meditation do not, therefore, prove the independent, autonomous existence of the mind or consciousness as the causal agent of neuroplastic change.

Nature of the self: emptiness

The Buddhist teaching known as *anatman* asserts the absence of any essence – any permanent, eternal, absolute, or unchanging self in either persons or objects. Since

Schopenhauer's interpretations of Buddhism and Hinduism, *anatman* has been largely interpreted as having psychological reference, as an assertion that the ego or self does not exist. This psychological interpretation has been widely extended into contemporary psychotherapeutic and self-help literatures (e.g. Epstein 1995). Despite the almost exclusively psychologized interpretation, the doctrine is more fundamentally ontological, as indicated by the inclusion not only of persons, but also of objects as lacking any permanent, eternal, absolute, or unchanging "self." Hence this teaching is not just about personal "selves," but is more generally a denial of any essence.

It is, however, in the area of the personal self that there is a connection with cognitive science. As discussed by several cognitive scientists, the personal self does not appear to have any substantive existence. Flanagan, for example, says "the self is a fiction in the sense that it is constructed and because it unfolds like a story that is not yet completed" (Flanagan 1991: 355). Although this idea can be traced in Western thought at least back to Hume's famous assertion regarding the introspective absence of any self, this has until more recently been considered a part of Hume's skepticism that can be dismissed.

Buddhist discussions acknowledge that we experience ourselves as a singular, continuous, autonomous, enduring agent. The response is that such a perception is illusory. Nagarjuna give eight analogies for this illusory status, including, for example, the circle of fire that we see when a firebrand is whirled around and around (Nagarjuna 1987: 94, §66). These analogies serve to make evident how it is that any actually existing entity – dependent on causes and conditions, impermanent, composed of parts, or conventionally designated – can give the appearance of being a singular, continuous, autonomous, enduring agent.

Binding problem

The "binding problem" is the question of how it is that disparate sensory information is brought together to form the kinds of whole that constitute our ordinary experience. Broadly, how is it that, when we are holding a rose, the red color, the flower shape, the subtle smell, and the thorn pricking our finger all come to be experienced as part of one thing – the rose in our hand? At a finer level of analysis, the problem becomes even more complex as, for example, visual shapes and colors are processed in distinct and segregated cortical areas (Hardcastle 1998).

Again, in the history of Western philosophy, Hume was perhaps the first to call attention to this problem. Working from Locke's conceptions of primary and secondary qualities, Hume realized that simple association was not an adequate explanation. Yogacara thinkers also recognized this problem. Following on the analytic of *abhidharma*, they hypothesized that the different sensory inputs – those from the six senses – were brought together to form an experienced whole in the *manas* (also *klishtamanas*, defiled awareness).

Continuity of consciousness

Given the composite and impermanent nature of the ego, how then does it continue across gaps of consciousness, such as dreamless sleep? How is it reconstituted after a break in continuity? In more explicitly Buddhist terms, how is it that *karma* is effective, that the consequences of one's actions are of consequence to oneself? Here we see a moral dimension of Buddhist thought – if that future person who may suffer the consequences of any present actions is not the same person as my present self contemplating those actions, why should that person's future suffering be of any concern to me in the present? (Guarisco 2005: 20–23). Although expressed in the language of action (*karma*) and its consequences, this was also a more general concern with the continuity of consciousness.

It is the eighth cognitive function, the "comprehensive ground of cognition" (*alayavijnana*, sometimes rendered from the Chinese as "store consciousness" or "storehouse consciousness," Schmithausen 2007 [1987]: 1) that was hypostatized to provide this continuity – not just across dreamless sleep, but from one lifetime to another. Despite this function, the comprehensive ground of cognition is itself a composite, conditioned entity and therefore is not an eternal, unchanging, permanent, or absolute soul or self, any more than any of the other seven cognitive functions. In addition, though its activity contributes to the ongoing process of cognizing existing entities, it is not a creator deity as some Indian opponents of Buddhism asserted.

I and me: self-reflective awareness

The last area of overlap to be considered here is the self-reflective character of consciousness. This is a long-standing issue in Western philosophy of mind, dating at least from the works of Locke and Kant. Darwin identified it as a central issue, and it is now suggested to be part of the social character of human consciousness (Cheney and Seyfarth 2007: 199–216).

Self-reflective awareness is known in Sanskrit as *svasamvedana* (or *svasamvitti*). It became a topic of discussion for epistemologists, and continued to be actively argued into the nineteenth century with the work of Mipham (1846–1912) in Tibet (Williams 1998; Yao 2005). The views involved have been interpreted as distinguishing between "mere" reflexivity and self-awareness. Mere reflexivity refers to the fact of consciousness having a sense of its own intentional structure, that when one is aware of some object, one is at the same time aware that it is one's own awareness – when one is happy, one is aware of being happy, for example. Self-awareness is the awareness of consciousness itself. It was the latter that provided grounds for debate within the Buddhist tradition.

What classical Buddhist philosophy of mind does not do

Buddhist philosophy of mind does not share the same historical grounding that is common to both cognitive science and Western philosophy of mind. This means that there is little to be gained by simply interrogating Buddhist philosophy of mind from a pre-critical position within the horizon of which the questions, concerns, and issues of Western philosophy of mind and cognitive science appear unproblematically natural. At least some of the questions, concerns, issues of Western philosophy of mind and cognitive science may be simply historical artifacts, whose significance and weight have been gained because they have been asked repeatedly for centuries within the tradition of Western thought itself. The absence of certain questions, concerns, and issues from Buddhist philosophy of mind may easily be seen as a lack, a failing, an inadequacy, rather than an avenue toward resolution.

There is, in other words, nothing "natural" about the mind–body problem, or the problem of free will. These are problematic because of certain ways of structuring the discourse that pervade Western thought, and that may well deserve to be themselves problematized, rather than answered.

Mind–body dualism

As important as the mind–body problem is for Western philosophy of mind and cognitive science, that discussion is not a "natural" one, but rather a social one, with its roots in Western intellectual history; it does not arise in Buddhist philosophy of mind because that discourse does not share in the underlying assumptions regarding the insuperable dualism of mental and physical that is the common ground of spirit–matter, mind–body, brain–mind, etc. (cf. Flanagan's critique of McGinn: Flanagan 1991: 338–39). Having never been apart, there is no motivation to put them back together.

This is, of course, not to say that there are not discussions of the interrelations of mind or consciousness (*citta*) and material aspects of existence (*rupa*), but rather that the specific configuration that motivates the mind–body problem in terms of two autonomous, ontological categories was not a part of the intellectual horizons of Buddhist philosophy of mind. An "answer" may be squeezed out of Buddhist thought, but that does not make the question a universal one.

The Buddhist view would seem to be something like a "pre-Cartesian" version of the existential phenomenological view of Merleau-Ponty, particularly as explicated by Evan Thompson, which identifies the mind–body and the subject–object dichotomies as abstractions (the inevitable and insurmountable consequence of definitions) and displaces this with a phenomenology of the lived-body/living-body, which is "neither purely first-personal (subjective) nor purely third-personal (objective), neither mental nor physical [but rather] existential structures prior to and more fundamental than these abstractions" (Thompson 2007: 248).

Free will versus determinism: the nature of karma

The philosophic problem of free will as it has come into cognitive science may be traced to the rise of a mechanistic world-view following Descartes, but more specifically attributable to Pierre-Simon Laplace. It is only within this frame of reference, one in which "if I know the location and motion of all particles, I can predict the future absolutely," that the philosophic debate over free will and determinism can arise or make sense. Although *karma* has often been likened to determinism, it is more productively interpreted as a naturalistic understanding of the relation between actions and consequences (as distinguished from causes and effects). That actions have consequences does not entail the absence of free will, and hence does not necessarily create the "problem." Some Buddhist thinkers interpret *karma* moralistically (What actions have karmic consequences? Is intent the determining factor?)

rather than naturalistically. However, even under these interpretations, the concerns about *karma* are existentially based in embodied human cognition and action.

Some closing thoughts regarding the "problem of consciousness": concept, function

From the critical perspective of Madhyamaka, it is possible to call into question the status of problems and ask whether they are not in fact pseudo-problems. The problem of consciousness may be just one such pseudo-problem.

Consciousness is an intersubjective entity, that is, it is simply a socially constructed concept. There is no such thing as consciousness, only (a lot of) talk about it. This is, of course, not to say that people are not conscious, but rather to point out that it is illegitimate to reify a characteristic of experiences into an autonomous object of some kind. The analogy would be that we have lots of blue experiences, but we know that blue is not some kind of independently existing object. Blue is a concept abstracted from a set of experiences, and identified and employed according to a set of socially determined categories. Consciousness is fundamentally the same kind of thing.

Conclusion

A full explication of Buddhist systems of thought would require tracing not only the line of developing thought from Śakyamuni forward to the systems we are considering here, but also provide information on the broader intellectual context within which these developments took place – the ideologies developed in the *Upanishads*, the "orthodox" schools (*astika*), and the broader cultural milieu as found in the epics, for example (Ganeri 2007: 6). That background falls beyond the scope of this article, but the interested reader who wishes to pursue these matters in greater detail is advised to include these perspectives in their studies as well.

References

Austin, James H. (2006) *Zen–Brain Reflections: Reviewing Recent Developments in Meditation and States of Consciousness*, Cambridge, MA and London: MIT Press.

——(2009) *Selfless Insight: Zen and the Meditative Transformations of Consciousness*, Cambridge, MA and London: MIT Press.

Begley, Sharon (2007) *Train Your Mind, Change Your Brain: How a New Science Reveals Our Extraordinary Potential to Transform Ourselves*, New York: Ballantine Books.

Cheney, Dorothy L. and Robert M. Seyfarth (2007) *Baboon Metaphysics: The Evolution of a Social Mind*, Chicago, IL and London: University of Chicago Press.

Cox, Collett (1995) *Disputed Dharmas: Early Buddhist Theories on Existence*, Tokyo: International Institute for Buddhist Studies.

Doidge, Norman (2007) *The Brain that Changes Itself: Stories of Personal Triumph from the Frontiers of Brain Science*, New York: Penguin.

von Eckardt, Barbara (1995) *What is Cognitive Science?*, Cambridge, MA: MIT Press.
Epstein, Mark (1995) *Thoughts without a Thinker: Psychotherapy from a Buddhist Perspective*, New York: Basic Books.
Flanagan, Owen (1991) *The Science of Mind*, 2nd edn, Cambridge, MA and London: MIT Press.
Ganeri, Jonardon (2007) *The Concealed Art of the Soul: Theories of Self and Practices of Truth in Indian Ethics and Epistemology*, Oxford: Oxford University Press.
Groopman, Jerome (2001) "God on the Brain: The Curious Coupling of Science and Religion," *New Yorker Magazine*, 17 September.
Guarisco, Elio (2005) "Introduction," in Jamgön Kongtrul Lodrö Tayé, *The Treasury of Knowledge, Book Six, Part Four: Systems of Buddhist Tantra, The Indestructible Way of Secret Mantra*, Kalu Rinpoché Translation Group (trans.), Ithaca, NY and Boulder, CO: Snow Lion Publications, 20–23.
Hardcastle, Valeri Gray (1998) "The Binding Problem," in *A Companion to Cognitive Science*, William Bechtel and George Graham (eds), Malden, MA: Blackwell.
Hopkins, Jeffrey (1996 [1983]) *Meditation on Emptiness*, Boston, MA: Wisdom Publications.
Jiang, Tao (2006) *Contexts and Dialogue: Yogacara Buddhism and Modern Psychology on the Subliminal Mind*, Honolulu: University of Hawai'i Press.
Lusthaus, Dan (2002) *Buddhist Phenomenology: A Philosophical Investigation of Yogacara Buddhism and the* Ch'eng Wei-shih Lun, London and New York: RoutledgeCurzon.
Nagarjuna (1987) *Nagarjuna's* "Seventy Stanzas:" *A Buddhist Psychology of Emptiness*, David Ross Komito (trans.), Ithaca, NY: Snow Lion.
Nyima, Thuken Chökyi (2009) *The Crystal Mirror of Philosophical Systems: A Tibetan Study of Asian Religious Thought*, Lhundub Sopa (trans.), Roger Jackson (ed.), Boston, MA: Wisdom Publications.
Schmithausen, Lambert (2007 [1987]) *Alayavijnana: On the Origin and the Early Development of a Central Concept of Yogacara Philosophy*, two volumes, reprinted with addenda and corrigenda, Tokyo: International Institute for Buddhist Studies.
Schwartz, Jeffrey M. and Sharon Begley (2003) *The Mind and the Brain: Neuroplasticity and the Power of Mental Force*, New York: Harper Perennial.
Spivey, Michael (2007) *The Continuity of Mind*, Oxford: Oxford University Press.
Staal, Frits (1962) "Negation and the Law of Contradiction in Indian Thought: A Comparative Study," *Bulletin of the School of Oriental and African Studies* 25(1): 52–71; reprinted as chapter 6 in Frits Staal (1988) *Universals: Studies in Indian Logic and Linguistics*, Chicago and London: University of Chicago Press.
Thompson, Evan (2007) *Mind in Life: Biology, Phenomenology, and the Sciences of Mind*, Cambridge, MA and London: Harvard University Press.
Williams, Paul (1998) *The Reflexive Nature of Awareness: A Tibetan Madhyamaka Defense*, Richmond, UK: Curzon.
Yao, Zhihua (2005) *The Buddhist Theory of Self-Cognition*, London: Routledge.

Further reading

Buddhist philosophy of mind is central to the entirety of classical Buddhist thought. The teaching that the self does not exist autonomously is foundational, and the treatment in the early period is the focus of Steven Collins, *Selfless Persons: Imagery and Thought in Theravada Buddhism* (Cambridge University Press, 1990), and of two works by Sue Hamilton, *Early Buddhism – A New Approach: The I of the Beholder* (RoutledgeCurzon, 2000) and *Identity and Experience: The Constitution of the Human Being According to Early Buddhism* (Luzac Oriental,

2001). How the self is conceived is intimately related to the conception of the goal of practice, that is, *nirvana*, a relation explored by Peter Harvey in his *The Selfless Mind: Personality, Consciousness and Nirvana in Early Buddhism* (RoutledgeCurzon, 1995). For a broader treatment of the metaphysics foundational to these ideas, see Noa Ronkin, *Early Buddhist Metaphysics: The Making of a Philosophical Tradition* (RoutledgeCurzon, 2005).

The rise of Mahayana Buddhism in early medieval India introduced new concepts in response to these issues. Although frequently treated as a kind of radical rupture, recent scholarship has focused on continuities. Particularly important in this regard is Richard King's essay "Vijnaptimatrata and the Abhidharma Context of Early Yogacara," *Asian Philosophy* 8(1) (1998): 5–18. Robert Kritzer also deals with the continuity of issues in his *Rebirth and Causation in the Yogacara Abhidharma* (Arbeitskreis für Tibetische und Buddhistische Studien, Universität Wien, 1999). J. Duerlinger focuses on the thought of one of the major transitional figures in his *Indian Buddhist Theories of Person: Vasubandhu's Refutation of the Theory of a Self* (RoutledgeCurzon, 2003). The concept that the mind has operations that are not part of conscious awareness, referred to as the *alayavijnana*, is one of the key developments. William Waldron's *The "Buddhist Unconscious": The Alaya-Vijnana in the Context of Indian Buddhist Thought* (RoutledgeCurzon, 2003) explores this concept and its relation to concepts of the unconscious in Western psychology. These ideas were also fundamental to the expansion of Buddhism outside of India, forming the basis of developments in East Asia. A key study of the spread of Indian Buddhist philosophy of mind is Diana Y. Paul, *Philosophy of Mind in Sixth-Century China: Paramartha's "Evolution of Consciousness"* (Stanford University Press, 1984).

28
CHRISTIANITY AND THE COGNITIVE SCIENCES

Charlene P. E. Burns

> No one has found God in the nervous system.
>
> (Hood *et al.* 2009: 66)

During the past two decades, a great deal of theological attention has been focused on the questions posed by the cognitive sciences. The issues are complex both scientifically and theologically because, as Spezio points out in Chapter 26, "cognitive sciences" is an umbrella term used to designate interdisciplinary exploration of the brain and consciousness via disciplines including neuroscience, philosophy, evolutionary biology, and psychology. A complete exploration is obviously far beyond the scope of this essay; because the most obvious challenges for theology fall into the realm of anthropology, I address here questions raised by the "embodied mind" for understandings of the soul and personhood.

Neurotheology: theology without theologian

"Neurotheology" aims to integrate neuropsychological research and theology, and provides an example of the important issues at stake in reflecting on the relation of theology and cognitive science. The pioneers in the field, James Ashbrook and Carol Rausch Albright, suggested that we are "hard-wired" for religious experience because the brain is itself in some sense revelatory of the divine (Ashbrook and Albright 1997).

In a 1999 book, two physicians, Eugene d'Aquili (psychiatrist) and Andrew Newberg (radiologist), attempted to redefine neurotheology on the basis that Ashbrook's and Albright's assertions had not been established through "a substantive integration" of neuropsychology and theology. For d'Aquili and Newberg (1999), neurotheology is study of "how the mind/brain functions in terms of humankind's relation to God or ultimate reality." They offered a model for understanding how God is generated by the brain and yet at the same time is generative of material reality.

d'Aquili and Newberg used single-photon emission computed tomography (SPECT) to monitor a small group of Tibetan Buddhist practitioners in meditation and Catholic Franciscan nuns in prayer. SPECT imaging measures blood flow to the brain, and studies have demonstrated that blood flow increases to activated areas of the brain. In the meditating Buddhists, blood flow increased to areas associated with attention, and decreased to areas of the parietal lobe that inform us about position and movement of the body. When the nuns prayed, their parietal lobes showed the same decrease in blood flow as in the Buddhists, while areas associated with language showed increased flow. This finding is considered significant as Christian forms of prayer tend to be more verbal than Buddhist meditation. The researchers took this to support their proposed model: An altered state of consciousness, Absolute Unitary Being (AUB), a state in which the practitioner "loses all awareness of discrete limited being and of the passage of time," is generated when areas of the brain experience alterations in blood flow. When areas of the brain that function to maintain self–other distinction are not stimulated, a sense of "oneness" ought to ensue. At the same time, heightened awareness would result from stimulation of areas related to increased concentration. If associated with positive emotion, AUB tends to be interpreted as experience of God; if associated with neutral emotion, it tends to be interpreted as encounter with the nameless Absolute or with Nirvana (*ibid*.).

d'Aquili's and Newberg's claims have empirical grounding, but they are speculative and go beyond science in offering theological interpretations of the data. Neurotheology, they say, can be the basis for a sort of "megatheology" acceptable to all religious traditions, a basis upon which to build genuine ecumenical dialogue.

Major criticisms of neurotheological approaches from the standpoint of science revolve around the starting point. Both teams of theorists discussed above assume the reality of the divine. They use cognitive science and neurosciences to illuminate what is, for them, the unquestioned divine–human relationship. This is valid for theological reflection, but is questionable as the starting point for something purporting to be science. For this and other reasons, neurotheology has been called "quasi-science" (Feit 2003).

d'Aquili and Newberg said they offered a model for understanding how God/AUB is generated by the brain, and at the same time is generative of material reality. But from the scientific standpoint, all that can be said is that reports of encounters with the divine, or a sensation of "oneness" with creation, accompany certain brain states which are also correlated with motivation, emotions, and sexual acts. Nothing can be said about the source of material reality itself.

Another problem arises from their conflation of "God" and AUB. Buddhism is a non-theistic religion; there is no God and the cosmos is eternal, without beginning. The ultimate goal of practitioners is to achieve Nirvana, a state that cannot be described, since one who achieves it ceases to exist in any normal sense of the term. The Christian God is a personal deity who not only created material reality, but sustains it and will at some future point radically transform it into the *baseleia*, a realm of actual existence that perfectly reflects the divine. To claim to have made discoveries about God through the study of meditating Buddhists whose goal is "extinguishment" as a life force is at minimum, disrespectful of Buddhist teachings, and at worst, Western monotheistic arrogance.

Other problems arise from the fact that the research can be used to support diametrically opposite conclusions. The data might lead us to say that religious experience is merely one of many brain states. The fact that certain areas of the brain are activated during meditation, prayer, and ritual practice actually tells us nothing about the reality of God. Or, oddly enough, we might reach the opposite conclusion. Since there is no distinction between AUB and God, one might conclude that human consciousness and God are indistinguishable. In fact, Newberg sometimes seems to echo Tillich's description of God as the Ground of Being: "So, if Absolute Unitary Being truly is more real than subjective or objective reality – more real, that is, than the external world and the subjective awareness of the self – then the self and the world must be contained within, and perhaps created by the reality of Absolute Unitary Being" (2001).

Ilia Delio argues that without philosophical exploration of the nature of reality and God's relation to it to guide research, neurotheologians have committed a "fallacy of misplaced contingency" wherein God's reality is contingent upon one's experience of God. Here we have a "new anthropic principle – in order for God to exist, we must exist, because it is we humans who give a conscious voice to the existence of God" (Delio 2003).

In d'Aquili and Newberg's work, the methodological difficulties compound because two *scientists* have developed a useful but highly speculative scientific framework, then used it to speak of *theological* concerns. Apparently unaware of the varieties of religious experience, they apply the theory to all forms of mystical experience, even though they studied only intentionally generated meditative experiences. Religious experiences are in fact quite diverse, as first documented by William James in his classic work *The Varieties of Religious Experience* (James 1902), and today widely acknowledged among scholars of religious studies and the psychology of religion. Religion is extremely diverse across individuals and cultures, so it is not clear how generalizable the findings of neurotheology might be. Any theory of religion must be multi-level and mindful of the entire structural system of human cognition.

Reports of spontaneous mystical encounters are relatively common; there is no way to determine whether unplanned experiences differ from the forms studied. Religious experience, particularly mystical, is deeply subjective. We know it exists only because of believers' reports. Proving that specific changes in neurological blood flow are always associated with all types of mystical experience is, therefore, likely impossible.

More serious problems stem from confusion of methodologies, because the vast majority of what is being written on this so-called theology is by scientists, not theologians. Hopefully, recent trends to include cognitive sciences in graduate degree programs focused on religion (e.g. University of California Santa Barbara, Emory, Oxford, and Queen's University Belfast), and efforts such as this volume, will lead to development of more complete and truly interdisciplinary theories in the near future.

Michael Spezio (Chapter 26) rightly argues that the current state of research is not adequate for making inferences about cause. It is unfortunate that much scientific literature displays a problematic trend – the use of reverse inference to explain results. This type of reasoning muddies the waters of discussion, since we have not yet achieved the degree of sophistication in mapping neural processes required in order to be certain that specific patterns of brain activation always and only occur with particular experiences.

Methodological criticisms aside, it cannot be denied that mental states are intimately related to neurochemistry. Even though the hard problems of consciousness have not been solved, theology must grapple with the implications of this research, since there does appear to be a consistent array of brain structures that are activated in religious activity. "[A]cross many different types of religious practices and different participants, the prefrontal lobes […], the temporal lobes, the limbic system […] and the [dopamine activation] systems all appear to undergo increased levels of activation during the religious practice. There is also a trend at the cortical level for activation increases to be right-sided" (McNamara 2009). As Spezio outlines, although the methods of cognitive science are reductive, this does not invalidate the approach for understanding human nature. Our personalities and emotions, indeed consciousness itself, are in some sense by-products of the physical brain.

Neuroscience and the Christian soul

"Soul" in Christian thought is a concept that has functioned in at least two ways: to designate that which in some sense survives death; and as a label for that aspect of the human that is accountable for moral choices and capable of communion with God (Brown *et al.* 1998). Traditional Western concepts of the soul and life after death have been under attack for many years, from many directions. Thomas Hobbes (1588–1679) argued there is no such thing as incorporeal substance, and nothing of the human survives death without divine intervention. The nineteenth century brought with it Marxist humanism and its insistence that all religious teachings are oppressive tools of the powerful, designed to placate the masses with promises of fulfillment in a life-to-come. Some twentieth-century feminists and environmentalists insisted that belief in a survivable soul is a dualist deprecation of material creation.

The problem for theology is that of accepting the truths of science without compromising important theological truths. Although there are divergent opinions on the details (ranging from dualism to reductive materialism), one assumption among some philosophers and scientists regarding religious ideas of the soul is that if the "Cartesians can no longer live in their disembodied souls," neither can the Christians consider their souls to be immortal (Peters 1999). But just as scientists do not agree on the mind/body problem, there has never been theological consensus on the number and kind of "ontological ingredients" it takes to make a person (Cooper 2000). Trichotomy (body, soul, and spirit), dichotomy (body and soul), and monism (body–soul unity) have all been proposed.

For most of Christian history, dualist language has tended to predominate, even though a strong dualism (material body and separable, inherently immortal soul or spirit) is alien to the scriptures (Cullman 1958). Christian teachings on the afterlife do not require body/soul dualism, but they do insist on a future bodily resurrection. As we shall see, the tendency to speak of a dual human nature is driven by the claim that the essence of the person in some sense resides with Christ prior to the final transformative bodily resurrection.

Joel Green has shown that, while there are diverse views of the person in the scriptures, the dominant theme is an "ontological monism" that precludes any sort of disembodied existence. Belief in an intermediate state after death does not, he says, necessitate an immaterial separable soul. When body and soul are contrasted in the scriptures it is in the context of soteriological value: that which upholds the spiritual versus that which upholds the selfish use of material reality. What seems to have mattered more to New Testament writers than clearly developed theological anthropologies was the person's relationship to others and to God. "[W]ho we are, our personhood, is inextricably tied to the cosmos God has created, and in the sum of our life experiences and relationships […] the relationality and narrativity that constitute who I am are able to exist apart from neural correlates and embodiment only insofar as they are preserved in God's own being" (Green 2008: 179–80).

Theological difficulties arise when reductionist claims lead theorists to confuse the two functions of the soul concept noted above. For many, anything implying the soul lacks substantiality/independence from the body eliminates moral accountability and the possibility of life after death. This is an unfortunate misinterpretation. If it were true, it would certainly be problematic, since one central aspect of Christian doctrine includes the promise of life after death in communion with God. In fact, it is more theologically consistent with scripture and tradition to accept the claims of science for the embodied nature of the human self than to claim soul and body are distinct entities.

Christian theologians interested in science-and-religion dialogue have begun to re-examine the scriptures to explore ways of speaking about the soul that are true to the tradition and also scientifically coherent. These "sophisticated conciliationists" (Flanagan 2002) offer a philosophical framework of non-reductive physicalism in place of dualism. Non-reductive physicalism posits that all causation of functional properties is physical, even though the functional cannot be reduced to the physical. The position is predicated on acceptance that this is preferable to eliminative or reductive physicalism, which defines the person as nothing but a physical being, all of whose experiences will eventually be explained by science (Brown *et al.* 1998). The person is "a physical organism whose complex functioning, both in society and in relation to God, gives rise to 'higher' human capacities such as morality and spirituality." In this framework, the soul and consciousness become circumstantially supervenient emergent properties of the brain that exert causal influence on the body in a top-down direction.

Nancey Murphy argues that circumstantial supervenience avoids causal reductionism. In circumstantial supervenience, mental properties are what they are not just by reason of the neurochemistry that brings them about, but also by reason of their function (Murphy 1999). This allows for the possibility that identical events occurring under different circumstances might not produce the same outcome (*ibid.*). To claim that the soul is an emergent property is to say that an exhaustive description of the underlying physical state of the human is necessary, but not sufficient, for explaining the soul's existence. An emergent property is an unanticipated outcome or by-product, a "something more:" whereas normally $a + b$ should $= c$, if the relation between a and b is one of emergence, $a + b = c^{+1}$ (Murphy and Ellis 1996).

Advocates say that supervenience helps explain causation in the direction of physical to mental, but experience tells us that mind/body causation is not a one-way street. "Bottom-up" causation in firing neurons and neurochemical transfer across synapses is certainly necessary, as far as we now know, for any mental or physical event. But evidence indicates that causation flows from the top down as well. This has been most clearly demonstrated in perception studies. How we perceive sensory input is determined both by the stimulus itself, and by individual expectations regarding the stimulus. We very often see what we expect to see, rather than what is really there. Non-reductive physicalists say this means the physical determines initial emergence of the mental, but does not fully determine the outcome of the mental after its emergence. If the mental life is an emergent feature of the complex biological structure of the brain's interaction with its environment, a person is a physical being whose multifaceted functioning gives rise to "higher" human faculties like the moral and spiritual. The soul is a property, a quality, or a phenomenon, not a substance: the physical brain causes but does not determine it. The non-reductive physicalist's soul is the higher-level cognition that emerges out of, and supervenes upon, the physical brain, and is in some sense capable of freedom and moral accountability.

While this approach might overcome some of the difficulties, it does not solve all our problems. It may, in fact, concede too much too soon to science. There are philosophical, practical, and theological issues at stake here, and the territory is not well mapped. According to Huston Smith, the non-reductive physicalists are earnest Christians who do not believe they are surrendering to the scientific world-view, but they are doing just that. Their God is "(1) the world's first and final cause, who (2) works in history by controlling the way particles jump in the indeterminacy that physicists allow them" (Smith 2001).

In a very real sense, we are all non-reductive physicalists when it comes to the things of everyday life. A non-reductive physicalist interpretation of the self is no more revelatory than the claim that we cannot adequately explain what a pizza is by talking about its quantum structure (Wacome 2004). And it is not at all clear how, even with circumstantial supervenience, this frees the soul from the bonds of physical causation. Finally, in attempting to free theology of an immaterial soul, non-reductive physicalists intensify the problem of free will. In a recent work, Murphy and Brown conclude that reconciliation of free will and biology is a problem more for neuroscience than for philosophical reflection. They issue a challenge to cognitive scientists to develop better accounts of how "our neural equipment provides for the cognitive and behavioral capacities that go into responsible action" (Murphy and Brown 2007: 306).

Theologically, it is problematic to reduce all aspects of human life to the physical. What is the moral status of someone who suffers from Alzheimer's disease, severe brain damage, or congenital cognitive disability, if that which makes us persons is nothing more than neurochemistry? On the other hand, strongly dualist accounts are problematic in overemphasis on the survival of the spiritual to the detriment of the physical. Taken too far, this ends in Gnostic portrayals of the physical world as a prison from which we must escape. Theology must seek the middle ground here, while acknowledging that the urge to dualism is a reflection of the intuition that subjective experience is not reducible to the physical.

By entering the brain/mind fray from the standpoint of the individual mind, conciliationists accept a basic premise of science that compromises important theological points. This requires that the object of study be the individual mind in isolation, a necessarily solipsistic enterprise. No solipsistic enterprise can adequately support the communal imperative of Christian theology. A methodology wherein we start with scripture and theological anthropology, not science, allows us to hold in tension the tenets of Christian faith and the discoveries of science without granting too much to scientific speculation. Even more importantly, it allows us to reach conclusions that capture the gist of non-reductive physicalism and eliminate dualistic errors that have crept into Christian thought over the centuries without compromising theological priorities.

The embodied Christian soul

The Christian soul is a relational moral concept, the product of evolving thought traceable in the biblical texts. In the Hebrew Bible, the person is a unity of body and soul, a "functional holism" in which there is a duality of ingredients. We do not "have" souls; the human is human only as body-and-soul (Cooper 2000). A detailed examination of the Hebrew terms goes beyond the scope of this essay, and there is some question as to the usefulness of this enterprise for uncovering theological anthropology in the scriptures. We can say, however, that there is nothing in the terms themselves that unquestionably supports dualist anthropologies.

The Hebrew texts do not offer much about what happens to us after death, but some general comments are possible. The person survives, although whether consciously or unconsciously is unclear, apparently in Sheol, the resting place for all who die. Sheol is sometimes confused with later conceptions of Hell, but one's moral standing has nothing to do with it. Sheol is a place of waiting for all who have died (*ibid.*). Moral responsibility is a communal concept at this stage; subsequent generations bear liability for the sins of the present (cf. Exodus 20: 5; Deuteronomy 5: 9). In later texts, this is replaced by individual accountability for sin (cf. Jeremiah 31: 29–30; Ezekiel 18: 2–4).

As ideas of individual responsibility took shape within the Jewish community, theological ideas of the human being expanded to allow space for the individual to stand in personal relationship with God, and the soul concept that evolved alongside the individualization of moral responsibility is an expression of this. During the intertestamental period, beliefs about life after death develop more clarity as well as variety.

In the Hebrew Bible, the heart is the seat of conscience whereas the emotions (also firmly seated in the body) are "located" in the gut. The heart is the "place" of relation to God: Hardening the heart separates us from God, and having a new heart signifies spiritual rebirth. In the New Testament, heart is synonymous with the inner being or whole self. It is the ethical center and seat of memory. This "cardiac anthropology" implies a kind of holism: the literal physical organ is the center of spiritual and psychic integration of the person in relation to God (Ware 2002).

Evaluating theological anthropology of the New Testament is made difficult because in the Gospels, soul language functions primarily in the context of teachings on salvation, not as a technical theological or philosophical concept. Complicating things further, Paul uses a variety of terms that some have taken to mean we are a trichotomy of body, soul, and spirit; body and soul are part of the natural human, and spirit is said to be some commodity added upon conversion to the faith. But since Paul's surviving letters are "occasional" pieces, written to small communities to address particular and personal concerns, theological caution is in order.

Adding to the picture is the fact that the New Testament gives more attention than earlier texts to resurrection of the body and an intermediate state after death. Since the idea of an intermediate state does appear in the New Testament (cf. Luke 16: 19–31; 23: 40–43; 24: 36–49; 2 Corinthians 5: 1–10), attempts to eliminate it from the discussion are misguided. The idea is there, but without speculation as to specifics. Some sort of intervening status, which represented union with Christ, was expected (Cullman 1958). "All we know from Scripture is that in God's providence human beings can exist in fellowship with Christ without earthly bodies" (Cooper 2000).

Biblical scholarship shows that early Christian soteriologies included the whole person – body and soul. The clearest illustration of this is Jesus' own resurrection and ascension. Christ really died. If his soul had been immortal and separable, what was the point of the resurrection? As Adrian Thatcher so drolly put it, "What then is the ascension [if dualism is correct]? A highly visual way of saying cheerio? It is, rather, the return of the transformed, transfigured, glorified, yet still *embodied*, Christ to the Father" (Thatcher 1987).

Human nature is portrayed in the scriptures as dual – made up of a physical body and an aspect with the capability of communion with God such that it can survive death of the body. This does not, however, necessitate a Platonic or Cartesian dualism of substances. Historians sometimes wrongly claim that the earliest theologians were dualists – in fact, the separable soul did not become doctrine until the Middle Ages, when teachings on purgatory and the sale of indulgences made elaboration necessary.

Early theologians examined the difference between the Platonist's inherently immortal soul and the scriptural soul's immortality as gift of God's grace. Justin Martyr (d. 165 CE) says, "I pay no regard to Plato" in speaking of the soul, for it "lives not as being itself life, but as the partaking of life" because "God wills it to live […] for it is not the property of the soul to have life in itself" (Wolfson 1993). The scriptural imperative that God alone possesses immortality was unquestioned in the early decades of Christian theology.

During the third through fifth centuries, theologians worked out their thought in conversation with the predominant philosophies of the day. Augustine of Hippo argued in *City of God* that the human is "constituted by body and soul together […] the soul is not the whole man; it is the better part of man, and the body is not the whole man; it is the lower part of him. It is the conjunction of the two parts that is entitled to the name of 'man'" (Augustine 1980: XIII: 24). The human is a combination of body and soul, the relationship of which an inexplicable "miraculous combination" wrought by God (*ibid.*: XXII: 24).

Variance of opinion continues into the Middle Ages. In the thirteenth century, Thomas Aquinas incorporated Aristotelian metaphysics into theology in what would become the orthodox Catholic doctrine of the soul as the form of the body. He said the rational soul (which only humans have) is a simple substance with a spiritual nature that is incomplete until united with the body. Through a special act of creation, God replaces the human embryo's "vegetative" with a rational soul, making possible higher cognitive functions (Aquinas 1964: 1.Q 75–76).

In the seventeenth century, Descartes recovered Platonic dualism with a vengeance. For him, there were two kinds of reality: "thinking" substance (the mind, angels) and "extended" substance (material things). "The soul by which I am what I am, is entirely distinct from body, and is even more easy to know than the later; and if body were not, the soul would not cease to be what it is" (Descartes 1970 [1637]). Drawing such a hard line between soul and body set the stage for the difficulties that plague us today.

The relational embodied soul

The solipsistic pull we noted in attempts to incorporate neuroscientific claims into theology is a problem for Christian theology. This is so because, although the gift of the incarnation is salvation for the individual person, it is meaningful only in the context of relationship. God as Trinity is an expression of the intuition that person-in-relation is the very existence of God (Zizioulas 1985). We are held individually accountable for our choices, and what makes those choices meaningful is how we live in relation to others and to God.

Our development as a species is a dual process of biological and cultural evolution, our minds a hybrid outcome of biology and culture. Evolutionary sciences tell us that cognitive skills in the human cannot have evolved without the simultaneous development of cultures. By means of symbol systems like language, human minds can learn "not just *from* the other [as other species do] but *through* the other" (Tomasello 1999). The "symbolic technologies" of our cultures "liberate consciousness from the limitations of the brain's biological memory systems" and enable us to break the bonds of biology (Donald 2001).

The soul, then, is the organizational structure that makes the individual person possible, and culture is the organizational structure that makes humanity possible. Individual minds become persons in and through relationship – to one another in cultures and to God in spiritual communion. God's own being is an act of communion. Humanity reflects this reality; communion is likewise constitutive of what it means to be a person. In and through cultures, humanity pools its resources, thereby fulfilling its potential. In communion with other minds, we learn what it means to be created in the image of God and we are made capable of living that reality. The soul is the seat of relationship, the locus of God's action within the individual.

A theology of cultures added to reflections on soul allows us to say that culture is the guardian of our souls. In and through cultures, we learn moral behavior even when individual role models fail. The souls of those who suffer from diseases which challenge all our assumptions about what it means to be a person are preserved in communities of memory. The biblical truth that immortality is a gift from God is preserved, since the soul is both "within" the individual and "outside" in the community. Survival of death is both "objective immortality," the cumulative effects of one's life on the cultural and communal memory, and "subjective immortality," the gift given by God in God's own time. The Christian idea of the afterlife finds its fullest expression in eschatological hope. The promise of life after death can be understood only in the context of Jesus' resurrection, and the resurrection can be understood only within the framework of Jesus' teachings about the world to come, or the Kingdom of God. And what is the "Kingdom of God" if not an ethical, relational concept? The soul – as the sum total of who each of us has been, is, and will be in this earthly life – is an ethical, future-oriented concept, a product of the relational character of human being. What this means can be illuminated to some extent by the sciences. But in the end, the very neurological and cultural realities that make our spirituality possible are the same realities that give us our limitations (Teske 1996).

References

Ashbrook, J. (1984) "Neurotheology: The Working Brain and the Work of Theology," *Zygon: Journal of Religion and Science* 19: 331–50.

Ashbrook, J. and Albright, C. (1997) *The Humanizing Brain: Where Religion and Neuroscience Meet*. Cleveland, OH: Pilgrim Press.

d'Aquili, E. and Newberg, A. (1999) *The Mystical Mind: Probing the Biology of Religious Experience*, Minneapolis, MN: Fortress Press.

Aquinas, T. (1964) *Summa Theologia* Book I, Questions 75 and 76, Blackfriars Edition, New York: McGraw-Hill.

Augustine (1980) *City of God*. H. Bettenson (trans.), New York: Penguin Books.

Brown, W. S., Murphy, N. and Malony, H. N. (eds) (1998) *Whatever Happened to the Soul? Scientific and Theological Portraits of Human Nature*, Minneapolis, MN: Fortress Press.

Burns, C.P.E. (2002) *Divine Becoming: Rethinking Jesus and Incarnation*, Minneapolis, MN: Fortress Press.

——(2005) "Cognitive Science and Christian Theology," in *Soul, Psyche, Brain: New Directions in the Study of Religion and Brain-Mind Science*, K. Bulkeley (ed.), New York: Palgrave Macmillan, 346–88.

Chalmers, D. J. (1995) "Facing up to the Problem of Consciousness," *Journal of Consciousness Studies* 2: 200–209.

Cooper, J. W. (2000) *Body, Soul, and Life Everlasting: Biblical Anthropology and the Monism–Dualism Debate* Grand Rapids, MI: William B. Eerdmans.

Cullman, O. (1958) *Immortality of the Soul or Resurrection of the Dead?*, London: Epworth Press.

Damasio, A. (1999) *The Feeling of What Happens: Body and Emotion in the Making of Consciousness*, San Diego, CA: Harcourt.

Delio, I. (2003) "Brain Science and the Biology of Belief: A Theological Response," *Zygon: Journal of Religion and Science* 38: 573–85.

Descartes, R. (1970 [1637]) *The Philosophical Works of Descartes*, Vol. 1., Elizabeth S. Haldane and G.R.T. Ross (trans.), New York: Cambridge University Press.

Donald, M. (2001) *A Mind So Rare: The Evolution of Human Consciousness*, New York: W.W. Norton.

Feit, J.S. (2003) "Probing Neurotheology's Brain, or Critiquing an Emerging Quasi-Science," paper presented to the Critical Theory and Discourses on Religion Section, American Academy of Religion, 2003 Annual Convention, Atlanta, GA, November 22–25, 2003.

Flanagan, O. (2002) *The Problem of the Soul: Two Visions of the Mind and How to Reconcile Them*, New York: Basic Books.

Grandqvist, Pehr, Mats Fredrikson, Dan Larhammar, Marcus Larsson and Sven Valind (2005) "Sensed Presence and Mystical Experiences are Predicted by Suggestibility, Not by the Application of Transcranial Weak Complex Magnetic Fields," *Neuroscience Letters* 379(1): 1–6.

Green, Joel B. (2008) *Body, Soul, and Human Life: The Nature of Humanity in the Bible*, Grand Rapids, MI: Baker Academic.

Gillman, N. (1995) *The Death of Death: Resurrection and Immortality in Jewish Thought*, Woodstock, VT: Jewish Lights Publications.

Hood, R., Hill, P. and Spilka, B. (2009) *The Psychology of Religion* 4th edn, New York: Guilford Press.

James, W. (1902) *The Varieties of Religious Experience*, Cambridge, MA: Harvard University Press.

Jeeves, M. and Brown, W. (2009) *Neuroscience, Psychology, and Religion: Illusions, Delusions, and Realities about Human Nature*, West Conshohocken, PA: Templeton Foundation Press.

Jewett, P.K. (1996) *Who We Are: Our Dignity as Human*, Marguerite Shuster (ed.), Grand Rapids, MI: William B. Eerdmans.

Kim, J. (1996) *Mind in a Physical World: An Essay on the Mind–Body Problem and Mental Causation*, Cambridge, MA: MIT Press.

McNamara, P. (2009) *The Neuroscience of Religious Experience*, New York: Cambridge University Press.

McWilliam, D.J.E. (1986) *Death and Resurrection*, Wilmington, DE: Michael Glazier.

Murphy, N. (1999) "Downward Causation and Why the Mental Matters," *CTNS Bulletin* 19(1).

Murphy, N. and Brown, W.S. (2007) *Did My Neurons Make Me Do It? Philosophical and Biological Perspectives on Moral Responsibility and Free Will*, Oxford: Oxford University Press.

Murphy, N. and Ellis, G. (1996) *On the Moral Nature of the Universe*, Minneapolis, MN: Fortress Press.

Newberg, A. and d'Aquili, E. (2002) *Why God Won't Go Away: Brain Science and the Biology of Belief*, New York: Ballantine Books.

Persinger, M. (1987) *Neuropsychological Bases of God Beliefs*, New York: Praeger Books.

Peters, T. (1999) "Resurrection of the Very Embodied Soul?," in *Neuroscience and the Person: Scientific Perspectives on Divine Action*, Russell, R.J., Murphy, N., Meyering, T.C. and Arbib A.E. (eds), Notre Dame, IN: University of Notre Dame Press.

Russell, R.J., Murphy, N., Meyering, T.C. and Arbib, A.E. (eds) (1999) *Neuroscience and the Person: Scientific Perspectives on Divine Action*, Notre Dame, IN; University of Notre Dame Press.

Smith, H. (2001) *Why Religion Matters: The Fate of the Human Spirit in an Age of Disbelief*, San Francisco, CA: HarperSanFrancisco.

Teske, J. (1996) "The Spiritual Limits of Neuropsychological Life," *Zygon: Journal of Religion and Science* 31: 209–34.

Tomasello, M. (1999) *The Cultural Origins of Human Cognition*, Cambridge, MA: Harvard University Press.

Thatcher, A. (1987) "Christian Theism and the Concept of a Person," in *Persons and Personality: A Contemporary Inquiry*, A. Peacocke and Grant Gillett (eds), Oxford: Basil Blackwell, 180–96.

Wacome, D.H. (2004) "Reductionism's Demise: Cold Comfort," *Zygon: Journal of Religion and Science* 39: 321–38.

Ware, K. (2002) "How Do We Enter the Heart?," in *Paths to the Heart: Sufism and the Christian East*, James Cutsinger (ed.), Bloomington, IN: World Wisdom, 2–23.

Wolfson, H.A. (1993) "Immortality and Resurrection in the Philosophy of the Church Fathers," in *Doctrines of Human Nature, Sin, and Salvation in the Early Church*, Vol. X, Studies in Early Christianity, Everett Ferguson, David Scholer and Paul Finney (eds), New York: Garland Books, 301–36.

Zizioulas, J.D. (1985) *Being as Communion*, Crestwood, NY: St Vladimir's Press.

29
HINDUISM AND THE COGNITIVE SCIENCES
Challenges, contrasts, and confluences

Stephen Kaplan

Setting the stage

Describing the U.S. Army's "Warrior Reset Program," *BBC America* (April 21, 2010) reports "[t]welve soldiers sit on the floor, with eyes closed, focusing on their sacral *chakra*. They chant in unison." This program is training soldiers with post-traumatic stress disorder (PTSD) in the ways of yoga and meditation. Some are learning techniques to raise the energy (*kundalini*) that runs through the various *cakras* (wheels, energy centers), which are located along the spine starting at the base and ascending to the top of the head. The U.S. military, or at least some elements, believe that these types of program can be tested and replicated for their biological–psychological effectiveness and benefits. This particular report praised the success of the program for its stress and anxiety reduction, and cited the need for its expansion in light of the fact that approximately 10–15 per cent of soldiers returning from Iraq and Afghanistan are reporting symptoms of PTSD (news.bbc.co.uk/1/hi/world/Americas/8634277.stm).

The use of meditation techniques, from Transcendental Meditation to mindfulness, to deal with a variety of medical conditions, from high blood pressure to anxiety, has been reviewed for years in the medical and scientific literature, and often found to be effective (Anderson *et al.* 2008). Such studies, championed by Herbert Benson (Emeritus Director, Benson-Henry Institute), Jon Kabat Zinn (Professor Emeritus, University of Massachusetts Medical School), Richard Davidson (University of Wisconsin), and others, can be labeled therapeutic studies. A second type of study has aimed at correlating the particular mental states produced by specific meditative practices with their concomitant neurophysiological activity in order to understand what is going on in the brain of meditators as they report their meditative experiences. For example, early electroencephalography (EEG) studies contend that some types of meditative practice may lead the reticular activating system to "shut down" repetitive neural input, producing a state of "void" or "oneness" (Naranjo and Ornstein 1974). More recently, d'Aquili and Newberg (1999) have looked at the impact of particular meditative techniques on the parietal lobe in order to understand the neuropsychology of the experience of non-duality. Their contention is that particular types of concentrative meditation decrease the level of activity in the parietal lobe, which is responsible for locating "me-as-subject" embodied in a world-of-objects. Allegedly, such hypo-activation of the parietal lobe is concomitant with a diminished or eliminated sense of subject–object dualism, which the authors posit is a state of consciousness labeled Absolute Unitary Being (AUB), identified as the highest state of mystical knowledge. These studies, to which we will return, operate at the border between methodological and ontological reductionism – methodologically looking for the neurophysiological correlates concomitant with meditation practice, while raising the possibility that such meditative experiences are ontologically reducible to their neurophysiological correlates.

Taken as an aggregate, these two types of study ask us to contemplate how Hindu sciences of mind/body and their associated techniques for health and wholeness can be understood and evaluated in contemporary cognitive terms. This literature often grabs public attention with the idea that meditation and yoga techniques, arising out of ancient India, hold secrets that need to be more deeply explored and more widely disseminated. This literature sometimes leads us to contemplate whether the contemporary cognitive sciences are verifying the wisdom already discovered by Hindu cognitive sciences – or are these cognitive sciences illuminating the true neuropsychological meaning of the ideas emanating from traditional Hindu thought? Following Spezio's lead (Chapter 26 in this volume), this essay suggests that generalizations regarding Hindu cognitive theories often mask significant differences between contemporary cognitive theories and their Hindu counterparts; however, delving into the specificities of each might open new avenues for thought.

Raising some of the challenges

There are enormous challenges in trying to relate the cognitive sciences to Hinduism. On the one side, Spezio's essay (Chapter 26) illuminates the diversity of foci of the cognitive sciences, which include sensation, perception, attention, language, and reasoning, and he illuminates the diversity of methodological approaches that are part of the cognitive sciences. On the other side, we begin by acknowledging that "Hinduism" is a controversial term whose usage is anachronistically applied to much of the material reviewed here (Llewellyn 2005). The term Hinduism, arising as a foreign appellation relating to a geographical demarcation, namely the Sindhu River, functions here as an umbrella for an enormous diversity, over 3500 years in the making, of philosophical positions, theological beliefs, and religious practices. The endeavor to relate the cognitive sciences to Hinduism would be extraordinarily complex if we constricted this discussion to the so-called six major philosophical schools of Hinduism and the view of each on the different foci listed above. However, each school is itself an umbrella for historical and philosophical diversity, and these six schools exclude at least as many positions that fall under the umbrella of Hinduism as they include. The entire Ayurvedic medical tradition, the Tantric traditions, and the Hatha yoga traditions, to name only three, fall outside of the aforementioned six schools, although each shares characteristics with those schools. If a simple mapping or correlating of cognitive science positions to Hindu positions were possible, the task would be daunting, yet still insufficient, since such a mapping would not reveal the broad philosophical and systematic differences between the disciplines related to the cognitive sciences and the disciplines or schools under the umbrella of Hinduism. It is to the latter that we turn first.

The cognitive sciences are not limited to the neurosciences, but they certainly revolve around the neurosciences. The Hindu positions are historically not oriented toward the neurosciences. First, to state the obvious, the tools of the cognitive sciences such as EEG and functional magnetic resonance imaging (fMRI) were not available. Second, the primary methodology of the cognitive sciences, as described by Spezio in Chapter 26 of this volume, entails "those measures that are directly observable, measurable, and sometimes quantifiable from the crucial third-person perspective." Methodologically, the Hindu systems were focused on establishing the valid means of knowledge (*pramana*) and ascertaining the legitimate definition for each means of knowledge in order to arrive at what type of cognition (*jnana*) could be labeled true. Among the different schools, Vedanta and some segments of the Mimamsa school, for example, accept six valid means of knowledge – perception, inference, verbal testimony, comparison, postulation, and non-perception – but other schools, such as Samkhya, accept only the first three of the aforementioned, while Nyaya accepts four *pramanas*. Furthermore, the definition that each uses to describe the different means of knowledge may differ. For example, while the Buddhist Dignaga defined perception as being free of all concepts, the Hindu Bhartrhari, a grammarian, contended that all perceptions have a linguistic component; and the Vedantins distinguished perceptions with mental concepts from perceptions without concepts (*savikalpa* and *nirvikalpa*, respectively). The texts of each of these schools are filled with logical arguments to prove the position of that school, and are filled with polemical debates to discredit the positions of the other schools. These different theories of valid cognition were not created in empirical laboratories with control groups and third-person observations. Rather, Hindu cognitive theories proposed by each of the different schools and sub-schools were developed through hotly debated arguments rooted in logical disputations tinged by differing ontological commitments and a diversity of first-person epistemological experiences that included a variety of states of consciousness, from waking to dreaming, to dreamless sleep, to a fourth state, *turiya*, a state of self-illuminating consciousness. There is some debate over the "empirical, scientific" nature of Ayurvedic medicine (Engler 2003), and there is a growing voice, especially related to His Holiness the Fourteenth Dalai Lama and the Mind & Life Institute, that first-person, meditative experiences should be treated as empirically trained statements. Nonetheless, the methodology that is presented in Hindu texts related to the different schools is decidedly philosophical, and not empirical in the sense in which Spezio uses the term.

From the Upanisads to the Samkhya–Advaita–Nyaya dialogues

In distinguishing contemporary cognitive sciences from the Hindu systems, the roles of the heart and brain cannot be ignored. There is no doubt that the brain and the nervous system, as envisioned in the Ayurvedic, Tantric, and many associated schools, are part of a map of the human person, which includes a series of *cakras* and channels (*nadis*) running to the top of the skull. This map of the human person, which is itself a microcosm of the cosmological map, depicts a mind and body fully integrated. In addition, numerous Hindu references declare that the true self (*purusa*), the mind, and the different states of consciousness reside in the heart (*Chandogya Upanisad* 3.14.3, Anon. 1996). The *Taittiriya Upanisad* (1.6) declares that the immortal person consisting of mind and residing in the heart travels to and through the skull in the process of self-realization. A similar image is provided in the *Katha Upanisad*

> One hundred and one, the veins of the heart,
> One of them runs up to the crown of the head.
> Going up by it, he reaches the immortal.
> The rest, in their ascent, spread out in all directions.
>
> (*Katha Upanisad* 6.16)

The realization of true self involves cutting the ties that bind the individual to the heart and ascending the channel that reaches to the top of the skull, from which liberation (*moksa*) can be achieved.

Stepping back from this anatomical issue, an overview of the psychic apparatus will allow us to present some of the key issues within the Hindu schools. (A note of caution is in order: the Sanskrit terms that follow are understood in particular ways with very particular functions and should not simply be conflated with the English equivalents initially provided.) The *Katha Upanisad*, employing the analogy of a chariot, provides one of the classic images of the Indian cognitive apparatus.

> Know the self as a rider in a chariot, and the body, as simply the chariot. Know the intellect as the charioteer, and the mind, as the reins. The senses, they say are the horses, and sense objects are the paths around them; He who is linked to the body (*atman*), senses, and mind, the wise proclaim as the one who enjoys.
>
> (*ibid.* 3.3–4)

The rider, the true self (*atman*), and the charioteer, the intellect (*buddhi*), are distinguished from each other and from the mind (*manas*) as well as from the body and the senses (*indriyas*). The latter are like wild horses that need to be controlled by the reins of the mind, and the mind is steered by the intellect, the *buddhi*. The true self (*atman*) is not engaged in any activity; it is a passenger/rider, the witness (*saksin*), the eternal, unchanging self.

In the Samkhya school, this true self is referred to as *purusa*. The fundamental nature of each *purusa* is pure, contentless consciousness, the passive, inactive witness [*Samkhya Karika* (*SK*) 19, Larson 1978]. There are a multitude of *purusas*; each *purusa* is individual, yet not personal, since each lacks any distinguishing characteristics as it is pure illuminating awareness (*SK* 18). For Samkhya, there is consciousness and there is matter/nature (*prakrti*). In this schema, *purusa* and *prakrti* are ontologically distinct and separate, yet somehow brought into sufficient proximity such that *purusa* illuminates the workings of the non-conscious (*acetanan*), material, internal psychic organ (*antahkarana*) (*SK* 20). Here, the false identification of *prakrti* with *purusa* is the fundamental human problem leading to rebirth (*samsara*). As in so much of Hindu thought, the fundamental human problem is cognitive; it is not moral, not a question of improper acting, but incorrect knowing.

The internal cognitive organ (*antahkarana*), part of *prakrti* (matter), is both individual and personal. It is comprised of *buddhi*, *ahamkara*, and *manas*. The *buddhi* (intellect), the most direct involution of primordial matter (*mulaprakrti*), is the closest to the true self and engages in the act of discernment. It is characterized as insight, ascertainment, and wisdom (*prajna*). Arising from the *buddhi* is the *ahamkara*, (the maker of the I, the ego). *Ahamkara* is associated with self-awareness and conceit (*abhimano*). The *ahamkara* gives rise to the mind (*manas*) as well as the five sense organs, such as the eye and ear, and the five organs of action, such as hands and feet. *Manas* is identified with intentionality (*samkalpaka*) (*SK* 22–29). Illustrating a fragment of the diversity within Hinduism, Advaita Vedanta adds to the *antahkarana* a fourth element, *citta*. While *citta* is routinely translated and understood, generically, as "mind" in numerous Sanskrit texts, the *Vedantaparibhasa* (*VP*) defines *citta* as memory, recollection (*VP* 1: 58, Dharmaraja 1971). K. C. Bhattacharyya describes it as "the faculty of intellectual synthesis as distinct from mere apprehension" (1956: 46). In the *VP*, *manas* is related to doubt (*samsaya*), by both asserting and negating, while *buddhi* is fundamentally involved in determination, an assertion without yet the notion of I and not I. *Ahamkara* is identified by pride (*garvas*).

While Samkhya is both dualistic (*purusa* and *prakrti*) and pluralistic (a multitude of *purusas*), Advaita Vedanta is neither pluralistic nor dualistic. Advaita is non-dualistic. Advaita contends that there is only one true self (*atman*), not a multitude of selves. Advaita declares that *atman* is Brahman, the Being of all that has ever existed and that will ever exist. Brahman is one unchanging, eternal Self which is Being, Consciousness, and Bliss. The failure to recognize that all is *atman* is ignorance (*avidya*). This *avidya* is the imposition (*adhyasa*) of duality, the duality of subject and object, on that which is not dual. This cognitive problem is the cause of rebirth according to Advaita.

Nyaya disagrees with the Samkhya and Advaita positions, which assert that the true self (*purusa* or *atman*, respectively) is conscious. For Nyaya, the self is not by nature conscious. Consciousness is a quality of the self that only arises under the appropriate conditions of the mind/body complex [*Nyaya-Sutra* (*NS*) i.1.22, Gautama and Vatsyayana 1982).

In fact, for Nyaya the liberated soul is not conscious, not in a state of self-illuminating awareness (*NS* iv.2.44). Nyaya also contends that consciousness does not illuminate itself in the act of illuminating a cognition. It is *paraprakasa* (illuminating an other). One may be conscious of an object, such as computer, without knowing one knows it. Advaita maintains that such an idea would lead to an infinite regress. J. N. Mohanty also questions Nyaya on this by pondering: "To be able to desire to reflect upon the just gone state of consciousness, one needs to have some acquaintance with the latter. You cannot desire to know what you simply have no acquaintance with" (Mohanty 1993: 64). In contrast, Advaita declares that consciousness (*cit*) is self-illuminating (*svaprakasa*). The conscious knowing of an object entails the knowing that one knows that object. In addition to being *svaprakasa*, Advaita claims that consciousness is without form (*nirakara*), without an object (*nirvisaya*), and without a locus (*nirasraya*). Understanding consciousness (*cit*) with these four qualities is concomitant with the Advaita understanding of *cit* as *atman*. Since *atman* is everywhere, it cannot have a locus. It can not be one place and not another place. Nor could consciousness have an object, as that would imply intentionality, and that which is non-dual cannot seek an other and remain non-dual. Similarly, *cit* cannot have a form, because it would then be distinguished from a second, an other form.

While consciousness has no form, Advaita declares that the *antahkarana* takes a form in the process of perception (*pratyaksa*). In this process, the object as it is known is the mind in the form of the object. Likewise, as the individual is known to itself as an object (my body), the mind simultaneously becomes both the subject (*grahaka*, literally the grasper) and the object (*grahya*, literally that which is grasped) [*Mandukyopanisad* (*MK*) 4: 72, Gaudapada 1989]. The duality of mind as both subject and object, grasper and grasped, is produced by the movement of the mind (*cittaspandita*) and this duality is, for the Advaitins, *maya*, an illusion. In this context, it is the illusion that what is presumably known as the object itself is instead the mind in the form of the object (Kaplan 1987). Like Samkhya and Nyaya, Advaita contends that the mind must go out through the appropriate sense organ and assume the form of the object as known. In smell, taste, and touch, the object is in contact with the body, but for sight and hearing, the mind must reach out to the object (*prapyakarin*); the *antahkarana* is projected into the world. As evidenced by the Advaita understanding of illusory perception, wherein a faulty sense organ is cause for a mistaken perception (*VP* 1: 83–85), this theory of projection does not discount the role of the sense organs in receiving sense data. Rather, it affirms common sense experiences – for example, (1) "I" look *into the world* and see a car *out-there*, in front of me; and (2) I "feel" someone looking at me, as if their sight has touched me (Eck 1985). The cognitive sciences rarely engage a theory of projection in which the mind goes out, beyond the brain. An exception can be found in the work of Karl Pribram (1977), who proposed a holographic theory of mind/brain, which has some connection to this Hindu *prapyakarin* notion (Kaplan 1987).

Nyaya formally defines perception as non-linguistic, direct object contact that entails a relation to a specific object that is not conflated with nor confused with other objects (*NS* i.1.4). In their definition, we not only see the notion of the mind reaching out to make direct contact, but we see the beginning of a distinction between non-linguistic and linguistic perceptions. Nyaya, Advaita, and others, in varying ways, distinguish perceptions without constructions (*nirvikalpa*) and perceptions with constructions (*savikalpa*). Perception without mental constructions refers to a perception whose character has not been overlaid with linguistic, conceptual categories. Perceptions with mental constructs would be those in which one attributes qualities and characteristics to the perception.

> Now Nyaya says that for this sort of conceptual cognition to occur, there must first occur a non-conceptual perception, one that is not attributive in character. In this sort of cognition what we perceive are the individual

> constituents of the conceptual cognition by themselves, separately. So in order to have the conceptual perception of Flossie as a cow, I must first non-conceptually perceive Flossie just as such, *cowness* just as such, and the inherence that connects Flossie and cowness just as such. Of course we are never aware that we are doing this. We couldn't be, since the contents of non-conceptual cognitions can never be expressed. To express something requires making a judgment, attributing a character to the object. But, Nyaya argues, there must be this non-conceptual perception before every conceptual perception, since otherwise we would be unable to connect the object and the character we attribute to it.
>
> (Siderits 2007: 94)

Leaving aside the possibility of perceiving universals such as "cowness" and what that would entail, the Nyaya distinction between *nirvikalpa* and *savikalpa* cognitions calls to mind Spezio's point (Chapter 26 in this volume) that not all cognitions are conscious.

Conflicts and confluences

In bringing Hinduism and the cognitive science into dialogue, the Samkhya dualism of *purusa* and *prakrti* needs to be distinguished from the dualism that appears in Western philosophical thought, such as the dualism of Descartes' mind and body. In Western thought, mind and consciousness are often conflated and the terms are frequently used interchangeably. Many in the cognitive sciences either reduce mind and consciousness to brain, or see mind and consciousness as a property or function of the brain. In either case, mind and consciousness are connected. Samkhya, on the other hand, declares that the entire mental apparatus, comprising *buddhi*, *ahamkara*, *manas*, and the brain, is *prakrti* (matter). Some elements are constituted by subtle matter (*suksma*) and other elements are constituted by gross matter (*sthula*), but all of these elements are non-conscious matter. *Purusa* is consciousness, and it is ontologically distinct from matter, brain, and mind. This is a different form of dualism from that associated with Western thought.

Western theology, confronting the cognitive sciences, faces different concerns from those that Samkhya and Advaita face. The fear of reducing mind and consciousness, or soul, to brain – a reductionism which, according to Slingerland (2008), undermines the religion–science interchange – is not relevant to Samkhya or Advaita. For Samkhya, since mind is presumed to be unconscious matter, there is no fear of reducing mind to brain. Furthermore, as stated, *purusa* can never be reduced to matter for Samkhya; it is eternally ontologically distinct from matter. For the Advaitin, mind, brain, and everything else is *atman*/Brahman, Being and Consciousness, and therefore there can be no fear of reducing the mind to non-conscious brain, since all is *atman*.

While these Hindu systems have no need to fear a mind-to-brain reductionism, the Samkhya notion that *buddhi*, and the rest of the *antahkarana*, is the initial manifestation of primordial matter (*mulaprakrti*) poses an issue for discussion. Cognitive sciences, rooted in evolutionary biology, do not see individuals developing from subtle matter (*suksma*) beginning with the intellect (*buddhi*) and "progressing" to gross matter (*sthula*) with physical bodies and brains. The opposite would be their contention. So, does this end any chance of dialogue? With regard to the cognitive sciences, I think not. *The Samkhya Karika* (1) presents this notion of the development of the individual within the context of *duhkha* (suffering) and previous births (*SK* 40). An individual is embodied in a gross body, which is connected to the nature of one's parents (*SK* 39), because one already has a subtle body trapped in *samsara*. Since the individual's cycle of births is without a beginning, the Samkhya ideas cannot constitute a declaration of an initial, first moment of individual, psychological creation. Embodiment is re-embodiment, and re-embodiment begins with one's karmic residues. There must be a previously existing psychic apparatus or there would be no rebirth, no gross body with a neurological structure. Since the issue of rebirth is absolutely not on the plate of the cognitive sciences – not to be rejected, nor accepted – the Samkhya notion of the involution from *buddhi* to brain is therefore also not on the table to be rejected or accepted. (For a fuller analysis regarding the psychological and/or cosmological nature of the Samkhya position, see Parrott 1986 and Larson 1979, whose view seems more aligned with the position expressed here.)

Shifting from the development of mind to the nature of consciousness, Samkhya and Advaita declare that consciousness (*purusa*, *cit*) is not a product of a long evolutionary development from the inorganic to the organic and from the non-conscious to the conscious. The latter notion underlies the evolutionary aspect of the cognitive sciences. As we have seen, according to Samkhya and Advaita, consciousness is a fundamental ontological reality, eternal, unproduced. This point of difference between the Hindu systems and cognitive sciences manifests itself in those studies, briefly noted, in which cognitive methods such as the use of fMRIs are employed to analyze meditative states. When, for example, d'Aquili and Newberg "uncover" that the neurophysiological correlates of AUB – the meditative state of non-dual consciousness – are concomitant with the "hypoactivation of the parietal lobe," can one declare that the meditative state of pure consciousness (*cit*) is reducible to a brain state? Conversely, can one declare that the cognitive sciences have uncovered the reality of the non-dual state of consciousness, of *atman*, *purusa*? Adjudicating between these two ontological positions would demand, as Spezio points out, that the cognitive sciences move from methodological reductionism to ontological reductionism, and such a move is questioned not only by Spezio, but also by d'Aquili and Newberg (1999: ch. 10). In the context of the Hindu–cognitive science dialogue, this is the "grand ontological question" regarding human nature. It is a question that frequently becomes the focus of such cognitive studies, but it remains a question that cannot escape its own presuppositions, namely, (1) consciousness is produced by brain states; or (2) consciousness is eternal and appears with brain states.

The Hindu–cognitive science interchange needs to go beyond, without abandoning, the two types of studies mentioned in the opening paragraphs – the therapeutic studies and the studies on meditation that dance around the issue of methodological and ontological reductionism. Shifting away from the meditation and yoga focus of the first two types, a third type of study, which engages the theoretical insights of both disciplines, needs to be explored. Two examples must suffice. First, building upon the meditational research of d'Aquili and Newberg, my research (Kaplan 2009) has led to an interdisciplinary analysis of grasping and the constructed nature of the subject–object dichotomy. On the one side, the parietal lobe provides us our sense of an embodied subject in a world of external objects. "There is a mass of converging evidence […] that the right inferior parietal lobe plays a key role in the process of self/other distinction" (Ruby and Decety 2003: 2479). Some of this ability to distinguish self and other is traced to the act of grasping. On the other side, Advaita identifies the subject as *grahaka*, the grasper, and the object as the *grahya*, that which is grasped. Grasping (*grahaka*) simultaneously produces both subject and object. In addition, both Advaita and the cognitive sciences inform us that alterations to this process of grasping change our sense of the subject–object relation. Specifically, each informs us that too much grasping, a hyper-activation of grasping, leads to a confusion about who or what is the subject and the object of experience. Too much grasping and one is "possessed." Conversely, each informs us that the hypo-activation of grasping, either neurophysiologically defined or achieved through *asparsayoga* (yoga of no-contact), leads to a diminution or elimination of the duality of subject and object, an experience of the non-duality of consciousness. In spite of these glaring similarities, this research does not lead to an identity of thought, but to a confluence of insights growing out of divergent methodologies with divergent concerns. This research, which does not grant epistemological primacy to either disciple, produces an appreciation of the constructed nature of the subject–object relation. Maybe it will enhance our sense of wonder as we watch an infant grasp for their toes and marvel at the otherness of these wiggly creatures. The concreteness of the neurosciences provides a new perch from which to understand the Advaita analysis of grasping and the concomitant presentation of duality. The insights of Advaita may offer other insights to the neuroscientist, but that I leave to members of that discipline.

A final example to illustrate this type of research comes from the discussions above. Specifically, can the issue of "blind sight" illuminate the Nyaya understanding of *nirvikalpa* and *savikalpa* perceptions – perception without concepts and with concepts? Blind sight is a condition in which neurological deficits to visual centers leave an individual proclaiming that he is blind, yet that individual is able to walk through a room filled with furniture. Some level of visual processing is occurring, but the individual is not aware that such processing is occurring. Recall the quote from Siderits, in which Nyaya maintains that perceptions begin non-conceptually, but we are not aware of this stage of perception. Is blind sight an example of Nyaya's *nirvikalpa* perception? Can we use blind sight to help us understand the Nyaya discussion? Conversely, is there anything in the Nyaya position that could illuminate the work of contemporary cognitive scientists in their attempt to understand "blind sight"? These questions must be answered elsewhere.

References

Anderson, James W., Chunxu Liu and Richard J. Keyscio (2008) "Blood Pressure Response to Transcendental Meditation: A Meta-Analysis," *American Journal of Hypertension* 21: 310–16.

Anon. (1996) *Upanisads*, Patrick Olievelle (trans.), Oxford: Oxford University Press.

Bhattacharyya, Krisnachandra (1956) *Studies in Philosophy*, Vol. 1, Gopinath Bhattacharyya (ed.), Calcutta: Progressive Publishers.

Dharmaraja (1971) *Vedantaparibhasa*, Suryanarayana Sastri (ed. and trans.), Madras: The Adyar Library and Research Centre [*VP*].

Eck, Diana L. (1985) *Darsan: Seeing the Divine Image in India*, Chambersburg, PA: Amina Books.

Engler, Stephen (2003) "'Science' vs. 'Religion' in Classical Ayurveda," *Numen*, 50: 416–63.

Gaudapada (1989) *The Agamasastra of Gaudapada*, Vidhushekhara Bhattacharya (ed.), Delhi: Motilal Banarsidass Publishers.

Gautama and Vatsyayana (1982) *Nyaya-Sutra* with Vatsyayana's Commentary, Mrinalkanti Gangopadhyaya (trans.), Calcutta: Indian Studies [*NS*].

Gupta, Bina (2003) *Cit Consciousness*, New Delhi: Oxford University Press.

Kaplan, Stephen (1987) *Hermeneutics, Holography and Indian Idealism*, New Delhi: Motilal Banarsidass.

——(2009) "Grasping at Ontological Straws: Overcoming Reductionism in the Advaita Vedanta–Neuroscience Dialogue," *Journal of the American Academy of Religion* 77: 238–74.

Larson, Gerald James (1978) *Classical Samkhya: An Interpretation of its History and Meaning*, Delhi: Motilal Banarsidass [*Samkhya Karika, SK*].

Larson, Gerald James and Ram Shankar Bhattacharya (1987) *Encyclopedia of Indian Philosophies: Samkya, A Dualist Tradition in Indian Philosophy*, Princeton, NJ: Princeton University Press.

Llewellyn, J. E. (ed.) (2005) *Defining Hinduism, A Reader*, New York: Routledge.

Mohanty, J. N. (1993) *Essays on Indian Philosophy Traditional and Modern*, Purusottama Bilimoria (ed.), Delhi: Oxford University Press.

Parrott, Rodney J. (1986) "The Problem of the Samkhya Tattvas as Both Cosmic and Psychological Phenomena," *Journal of Indian Philosophy* 14: 55–77.

Pribram, Karl H. (1977) *Languages of the Brain: Experimental Paradoxes and Principles in Neuropsychology*, Pacific Grove, CA: Brooks/Cole Publishing Co.

Ruby, Perrine and Jean Decety (2003) "What You Believe Versus What You Think They Believe: A Neuroimaging Study of Conceptual Perspective-Taking," *European Journal of Neuroscience* 17: 2475–80.

Sankara (1995) *The Bhagavad Gita with the Commentary of Sri Sankaracharya*, Alladi Madadeva Sastry (trans.), Madras: Samata Books.

Siderits, Mark (2007) *Buddhism as Philosophy*, Indianapolis, IN: Hackett.

Slingerland, Edward (2008) "Who's Afraid of Reductionism? The Study of Religion in the Age of Cognitive Science," *Journal of the American Academy of Religion* 76: 375–411.

Further reading

Jadunath Sinha's *Indian Psychology, Cognition Volume 1* (Sinha Publishing House, 1958) and D. M. Datta's *Six Ways of Knowing* (University of Calcutta, 1972) provide comprehensive overviews of the cognitive issues with which the major schools of Hindu thought wrestle – issues ranging from perception, to dreams, to memory, to illusions – and each provides a sense of the diversity of opinion within each school and between schools. Bimal K. Matilal, *Perception: An Essay on Classical Indian Theories of Knowledge* (Clarendon Press, 1986), focusing on Nyaya and Buddhist thought, also engages contemporary Western philosophy in an analysis of different *pramanas*. Finally, Joseph Alter's *Yoga in Modern India* (Princeton University Press, 2004) presents a wonderful array of studies arising out of India that focus on physiological changes such as alterations in oxygen levels, blood pressure, and neurochemical changes concomitant with the practices of yoga and meditation. Among the individuals discussed are Sri Yogeshwaranand Parmahans, Swami Kuvalayananda, Swami Sivananda, and Dr. K. N. Upupa.

(vi) Ecology and the integrity of nature

30
FRONTIERS IN RELIGION AND ECOLOGY

Notes on the new ecology and the creation of value

Nathaniel F. Barrett and William R. Jordan, III

Mainstream religion and ecology, and its critics

One of the most promising cultural developments of the past few decades has been the spread of environmental concern to an increasingly diverse range of religious traditions and communities (Jenkins 2009). The growth of religious environmentalism in society at large is reflected within the academy by the recent blossoming of religion and ecology as a distinct sub-field of theology and religious studies (Gottlieb 2006: 16–17). Joined together and energized by an acute sense of social and environmental crisis, these parallel movements present a wealth of opportunities to catalyze new working relationships between diverse cultures, disciplines, scholars, and practitioners.

However, despite what the name suggests, the field of religion and ecology presently exhibits little of the interdisciplinary spirit that animates self-described "religion and science" types of inquiry. Indeed, newcomers may be surprised to learn how little it has to do with the science of ecology, the branch of biology that deals with the relationships between organisms and their environments. This is not necessarily a case of false advertising, as the term "ecology" has taken on a bewildering variety of meanings since it gained currency in the 1960s and 1970s, and is now as likely to refer to a recycling program, a new kind of light bulb, or simply to "nature" in general, as to a particular branch of the life sciences (cf. Foltz 2003: xiv). Contributing to this semantic pluralism, a majority of those working in the field of religion and ecology use "ecology" as a synonym for environmental ethics, and focus their attention on religious cosmologies as resources for improved relations between humanity and the rest of nature (e.g. Tucker and Grim 1994: 12–13).

Besides the neglect of science, what is salient in the dominant ethical orientation of religion and ecology is the abstractness of its approach to human–Earth relations.

This approach is, of course, deeply congenial to academic culture, but it also has a venerable precedent in the writings of Aldo Leopold (1966), often regarded as the *fons et origo* of much of the environmentalist thinking of the past three-quarters of a century. Leopold's fundamental contribution in this area was to take the metaphor of community, which ecologists had adopted as a model for relationships among associations of species (Odenbaugh 2006), seriously enough to consider its moral implications.

The idea of community that Leopold brought to bear on questions of conservation and relationships with the environment was, however, seriously limited. Most of his observations about human relationships with nature were framed in abstract terms, such that, as in one well known story, even the killing of a wolf is an occasion for insights into predator–prey relations rather than the emotional and moral ambiguity we might expect to accompany such an experience. Making community a cornerstone of his "land ethic," and stressing that, as in a human community, this entailed a "limitation on freedom of action" and "a differentiation of social from anti-social conduct" (1966: 238), Leopold had little to say about the more challenging psychological implications of these strictures, about the tensions inherent in relationships, or about the fact that community, from the time of Cain and Abel on, has always been a cockpit of rivalry, dissention, anxiety, resentment, and conflict of interest. In articulating his ideas about the relationship between humans and their environment in abstract terms of right and wrong, Leopold in effect rose above all this and laid the foundation for an environmentalism that has been reformist in character, promoting an idea of relationship based on a sentimental idea of community as fundamentally unproblematic – that is, emotionally unchallenging and morally unambiguous – apart from human error and transgression.

Congenial to the intellectual habits of academic philosophers, and deeply resonant with a culture imbued with the biblical idea that nature is inherently good apart from human interference, this idea has underlain a good deal of the environmental thinking of the past half century. The result is an environmentalism based not only on the dubious ideal of a universal community, but also on the expectation that it might be achieved without emotional expense.

To the extent that it deals with human experience more comprehensively and in more concrete terms than ecology or philosophy, religious studies is in a position to correct this habit of moralizing and top-down theorizing. But here again, the habit of focusing on abstract ideas, exemplified in Lynn White's hugely influential indictment of Christian cosmology as the "root of our environmental crisis" (White 1967), has generally prevailed (Jenkins 2009). Religion and ecology has, in large part, been guided by the dual assumptions that religious traditions, as cosmologies or worldviews, are important to environmentalism primarily as moral frameworks and, consistent with this, that the idea of community implicit in Leopold's thinking is the moral framework *par excellence*.

Accordingly, leaders of the religion-and-ecology field see themselves as the intellectual vanguard of a new movement that promotes a more inclusive and egalitarian Earth community, much as the civil rights movement of the mid-twentieth century promoted a more inclusive human community (e.g. Foltz 2003: 5–6; Tucker 2003: 9, 22–23; Kearns and Keller 2007: 12). The importance of this Earth community ideal can hardly be overstated, as it guides and unites the most common themes of religion-and-ecology literature: the emphasis on holism and interconnectedness; the championing of eco-centrism over anthropocentrism; the preference for meta-ethical theories that affirm the intrinsic values of nature; and the idealization of ecosystems in their "natural" state – perceived as having the virtues of harmony, balance, diversity, and stability – as sources of moral inspiration. Insofar as these themes are united, there is reason to suspect that the religious cosmologies selected by religion-and-ecology scholars from diverse traditional sources are actually variants of a single communitarian cosmology, what one critic has dubbed the "religious environmentalist paradigm" (Kalland 2005).

As the field of religion and ecology matures, however, a growing number of its members are questioning this mainstream orientation and at least some of its premises. Most notably, Bron Taylor, a prominent historian of religious environmentalism and executive editor of the *Encyclopedia of Religion and Nature*, complains of the narrow focus on religious traditions privileged as "world traditions" and, within those traditions, on historically dominant forms at the expense of new, hybrid, and marginal varieties of religious environmentalism. Taylor also argues for the need to balance the activist fervor of what he calls the "confessional/ethical" approach with the critical distance and attention to practice characteristic of more "historical/social scientific" approaches (Taylor 2005: 1379). In response, the religious ethicist Willis Jenkins suggests that scholars can advocate for religious environmentalism with greater sensitivity to its budding diversity by allowing environmental problems and social practices to drive the reform of religious cosmologies rather than *vice versa* (Jenkins 2009). And, pointing to a more practice-based approach to environmental ethics, philosopher Jim Cheney and his colleagues have explored the idea of an etiquette-based approach in which ethical principles emerge from direct, respectful interaction with other species (Cheney and Weston 1999; Peterson 2001).

Meanwhile, a few scholars have begun to call for closer attention to evolutionary science and ecology (e.g. Sideris 2003, 2006; Lodge and Hamlin 2006; O'Brien 2007), and in particular to evidence from these sciences that the moral example presented by nature is ambiguous at best. In *Environmental Ethics, Ecological Theology, and Natural Selection* (2003), for example, Lisa H. Sideris exposes a widespread neglect of evolutionary science in the works of prominent Christian ecotheologians. Sideris argues that this neglect coincides with the promotion of "a model of nature as a harmonious, interconnected, and interdependent community" (Sideris 2003: 2), the very same communitarian ideal described above. However well intentioned, it seems that attachment to this ideal has reinforced "a persistent reluctance to accept the disequilibrium, moral ambiguity, and ineradicable suffering and death that natural selection entails" (*ibid.*: 5).

Sideris' critique raises the question of how the greening of religion might proceed without the whitewashing of nature. Surely the attempt to forge healthier relationships with nature should not dispense with complexity for the sake of moral certainty. But then what kind of universal community can be modeled on a natural world in which an estimated 99.9 per cent of all species that have ever lived are now extinct?

This figure – or rather the challenge it presents to mainstream environmentalism – is a token of how wide the gap between ethical and scientific views of nature has become. To be fair, this divergence is partly the consequence of a development in ecological thought that occurred shortly after the environmental movement began in the 1960s. A clear-cut if perhaps somewhat simplified way to describe this development is to say that ecology has since transitioned from a balance model of ecosystems to a flux model. In his landmark book *Discordant Harmonies: A New Ecology for the Twenty-first Century* (1990), the ecologist Daniel Botkin describes this transition as a fundamental shift in Western ideas of nature, which for thousands of years had been rooted in the conviction that nature is constant unless disturbed, and that change – especially when caused by human interference – is bad (Botkin 1990: 12–13). This bias affected even the science of ecology, which until the 1970s was dominated by concepts of ecosystems as self-regulating, homeostatic systems.

> Until the past few years, the predominant theories in ecology either presumed or had as a necessary consequence a very strict concept of a highly structured, ordered, and regulated, steady-state ecological system. […] Change now appears to be intrinsic and natural at many scales of time and space in the biosphere. Nature changes over essentially all time scales, and in at least some cases these changes are necessary for the persistence of life, because life is adapted to them and depends on them.
>
> (Botkin 1990: 9)

The flux model is clearly a curve ball for any moral framework based on the idea that nature itself, as represented by a "natural" ecological association, is characteristically stable, orderly or predictable. As Botkin acknowledges:

> Clearly, to abandon belief in the constancy of undisturbed nature is psychologically uncomfortable. As long as we could believe that nature undisturbed was constant, we were provided with a simple standard against which to judge our actions, a reflection from a windless pond in which our place was both apparent and fixed, providing us with a sense of continuity and permanence that was comforting.
>
> (*ibid.*: 188)

This shift, and its troubling implications, has not entirely escaped the attention of the religion-and-ecology community. In their introduction to a recently published collection of reflections on the moral and ethical implications of the new ecology, David M. Lodge and Christopher Hamlin corroborate Sideris' claim that neglect of the science of ecology has contributed to its idealization as a guide to morally untainted human–Earth relations, "a locus of faith and hope for an earth in which we can live with joy and without guilt" (Lodge and Hamlin 2006: 9). In contrast, they argue that the "new paradigm" of ecology exposes a host of moral uncertainties in our dealings with nature, perhaps leading to a "more honest ecology by ceasing to disguise those moral problems as somehow resolved in the natural order of things" (*ibid.*: 8–9). Whatever knowledge the new ecology and its successors will bring, we can no longer anticipate that science will provide us with "a cognitive basis for being comfortable in our world" (*ibid.*: 280).

As pertinent as these criticisms are, we believe that they have not gone far enough. Those who have identified the moral problems posed by the flux model rightly question the adequacy of the Earth community ideal. But they leave unquestioned the sentimental conception of community and relationship that underlies much environmental thought and, concomitant with this, the basic assumption that the role of religion is, first and foremost, to provide a moral framework for dealing with the environmental crisis. Thus, J. Baird Callicott is able to retro-fit Leopold's land ethic in response to the new ecology by "dynamizing" it, pointing out that human communities, too, are dynamic and unpredictable but, like Leopold, saying nothing about the emotionally and morally problematic aspects of such dynamism (entailing losses of whole populations and cultures) or of life in community generally (Callicott 1999). At the same time, Sideris and Hamlin and Lodge react to the "bad news" of the new ecology – namely that nature is so messy as to confound any simple or emotionally unchallenging notion of communion with it – by retreating from the Earth community ideal, instead recommending that we "cultivate our inward compass" (Hamlin and Lodge 2006: 307) or restrict our management of nature to a minimum (Sideris 2006: 461).

What these authors fail to appreciate is that the realization of the inadequacy of moral frameworks in the face of the complexity of nature may itself be a profound type of religious experience. For example, when Hamlin and Lodge remark, "the new ecology is terrifying because it exposes the inadequacy of our normative systems" (2006: 9), they fail to remark on the many religious precedents for this kind of terror. What of Job's terror before the whirlwind, or Arjuna's terror before the revelation of Krishna's true form? What of the *Daodejing*'s claim that "Heaven and Earth are not humane; they regard all things as straw dogs" (Chan 1963: 107)?

Such experiences are more than just phenomenological curiosities. By highlighting the limitations of our most cherished values, including the value of community, experiences of moral inadequacy open an opportunity for a more authentic communion with nature, one that does not shun the difficulties that arise from engagement with the complexities of ecology or the moral ambiguity of our actual experiences of nature. In fact, as we describe below in the context of restorative practices – practices that require intimate involvement with the complexities of particular ecosystems – experiences of nature's moral intractability can become occasions of religious meaning-making that allow us to acknowledge the inadequacy of our moral frameworks without coming to despair.

Experiences of "existential shame"

Here we wish to make the case for the importance of experiences that are not well served by the conception of religion as a moral framework. This is not an argument about the essence of religion. Rather, it is an attempt to expand the scope of experiences that are relevant to religious environmentalism. We wish to spotlight experiences that have hitherto remained in the shadows, not because they are troubling, disturbing, or even terrifying – after all, environmentalism has plenty of guilt and fear to go around – but because they cannot be understood in moral terms.

These experiences of moral inadequacy are, in one sense, the most poignant moral experiences one can have. But in another sense they point beyond the moral, because they expose the limitations and contingency of our moral frameworks. We are not speaking here of guilt – that is, of experiences of inadequacy with respect to some set of moral standards. However troubling it may be continuously to fail by our own standards, there is yet another experience of inadequacy that arises when we confront *the limitations of these standards*, over and against an infinitely larger – and infinitely messy – world. This is not the confrontation of our anthropocentric world-view with an ecocentric world; it is our confrontation with a world that *has no* center. Such experiences appear to be nihilistic only if we forget that their poignancy stems from an acute sense of a world filled with things of unique and intrinsic value, each of them shaming us by dramatizing our inadequacies. It is the sense that simply to exist is to displace others who are no less worthy than us, including the many other selves we might have become. "I am ashamed," Sartre writes, "of what I am" (1956: 197). To capture the peculiarly pre-moral character of this experience, and to distinguish it from the shame associated with wrongdoing, we have termed it *existential shame*.

Is there room for this dark side of our experience of nature in religion and ecology? Whatever its validity in other contexts, does it belong in a movement that is defined by such urgent moral purpose? Though it may seem counter-intuitive, we believe that any communitarian ethics, but especially an ethics that takes the entire Earth community as its focus, actually *demands* greater attention to this experience, as it cannot be authentic – or, ultimately, effective – without it.

Ideas for a new communion with nature

What we propose here is a direct, if in some ways unorthodox, response to the challenge posed by the new ecology. For, while the moral incoherence of the ecology of flux may deny us the comfort of nature as a *model* for human–Earth relations, by the same token it helps us to confront the morally problematic context in which core values of human–Earth relations must be *created* rather than derived from some pre-existing source, and the profound existential difficulties that accompany this work of value creation.

Our proposal is drawn principally from the work of the literary critic Frederick Turner (1991), though it is supported in various ways by material from a wide range of disciplines and areas of human experience (e.g. Glaude 2007). Its principal points are as follows.

- First, that a fundamental problem for humans is the apprehension of what might be called a plurality of goods – that is, the goodness of many, or even all, things, so that any act causes harm as well as benefit and no act, however "natural" or well intentioned, is entirely good in its effects. This is experienced most immediately in the apprehension of the goodness of the other as distinct from the self, an unavoidable condition of life that forces us to choose not between good and evil, but between two goods. This not only implies the need for fundamental moral trade-offs, it also elicits a feeling of shame in this experience of our inadequacy in the face of the valuable other.

- Second, that this is an intractable problem, an irreducible scandal to the imagination that arises from the conditions of existence itself and cannot be solved in literal terms, but only through the technologies of the imagination, commonly grouped under the headings of myth, symbol, art, ritual, and, most comprehensively, religion.
- Third, that the "products" of these technologies are the experiences of higher values such as meaning, beauty, community, and the sacred.

In contrast with the approach that currently dominates religion and ecology, which derives ethical principles from pre-established cosmologies, the above points argue that values not only precede ethical principles, they emerge from experience intensified and made reflexive through performances of ritual and the arts. More specifically, they arise from precisely those experiences that call whatever ethical systems we have into question: experiences that evoke feelings of shame in the encounter with the other.

Keep in mind here that we are making a clear distinction between guilt, which is the response of conscience to wrongdoing, and shame, which arises from our experience of limitations, including those limitations that provide the basis for identity: mammal (not bird or fish); primate (not squirrel or bear); Asian (not European or Australian); Japanese (not Chinese), and so forth.

This distinction is crucial for us – and easily missed. As Rosemary Radford Ruether has pointed out, the biblical characterization of both disobedience *and* limits (or finitude) as sinful "has imparted a mixed heritage to the Western world" (Ruether 1992). In our terms, it has resulted in a world-view that consistently confuses existential shame, which arises from the limitations inherent in life itself, with guilt, which is the response of the conscience to disobedience, transgression, or wrongdoing. We believe that this is a serious – even tragic – mistake. The distinction between these emotions is crucial, and *we are speaking here not of guilt but of shame.*

"What we are" – Sartre's occasion for shame – is most evident to us when we apprehend what we are not and recognize attributes of the other that we do not share. This is especially true when we are not only aware of that other, but find ourselves dependent on it, as we do constantly in every dimension of our lives, from birth to death, the ultimate limits that bookend every life.

A classic example, from the prime of adult life, is the need to kill in order to live. As an Iglulik shaman says, "life's greatest danger […] lies in the fact that man's food consists entirely of souls" (Briggs 1982: 115). The danger, of course, lies most obviously in the fact that eating means taking life, privileging one good (my life) to that of another (the life of a seal or whale), a matter of self-interest that surely compromises the hunter's judgment in setting out deliberately to kill another "soul." It also lies in the apprehension of the radical dependence this killing dramatizes: the shameful limit of the hunter as a carnivore, a heterotroph incapable of the innocent way in which plants nourish themselves by photosynthesis. Thus Turner suggests that one function of sacrifice is to formalize the act of necessary killing – the killing on which life depends – in order to focus the shame of the act, making it overt and public, and concentrating it in a time and place as a first step in dealing with it in a psychologically and spiritually productive way (cf. Smith 1987).

Such experience is also, in Turner's reading, the context for the creation of new value – specifically the transcendent values that provide the moral and psychological foundation for conscience. This, however, does not happen – or at any rate cannot be counted on to happen – spontaneously, but is, he argues, achieved through the psychological work of ritual and art, which provide the essential means for the passage "through shame to beauty" (Turner 1991).

In light of the importance of this work, it is not the "positive," emotionally easy experiences of nature and others – the butterflies and babbling brooks – we must seek out for the creation and transmission of values such as meaning, community, or beauty, but precisely those that are emotionally troubling. This is why eating is universally an occasion for ritual, the result of which is communion, the psychological basis for community (Visser 1991). It is also why occasions of life passage – birth, coming of age, marriage, and death – are also commonly ritualized, as each of these entails an encounter with limits in the form of a beginning or ending, or the closing-off of possibilities (Grimes 2000). These rituals, in other words, do not merely mark or celebrate the occasion, but arguably provide a context for confronting the shame that arises from it and "transmuting," as Turner says, this shame into values such as meaning, identity, community, beauty, and the sacred.

When we describe environmental thinking as consistently sentimental, what we mean is that it consistently neglects or downplays these irreducibly problematic aspects of experience – or, alternatively, that lacking the wherewithal to deal with them productively, it dwells on them in a merely morbid spirit.

Ecological restoration as performing art

The rituals of dinner arise from our encounter with individual animals or plants, or perhaps with populations representing a few selected species. Turning to the relationship with whole ecosystems, which has been a major concern of environmentalists for the past few generations, we might look for precedents in land management practices of pre-modern peoples, which commonly center on rituals of "world renewal" undertaken to re-energize a world understood to be not only in flux, as the ecologists now tell us, but in decay, and dependent on deliberate human effort, in the form of ritual, for renewal.

Such rituals may apply to and inform practices associated with the management of working as well as "natural" landscapes. Here we offer some reflections on a particular form of land management – the attempt to restore or re-create whole historic habitats for their own sake – and its value as a context for the creation of value-generating ritual. This form of land management, which could be termed "ecocentric restoration," is of special interest here for two reasons. One is its interesting relationship with science, especially ecology, by which it is directly informed, but which does not define its aims – the reassembly of altered or degraded ecosystems. When coupled with scientific expertise, these aims anchor the practice of restoration in the concrete, rescuing it from the disinterested relationship with nature for which scholars have criticized classical science (Merchant 1980). At the same time, though this form of land management explicitly rejects self-interest in deference to the ecosystem being restored, it nevertheless provides innumerable occasions for experiencing the moral ambiguity of our relationship with nature and the shame that arises from this (Jordan 2003).

Indeed, ecocentric restoration is instructive precisely *because* it is entirely positive in its aims so far as the ecosystem is concerned – to the extent that it could be termed "altruistic restoration" – and yet entails encounters with shame in many ways. To begin with, by definition and most fundamentally, ecocentric restoration entails an encounter with an *other* that owes nothing to us, an experience that dramatizes our limitations as partners or participants in creation. Besides this, this encounter with the other entails a systematic attempt to identify ways in which "we" have influenced a habitat and to find ecologically effective ways of compensating for, or reversing, these influences – an attempt, really, to disappear from the landscape. The result is a precise definition, in ecological and negative terms, of who we are, each restorative act – the reintroduction of fire to restore a prairie, the reflooding of a drained marsh, the reintroduction of an extirpated species, and so forth – dramatizing an element in the definition. The picture that emerges may or may not be flattering in moral or esthetic terms. But quite apart from that, by *defining* us, it draws attention to our limitations: Europeans did not, as pre-Columbian peoples did, burn the prairies; they plowed them up and planted wheat instead: not a bad thing, only a different thing, and therefore shameful.

Besides this, ecocentric restoration entails discrimination and killing, choosing one suite of species in preference to another, a direct experience of the conflict of goods mentioned above. The restorationist also encounters shame in her awareness of the inadequacy of the gift – the imperfectly restored ecosystem – she offers back to nature in recompense for what she has taken from it – that is, everything she has or is. And she encounters shame in the awareness that restoration, in the strictest sense, is impossible – an encounter with the tragic irreversibility of ecological time, and so of life itself.

Altogether, this clearly shows the value of ecocentric restoration as a context for encountering the existential shame that is inseparable from our experience of nature, and so as an occasion for the invention of rituals, many of them resonant with traditional rituals such as world renewal, sacrifice, initiation, and artistic genres such as pastoral art, for passing through that shame to values such as identity, community, and beauty. At this point, practitioners have done relatively little to take advantage of this, the discovery and development of restoration as a context for performance lagging well behind the discovery of its environmental and heuristic value. This is hardly surprising in a puritan culture that has decisively rejected the idea that ritual has ontological power – power, that is, to make and restore the world – and so has greatly diminished its resources for dealing productively with existential shame (cf. Seligman *et al.* 2008). But there have been modest steps in this direction. One is the salmon reproduction ceremony Freeman House beautifully describes in his account of a decades-long attempt to restore salmon habitat in Northern California (1999). Another, arising from the killing (of exotic trees and shrubs) that accompanies the restoration of grasslands in the U.S. mid-west, is the "Bagpipes and Bonfires" festival conducted each year in Lake Forest, Illinois around the time of the autumn equinox (Holland 1994). Still another, riffing on the prescribed burns that are the strong moment in the restoration cycle on the prairies, dramatizing dependence (in this case of the prairie on us) and evoking archetypes of creative destruction, are the night burns that restorationists occasionally undertake to enhance the spectacle of a burn for an audience.

Small beginnings, perhaps. But strikingly beautiful. And opportunities, at the very least, to try out ideas such as those we have outlined here.

Acknowledgments

This article is an outcome of the work of the Values Project Roundtable a joint program of the New Academy for Nature and Culture and DePaul University's Institute for Nature and Culture, and reflects contributions from Randy Honold and Liam Heneghan (DePaul University), Todd Levasseur and Les Thiele (University of Florida), and Gretel Van Wieren (Michigan State University).

References

Botkin, Daniel (1990) *Discordant Harmonies: A New Ecology for the Twenty-First Century*, New York: Oxford University Press.

Briggs, Jean L. (1982) "Living Dangerously: The Contradictory Foundations of Value in Canadian Inuit Society," in *Politics and History in Band Societies*, Eleanor Leacock and Richard Lee (eds), Cambridge: Cambridge University Press, 109–31.

Callicott, J. Baird (1999) "Do Deconstructive Ecology and Sociobiology Undermine the Leopold Land Ethic?" in *Beyond the Land Ethic: More Essays in Environmental Philosophy*, J. Baird Callicott (ed.), Albany, NY: SUNY Press, 117–42.

Chan, Wing-tsit (1963) *The Way of Lao Tzu (Tao-te ching)*, Upper Saddle River, NJ: Prentice Hall.

Cheney, Jim and Anthony Weston (1999) "Environmental Ethics as Environmental Etiquette," *Environmental Ethics* 21(2): 115–34.

Foltz, Richard C. (ed.) (2003) *Worldviews, Religion, and the Environment: A Global Anthology*, Belmont, CA: Wadsworth.

Glaude Jr., Eddie (2007) *In a Shade of Blue: Pragmatism and the Politics of Black America*, Chicago, IL: University of Chicago Press.

Gottlieb, Roger S. (2006) "Introduction: Religion and Ecology – What Is the Connection and Why Does It Matter?" in *The Oxford Handbook of Religion and Ecology*, Roger S. Gottlieb (ed.), Oxford: Oxford University Press, 3–21.

Grimes, Ronald L. (2000) *Deeply into the Bone: Reinventing Rites of Passage*, Berkeley, CA: University of California Press.

Hans, James (1991) *The Origins of the Gods*, Albany, NY: SUNY Press.

Holland, Karen (1994) "Restoration Rituals: Transforming Workday Rituals into Inspirational Moments," *Restoration & Management Notes* (now *Ecological Restoration*) 12(2): 121–25.

House, Freeman (1999) *Totem Salmon: Life Lessons from Another Species*, Boston, MA: Beacon Press.

Jenkins, Willis (2009) "After Lynn White: Religious Ethics and Environmental Problems," *Journal of Religious Ethics*, 37 (2): 283–309.

Jordan, William R., III (2003) *The Sunflower Forest: Ecological Restoration and the New Communion with Nature*, Berkeley, CA: University of California Press.

Kalland, Arne (2005) "The Religious Environmentalist Paradigm," in *The Encyclopedia of Religion and Nature*, Vol. 2, Bron R. Taylor (ed.), London and New York: Thoemmes Continuum, 1367–71.

Kearns, Laurel and Catherine Keller (eds) (2007) *Ecospirit: Religions and Philosophies for the Earth*, Bronx, NY: Fordham University Press.

Leopold, Aldo (1966) *A Sand County Almanac, with Essays on Conservation from Round River*, New York: Ballantine Books.

Lodge, David M. and Christopher Hamlin (eds) (2006) *Religion and the New Ecology: Environmental Responsibility in a World in Flux*, Notre Dame, IN: Notre Dame University Press.

Merchant, Carolyn (1980) *The Death of Nature: Women, Ecology and the Scientific Revolution*, San Francisco, CA: Harper & Row.

O'Brien, Kevin J. (2007) "Toward an Ethics of Biodiversity: Science and Theology in Environmentalist Dialogue," in *Ecospirit: Religions and Philosophies for the Earth*, Laurel Kearns and Catherine Keller (eds), Bronx, NY: Fordham University Press, 178–95.

Odenbaugh, Jay (2006) "Ecology," in *The Encyclopedia of Science: An Encyclopedia*, Vol. 1, Sahotra Sarkar and Jessica Pfeifer (eds), New York and London: Routledge, 215–24.

Peterson, Anna L. (2001) *Being Human: Ethics, Environment and Our Place in the World*, Berkeley, CA: University of California Press.

Ruether, Rosemary Radford (1992) *Gaia and God: An Ecofeminist Theology of Earth Healing*, New York: HarperCollins.

Sartre, Jean-Paul (1956) *Being and Nothingness: An Essay in Phenomenological Ontology*, Hazel E. Barnes (trans.), New York: Citadel Press.

Seligman, Adam B., Robert P. Weller, Michael J. Puett and Bennett Simon (2008) *Ritual and Its Consequences: An Essay on the Limits of Sincerity*, Oxford: Oxford University Press.

Sideris, Lisa H. (2003) *Environmental Ethics, Ecological Theology, and Natural Selection*, New York: Columbia University Press.

——(2006) "Religion, Environmentalism, and the Meaning of Ecology," in *The Oxford Handbook of Religion and Ecology*, Roger S. Gottlieb (ed.), Oxford: Oxford University Press, 446–64.

Smith, Jonathan Z. (1987) "The Domestication of Sacrifice," in *Violent Origins: Walter Burkert, René Girard and Jonathan Z. Smith on Ritual Killing and Cultural Formation*, Robert G. Hamerton-Kelly (ed.), Stanford, CA: Stanford University Press, 191–205.

Taylor, Bron R. (2005) "Religious Studies and Environmental Concern" in *The Encyclopedia of Religion and Nature*, Vol. 2, Bron R. Taylor (ed.), London and New York: Thoemmes Continuum, 1373–79.

Tucker, Mary Evelyn (2003) *Worldly Wonder: Religions Enter Their Ecological Phase*, Chicago and La Salle, IL: Open Court.

Tucker, Mary Evelyn and John A. Grim (eds) (1994) *Worldviews and Ecology: Religion, Philosophy, and the Environment*, Maryknoll, NY: Orbis.

Turner, Frederick (1991) *Beauty: The Value of Values*. Charlottesville, VA: University of Virginia Press.

Visser, Margaret (1991) *The Rituals of Dinner: The Origins, Evolution, Eccentricities, and Meaning of Table Manners*, New York: Grove Weidenfeld.

White, Lynn Townsend, Jr. (1967) "The Historical Roots of Our Ecologic Crisis," *Science* 155 (3767): 1203–7.

Further reading

Lynn White Jr.'s seminal essay (1967) and excerpts from Leopold's *Sand County Almanac* (1966) can be found in Roger Gottlieb's fine collection, *This Sacred Earth: Religion, Nature, Environment*, 2nd edn (Routledge, 2004). Excellent discussions of the new ecology and its implications for religious environmental ethics can be found in Lisa Sideris, *Environmental Ethics, Ecological Theology, and Natural Selection*, and David M. Lodge and Christopher Hamlin (eds.), *Religion and the New Ecology: Environmental Responsibility in a World in Flux* (both cited above). For an overview of ecological restoration as a performing art, see William R. Jordan III, *The Sunflower Forest: Ecological Restoration and the New Communion with Nature* (also cited above), especially chapter 7.

31
JUDAISM AND THE SCIENCE OF ECOLOGY

Hava Tirosh-Samuelson

Introducing a Jewish perspective

Nathaniel F. Barrett and William R. Jordan, III are right to claim that the science of ecology has exerted a limited impact on the discourse of religion and ecology. In that discourse the term "ecology" is not a "branch of biology that deals with the relationships between organisms and their environments" but a "synonym for environmental ethics, [which focuses its] attention on religious cosmologies as resources for improved relationship between humanity and the rest of nature" (Chapter 30 in this volume). The discourse of religion and ecology is scientifically flawed, because Christian ecotheologies have promoted a model of nature as "harmonious, interconnected, and interdependent community" (Sideris 2003: 2), which the science of ecology has falsified. An accurate understanding of the theory of evolution, the core of the science of ecology, makes clear that nature is not governed by balance and order, but by flux and disorder.

Barrett and Jordan wish to advance the discourse of religion and ecology as follows. First, they call on scholars to adopt the "new ecology" that offers a more accurate understanding of the theory of evolution, exposing the "dark" science of nature with its predation, conflict, and strife. Second, they claim that the appropriate response to the "new ecology" is not the concept of guilt but the concept of "existential shame" that can respond to "our confrontation with a world that has no center […] a world filled with things of unique and intrinsic value, each of them shaming us by dramatizing our inadequacies." Third, they maintain that by means of "technologies of the imagination" shame can turn into "myth, symbol, art, ritual, and, most comprehensively, religion" that can provide "ecological restoration" (Chapter 30 in this volume). Such restoration will involve rituals of "world renewal, sacrifice, initiation, and artistic genres such as pastoral art, for passing through that shame to values such as identity, community, and beauty." By dramatizing human–nature dependence and evoking "archetypes of creative destruction," humanity could presumably come to terms with the "dark" and terrifying picture of nature.

To invite a Jewish response to the essay by Barrett and Jordan necessarily changes the terms of the discussion. A Jewish perspective is unavoidably historical, taking into consideration not only Judaism as a belief system, but also the historical context of the Jews, as a minority, as a sovereign nation, or as individuals. Such historical perspective is conspicuously missing from the essay by Barrett and Jordan. Although Judaism evolved over time and speaks in many voices, there are certain foundational beliefs that frame the Judaic world-view: that God created the world; that God revealed his Will to Israel in a form of Law, the Torah; and that God will redeem the world and the Jewish People. To engage the science of ecology from a Jewish perspective requires reflections on these beliefs, but the essay by Barrett and Jordan cannot accommodate them because its approach to religion is decidedly secular, undermining the Judaic notion of revelation. Finally, although the authors correctly hold that rituals provide social context, they mistakenly promote *shame* as the point of departure for their "restorative ecology." In Jewish ecological thought, *responsibility* is the paramount value, but responsibility requires awareness of culpability which Barrett and Jordan consider a "tragic mistake." The following remarks engage the essay by Barrett and Jordan from a Jewish perspective.

Contemporary Jewish environmentalism

The Jewish religious tradition is replete with ecological wisdom, but Jews began to encounter this fact only in the 1970s, with the rise of a Jewish environmental movement (Tirosh-Samuelson 2006). It emerged as an apologetic response to the accusation of Lynn White Jr. that Judeo-Christian tradition was the root of the current ecological crisis. In defense of Judaism, Jewish theologians have argued that White and other environmentalists either misread the Hebrew biblical text, or lack any knowledge of post-biblical Judaism. An accurate and informed reading of Jewish sources shows that the Jewish religious tradition, and especially the Bible, can be the basis for sound environmental policies. Jewish environmental activists began to explore ways to integrate their environmental sensibilities with their desire to live a more meaningful Jewish life. Guided by Zalman Schachter-Shalomi's Jewish Renewal Movement (Schachter-Shalomi 1993), environmentally concerned Jews began to mine the Jewish literary tradition for its ecological wisdom, reinterpreting the Jewish heritage in light of environmental concerns and values (Bernstein 1997). The prophetic commitment to social justice led Arthur Waskow, the most important Jewish environmentalist, to promote a Jewish, religious, progressive environmentalism under the broad concept of "Eco-Kosher" (Waskow 1995, 1996).

In 1993, several Jewish environmental organizations coalesced into the Coalition on the Environment and Jewish Life. This umbrella organization has attempted to educate Jews about environmental matters, inspiring Jews to lead an environmentally sound communal life, beginning with the greening of synagogues, and calling Jews to lend their support to various legislative initatives and to enter inter-faith dialogue on environmental matters. Other small, non-profit organizations (e.g. Hazon, Teva, Isabella Freedman Learning Center, and Kanfei Nesharim) attempt to frame an environmentally aware Jewish way of living, but their impact on mainstream Jewish denominations is still very limited. The message that Judaism can be part of the solution to the ecological crisis, and that Judaism approaches the crisis in its own distinctive manner, has been slow to spread. Jews either assume that Judaism has little to say about environmental matters, or presuppose that Judaism and environmentalism are inherently incompatible.

There are historical and cultural reasons for this perception. The exile of the Jews from the Land of Israel has brought about major economic transformation in the life of the Jewish people. Urbanization of the ancient world, the occupational shift from agriculture to commerce in the Islamic world, and the restriction on Jewish ownership of land in the Christian world brought about growing alienation of Jews from their physical surroundings and a growing indifference toward the natural world. These historical conditions were exacerbated by the scholastic and bookish culture of Rabbinic Judaism that placed Torah study as the overarching ideal of Jewish religious life. Governed by study and ritual, Jewish religious life was text-centered rather than nature-oriented. For observant Jews in the pre-modern world, nature was good, but not holy; it could be made holy, or sanctified through the observance of divine commands that pointed to the divine Creator as the source of meaning and value, rather than to nature. Nature does not dictate what ought to be; only divine revelation articulates the moral norm. This is why Steven Schwarzschild spoke about the "unnatural Jew," (Schwarzschild 1984), a position that angered several Jewish environmentalists who missed the Kantian aspect of his claim. For Schwarzschild, as for many nineteenth-century Jewish theologians who were influenced by Kantian philosophy and were associated with the movement for religious reform, Judaism supersedes pagan religions. Whereas these traditions identify God with nature, Jewish monotheism expresses universal, rational morality that stands as a critique of nature. Unlike Spinoza, most modern Jewish thinkers regarded nature, especially as interpreted by Darwin's theory of evolution, to be amoral. Whereas nature has no room for the weak and the marginal, Judaism enjoins humanity to defend the weak and the socially marginal. In Judaism, what "ought" to be (morality) determines how humans relate to what "is" (nature). The Romantic infatuation with nature influenced modern Hebrew literature, especially Zionist literature, but not modern Jewish philosophy.

The science of ecology and the theory of evolution

Why has the science of ecology failed to inform Jewish reflections on the interaction between humanity and nature? One answer is found in the growing separation between Judaism and science during the modern period. The granting of civil rights to Jews in the nineteenth century enabled them to enter the universities that previously had excluded them. As part of the Jewish drive to integrate in European society and culture, Jews flocked to the natural sciences, especially the new disciplines of chemistry, microbiology, and medical biology (Charpa and Deichmann 2007: 5–36). In some scientific fields, Jews were disproportionately represented and reached outstanding achievements; other fields were shaped entirely or mainly by Jewish scientists. For Jews who wished to become part of European culture, modern science became a substitute for religion, although, ironically enough, it was the lifestyle of traditional Judaism, with its insistence on meticulous observance of laws and commitment to the pursuit of truth, that generated the personality type suitable for the rigors of scientific inquiry.

But no less important is the fact that the science of ecology, from its inception, was a Christian (and more specifically Protestant) discourse (Worster 1994; Cittadino 2006, Stoll 2006), a fact that Barrett and Jordan fail to mention. The science of ecology took shape in Lutheran countries (such as Germany and Denmark) and was planted in America in Congregationalist and Presbyterian denominations. For Protestant contributors to the science of ecology (such as John Muir), nature, which was viewed as pure, ongoing creation of God, served as the foil for human corruption. They all shared the view that the environment was an organism, and their holistic outlook was colored with mystical overtones. Since the science of ecology was configured within a Christian matrix, it is no wonder that Jews did not engage it, and instead chose to pursue natural sciences that were devoid of religious undertones (such as chemistry). Yet Jews did not ignore the core theory of the science of ecology – evolution. Informed of Darwin's variant of the theory of evolution by random selection, Jewish scholars were aware that natural selection challenges traditional Judaism. Only a handful of Jews engaged the scientific details of the theory of evolution; most focused on the *implications* of evolution for Judaism (Cantor and Swetlitz 2006). However, the debate was not merely theological; it also reflected diverse attitudes towards modernity, assimilation, and acculturation, pluralism within modern Judaism, and changing conceptions about the desired relationship between the Jewish minority and Christian majority.

In America, the Jewish engagement with Darwinian evolution came mainly after the publication of Darwin's *Descent of Man* in 1871 (Swetlitz 1999, 2006). A rigorous dispute erupted between leading Jewish theologians, who promoted the reform of Judaism. Rabbi Kaufmann Kohler endorsed Darwin's theory because he viewed it as a scientific proof for Reform Judaism: Judaism is a progressive religion that evolved over time; yet Kohler ignored Darwin's theory of natural selection. His opponent, Rabbi Isaac Mayer Wise, understood natural selection to be a natural law in which survival of the strongest prevails. Nature was indeed a "battle ground" which robbed the moral law, as taught by Judaism, of all its legitimacy. Rejecting Darwin, Wise developed his own theory about the history of life, one that acknowledged that the Jewish religion, like nature, is bound by the law of evolution, that is, progression from lower to higher forms. However, Wise did not adopt the theory of progressive revelation, and opposed the notion of graduate continuous transmutation of species. A few Reform rabbis followed Wise in rejecting evolution on the ground that it is improbable, but several more traditional rabbis among the reformers began to consider arguments against evolution on the basis of specific references in Genesis.

The debate between those who appealed to evolution to explain the progressive nature of Judaism, and the traditionalists who rejected evolution because it challenged Jewish observance, resulted in the emergence of a new Jewish denomination, Conservative Judaism. It would enable millions of Eastern European Jewish immigrants to America to modernize while remaining loyal to traditional Judaism. In the 1930s, Rabbi Mordecai Kaplan (1881–1983) elaborated the notion of Judaism as an evolving civilization, even though he did not accept key elements of Darwin's theory of evolution (Swetlitz 2006: 52–55). Similarly, Kaplan failed to draw the implications of the theory of evolution for belief in God, although he did develop a naturalistic world-view that viewed the universe as an organic totality. Ironically, when Kaplan articulated his new view of Judaism (Kaplan 1934), the science of ecology began to move away from its religious roots, with the rise of utopian visionaries who viewed ecology as the scientific underpinning of a new social order and the antidote to the excesses of modern civilization. In the mid-1930s, the term "ecosystems" replaced the term "ecology" in order to dissociate ecology from organic holism, which generated objectionable political implications on the political left (Communism) and on the political right (Fascism). After the Second World War, the study of ecosystems became increasingly mathematical, as concepts and metaphors from cybernetics and information science gave it a new flavor and direction (Stoll 2006: 64). Thus the *religious* "old ecology" was gradually replaced with *secular* "new ecology."

Ecological strands in modern Judaism

The distinction between "old ecology" and "new ecology" does not capture the nuanced reflections on the interplay between God, humanity, and nature in modern Jewish thought. Nonetheless, several Jewish thinkers can be labeled "ecological" because they highlight interaction and connectedness between all living and nonliving things; they reject the notion that nature has only instrumental value as a resource utility for human beings; and they promote a view of nature as a source of moral obligation and/or spiritual vitality. A few examples will illustrate ecological tendencies in Modern Orthodoxy, Zionism, and the Jewish Renewal Movement. The impetus for these ecological reflections did not come from the science of ecology, as some views held nature to be holistic, stable, and balanced, while others recognized nature as dynamic, perpetual flux.

Modern Orthodoxy

Modern Orthodoxy was founded in Germany by Samson Raphael Hirsch (1808–88), as a response to the movement for religious reform. While Hirsch endorsed the Jewish struggle for emancipation, and advocated openness toward European secular culture, he defended the traditional doctrine of "Torah from Heavens." He rejected the reformers' critique of rabbinic Judaism or their tendency to discard traditional practices and introduce new rituals. In continuation with rabbinic Judaism, Hirsch argued that God, the Creator of the world, gave humans the *right* to rule nature, but that this right came with the *duty* to treat God's created order in accordance to divine will. According to Hirsch, the human is part of nature, indeed a "brother to all creatures," but, like the first-born in a Jewish family, the human also has special privileges and obligation. Hirsch held that human mastery over nature is about the fulfillment of the human, rational, God-given free will, but the human right of mastery over nature depends on the extent to which the human will corresponds to God's will. The Torah itself thus discloses how nature is to be treated with justice and respect.

In his classification of Jewish laws, Hirsch placed the commandment "Do not destroy" at the head of the section on the *Hukkim*, which he defined as "statements concerning justice toward subordinate creatures by reason of the obedience due to god; that is, justice toward the earth, plants, and animals, or, if they have become assimilated to your own person, then, justice toward your own property, toward your own body and soul and spirit" (Hirsch 1969: 75). The *Hukkim* were legislated by God primarily for the protection of nature from human avarice and exploitation. Heedless destruction of nature reflects human arrogance and rebellion against God, but the laws of the Torah assure that humans behave wisely and judiciously to protect the integrity of the natural world and its perpetuation. For Hirsch, the created world exhibits not only inherent purpose, but also orderliness, intelligence, and interdependence. Given the remarkably wise design of the universe, humans have an obligation to protect the natural world. Indeed, Scripture prohibits copulation of diverse animals, grafting of diverse trees, yoking together of diverse animals, wearing of wool and flax, and mixing of milk and meat. These laws are rooted in the act of creation when God separated His creatures "each according to its kind." Through the Torah, the Creator of the world functions as the "Regulator of the world;" the human who was appointed as the "administrator" of God's estate executes the rules that ensure protection of nature. In Hirsch's analysis of the *Hukkim*, nature serves as a model for observance of divine commands and places its own demands or commandments on humans. Hirsch is an example of how Modern Orthodoxy can support Jewish religious environmentalism.

Zionism

Jewish religious environmentalism accords a place of honor to the Land of Israel, the Holy Land, whose well-being reflects the dynamic relationship between God and the People of Israel. The Bible makes clear that the Land of Israel was given to Israel conditionally: so long as Israel observes God's Will and follows His commandments, including the commandments for the treatment of nature, the land remains fertile, providing the People of Israel with abundance. But when Israel rebels against God and sins against God, the Land becomes infertile and desolate; when sinfulness abounds, God exiles Israel from the Land of Israel. Throughout their long exilic existence, Jews have yearned to return to the Land of Israel, but they postponed the fulfillment of this dream to the Messianic Age of the remote future. At the end of the nineteenth century, however, Zionism rebelled against traditional Jewish messianism by insisting that Jews leave their country of residence and settle in their ancestral home. Only in the Land of Israel could the Jews become a normal nation with its own political sovereignty, spoken language, and unique culture. For Zionist ideologues, the return of the Jews to the Land of Israel was not only a secularization of the messianic dream, it was also a call for the return of the Jews to nature in order to create a new "muscular Jew," a physically strong, fearless Jew who celebrates the rhythms of nature and derives vitality from nature.

The return to nature played a central role in the original and highly creative thought of Aaron David Gordon (1856–1922), the spiritual leader of Labor Zionism (Schweid 1985: 157–70). Although Gordon grew up in an Orthodox home in Russia, on his own he studied European philosophy and literature, and was particularly influenced by Friedrich Nietzsche, Henri Bergson, and Leo Tolstoy. Settling in Palestine in 1904, Gordon joined the agricultural settlements and experienced the hardship of pioneers' life in order to exemplify his call not just for the Jews, but for all of humanity. For Gordon, the Jews' return to their land symbolized humanity's return to nature and the renewal of the relationship (indeed the covenant) between humanity and nature which was destroyed by culture, especially modern, urban, industrialized culture.

Gordon contended that human beings stand outside nature by developing three major postures: as artists, humans express love of nature's beauty; as scientists, they explore nature's mysteries; and as engineers, they use human technology to exploit nature's resources. All three postures are mistaken because they deny that humans are part of nature. Instead, humans should strive "to live with and in nature," because the universe is an organic totality enlivened by divine energy that pulsates through all levels of reality. Emerging out of the organic totality, humans have reached the most developed state of being: culture and self-consciousness. Yet these are also the causes of human alienation from nature. The human tragedy is especially severe in the case of Jews because they seek to assimilate into Western Christian culture, denying their roots in the Land of Israel, the Jewish nation, and the Hebrew language. Only agriculture and farming could reconnect modern, alienated Jews to the sources of cosmic creativity, enabling them to live most authentically as Jews as well as human beings, an ideal he exemplified in his own life.

A. D. Gordon's thought has a strongly pantheistic character, which could be traced to various intellectual sources, both Jewish (Kabbalah and Hasidism) and non-Jewish (Bergson and Tolstoy). He viewed nature as an organic totality out of which emerges human consciousness, and he called the totality of nature *havaya*. Literally, this means "being," but it is in fact the four letters of the Tetragrammaton arranged in a different order. Secularizing the notion of divine immanence, Gordon understood Being as a dynamic, ever-changing, living force in constant flux that pulsates throughout all levels of reality. Humans can experience the hidden aspect of nature only through direct intuition, but such experience can be attained only by means of manual labor that overcomes the alienation of mankind from nature. For Gordon, the regeneration of humanity and the regeneration of the Jewish people could come only through the development of a new understanding of labor as the source of genuine joy and creativity. Gordon's holistic views are susceptible to the critique of "old ecology" put forth by Barrett and Jordan, and others (Sideris 2003), but this critique cannot address the religious assumptions of Gordon's world-view.

Jewish Renewal Movement

The Zionist call for the return of the Jews to nature illustrates the traditional Jewish idea of *teshuvah*. The term is usually translated as "repentance," but its Hebrew stem connotes both "to return" and "to reply," so that *teshuvah* means both a movement of return to one's source, to the original paradigm, and simultaneously a response to a divine call. *Teshuvah* thus involves a spiritual reorientation or a transformation of the self away from an inauthentic way of life, lacking creative force, toward the authenticity that is characterized by continual creativity and renewal. In America during the second half of the twentieth century, this concept gave rise to the Jewish Renewal Movement.

The catalyst for it was Rabbi Abraham Joshua Heschel (1907–72), a Polish Jew who was born into a Hasidic family, but who also received modern university training. Heschel managed to flee Nazi-occupied Poland and settled in 1941 in America, where he inspired scores of alienated American Jews to find their way back to the sources of Judaism in order to heal the atrocities of modernity, which culminated in the Holocaust. Heschel's ecologically sensitive Depth Theology spoke of God's glory as pervading nature, leading humans to radical amazement and wonder; viewed humans as members of the cosmic community; and emphasized humility as the desired posture toward the natural world (Kaplan 1996). Another product of Hasidism, and a refugee from Nazi-occupied Europe, was Zalman Schachter-Shalomi (b. 1924), who founded the Jewish Renewal Movement in the late 1960s. His creative reinterpretation of Judaism combined a "Gaia consciousness" with psychological interpretation of Lurianic Kabbalah and New Age spirituality. Schachter-Shalomi urged a paradigm shift from monotheism to pantheism within Judaism, but did not intend to revive neo-pagan pantheism. Instead, he offered contemporary Jews a new way to infuse Jewish life with rituals that envision "a God who is an integral part of all human civilization and all of humanity has a specific responsibility for that relationship" (Magid 2006: 65). Unlike the rituals discussed by Barrett and Jordan, the rituals of the Jewish Renewal Movement are all contemporary variants of traditional Jewish practices (for example, the pilgrimage festivals). Schachter-Shalomi's ideas were systematized into Jewish ecology by Arthur Green (b. 1941), who, under the influence of Kabbalah, presented a holistic view of reality in which all existents are in some way an expression of God and are to some extent intrinsically related to each other (Green 1992, 2003). From the privileged position of the human, Green derives an ethics of responsibility toward all creatures that acknowledges the differences between diverse creatures, while insisting on the need to defend the legitimate place in the world of even the weakest and most threatened of creatures. For Green, a Jewish ecological ethics must be a set of laws and instructions that truly enhances life. Green's ecotheology does not pay sufficient attention to the "dark" of nature, and does not explain how human conduct, guided by divinely revealed law, may actually address it. Thus Green, like Gordon and Heschel, is open to the criticism leveled by Barrett and Jordan.

Ecology and the Jewish imperative of responsibility

To some extent, the Jewish Renewal Movement and all late-twentieth century Jewish ecological thinking can be viewed as a belated response to the catastrophe of the Holocaust, a determination of the Jewish people to renew themselves so as "not to give Hitler a posthumous victory," to use the famous formulation of Emil Fackenheim. The Nazis' attempt to exterminate the Jewish People because of their regard for the Jews as sub-human was the most distorted application of evolutionary theories. Treating Jews as vermin, the Nazis applied Zyklon-B gas with the aim of totally eradicating them, using bureaucratic efficiency and the most advanced science and technology for demonic purposes. The struggle between Nazism and Judaism raises some poignant questions about paganism as a world-view that does not allow for the possibility of transcendence, and that takes the world of the senses to be ultimate reality. The horrendous results of Nazism for Jews remind us that Nazism was the most consistent assault on the Jewish notion that physical environment is *not* inherently sacred, and that only when humans act in accord with divine commands can nature become holy. While nature can be a source of spiritual inspiration, it is important to remember that nature is also violent, competitive, ruthless, and destructive, precisely as the "new ecology" teaches. Nature, indeed, does not care about the sick, the weak, and the deformed; it disposes of them in the relentless struggle for survival. Nature does not establish moral values that can create a just society in which the needs of the sick and the poor are addressed. These moral values, which constitute the Jewish ethics of responsibility, are revealed by God and implemented by humans who wish to sanctify nature as they strive to become like God.

No-one understood the lessons of the Holocaust better than Hans Jonas (1903–93), a German Jewish Zionist who fled Nazi Germany in 1934 and settled in Palestine in 1935 (Wiese 2007). During the Second World War, Jonas volunteered with the Jewish Brigade of the British army, which brought him back to Germany as a victor. Yet the war experience made him shift to philosophy of biology, or more precisely to the philosophy of organic life. Jonas' philosophic response to the total destruction practiced during the Second World War was to invest matter itself with *inherent moral meaning*, presenting the human as the final manifestation of nature's "needful freedom" (Jonas 1966, 1984, 1996). His philosophy of organism starts with the phenomenon of metabolism, and interprets organic life and individual organisms in terms, concepts, and categories that transcend Cartesian dualism, idealism, and physicalist materialism. For Jonas, organic life itself is an ontological revolution in the history of matter, a radical change in matter's mode of being. By giving organisms on all levels their philosophical and moral due, animate nature was philosophically rehabilitated. The radical split between nature and ethics, between "is" and "ought," was thereby bridged. Jonas asserted that value and disvalue are not human constructs, but "essential to life itself [since] every living thing has a share in life's needful freedom." Jonas did not appeal to revelation, even when he reworked traditional Jewish concepts such as creation in the "image of God." Yet Jonas' insights were profoundly Jewish; they resonate with traditional Jewish moral passion and the prophetic call to protect the needy and powerless. Jonas was less stunned by the innumerable material forms and processes of life than by the very fact of life itself, and especially by organic *life's capacity for moral responsibility, evidenced in human beings*. The very fact that, in a vast universe characterized largely by inorganic, dead matter, there has emerged animal and moral being as a revolt against death and valuelessness led Jonas to enjoin us to protect organic life into the indefinite future. Jonas is the best proof that the particular historical circumstances of Jews could inspire an environmental philosophy for humanity that attempts to cope with an ecological crisis of its own making. Since human activities are largely, although not exclusively, responsible for the current ecological crisis, humans have the *responsibility* to mend the world that belongs to God, precisely as traditional Judaism teaches.

In contrast to the Jewish emphasis on responsibility, Barrett and Jordan maintain that the only way to come to terms with the truths of the science of ecology is for humans to acquire a sense of shame. The authors invoke Jean Paul Sartre, who held that the very existence of an onlooker implies shame. However, Sartre did not explain shame; he only explained it away. What is lacking in Sartre's analysis of shame, as Christian critics have already noted, is an adequate accounting for the sense of culpability that is inseparable from shame: if the Other is merely an intruder, we would only feel annoyed and attempt to eliminate the intruder. But the glance of the Other does not generate shame unless it falls upon some sin that exists objectively within the shamed one. Barrett and Jordan consider the traditional Christian notion of guilt and sinfulness a "tragic mistake" in our framing of human relationship to nature, but the horrific experience of Jews in the Holocaust attests that it is much more tragic when human beings dispense with notions of guilt, culpability, and sinfulness occasioned by one's harming of the Other. After all, these are the values that Nazi ideology and culture conspicuously lacked, leading the Nazis to commit unspeakable atrocities. Sartre's concept of existential shame is not a promising point of departure for restorative ethics. Biblically rooted Christian ecotheologies are more in accord with the Judaic imperative of responsibility than the secular views promoted by Barrett and Jordan.

We must never abandon this responsibility, even though we will continue to debate how to translate the idea of responsibility into sound environmental policies in light of the science of ecology.

References

Bernstein, Ellen (ed.) (1997) *Ecology & The Jewish Spirit: Where Nature and the Sacred Meet*, Woodstock, VT: Jewish Lights Publishing.

Cantor, Geoffrey and Marc Swetlitz (eds) (2006) *Jewish Tradition and the Challenge of Darwinism*, Chicago, IL: University of Chicago Press.

Charpa, Ulrich and Ute Deichmann (2007) *Jews and Science in German Contexts*, Tübingen: Mohr Siebeck.

Green, Arthur (1992) *Seek My Face, Speak My Name*, Northvale, NJ: Aronson.

——(2003) *Ehyeh: A Kabbalah for Tomorrow*, Woodstock, VT: Jewish Lights Publishing.

Hirsch, Samson Raphael (1969) *The Nineteen Letters on Judaism*, New York: Feldheim.

Jonas, Hans (1966) *The Phenomenon of Life: Toward a Philosophical Biology*, New York: Harper & Row.

——(1984) *The Imperative of Responsibility: In Search of an Ethics for the Technological Age*, Chicago, IL: University of Chicago Press.

——(1996) *Mortality and Morality: A Search for the Good after Auschwitz*, Lawrence Vogel (ed.), Chicago, IL: Northwestern University Press.

Kaplan, Edward K. (1996) *Holiness in Words: Abraham Joshua Heschel's Poetics of Piety*, Albany, NY: SUNY Press.

Magid, Shaul (2006) "Jewish Renewal, American Spirituality, and Post-Monotheistic Theology," *Tikkun* (May/June): 62–66.

Rosenblum, Noah H. (1976) *Tradition in an Age of Reform: The Religious Philosophy of Samson Raphael Hirsch*, Philadelphia, PA: Jewish Publication Society.

Schwarzschild, Steven S. (1984) "The Unnatural Jew," *Environmental Ethics* 6: 347–62; reprinted in Yaffe, Martin D. (2002) *Judaism and Environmental Ethics: A Reader*, Lanham, MD: Lexington Books, 267–82.

Schweid, Eliezer (1970) *The World of A.D. Gordon* (in Hebrew), Tel Aviv: Am Oved.

Sideris, Lisa (2003) *Environmental Ethics, Ecological Theology and Natural Selection*, New York: Columbia University Press.

Stoll, Mark (1999) "American Jewish Responses to Darwin and Evolutionary Theory, 1860–90," in *Disseminating Darwinism: The Role of Place, Race, Religion and Gender*, Ronald L. Numbers and John Stenhouse (eds), Cambridge: Cambridge University Press, 209–46.

——(2006a) "Creating Ecology: Protestants and the Moral Community of Creation" in *Religion and the New Ecology: Environmental Responsibility in a World in Flux*, David M. Lodge and Christopher Hamlin (eds), Notre Dame, IN: University of Notre Dame Press, 53–72.

——(2006b) "Responses to Evolution by Reform, Conservative and Reconstructionist Rabbis in Twentieth-Century America," in *Jewish Tradition and the Challenge of Darwinism*, Geoffrey Cantor and Marc Swetlitz (eds), Chicago, IL: University of Chicago Press, 47–70.

Tirosh-Samuelson, Hava (2006) "Judaism," in *The Oxford Handbook of Religion and Ecology*, Roger S. Gottlieb (ed.), Oxford and New York: Oxford University Press, 25–64.

Waskow, Arthur (1995) *Down-to-Earth Judaism: Food, Money, Sex and the Rest of Life*, New York: W. Morrow.

——(1996) "What Is Eco-Kosher?," in *This Sacred Earth: Religion, Nature, Environment*, Roger S. Gottlieb (ed.), New York: Routledge, 297–300.

——(ed.) (2002) *Torah of the Earth: Exploring 4,000 Years of Ecology in Jewish Thought*, Woodstock, VT: Jewish Lights Publishing.

Worster, Donald (1994) *Nature's Economy: A History of Ecological Ideas*, 2nd edn, Cambridge: Cambridge University Press.

Yaffe, Martin D. (ed.) (2002) *Judaism and Environmental Ethics: A Reader*, Lanham, MD: Lexington Books.

Further reading

The best overview of Judaism and environmentalism is Manfred Gerstenfeld, *Judaism, Environmentalism and the Environment: Mapping and Analysis* (Jerusalem Institute of Israel Studies and Rubin Mass, 1998). Two excellent examples of Jewish religious environmental discourse are Ellen Bernstein, *The Splendor of Creation: A Biblical Ecology* (Pilgrim Press, 2005) and Jeremy Benstein, *The Way into Judaism and the Environment* (Jewish Lights Publishing, 2006). For an ecological reading of the Bible, the point of departure for Jewish religious environmentalism, consult Evan Eisenberg, *The Ecology of Eden* (Alfred A. Knopf, 1998) and Ellen F. Davis, *Scripture, Culture and Agriculture: An Agrarian Reading of the Bible* (Cambridge University Press, 2009). The complex place of the Land of Israel in Jewish history and culture is explored in Leonard J. Greenspoon and Ronald A. Simkins (eds) "*A Land Flowing with Milk and Honey*": *Vision of Israel from Biblical to Modern Times* (Creighton University Press, 2001) and in Lawrence A. Hoffman (ed.), *The Land of Israel: Jewish Perspectives* (University of Notre Dame Press, 1986). For engagement with diverse philosophical and theological problems that confront Jewish environmentalism, consult Hava Tirosh-Samuelson (ed.) *Judaism and Ecology: Created World and Revealed Word* (Harvard University Press, 2002). For in-depth analysis of Hans Jonas's thought, see Tirosh-Samuelson and Christian Wiese (eds.) *The Legacy of Hans Jonas: Judaism and the Phenomenon of Life* (Brill, 2008).

32
ASIAN RELIGIONS, ECOLOGY, AND THE INTEGRITY OF NATURE

Christopher Key Chapple

Asian religions span a vast continent, from its dry western expanse, south to the Indian subcontinent, rising up northward over the Himalayas to the Arctic, and east to the shores of China and Vietnam, the Korean peninsula, and the Japanese islands. Asia gave birth to many of the world's great religions: Confucianism, Zoroastrianism, Hinduism, Judaism, Daoism, Jainism, Buddhism, Christianity, Islam, and Sikhism. This chapter examines some key themes from just a few of these faiths in light of their relationship with nature and issues of ecological concern.

In the introduction to this section (Chapter 30), Barrett and Jordan cite Daniel Botkin's (1990) call for ecologists to recognize that human intervention has long altered the landscape, and that what might have seemed to be self-regulating communities in fact have been repeatedly changed by planned burns in the forest or agricultural practices. They suggest that working with hard data, historical and scientific, is essential in order to develop a credible approach to environmental ethics. Botkin's work highlights the notion that virtually no landscape has remained untouched by human contact, citing as one example the Genesee Valley where I grew up in western New York State. Remarkable sweeping vistas, stretching for miles from one side of the valley to the other, punctuated by massive oak trees, were created hundreds of years ago by the tradition of annual burns implemented by the indigenous Seneca peoples. Now that I live in southern California, I hear similar stories from my native Tongva friends, who tell of how the cultivation of specific plants helped shape a landscape that the Spanish settlers deemed "natural." Botkin's point is well taken. Barrett and Jordan are correct. Without careful analysis that entails a detailed study of history and biology, it is all too easy to fall into a top-down environmental ethic that ignores local circumstances, opting for what Bruun and Kalland (1995) refer to as "western tendencies to dichotomize the universe and stress the absolute." In Asia, it has often been observed that understanding context is crucial before a decision can be rendered. Ecological activism in Asia combines guiding principles and traditions applied within local circumstances.

This essay seeks to explore the particularity of and differences among Asian traditions on ecology and nature. Though some mention is made of East Asian traditions, the primary focus of this chapter is on India. In doing so, it looks at the proto-science of select traditions, from both philosophical and narrative texts.

Asian religions and the environment

From the Vedas, the Upanisads, Jaina literature, the Buddhist Abhidharma texts, as well as later Hatha Yoga manuals, we can gather a sense of the complexity with which the Indian traditions discussed the natural world. From the *Dao De Jing* and the *Analects* of Confucius, we can also catch a glimpse into the ancient Chinese world-view. The Jaina *Acaranga Sutra* and the Buddhist *Jataka Tales* (*c.* 300 BCE) include narratives that describe the destruction of forests and consequent ecological upheaval due to the rapid growth of trade and of cities. For instance, the Jaina teacher Mahavira, warning against the allure of commerce, tells the monks and nuns to "change their minds" about looking at big trees. He says that rather than seeing them as "fit for palaces, gates, houses, benches, boats, buckets, stools, trays, ploughs, sets, beds, cars, sheds," one should see and speak of them as "noble, high, round, big" (*Acaranga Sutra*, Jacobi 1968: 2.4.2.11–12). This lesson encourages his disciples not to fall prey to consumerist, exploitive impulses. In the *Vyaddha Jataka*, the Buddha tells that the tree spirits of a particular forest were repelled by the stench of rotting meat left repeatedly by an over-zealous lion and tiger. They arranged to scare away the predators. However, the villagers who were previously too afraid to enter the forest noticed that the felines were gone, and quickly chopped down the forest and put it under cultivation, depriving the forest spirits of their habitat. Due to their folly, the denizens of the forest were chased from their native habitat (*Jataka* 272 in Cowell 1895–1907: 3: 244–46). Though later transcendentalist and orientalist thinkers tended to develop a grand romantic narrative from early materials such as these, the texts themselves are actually quite earthy and practical. A tree is seen as a tree, a forest as a forest, and a field as a field, in contrast to the later poetry of Wordsworth and Whitman and the elevated prose of Emerson and Thoreau, which are laden with rhapsody about nature over and beyond the reality of nature itself. In India, people do not tend to romanticize nature, but seek to survive within it.

The "face" of environmentalism in India differs from that elsewhere. As articulated by Ramachandra Guha and Madhav Gadgil, the standard Western categories of nature reserve, or even national parkland, do not fit the complex geography and human landscape. Due to the extensive population and the increasing divide between urban and rural cultures, as well as the many changes imposed on India by British colonial rule, it is more useful to think of any discussion of nature and animals in terms of social ecology than attempting a purely scientific approach (see Gadgil and Guha 1992; Guha 2006).

Meera Nanda warns that the Hindu nationalist movement has taken up the cause of religious environmentalism to advance its own political agenda, as discussed below. However, as will be seen, the emphasis on nature in early Indian literature pre-dates nationalist concerns, and the nature of environmental activism world-wide, especially in India and China, seems to be repeatedly at odds with governmental national policy, as seen in the struggle over the Narmada dam projects in India and the Three Gorges displacements in China. This chapter includes three examples demonstrating that protection of land and animals is an old tradition in India, predating modern times and yet being carried forward into the future by the Bishnois, the Chipko movement, and the advocacy of M. C. Mehta.

The methodology of this essay draws from the tradition of theological ethics, not as applied to the Bible or casuistic texts, but as constructed through a process of examining traditional Asian literature and religious practice that makes suggestions for correct ethical behavior utilizing directives, parables, and rhetorical arguments. This method requires a study of culture, world-view, and history. It was inspired largely by the example of Thomas Berry (1914–2009). Berry, a Catholic monk and priest, studied Thomas Aquinas and Giambatista Vico in the original Latin for many years. He then learned classical Chinese to probe the teachings of Confucius, Mencius, Lao Tzu, and Chuang Tzu. Next, he studied Sanskrit to gain an in-depth understanding of Hinduism and Buddhism. Later in life, he studied Native American traditions and scientific accounts of the origins and development of the universe and life itself, a process that included decades of immersion in the work of Pierre Teilhard de Chardin. This essay involves a study of the history of religions and the application of comparative ethics.

As noted above, Barrett and Jordan (Chapter 30 in this volume) suggest that the field of religion and ecology has neglected the inclusion of hard scientific data. Berry wove and retold the scientific story in a comprehensive way, particularly as seen in his collaborative work with Brian Swimme (Berry and Swimme 1992). Another early work in the emerging genre of studies in religion and ecology, *Ecological Prospects: Scientific, Religious, and Aesthetic Perspectives* (Chapple 1994) includes essays on cosmology (Sagan/Margulis), ecological restoration in Madagascar (Wright), reflections on invasive botany and insect populations worldwide (Crosby), and the challenges of wilderness management (Callicot, Botkin). The book offers several ethical responses to these and other issues from the perspectives of Confucianism and neo-Confucian organicity (Tucker), Christian panentheism (McDaniel), eco-feminism (Ruether), and Earth First!'s radical environmental activism (Taylor). *Worldviews and Ecology: Religion, Philosophy, and the Environment* (Tucker and Grim 1994), although not dwelling extensively on scientific material, presents ecological approaches from the world's religious traditions, including Native American perspectives (Grim), Judaism (Timm), Baha'i (White), Hinduism (Chapple), Buddhism (Brown), Jainism (Tobias), Whitehead (Griffin), and more.

The field of the study of the world's religions and ecology, which had some of its beginnings in the gatherings that inspired the books described above, blossomed into a series of twelve conferences held at Harvard University, the United Nations, and the American Museum of Natural History from 1997 to 2001. More than 600 scholars from ten religious traditions discussed the "premise that the religions of the world may be instrumental in addressing the moral dilemmas created by the environmental crisis." In a series of ten volumes, multiple perspectives emerged. Even within traditions, no single approach emerged with the definitive answer to how religions might best develop an ethical response to ecological degradation. Some scholars took a purely historical approach, citing instances from within religious scriptures that encourage and delineate best practices when interacting with nature. Others provided concrete examples of historical figures who established laws mandating kindly treatment of animals, rotation of crops, and forest preservation. Some scholars were quite skeptical that religions could play a role in this arena.

From traditional Asian religious literature, we can arrive at a sense of the complexity with which the Indian and Chinese traditions regard the human relationship with nature. The *Vedas* include numerous hymns that extol the power and majesty of Earth, the waters, and the winds. The poets of the *Rig Veda* (*c.* 1500 BCE) saw continuity between the human experience and cosmic forces. The feet of the cosmic person are rooted in the Earth. The right eye correlates to the radiance of the Sun, the left eye to the Moon. The monsoon rains, released by Indra, the god of the thunderbolt, bring crops and sustenance. The composers of the *Atharva Veda* (*c.* 500 BCE) praise the Earth for her bounty and generosity, ask for her protection, and advise humans to avoid polluting her waters. In the *Chandogya Upanisad* (*c.* 800 BCE), Satyakama Jabala, one of the great teachers of his day, receives his spiritual instruction from animals, birds, and the forces of nature. A bull teaches him the significance of orienting oneself in space. A fire teaches him about the three realms of earth, atmosphere, and sky, and the fourth realm of the vast ocean. A heron or egret teaches him about the significance of the many forms of light and fire. Finally, a diving bird, perhaps an Indian variant of the pelican, teaches Satyakama about the body and breath, seeing, hearing, and thinking. These lessons, all taught outdoors, indicate the ongoing importance of rural life in India, particularly as documented by Gadgil and Guha (1992); Guha (2006).

In the philosophical period of Indian culture (*c.* 500 BCE), three movements arose that share a common interest in understanding the natural world: Samkhya, Jainism, and Buddhism. Samkhya sets forth twenty-five principles that govern and explain the human connectivity with the grander forces of the cosmos. These include the Great Elements of earth, water, fire, air, and space; the Subtle Elements linked to smelling, tasting, seeing, touching, and hearing; the sense organs (nose, mouth, eyes, skin, and ears); and the actions that the human can perform: evacuating waste, reproduction, grasping, walking, and talking. Each individual human being moves through life using the mind and body to gather and present data to an ever-present witness consciousness. A purified being (*sattva*) sees things as they are; a being laden with *karma* views the world lethargically (*tamas*) or through selfish greed (*rajas*). By purifying one's intentions through ethical behavior and meditation, one can leave behind attachment and live in a state of blessed immediacy. The beginning point of ascent toward this spiritual vision can be found through intimacy with the great elements of nature.

Jaina philosophy accepts this general assessment of the elements, and adds the assertion that all realms are suffused with countless souls. According to their early literature (the *Acaranga Sutra*, *c.* 300 BCE), Mahavira, a great teacher, closely inspected life and discovered its presence in a variety of places. Its elemental, microbial, and botanical forms possess the faculty of being able to feel the touch of other beings. According to this system, worms possess an individual soul consciousness that expands beyond mere touch to the ability to taste. Bugs can touch, taste, and smell. Flying insects can touch, taste, smell, and see. Higher life forms, including mammals, reptiles, birds, and humans, add hearing and thinking to the four foundational sensory capacities. Extensive Jaina biological texts emerge in the medieval period that provide meticulous detail about the nature of life in its myriad forms (see Chapple, "The Living Earth of Jainism and the New Story," in Chapple 2002: 119–40). Care is taken to ensure humans inflict as little harm as possible in the course of daily life, resulting in the development of a vegetarian diet routinely observed by all Jainas, as well as the establishment of thousands of bird and animal shelters all over India.

Whereas the Hindus see nature as emerging from, and inseparable from, universal consciousness, and the Jainas describe a multiplicity of countless individual souls progressing on a distinct journey, Buddhists eschew the notions of one-ness and many-ness in favor of a refusal to speculate on the nature of nature, preferring to direct the attention of their followers toward self-improvement. Nonetheless, many of the Buddha's early stories that narrate his past lives (*Jataka Tales*) include information of interest to naturalists and often serve as parables urging prudent behavior, not only in the company of human beings, but also when dealing with animals, fields, and forests.

From the *Dao De Jing* and even the *Analects* of Confucius, we can catch a glimpse into the ancient Chinese view toward nature. The *Dao* repeatedly employs nature metaphors to encourage attention to the flow and selfless unfolding of life when lived untrammeled by human interference. Confucianism, by contrast, advocates anthropocentricism, putting humans before horses, and declaring that the human being provides the critical balancing point between heaven and earth. Both systems arise from an earlier philosophy of *yin* and *yang* that seeks to harmonize and balance these two complementary forces. The *yin* represents the feminine, the cool, the unseen aspect of reality; the *yang* represents the masculine, the hot, and the apparent. In Daoism, one retreats to allow for their natural union. In Confucianism, one exerts effort to cultivate harmony through the practice of virtues and the active cultivation of self.

The volumes that arose from the Harvard conferences (1997–2002) paint a complex picture, enhanced by the even more inclusive *Encyclopedia of Religion and Nature* edited by Bron Taylor (2005). The Buddhist volume suggests various paradigms for environmental activism that have been developed in Buddhist communities worldwide, from the protection of trees through their initiation as monks in Thailand, to the recycling strategies employed at Zen Mountain Monastery in Idyllwild, California. The book also presents the perspective that the original teachings of Buddhism would consider protection of nature a distraction from the required practices of meditation.

The Hindu volume examines a variety of texts, from Vedas and Upanisads to the *Mahabharata* and *Ramayana* epics, finding examples and counter-examples of ecological concern. It also includes histories of kingdoms in the early modern period that emphasized protection of resources, and provides details on the recent campaigns (ultimately unsuccessful) to stop the damming of rivers in the Himalayas and in Central India. A critical look at traditional Indian literature is also included, raising the question whether the world-renouncing ethic espoused in the *Bhagavad Gita* and elsewhere contradicts an ecological ethic.

The Jaina volume, similarly to the others, includes the voices of academics, activists, and practicing adherents to the faith. The Jaina philosophy of innumerable souls constantly changing bodies, seeking ascent, and eventually moving toward release in many ways lends itself to an ecological view due to the careful attention to the protection of all life forms as the path of purification of one's soul. The tradition claims that even particles of earth and water contain sparks of awareness. Because of its doctrines that teach minimizing harm to all life forms, contemporary Jainas proclaim their faith to be inherently Earth-friendly (see essays by Sadhvi Shilapi, Bhagchandra Jain, and Satish Kumar in Chapple 2002). However, some scholars also point out that specific instances, such as the restrictions against helping predatory or even grazing animals survive, and the Jaina involvement with the mining industry, can in fact produce imbalances within larger ecosystems (see Cort, Dundas, and Jaini in Chapple 2002). The Daoism, Confucianism, and Shinto volumes present similarly balanced accounts of how these respective faiths hold both resources for inspiring environmental concern and an occasion to pause for further reflection.

Since these volumes were published, several books have appeared that ask for further probing and reconsideration of the presumed relationship between Asian world-views and the application of their ethical systems to ecological issues. As early as 1972, Protestant theologian John Cobb wrote that Eastern philosophy did not hold the solutions needed for ecological problems. Several experts on Asian thought contributed to *Nature in Asian Traditions of Thought* (Callicott and Ames 1989), a volume that similarly advises prudence when making blanket statements that Asian philosophy is Earth-friendly in contrast to the exploitive nature of Western thought. Lance Nelson has suggested that the world-denying aspect of the *Bhagavad Gita*, as well as India's overall emphasis on religious asceticism, must be critiqued. He writes that "Nature, however, is finally irrelevant in the *Gita*'s soteriological goals. […] the *Gita* teaches that our true self is outside the world of nature" (Nelson 2000: 127–64). Meera Nanda suggests that a danger lies in the misappropriation of traditional Vedic ideas and their rebranding as science. She also warns that eco-Romanticism can lead to Hindu nationalism, and perhaps down a slippery slope to fascism. She is very suspicious of what she refers to as "the Hindu–neo-pagan dialogue," though Emma Tomalin comments that "pagan environmentalists […] are sharply critical of hierarchy and oppression," the aspects of Hinduism that most rankle with Nanda (Tomalin 2009: 172–74).

Important thinkers and movements

Of particular note in the field of religion and ecology is the life work of O. P. Dwivedi, Professor Emeritus at Guelph University and Fellow of the Royal Society of Canada. Dwivedi co-authored the first book on Hinduism and ecology, *Environmental Crisis and Hindu Tradition* (Dwivedi and Tiwari 1987), and has contributed to numerous subsequent collections of essays and has written additional books. His work starts with an examination of the importance of nature in the *Rig Veda*, the Upanisads, the *Mahabharata*, the *Ramayana*, and various Puranas. Mindful of the particular ecology of the subcontinent, and in a certain way anticipating and responding to the astute observations of Ramachandra Guha that Western-style environmentalism will not work in India, Dwivedi outlines five major issues: (1) land degradation; (2) shortage of wood and fodder; (3) forest depletion; (4) excessive use of pesticides and chemical fertilizers; (5) poor environmental regulations. He address specific imbalances that plague both rural and urban India, and suggests four areas of traditional Hinduism that might be instructive for motivating individuals and policy-makers to make improvements: the principle that the supreme being resides in all things, as articulated in the *Srimad Bhagavata Mahapurana* (2.2.41, quoted in Dwivedi 2000: 5); the continuity between human and animal life forms, as taught in the doctrine of reincarnation; the "family" aspect of ecosystems, as described in the *Prthivi Sukta* of the *Atharva Veda*; and the teaching in the *Bhagavad Gita* that humans need to be constantly mindful of the welfare of all beings. Dwivedi makes a specific link between the Western concept of environmental stewardship and the Hindu notion of *dharma*, which he seeks to reinterpret in light of appropriate environmental activism.

Dwivedi (Dwivedi and Tiwari 1987; Dwivedi 2000); Guha (Guha 1989, 2006; Gadgil and Guha 1992); Vandana Shiva (1988, 1999); Pankaj Jain (2011), and others have written about the significance of two movements that have developed local responses to specific environmental problems over the course of India's history: the Bishnois, established in the fifteenth century by Guru Maharaj Jambaji, who continue to enforce firm protection of animals and trees in their region of Rajasthan; and the Chipko movement (Guha 2006), which in the early 1970s successfully resisted logging in Uttar Pradesh. Women served in leadership positions in both. India today has thousands of non-governmental organizations dedicated to ecological restoration, many of which draw inspiration from traditional religious ideas. Some of these organizations critique instances where religious rituals themselves can cause environmental harm. Fireflies Ashram near Bangalore has educated people regarding the ill effects of immersing Ganesh images in water at the end of the festival period. These statues, which can be quite large, in the past have been covered with a highly toxic lead-based red paint. As an alternative, a tradition has been initiated to leave the terracotta statues unpainted so that when they are ceremonially submerged in local ponds, they will not taint the water.

Another example of environmental activism can be found in the work of the lawyer M. C. Mehta, founder and director of Eco Ashram near Rishikesh in northern India and winner of the 1996 Goldman Environmental Prize. He has argued successfully for environmental causes in India's Supreme Court, winning cases for air-quality protection at the Taj Mahal, the conversion of public transport vehicles to compressed natural gas in New Delhi and other cities, and reduced pollution in the Ganges River. At Eco Ashram, a retreat facility on twelve acres in the Himalayan foothills, he trains lawyers from throughout South Asia to face the challenges presented by environmental conditions. In 1989, he initiated the annual Green Marches in the tradition of Gandhi's Salt Marches to raise public awareness of environmental issues. He is also a passionate advocate for children's welfare, seeking to protect child workers employed in toxic industries such as mining and electroplating, with the hope of returning them to the nurturing environment of the classroom. Mehta is currently working on the problem of Himalayan glacier melt. He credits religion with playing an important role in his formation as a child, noting that: "When I was a child my father was a very learned person in the sense that he knew the Quran and he knew all about the Hindu religion and used to read the Gita everyday. My father said that we are all human beings; we should all live happily, and should not discourage each other."

Asian religions in a global context

The religions of India have influenced world culture deeply and widely. Hinduism and Buddhism spread throughout Southeast Asia and Indonesia over a thousand years ago. Buddhism has been influential for centuries throughout Central Asia, China, Korea, and Japan, and the forms of Islam that now prevail in Malaysia and Indonesia bear the mark and form of their South Asian origin. Starting with the European romantics, the Dutch and German philosophers such as Schopenhauer and Nietzsche, and the New England transcendentalists, Indian philosophy has become globally influential in many ways. Buddhist forms of meditation and the practice of Hatha Yoga have become commonplace for Christians and Jews. Many prominent American Buddhists are actively involved in environmental philosophy, linking the Asian tradition of engaged Buddhism with eco-friendly lifestyle changes. Stephanie Kaza's book *Hooked! Buddhist Writings on Greed, Desire, and the Urge to Consume* has been a top seller for Shambhala Press (Kaza 2005).

Similarly, the far-flung Yoga community has linked its chosen form of practice with the ideals of environmentalism, giving rise to organizations, online communities, conferences, special magazine issues, and books devoted to the adoption of environmental ideals, including vegetarianism, as part of the practice of Yoga. With over 18 million individuals practicing Yoga in the United States, this can have a far-reaching effect. On the more philosophical side of Yoga, the founder of the Deep Ecology, Arne Naess, was a Gandhian scholar, deeply influenced by Yoga as described in the *Bhagavad Gita* (see Jacobsen in Chapple 2009). Philosopher Henryk Skolimowski (1991, 1994) wrote extensively about the relationship between meditation, Yoga, and ecological values. Several scholars offer reflections on Yoga and ecology in the book *Yoga and Ecology: Dharma for the Earth*, (Chapple 2009), in which Yoga may be seen as a modern application of proto-science through progressive meditations on correlations between body and universe. Practitioner David Frawley (2004) and scholar Georg Feuerstein (2007) have offered deeply personal accounts of their commitment to environmentalism in relationship to Yoga practice.

If one were to generalize about the nature of religion and ecology in light of Asian religions, one would begin by emphasizing the plurality of approaches. In India, each village would be cognizant of the major deities, such as Vishnu the Preserver and his *avataras*. These include Krishna and his wife Rukmani, and consort Radha and the thousands of his cowherd girl Gopi devotees. Another well known *avatara* of Vishnu is Rama, always seen with his wife Sita. The iconography of these incarnations includes the companion animals associated with each: the cow with Krishna, and the monkey Hanuman with Rama. The many theologies associated with Krishna find multiple proclamations of his intimacy with nature, such as "space, air, fire, water, earth, planets, all creatures, directions, trees and plants, rivers, and seas, all are organs of God's body." Similarly, one can find an abundance of nature imagery in the holy family of Lord Siva, the god of meditation and death. His companion animal, the bull, evokes both strength and the economic significance of the symbiotic relationship between cattle and humans throughout the subcontinent. His wife, Devi or Sakti, takes multiple forms, beautiful and horrific, from Bhu Devi the earth goddess to Kali the bringer of death. Through their union, all material existence emerges. One of their sons, Ganesh, has the head of an elephant and rides a mouse. The other son, Skandha or Kartikeya, has a peacock as his mount. The boundary between animal and human throughout the Indian subcontinent continues to be quite fluid, with animals, real and mythic, entering one's awareness and experience on a daily basis.

In addition to these pan-Indian deities, each of which exhibits numerous pastoral connections indicating intimacy with nature, every village will also have deities known only within its particular locale. One very popular residence for these deities is in trees, which Albertina Nugteren describes as possessing five primary symbolic meanings: verticality, centrality, immortality, fertility, and generosity (Nugteren 2005). Throughout India, one can witness trees under worship, venerated for their medicinal properties, for their wish-granting qualities, and for their sheer beauty. Similarly, each river becomes a locus for worship. Abundant classical and vernacular literature attests to the presence of the goddess in rivers. Despite their initial rejection of the idea that any river could be sullied, many religious leaders have advocated for the clean-up of industrial waste that has polluted most of India's rivers.

As the world continues to grapple with an expanding list of environmental dilemmas, from chemical pollution to food issues, climate change, and species loss, religions will continue to be a source of solace, providing meaning and ethical encouragement to improve human behavior. Traditional religions will be challenged by the theological shifts required. No longer can a sole concern with human salvation be sufficient as a religious paradigm. For the prophetic monotheisms, whose creation narrative has already been challenged by modern science, an interest in panentheism, incarnationalism, and a renewed emphasis on the immanence of God are emerging. For shamanic and Asian faith traditions, whose world-views are, in some instances, a bit more Earth-friendly, a new approach to ethics is needed. The asceticism of Hinduism, Buddhism, and Jainism, generally associated with religious renunciation, can be instructive and helpful for coping with the looming issues of over-consumption and increased levels of pollution as the Asian world continues to model itself on the Western consumerist paradigm. Mahatma Gandhi pioneered in this new frontier of abstemiousness, advocating and modeling adherence to non-violence, truth, non-hoarding, sexual restraint, and living with minimal possessions. Though not a particularly popular figure at present, the path he forged remains instructive as the religions of Asia seek models to understand the integrity of nature and the human place within ecology.

In summary, Asian traditions present a rich challenge to thinking about nature and ecology. On the one hand, the traditional lore and literature, particularly in India, speaks of nature and animals with great fondness and intimacy. On the other hand, some aspects of contemporary urban Asia seem to be crowding out animals, shutting out nature. As we examine not only ancient texts, but also modern movements and practices, we see many avenues for dialogue. By emphasizing the relationship between humans and the natural world, Asian traditions may selectively be seen as "Earth-friendly" and perhaps useful as source of inspiration in the emerging ecological age.

References

Alley, Kelly D. (2000) "Separate Domains: Hinduism, Politics, and Environmental Pollution" in *Hinduism and Ecology: The Intersection of Earth, Sky, and Water*, Christopher Key Chapple and Mary Evelyn Tucker (eds), Cambridge, MA: Center for the Study of World Religions and Harvard University Press, 355–88.

——(2002) *On the Banks of the Ganga: When Wastewater Meets a Sacred River*, Detroit, MI: University of Michigan Press.

Berry, Thomas and Brian Swimme (1992) *The Universe Story: From the Primordial Flaring Forth to the Ecozoic Era*, San Francisco, CA: HarperSanFrancisco.

Botkin, Daniel (1990) *Discordant Harmonies: A New Ecology for the Twenty-First Century*, New York: Oxford University Press.

Bruun, Ole and Arne Kalland (1995) *Asian Perceptions of Nature: A Critical Approach*, Richmond, UK: Curzon Press.

Callicott, J. Baird and Roger T. Ames (1989) *Nature in Asian Traditions of Thought: Essays in Environmental Philosophy*, Albany, NY: SUNY Press.

Chapple, Christopher Key (ed.) (1994) *Ecological Prospects: Scientific, Religious, and Aesthetic Perspectives*, Albany, NY: SUNY Press.

——(ed.) (2002) *Jainism and Ecology: Nonviolence in the Web of Life*, Cambridge, MA: Center for the Study of World Religions and Harvard University Press.

——(2008) "Asceticism and the Environment: Jainism, Buddhism, and Yoga," *Crosscurrents* 57 (4): 514–26.

——(ed.) (2009) *Yoga and Ecology: Dharma for the Earth*, Hampton, VA: Deepak Heritage Press.

Chapple, Christopher Key and Mary Evelyn Tucker (eds) (2000) *Hinduism and Ecology: The Intersection of Earth, Sky, and Water*, Cambridge, MA: Center for the Study of World Religions and Harvard University Press.

Cobb, John B. (1972) *Is It Too Late?: A Theology of Ecology*, Beverly Hills, CA: Bruce.

Cowell, E. B. (ed.) (1895–1907) *The Jataka or Stories of the Buddha's Former Births*, six volumes, London: Pali Text Society.

Dwivedi, O. P. (2000) "Dharmic Ecology," in *Hinduism and Ecology: The Intersection of Earth, Sky, and Water*, Christopher Key Chapple and Mary Evelyn Tucker (eds), Cambridge, MA: Center for the Study of World Religions and Harvard University Press.

Dwivedi, O. P. and B. N. Tiwari (1987) *Environmental Crisis and Hindu Religion*, New Delhi: Gitanjali Publishing House.

Feldhaus, Anne (1995) *Water and Womanhood: Religious Meanings of Rivers in Maharashtra*, New York: Oxford University Press.

Feuerstein, Georg (2007) *Green Yoga*, Eastend, Saskatchewan: Traditional Yoga Studies.

Frawley, David (2004) *Yoga and the Sacred Fire: Self-Realization and Planetary Transformation*, Twin Lakes, WI: Lotus Press.

Gadgil, Madhav and Ramachandra Guha (1992) *This Fissured Land: An Ecological History of India*, Delhi: Oxford University Press.

Guha, Ramachandra (1989) "Radical American Environmentalism: A Third World Critique," *Environmental Ethics* 11(1): 71–83.

——(2006) *How Much Should a Person Consume?: Environmentalism in India and the United States*, Berkeley, CA: University of California Press.

Haberman, David (2006) *River of Love in an Age of Pollution: The Yamuna River of Northern India*. Berkeley, CA: University of California Press.

Jacobi, Hermann (trans.) (1968) *Acaranga Sutra*, in *Jaina Sutras, Part I: The Akaranga Sutra, The Kalpa Sutra*, New York: Dover.

Jain, Pankaj (2011) *Dharma and Ecology of Hindu Communities: Sustenance and Sustainabililty*, Surrey, UK: Ashgate.

Kaza, Stephanie (2005) *Hooked! Buddhist Writings on Greed, Desire, and the Urge to Consume*, Boston, MA: Shambhala.

Nanda, Meera (2002) *Breaking the Spell of Dharma and Other Essays*, New Delhi: Three Essays Collective.

——(2005) *The Wrongs of the Religious Right: Reflections on Science, Secularism, and Hindutva*, New Delhi: Three Essays Collective.

Nelson, Lance (2000) "Reading the *Bhagavadgita* from an Ecological Perspective" in *Hindusim and Ecology: The Intersection of Earth, Sky, and Water*, Christopher Key Chapple and Mary Evelyn Tucker (eds), Cambridge, MA: Center for the Study of World Religions and Harvard University Press, 127–64.

Nugteren, Albertina (2005) *Belief, Bounty and Beauty: Rituals around Sacred Trees in India*, Leiden: Brill.

Panditaraja Jagannatha (2007) *The Saving Waves of the Milk-White Ganga*, John Cort (trans.), Calcutta: Writers Workshop.

Shiva, Vandana (1988) *Staying Alive: Women, Ecology, and Development*, London: Zed Books.

——(1999) "Women in the Forest," in *Ethical Perspectives on Environmental Issues in India*, George James (ed.), New Delhi: A.P.H. Publishing, 73–114.

Skolimowski, Henryk (1981) *Eco-philosophy: Designing New Tactics for Living*, Boston, MA: M. Boyars.

——(1993) *A Sacred Place to Dwell: Living with Reverence upon the Earth*, Rockport, ME: Element Books.

——(1994) *EcoYoga: Practice and Meditations for Walking in Beauty on the Earth*, London: Gaia Books.

——(1999) *Dharma, Ecology, and Wisdom in the Third Millennium*, New Delhi: Concept Publishing.

Taylor, Bron R. (ed.) (2005) *The Encyclopedia of Religion and Nature*, London and New York: Thoemmes Continuum.

Tomalin, Emma (2009) *Biodivinity and Biodiversity: The Limits to Religious Environmentalism*, Surrey, UK: Ashgate.

Tucker, Mary Evelyn and John Grim (eds) (1994) *Worldviews and Ecology: Religion, Philosophy, and the Environment*, Maryknoll, NY: Orbis.

——(1997) "Series Foreword" in *Buddhism and Ecology: The Interconnection of Dharma and Deeds*, Cambridge, MA: Harvard University Center for the Study of World Religions, xv-xxxi.

Further reading

For an overview of Asian religions in relation to environment, see my *Nonviolence to Animals, Earth, and Self in Asian Traditions* (1993). For in-depth Hindu perspectives, see *Purifying the Earthly Body of God: Religion and Ecology in Hindu India*, edited by Lance Nelson (1998). For details on the context of India, see Madhav Gadgil and Ramachandra Guha, *This Fissured Land: An Ecological History of India* (cited above) and *Ecology and Equity: The Use and Abuse of Nature in Contemporary India* (1995). The Harvard Religions of the World and Ecology series includes volumes on Buddhism, Hindusim, Jainism, Confucianism, and Shinto, some of which are cited in this chapter. Additionally, the website of the Forum on Religion and Ecology at Yale (http://fore.research.yale.edu) and the *Encyclopedia of Religion and Nature*, edited by Bron Taylor (cited above), are valuable resources. Two academic journals publish important articles in this field: *Worldviews: Global Religions, Culture, and Ecology* (Brill) and *Journal for the Study of Religion, Nature, and Culture* (Equinox).

Popular periodicals such as *Yoga Journal* and *LA Yoga* include monthly features on Yoga and ecology. The website of the Green Yoga Association (www.greenyoga.org) indicates a range of activities.

33
MEANING-MAKING PRACTICES AND ENVIRONMENTAL HISTORY

Toward an ecotonal theology

Whitney A. Bauman

In the introduction to this section (Chapter 30), Barrett and Jordan make a valid point in identifying the problem of trying to make meaning in a world that is constantly in flux from within meaning-making systems that assume some amount of stasis and universality. The problem of how to make meaning in a world that is now globalized, culturally and economically, and in the face of planetary environmental crises – such as global climate change – is a relatively new one for humanity. Furthermore, the critique of an idealized understanding of "nature" as static and/or wilderness is important in locating the ways in which cultures co/construct understandings of "nature." This means that our understandings of "nature" can adapt and change according to how well they promote the well-being of the planetary community. Destabilizing concepts of nature is also important because it counters the multiple sites of identity oppressions that are coded as "natural:" sexism, racism, heterosexism, etc. Although I don't think the authors' sweeping critique of "religion and ecology" to date is entirely accurate – there are, for example, many thinkers in the field who have thought about "existential shame," sin, and the tragic side inherent in life (such as the fact that something must die for something else to live), and who have thought of nature/ecology as "in flux" (e.g. McDaniel 1989; Ruether 1992; Wallace 1996; Gebara 1999; Keller 2003; Kaufman 2004) – I do think that the charge to rethink how and where meaning-making processes materialize in the world is very important. It is this task to which the rest of this chapter is devoted.

In what follows, I put forward a proposal for evaluating meaning-making practices that could be understood as the practice of "spiritual cartography" (Tweed 2006: 112–13). As such, the analysis of meaning-making (both within and outside of the context of "traditional" religions) becomes a component of environmental history that charts how meaning making *matters* (in and to) the world in three basic ways, which I am calling theo-metaphorical materializations, institutional materializations, and moral/ethical materializations. What I am arguing for is what many other scholars have described as a "post-foundational" understanding of religion and nature (van Huyssteen 1996; Kaufman 2004; Taylor 2007; Bauman 2009). This chapter is a small effort to develop an ecotonal theology from what others and I describe as common, shifting grounds, rather than an ecotheology based on foundations (Keller and Kearns 2007: 1–20). Common grounds suggest movement, shifts and tectonic plates, shaking, and change, yet ground is all we have to live and stand on. We do make claims about meaning and value, but from these common shifting grounds, rather than from eternal, ethereal foundations. An ecotone is a transition space between two different ecosystems, in which a blending of the two ecosystems occurs. To extend this metaphor for the purposes of this chapter, we live in a time of the "in-between," of flux and change. The planet is currently in an "ecotonal" phase, the evidence of which is the process of economic and cultural globalization and planetary environmental problems such as global climate change. In such an ecotonal period, meaning-making practices have the capacity to be intentionally transformative: they are practices that highlight the perforated boundaries between self–other, human–nature, male–female, religion–science, etc. Because they highlight the boundaries that make up our identities, places, and spaces, they can also help to renegotiate these boundaries. This type of ecotonal meaning is important for a world "on the move" due to forces of globalization, technology, and an emerging planetary conscience. It is to these three aspects of our contemporary context that I now turn.

The postmodern, planetary context

Globalization and the localization of meaning

Though intercultural exchange has always existed, the amount of intercultural exchange began to explode exponentially with the process of European colonization. On the heels of this forced exchange, the scientific revolution began significantly to improve instruments by which we could understand the natural world and, as a result, "make use" of the rest of the natural world via more and more complex technologies. Fast-forward to our current context, where we can travel, communicate, and exchange goods globally (assuming one has the economic status to do so). We can, quite literally, move goods and affect places all over the globe just with a few clicks of the mouse or taps on a touch-pad. Furthermore, we can obtain multiple perspectives on just about any area of inquiry imaginable. In this context, meanings are communicated and reproduced with great ease. Barrett and Jordan write of "a world that has no center" (Chapter 30 in this volume). Whereas the extant religious traditions emerge from the axial age, a time when universal meaning was much easier to proclaim and assume because people's worlds were much smaller and news traveled much more slowly, our contemporary context is one of multiple meanings, multiple truth claims, and multiple meaning-making systems (many of which are not complementary). What is one to do with the proliferation of meanings available when addressing questions such as "what is good?," "what is valuable?," or "what is most meaningful in life?" Surely, and as many have suggested, we can't merely transpose the same universal meaning-making practices onto such a radically altered context. Perhaps then, meaning-making practices ought to be understood as located within specific contexts. This is not giving up universalism for relativism. In fact, the universal versus relative dualism is a false one (Warren 2000: 156). Both universalism and relativism ignore living contexts: one suggests the same everywhere, regardless of context; while the other suggests anything goes, again regardless of context. A contextual understanding of meaning-making suggests that meaning evolves from within living human communities over time, and that these meanings in turn materialize in social relationships, institutions, and human–Earth relations.

Finally, such a proliferation of meaning-making practices means that there is room to converse, persuade, and dialogue toward alternative futures, and that these practices can be held accountable. This type of dialogue has largely been the project of "religion and ecology" as a field since the 1970s. The work of the Forum on Religion and Ecology has been particularly important here (Tucker and Grim 1997–2003). Expanding on this work to include meaning-making practices outside of the world's religion are the International Society for the Study of Religion, Nature & Culture, and *The Encyclopedia of Religion and Nature* (Taylor 2005). Both of these organizations and the publications emerging from them are about reshaping meaning-making practices from within a planetary consciousness.

The industrial revolution, technology, and the "double-death" of nature

A second major factor affecting contemporary meaning-making practices is the industrial revolution and the rapid development of technologies. Currently, more people on the face of the Earth (for the first time in history) live in urban rather than rural areas. Couple this with the fact that most environmental ethics, including those emerging from "religion and ecology," are in large part developed with the idea of a pre-industrial, euro-western understanding of nature as wilderness, or at least "without humans." This romantic understanding of nature was a direct response to the industrial revolution and was efficacious in drawing attention to the ways in which technology and industrialization affect the rest of the natural world and our understanding of humanity. However, just as meaning-making projects in the West have gone through the "Death of God" (read death of the omni-male God in the sky), so now we have gone through what Carolyn Merchant refers to as the Death of Nature, and what Bill McKibben refers to as the End of Nature (Merchant 1980; McKibben 1989). This "double-death" means that "nature," through the scientific revolution, changed from a living thing into dead matter for use in the "progress" of human civilization *and* that some sort of "pure" nature no longer exists (if it ever did). The processes of genetic manipulation of animals and plants, global climate change, and the movement of species of plants and animals all over the globe, among other things, all make it impossible to "return" to some pre-modern nature, and impossible to maintain the false distinctions between human–Earth, culture–nature, and history–biology. In other words, we exist in an evolving world always, already, as natural–cultural beings (Haraway 1990; Kaufman 2004; Latour 2004). Rather than thinking human projects such as "culture" and "technology" outside of the rest of the natural world, perhaps they are better seen (as are humans in general) as emerging out of the process of planetary evolution. Rather than maintaining some sort of human exceptionalism from the rest of the natural world, we might begin to re-narrate ourselves back into the planetary community as meaning-making creatures (Peterson 2001). Nature, human, technology, other animals, plants, minerals, atoms, genes, chemicals: all are a part of the ongoing process of nature naturing, and how we as meaning-making creatures make sense out of this process matters in, and to, the rest of the planetary community. This brings me to the third aspect of our contemporary context: the image of a single planet.

The "Earth Rise" image: sciences and the emergence of planetary consciousness

Again, most extant meaning-making practices have their historical roots in a time before the scientific revolution. Most of them, especially within the world religions, adopted the cosmological thinking of the time and read meaning into the world through these cosmological lenses. Fast-forward to the Copernican and Galilean revolutions, the Darwinian and evolutionary revolution, and the quantum, cosmological, and genetic revolutions of the last century, and the world looks a lot different. Much of the dialogue in religion and science addresses these issues. Yet still, meaning-making practices have not sufficiently adapted to these new understandings of the world. Religion and ecology, and other forms of religious naturalisms that take these sciences seriously, provide us with ways to re-create meaning in this planetary context.

Finally, the image of "Earth Rise," which allows me to speak of the planetary context, has not yet fully taken hold of our imagination. The fact that the "Earth Rise" image of 1969 marks the first time that human beings saw the "little blue ball" floating through space has radical implications. All histories, civilizations, scientific knowledge, religions, art, evolution, etc. take place on this one, small planet. This is well described in a recent documentary by Zeitgeist Films, *Earth Days* (2009), which explores the history of the modern, Western environmental movement. A planetary consciousness is not a call for the leveling of difference between humans, nor of life on Earth in general. Rather, it gives us a common ground, a planetary context, a sense of humility about all of our technological and meaning-making projects. The effect of the image may aesthetically persuade us (as many religions do) to expand our circle of ethical and moral concern past that of self, kinship, nation, and even species, and toward that of the planetary. We are "in" Earth rather than merely "on" it. All of the evolutionary and cultural processes that lead up to me typing this chapter out on my computer take place in this context. In fact, without the things we refer to as "nature," as "culture," as "science," and as "technology," this image of the Earth from space would not be possible. Our ideas, and our technologies, and we ourselves are radically *of* this planet. It is from within this context – globalized, technologized, and planetary – that we might begin to articulate a type of ecotonal meaning-making project.

Mattering values and ideas

Historically, human projects of epistemology and ontology have found their justification in some version of transcendent ideas or ideals (e.g. philosophy and religion), or in some sort of natural essence (e.g. material reductionisms in the sciences), so that either the transcendent realm of ideas/ideals *or* the material world is "the really real." From this perspective, once either the material or the ideal is wed with political, economic, and/or cultural power, they become the site at which knowledge is written over the world. It is in this place of justification where the immaterial is written into the material world. I argue that an integrated approach to environmental analysis and study must include study of the processes by which religious ideals, religious values, religious imaginings of a "better" future, and religious understandings of hope help "matter" our bodies and the worlds around us. Regardless of the truth of various religious beliefs and traditions, religions "matter" the world around us. That is, religious ideas and institutions have very material-real ways of shaping human bodies, other Earth bodies, and human–Earth relations.

On the one hand, this insight is not so new. Ever since Terrance Glacken's *Traces on the Rhodian Shore* and Lynn White's critique of Christianity were published, religious and environmental scholars have tussled over the ways in which ideas "matter" the world around us (Glacken 1967; White 1967). However, this tussling often involves apologetics on the side of religious studies, and supersessionist arguments on the side of environmental and other scientists. These are both, perhaps, appropriate initial responses, but the evolution of the implications requires more sophisticated analyses. In a modest attempt to bring new intellectual tools to bear on these relationships, I argue for at least three levels of analysis: (1) theo-metaphorical materializations; (2) institutional–ritual materializations; and (3) moral–ethical materializations. All of these materializations assume that human beings, if nothing else, are meaning-making creatures, and that the meanings, narratives, ideas, and values that are fashioned "matter" the human and "more-than-human" world.

Theo-metaphorical materializations

Theo-metaphorical materializations are perhaps the most familiar way in which religions "matter" the world. From Roderick Nash's *Wilderness and the American Mind*, through Carolyn Merchant's *Reinventing Eden*, to my own work that analyzes how the Christian doctrine of "creation out of nothing" materializes in colonial understandings of *terra nullius* and private property, and many others, theo-metaphorical materializations recognize the ways in which ideas shape the more than human world and our understandings thereof (Nash 1967; Merchant 2003; Bauman 2009).

On the flip side of this understanding, natures also shape our theo-metaphorical projects. Theodor Hiebert's *The Yahwist's Landscape: Nature and Religion in Early Israel* (1996) and Daniel Hillel's *The Natural History of the Bible: An Environmental*

Exploration of the Hebrew Scriptures (2006) are two good examples of this. The work of Sean Esbjörn-Hargens and Michael Zimmerman in *Integral Ecology* captures this aspect of theo-metaphorical materializations well. They write, "Integral Ecology is the study of the subjective and objective aspects of organisms in relationship to their intersubjective and interobjective environment at all levels of depth and complexity" (Esbjörn-Hargens and Zimmerman 2009: 168–69). In other words, ideas, values, and the other "invisible" components of human thought and culture are just as real and should not be left out of scientific analyses. This aspect of an environmental history of religious studies is significant because it grounds our meaning-making practices within the planetary community.

As Judith Butler notes, "To know the significance of something is to know how and why it matters, where 'to matter' means at once 'to materialize' and 'to mean'" (Butler 1993: 32). This focus on the materiality of ideas may help us to understand better how ideas unfold and shape the natural–cultural worlds around us. Thus it provides a way of analyzing environmentally how meaning-making matters in the world for better or worse.

Finally, the understanding of meaning as theo-metaphorical materializations navigates between the false distinction of ideas/matter or spirit/body that have arguably been one of the sources of anthropogenic forcings of environmental problems. This move suggests that understanding religion as projection is not a demotion of religion, rather that ideas are very real and "matter" the world around us in important ways. They are indeed a type of communal, socio-cultural projection, that shape, and are shaped by, the living communities of peoples in the present. Equally important, they shape, and are shaped by, the rest of the natural world around us. Without getting too technical, one might say that "religions" and "meaning-making" processes in general are akin to what Deleuze and Guattari (1987) mean when they talk about the virtual as real. Though the "virtual" has multiple meanings for Deleuze, one such meaning is the way in which the immaterial is diverse and constitutive of the material (Deleuze 1994: 183).

As an example, let us focus for a moment on the world-wide web. From *Facebook* to *Amazon*, *Wikipedia* to *Google News*, *Second Life* to *eBay*, the diverse and complex virtual is shaping the world in very material-real ways. It can be as indirect as the sense of well-being one feels from communicating with far-away friends on *Facebook*, that then carries over into his/her interactions with others throughout the day. Or it can be as direct as the fact that one can literally move energy, materials, and goods around the world through the virtual web. Or think of the energy grid used to support the world-wide web, or the materials that go into computer technologies. The list goes on. My point is that religions and meanings, too, have their virtual technologies that "matter" the world around us. I have just mentioned the more conceptual and theological technologies of meaning-making practices, and now move to the institutional and ethical/moral materializations.

Institutional materializations

Both "organized" religions and other modes of meaning-making practices support, and are supported by, institutions. These institutions often affect directly the local natures/bodies that they inhabit. Taking just one example from the tradition that I am most familiar with, the spread of Christianity through Europe during the Middle Ages saw the razing of sacred forests and the building of cathedrals. These cathedrals literally moved mountains. Ornate silver and gold decorations of the Catholic Church aided mining projects. Another example might be the ways in which plants, water, food, animals, etc. are used in religious ceremonies and rituals. How have certain ritualistic foci on specific elements changed the natures inhabited by specific religions?

Again, the flip side of this is that specific geographic regions in which meaning-making institutions emerge shape the very architecture and ritual of those traditions. Think of the distinct architecture and rituals associated with a mosque, Hindu temple, Shinto shrine, or Catholic cathedral. How might the various contexts out of which these institutional architectures emerged contribute to their differences? Again, this second aspect is important in that it grounds institutional aesthetics, cultural aesthetics, within a planetary, if not bio-regional, context.

It is this aspect of meaning-making that is the most overtly "performative" (Butler 1994). The rituals and institutions shape bodies in the world: whether it be the rock used to build the cathedral, or the human bodies participating in the ritual. These are the practices by which the power structures of a religion (or other meaning-making adventure) quite literally persuade and enforce their power in the world (Foucault 1972). Again, let me provide a somewhat alternative example: technology as a religion (cf. Noble 1997).

Most people will probably not understand "technology" as a "religion" in any traditional sense of the word. Here, I understand technology as a meaning-making practice of the sciences. How is it that the balance of power shifted away from religions and toward that of the sciences, especially in Western countries during the twentieth century? Through analyzing the persuasive power of science – through its technologies – one can begin to see how scientific technologies are meaning-making practices. The sciences are more directly able to create things that improve human life: they allow us to see better, hear better, heal better, communicate better, eat better, etc. They are, then, much more persuasive than, say, the tools of theology or philosophy. The materializations of the latter two are much less direct than, say, a new Mac PowerBook that enables you to do your job effectively and communicate with the rest of the world. However, these very technologies indeed change what it means to be human and what it means to be alive (Hefner 2003). Try to get through one day without the use of any modern technology, and I think you will find it impossible to do. In fact, even though many environmentalists are luddites, environmentalism would be impossible without these technologies. We make meaning out of the world through these technologies and they, in turn, allow us to perform the understanding of the world that science provides us with.

One could also point out the negative meanings associated with technology, particularly those of the fossil fuel and nuclear industries. Or, moving beyond technology, one can think of "consumerism" or "free market capitalism" as meaning-making processes that make meaning through institutions and practices (e.g. Cobb and Daly 1989). Institutions and practices *persuade* us to perform certain identities, including what it means to live a "good" life and what it means to live a "bad" life.

These rituals and practices then crystallize into ethical and moral shorthand, or guides for daily living. It is to this final materialization of meaning-making practices that I now turn.

Moral/ethical materializations

Exploring moral/ethical materializations involves examining specific habits and ethical mandates supported by various religions/meaning-making programs. More specifically, it takes seriously that the distinctions we have made between self–other (identity), human–animal (human uniqueness), culture–nature (exceptional dualism), are all the result of enacted boundaries, and some of these have been to the peril of the planetary community. Thus the habits and ethical mandates enacted by humans from within systems of meanings are the very means by which "imagined communities" materialize and reinforce bodies in the world (Anderson 1983). "Mattered" bodies are not, then, the foundational point from which inquiry begins; rather, matter is "a process of materialization that stabilizes over time to produce the effect of boundary, fixity, and surface we call matter" (Butler 1993: 9). These habits and ethical mandates, these actions, then "matter" bodies, and this mattering returns to institutions for their justifications, which further rely on theo-metaphorical matterings for their successes and failures: the three matterings are interrelated.

In terms of habits and ethical mandates, and according to much scholarship in religion-and-ecology, extant world religions have done a good job of reinforcing habits and practices that write humans outside of the rest of the natural world. Many in this field are now looking to reshape not only religious thinking (the topic of theo-metaphorical materializations), but also ritual and practice. The transformation of kosher to eco-kosher would be one example of this. Emerging "religious naturalisms" – I would include the practice of restoration ecology here – are also very much involved in creating new habits and ethical mandates that re-place humans within the rest of the natural world: that re-write our bodies as Earth-bodies. What practices might develop from an understanding of human beings as an emergent part of the evolutionary history of the planet, and how would these practices "matter" our bodies and other Earth bodies differently? What institutions will emerge to support these practices, and through what theo-metaphorical materializations will these institutions be justified?

Conclusions: ecotonal meaning-making

For a planetary community that is "on the move," meaning-making practices will be more effective if they address us in our emerging contexts as varied communities of evolving planetary creatures. In this sense, meaning-making practices need to be, in part, about the process of deterritorializing and reterritorializing (Deleuze and Guattari 1987). That is, religions and meaning-making practices are not merely about creating a sense of well-being, wholeness, and stability. They are also about destabilizing structures that do not promote the health of the planetary community. As

Latour notes, "religion […] does everything to constantly redirect attention by systematically breaking the will to go away, to ignore, to be indifferent, blasé, bored" (Latour 2003: 7). Religion is precisely of this world and focuses our senses on the contours of the planet and our relations therein. Focusing on the contours of the planet means precisely paying attention to the diverse, evolving contexts of which we are a part. This understanding of transitional or ecotonal meaning-making has the capacity to break open ossified meaning-making practices onto the contours of the diverse, evolving planetary community.

It is my hope that this method of analysis will enable us to move beyond seeing "religion and ecology" as having to do merely with "environmental ethics." Ethical systems are touchstones that are useful, given our finitude and inability to constantly rethink all aspects of life. Ethics are important, but there are also many other ways in which "religion" and meaning-making are relevant from an ecological perspective. Religion, and even more broadly, meaning-making practices, help to re-matter humans and re-think the Earth.

It *already is* the case that humans are beginning to think themselves into the rest of the natural world: globalization, planetarity, social geography, nature–culture, religious naturalism, religion and ecology, terrapolitanism, global citizens, and other tropes are evidence of this. The movement in governments, academics, and in at least international politics is toward some type of understanding of humans-as-primarily-earthlings. The questions now for religious reflection as environmental history are: How do we want to become? What visions of future-nature do our theo-metaphorical, institutional, and moral/ethical materializations work toward? How have our traditions emerged from planetary evolution, and how do they return to affect it? How will our own habit formations and ethical actions help shape future co-creations of the planetary community? Religion understood as meaning-making, if nothing else, is a very real part of the planetary community, and it is ignored at the peril of the future of that community. In this sense, religion and science desperately need one another in the project of transforming human identities into planetary creatures.

References

Anderson, Benedict (1983) *Imagined Communities: Reflections on the Origin and Spread of Nationalism*, London: Verso.

Bauman, Whitney (2009) *Theology, Creation and Environmental Ethics: From* Creatio ex Nihilo *to* Terra Nullius, New York: Routledge.

Butler, Judith (1993) *Bodies that Matter: On the Discursive Limits of Sex*, New York: Routledge.

Castree, Noel and Bruce Braun (eds) (2001) *Social Nature: Theory, Practice and Politics*, Malden, MA: Blackwell.

Cobb, John and Herman Daly (1989) *For the Common Good: Redirecting the Economy Toward Community, the Environment, and a Sustainable Future*, Boston, MA: Beacon.

Deleuze, Gilles (1994) *Difference and Repetition*, first English translation, New York: Columbia University Press.

Deleuze, Gilles and Felix Guattari (1987) *A Thousand Plateaus: Capitalism and Schizophrenia*, Minneapolis, MN: University of Minnesota Press.

Esbjörn-Hargens, Sean and Michael Zimmerman (2009) *Integral Ecology: Uniting Multiple Perspectives on the Natural World*, Boston, MA: Integral Books.

Foucault, Michel (1972) *The Archeology of Knowledge and the Discourse on Language*, first English translation, New York: Pantheon Books.

Glacken, Terence (1967) *Traces on the Rhodian Shore*, Berkeley, CA: University of California Press.

Haraway, Donna (1990) *Simians, Cyborgs and Women: The Reinvention of Nature*, New York: Routledge.

Hefner, Phil (2003) *Technology and Human Becoming*, Minneapolis, MN: Fortress.

Hiebert, Theodor (1996) *The Yahwist's Landscape: Nature and Religion in Early Israel*, Oxford: Oxford University Press.

Hillel, Daniel (2006) *The Natural History of the Bible: An Environmental Exploration of the Hebrew Scriptures*, New York: Columbia University Press.

van Huyssteen, J. Wentzel (1996) *Essays in Postfoundational Theology*, Grand Rapids, MI: William B. Eerdmans.

Kaufman, Gordon (2004) *In the Beginning ... Creativity?*, Minneapolis, MN: Fortress Press.

Keller, Catherine (2003) *Face of the Deep: A Theology of Becoming*, New York: Routledge.

Keller, Catherine and Laurel Kearns (eds) (2007) *EcoSpirit: Religions and Philosophies for the Earth*, New York: Fordham University Press.

Latour, Bruno (2004) *The Politics of Nature: How to Bring the Sciences into Democracy*, Cambridge, MA: Harvard University Press.

——(2003) "'Thou Shall Not Freeze-Frame' or How not to Misunderstand the Science and Religion Debate," www.bruno-latour.fr/articles/article/86-FREEZE%20new.html.

McDaniel, Jay (1989) *Of God and Pelicans: A Theology of Reverence for Life*, Louisville, KY: Westminster John Knox.

McKibben, Bill (1989) *The End of Nature*, New York: Anchor Books.

Merchant, Carolyn (1980) *The Death of Nature: Women, Ecology and the Scientific Revolution*, New York: Harper Collins.

——(2003) *Reinventing Eden: The Fate of Nature in Western Culture*, New York: Routledge.

Morton, Timothy (2007) *Ecology Without Nature: Rethinking Environmental Aesthetics*, Cambridge, MA: Harvard University Press.

Nash, Roderick (1967) *Wilderness and the American Mind*, New Haven, CT: Yale University Press.

Noble, David (1997) *The Religion of Technology: The Divinity of Man and the Spirit of Invention*, New York: Penguin.

Peterson, Anna (2001) *Being Human: Ethics, the Environment and our Place in the World*, Berkeley, CA: University of California Press.

Ruether, Rosemary R. (1992) *Gaia and God: An Ecofeminist Theology of Earth Healing*, New York: HarperCollins.

Taylor, Bron (2005) *The Encyclopedia of Religion and Nature*, two volumes, New York: Continuum.

Taylor, Mark C. (2007) *After God*, Chicago, IL: University of Chicago Press.

Tucker, Mary Evelyn and John Grim (eds) (1997–2003) *Religions of the World and Ecology*, nine volumes, Cambridge, MA: Harvard University Press.

Tweed, Thomas (2006) *Crossing and Dwelling: A Theory of Religion*, Cambridge, MA: Harvard University Press.

Wallace, Mark (1996) *Fragments of the Spirit: Nature, Violence, and the Renewal of Creation*, New York: Continuum.

Warren, Karen J. (2000) *Ecofeminist Philosophy: A Western Perspective on What it is and Why it Matters*, Lanham, MD: Rowman & Littlefield.

White, Lynn (1967) "The Historical Roots of Our Ecological Crisis," *Science* 155 (3767): 1203–7.
Zizek, Slavoj (2008) *In Defense of Lost Causes*, London: Verso.

Further reading

For in-depth analysis of world religions and ecology, see the nine-volume series *World Religions and Ecology* (Tucker and Grim 1997–2003, cited above). Each volume brings together a number of scholars to address a specific tradition (Buddhism, Hinduism, Islam, etc.) and ecology. Also helpful as a reference is the *Encyclopedia of Religion and Nature* (Taylor 2005). For those interested in reading more about postfoundational understandings of nature, a good collection of essays is *Social Nature: Theory, Practice, and Politics* (Castree and Braun 2001). There is also an excellent volume that addresses "religions and the ecology of flux," David M. Lodge, Christopher Hamlin and Peter Raven (eds) *Religion and the New Ecology: Environmental Responsibility in a World in Flux* (University of Notre Dame Press, 2006). For a good example of an "environmental history" of religious beliefs, see Carolyn Merchant's (2003) *Reinventing Eden*. Finally, for those interested in various approaches to "ecotheology", a good, accessible survey is Stephen Bede Scharper, *Redeeming the Time: A Political Theology of the Environment* (Continuum, 1998).

Part III

RELIGION AND SCIENCE, VALUES, AND PUBLIC POLICY

(i) Origins

34
ORIGINS

Michael Ruse

Before Charles Darwin

The big-name Greeks had no interest in origins, mainly because there were none! Plato and Aristotle believed in an eternal world, where there may be limited change, but essentially all was as it was in the beginning and will always be in the future (Sedley 2008). There were some who challenged this vision, Empedocles for example, but generally they were few, and were regarded as muddled and misguided. The ancient Jews, of course, did have their creation story, and it was this that governed Western thinking right through the scientific revolution of the sixteenth and seventeenth centuries. This persistence was not so much a fact that no-one wanted to go against Holy Scripture – Augustine, around 400 AD, had argued that if the evidence shows otherwise, literalistic interpretations of the Bible must be relinquished (McMullin 1985). It was rather that there was no reason to dispute the accuracy of the Genesis accounts of origins.

Things started to change in the eighteenth century, in part because of new discoveries – fossils, embryological details, species from around the world – but even more because of the ideology of progress (Ruse 1996, 2005). The Reformation had firmly established the significance of Providence for the believer. We humans are fallen sinners and without God's help we can do nothing. Progress counters this. It is the claim that unaided we can, through our own abilities and efforts, improve knowledge and health and living generally. We can go from ignorance to understanding, from sickness to vibrancy, from poverty to wealth. In other words, we can go from lesser to greater, we can go upwards. Progressionists (perhaps the earliest was the French novelist and encyclopedist Denis Diderot) took this cultural idea, and read it into the biological world – from blob to sophisticated organism, from (as they used to say) monad to man. Erasmus Darwin, the physician grandfather of Charles Darwin, was a paradigm.

> Imperious man, who rules the bestial crowd,
> Of language, reason, and reflection proud,
> With brow erect who scorns this earthy sod,
> And styles himself the image of his God;
> Arose from rudiments of form and sense,
> An embryon point, or microscopic ens!
>
> (Darwin 1803: 1, ll. 295–314)

One can hardly speak of any of this as serious science. Certainly back then, when Erasmus Darwin – and even more famously the French biologist Jean-Baptiste Lamarck (in his *Philosophie zoologique* of 1809) – were speculating in this fashion, critics thought that they were promoting the crudest kind of pseudo-science. Right through to the middle of the nineteenth century, although few now wanted to subscribe to a literalist view of Genesis – apart from anything else, geology had shown that the world is way older than one can infer from the genealogies of the Old Testament – serious thinkers, and this included almost all of the scientific community in Britain, France, and Germany, rejected the idea of evolution or (as they then called it) transmutation.

On the Origin of Species

The English naturalist Charles Robert Darwin changed all of this. In his great work, *On the Origin of Species*, published in 1859 but drawing on ideas he had first formulated some twenty years earlier, Darwin did two things. First, he established the serious respectability of evolutionary ideas. He did this by providing what the British historian and philosopher of science William Whewell (1840) called a "consilience of inductions." Whewell argued that when you are trying to establish a hypothesis about unseen events or phenomena – in his case, he was particularly interested in the unseen waves postulated by the then-conquering theory of light – you must show that the hypothesis explains many different "clues" (like the interference patterns of Young's double-slit experiment) which, in turn, support the cause at the center of the hypothesis. Darwin analogously argued that evolution explains many facts in the biological world – that the fossil record is roughly progressive, that the birds and reptiles of the Galapagos archipelago are similar although slightly different from island to island, that the forelimbs of humans, horses, porpoises, bats have similar bones ("homologies") even though the functions of the limbs are very different, that the embryos of organisms very different as adults (such as dogs and humans) are nevertheless very similar. Conversely all of these facts, these clues, point to the truth of evolution (see Ruse 2008).

The second thing that Darwin did in the *Origin* was to provide a mechanism or cause of change, natural selection. He provided a two-part argument. First, something the English political economist (and Anglican clergyman) Thomas Robert Malthus (1914 [1826]) had called a struggle for existence: "as more individuals are produced than can possibly survive, there must in every case be a struggle for existence, either one individual with another of the same species, or with the individuals of distinct species, or with the physical conditions of life" (Darwin 1859: 63). Second, from the struggle, and taking in the differences between organisms, to natural selection: "can we doubt (remembering that many more individuals are born than can possibly survive) that individuals having any advantage, however slight, over others, would have the best chance of surviving and of procreating their kind? On the other hand we may feel sure that any variation in the least degree injurious would be rigidly destroyed. This preservation of favourable variations and the rejection of injurious variations, I call Natural Selection" (*ibid.*: 80–81).

What was crucially important was that natural selection leads not simply to change, but to change of a particular kind, namely in the direction of increased adaptation. The features of organisms do not exist randomly without rhyme or reason. They are as if designed for the survival and reproduction of their possessors. Eyes, teeth, noses, penises, vaginas, bark, leaves, roots, wings, fins, legs – all of these features, these adaptations, serve the ends of the organisms that have them (Ruse 2003).

Reactions and developments

What was the reaction to the *Origin*? We can say two things. First, evolution was accepted very rapidly by almost everyone. Both scientists and laypeople, in Britain, on the Continent, across the Atlantic in the USA, accepted evolution as true. This was an almost overnight phenomenon. Darwin's argument convinced people. But what about those causes? This is the second point. No-one wanted to deny natural selection. Almost no-one wanted to accept it as the main cause of evolutionary change. People were unimpressed by selection. Indeed, generally people were not that interested in causes at all. Much more exciting was the working out of the paths of evolution – phylogenies – aided first by (often suspect) analogies between the development of individual organisms and of evolving lines, and second by increasingly fabulous fossil finds, most from the American West. Evolution became very much a science of the public domain. It wasn't something tucked away in the laboratories, clothed in the mysteries of mathematics. It was rather a museum subject, housed in institutions where families could go on Sundays and marvel at the glories of the past.

There were good scientific reasons why natural selection did not catch fire after the *Origin*. The chief one was that Darwin had no adequate theory of heredity, what we today call genetics (Vorzimmer 1970). However good a new variation might be, there was no guarantee that it would be preserved and transmitted to future generations. It was not until the beginning of the twentieth century that things really started to move on this front, thanks then to the discovery of the principles of heredity first formulated back in the 1860s by the obscure Moravian monk Gregor Mendel. By the third decade of the twentieth century, genetics was a fully formed science, and it was then that people started to realize that it offered the missing piece in the evolutionary causal picture. Natural selection could work on units of heredity, genes, preserved from generation to generation, occasionally changing (mutating) and thus providing the building blocks of overall evolution (Provine 1971).

These insights were formalized by a number of mathematically gifted biologists – Ronald Fisher and J. B. S. Haldane in Britain and Sewall Wright in the USA. Soon after, the naturalists and experimentalists came along and put empirical flesh on the "population geneticists'" mathematical skeletons. Notable in Britain was E. B. Ford (who founded the school of "ecological genetics"), and in the USA the Russian-born geneticist Theodosius Dobzhansky, who synthesized his thinking in a very influential work, *Genetics and the Origin of Species* (Dobzhansky 1937). In Britain, Julian Huxley (grandson of Darwin's great supporter Thomas Henry Huxley) provided an influential overview, *Evolution: The Modern Synthesis* (Huxley 1942), and in the USA a group around Dobzhansky fleshed things out greatly. Notable were Ernst Mayr, ornithologist and systematist and author of *Systematics and the Origin of Species* (1942); paleontologist George Gaylord Simpson, author of *Tempo and Mode in Evolution* (1944); and botanist G. Ledyard Stebbins, author of *Variation and Evolution in Plants* (1950).

In Britain this newly invigorated theory was known as neo-Darwinism, in the USA as the synthetic theory, presumably because it was a synthesis of Darwin and Mendel. It is the updated version of this theory that rules professional evolutionary studies today. The coming of molecular genetics in the 1950s at first seemed threatening to the ideas, but soon it was seen that molecular tools are friends, offering very powerful ways of analyzing the mysteries of nature. It is true that molecular thinking led to the hypothesis that, at the level of the gene (now of course translated into the language of molecules and identified with the strands of DNA, twisted into a double helix), it is possible that selection does not have great effects and that gene types (alleles) drift randomly. But this "neutral theory" of evolution is seen as a complement to the neo-Darwinian theory that rules at the level of physical characteristics (Kimura 1983).

Not that the science has been controversy-free. Let it be emphasized that no-one today, within the scientific community, wants to challenge evolution. But there have been, and probably always will be, those who wonder about the scope and power of natural selection. Notorious was the late Stephen Jay Gould, Harvard paleontologist and popular writer beyond compare, who argued that in the fossil record we see non-selection-fueled jumps, taking us from one form to another (Eldredge and Gould 1972). Explicitly, he contrasted his jerky theory of "punctuated equilibrium" with the smoothness of Darwinian "phylotic gradualism." Equally notorious have been the critics (who counted Gould as a leader) who wondered about the applicability of Darwinian thinking to humankind (Allen *et al.* 1975). Again, let it be stressed that no-one denied that humans have evolved, or that selection would have been a major causal factor. Getting on one's hind legs and having big brains are paradigmatic examples of selection-caused adaptations. But how far selection has molded, and continues to affect, human thinking and actions has been a matter of bitter controversy.

Science and religion

Let us pull back now and look specifically at the science–religion relationship. As already intimated, the early years – let us say from 1700 to 1859 – were framed by the conflict between progress and Providence. Cultural progress was rightly and explicitly seen as a challenge to the doctrine of Providence and, inasmuch as evolution (correctly) was seen as a child of progress, then evolution was seen as going against Christianity. By and large, the worry about biblical literalism was not a big issue, and by and large neither was atheism. Diderot and other French thinkers may have been close to total non-belief, but most evolutionists – certainly Erasmus Darwin and Lamarck – were deists, that is, believers in a god who works through unbroken law. An Unmoved Mover. This incidentally was Charles Darwin's religious position for most of his life. He started as a fully committed Anglican, but then on the *Beagle* voyage moved to deism. Later in life, probably under the influence of T. H. Huxley, Darwin joined many Victorians in becoming more of an agnostic.

Anglican or not, his background was important for Darwin in becoming a Darwinian, meaning the discovery of natural selection. The struggle for existence comes right from Malthus' theological concerns about how God has got us to work for our living and not just laze things away. With the reproductive powers stronger than the food and space supplies can handle, we have to work. This is all part of God's forethought. Of course, Darwin was to make something very different of all of this, but in the case of Archdeacon William Paley, another Anglican clergyman, the story is much more direct and continuous. Paley, in his *Natural Theology* (1819 [1802]), a work that Darwin read as a student at Cambridge, offered the classical case for the argument from design. The eye is like a telescope. Telescopes have telescope-makers. Therefore the eye has an eye-maker, the Great Optician in the Sky. Right through the time of writing the *Origin*, Darwin accepted that a god was responsible for the eye, although for him it had to be a god who works through unbroken law. More importantly, Darwin always accepted Paley's premise that the eye seems as if designed. It is not just randomly thrown together without function. Eyes work for the good of their possessors (Ruse 2003).

After the *Origin*, religious people – who were already, particularly under the influence of German biblical scholarship, starting to move towards a less interfering, no longer quasi-magical god – could find within Darwinism much to admire and possibly accept. And so it proved. For all of the initial opposition, it was not long before Christians, in Britain, on the Continent, and in much of the USA, embraced evolution (Roberts 1988). By now far less worried about thoughts of progress and more inclined to think that God does expect us to do things for ourselves, they took adaptation and turned it to their own ends. For instance, Frederick Temple, future Archbishop of Canterbury, writing in the 1880s, was quite explicit on the need to make a shift from an old-style, natural theology to a new-style, evolution-informed substitute. He stressed that, after Darwin, if one were rewriting Paley's *Natural Theology*, the emphasis would be different. "Instead of insisting wholly or mainly on the wonderful adaptation of means to ends in the structure of living animals and plants, we should look rather to the original properties impressed on matter from the beginning, and on the beneficent consequences that have flowed from those properties" (Temple 1884: 118–19). Likewise John Henry Newman, the greatest English-speaking theologian since the Protestant Reformation. Asked if he thought that Darwin should be offered an honorary degree at Oxford, he replied: "Is this [Darwin's theory] against the distinct teaching of the inspired text? If it is, then he advocates an Antichristian theory. For myself, speaking under correction, I don't see that it does – contradict it" (Letter of June 5, 1870, in Newman 1973: 137).

Fueling the conflict

What is objected to, even by Christians such as these, is the use of Darwinian ideas to promote humanism, or secularism, or outright atheism. There is reason for complaint. From the first, from 1859 when the *Origin* was published, many evolutionists used their theory as a tool in a battle between religion and science that was, to a great extent, of their own making (Ruse 2005). Thomas Henry Huxley led the troops, ably assisted in Germany by Ernst Haeckel. For these people, evolution was a substitute theory of origins, one that put humans at the top (given the progressive nature of the evolutionary process), and generally one with a strong cultural agenda. This is "social Darwinism," the idea that one can base moral and social norms on the evolutionary process.

There were social reasons why the scientists argued for a secular vision in the name of science, of evolution specifically. People like Huxley were trying to upgrade Britain (Haeckel in Germany) from what they rightly saw as a near-feudal society with power in the hands of a few, and the benefits likewise flowing disproportionately to a minority, to a modern state based on democracy, with education and health for all, and with the benefits of industry backing a world in which everyone can realize their full potential. Positively, they were for science; negatively, they were against the forces that they felt stood in their way, and foremost was organized religion, which they saw as a lackey of the establishment. Hence the promotion of the warfare – an attitude that persists to this day. The Harvard entomologist and sociobiologist Edward O. Wilson openly promotes the naturalism behind evolution as a substitute for conventional religion: "the final decisive edge enjoyed by scientific naturalism will come from its capacity to explain traditional religion, its chief competition, as a wholly material phenomenon. Theology is not likely to survive as an independent intellectual discipline" (Wilson 1978: 192). More frenetic in their shrill atheism are Richard Dawkins' *The God Delusion* (2007) and philosopher Daniel Dennett's *Breaking the Spell* (2006). Science generally, evolution particularly, is promoted as a world picture, and it is this that counts rather than the minutiae of the movements of the genes. Evolution stands for a philosophy, a way of life.

Evangelical literalism

The same is true on the other side. The leading founding fathers, almost to a person, were deists (Noll 2002). But the USA is a religious country, and as the new nation found its way in the nineteenth century, the preachers moved in – particularly in the south and as the country moved westward – and offered an ideology for a people whose lives were hard and often dangerous, but who were convinced that they were the new Israelites, chosen by God for this purpose. People moved towards a literalism of biblical interpretation, one that gave ready and simple answers to life's problems, and one (this was very important) that was accessible to all, without the need of sophisticated teachers to explain and guide.

The US Civil War was of crucial significance. The North won. After this, it moved forward, industrializing and building what was to become the dominant world society of the twentieth century. Modernism, in culture, in science, in religion, was all. The South lost. It turned inwards and to the Bible for solace and comfort – after all, as preacher and politician stressed in harmony, the work justifies slavery. Did not Paul tell the slave to return to his master and obey? Likewise, the story of the Israelites in captivity became a sermon favorite. God afflicts most those whom he loves the most. So as the century started to draw to a close, biblical literalism – not a traditional Christianity, but an idiosyncratic creation of nineteenth-century, Protestant America – grew and flourished. In the South, in the West as the country opened up, and increasingly in the stressed pockets of the North. City-dwellers, who were used by the industrial barons, felt threatened by the influx of immigrants from Europe, often doubly alien in their Catholicism or Judaism, who likewise looked for simple solutions to their lives and problems.

As was the case for the modernists, evolution became a signal or a flag. Few lay awake at nights worrying about the gaps in the fossil record. Many lay awake worrying about the effects of modern society on themselves and on their children, and evolution was seen to symbolize the rottenness at the heart of this society. That it opposed Genesis was bad. That it promoted loose living was worse. The great preacher of the age, the Billy Graham of the late nineteenth century, Dwight L. Moody, preached on the "four great temptations that threaten us today." These are the theater, ignoring the Sabbath, Sunday newspapers, and atheism including evolution (Marsden 1980: 35).

The battles of the twentieth century between the evangelical literalists and the evolutionists are well known. Most famously, there was the Scopes monkey trial in Dayton, Tennessee, where a young evolution-teaching school teacher was prosecuted by three-times presidential candidate William Jennings Bryan and defended by famous agnostic Clarence Darrow (Larson 1997). Then, in the years after the Second World War, there was the growth of so-called scientific creationism (or creation science), spurred by *Genesis Flood*, a work authored by a Princeton-trained theologian, John C. Whitcomb Jr. and a hydraulic engineer, Henry M. Morris (Whitcomb and Morris 1961). Here one had full-blown "young Earth creationism" promoting an Earth span of 6000 years, a six-day creation of organisms leading to humans, and a world-wide flood. (This last is a vital part of creationist eschatology, marking the end of the first of the dispensations – successive periods of God's dealings with humankind – the last of which will end with the battle of Armageddon.) Attempts to get the claims of this book into schools came crashing down in 1981, when a federal judge in Arkansas ruled that creation science is religion, not science, and hence is constitutionally barred from state-supported public schools (Ruse 1988). Minimally deterred, like the phoenix, anti-evolutionary doctrines arose again almost immediately, this time in the guise of intelligent design theory. Promoted by Harvard-trained Berkeley law professor Phillip Johnson (*Darwin on Trial*, 1991); ably articulated by Lehigh University biochemist Michael Behe (*Darwin's Black Box*, 1996); defended by Chicago-trained mathematician and philosopher William Dembski (*The Design Inference*, 1998); and funded by conservative Seattle think tank The Discovery Institute, intelligent design theory has had considerable success and influence.

Intelligent design theory met its Waterloo at Dover, Pennsylvania in 2005, when another federal judge ruled that it truly is religion not science, and hence has no place in the publicly funded classroom (Pennock and Ruse 2008). No doubt it will persist in this or some other form. Significant for us here is that one can trace a line from Dwight Moody, via William Jennings Bryan and Henry M. Morris, to Phillip Johnson. They are not really that bothered by evolution as such. Historian of the field Ronald Numbers (2006) – who himself grew up as a creationist – has pointed out amusingly that most creationists in fact accept a huge amount of evolution, believing that after the Flood the surviving animals diversified into many different forms (this cuts down on the number you need on board). Johnson (1991) is positively cavalier about *Archaeopteryx*, the bird–reptile. "Score one for the evolutionists" is his attitude. It is true that most want to hold to a literal Genesis (Behe, a Catholic, is much more inclined to accept some form of guided evolution), but literalism is a very fluid and creative concept in the hands of creationists. When it comes to the second-favorite book of the Bible after Genesis, namely Revelation, imagination runs riot. No-one thinks the whore of Babylon was a woman – speculation ranges from the Pope to the Catholic Church generally. Or one can go farther east. Saladin used to be a favorite; then Saddam Hussein became a top candidate.

What do link and motivate all of these people are the moral issues (Ruse 2005). Bryan was open in his fear that Darwinism promotes militarism, not to mention the vile ways of the 1920s – jazz, liquor, short skirts, and bras that made the chests of young women look like those of their boyfriends. Morris worried non-stop about the degeneracy of the modern world, accusing "notorious Darwinian philosopher Michael Ruse," apparently a well known "atheistic humanist," of contributing to the moral rot. "It is rather obvious that the modern opposition to capital punishment for murder and the general tendency toward leniency in punishment for other serious crimes are directly related to the strong emphasis on evolutionary determinism that has characterized much of this century" (Morris 1989: 148). Johnson obsesses about gay marriage, abortion on demand, and – of all things – cross-dressing. This last stems not from a fear that the average male evolutionist goes home and slips into something smooth, silky, and pink, but from a loathing of feminism. Hillary Clinton in her pant suits are the objects of his ire.

Things are never quite as straightforward as they seem. That is what makes them interesting. The Greeks did not care about origins. Thanks to the Jews, we do, and at no time more so than today. Although for the past century, at the interface between science and religion, this has overwhelmingly been an American issue, today it is spreading, with creationist anti-evolutionist sympathies rising in Europe, South America and other parts of the world where American evangelicals have made, and are making, their mark (South Korea for instance), and most recently in the Muslim world where opposition to Western modernism often takes the familiar form of highlighting evolution as particularly pernicious. No end is in sight to conflicts over origins; but, if this essay has shown anything, it is that although it may ostensibly be a science–religion question, in fact it is much broader, resting ultimately on the most basic questions and convictions about the kind of culture and society that we want for ourselves and our fellow humans.

References

Allen, E., and others (1975) "Letter to the Editor," *New York Review of Books*, sec. 22, 18, 43–44.

Behe, M. (1996) *Darwin's Black Box: The Biochemical Challenge to Evolution*, New York: Free Press.

Darwin, C. (1859) *On the Origin of Species by Means of Natural Selection, or the Preservation of Favoured Races in the Struggle for Life*, London: John Murray.
Darwin, E. (1803) *The Temple of Nature*, London: J. Johnson.
Dawkins, R. (2007) *The God Delusion*, New York: Houghton, Mifflin, Harcourt.
Dembski, W.A. (1998) *The Design Inference: Eliminating Chance through Small Probabilities*, Cambridge: Cambridge University Press.
Dennett, D.C. (2006) *Breaking the Spell: Religion as a Natural Phenomenon*, New York: Viking.
Dobzhansky, T. (1937) *Genetics and the Origin of Species*, New York: Columbia University Press.
Eldredge, N. and Gould, S.J. (1972) "Punctuated equilibria: an alternative to phyletic gradualism," in *Models in Paleobiology*, T.J.M. Schopf (ed.), San Francisco, CA: Freeman, Cooper, 82–115.
Huxley, J.S. (1942) *Evolution: The Modern Synthesis*, London: Allen & Unwin.
Johnson, P.E. (1991) *Darwin on Trial*, Washington, DC: Regnery Gateway.
Kimura, M. (1983) *The Neutral Theory of Molecular Evolution*, Cambridge: Cambridge University Press.
Lamarck, J.B. (1809) *Philosophie zoologique*, Paris: Dentu.
Larson, E.J. (1997) *Summer for the Gods: The Scopes Trial and America's Continuing Debate over Science and Religion*, New York: Basic Books.
Malthus, T.R. (1914 [1826]) *An Essay on the Principle of Population*, 6th edn, London: Everyman.
Marsden, G.M. (1980) *Fundamentalism and American Culture: The Shaping of Twentieth Century Evangelicalism 1870–1925*, Oxford: Oxford University Press.
Mayr, E. (1942) *Systematics and the Origin of Species*, New York: Columbia University Press.
McMullin, E. (1985) "Introduction: Evolution and Creation," in *Evolution and Creation*, E. McMullin (ed.), Notre Dame, IN: University of Notre Dame Press, 1–58.
Morris, H.M. (1989) *The Long War Against God: The History and Impact of the Creation/Evolution Conflict*, Grand Rapids, MI: Baker Book House.
Newman, J.H. (1973) *The Letters and Diaries of John Henry Newman, XXV*, C.S. Dessain and T. Gornall (eds), Oxford: Clarendon Press.
Noll, M. (2002) *America's God: From Jonathan Edwards to Abraham Lincoln*, New York: Oxford University Press.
Numbers, R.L. (2006) *The Creationists: From Scientific Creationism to Intelligent Design*, 2nd edn, Cambridge, MA: Harvard University Press.
Paley, W. (1819 [1802]) *Natural Theology (Collected Works: IV)*, London: Rivington.
Pennock, R., and Ruse, M. (eds) (2008) *But is it Science? The Philosophical Question in the Creation/Evolution Controversy*, 2nd edn, Buffalo, NY: Prometheus.
Provine, W.B. (1971) *The Origins of Theoretical Population Genetics*, Chicago, IL: University of Chicago Press.
Roberts, J.H. (1988) *Darwinism and the Divine in America: Protestant Intellectuals and Organic Evolution, 1859–1900*, Madison, WI: University of Wisconsin Press.
Ruse, M. (ed.) (1988) *But is it Science? The Philosophical Question in the Creation/Evolution Controversy*, Buffalo, NY: Prometheus.
——(1996) *Monad to Man: The Concept of Progress in Evolutionary Biology*, Cambridge, MA: Harvard University Press.
——(2003) *Darwin and Design: Does Evolution Have a Purpose?*, Cambridge, MA: Harvard University Press.
——(2005) *The Evolution–Creation Struggle*, Cambridge, MA: Harvard University Press.
——(2008) *Charles Darwin*, Oxford: Blackwell.
Sedley, D. (2008) *Creationism and its Critics in Antiquity*, Berkeley, CA: University of California Press.

Simpson, G.G. (1944) *Tempo and Mode in Evolution*, New York: Columbia University Press.
Stebbins, G.L. (1950) *Variation and Evolution in Plants*, New York: Columbia University Press.
Temple, F. (1884) *The Relations Between Religion and Science*, London: Macmillan.
Vorzimmer, P.J. (1970) *Charles Darwin: The Years of Controversy*, Philadelphia, PA: Temple University Press.
Whewell, W. (1840) *The Philosophy of the Inductive Sciences*, London: Parker.
Whitcomb, J.C. and Morris, H.M. (1961) *The Genesis Flood: The Biblical Record and its Scientific Implications*, Philadelphia, PA: Presbyterian and Reformed Publishing Company.
Wilson, E.O. (1978) *On Human Nature*, Cambridge, MA: Harvard University Press.

Further reading

David Sedley's *Creationism and its Critics in Antiquity* (University of California Press, 2008) is a superb discussion of early thinking about origins. My *Monad to Man* (cited above) covers in some detail the history of evolutionary thinking for the 300 years beginning at the start of the eighteenth century. Janet Browne's biography of Darwin is definitive: *Charles Darwin: Voyaging* (Knopf, 1995); *idem*, *Charles Darwin: The Power of Place* (Knopf, 2002). Ronald Numbers' *The Creationists: From Scientific Creationism to Intelligent Design* (Harvard University Press, 2006), is very good on the history of American biblical literalism, and my *The Evolution–Creation Struggle* (also cited above) puts in context the whole question of secular and religious approaches to origins.

35
CREATION AND LIBERATION
The ontology of American Indian origins

Scott L. Pratt

In his two most recent books, American Indian theologian George Tinker proposes that the affirmation of the created character of the universe is a necessary condition for the praxis of liberation. Origin stories provide crucial information for American Indians living there, and provide a starting point for European-descended peoples to find their place as well. Even as Euro-American historians and scientists seek to explain the shared history and problems faced by the diverse peoples of North America, Tinker argues that it is indigenous knowledge that will make sense of the past and point to a future in which all peoples have a chance to survive. "American Indians and other indigenous peoples," Tinker writes, "have a long-standing confidence that they have much to teach European and north American peoples about the world and human relationships in the world." He argues that much is at stake in learning these lessons: American Indians are "confident that those foundations can become a source of healing and reconciliation for all human beings and ultimately for all of creation" (Tinker 2008: 47). This confidence is affirmed by a wide range of American Indian writers, including Luther Standing Bear, who concluded in his 1933 autobiography "it is now time for a destructive order to be reversed […] America can be revived, rejuvenated, by recognizing a native school of thought. The Indian can save America" (Standing Bear 1978 [1933]: 255). Daniel Wildcat, an American Indian philosopher at Haskell Indian Nations University, argues in his recent book on global climate change that the key to survival in the long run will be found in indigenous knowledge. He concludes, "Because indigenous peoples have paid attention to our Mother Earth, it is important to listen to what we can share with humankind" (Wildcat 2009: 17; also see Deloria 1970).

The discussion that follows is an attempt by a European-descended American to listen closely to American Indian thinkers and the traditions they present in an effort to understand the connections between creation and liberation; between an understanding of the world grounded in the idea of creation and ways of life that can respond to the accumulated problems of the present globalized, militarized, and industrialized world. What connects these ideas is a conception of indigenous knowledge, or better, an alternative conception of knowing that has room for both indigenous knowledge and knowledge produced within the Western or European-descended tradition. I argue that, while the epistemology of the West cannot make room for indigenous knowledge (except on terms that undercut the possibility of liberation), epistemology grounded in the American Indian tradition can make room for scientific knowledge. I first present Tinker's claims regarding the idea of liberation and, in the second part, what it means to affirm creation. In the third section, I consider the relation between creation and liberation in terms of the meaning of origin stories and the ways in which origin stories provide a means of achieving libratory praxis. This argument, I think, supports the claim that the affirmation of creation is a sufficient condition for liberation of the kind sought by Tinker. I conclude by considering the relation between knowledge claims of Western science and those generated within American Indian thought, argue for a particular kind of compatibility, and suggest its implications for libratory praxis. The final section points toward an argument for Tinker's stronger claim that the affirmation of creation is a necessary condition for liberation.

The meaning of liberation

In his 2008 volume *American Indian Liberation: A Theology of Sovereignty*, Tinker defines liberation as "freedom to practice, recover, restore, and reinvent whatever tribal/indigenous practices and life ways are enriching, healing, and life-sustaining" (Tinker 2008: 143). While Tinker develops his notion in relation to liberation theology as it emerged in the 1970s in Central and South America, he argues that American Indian liberation moves sharply away from the basic commitments of the earlier liberation theology and toward a view that is more responsive to the historical circumstances of indigenous Americans. Citing the work of Gustavo Gutiérrez as defining the idea, Tinker observes that liberation theologies "have been characteristically theologies of resistance and struggle and have engaged the colonizer's missionary theology by way of challenge and deconstruction" (*ibid.*: 34). It is this character of liberation theology that Tinker finds relevant to the future of American Indians. At the same time, liberation theologies "begin with a radical interpretation of Jesus and the gospel" (*ibid.*: 129). "For American Indians," Tinker continues, "on the contrary, radical interpretation of Jesus would be an unproductive and even counterproductive starting point for a liberation theology because the first proclamation of Jesus among any Indian community came as the beginning of a colonial conquest that included the displacing of centuries-old religious traditions" (*ibid.*: 129). While the liberation theology of Gutierrez affirms that "the liberating action of Christ […] is at the heart of the historical current of humanity" (Gutierrez 1973: 168), Tinker argues that liberation is rather a practice of establishing diverse communities not dependent on Christian history or ideals. Liberation, in this sense, is a process that will allow "Indian communities to resuscitate old, communal ways of relating to the Sacred, to find life for the peoples in those ceremonial ways and cultural values" (Tinker 2008: 140). In short, liberation is a process of cultural restoration involving the reassertion of a community's connections with traditional lands and the recovery and revitalization of traditional knowledge.

Common ground between Western colonial beliefs and ways of life with those of indigenous peoples is the presumed affirmation by both the colonizers and the colonized that the world is a creation. In order to begin the process of liberation, American Indians opt for an approach that "affirms the 'old covenant' promises that the Creator has given Indian peoples and presumes those promises are still good and appropriate" (*ibid.*: 137). The recognition or affirmation of creation is "the affirmation that all of life is sacred, and therefore I am sacred as a part of the created whole." Put another way, Tinker says, "I begin by affirming myself and all of life, especially every other human being, as a sacred and good part of creation" (*ibid.*: 43). In contrast to this spiritual starting point in indigenous traditions, Christian notions of liberation begin with a New Testament affirmation of sin and evil "that taints all human beings from birth and becomes the *prima facie* logic for a presumed need of salvation. [… T]hat schematic then becomes the major impetus for the colonial and imperial missionary outreach of the nineteenth and twentieth centuries" (*ibid.*: 45).

Yet, despite its focus on sin, Tinker argues that Christianity has the resources to recognize the American Indian starting point as well. He observes that the Judeo-Christian tradition and the Christian sacred texts begin with creation. As Christianity developed, the emphasis shifted to the act of reconciliation that came with Jesus and the fall-and-redemption process that divided the world between good and evil, sin and salvation. "As a result, not only did euro-western Christians lose sight of a theology of creation […] [but] on this continent, […] were blinded […] to any appreciation of cultural difference they met in indigenous people." By recognizing the history of Christian belief and practice, Tinker argues that Christians could recover a theology of creation and come to affirm the good of creation and its implications for human life. The received idea of liberation theology, transformed by taking creation as a starting point, would do the double duty of providing a critical common ground among peoples and acknowledgement of divergent approaches to liberation grounded in American Indian origins.

In sum, liberation involves two sides. On one, liberation is a matter of indigenous sovereignty. Since indigenous peoples are a part of the created universe, they are good and worth fostering. At the same time, liberation involves repentance and reconciliation by colonizers and their heirs to the communities that they have oppressed. Sovereignty requires external acknowledgement; and for those who have participated in the destruction of indigenous communities, acknowledgement amounts to taking responsibility and seeking ways to sustain and foster growth in those parts of creation that were formerly under attack.

To these two aspects of liberation, a third dimension is suggested by Tinker when he concludes, "we must begin to dream together, Indian and non-Indian, White and color, to dream a new vision of the world in which domination and privileging lose their seemingly natural prominence in structuring a world society" (*ibid.*: 162). This "dreaming together" marks a practical response to shared problems of environmental destruction and turns on finding ways to learn from indigenous peoples. "American Indian cultures and values have much to contribute," he says, "to the systemic reimagining of euro-western peoples and the value system that has resulted in our contemporary crisis of ecojustice" (*ibid.*: 81). The praxis of liberation finally depends, as Wildcat claims, on recognizing "that the earth can be saved through indigenous knowledges" (Wildcat 2009: 135). Ultimately, the principle Wildcat identifies, that affirms diverse indigenous knowledges, is exactly the issue at stake in the relation between Western science and indigenous origin stories. If Tinker and Wildcat are right, the key to libratory praxis is to find a way for diverse knowledges to interact and frame new action.

The meaning of creation

The affirmation of creation can be understood as two related notions of what the affirmation leads to in the way of belief and action. The first condition of affirming creation is that it commits one to a disposition that affects all of one's activities, that is, creation is a universal term. Tinker represents this disposition to act in certain ways as one expressed in the Lakota phrase "*mitakuye oyasin*." The phrase, often used in the same way as "Amen" in Christian practices, is usually translated "for all my relations." As a prepositional phrase indicating the direction of action, *mitakuye oyasin* marks a disposition to act in ways that are toward others and for purposes beyond one's own. The disposition is not simply a commitment to related humans, but to the whole of creation. In this sense, the affirmation of creation is like a universal quantifier that requires the application of what follows to everything and everyone encountered and is, at the same time, bound up with the care and obligation that is part of being related to others.

The second condition of the affirmation of creation is that creation is a local or particular term. Even as Tinker stresses the value of creation as a starting point for liberation, he also recognizes key limitations on the idea. The term "creation," he says, names a "euro-western" idea and has a "distinctly borrowed flavor" (65) when taken up by American Indians. The problem is that the received notion of creation from Western religious traditions is one where creation "is objectified as something quite apart from human beings and to which humans relate from the outside" and over which human beings have, according to tradition, been given dominion. In contrast, "every tribe has several creation stories (sometimes clan-specific)" (64–65) that mark the beginning of a part of the whole and that usually assume the pre-existence of the world in some form. In this case, the affirmation of creation is like an existential quantifier, affirming the existence of particular beings as active agents in particular relations. Creation, in this sense, is a particular term. "Rather than conceiving of an initial creation that was long ago and has little continuing relevance in a world in which only human redemption is in process," Tinker says, "Indian intellectual traditions conceive of the world in a constant creative process that requires our continual participation – just as it requires that of trees, for instance, and buffalos continually fulfilling their prescribed part" (65). In short, the affirmation of creation that serves as the starting point for liberation is characterized at once as a universal disposition to act toward the whole of creation "for all my relations" and, at the same time, the affirmation of the existence of particular beings and relations that are only part of the whole.

Both conditions have implications for the relationship between American Indians and other peoples. The first condition, that involves a disposition to act toward all of creation, also requires that liberation will proceed as a matter of practice and it will necessarily go beyond the oppressed peoples whose struggle is to attain recognition as a community and extend to the communities of the oppressors. Tinker concludes, "our liberation is not possible without the liberation of our White relatives who share this continent with us" (141). At the same time, affirmation of creation requires the recognition of diverse particular communities marked by distinct (and sometimes multiple) origins. Here, liberation amounts to fostering the lives of diverse, bounded communities that lead to "the goal of every indigenous community" "to be recognized as a community" (137).

The second aspect of creation seems at odds with the first. Even as one recognizes the relatedness of all things, one also recognizes the diversity of things in their particular relations. In this case, creation is not about the universe as a whole, but about the emergence of distinct places, individuals, and groups, that is, creation is a local term that recognizes differences and boundaries. It appears that the affirmation of creation, rather than providing a clear way to liberation, begins with dispositions at cross-purposes. The apparent tension, however, can be addressed to some degree by considering the knowledge that emerges from the affirmation of creation and aims to foster diverse and flourishing communities.

Origin stories

Tinker focuses in particular on the need for American Indian communities to recover and restore traditional ways of life and knowing. Such a process involves both a certain kind of thinking and the need to establish ways of life in a spatial or placed context. At the same time, Tinker argues that white culture needs to recognize its history of destruction and disrespect, admit responsibility, and find ways of reconciling this history of devastation with the living communities of American Indians. If European-descended and American Indian groups are successful in fostering these two processes, he concludes, they will be able to engage in the construction of shared vision of life. Although not responding directly to Tinker, Wildcat proposes that the shared vision must be one that somehow brings together not just mutual respect and coexistence, but a larger process of co-action in response to the immanent destruction of the ecosystems of the planet. This sort of cooperative work will require the ability to integrate the products of Western science and what Deloria and others call Native Science. While the former is typically offered as "facts" framed by theory and confirmed by experimentation, the latter are offered as stories, less clearly framed by theories, but are explicitly offered as confirmed by experience. In effect, the bridge from a shared affirmation of creation – the understanding of the relatedness of all things – to a praxis of liberation involving the mutual flourishing of diverse communities, will require an epistemology that can integrate diverse knowledges in a way that does not undermine diverse communities or mutual survival. The worry is that such diverse knowledges are incompatible, and integration will require the reduction of claims to one epistemic system or another.

Consider the following story from one of the Salish tribes, the Skykomish, on the eastern shore of Puget Sound, called "Why Rivers Flow But One Way." "Before the world changed," the story begins, "the Snoqualmie, Snohomish, Swinomish and all other tribes came together. Eagle was the headman of the gathering. He was a great man and lived up in a tree. When the people wanted to decide an important question they called up to him as he sat in his tree, and in the conference that followed, each one of the people below was allowed to give his opinion" (Haeberlin and Boas 1924: 396). At issue at this gathering was the question of how rivers should flow. The proposal, accepted by everyone but Raven, was that "the rivers should go up to the falls and turn around there. Eagle wanted this so that the people would have an easy time travelling both up and down stream" (*ibid.*: 396). Raven, a "trickster" in Northwest traditions, appears in different forms in different stories. Here, he appears as a slave known for his wisdom. His appearance is significant because "slaves" in Northwest tribes were typically outsiders captured in war and made a part of the tribe, usually in the lowest class (see Donald 1997). From this position, Raven disagreed with Eagle and his people: "If the rivers turn around at the falls, salmon will have no chance to stop. They will go up as far as the falls, and then they will come right back again. Where will they spawn? And how will the new people catch them?" (Clark, 1953: 86). He proposed that the rivers flow one way, with eddies at various places where the salmon can slow down and where people will have a chance to catch them. "Now Raven had fine judgment […] and convinced the other people that the only proper thing to do was to adopt his plan. So now the rivers only run one way and the salmon have a chance to go upriver and spawn" (Haeberlin and Boas 1924: 396).

An alternate account of river flow is captured in a webpage designed to answer questions for school children. "Rivers always flow downhill, of course! A stream, or a river, is formed whenever water moves downhill from one place to another" (http://chamisa.freeshell.org/flow.htm). The first claim affirms what we expect and the second explains the direction of flow as (more or less) caused by gravity. If the cause of rivers flowing one way is as given by the Skykomish story, then it is clearly at odds with the claims made in the school account. Unless gravity is the force used by Eagle and his people to direct the flow, the two stories give different causal accounts. There are ways of resolving the differences, of course. Given the universal acceptance of the school account, the Skykomish story might not be about rivers at all. It might be taken as an instructive story about the process of collective decision-making. It might be seen as a quaint story told by people in the past, before they understood the role of gravity in controlling the flow of water. Or perhaps the story is an entertaining tale, radio theatre of ancient times, with no claims on the state of the world. Yet, even as we look at ways of resolving the incompatibility of the accounts, it is worth keeping in mind that, for Wildcat and others, stories of this sort are at least candidates for indigenous knowledge that have the potential to assist human beings in fostering cooperation in response to shared problems. I propose that the characteristics of affirming creation provide another frame for understanding the story.

Origin stories can be understood to have two aspects that parallel the two aspects of the affirmation of creation. In each case, the meanings of stories are understood pragmatically as a matter of what they lead to. First, an origin story's meaning is general, that is, not confined to a particular situation, but taken as something that is operative in any situation. This aspect of origin narratives provides models of behavior and practice that help to foster certain dispositions and interests in the community. From this angle, the claims of origin stories are not intended to be literal "facts," but rather claims that produce attitudes whose truth has do to with their effectiveness in fostering a flourishing community life. In the Skykomish story, the practice of the people led by Eagle models a process of deliberation framed by a problem and carried out through conversation and reason-giving. The epistemic position of Raven is particularly important since it represents as valuable the perspectives of those who are "other," both as members of the lowest class within the tribe and as people who are from outside the tribe. All members of the community are listened to and the community offers its approval after considering the reasons offered. The reasons offered are ones that aim to balance the interests involved. While it would be, on the whole, more convenient for the local humans if the river circulated, it would not be good for the salmon because salmon would find it hard to spawn, and this would have implications for the wider community that depended on the salmon. By sending the river only downhill, the salmon can still flourish; by providing for eddies along the way, humans and others would have the chance to catch some of the salmon. The story models decision-making and gives a general standard for deciding courses of action that reflect the ideas of reciprocity and respect. In light of the general character of creation, origin stories are not efforts to present the particular "facts" of origin, but rather contribute to the cultivation of a disposition that presumes that the world is a created one in which diverse agents are all related.

Second, and at the same time, origin stories have a particular meaning as well. Even as stories cultivate a general disposition, they also can be seen as making existential claims about a particular way of life in an actual place. The Skykomish story, despite its apparent metaphorical character, also contains a range of concrete "facts" based on the experience of living on the eastern shore of Puget Sound. The reference to "rivers" in the story probably points to the rivers in the Skykomish lands that, when followed upstream, proceed into the coastal mountains and eventually reach waterfalls from which they receive rain and melt water from the higher mountains. The waterfall practically divides the river between the part accessed by the people and the part that is reserved for the salmon. The salmon require a transit upstream in order to spawn; eddies are good places to fish because fish hold there on their return to spawn, and so on. The story is more than a fictional illustration of decision-making, it also reflects on the character of the place where the people live and identifies key pieces of information that help one to flourish in that place. Even as creation marks a general disposition, it also marks the division of the world into local places characterized by particular ways of life. The route from the recognition of creation to liberation involves knowledge that fosters both a disposition and a distinctive cultural community.

The account of river flow helpfully presented by the school website, in contrast, begins with the general claim that rivers always flow downhill. The truth of the claim follows from the very nature of rivers: they are formed when water flows downhill in response to the force of gravity. The general claim about rivers is taken as a "fact" that is part of a system of facts about the flow of water and gravity, and a still wider system of knowledge that involves gravity and other natural phenomena. Claims about particular rivers are then understood as instances of these general principles. What is lost in the school account of the river is the model of decision-making, that is, the attempt to teach a disposition (of inquiry as it turns out) and an account of the important local relations that characterize rivers in the area. At the same time, the Skykomish story lacks the universal character of the school account as knowledge that can be applied to all rivers. It is clearly not the case that the Skykomish story would apply, for example, to the Rock River in northern Illinois and southern Wisconsin. Here, there are no salmon and while the flow is one way, it is slow with no waterfalls and surrounded by a flat terrain. The Skykomish story would be of little use here, even as the school account would still apply.

The differences between the two accounts are not simply a matter of generality. It is important to see that for Tinker, the contrast between colonizer peoples and indigenous peoples is not simply one of emphasis on creation over sin, but also reflects a different set of expectations regarding what has been created. The first aspect of creation, the idea of universal relatedness, leads to an ontology that is, at least at first, sharply opposed to the ontology widely presumed in Western philosophy and science. The West (at least much of Western knowledge from an indigenous perspective) presumes a materialist starting point for understanding the character of creation, and sees purpose either as a product of evolution (or some other material process) or as something made part of creation from outside (by God or some other transcendent being). In either case, much or all of creation is not purposive in its activities and lacks anything like a soul or spirit. As a result, efforts to understand the world are taken as efforts of purposive human beings investigating a purposeless world of things. The alternative American Indian view is one that can be called "agent ontology," that is, a view that presumes that creation is made up of agents who bring to their interactions diverse purposes. In this case, the process of knowing is better seen as a process like that of coming to know other people, while the practices of knowing in Western science look like coercion and violence.

Deloria and Wildcat, in their book *Power and Place* (2001), bring together these two implications of the affirmation of creation in the context of their conception of personhood. Persons, on their account, are the intersection of power and place. Personhood is not limited to human beings, but rather emerges wherever power (sometimes called *Manitou*, *wakonda* or *orenda*) intersects with place (understood as particular relations with other persons). The resulting view is an agent ontology that recognizes that the universe is made up of persons (see Pratt 2006). This general claim (like the first aspect of creation) is meant to apply to everything encountered, and so is universal in its application. Its meaning, however, is to be understood in terms of the disposition it establishes for processes of interaction with others. At the same time (in parallel to the second aspect of creation) personhood requires particular instantiations: power manifested through relations that mark persons as both something distinctive and something dynamic.

The connection between creation and liberation is maintained through shared knowledge, often expressed as origin stories (though it may be expressed ceremonially, through ritual practice and other kinds of activities that do not produce spoken narratives). These stories provide a means of understanding and acting in light of the affirmation of creation in ways that are libratory.

The relation of indigenous knowledges and Western science

Taken together, it may still not be clear that Western and indigenous epistemologies are as opposed as I have suggested. Even though they adopt alternative ontologies (agential versus material), if one stipulates these differences, perhaps the resulting knowledge claims can be understood as claims that can be compared, criticized, and adopted. The problem with the attempt to make these epistemologies compatible in this way, however, is that the comparison and criticism of the alternative claims is still one that reduces the character of indigenous knowledge claims to ones that are primarily "matters of fact." From the perspective of Western epistemology, what is taken as general in indigenous knowing is viewed as problematically particular, and what is particular in indigenous knowing is taken as inadequately general.

The dispositional aspect of origin stories that foster a particular attitude toward others as relatives in the American Indian tradition seems to function as narrowing prejudices from the Western perspective. To motivate knowing through an attitude of caring that produces claims to benefit others in particular ways would seem to give up the neutrality of knowing and its potential for the development of claims that can be universally applied. At the same time, in Western epistemology, knowledge is best represented by claims that are general "facts" that either draw on particulars for their justification or allow one to make predictions about particulars. Claims that pass as indigenous knowledge seem to fail as candidates for knowledge in this sense because they stop with situated or local claims and resist generalization. Such limited claims on the way to knowledge must be treated as partial and incomplete and, ideally, are to be replaced by universal claims that operate across all situations. In this light, Western and Indian epistemologies are clearly at odds.

This tension can be seen in the Skykomish story as well. General dispositional claims about relatedness and concern can be seen, from the Western perspective, as dispositions that compromise the process of knowing. The story focuses on the interests of the various people concerned with the flow of local rivers, and the reason that rivers flow one way is the result of a consideration of these interests. Rivers flow one way because the people decide that they *should*. Such dispositions, however, confuse the account – it doesn't matter what the people want, since rivers flow the way they do because of processes that are independent of such concerns. Dispositional aspects of the story that mark interests and relations can therefore be taken as fictional, or as a kind of prejudicial narrowness that needs to be rejected as incompatible with knowledge.

At the same time, the claims that are taken as particular in the Skykomish story (the claims about salmon and rivers) can be extracted as truth claims independent of the point of view (the situation) of the story. Situation-specific knowledge claims are taken in support of general truths. From this angle, it is clear that indigenous knowledges can be taken up into Western systems of knowledge by setting aside the dispositional aspect and converting local knowledge into general claims. The problem is this: rejecting these key elements of indigenous knowledge means that it loses its connection with creation, and so its potential for fostering libratory praxis. By discounting the dispositional aspect of knowledge, the relatedness of all things can be lost. By taking particulars as data for general claims, local places become mere instances of larger laws and lose their distinctiveness. Again, liberation – at least of the sort sought by Tinker – is blocked.

Indigenous knowing, however, can provide a perspective that can preserve Western knowledge to some extent is consistent with libratory praxis. From this perspective, one can see that Western knowledge claims set aside the general dispositional element by assuming that, in effect, everyone shares a single disposition toward the world and then generates knowledge that is situated. However, since people have lost track of the dispositional element, they imagine that the situation specific knowledge of Western science is the only kind of knowledge to have, and every other sort of knowledge is an attempt to achieve the same standard. In this light, it should be clear that the indigenous conception of knowledge framed by an affirmation of creation provides both a critical angle on Western knowledge and a route to move from creation to liberation.

As criticism, indigenous knowledge can recognize the role of dispositions at work in the process of science. Deloria, for example, identified one version of the dispositional contrast: "Science *forces* secrets from nature by experimentation, and the results of the experiments are thought to be knowledge. The traditional peoples *accepted* secrets from the rest of creation" (Deloria and Wildcat 2001: 64). Western processes of knowing mark a disposition to set aside the interests and interactions of agents other than those recognized by the knower as human. As a result, the purposes of non-human agents, and human agents believed to be less mature or rational, may be discarded in the knowing process. When the role of dispositions is recognized, Western knowledge that claims general application can be seen as a situated knowledge, but one situated in a hyper-extended place that aims to include everything. Western epistemology then mirrors the designs of colonization by overriding boundaries and cultivating a disposition that fails to respect the diversity of creation. Again, from this angle, one can credit Western knowledge with fitting the pattern of knowing that can be identified with the affirmation of creation, and see that the resulting claims are situated in some sense.

Even as indigenous knowing can account for and critique Western epistemology, it can also accept at least some of its findings. Wildcat, for example, argues for a view he calls "indigenous realism" that challenges Western forms of knowledge but "refuses to be placed in an exclusively negative critique of or reactive mode to colonial institutions infatuated with human-centered design and technique" (Wildcat 2009: 102). Instead, "The necessary and sufficient condition for life-enhancing [libratory] knowledges requires paying attention to the life surrounding us [creation], what I call a deep spatial experiential body of knowledge [including origin stories] complemented by scientific information and knowledge" (*ibid*.: 15). From the perspective of indigenous realism and Tinker's idea of affirming creation, one can (and perhaps must) engage both indigenous knowledge and Western science in a way that recognizes the boundaries of situations. For example, Wildcat begins his discussion by quoting Bill McKibben, a well known author and environmentalist, "the most fundamental chemistry lesson for the twenty-first century [is that] burning one gallon of gasoline in your automobile inevitably results in the placement of five and a half pounds of carbon dioxide into the atmosphere" (*ibid.*: 4). This lesson and its relation to climate change arise in the context of Western knowledge. By maintaining the dispositional component of the affirmation of creation, such knowledge can be taken up as a situated knowledge bound by the concerns of the shared place of Earth without undermining the local knowledge that binds people to places. The claim here is not that Western science ought to be rejected, but rather that it can be credited as another situated knowledge whose results are potentially valuable in addressing present and local problems. This does not mean that if one is in for a penny, one is also in for a pound, because the knowledge taken up is framed by the openness that comes from recognizing creation as a whole and by the reality of places. Where Western science is driven to reject the dispositional mandates of *mitakuye oyasin* as primitive or prejudiced, an indigenous perspective can gain a higher ground by recognizing the ways in which both Western and indigenous people are in the same boat.

The real lesson of Tinker's assertion of the connection between creation and liberation is that it opens up the recognition of both the limits of Western knowledge and culture, and the potential for listening to others. Tinker's argument is that if Christians organized their understanding of the world in terms of creation rather than the "Christ event," then they would be better prepared to treat the non-human parts of the world with respect and care, and would be disposed to recognize and coexist with differences (human and otherwise). Liberation would be fostered for American Indians because the relation of respect and recognition could lead to repentance and reconciliation that would help to restore a balance between European peoples, indigenous peoples and the other agents who are part of these diverse communities. Liberation would be afforded by retelling origin stories, remembering the past of each people, and projecting a future life framed by this creationist understanding.

References

Clark, Ella A. (1953) *Indian Legends of the Pacific Northwest*, Berkeley, CA: University of California Press.

Deloria, Jr., Vine (1970) *We Talk, You Listen: New Tribes, New Turf*, New York: Macmillan.

——(1995) *Red Earth, White Lies: Native Americans and the Myth of Scientific Fact*, New York: Scribner.

——(1999) *For This Land: Writings on Religion in America*, New York: Routledge.

Deloria, Jr., Vine and Daniel R. Wildcat (2001) *Power and Place: Indian Education in America*, Golden, CO: Fulcrum.

Gutierrez, Gustavo (1973) *A Theology of Liberation*, Maryknoll, NY: Orbis Books.

Haeberlin, Hermann and Franz Boas (1924) "The Mythology of Puget Sound," *Journal of American Folklore* 37(145/146): 371–438.

Johnson, Mark (2007) *The Meaning of the Body: Aesthetics of Human Understanding*, Chicago, IL: University of Chicago Press.

Mendieta, Eduardo (2009) "From Imperialism to Dialogical Cosmopolitanism," *Ethics and Global Politics* 2(3): 241–58.
Mohanty, Chandra Talpade (2004) *Feminism Without Borders: Decolonizing Theory, Practicing Solidarity*, Durham, NC: Duke University Press.
Pratt, Scott L. (2006) "Persons in Place: The Agent Ontology of Vine Deloria, Jr.," *APA Newsletter on American Indians in Philosophy* 6(1): 4–9.
Standing Bear, Luther (1978 [1933]) *Land of the Spotted Eagle*, Lincoln, NE: University of Nebraska Press.
Tinker, George E. (2004) *Spirit and Resistance: Political Theology and American Indian Liberation*, Minneapolis, MN: Augsburg Fortress.
——(2008) *American Indian Liberation: A Theology of Sovereignty*, Maryknoll, NY: Orbis Books.
Wildcat, Daniel R. (2009) *Red Alert: Saving the Planet with Indigenous Knowledge*, Golden, CO: Fulcrum.

Further reading

In addition to the works discussed above, there are several key resources for thinking about the intersection of Native American traditions and Western science, including Gregory Cajete, *Native Science* (Clear Light, 2000) and *Look to the Mountain* (Kivaki Press, 1994); Vine Deloria, Jr., Parts I and V of *Spirit and Reason* (Fulcrum, 1999) and his book *Evolutionism, Creationism, and Other Modern Myths* (Fulcrum, 2002); Thomas Norton Smith's *The Dance of Person and Place* (SUNY Press, 2010); and *Blackfoot Physics* by F. David Peat (Weiser Books, 2002).

36
ORIGINS
The Hindu case

C. Mackenzie Brown

Before British colonialism

In ancient India there was a profusion of views regarding the question of origins. A few thoughtful sages of Vedic times (1200–500 BCE) doubted that the origin of the universe was knowable, something even the gods were uncertain about and perhaps even the Supreme Being could not discern. Most thinkers of those times, however, were less skeptical, more audacious, willing to set forth their conjectures regarding origins in a diverse set of cosmogonic myths and cosmological speculations (Halbfass 1992). Some of the Vedic seers assumed that behind the universe, a master craftsman or architect was at work. Others speculated that the world emanated from a primordial being, or hatched from a cosmic egg. Some pondered the possibility that the physical realm evolved from an original substance or from the material elements earth, water, fire, and air. There were those who insisted it happened all by chance. Others saw the inherent nature of the elements themselves as responsible for their coalescing into new combinations from which consciousness might emerge (Mittal 1974). A few came to think that the process was simply a divine dream. Most of these viewpoints centuries later were systematized in the so-called "orthodox" philosophical schools.

Three perspectives are especially relevant to the question of origins. The ancient theme of an extra-cosmic creator came to be represented in the theistic school of Logical-Atomists (Nyaya-Vaisheshika). While originally non-theistic, the school encountered difficulties in explaining how insentient atoms could form complex, ordered compounds without divine guidance. Accordingly, they came to incorporate a supervening deity, developing in the process sophisticated versions of the design argument (Chemparathy 1972). Among these is the claim, put forth by the greatest of all Hindu rational theologians Udayana (tenth to eleventh century CE) that all human culture, language skills, arts, and crafts must have been devised by a divine curriculum-planner. This designer of culture, identical with the creator of the universe, taught such knowledge to the first humans at the time of creation a few billion years ago (Brown 2008). This view that humankind, like an infant, would be forever ignorant without divine instruction militates against the idea that knowledge is cumulative, something that humans can discover on their own.

The Vedic idea of evolutionary transformation is exemplified in the non-theistic Samkhya founded by the legendary sage Kapila. The school regards all mental, psychological, and gross material elements in the universe as evolutes from Primordial Nature, but it is not a materialist philosophy. It is radically dualistic, supposing that alongside Nature there is Spirit, constituted by innumerable souls. An individual is the intermingling of a soul with the evolved elements of Nature. Nature acts on behalf of souls to liberate them from entanglement with itself. But the Samkhya never explains how souls and Nature came to be co-mingled in the first place, since Nature is insentient, and souls, being ever inactive, could not have initiated the evolutionary process.

The third perspective, that the universe is a manifestation of ultimate consciousness, is systematized in the Advaita Vedanta (the non-dualist school based on the teachings of the Vedanta or Upanishads) of Shankara (eighth century CE). Ultimate reality, the one Pure Consciousness called Brahman, is both the material and efficient cause of the universe. But the material universe is not what it seems, appearing as different from consciousness and multiple in form. Thus the empirical universe is a kind of illusion (*Maya*). While Shankara himself used the design argument against his non-theistic opponents (like the Samkhya), he ultimately regarded it as applying only to the lesser realm of *Maya* – even the designer god is an illusion of sorts.

The design argument was not left unchallenged. Buddhists and Jains, as well as many Hindus, anticipated most of the refutations of David Hume and Immanuel Kant by several centuries (Murty 1959). The thirteenth-century Hindu theologian Ramanuja rejected the argument on the grounds that it fails to establish only one creator, nor does it explain how a disembodied being can interact with matter. Most significantly for Ramanuja, the argument compromises the infinite goodness of God since it requires a close similarity between imperfect human artificers and the divine creator (Smart 1964).

The orthodox schools shared a sense that humankind, indeed all sentient beings, stand in need of spiritual release from this misery-laden world of birth, death, and rebirth. The schools generally viewed the cosmos as subject to never-ending cycles of creation and dissolution. Even theists assumed that God recreated the universe periodically, using pre-existing materials left over from previous cycles. The orthodox were also unanimous in rejecting the materialists, denouncing them for their repudiation of Vedic and priestly authority, their denial of an afterlife and karmic compensation, and their supposed promotion of immorality.

While ancient and medieval Indians developed several sciences, making significant discoveries in astronomy, mathematics, and medicine, such advancements were not particularly Hindu (Nanda 2003). The natural sciences languished as Indian philosophical inquiry, driven by spiritual concerns, focused increasingly on metaphysics and matters relating to the soul's destiny. As a result, Hindu intellectuals, although lacking interest in science, were well stocked with various theological and philosophical perspectives when, beginning in the sixteenth century, their civilization was faced with unprecedented challenges instigated by the arrival of European traders, imperialists, and missionaries. Among these challenges, the most momentous was that posed by modern science and technology (Halbfass 1988).

The colonial context

With the growing dominance of the British colonial enterprise in India in the nineteenth century, Western literary, philosophical, political, social, and theological ideas came streaming into the sub-continent. Enlightenment ideals of rationalism, social equality, tolerance, faith in science, and progress arrived alongside British cultural pretensions of superiority and Protestant missionary condemnations of all things Hindu. Deistic ideals of an intelligently ordered universe and a universal rational religion competed with Christian notions of humankind's fallen state and need for divine absolution. Yet the missionaries provided the Indian elites opportunities for English education, highly desired by Hindus as a means of advancement under British employment. Among the subjects taught were the natural sciences, initially intended to undermine traditional Hindu views, thereby preparing the way for conversion (Gosling 1976; Killingley 1995).

Until the 1890s, many Indian intellectuals looked upon the coming of the British as providential, enabling Indians to cast off age-old superstitions, reform their caste-bound society, and improve material life (Raychaudhuri 1999). Some Hindu reformers such as Rammohan Roy (1772?–1833), founder of the Brahmo Samaj, called for the introduction of the natural sciences into the Indian curriculum, while claiming that India was the source behind all human knowledge, including science. Roy took seriously the claim of Orientalists such as William Jones that India had once enjoyed a Golden Age (the time of the Vedas and Upanishads) in which the sciences, arts, and a primitive form of monotheism had flourished (Kopf 1969; Trautmann 1997). This peaceful and prosperous civilization, according to some versions of the Orientalist story, was gradually corrupted by popular superstitions, apathy, and foreign invasions.

Roy searched the Vedic literature looking for aspects of his tradition admired by the British, and found them. In particular, he discovered a rational monotheism purer than the corrupted theology of polytheistic (Trinitarian) Christianity (Killingley 1981, 1993). In defense of a pristine Hindu monotheism, Roy combined the classical Hindu design argument of Shankara with European natural theology, creating a Vedantic deism. His Brahmo Samaj became a major player in the cultural negotiations between Hindu traditionalism and the twin forces of liberal modernism and Christian evangelism.

By the end of the nineteenth century, Hindus had become disillusioned with many aspects of the British Raj. Especially following the Revolt of 1857, British rule grew increasingly oppressive. Hindus realized that, despite the capacity of science to improve life, science had also created the military technology that enabled the British conquest of India. The hypocrisy of the British rulers, with their ideals of social justice that applied only to Europeans, was duly noted.

In the religious arena, Roy's successors in the Brahmo Samaj, Debendranath Tagore (1817–1905) and Keshab Chandra Sen (1838–84), had misgivings regarding the thoroughgoing rationalism of his Vedantic deism. Apprehensive about the atheistic potential of deistic views, Tagore and Sen might have been expected to turn to an uncritical reliance on Vedic scriptures. But the historical and literary critique of the Bible in the West had its own impact on English-educated Hindus. Under

Debendranath's leadership, the Brahmo Samaj renounced the idea of Vedic infallibility, emphasizing instead an emotional approach to God relying on inner, intuitive awareness. In addition, Hindus by mid-century were no longer satisfied with pleading for the equality of Hinduism with the religion of their rulers. They began to proclaim the superiority of Hinduism to Christianity, and to all other religions – a view put forth by Rajnarain Bose (1826–99), a member of Debendranath's conservative wing of the Brahmo Samaj. Intermingling with these religious issues was the emergence of Hindu cultural nationalism – Rajnarain has been called the Grandfather of Indian Nationalism (Kopf 1974, 1979). Such views created considerable tension with the universalistic outlook championed by Roy and Sen. The Hindu reception of Darwinism in the latter three decades of the nineteenth century can be fully understood only in the context of these complex, interacting trends.

Responses in the late nineteenth and early twentieth centuries

One of the earliest Hindu responses to Darwinism was that of the Vedic revivalist Dayananda Saraswati (1824–83). Founder of the Arya Samaj, Dayananda is well known for his Orientalist-inspired view that the Vedas contain all knowledge, including modern science (Jordens 1998). But, for Dayananda, Darwinian evolution is not part of modern science because it is not scientific. In an 1878 public lecture dealing with Western philosophy and Darwin's theory, Dayananda characterized English philosophy as that of worms and insects (Singh 1971). He held that if Darwin were correct, then there should be examples of contemporary monkey–human transformations. Further, he argued, the copulation of one animal species with another results in sterility – thereby confusing hybridism with transmutation.

Underlying Dayananda's anti-evolutionism is his theistic world view. Dayananda refurbished the classical Logical-Atomist design argument, using its assumption of the eternal nature of material atoms and souls as well as of God to ridicule the Christian doctrine of *creatio ex nihilo* (Saraswati 1970). His anti-evolutionism is elaborated in the writings of his early followers, who revived the Logical-Atomist argument for a divine tutor:

> We have […] little respect for a theory such as that of Darwin which propounds that human species are a development of an inferior animal nature. For, if we were to accept this, we would be at a loss to trace the origin of human language and the possession of Divine knowledge, which are peculiar to mankind only, and which […] are not self-acquired, but can only be learnt from others.
>
> (Quoted in Singh 1971: pt. 2, 5n)

Another early Hindu response, but more favorably disposed to Darwin, was that of Keshab Chandra Sen. Sen (1940a) avoided detailed discussion of organic evolution and natural selection, relegating them to an inferior status and focusing on a higher, progressive spiritual evolution intermingled with notions of cultural and religious evolution. He interpreted the history of religion as a succession of ever more enlightening revelations, culminating in his own New Dispensation, a blend of Christian and Hindu ideas. Particularly noteworthy is Sen's (1979) idea – probably inspired by the writings of Helena Petrovna Blavatsky, co-founder of the Theosophical Society – that the traditional avatar mythology of the Hindus, involving successive incarnations of the god Vishnu in fish, tortoise, boar, half-man/half-lion, dwarf, and fully human forms, anticipated the stages of Darwinian evolution. But the Hindu version was superior as it included higher stages of cultural and spiritual evolution, as seen in the incarnations of Buddha and Krishna (Brown 2007a). Such evolutionary truths had been discovered by the ancient seers not by empirical methods, but by means of yogic intuition, or "scientific yoga vision" (Sen 1940b: 540).

Most of the early Hindu assimilations of evolutionary thinking were responses not so much to Darwin's theory as to Lamarckian and various socio-cultural versions of evolution. Noteworthy are the theories of Auguste Comte and especially Herbert Spencer. Spencer's theory of cosmic evolution (elaborated in his *First Principles*), with its insistence that the universe went through periodic cycles of evolution and dissolution, seemed to provide scientific warrant for the Hindu notion of recycling cosmic ages. His appeal to the law of energy conservation and the indestructibility of matter to oppose the Christian claim of God's creating the universe *ex nihilo* bolstered Hindu self-affirmation *vis-à-vis* the "anti-scientific" dogmas of the Christian missionaries. Further, Spencer's idea that science is a quest for unity and merely the opposite side of a similar religious quest confirmed for many Hindus the monistic ideals of Shankara.

The foremost advocate of a scientized Advaita compatible with evolution was the Bengali monk Swami Vivekananda (1863–1902). Influenced by Spencer's views of evolution and the harmony of science and religion, Vivekananda regularly appealed to the law of energy conservation to proclaim to audiences in the West, as well as in India, that science confirmed the truth of Advaita, that we are all manifestations of one Reality, call it God or Brahman. Vivekananda (2003: 3: 111, 4: 348–49, 5: 533) portrayed Christianity as anti-scientific and crumbling under the onslaught of modern evolutionary theory.

At the same time, Vivekananda was disquieted by Spencer's insistence that the highest reality, uniting science and religion, must ever remain unknown. Inspired by ideas of yogic perception, he claimed that, unlike Western scientists who feared the Unknown, ancient Vedic seers and contemporary sages have made the leap and conquered through inner vision (*ibid.*: 6: 104). Yogic perception explains how the Samkhya teacher Kapila discovered the truth of organic evolution without using microscopes or telescopes, how the Yoga teacher Patanjali discerned the truth of spiritual evolution, and the Advaita teachers realized the ultimate unity beyond spirit and matter. For Vivekananda, evolution of the soul in various animal forms, from amoeba to enlightened Buddha, is simply the reverse of an involution of spirit by which the Consciousness of Brahman becomes involved in matter – a notion likely borrowed from Blavatsky. This dual process of spiritual involution and evolution is a hallmark of Vivekananda's modern Vedic evolutionism (Killingley 1990). Spiritual evolution, accordingly, trumps organic evolution: a soul with sufficient spiritual merit can transform the body it inhabits into a higher organism without waiting for rebirth, by yogic manipulation of the body's molecules (Vivekananda 2003: 1: 290, 6: 113).

Variants of Vivekananda's Vedic evolutionism abound. Perhaps the most famous is that of the Bengali nationalist turned mystic Aurobindo Ghose (1872–1950). Like Vivekananda, Aurobindo propounded a notion of spiritual involution–evolution and chastised Darwinism for its ethical shortcomings in emphasizing competition over love. And, like the Swami, Aurobindo could not accept that Darwinism was the whole story. He believed that gradual Darwinian evolution failed to explain gaps between species, arguing for a kind of punctuated equilibrium dependent upon "sudden and rapid outbursts" of the Divine to produce higher life forms (Ghose 1944: 9). Each species has its own inherent nature modifiable only within small limits, an early Hindu instance of anti-macroevolutionism. For Aurobindo, spiritual evolution seemed destined to result in Supermanhood, but the teleological implications of this view were problematic. On the one hand, he acknowledged a lack of scientific evidence for purpose in nature. On the other, he feared that any notion of intent would suggest that the divine lacks something it desires. Accordingly, the attainment of Supermanhood is simply the play of Godhead/Brahman and "only the realisation of the totality in the part" (Ghose 1982: 835).

The post-colonial period

The spectrum of late nineteenth and early twentieth-century Hindu responses to Darwinism continued to reverberate among educated Hindus long after Indian independence in 1947 and into the twenty-first century. In the post-colonial era, two important trends have emerged affecting the Hinduism–origins discourse. First is the accelerating number of Hindus living outside India, generally constituting a well educated, prosperous minority concerned with preserving cultural traditions (Eck 2000; Knott 2000). Second is the development within India itself, beginning in the 1920s, of an exclusivist Hindu nationalism focused not on British imperialism, but on Hindu identity in opposition to corrupting foreign elements – from Western culture in general to alien religions, especially Christianity and Islam (Bhatt 2001). In their shared concern for cultural self-affirmation, Hindus of the diaspora and of the old country occasionally interact in advancing the idea that two centuries of European colonization of India have bequeathed to Western-educated Hindus a colonized mind sullied by the influences of "Western" Enlightenment thinking, "Western" science, and "Western" materialism.

Until the mid-1960s, the major strand of Hinduism known to most westerners was the Vedanta of Shankara as filtered through the Neo-Vedanta of Vivekananda. The steady growth of his world-wide Ramakrishna Mission helped to spread his scientized, evolution-accommodating Neo-Advaita. But, with the arrival in New York in 1965 of Swami A. C. Bhaktivedanta Srila Prabhupada, evangelist for the Gauḍiya Vaishnava sect focused on Krishna, another important aspect of Hinduism began to be noticed in the West. The society that Prabhupada founded, the International Society for Krishna Consciousness (ISKCON), while initially attracting disillusioned Western youth, gradually gained attention from conservative members of the Hindu diaspora steeped in theistic traditions from the old country. In recent decades, other theistic Hindu movements have found a home in the diaspora.

Regarding origins, the theistic schools are generally anti-evolutionist. Reminiscent of Dayananda's anti-evolutionary views, they often accept the idea of cosmic evolution but reject organic evolution, incorporating strategies and arguments developed by Christian anti-evolutionists (Brown 2002). Prabhupada (1979) is well known for his opinion of Darwin as a rascal, and that Darwin and other evolutionists were monkeys in their former lives. Prabhupada's more scientifically minded American disciples, Richard L. Thompson (1981) and Michael A. Cremo (2003), have developed elaborate Krishnaite versions of the design argument.

An unexpected ally of the Hindu creationist cause is the celebrated New Age promoter of Ayurvedic medicine, Deepak Chopra. While bemoaning the "hijacking of the whole notion of intelligent design" by Christian fundamentalists, he readily affirms the oft-repeated Christian creationist argument taken over from Fred Hoyle that the universe randomly producing DNA is like a hurricane producing a jet plane by blowing through a junkyard (Chopra 2005).

Like Christian creationism, Hindu creationism has come to accept much of modern evolution. For example, the comparative historian of philosophy Kisor Kumar Chakrabarti (1999: 211), in sympathizing with the Logical-Atomists (referred to below as Nyaya), argues:

> the evolution of higher animals from lower animals and that of the latter from inanimate matter is evident and raises no problems for the Nyaya […] Life forms are typically supposed to emerge later and evolve from the lower to the higher. But that does not imply that the Darwinian type of evolution can be the whole story. For that leaves the evolution of conscious states to a process of natural selection without the guidance of intelligence – and this is not acceptable to the Nyaya.

ISKCON's Michael Cremo (2003) claims that the Vedic account of what he calls "human devolution" incorporates elements of Darwinism, specifically, "reproduction with modification." But the process is top-down, rather than bottom-up, humans devolving from higher subtle and more complex forms through a process of intelligently guided genetic engineering.

Science and religion

Common to most Hindu responses to Darwinism is respect for science. Few educated Hindus today question the idea that Hinduism is scientific. If Hinduism is regarded as harmonizing with Darwinism, this simply reaffirms the scientific credentials of Hinduism. If Hinduism is seen as conflicting with Darwinism, this certifies the non-scientific nature of the latter. But how is science understood by Hindu apologists? The meaning assigned to or assumed for science is critical to the way religion and science are harmonized and integrated. Generally Hindus have viewed science as a rational, consistent body of knowledge gained through study and practice, but with relative disregard for science as a particular method of discovery (cf. Rambachan 1987).

The basic apologetic strategy, then, is to distinguish two levels of knowledge, higher and lower, spiritual and material. The achievements of modern science based on limited sensory experience – the lower science – are read back into the sacred texts, thereby scientizing the tradition. The truths of the higher, spiritual science are confirmed by one of two basic means of knowing. For Neo-Advaitins such as Vivekananda, the validating authority is supra-conscious perception – the inner yogic intuition – of qualified teachers. Such supra-conscious experience is both conflated with scientific empiricism and praised as superior to outward empirical confirmation as it has the warrant of inner certainty. Neo-Advaitins rarely acknowledge the social and psychological conditioning of all experience, internal or external. For theistic Hindus, the ultimate warrant for truth is not yogic perception, but divine revelation. Thus, in the case of ISKCON, there is nothing in the Vedas, the *Bhagavata Purana*, or the *Bhagavad-Gita* that is not scientific – their teachings all reveal the higher dimensional science of Krishna consciousness.

The Hindu accommodation of evolutionary theory has been accomplished by the complementary interpretive processes of scientizing the tradition and spiritualizing science. Where the two processes are not integrated, success is minimal, as illustrated in the case of Narayan B. Pavgee (1854–1935), a Marathi nationalist who eagerly read into Puranic accounts of Vishnu's avatars the whole of geologic history, equating various geologic eras with the various incarnations (Brown 2007b). Most significant was Pavgee's insistence that the ancient Vedic seers made these discoveries through thoroughly empirical, scientific means, discovering fossils such as trilobites. But Pavgee, more interested in political than mystical goals, found little acceptance of his ideas – due at least in part to his refusal to spiritualize science.

The situation today

Michael Ruse (Chapter 34 in this volume) refers to the tension in the West, from 1700 to 1859, between the ideals of providence and progress. A variant of this tension developed in India with the introduction of European ideas. In the Hindu case, however, the perspective opposing the idea of progress was not that of divine providence, but that of cosmic destiny manifest in the great cosmic cycles. Especially relevant here is that within any one basic cycle, lasting millions of years, the temporal process is one of decline and degeneration. This interpretation of history leads to the idea that all knowledge (in the current cycle) was known in the past but gradually forgotten, so that any modern breakthroughs are simply rediscoveries. There is no real openness to new discoveries or revisions of knowledge about the world, for even supra-conscious perception only confirms the teachings of the ancients.

As in the West for Christians, the issues surrounding the question of origins for Hindus reflect the larger conflict between tradition and modernity. But for Hindus today, the conflict is enormously complicated by the extent to which modernization is identified with westernization. Technology is commonly embraced, but the

"Western" secular attitude of mind, the skepticism towards all traditional authority that characterizes the scientific temperament, is often rejected. The result is what Nanda (2003) refers to as reactionary modernism. For Christianity, the crisis with modernity came from within; for Hindus and Asians generally, it came from without. Hindu responses to modern science and evolutionary theory are thus equally responses to Western imperialism, Christian exclusivism, and their postcolonial legacies. There is no end in sight to these conflicts. Thus, to rephrase Ruse's conclusion for the Hindu context (Chapter 34 in this volume): While ostensibly the controversy regarding origins may seem to be a science–religion question, for Hindus it is a much broader concern not only about what kind of culture and society Hindus want for themselves, but also about what it means to be Hindu in the contemporary, pluralistic world.

References

Bhatt, C. (2001) *Hindu Nationalism: Origins, Ideologies and Modern Myths*, Oxford: Berg.

Brown, C.M. (2002) "Hindu and Christian Creationism: 'Transposed Passages' in the Geological Book of Life," *Zygon: Journal of Religion and Science* 37: 95–114.

——(2007a) "The Western Roots of Avataric Evolutionism in Colonial India," *Zygon: Journal of Religion and Science* 42: 423–47.

——(2007b) "Colonial and Post-Colonial Elaborations of Avataric Evolutionism," *Zygon: Journal of Religion and Science* 42: 715–47.

——(2008) "The Design Argument in Classical Hindu Thought," *International Journal of Hindu Studies* 12(2): 103–51.

Chakrabarti, K.K. (1999) *Classical Indian Philosophy of Mind: The Nyāya Dualist Tradition*, Albany, NY: SUNY Press.

Chemparathy, G. (1972) *An Indian Rational Theology: Introduction to Udayana's Nyāyakusumāñjali*, Vienna: Indologisches Institut der Universität Wien.

Chopra, D. (2005) "Intelligent Design without the Bible," www.huffingtonpost.com/deepak-chopra/intelligent-design-withou_b_6105.html.

Cremo, M.A. (2003) *Human Devolution: A Vedic Alternative to Darwin's Theory*, Los Angeles: Bhaktivedanta Book Publishing.

Eck, D.L. (2000) "Negotiating Hindu Identities in America," in *The South Asian Religious Diaspora in Britain, Canada, and the United States*, H. Coward, J. R. Hinnells and R. B Williams (eds), Albany, NY: SUNY Press, 219–37.

Ghose, A. (1982) *The Life Divine*, Pondicherry: Sri Aurobindo Ashram.

——(1944) *Evolution*, Calcutta: Arya Publishing House.

Gosling, D. L. (1976) *Science and Religion in India*, Madras: Christian Literature Society.

Halbfass, W. (1988) *India and Europe: An Essay in Understanding*, Albany, NY: SUNY Press.

——(1992) *On Being and What There Is: Classical Vaiśeṣika and the History of Indian Ontology*, Albany, NY: SUNY Press.

Jordens, J. T. F. (1998) *Dayananda Sarasvati: Essays on His Life and Ideas*, New Delhi: Manohar.

Killingley, D. (1981) "Rammohun Roy on the Vedānta Sūtras," *Religion* 11: 151–69.

——(1990) "*Yoga-Sūtra* IV, 2–3 and Vivekānanda's Interpretation of Evolution," *Journal of Indian Philosophy* 18: 151–79.

——(1993) *Rammohun Roy in Hindu and Christian Tradition; The Teape Lectures 1990*, Newcastle upon Tyne, UK: Grevatt & Grevatt.

——(1995) "Hinduism, Darwinism and Evolution in Late Nineteenth-century India," in *Charles Darwin's The Origin of Species: New Interdisciplinary Essays*, D. Amigoni and J. Wallace (eds), Manchester, UK: Manchester University Press, 174–202.

Knott, K. (2000) "Hinduism in Britain," in *The South Asian Religious Diaspora in Britain, Canada, and the United States*, H. Coward, J. R. Hinells and R. B Williams (eds), Albany, NY: SUNY Press, 89–107.

Kopf, D. (1969) *British Orientalism and the Bengal Renaissance: The Dynamics of Indian Modernization 1773–1835*, Berkeley, CA: University of California Press.

——(1974) "The Missionary Challenge and Brahmo Response: Rajnarain Bose and the Emerging Ideology of Cultural Nationalism," *Contributions to Indian Sociology* 8: 11–24.

——(1979) *The Brahmo Samaj and the Shaping of the Modern Indian Mind*, Princeton, NJ: Princeton University Press.

Mittal, K. K. (1974) *Materialism in Indian Thought*, New Delhi: Munshiram Manoharlal.

Murty, K. S. (1959) *Revelation and Reason in Advaita Vedānta*, Waltair: Andhra University.

Nanda, M. (2003) *Prophets Facing Backward: Postmodern Critiques of Science and Hindu Nationalism in India*, New Brunswick, NJ: Rutgers University Press.

Prabhupada, A. C. B. (1979) *Life Comes from Life: Morning Walks with His Divine Grace A. C. Bhaktivedanta Swami Prabhupada*, Los Angeles, CA: Bhaktivedanta Book Trust.

Rambachan, A. (1987) "The Place of Reason in the Quest for *Moksha* – Problems in Vivekananda's Conceptualization of *Jñānayoga*," *Religious Studies* 23: 279–88.

Raychaudhuri, T. (1999) *Perceptions, Emotions, Sensibilities: Essays on India's Colonial and Post-Colonial Experiences*, Oxford: Oxford University Press.

Saraswati, D. (1970) *An English Translation of the Satyarth Prakash, Literally: Exposé of Right Sense (of Vedic Religion) of Maharshi Swami Dayananda Saraswati, "The Luther of India," Being a Guide to Vedic Hermeneutics*, 2nd edn, D. Prasad (trans.), New Delhi: Jan Gyan Prakashan.

Sen, K.C. (1940a) "Philosophy and Madness in Religion," in *Life and Works of Brahmananda Keshav*, P. S. Basu (ed.), Calcutta: Navavidhan Publication Committee, 334–45.

——(1940b) "Yoga – Objective and Subjective," in *Life and Works of Brahmananda Keshav*, P. S. Basu (ed.), Calcutta: Navavidhan Publication Committee, 535–55.

——(1979) "That Marvelous Mystery – The Trinity," in *Keshub Chunder Sen*, D. C. Scott (ed.), Madras: Christian Literature Society, 219–47.

Singh, Bawa Chajju (1971) *Life and Teachings of Swami Dayanand Saraswati*, New Delhi: Jan Gyan Prakashan.

Smart, N. (1964) *Doctrine and Argument in Indian Philosophy*, London: George Allen & Unwin.

Thompson, R. L. (1981) *Mechanistic and Nonmechanistic Science: An Investigation into the Nature of Consciousness and Form*, Los Angeles, CA: Bhaktivedanta Book Trust.

Trautmann, T.R. (1997) *Aryans and British India*, Berkeley, CA: University of California Press.

Vivekananda. (2003) *The Complete Works of Swami Vivekananda*, nine volumes, in *Swami Vivekananda: Life, Works & Research* [multimedia CD], Kolkata: Advaita Ashrama.

Further reading

My essay "Hindu Responses to Darwinism: Assimilation and Rejection in a Colonial and Post-Colonial Context" (*Science & Education* (2010) 19: 705–38) surveys traditional and modern Hindu perspectives on origins. My article "The Design Argument in Classical Hindu Thought" (cited above) surveys major arguments for and against the concept of a divine designer in classical Hindu philosophical–theological literature. Forthcoming from Routledge (2012), my book, *Hindu Perspectives on Evolution: Darwin, Dharma, and Design*, gives a detailed historical analysis of Hindu views on evolution and creationism from Vedic times to the twenty-first century. From the works cited above, Wilhelm Halbfass's *India and Europe: An Essay in Understanding* is a masterful discussion of the political–cultural contexts in which Indians responded to the challenges of modern science. David Gosling's *Science and Religion in India* summarizes developments in the Hindu–science discourse in the nineteenth and twentieth centuries. Dermot Killingley's "*Yoga-Sūtra* IV, 2–3 and Vivekānanda's Interpretation of Evolution" nicely analyzes Vivekananda's evolutionary thought. Also very informative is Killingley's "Hinduism, Darwinism and Evolution in Late Nineteenth-century India". My essay "Hindu and Christian Creationism: 'Transposed Passages' in the Geological Book of Life" details ISKCON creationism and its relation to late twentieth-century Christian creationism. Meera Nanda's *Prophets Facing Backward: Postmodern Critiques of Science and Hindu Nationalism in India* gives an astute critique of Hindu nationalist abuse of science in its advocacy of the "Vedic science" pioneered by Vivekananda.

37
CHRISTIAN RESPONSES TO EVOLUTION

Chris Doran

While it may be a bit over-simplistic to say that Christian responses to evolution are divided between those who take what science says seriously and those who do not, this claim would not be far from the mark. From the scientific creationists, to intelligent design theorists, to those who believe that God indeed creates the world through evolutionary processes, Christians have either made some sort of peace with evolution, or they continue to challenge its scientific legitimacy in spite of its overwhelming success in explaining the rise of biological complexity. For those in the former group, the task now is to describe not only how God creates via evolution, but also to examine any potential trouble one runs into by making such an assertion. For those in the latter group, the battle to dislodge it as the organizing theory of biology rages on still today.

Scientific creationism

The scientific creationist movement led perhaps the prominent twentieth-century American Christian challenge of the legitimacy of evolutionary biology. Invigorated by Henry Morris (1985), scientific creationists rely on a form of biblical literalism that views much of the Bible as a literal report of historical events. Genesis 1–11, in particular, is viewed as a scientific account of how God created the world. So, for example, Morris rejects the standard age of the universe, the gradual formation of the fossil record over time, and the idea that predation and death are intrinsic to the structure of the biological world. Instead he believes that the universe is about 6000 years old, a singular world-wide flood explains the fossil record, and lions and Venus flytraps were vegetarians before Eve took her fateful bite from the apple. It is easy to criticize scientific creationists for what seems to be an irrational position in light of the contemporary scientific understanding of the world; yet it is important to realize that underlying their position is a fundamental epistemological concern that still drives their movement today: If the first chapters of the Bible are not true, then the remainder of the text cannot be trusted either. While one can sincerely sympathize with their concern, it is important to question the peculiar way that they have chosen to address the issue, since their primary contention about Genesis values scientific truth over other forms of truth. In other words, the theological truths of Genesis 1–11 (the universe's utter dependence on God, the awesomeness of divine power, the human condition, etc.) have no veracity unless they are first proven true scientifically. This not only makes theology a slave to science, but also makes science into an arbiter of claims that, by definition, it has no right to discuss. As we shall see, the topic of what science can or cannot adjudicate seems to be of perennial importance as Christians talk about evolution.

Intelligent design

While the 1987 US Supreme Court decision Edwards *v.* Aguillard effectively stopped scientific creationism from being taught in American public schools, it did not halt popular challenges to evolution. In 1991, this challenge reached a previously unseen level in the United States with the publication of the widely popular *Darwin on Trial*, in which Philip Johnson laid out the central ideas that would give birth to the intelligent design (ID) movement. While Johnson did little to provide the details of the proposed ID scientific research project, he made attacking evolution and the way scientists do science an acceptable practice for his followers. His chief argument is that, since the scientific method is committed to analyzing the world through natural causes only, God is by definition excluded from scientific investigation. As such, it's not that science directly denies the existence of God, but by definition treats divine action as if it has no measurable impact on the universe. Once this move is made, then in all practicality God's existence is denied and scientists, most of whom Johnson thinks are atheistic, are left to fashion the story of how the universe came to be. This "scientific priesthood," as he puts it, has proclaimed evolution, conceived of as a completely naturalistic and purposeless process, to be the story of how the universe came to be (Johnson 1993: 159). Moreover, in order to prevent this creation story from being displaced from its perch, these scientific priests set the rules of science. One of the most important rules is that theories, like evolution, cannot be disputed unless they can be replaced with an acceptable substitute. So if someone challenges evolution without offering a replacement, scientists can merely dismiss the person for not understanding how science works.

With the dominant origin story in hand and the rules to maintain its hegemony, Johnson insists that it is a short step for scientists to say that something outside of the scope of science is in fact not real. That is why scientists can, in good conscience, say in one breath that science does not deal with God, and then in the next breath make sweeping pronouncements about the purposelessness of the cosmos. What other people understand to be the limitations of science become twisted into limitations upon reality, because to these scientific priests the notion that there could be a reality outside of science is literally unthinkable. Anything outside of the realm of science amounts to nothing more than superstition, which is seen as a blatant abandonment of a rational and objective system of thought for something completely irrational and subjective.

While it is true that science explains physical phenomena using only natural causes (methodological naturalism), it is quite a leap to say that this rule makes science functionally atheistic. This rule does not take away from the idea of God sustaining or acting within the universe, but merely indicates that science is agnostic on this point. Any scientist that turns this methodological principle into a philosophical world-view, as Johnson suggests many scientists do, should be reminded that she is no longer engaging in the scientific enterprise, but rather in philosophy. Furthermore, Johnson obviously believes that scientific knowledge (which by his assessment is not merely ambivalent about but rather antithetical toward God) enjoys hegemonic authority in our culture. This assertion would be quite disturbing if it was in fact true, but for many this is certainly not the case. Yet, even if Johnson were right, it is not the rules of science that should be questioned, but rather our culture's insistence upon listening to "scientific priests" when they pontificate on matters outside of science.

While the ID movement could not have begun without Johnson, it would have not blossomed into the worldwide phenomena it is today without the work of at least two other people. The first key person to join Johnson's movement was biochemist Michael Behe. In his widely popular book *Darwin's Black Box*, Behe introduced the fundamental ID concept: irreducible complexity. "By irreducibly complex I mean a single system composed of several well-matched, interacting parts that contribute to the basic function, wherein the removal of any one of the parts causes the system to effectively cease functioning" (Behe 1998: 39). He goes on to say that these irreducibly complex biological features could not have evolved by gradual evolutionary processes and thus must have been designed by a designer. While his theoretical model is intriguing, Behe of course has to overcome a considerable hurdle – he has to provide examples of irreducibly complex features that occur in nature. He believes there are at least five such examples; perhaps the best known of these is the bacterial flagellum. The idea is that the "tail" that so many bacteria use to swim could not have evolved through a gradual process because no intermediate tail-like structure would have been of any advantage to a bacterium. Therefore the flagellum must have been designed in one fell swoop. For most members of the science-and-religion dialogue, Behe's concept of irreducible complexity is nonsensical. For instance, Kenneth Miller (1999) demonstrates in great detail how this idea falls apart, both conceptually and scientifically, when one considers how things have actually evolved. For example, Miller shows how intermediate tail-like structures did exist, yet were not used as flagella for locomotion but instead provided other functionality. In other words, evolutionary theory does not dictate that the function of a biological structure we see presently be the same as the function we observe in a "transitionary" feature of the past.

While Johnson is undoubtedly the father of the movement, in many ways William Dembski is the most important thinker in ID today. With doctoral degrees in mathematics and philosophy, as well as a master of divinity degree, Dembski provides many of the scientific, philosophical, and theological details of the larger research program that Johnson envisioned in the early 1990s. Eager to find a repeatable method that definitively shows that irreducibly complex or designed features exist in nature, and thus the existence of a designer, Dembski created his famous, or perhaps infamous, Explanatory Filter (Dembski 1999: 122–52). The Filter is supposedly capable of distinguishing biological features that were created by necessity, chance, or design. The Filter is fallible, even Dembski admits that; it will likely yield both false negatives and false positives. For example, the designer might in fact be deceptive and make a biological feature look like one created by chance, even though it was in fact designed. Ultimately, the Filter acts as a net that catches designed things, but lets through non-designed things. Furthermore, and perhaps most importantly to the efficacy of the entire ID project, is the insistence that ID does not have to speculate as to the identity of the designer in order for the Filter to operate properly. "Intelligent design is therefore not the study of intelligent causes per se but of informational pathways induced by intelligent causes. As a result, intelligent design presupposes neither a creator nor miracles. Intelligent design is theologically minimalist. It detects intelligence without speculating about the nature of the intelligence" (Dembski 1999: 107).

Dembski's own admission about the fallibility of the Filter does not begin to address one of its deepest flaws. The Filter makes a person choose between three mutually exclusive options, when most would agree that biological features are a product of necessity and chance working together, not independently of each other. More troubling, however, is his last assertion about not needing to make statements about the nature of the intelligence of the designer. ID has to speculate about the identity of the designer, and in fact already does implicitly. For example, Dembski says that ID abides by the scientific rules of such disciplines as forensics, cryptography, and anthropology in order to perform its research. The significant problem that ID fails to recognize is that these sciences presuppose that a certain kind of intelligence is operating behind the scenes, namely human intelligence. If these types of science can lend aid to design investigation, then ID proponents are actually presuming that the designer acts in a similar manner to human beings, which is a violation of their very own precept that they are not speculating about the nature of the designer, and leads one to consider whether ID can actually deliver on its promise.

Following in the footsteps of Johnson, Dembski also believes the scientific method constricts inquiry into design, since it is limited to natural causation. Since the rules of science are functionally atheistic, one is prevented from legitimate investigation into whether or not divine action is scientifically detectable. Operating under the assumption that divine action is in some manner detectable by scientific means, one can see that the potential payoff for the ID movement is quite substantial. If ID is correct, then there is scientific evidence that supports the existence of God. Dembski takes this particular point and runs with it, saying that ID is the bridge between science and Christian theology (Dembski 1999). If ID is seen as a legitimate scientific research enterprise, then ID and Christian theology are mutually supportive in their claims about the origin of the universe and the deity behind it. The potential theology of ID has yet to be worked out in careful detail, but it is readily assumed by many ID proponents that the God of Jesus Christ and the designer behind ID are one and the same.

This association is dangerously cavalier, for at least two reasons. First, as discussed already, Dembski himself admits that the designer may in fact be deceptive. If that's the case, then we are forced to ask, do Christians really want to attribute that particular characteristic to God? Second, it is clear that ID has to assume that the designer acts like a human, if forensics, cryptography, and anthropology are to be at all useful. The ability to use those scientific disciplines in service of ID implicitly presupposes an analogy between divine action and human action. While ID proponents have yet to justify this analogy theologically, it appears that such a direct analogy violates any sense of divine transcendence, which is fundamental to the Christian doctrine of God (see Doran 2010).

Theistic evolution

Those who are convinced that evolution really is supported by the data, and believe that God uses and/or directs evolution to bring about the divine *telos* of the universe, are often called "theistic evolutionists." Ironically, this term was used first as a pejorative label by scientific creationist Henry Morris (1985: 215). The range of scholars who fall in this camp are many, and the scope of explaining how God actually works through evolutionary processes is vast. Below are four examples that are representatives of the key contributions to this topic.

Robert John Russell (2008) argues that what we see around us is the direct effect of God working through evolutionary processes to bring creation toward the divine end, and what's more, God does it without breaking the laws of nature that God laid out in the very beginning of the universe. This non-interventionist objective divine action, as he calls it, works at the level of quantum events. Relying on an indeterministic interpretation of quantum mechanics that holds there are ontological gaps in the very framework (the quantum level) of the universe, Russell believes that Christians can maintain that God works in these openings to affect the direction of evolutionary history, since quantum events are ultimately the causal factors in genetic mutations that lead to evolutionary change. While this is obviously a "bottom-up" understanding of divine action (meaning God's activity at the bottom level "multiplies" into effects we can see at an upper level), Russell maintains that this description of divine action is not exhaustive, nor does it preclude other descriptions of divine action (e.g. "top-down" or "whole–part"). This particular account of divine action depends upon a particular interpretation of scientific knowledge and thus is subject to alteration, if not complete dismissal, if the science changes. While Russell is willing to take this gamble, since he believes a doctrine of creation and God's activity within it is dependent at some level on the science of the day, some desire a theology of divine action that does not rely so heavily on science.

Arthur Peacocke sees Russell's proposal as mistaken because God is somehow viewed as a supplemental figure to the world's processes. Instead, he believes that the natural processes revealed by evolutionary biology and other sciences are in fact God acting as Creator. "God, to use language usually applied in sacramental theology, is 'in, with, and under' all-that-is and all-that-goes-on" (Peacocke 1998: 360). According to Peacocke, God voluntarily limits Godself to allow room for creation to become itself. This divine self-limitation plays out particularly in his understanding of the interplay of law and chance in the creative process. If the universe were only governed by law, then we would only see a rather uncreative, repetitive order; yet, if the universe was ruled only by chance, chaos would reign because order would never develop. Thus at the intersection of just enough law to create order and just enough chance to create novelty, the universe continues to be created. "For a theist, God must now be seen as acting to create in the world *through* what we call 'chance' operating within the created order, each stage of which constitutes the launching pad for the next" (Peacocke 1998: 364). While divine self-limitation has become quite popular in the science-and-religion dialogue as a way of supposedly making room for the creation to be itself, it seems strange to me, at least, that God must in any way limit Godself in order to make room for creatures to exist. Such a theological move seems to be made on the faulty presupposition that God and creatures are in competition when they act at the same moment. If God is truly transcendent, though, God does not compete with creatures because divine action is of a different kind than creaturely action.

Blending his Roman Catholic background with process philosophy, John Haught asserts that Darwin actually gave a great gift to Christian theology. "Evolutionary biology not only allows theology to enlarge its sense of God's creativity by extending it over measureless eons of time; it also gives comparable magnitude to our sense of the divine participation in life's long and often tormented journey" (Haught 2008: 50). Evolution shows us that life in this universe is much messier than Christians before Darwin could have ever imagined, and therefore we must now focus more explicitly on suffering love as the central attribute of God. With that as his controlling theme, he renounces the classical attributes of omnipotence and impassibility, instead maintaining that God lures creation toward a better future through a persuasive rather than coercive love and suffers along with the world, as creativity is often expressed through the tragedy of pain, death, and extinction. For Haught, the divine goal of the universe is beauty, which he defines as "a delicate synthesis of unity and complexity, stability and motion, form and dynamics" (*ibid.*: 139). While Haught forces us to think about the purpose of the universe in a much different way with the introduction of an aesthetic *telos*, the link between beauty and tragedy is somewhat overwhelming. Does he mean to say that God cannot create something beautiful without an element of the tragic?

Theologian Ted Peters and scientist Martinez Hewlett consider God's work in creation from a much different perspective. Even though the dominant Darwinian interpretation of nature rules out an inherent *telos*, they argue it has nothing to say about whether or not there is a divine purpose for nature. The purpose for creation comes not from the origin of the universe, but instead from God's plan of eschatological consummation. For them, God's redemptive activity gives creation its meaning, and so purpose can only be ascertained from an eschatological vantage point. "It is omega that determines alpha" (Peters and Hewlett 2003: 160). God creates, sustains, and directs the universe by giving it a future. In other words, God's creative activity is constant as God gives the universe each moment of its existence in such a way that it is open to what might come next, and thus open to novelty that is not determined by the past. This understanding of God's interaction with the universe relies on Thomas Aquinas' understanding of primary and secondary causality. God is the primary cause from which all other secondary causes proceed and derive their efficacy. While this tag-team approach to God's activity may not have the precise detail of some of the other proposals, one wonders if this is all that we can really say about the mystery of divine action.

Theodicy

Merely saying that God creates through evolutionary processes does not necessarily get a Christian where she wants to go. If God really does create via evolution, then does a world that seems to exhibit so much suffering and death say anything meaningful about God? We find ourselves up against the age-old theodicy problem, but this time with an evolutionary twist. In particular, if the issue of human or moral evil is set aside, the question of natural evil, whether that be physical (volcanoes, earthquakes, tsunamis, etc.) or biological (pain, predation, extinction, etc.), is still hugely problematic because such evil existed for billions of years before humans ever arrived on the scene. Before we turn to the various responses to this topic, it is important to say up front that theodicy is not so much a problem to be solved *per se*, but instead we are engaging in the exercise of faith seeking understanding.

One way to approach this issue is to say that natural evil is not a problem at all, since non-human suffering and extinction are just the facts of life and as such they have no moral content other than what humans project onto them. In other words, the cat batting the mouse around before she kills it is just the way it is – it's neither good nor bad. Kenneth Miller puts it this way, "Like beauty, the brutality of life is in the eye of the beholder […] The reality of life is that the world often lacks mercy, pity, and even common decency" (Miller 1999: 246). While in one sense Miller "solves" the theodicy by suggesting that natural evil is not really evil at all, it seems like a bit of a stretch to say that the same God who created the universe and proclaimed it very good would not in fact consider the mouse's suffering to be real and thus in need of redemption.

Another way to approach this issue is to admit that natural evil really exists, but ultimately it is part of a greater good that God desires for the universe. In many ways, this position is the free-will defense of the existence of moral evil extended into the realm of natural evil. John Polkinghorne (2005), for example, calls it the "free-process" defense. Since God loves creation, God voluntarily limits divine power in order to allow creation the space to be itself and thus "create" itself. Through the interplay of natural laws and evolutionary processes, we observe the heights of biological complexity, but also the depths of suffering involved with predation. In the end, it is in this space that God displays divine love, and the possibility of human free will is allowed to arise. One is still left to wonder, though, whether this means-to-an-end argument is ultimately fitting of a God of love. In other words, is human free will worth hundreds of millions of years of non-human predation and extinction?

Christopher Southgate goes in a different direction completely, and constructs a four-part evolutionary theodicy. First, he says Christians cannot shy away from the ontological aspect of theodicy. Christians must admit to, and somehow how attempt to make sense of, the fact that God gave existence to and continues to sustain a universe that not only contains non-human suffering, death, and extinction, but uses it to generate novelty and new life. Second, Christians must confront the teleological aspect, which he thinks may be the "sharpest edge" of the problem (Southgate 2008: 9). If God has a long-term *telos* for creation, then the creaturely suffering, death, and extinction that have existed for millions of years appear to be a rather gruesome means to whatever divine end, no matter how glorious. Third, he adds a kenotic feature to this proposal by maintaining that God the Father fact suffers alongside of creation through a self-emptying love that is demonstrated by the Cross. Finally, at the level of soteriology, the significant question remains: Does God's plan of salvation include the redemption of non-human creatures through Christ as well? Moreover, is God really a good and loving God if there is no measure of redemption for non-human suffering? Therefore Southgate asserts that God must redeem non-human suffering if one is to maintain that God is indeed omnibenevolent. Southgate's proposal should be strongly commended for showing us what it really means theologically to proclaim that God creates via evolution; however, the question remains: How does patripassianism helps us "solve" the theodicy problem? While I see this turn to divine suffering (common among participants in the science-and-religion dialogue) primarily as a misunderstanding of the traditional doctrine of divine impassibility, I fail to see how God the Father suffering with creation is any more redemptively efficacious than God the Father staying resolute despite creaturely suffering in bringing the universe to a glorious consummation.

Drawing upon the insights of the process philosophers, process theologians such as Ian Barbour come at theodicy from a different starting point from those mentioned above. Unlike Polkinghorne, who, for example, believes in voluntary divine self-limitation, Barbour understands God to be metaphysically limited. Barbour clearly points out that this does not mean God is limited by a force outside of God, but rather that the traditional attributes of omnipotence, omniscience, and impassibility must be reinterpreted in light of what science says about how the universe works. For example, in contradistinction to the traditional case for divine impassibility, Barbour believes that God suffers along with creation as God tries to bring about divine goals, since change is a metaphysical fact of this particular universe from which not even God is immune. This viewpoint, then, has a particular payoff. "In an evolutionary world, struggle and conflicting goals are integral to the realization of greater value. By accepting the limitations of divine power we avoid blaming God for particular forms of evil and suffering; we can acknowledge that they are contrary to the divine purposes in that situation" (Barbour 1997: 323). He openly admits that the process understanding of suffering is unpalatable to many because it calls into question whether good ultimately triumphs over evil. Instead, he says God does not abolish evil once and for all, but transmutes it into something that can be integrated into the larger pattern of beauty God is weaving. The standard objection to process theology, of whether or not the Christian faith, and particularly the doctrine of God, is capable of being described purely in metaphysical categories, is valid. More to the particular point about theodicy, it seems rather difficult from the vantage point of the Easter event to argue that the resurrection is not the definitive symbol of God's ultimate triumph over evil. If that is the case, then process theologians have given up too much in an attempt to absolve God from creating a world that includes suffering and death.

Why all the fuss?

After all of this, it seems natural to ask: Why all the fuss over the theory of evolution anyway? What makes it so different from the theories of gravity, plate tectonics, or relativity? Part of the reason why evolution stirs people up so much, in America at least, comes from how the news media often portray the subtleties of the science-and-religion dialogue as "evolution and creation" or, worse, "evolution versus creation." While this stark dichotomy may make for explosive television programming, it does not take into account the sophistication of Christian thought that this dialogue has brought to the table. That aside, there are at least three reasons why a discussion of the theory of evolution differs from one about gravity. First, as seen with the scientific creationists, at first glance it is easy to read the opening passages of Genesis as if they are eyewitness accounts to the creation of the world, but upon a deeper reading significant textual issues become rather prominent. For example, how does one make sense of the discontinuity of the Genesis 1 and 2 creation stories without performing quite sophisticated mental gymnastics? Once again taking their cue from scientific creationists, many Christians unwittingly assume that if the first pages of the Bible are not historically accurate, then the rest is untrustworthy as well. Christian theologians as early as Augustine, though, have proclaimed that scripture tells the story of how to get to heaven, not how the heavens work. Put another way, the Bible is not a science textbook and as such does not have to be scientifically accurate in order to be theologically accurate. Christians must consider carefully why there is an insistence on treating the hermeneutical challenges of Genesis so differently from the hermeneutical difficulties of other biblical passages.

Second, ironically enough, many American Christians have uncritically bought into the following world-view, created by atheists: evolutionary processes adequately explain the biological world around us and thus an appeal to divine action is no longer needed. This, however, is a false dichotomy and one that Christians must not be afraid to refute. As seen in the descriptions of divine action by Russell, Peacocke, Haught, and Peters and Hewlett, above, there is no reason to believe that the success of evolution in explaining the rise of biological complexity gives it (or evolutionary biologists, for that matter) the ability to deny the existence of God or God's *telos* for the universe. The very idea of what power holds the universe in existence does not fall within the purview of evolutionary theory, or science as a whole. As more Christians are exposed to theistic evolution, the atheist rejection of divine action by merely appealing to Occam's razor becomes harder and harder to defend.

Third, I suspect the most troubling aspect of evolution to many Christians is actually this: common descent seems to be saying that humans are not really all that special in the grand scheme of things. This, then, is seen as a denial of human uniqueness spoken about in Genesis 1 and 2. There are, of course, considerable textual issues when discussing what it means to be created in the image of God. While not minimizing the finer details of this important discussion, I maintain that Christians often too quickly assume that being made in the image of God means that we are so unique that we are more unlike the rest of God's creation than we are like it. This is hubris in its worst form. While humans do exhibit qualities that are unique in comparison with other creatures, evolution's emphasis on common descent should spur us to remember two pre-Darwinian theological truths. The story of Genesis 1 tells us that we are profoundly related to everything else that God created in the universe, since everything derives its existence from God. Should it come as a surprise, then, that common descent describes in the language of science what Christian theology has affirmed for two millennia? Moreover, the Genesis 2 account tells us that God created Adam from the dust of the ground, the same ground from which the rest of creation arose. The Genesis writer's point that we are made from the same stuff as the rest of creation should be a keen reminder that we humans should remain humble when we consider our place among creation. In other words, evolution's ability to humble us may have more to do with why so many American Christians have been so aggressively distrustful of this theory than anything else.

References

Barbour, Ian (1997) *Religion and Science: Historical and Contemporary Issues*, New York: HarperCollins.

Behe, Michael (1998) *Darwin's Black Box: The Biochemical Challenge to Evolution*, New York: Touchstone Press.

Dembski, William (1999) *Intelligent Design: The Bridge Between Science & Theology*, Downers Grove, IL: InterVarsity Press.

Doran, Chris (2010) "Intelligent Design: It's Just Too Good to be True," *Theology & Science* 8 (2): 223–37.

Haught, John (2008) *God After Darwin: A Theology of Evolution*, 2nd edn, Boulder, CO: Westview Press.

Johnson, Philip (1993) *Darwin on Trial*, 2nd edn, Downers Grove, IL: InterVarsity Press.

Miller, Kenneth (1999) *Finding Darwin's God: A Scientist's Search for Common Ground Between God and Evolution*, New York: HarperCollins.

Morris, Henry (1985) *Scientific Creationism*, Green Forest, AR: Master Books.

Peacocke, Arthur (1998) "Biological Evolution – A Positive Theological Approach," in *Evolutionary and Molecular Biology: Scientific Perspectives on Divine Action*, Robert J. Russell, William R. Stoeger and Francisco J. Ayala (eds), Vatican City/Berkeley, CA: Vatican Observatory/Center for Theology and the Natural Sciences, 357–76.

Peters, Ted and Martinez Hewlett (2003) *Evolution from Creation to New Creation: Conflict, Conversation, and Convergence*, Nashville, TN: Abingdon Press.

Polkinghorne, John (2005) *Science and Providence: God's Interaction with the World*, Philadelphia, PA: Templeton Foundation Press.

Russell, Robert J. (2008) *Cosmology From Alpha to Omega*, Minneapolis, MN: Fortress Press.

Southgate, Christopher (2008) *The Groaning of Creation: God, Evolution, and the Problem of Evil*, Louisville, KY: Westminster John Knox Press.

Further reading

Responding to evolution from a Christian vantage point means dutifully considering the various textual issues of Genesis. One of the very best introductions into this is Conrad Hyers, *The Meaning of Creation: Genesis and Modern Science* (John Knox Press, 1984). For much more on the topic of how God works through evolution, see the edited work by Robert John Russell *et al.*, *Evolutionary and Molecular Biology: Scientific Perspectives on Divine Action* (Vatican Observatory/Center for Theology and the Natural Sciences, 1998). One very helpful contribution to the Christian responses from a more conservative theological viewpoint is *Perspectives on an Evolving Creation* (Eerdmans, 2003) edited by Keith Miller. Finally, if you are at all intrigued by process theology, then turn to the definitive introduction by John Cobb and David Ray Griffin entitled *Process Theology: An Introductory Exposition* (Westminster John Knox Press, 1976).

38
JEWISH ORIGINS
Cosmos, humanity, and Judaism

Shai Cherry

Cosmos

Although the ancient Greek philosophers agreed that nothing comes from nothing, they were every bit as interested in origins as were the ancient Israelites – and for the same reason. The Greeks denied *creatio ex nihilo* (creation out of nothing), and generally understood the world, or at least its material elements, to be eternal. But the prime cause (Aristotle) or demiurge (Plato) is ultimately responsible for the eternal laws of nature which keep the heavenly spheres in motion. The world has a design, and that design is sensible. Since nature has been ordered through reason, then the behavior of humanity, embedded within that natural order, should be in harmony with reason. Natural law is predicated on that very harmony. According to Plato's cosmogony (the creation of the cosmos) found in the *Timaeus*, the demiurge "planted reason in soul and soul in body." And just as our bodies have a soul, so, too, does the body of the universe (Plato 1965: 30). "The ultimate justification for the [ancient Greek] study of the world of nature is an ethical one" (Lloyd 1970: 71).

Ethics similarly drives the Israelite imaginings concerning the wonders of creation. To coin an ungainly phrase, cosmogony reflects theodicy; and theodicy, it need not be said, reflects ethics. For the Israelite authors of the Hebrew Bible and the Rabbis who later transform those writings into the Jewish Torah, what is compelling about cosmogony has nothing whatsoever to do with science and everything to do with its ethical implications.

Theological dualists, like Gnostics, accept the material world as evil. Alas, there's much evidence to support such a view. They then work backwards to argue that the creator of the world, too, must be evil. The heirs of the Hebrew Bible, however, have to contend with the word as well as the world – and the Torah describes God's evaluation of the cosmos in the very first chapter of the very first book, Genesis: "And God saw all that He had made, and found it very good" (Genesis 1: 31).

Does that evaluation include the snake that rears his ugly head to tempt Eve in the Garden of Eden? Or, did God not make the snake, thus excluding the serpent from the executive summary? But, if God did not make the snake, whence evil?

The prophet who penned the poetry of Isaiah was more concerned to preserve strict monotheism than to insist on unalloyed divine benevolence when he wrote that God is the author of all reality, the good and the bad: "I form light and create darkness, I make weal and create woe – I the LORD do all these things" (Isaiah 45: 7). Biblical scholars speculate that he was living in an environment (sixth century BC Babylonia) where a dualistic religion invoked both a good god and a bad god. Although that dualistic solution explains evil, it denies monotheism.

The opening of Genesis offers another response to the question of "whence evil?" Although translations like the Authorized King James usually obfuscate the theology of Genesis 1, the Hebrew actually suggests that God was *not* the creator of all.

> In the beginning, God created the heaven and the earth. And the earth was without form, and void; and darkness was upon the face of the deep. And the Spirit of God moved upon the face of the waters. And God said, Let there be light: and there was light.
>
> The Authorized King James Version

> When God began to create the heaven and the earth – the earth being unformed and void, with darkness over the surface of the deep and a wind from God sweeping over the water – God said, "Let there be light"; and there was light.
>
> The Jewish Publication Society TANAKH

When God began creating, according to the Hebrew and the Jewish Publication Society's translation, there were already material elements on the stage of creation. The translators of the TANAKH placed all those elements between dashes. Two of those elements were *tohu vavohu*, translated by the TANAKH as *unformed and void*, and by Everett Fox, a contemporary Bible scholar, as *wind and waste* (Fox 1995: 13). (You can almost hear the wild howling through the Hebrew *tohu vavohu*.) Although God went on to create light *ex nihilo*, material creation derives its origin not from God, but from that wild waste that God then ordered into a cosmos. On the stage of creation things were a-swirl as the curtain lifted. The claim of Genesis 1 is that chaos is the default state of creation (Levenson 1988). Without God imposing order on nature, and without humans behaving according to God's law, the cosmos would revert to chaos. This reversal to a watery chaos is exactly what happened during Noah's flood. The Torah says that, in addition to the heavens opening up from above, the Earth was inundated from the waters below (Genesis 8: 2), effectively undoing God's separation of the waters (Genesis 1: 6–7). This return to wild and waste was in response to creaturely recalcitrance (Genesis 6: 1–12).

In Genesis 1, chaos lurks just under the surface of the water in the form of those gigantic sea monsters (Genesis 1: 21) that in other Near-Eastern cultures challenge divine sovereignty. In the second creation story beginning in Genesis 2: 4b, which most biblical scholars assume was written earlier than Genesis 1, temptation is untamed. The question "Who let the snake into the garden?" is misplaced, or rather, it's anachronistic. Our earlier creation story in Eden simply assumes and accepts the existence of temptation as part and parcel of God's garden. Centuries later, Genesis

1 attempts to submerge evil in the abyss, where it could be domesticated only through human obedience to the divine (Levenson 1988).

The end of the second book of the Bible, Exodus, uses the same verb to describe the completion of the tabernacle as we have in Genesis for the completion of God's work of creation (Exodus 40: 33 and Genesis 2: 1). Literarily, the author, or editor, is signaling that creation is incomplete without God's presence on Earth as symbolized by the tabernacle (Kearney 1977). In the Garden of Eden, God is at home and humans are guests. In the world according to the priestly author of Genesis 1, we humans are responsible for making God a home here, and that occurs through constant dedication to righteous behavior (Klawans 2004). When our vigilance wanes, that's precisely when there is an opening for the forces of evil to rush into the ethical vacuum.

There are, then, three different cosmogonies preserved in the Hebrew Bible: (1) God is the author of all reality (Isaiah 45); (2) God ordered a pre-existent chaos (Genesis 1); and (3) there are multiple gods who are variously responsible for good and evil (Isaiah 45's implied disputant and, perhaps, the author of Psalm 82). Theodicy reflects cosmogony; each theory of the world's origins contains within it an explanation for the existence of evil.

These cosmogonies all appear in Rabbinic literature (first to eighth centuries AC). Yet there is a decided discomfort with allowing Genesis 1 to retain its plain sense. One midrash (c. fifth century AC) admits that there were elements on the stage of creation as the curtain rose, but insists that God had previously created those elements. Although this midrash doesn't explicitly address the claim that everything was created by God out of nothing, it is the clearest example within Rabbinic literature of the polemic between adherents of Genesis 1 (God created with pre-existent matter) and those of Isaiah 45 (God created everything).

> A philosopher inquired of Rabban Gamliel, saying to him: "Your God is a great artist, but he found good ingredients that helped him: wild and waste, darkness, wind, water and the deep."
>
> Rabban Gamliel said, "Drop dead! The verb 'create' is written about all those elements in other places in the Bible."
>
> (Genesis Rabbah 1: 9)

Table 38.1

	Cosmogony	*Theodicy*
Isaiah 45	God creates light and darkness (unlike Genesis 1, where God creates only light)	God is solely responsible for the evil in the world
Genesis 1	God creates the world from pre-existing material	The world is not perfect because God worked with what was available; we must be vigilant to obey God's will
Implied disputant of Isaiah 45	Multiple gods exist and an evil god fashioned the world	The good God has nothing to do with evil; God is purely good

Rabban Gamliel bases his retort on the relatively rare verb that is used for creation: *bara'*. The only character in the Hebrew Bible who "creates" is God. Thus Rabban Gamliel is arguing for a double creation that involves God having created all those elements that were swirling around chaotically on stage prior to the curtain rise. The philosopher is most likely representing a cosmogonic view found in Plato's *Timaeus* that bears striking similarity to that of Genesis 1. In both cases, God (or the demiurge) imposes order on the chaos. In neither text is the material cause of those pre-existing elements explicit. Rabban Gamliel exploits the lacuna.

The Gospel of Matthew (26: 41) wisely counsels us to avoid temptation since although the spirit is willing, the flesh is weak. The flesh may be weak, but, according to the implications of Rabban Gamliel's midrash, the flesh that God created is sufficiently strong to withstand temptation and to choose the good that God has commanded. The recalcitrance of matter is no excuse, in the Rabbinic world, for those who succumb to temptation. God commands humans who were created from material capable of fulfilling the divine will (Hirsch 1964; Genesis 1: 1.)

The most frequently cited cosmogony in the Rabbinic period was creation out of pre-existent material (Harvey 1992). Yet, to know what Judaism maintains about a given issue, look at Jewish law and liturgy, genres that embody a consensus. Within the narrative literature of Judaism, such as the Torah and midrash, one can find mutually exclusive opinions on all sorts of issues – as we have seen in regard to cosmogony. Even within the legal literature, disputes abound. So, it is all the more impressive when one finds an undisputed piece of law.

The Mishnah (c. 220 AC), Rabbinic Judaism's first literature in the wake of the Roman destruction of the Jerusalem Temple (69 AC), informs us that just as we are to gratefully acknowledge God as the source of goodness in our lives through reciting a blessing, so too must we recite a (different) benediction recognizing divine sovereignty upon hearing bad news (B'rachot 9: 2). The Jewish legal tradition, like Rabban Gamliel above, sides with Isaiah: God is the author of all reality. The morning prayer service similarly incorporates Isaiah 45's monotheistic manifesto. God is the creator of all – light and darkness.

The Rabbis of the Mishnah restrict the study of Genesis 1 and explicitly state that teaching it *requires interpretation* (Hagigah 2: 1). One simply cannot understand Genesis 1 through a literal reading. The Rabbis, for example, understood that we count days by our position *vis-à-vis* the Sun. But, if the Sun was not created until day four, how were the first three days measured? For good reason, then, there was a tradition not to read Genesis 1 literally. As with the Torah in general, the Rabbis often creatively recontextualized the words and sentences of Genesis in order to weave them into the fabric of their own lives (Cherry 2007).

Thus we see that Michael Ruse's claim that "there was no reason to dispute the accuracy of the Genesis account of origins" should be qualified when applied to the history of Judaism (Ruse, this volume, p. 381). First and foremost, the Rabbis eschewed a literal reading of the Hebrew Bible, especially concerning the account of creation (Cherry 2006). Secondly, although the ancient Rabbis generally accepted the reading of Genesis 1 which admits to pre-existent matter, the cosmogony of Isaiah 45 eventually eclipsed the cosmogony of Genesis 1, becoming nearly universal by the Middle Ages.

Moreover, while Isaiah 45 polemically claims that God is the *efficient* cause of both good and evil, *creatio ex nihilo* argues that God is the *material* cause of all reality, a claim not explicit in the Rabbinic sources. By the Middle Ages, Jewish philosophers and mystics rallied around the cosmogony of *creatio ex nihilo* to counter the corrosive influence of Aristotelian philosophy and its insistence on the eternity of the world (Fox 1990; Matt 1995). Jewish philosophers concurred that were the world eternal, as Aristotle claimed, laws of nature would never change. Since the Torah posits the divine reward of rain for obedience and drought for disobedience, an eternal universe operating through immutable laws of nature would "give the lie" to the Torah's incentive program (Maimonides, *Guide of the Perplexed*, II: 25).

The cosmogonic principle of *ex nihilo* was re-visioned by the mystics to mean creation from the divine Nothing, that infinite aspect of divinity about which nothing can be known or said. The Zohar, the thirteenth-century classic of Jewish mysticism, contends that Genesis 1 is not only an account of creation, but, more importantly, it's an account of divine self-disclosure through emanation. This image of cascading emanation will prove to be particularly accommodating to Jewish theologians seeking to incorporate biological evolution into Jewish thought.

Humanity

There are two different explanations for the origins of humanity offered in the two creation stories. Genesis 1, while identifying us with the rest of the land animals created on day six, also connects us to God through our creation in the divine image (Genesis 1: 26). Our name, *adam*, which is the generic name for humanity in this first story, is derived from being like (*domeh*) God.

Genesis 2 has Adam, a single human, created prior to the rest of the animal kingdom. Yet, in this account, Adam is so named because he is made from the earth, or *adamah* in Hebrew (Genesis 2: 7). In both stories, independently or taken together, the human is a volatile combination of the Creator and the created, of intelligence and will on the one hand, and ambition and appetite on the other. That volatility is felt when the serpent encircles Eve with his words and provokes her desires (Genesis 3: 1).

Although human frailty and the difficulty of obedience to the divine are highlighted in the Garden, the very next chapter has God assuring Cain that such temptations can be overcome (Genesis 4: 7). The stories of the first humans demonstrate a psychological predisposition to indulge our appetites, just as the animals do. But Rabbinic Judaism balanced that inclination with the value of, and capacity for, self-restraint. The Mishnah asks: "Who is mighty? One who controls his passions" (Avot 4: 1). Augustinian Christianity, however, turned that psychological predisposition to indulge into an ontological condition, beginning with Adam and Eve, and staining all future generations with their Original Sin in the Garden.

Original Sin is a Christian dogma with no precise counterpart in Jewish thought. Whatever punishment is doled out to the transgressors in the Garden of Eden does not stain the souls of Adam and Eve's progeny. Indeed, the Garden of Eden story, located in Genesis 2 and 3, is rarely referenced again in the Hebrew Bible. Genesis 1, with its culmination on the seventh day, becomes central to the Jewish observance of the Sabbath (Exodus 20: 11). When the scientific community began discussion of biological evolution in the second half of the nineteenth century, Judaism easily negotiated the textual challenges presented by a literal reading of the Genesis 1 narrative and ignored the Christian dogma of Original Sin. For Judaism, the challenges of evolution are theological, not textual.

The Jewish exegetical tradition was mined in order to demonstrate how consonant ancient Judaism was with the new theory of evolution. In particular, there is one explanation of a confounding biblical text that is particularly hospitable to an evolutionary reading. In the first twenty-five verses of Genesis, God creates in the singular. Then, in verse 26, God speaks in the first person plural. Genesis Rabbah, the fifth-century Rabbinic text in which we met Rabban Gamliel earlier, offers three different explanations for the plural. The most interesting, for our present purposes, is the interpretation that God is consulting with the works of the heaven and the Earth. A thirteenth-century mystic from Christian Spain, Moses Nachmanides, explains that the consultation involved material combinations and that humanity physically incorporates all that had been created earlier. By the time this tradition reaches a post-Darwinian rabbi, the Malbim (1809–79), he uses the fifth-century interpretation to explain that "let us *make* humans" in Genesis 1: 26 refers to the human form that contains within it all earlier life forms, while verse 27's "And God *created*" refers to the divine intellect that only God can create *ex nihilo*, which elevates humans to the divine image.

Although there were ways to interpret, or bracket, the text of Genesis in regard to Darwinian evolution, there was a pervasive concern among Jewish theologians that Darwin's theory left no room for God. Most Jewish theologians who dealt with evolution could accept the fact of evolution, and reconcile it with the text of the Torah if necessary, as long as there was a role for God in the unfolding of natural history. Materialism was the real threat, that and the attendant ethics of nihilism and relativism. As we saw with Rabbinic cosmogonic speculation nearly 2000 years before, it is the moral question that exercises the Jewish community.

The Jewish theologian who saw earliest and most clearly the threats of Darwin's mechanism to Jewish ethics was Isaac Mayer Wise (1819–1900), who became the institutional founder of American Reform Judaism. Like many opponents of Darwinism, Wise accepted the transmutation of species (although see Swetlitz 1995). Wise, influenced by the German philosophy of idealism, understood God to work within individual organisms to effect evolutionary changes and speciation. The struggle for survival that characterizes the engine of evolution for Darwin, however, was anathema:

> In a moral point of view the Darwinian hypothesis on the descent of man is the most pernicious that could be possibly advanced, not only because it robs man of his pre-eminence, which is the coffin to all virtue, but chiefly because it presents all nature as a battle ground, a perpetual warfare of each against all in the combat for existence, and represents the victors as those praiseworthy of existence, and the vanquished ripe for destruction. […] Peace in any shape is illegitimate and unnatural.
>
> (Wise 1876)

Michael Ruse is surely correct that opposition to Darwinism, at least in the Jewish community, stems from ethical concerns. Isaac Mayer Wise dubbed Darwinian evolution "Homo-Brutalism." The twentieth-century Jewish theologian Mordecai M. Kaplan emphasized humanity's "spiritual selection," as opposed to natural selection, whereby cooperation and kindness propel humanity's evolution (Kaplan 1948: 246–56).

The most common strategy of many early advocates of Darwinism was to identify evolution with progress, which contemporary scientists are careful to avoid (Gould 1989), and to show how that progressive element of evolution conformed to Jewish messianic belief. Rabbi Elijah Benamozegh of Italy (1822/23–1900) shifts the Garden of Eden from an idyllic past to a messianic future. The same approach was taken by Rabbi Kaufman Kohler as early as 1874. (Darwin's *Descent of Man*, which applies evolutionary theory to humanity, was published only in 1871.) Kohler went on to become the president of the Reform seminary, Hebrew Union College. Kohler pressed progressive evolution into service to support Reform ideology over Orthodoxy.

> Does not this idea of [the evolution of] life perfectly harmonize with our religion, whose history is one of internal progress, and whose aim is the highest future ideal of humanity? Does it not harmonize perfectly with our comprehension of religion, which we do not recognize in form, but in reform, which has its living power in the internal remodeling of Judaism and its Messianic mission in progress toward completing humanity?
>
> (Kohler 1874: 821)

In parallel fashion, some Orthodox thinkers emphasized evolution's slow, lawful changes to demonstrate evolution's affinity to Orthodoxy.

Other rabbis, influenced by the neoplatonic image of emanation within Jewish mysticism, see evolution as a physiological marker of the return to the One from whom we all emerged. The decades before the Second World War allowed Jews the illusion that cultural progress was sweeping the Jews toward a new dawn. The following excerpt from Rabbi Abraham Isaac Kook's (1865–1935) mystical diary summarizes his view toward evolution, though not the Darwinian mechanism of natural selection.

> The theory of evolution, which is increasingly conquering the world at this time, conforms to the kabbalistic secrets of the world more so than other philosophical theories.
>
> Evolution, which proceeds on a path of ascendancy, gives [us] reason to be optimistic in the world. How is it possible to despair at a time when we see that everything evolves and ascends? When we penetrate the inner meaning of ascending evolution, we find in it something divine which shines with absolute brilliance.
>
> (Kook 1938: II:537)

Rabbi Kook is here speaking of evolution as a philosophical theory, not a biological one. Yet elsewhere he admits the physiological descent of the human body from other animals, and sees in that unity testimony to the divine unity which permeates all of reality (Cherry 2003). As my teacher, Arthur Green, writes:

> Kabbalah shows us how deeply all levels of being are linked to one another. For the kabbalist, God and world, cosmic macrocosm and each individual human microcosm, all reflect the same structure. The "great chain of Being" approach to spirituality can be appreciated more than ever by post-moderns, not only for its beauty, but for a certain dimly perceived accuracy as well. Each human being contains the entire universe, claims the ancient myth. All the rungs of descent (and potential ascent) are contained in each soul. This is true even in a totally demythologized, biological form: all of our ancestors, each stage and mini-step in the evolution of life that brought us to where we are today are present within us. The DNA that constitutes the life-identity of each of us exists indeed *zecher le-ma'aseh bereshit*, "as a memory of the act of Creation."
>
> (Green 2003: 108)

Although there is an apocalyptic tradition within Jewish sources, the notion of progress is normative. (Interestingly, one of the very few groups to reject evolution, Lubavitch/Chabad, interpreted the catastrophe of the Jews during the Second World War as a harbinger of the messiah; Elior 1998.) In the traditional prayer service, recited thrice daily, the messiah is invoked to culminate the messianic process, not to initiate it. According to the Judaism of the liturgy, the Messiah will appear only when we humans have prepared the way in the desert (Hoffman 1998: 35f). Progress is a messianic prerequisite, and, as Kook and Green observe, is compatible with a mystical understanding of both the unfurling pageant of life from amoeba to human, and the moral and intellectual advances of human civilization. Thus Michael Ruse's comments on the antagonism between cultural progress and Christianity do not lend themselves to Judaism (Ruse, this volume, p. 384–85).

Judaism

There is one more origin to consider – the origin of Judaism. The Torah itself is conspicuously silent on why God chose Abraham as the father of the tribe. Rabbinic midrash fills in that gap and depicts Abraham as first monotheist. Rabbi Moses Maimonides, in 1180, provides more information about how Abraham turned from the religion of his fathers, polytheism, to monotheism. According to the philosopher Maimonides, Abraham realized through scientific speculation that there could only be one force behind the movement of all the celestial spheres. In other words, Abraham came to recognize God not through a vocal divine call, as we read in Genesis 12, but through his own philosophical and scientific reasoning. In order to know that God exists and to love God, as commanded in Deuteronomy 6: 5, Maimonides requires the Jew to study physics and metaphysics, preferably those written by Aristotle (Maimonides 1899: Laws of Idolatry, Chapter 1). By the Middle Ages, science and philosophy became religious pursuits and requirements (Davidson 1974)!

To be sure, few outside Maimonides' elite, philosophical circle agreed that the only way to love God is through the study of science and philosophy, but there did emerge such a tradition in the Middle Ages. In the decades prior to Darwin, when the emancipation of Jews in Western Europe and the Jewish Enlightenment were allowing and encouraging Jews to study the sciences, many followed the trail blazed by Maimonides (Harris 1987; Meyer 1997).

At roughly the same time, there was a religious renewal movement in Eastern Europe called Hasidism. One of the Hasidic masters recognized the necessity to study science himself, but he forbade his disciples from any such exposure. Science was far too dangerous to one's Jewish commitment. "The essence of Judaism," wrote Rebbe Nachman of Bratslav (1977: II: 12), "is to go only in wholehearted simplicity without any science." For other Hasidic leaders, even the image of Abraham demanded revision as one who knew God through devotion rather than speculation (Green 1989).

Today, it is precisely this population of Ultra-Orthodoxy (which includes Hasidism) which is resistant to evolution. The Modern Orthodox and non-Orthodox communities, which comprise more than 90 per cent of American Jewry, overwhelmingly support the teaching of evolutionary theory and are disproportionately involved in scientific pursuits (Heilman and Cohen 1989).

Conclusion

Although the Pentateuch gives no indication of the belief in resurrection of the dead, it becomes central for both Rabbinic Judaism and early Christianity. One scholar has argued that the doctrine of *creatio ex nihilo* originated in order to lend logical support to resurrection (Goldstein 1984). If God can create the world from nothing, all the more can God recombine pre-existent elements to revivify the dead and decomposed. Resurrection provides a venue to reward the righteous who died unrewarded. Resurrection is theodicy – it incentivizes righteous behavior in a seemingly indifferent world.

Yet the vast majority of American Jews no longer believe in resurrection of the dead. A new interpretation is in order, which understands God as the power that brings life to the inert and inorganic. God does not resurrect the dead; God vivifies that which has not yet emerged through the threshold of life.

Can the theodicy that resurrection had provided survive such a reinterpretation? If not, Judaism must once again wrestle with the question that has animated this essay: whence ethics?

References

Cherry, S. (2003) "Three Twentieth-Century Jewish Responses to Evolutionary Theory," *Aleph: Historical Studies in Science and Judaism* 3.

——(2006) "Crisis Management via Biblical Interpretation," in *Jewish Tradition and the Challenge of Darwinism*, G. Cantor and M. Swetlitz (eds), Chicago, IL: University of Chicago Press, 166–87.

——(2007) *Torah Through Time: Understanding Bible Commentary from the Rabbinic Period to Modern Times*, Philadelphia, PA: Jewish Publication Society of America.

Davidson, H.A. (1974) "The Study of Philosophy as a Religious Obligation," in *Religion in a Religious Age*, S. D. Goitein (ed.), Cambridge, MA: Association for Jewish Studies, 53–68.

Elior, R. (1998) "The Lubavitch Messianic Resurgence," in *Toward the Millennium*, P. Schafer and M. Cohen (eds), Leiden: Brill, 383–408.

Fox, E. (1995) *The Five Books of Moses*, New York: Schocken Books.

Fox, M. (1990) *Interpreting Maimonides*, Chicago, IL: University of Chicago Press.

Goldstein, J. (1984) "Origins of the Doctrine of Creation ex Nihilo," *Journal of Jewish Studies* 35(2): 127–35.

Gould, S. J. (1989) *Wonderful Life*, New York: W.W. Norton.

Green, A. (1989) *Devotion and Commandment*, New York: Hebrew Union College.

——(2003) *Ehyeh: A Kabbalah for Tomorrow*, Woodstock, VT: Jewish Lights Publishing.

Harris, J. M. (1987) "The Image of Maimonides," *Proceedings of the American Academy of Jewish Research* 54: 117–39.

Harvey, W. Z. (1992) "Rabbinic Attitudes Toward Philosophy," in "*Open Thou Mine Eyes ...*" *Essays on Aggadah and Judaica Presented to Rabbi William G. Braude*, Herman Blumberg (ed.), Hoboken, NJ: Ktav Publishing House, 83–101.

Heilman, S. C. and S.M. Cohen (1989) *Cosmopolitans and Parochials: Modern Orthodox Jews in America*, Chicago, IL: University of Chicago Press.

Hirsch, S. R. (1976) *The Pentateuch*, Isaac Levy (trans.), Gateshead, UK: Judaica Press.

Hoffman, L. A. (1998) *My People's Prayer Book*, Vol. 2, Woodstock, VT: Jewish Lights Publishing.

Kaplan, M. M. (1948) *The Future of the American Jew*, New York: Macmillan.

Kearney, P. J. (1977) "Creation and Liturgy: The P Redaction of Ex 25–40," *Zeitschrift fur die Alttestamentlische Wissenschaft* 89(3): 375–87.

Klawans, J. (2004) *Impurity and Sin in Ancient Judaism*, New York: Oxford University Press.

Kohler, K. (1874) "Science and Religion," *Jewish Times*, February 20.

Kook, A. I. (1938) *Orot HaKodesh*, Jerusalem: Mossad HaRav Kook.

Levenson, J. D. (1988) *Creation and the Persistence of Evil*, Princeton, NJ: Princeton University Press.

Lloyd, G. E. R. (1970) *Early Greek Science: Thales to Aristotle*, London: Chatto & Windus.

Maimonides, M. (1899) *Mishneh Torah*, Vilna.

——(1963) *Guide of the Perplexed*, S. Pines (trans.) Chicago, IL: University of Chicago Press.

Matt, D. C. (1995) "Ayin: The Concept of Nothingness in Jewish Mysticism," in *Essential Papers on Kabbalah*, L. Fine (ed.), New York: New York University Press, 67–108.

Meyer, M. A. (1997) "Maimonides and Some Moderns," *CCAR Journal* 44: 4–15.

Nachman of Bratslav (1977) *Likutey Mohoran*. Brooklyn, NY: Hasidei Breslav.

Plato (1965) *Timaeus*, Desmond Lee (trans.) Baltimore, MD: Penguin Books.

Swetlitz, M. (1995) "Responses of American Reform Rabbis to Evolutionary Theory," in *Interaction of Jewish and Scientific Cultures in Modern Times*, Y. Rabkin and I. Robinson (eds), Lewiston, NY: Edwin Mellen Press, 103–25.

Wise, I. W. (1876) *The Cosmic God*, Cincinnati, OH: Office of the American Israelite and Deborah.

Further reading

Noah Efron's *Judaism and Science: A Historical Introduction* (Greenwood Press, 2006) provides a comprehensive overview of Judaism and science. Hans Jonas' *Mortality and Morality: A*

Search for the Good after Auschwitz, ed. Lawrence Vogel (Northwestern University Press, 1996) is a collection of essays by the late philosopher of biology and religion, attempting to answer the question "whence ethics?" And Norbert M. Samuelson offers a specifically Jewish approach to our subject in his *Jewish Faith and Modern Science: On the Death and Rebirth of Jewish Philosophy* (Rowman & Littlefield, 2009).

(ii) Biotechnology and justice

39
BIOTECHNOLOGY AND JUSTICE

Ronald Cole-Turner

Before human beings discovered writing, or learned to live in cities, they practiced biotechnology in its simplest forms: agriculture, selective breeding of plants and animals, the use of yeast to produce bread and wine and beer, and the processing of plant extracts for medicinal purposes. These basic forms of biotechnology helped give rise to cities, laws, religions, philosophies, and eventually to the modern science of biology, which drives biotechnological advances to new levels.

Biotechnology alone has growing powers to remake living things, but today's biotechnology is anything but alone. Nanotechnology, and information technology, and a host of other new and exotic strategies have emerged – and some would say they are about to *converge* – in the human quest to transform nature, including human nature. These unprecedented powers may be used for good or ill. But even if they are used largely for good, they are profound in what they portend for our humanity and for our relationship with the natural world.

Today's biotechnology comes into existence within a Darwinian world-view, reflecting its assumptions and possibilities. Throughout the twentieth century, Darwinian evolution and molecular genetics were brought together into a "grand synthesis," culminating in massive projects in genetics research that allow precise genetic comparisons between species. Thanks to this synthesis, we now see the whole realm of living things as interrelated and evolving. We human beings now see ourselves as evolved creatures who share most of our genetic information with other species. For many, the theory of natural selection implies that there is no direction or purpose in evolution itself apart from the human purpose. If that is so, then paradoxically it might now be said that we human beings, who are nothing more than the unintended result of blind processes, are imposing our purposes on evolution by trying to modify nature to suit our will.

It is precisely this combination of a Darwinian world-view and rapidly emerging technologies that create such anxieties about biotechnology. The world of living things seems radically open to our manipulation. Nothing in nature seems to guide us or restrain us. The powers of technology are both expanding and converging. Never before in the history of nature has one species seemed poised to modify the natural world so radically and so quickly. Never before in human history have we been so powerful in our control over living things, including our own bodies and brains. It is no wonder that many today find themselves worrying whether our technology now poses an unmanageable risk to nature and to our own kind. If technology controls nature, who or what controls technology?

Recent advances in biotechnology

To approach such questions, it is first necessary to review the rise of biotechnology and its most recent advances. Biotechnology is not one narrow technique, but includes a range of technologies that interact with living systems in various ways, including areas such as stem cell research. In the past half century, however, the areas of genetics and genetic engineering occupied biotechnology's center stage. Until the pivotal work of Rosalind Franklin, Francis Crick, and James Watson, biotechnology was largely limited to selective breeding, which achieved sophisticated levels in the work of Luther Burbank, but which was limited to cross-breeding what nature had already created.

The 1953 discovery of the structure of the molecule of genetic inheritance, known as deoxyribonucleic acid (DNA), opened a new era for not just the selection but the manipulation of genes. In the 1960s and 1970s, researchers discovered how DNA codes for the construction of proteins, the building blocks of living cells. Soon, research led to techniques to manipulate this DNA, almost as one might edit a code or chemical message, opening the possibility of engineering at the genetic level through the modification of the DNA code.

Genetics and genetic engineering

One of the first applications of genetic engineering is in agriculture. The DNA of plants and farm animals has been modified in order to increase yields, alter the protein in crops, or change the appearance or storage features of produce. These changes have been controversial, especially in Europe, which has banned some of them from the market or required strict separation and labeling of all genetically modified (GM) food. Advocates of genetically engineered foods point to the advantages they see in crops that require less fertilizer, yield more protein, or grow in less favorable environments than traditional crops. Even so, the question of the morality of the patenting of GM seeds and their affordability remains a source of controversy around the world.

By the early 1980s, applications of genetic engineering to medicine seemed to be just around the corner. In the ensuing decades, however, new discoveries have given scientists a greater appreciation of the complexity and subtlety of living systems and of the challenges facing genetic engineering. If the technological advances have come more slowly that predicted, the fundamental science has advanced rapidly, revealing new challenges for technology, but also setting the stage for future technologies unforeseen decades ago.

The Human Genome Project

One context of advance in the basic science of genetics has been the Human Genome Project (HGP). Although the HGP was a federally funded project of the US government, the project itself was a joint effort involving international and private or for-profit partners, some of whom functioned more as competitors than team members. The result of the project, which in some ways is never complete, is the publication of the genetic detail of the entire human genetic code. Funding for the project was justified on the grounds that knowing the entire human genome would lead to breakthroughs in medical research, which is of course true, at least in part.

In the course of the project, researchers made major breakthroughs in automating the process of reading the genetic code and in storing and comparing the information contained in genes. The cost of gene sequencing, as it is called, has fallen dramatically since the project was first conceived. As a result, it is now increasingly common to sequence the genomes of other species, ranging from agricultural plants and animals to chimpanzees to long-extinct Neanderthals. Comparison of human with chimpanzee or Neanderthal DNA allows scientists to understand human evolution much more clearly and to close in, at least at a molecular level, on what makes human beings unique.

At the same time, human individuals can be compared with each other, giving science a clearer picture of human diversity. It turns out that what we call "races" are only superficial differences. Human beings are quite diverse across the species, but these differences are for the most part shared among all ethnic groups. Recent evolution, such as the impact of living for a few millennia with more or less sunshine, seems to have modified skin pigmentation rapidly, explaining how members of the same human family can look so different from each other.

Biological complexities

It was once thought that every protein had its own gene, but the HGP has shown otherwise. About 100,000 different proteins are produced in human cells. When the HGP began, researchers expected to find about 100,000 genes, but in the end found only about 22,000. These 22,000 genes or coding regions in the human genome somehow combine in various patterns to produce the RNA that actually provides the template that produces all these proteins. This finding suggests that a gene is not a closed bit of code so much as a dynamically generated combination of DNA segments that first play one role, then another.

In addition, basic research such as the HGP has revealed the importance of epigenetics, a term used to refer to various chemical processes by which the expression of DNA is regulated up or down. The epigenetic system involves modification of the DNA molecule, but the DNA code itself is not changed. As the name "epigenetics" suggests, these chemical changes are on top of the DNA, where they act somewhat like switches that turn the expression of DNA up or down. Epigenetic changes are inheritable with DNA, but they are more easily modified, and sometimes modifications can be passed from one generation to the next.

Epigenetics also plays a critical role in biological development, helping to explain how a single cell (the newly fertilized zygote) can develop into an organism of trillions of cells, each with the same DNA but each with highly specialized functions. Specialized function is largely a by-product of specialized epigenetic switching. It appears that when DNA is in the newly fertilized egg, many of the epigenetic "switches" are reset so that the DNA behaves as it should in the early embryo. But as cells divide, the switches are reset, variably in different parts of the developing body, so that most of the genes are switched off, allowing the body to develop as it should. Discoveries in epigenetics have led to greater insight as to why nuclear transfer or "cloning" is difficult to achieve, probably because epigenetic factors are not reset correctly. It has also led to a greater appreciation of the role of environment, even to consideration of the possibility that an environmentally induced resetting of an epigenetic factor can be transmitted from one generation to the next.

RNA interference (RNAi) is another system in cells related to gene expression. Essentially, nature has found a way for some RNA to control the function of other RNA. Normally, RNA provides the template for protein construction, but RNAi interferes with this process, reducing the amount of protein. As with discoveries in epigenetics, the science of RNAi reveals the unexpectedly complex systems in which genes do their work. These complexities create new hurdles for biotechnology, sometimes confounding earlier notions of simple success in controlling living processes just by controlling genetic information. But at the same time such discoveries lead to new technologies, for example when researchers learn how to modulate the RNAi system. Already it appears to be possible to use this technology to treat disease by introducing a partial "gene knock-down" through RNAi. In many diseases, including cancer, merely limiting the functional level of some genes may have significant benefit.

Genetics and medicine

When the HGP began, many thought that it would lead to an era of "gene therapy." The core idea of gene therapy is to treat a disease by disabling its genetic basis. Doing so involves modifying the DNA in the cells of the patient. The most commonly known genetic diseases, such as sickle cell anemia or cystic fibrosis, are caused by single genes, and it was believed in the early 1990s that scientists would soon learn how to treat, or maybe even cure, these diseases by repairing the underlying DNA.

The challenge facing gene therapy was to find a way to insert new or "healthy" DNA into many millions of cells in the patient's body without disrupting the function of other DNA. One strategy that has been used is to modify a virus by removing any of its genes that might cause disease, and inserting the desired DNA into the virus. Millions of copies of the modified virus might then be used to carry the DNA into the patient's body. This approach is complicated and not without its risks. Furthermore, even if the desired DNA is inserted, it is not clear that it will function as desired over a long period of time.

Even though gene therapy has proven more difficult than first thought, the field is still very promising. Furthermore, genetics has affected medicine in other important ways. For example, it is now possible to test individual patients for their own genetic risk factors. In the case of cancer patients, the tumor itself is tested to find which genes are especially active, and the choice of treatment is based on this information, leading to what has been called "personalized medicine."

It is also possible to conduct a genetic test of human embryos before they are implanted in the womb. The process is known as pre-implantation genetic diagnosis (PGD). The first step in the process is *in vitro* fertilization, a costly process that poses considerable risk for the woman involved. Once embryos have been created in the laboratory, the PGD procedure requires that the embryos are grown to eight or so cells. One of the cells is removed, leaving the rest of the embryo intact. The removed cell is tested for a genetic disease that the couple wishes to avoid, and embryos free of that disease are selected for implantation. PGD is opposed not just by any who oppose *in vitro* fertilization, but by others who object to the idea that future human lives should be screened and selected.

Some also are concerned that PGD might lead to human germline modification, fearing a gradual slide toward what they might call "designer babies." Germline modification is similar to gene therapy in its central concept of attacking disease by modifying its genetic base. Gene therapy, however, only modifies the DNA in some of the cells in the patient's body and is not passed to future generations. Germline modification, by contrast, affects all the cells and is passed on indefinitely.

Compared with PGD, the rationale for germline modification is obvious. Might it be possible not just to test embryos and select healthy ones, but to create a healthy embryo in the first place? Technically, however, PGD is relatively simple, while germline modification is full of risk, so much so that some believe it will never be safe enough even to test. Others object to germline modification because they believe that, if it becomes possible, medicine will not stop at creating merely healthy babies. This technology, many believe, will inevitably be used to create babies with desirable traits enhanced, and so the only moral strategy is to prevent the development of the technology in the first place. Some, however, regard the goal of helping couples have children free of a known disease to be justification enough for germline modification, provided it can be limited to therapy, while others find human enhancement itself to be a commendable goal.

Stem cells and regenerative medicine

As significant as genetics and gene modification may be for medicine, it is expected that in the next few decades stem cell research may have an even greater impact. Stem cells are cells that have the potential to divide and become more fully specialized or differentiated. Most of the cells of our bodies are fully differentiated. That is to say, they are functioning in a very particular way as skin cells, or brain cells. They have also lost their potential to multiply, to replace themselves, or to develop into other types of cells. However, hidden away in reserve in our bodies are stem cells, which can divide to replace differentiated cells that might be damaged or just simply die. The stem cells in our bodies have some limited potential to develop into various types of cells. They are sometimes called "precursor" cells because they have what is called "multipotency." For instance, multipotent brain cells may divide and produce the various cell types that make up the brain, but they cannot become skin cells or muscle cells.

In 1998, researchers isolated and cultured stem cells that possess a higher level of potency. They are called "pluripotent" because they have the potential to develop into any cell type in the body. Furthermore, they have the capacity to regenerate themselves indefinitely without losing their pluripotency. This step generated great excitement because researchers were suddenly provided with a seemingly inexhaustible supply of cells that could be guided down every pathway of development, towards brain, or blood, or muscle, or any other kind of cell.

Human pluripotent stem cells were isolated simultaneously by two independent research teams using quite different methods. The most widely known – human embryonic stem cells – were isolated from human blastocysts (embryos about the 100-cell stage). The process destroys the embryo. For some, that fact alone meant that human pluripotent cells from embryos were morally tainted and could never be used in research. The other research team used so-called germinal tissues from aborted embryos or fetus (weeks 5–9 post-fertilization, which bridges the usual transition from embryo to fetus). Few thought that this approach was morally preferable to the use of blastocysts, and most work on human pluripotent cells through 2007 was based largely on cells derived from blastocysts.

The quest for pluripotent cells

In 2007, however, human stem cell research changed dramatically. Based on work involving mouse cells, researchers learned how to turn fully differentiated cells into pluripotent cells. They referred to this procedure as inducing pluripotency, and the cells are known as induced pluripotent stem cells (iPS cells). Simply by adding genetic factors to a culture of skin cells, scientists were able to turn skin cells into what seemed to be the equivalent of embryonic cells, which passed every test by which pluripotency is assessed. Beginning in 2007, various teams of researchers were able to establish cell cultures of human pluripotent stem cells – appearing to be the functional equivalent of cells from blastocysts – without any resort to embryos as a source.

For many, this technical advance removed the premier moral problem that haunted the field of human pluripotent stem cell research from its inception, namely, the destruction of the embryo. The discovery of the iPS process, however, was largely based on knowledge gained through research conducted on stem cells derived from embryos. By studying embryonic cells, researchers learned how to mimic their pluripotency. Anyone wishing to avoid completely the moral taint of embryonic stem cell research will need to consider whether it is right to use the knowledge gained from research. Most experts in the field believe that cells from all sources should be studied in order to advance the field most quickly.

A more profound point to consider, however, is the fact that the iPS process turns potentiality into a technologically manipulable variable. Cells lacking in potentiality (the fully differentiated cell) can be driven backwards developmentally toward pluripotency, then forward developmentally through directed differentiation toward multipotency, perhaps as implantable brain precursor cells. In that regard, nuclear transfer or "cloning" is critically important. The announcement in 1997 of the birth of Dolly the sheep was met most commonly by the protests of those who feared the coming of cloned babies. From the standpoint of the power of technology to override the laws of nature, the greater significance of Dolly was that, for the first time in mammalian cells, scientists manipulated potency, in Dolly's case going not just back to pluripotent stem cells, but all the way back to the totipotent embryo. But it is induced pluripotency, a breakthrough achieved only a decade after Dolly, that makes fine-tuned control over cell potentiality even more useful for biotechnology.

From research to clinic

Moving stem cell research from the laboratory to the clinic, however, involves a whole new set of challenges. Foremost is patient safety. It is well known among stem cell researchers that there is a close relationship between pluripotency and cancer. This has led to advances in the understanding of cancer, but poses a serious risk for anyone who wants to insert stem cells into a patient. Another challenge is that inserted cells, if they come from a donor such as an unrelated embryo, are very likely to be rejected by the patient's immune system. One way to work around this problem is to use nuclear transfer to create a cloned, personalized stem cell line just for each patient. Even if nuclear transfer were to become relatively routine, this process is still highly complex. Furthermore, many are opposed morally, either because they want to avoid any form of cloning, or because they believe it is morally wrong to create and destroy a cloned embryo, even to save their own life. A more likely way to create immune-compatible stem cells is through iPS cells, but technical challenges must be resolved before it will be safe to implant these cells.

Induced pluripotency is also expected to play a major role in pharmaceutical research. Cells donated by patients with specific diseases can be used to create stem cells. The potency of these cells can be manipulated until clusters of cells in a dish mimic the progression of the disease. Pharmaceutical companies can use these disease-prone cells to test a wide range of possible drugs directly on human cells without involving human patients. Only the most promising drugs would be advanced to clinical trials.

If it turns out that pluripotent cells from any source may be safely implanted in patients, then the high promises of stem cell research might come to fruition, opening up a new era of regenerative medicine. Parts of the body that are damaged by illness or disease, or are simply wearing out with age, might be regenerated by the insertion of cells, some of which might replace lost cells and some of which might simply trigger the body to regenerate new cells on its own. Work with non-human animals has suggested that this strategy could be at least partly successful in renewing the function of nerve cells and other key tissues or cells. No-one can say how far this field might develop, but it is likely to be the basis of a major revolution in health-care, leading someday perhaps to the nearly-indefinite maintenance of the human body against the effects of aging or the damage of disease, even to the point where aging itself seems to be held at bay.

Emerging possibilities in biotechnology

While few would object to new forms of medicine to treat, for instance, neuro-degenerative disease, it may become possible not just to treat disease, but also to treat aging as if it were a disease. In the normal aging process, cells wear out and there are fewer remaining stem cells to replace them. Inserting stem cells into the aging body may not quite be a formula for perpetual youth, but it might extend the human lifespan.

It may also become possible in the not-too-distant future to use induced pluripotency as a new means of creating human gametes (eggs and sperm) for use in research, or possibly even in procreation. This would open new strategies for treating infertility, including the possibility of making fertility possible later in life. It also opens the possibility of germline modification without direct manipulation of the embryo. Pluripotent stem cells might be genetically modified, turned into sperm or egg precursor cells, and any pregnancy that might occur could carry the genetic modification. This is just one of many strategies that might lie ahead in the convergence of genetic engineering and reproductive technologies, sometimes called "repro-genetics," allowing the possibility of greater genetic control of future generations.

The initial justification for "repro-genetics" is, of course, to avoid the risk of disease. But technologies developed to avoid disease are easily adaptable for purposes of selecting, adding, or enhancing socially desirable traits. No-one knows yet what genes might be added or what biological modifications might be made to produce a child, for example, with enhanced cognitive abilities, but many expect that technically plausible strategies will be discovered and that prospective parents will show great interest.

The prospect of human enhancement via biotechnology is not limited to producing enhanced children. Many today look for ways to prevent the effects of aging or the other limits that arise from our biological nature. Already, there are technologies that claim to enhance our appearance, athletic ability, sexual performance, psychological mood, cognitive ability, and length of our lives. New and more reliable means towards these goals will surely be developed, given market demand and the pace of discoveries on the biological bases of cognition and aging. Some fear that, through these enhancements, we will modify ourselves not just "beyond therapy" but beyond recognition, turning ourselves into a "post-human" species. Others advocate the development and use of these technologies, wishing to be made "trans-human" in order to escape the limits of biology.

Biotechnology and religion

These recent and emerging developments in biotechnology pose new challenges to religious beliefs and morals, which are often based on now-outdated biological theories and technological assumptions. One example is the new insight being offered into human evolution. Detailed comparisons of modern human beings, Neanderthals, and the great apes show the close proximity between our species and other forms of life, suggesting that it is time to rethink philosophical and religious notions of human uniqueness and human dignity. Is it right for theology to regard only anatomically modern human beings as being made in the image of God? For Christian theology, is the presence of the Christ in humanity limited to our humanity, or inclusive of other hominids or other primates? Who is Jesus Christ, not just in the context of the past evolution of humanity, but in light of the prospect of a future of technologically driven evolution? Does the incarnation preclude technological manipulation? Or does it open before us a prospect of human transformation in which technology serves the purposes of God?

Theology must also learn to think anew about human diversity, differences not just in skin color, but also in behavior and character. Why do some human beings seem more inclined from birth to follow a religious or moral path through life? Christian theology has explained the differences in terms of either human freedom, or God's decision to save some but not all – explanations that have caused no end of controversy, largely mirroring the secular debate over nature *versus* nurture. Today, however, theology must take into account the results of genetic studies, which show that behavioral predispositions are at least strongly influenced by the interaction of genetic and environmental factors, and therefore that human beings vary in their moral and spiritual predispositions for reasons that have nothing to do with individual choice or God's grace. The current religious debate over the sources and the moral meaning of sexual orientation is just one context in which the interplay of genes, environment, freedom, and grace is being reconsidered.

As a result of advances in stem cell research and developmental biology, the moral and religious question of the human embryo is as divisive as ever, but now with a new twist. Not only is the human embryo accessible to technology by virtue of being in the Petri dish. The embryo's unique quality – its potential to develop into the fully differentiated cells of the body – is itself a manipulable variable, something that we are learning to control with such skill that we can imagine creating genetically modified embryos without beginning with naturally produced eggs or sperm. How far should we go in expanding our control of potentiality and our biotechnology of procreation?

The most pervasive issue raised by biotechnology, however, is that of social and economic justice. There is no doubt that biotechnology will continue to advance; that it will change fundamentally our relationship with the natural world in such sensitive areas as agriculture, the environment, and energy; and that it will therefore redefine our social and economic fabric, for good or ill. Whether tomorrow's advances in biotechnology come as a result of public funding or largely by private investment, the funding sources will originate in the world's wealthiest countries. The knowledge gained by these investments will be protected mostly by patenting or other forms of intellectual property protection, leading in time to greater concentrations of wealth and even more investment in research. Technologies aimed at human enhancement raise a special concern in this regard. Wealth might be used to buy biological improvements, so that today's economically disadvantaged suddenly find themselves to be tomorrow's biologically disadvantaged – to be not as healthy, long-living, or cognitively enhanced as their privileged counterparts.

Here, as elsewhere, technology seems, at least at first glance, to increase rather than reduce the inequities in the world. For this reason, it is perhaps helpful for religious communities to voice their concerns about systems by which the benefits and risks of advanced technologies are unfairly distributed. It is true, of course, that advances in biotechnology sometimes provide important benefits for the poorest or the most vulnerable. It is also true that much more could be done in that regard.

The concern for justice raises an even deeper question having to do with the role of religion in today's world. Our cultures are globally connected, pluralistic, largely secular, and highly technological. Technology is growing in its power to transform nature, and nature itself provides little or no guidance about the goal of our transformations. Perhaps living religious communities might draw again upon texts and traditions, rediscovering the relevance for today of ancient moral principles and spiritual longings, not to rule over technology or to restrict science, but to open up a space for a much-needed global conversation about the proper place of human beings in nature.

Further reading

Ronald Cole-Turner's *The New Genesis: Theology and the Genetic Revolution* (Westminster John Knox Press, 1993) is an early assessment of biotechnology from a Christian theological perspective, arguing for biotechnology in the service of God but warning about notions of "co-creation." Also, his edited volume *Design and Destiny: Jewish and Christian Perspectives on Human Germline Modification* (MIT Press, 2007) is a collection of essays that show surprising levels of religious support for the central idea of human germline modification, but warning of human enhancement. For a careful review of recent science, reflecting especially the virtue tradition in ethics, see Celia Deane-Drummond's *Genetics and Christian Ethics* (Cambridge University Press, 2006). Mark J. Hansen has edited *Claiming Power over Life: Religion and Biotechnology Policy* (Georgetown University Press, 2001), which reflects on the public role of religion in relation to biotechnology, public policy, and commercialization. C. Ben Mitchell, Edmund D. Pellegrino, Jean Bethke Elshtain, John Frederic Kilner and Scott B. Rae, *Biotechnology and the Human Good* (Georgetown University Press, 2007) provides a thorough assessment of biotechnology from conservative Protestant Christian perspectives, advocating limited uses, but warning of such things as genetic enhancement.

Contemporary Lutheran theologian Ted Peters offers essays on genes and behavior, including the questions of "original sin" and sexual orientation, in *Playing God? Genetic Determinism and Human Freedom* (Routledge, 1997). James C. Peterson's *Genetic Turning Points: The Ethics of Human Genetic Intervention* (William B. Eerdmans, 2001) is a comprehensive and generally positive assessment of human applications of biotechnology by a Protestant Christian scholar. For the classic statement about the value and the risks of human self-creation by a Protestant Christian moralist, see Paul Ramsey's *Fabricated Man: The Ethics of Genetic Control* (Yale University Press, 1970). Brent Waters offers a warning that postmodern society is unable to limit its own technology in *From Human to Posthuman: Christian Theology and Technology in a Postmodern World* (Ashgate, 2006). This book argues that Christianity places limits on human transformation through technology.

40
JUSTICE AND BIOTECHNOLOGY
Protestant views

Karen Lebacqz

Biotechnologies pose challenges for questions of justice. How do Protestants address those challenges? Three complexities confront us immediately. First, Protestants are a diverse lot, encompassing Lutheran, Calvinist, Anabaptist, Methodist, and numerous other emendations within the tradition. There will be no single normative Protestant view on any question. Indeed, within one denomination or branch, there will be conflicting views. Some Protestants use specifically religious language and address primarily other Christians; others may use religious terms such as covenant, but generally speak to the public sphere rather than specifically to a Christian audience; still others function in the public sphere without much reference to religious language, though their thinking may have been significantly informed by religious training or conviction. This breadth of approach makes it difficult to know what to count as a specifically "Protestant" view. Here, works by Protestants who do not take a deliberately "religious" approach are included, though the main focus is on those who articulate a theological vision for their views.

Second, the range of biotechnologies is enormous. From renal dialysis machines to new functional magnetic resonance imaging (fMRI) screening techniques, from genetic testing to stem cell research, from genetically modified foods to new surgical techniques – biotechnology is now an integral part of medical care, human living, and future prospects. What technologies should be included in a survey of Protestant concerns over justice? While the focus here is on newer technologies such as cloning or stem cells, justice discussions from earlier times are informative. Indeed, the matter is complicated by the fact that there are cogent and pointed discussions of justice with regard to some early technologies and issues, such as renal dialysis or distribution of healthcare resources in general, but discussions of newer technologies often focus on questions outside specifically justice concerns. For example, discussions of the ethics of stem cells have focused almost exclusively on the status of the embryo and whether its destruction is ethical; discussions of cloning focus on potential harms to the cloned child. Many contemporary Protestant texts carry no reference to "justice" in the index, and explicit discussions of justice are few and far between.

Thus we confront a third challenge: How is justice to be understood, and what constitutes a discussion of justice from a Protestant perspective? Lack of the specific term does not mean there is no attention to justice (cf. Lebacqz 1987). For instance, a pointed analysis of eugenics and racism in genetic screening, or a worried look at possible harms to developing nations from proposed developments in food biotechnology, suggest at least an implicit recognition that justice is at stake in the development and use of biotechnologies. In this regard, the 1979 conference of the World Council of Churches (WCC) on Faith, Science and the Future was prophetic: while mainstream bioethics at the time focused on abortion, sterilization, and *in vitro* fertilization (IVF), the WCC conference developed interfaith perspectives on biotechnology with concern for the "two-thirds" world (Shinn 1980). Economics, world hunger, global energy issues, disarmament – all these and other topics were part of the context for discussing the ethics of new biotechnologies. Not all the views presented were Protestant, but there were significant Protestant contributions with specific attention to the poor and to the issue of just distribution between rich and poor nations. This is one example of a creative approach to justice issues in new biotechnologies.

Given the links between justice and human rights, and the international grounding of human rights in concepts of human dignity, a discussion centering on human dignity may also implicitly be a discussion of justice. The former President's Council on Bioethics in the United States drew extensively on concepts of human dignity for several of its analyses, including significantly its attention to "enhancement" technologies (President's Council on Bioethics 2003). A recent European text also focuses on human dignity, but clearly intends its discussions to encompass justice concerns. Thus the approach to "justice" within Protestant traditions may be far-ranging, and may not focus on the categories and distinctions that are prominent in philosophical circles (Knoepffler *et al.* 2007).

For instance, religious thinkers have not given much attention to the impact of biotechnologies on commutative justice or retributive justice; they have tended to cluster discussions around distributive questions. In one famous case, researchers used discarded tissue from patient John Moore to develop a line of cells that proved lucrative. Moore sued, claiming lack of consent and a right to economic return for the use of his tissue. This classic case of commutative justice worked its way through the courts, but garnered little attention from Protestant ethicists. Similarly, DNA analysis is now used commonly in the criminal justice system, both to clear suspects and to establish putative guilt. Advances in neuroscience such as fMRI screening promise to create new dilemmas regarding the scope of moral responsibility in the retributive justice sphere. These questions about the impact of biotechnology on retributive justice have also garnered scant attention from Protestants.

By far the most attention has been to questions of distributive justice (e.g. Vigen 2006). Who should pay costs of biotechnologies, and who should reap benefits? How can fair access to beneficial technologies be assured? Does justice require certain basic human "rights" that should direct the development or use of new technologies? Most Protestants support stem cell research, for example, but some hold that the destruction of embryonic life violates the "image of God" in the embryo. To use one human being in the service of others is seen not only as a violation of the principle of respect for persons, but also as a violation of the demands of justice, which require that all humans be treated with equal respect. Thus justice concerns are sometimes used as an argument that new technologies should not be developed or used in certain ways.

In a famous public display, many Protestants joined with Roman Catholic, Muslim, and Jewish leaders to declare that human and animal life forms should not be patented. This approach was criticized by other Protestants, who charge that the signatories misunderstood the nature of patents. It is noteworthy, however, that the signers of the declaration included "animal" life forms in their statement; clearly, some Protestants take "justice" to apply to non-human animals as well as to humans. Discussing the use of animals as disease models, sources of organs for transplants, and other genetic engineering possibilities, and drawing generally on Christian affirmations about the goodness of creation and God's intentions, though not specifically on a developed theory of justice, the Society, Religion, and Technology Project of the Church of Scotland, for instance, puts animal welfare issues squarely within the purview of grounds for possible prohibition of particular biotechnologies and interventions.

When justice questions arise, do Protestants have a distinctive approach? Because many contemporary texts on biotechnologies do not address justice directly or develop a particularly "Protestant" approach to justice, it is instructive to turn to some earlier treatments of justice in healthcare generally, or treatments of Christian approaches to justice broadly construed. In the philosophical tradition, the formal statement of distributive justice is "treat similar cases similarly" or "give to each what is due." Arguments ensue about what cases are "similar" and what is "due." Should goods be distributed in accord with market forces (the liberal economic view), with need (the Marxist view), with merit or virtue (the Aristotelian view), or should they simply be distributed equally? An early classic on justice in healthcare by Lutheran ethicist Outka (1987) reviewed such proposals and opined that a Christian approach to justice in healthcare would focus on need with some attention to merit, but would reject ability to pay as a criterion for access. Other discussions stress the plight of the poor and vulnerable. Contemporary approaches to biotechnology often presume these earlier works.

What distinguishes a Christian Protestant approach is its beginning point and sources of authority. Protestants begin with God. They seek to do God's will. Drawing from the faith community and study of scriptures, Protestants affirm that God is the author of all creation, cares passionately for justice, and "so loved" the world that God was willing to sacrifice God's beloved child so that we might have abundant life. Some Protestants stress God as creator, particularly the notion that humans are created "in the image of God" and therefore have rights and dignity. Others draw from the life, death, and resurrection of Jesus to ground an approach to the requirements of justice, noting Jesus' call for liberation of the oppressed and his prioritizing of the poor. Still others turn primarily to eschatology – to the doctrine of "last things" or the ultimate statement of God's will and desire – to envision the fullness of life that would constitute the ends toward which Christian justice must move. The turn to Scripture rather than natural law distinguishes Protestant approaches to justice from Roman Catholic; the role of Spirit and community keeps Protestants from adopting wholeheartedly the individualistic or rationalistic approach common in Western philosophy.

From these roots, some affirmations follow. Because humans are created in the image of God and have equal dignity, justice requires equal treatment; any inequalities must be justified. When it comes to new technologies such as stem cells, only a global perspective on justice is sufficient: inequities in access around the globe are a matter of concern. Further, Protestants affirm God's special love for the vulnerable. Justice in biblical tradition as interpreted in contemporary Protestant theology means a "preference for the poor" and liberation of the oppressed. Thus all social arrangements must be judged in accord with their impact on the poor. In determining questions of access and distribution of goods, priority goes to the weakest, the marginalized, and the vulnerable (e.g. Townes 1998). Institutional reforms are therefore in order wherever disparities abound – for example, where black Americans receive inferior treatment to, or are less likely to have access to new technologies than, white Americans.

Finally, Protestants generally would say that, ultimately, justice depends on God: we can approximate justice but never fully attain it, given the sinfulness of the world in which we live. Thus every human arrangement is subject to judgment according to God's will. God's justice is not the same as human justice. Where human inclination might divide goods on the basis of merit, or achievement, or some other standard of what is "due," justice in God's eyes is always more than human imagination can conceive. Justice in Christian tradition must be tempered with the mercy associated with God.

These fundamental convictions about the centrality and meaning of justice cut across various branches of Protestantism. In an Anabaptist view of stem cell research, LeRoy Walters offers as one of three guidelines that one should "give special consideration to those who are the weakest and most vulnerable" and as another that one should "promote justice in the entire world and not just in advanced industrialized societies" (Walters 1985: 133–34). The same sentiment is echoed by Peters, Lebacqz, and Bennett (2008), representing Lutheran, United Church of Christ, and Church of the Nazarene traditions, respectively. Not all these representatives will agree on a social policy regarding stem cells, but all agree on the significance of the justice matters that must be addressed (for an approach that includes a useful summary of positions, see Chapman 1999).

A concern for the poor and oppressed raises issues regarding power. In Protestant perspective, justice is not simply about distribution of goods, but is also about the way in which distributions are affected by power arrangements. Does the very development of new biotechnologies create or contribute to an unjust redistribution of power? This issue was raised in at least preliminary form by feminist ethicists in early critiques of IVF. Although IVF increases options for women, many feminists opposed it on grounds that it took reproductive power away from women and put it in the hands of men. While Protestants generally support and approve new medical technologies, concerns about power redistribution have arisen in several contemporary spheres. African American bioethicists see technologies such as prenatal diagnosis as potentially new "backdoors" to eugenics. Anabaptist ethicist Kabiru Kinyanjui opines that the gap between Northern and Southern hemispheres is a concern of justice: "Bioethics operates in the context of power. Presently, this power is concentrated in the northern hemisphere. […] Developing countries, such as those in Africa, find themselves on the receiving end of that particular power (Kinyanjui 2005: 169)."

It may be the concern about power that most distinguishes Protestant views from several dominant philosophical theories with which most Protestant thinkers are familiar, and with which they are sometimes in dialogue. John Rawls' massive *A Theory of Justice* (1999) suggests that basic liberties must be shared "equally" while goods and services (income, positions) might fairly be distributed unequally, so long as the ultimate result is to the benefit of the "least advantaged." While Rawls grounds his argument in game- and decision-theory, George Parkin Grant (1985) has suggested that there are religious roots that inform his approach. Certainly, commentators from within Protestant Christian tradition have found it amenable, particularly since the concern for the "least advantaged" appears to cohere with Christian concerns for the "poor" and "oppressed."

A second theory that influences contemporary approaches to justice, including those of some Protestant commentators, is that of Michael Walzer (1983). Walzer argues that justice must be contextualized: what is required for "justice" will depend on what "sphere" of life is under consideration. Different communities will create a different sense of justice for each sphere, but within certain limits. In the sphere of healthcare, Walzer suggests that justice will require at least a common "floor" below which people do not fall. This view also coheres with Protestant approaches to justice in healthcare that focus on distribution in accord with need, and that find the existence of huge numbers of uninsured people in the United States to be unjust and unethical.

References

Chapman, Audrey (1999) *Unprecedented Choices: Religious Ethics at the Frontiers of Genetic Science*, Minneapolis, MN: Fortress, 1999.

Grant, George Parkin (1985) *English Speaking Justice*, Notre Dame, IN: Notre Dame University.

Kinyanjui, Kabiru (2005) "Crosscultural Approaches to Biotechnology," in *Viewing New Creations with Anabaptist Eyes: Ethics of Biotechnology*, Roman J. Miller, Beryl H. Brubaker and James C. Peterson (eds), Telford, PA: Cascadia Publishing House: 168–70.

Knoepffler, Nikolaus, Dagmar Schipanski and Stefan Lorenz Sorgner (2007) *Humanbiotechnology as Social Challenge: An Interdisplinary Introduction to Bioethics*, London: Ashgate.

Lebacqz, Karen (1987) *Justice in an Unjust World*, Minneapolis, MN: Augsburg.

Outka, Gene (1987) "Social Justice and Equal Access to Health Care," in *On Moral Medicine: Theological Perspectives in Medical Ethics*, Stephen Lammers and Allen Verhey (eds), Grand Rapids, MI: William B. Eerdmans.

Peters, Ted, Karen Lebacqz and Gaymon Bennett (2008) *Sacred Cells? Why Christians Should Support Stem Cell Research*, New York: Rowman & Littlefield.

President's Council on Bioethics (2003) *Beyond Therapy: Biotechnology and the Pursuit of Happiness*.

Rawls, John (1999) *A Theory of Justice*, Cambridge, MA: Harvard University Press.

Shinn, Roger (ed.) (1980) *Faith and Science in an Unjust World: Report of the World Council of Churches' Conference on Faith, Science and the Future; Volume 1: Plenary Presentations*, Geneva: World Council of Churches.

Townes, Emilie M. (1998) *Breaking the Fine Rain of Death: African American Health Issues and a Womanist Ethic of Care*, New York: Continuum.

Vigen, Aana Marie (2006) *Women, Ethics, and Inequality in U.S. Healthcare: "To Count Among the Living,"* New York: Palgrave Macmillan.

Walters, LeRoy (2005) "Ethical Issues in Biotechnology: Human Embryonic Stem Cell Research and the Anabaptist Vision," in *Viewing New Creations with Anabaptist Eyes: Ethics of Biotechnology*, Roman J. Miller, Beryl H. Brubaker and James C. Peterson (eds), Telford, PA: Cascadia Publishing House: 122–35.

Walzer, Michael (1983) *Spheres of Justice: A Defense of Pluralism and Equality*, New York: Basic Books.

Further reading

Overviews of the requirements of justice from a Protestant perspective can be found in John F. Kilner, *Who Lives? Who Dies? Ethical Criteria in Patient Selection* (Yale University Press, 1990). Discussions stressing power and its import will be found in Harley E. Flack and Edmund D. Pellegrino, *African-American Perspectives on Biomedical Ethics* (Georgetown University Press, 1992) and in an early work by Alastair V. Campbell, *Medicine, Health, and Justice: The Problem of Priorities* (Churchill Livingstone, 1978). Significant Protestant discussions of specific issues can be found in Michael C. Brannigan, *Ethical Issues in Human Cloning: Cross-Disciplinary Perspectives* (Seven Bridges Press, 2001); Ronald Cole-Turner, ed., *Human Cloning: Religious Responses* (Westminster John Knox, 1997); Brent Waters and Ronald Cole-Turner, eds, *God and the Embryo: Religious Voices on Stem Cells and Cloning* (Georgetown University Press, 2003). Significant individual contributions include Ronald Cole-Turner, *The New Genesis: Theology and the Genetic Revolution* (Westminster John Knox, 1993); Robert J. Nelson, *On the New Frontiers of Genetics and Religion* (William B. Eerdmans, 1994); and James C. Peterson, *Genetic Turning Points: The Ethics of Human Genetic Intervention* (William B. Eerdmans, 2001).

41
MUSLIM ETHICS AND BIOTECHNOLOGY

Ebrahim Moosa

Introduction

Muslim reflections on biotechnology are marked by vast discrepancies in the representations of reality (epistemology) that impact ethical deliberations. Due to the cultural and political diversity of Muslim societies around the globe, reaching meaningful consensus is difficult. Given major transitions that Muslim ethical practices experience under pressures of rapid modernization and globalization, with its accompanying agonies, debates about biotechnology show the vulnerability of Muslim ethics from a variety of perspectives.

When Professor Cole-Turner (Chapter 39 in this volume) links biotechnology to justice, it immediately triggers the question of the political, even though he does touch on a range of issues that go beyond it. Institutional politics do indeed connect and shape the life worlds inhabited by a differentiated humanity; so politics does indeed affect the most sensitive and deepest recesses of our beings. For a religious humanity, confronting a range of challenging and practical bioethical questions within larger structures of governance, from globalization to liberal capitalism, debates about biotechnology often sponsor a set of larger concerns. Such concerns are mediated by what one could best call "political theology:" how Muslims mediate and relate to the human–divine nexus. Humanity has always been challenged in how to deal with the larger forces beyond its control. How does God act in the world; how does divine power and influence intervene, and at what point does human responsibility and ownership begin? At more critical moments in the lives of human beings, in almost all traditions, believers struggle with questions about how divine justice (theodicy) works in the world, if at all. Or are humans always at the will of an omnipotent and omniscient Creator whose will we can only faintly descry, but never fully grasp? These questions become especially relevant when the vehicle of human life and vitality, the body, is afflicted with disease, illness, and disrepair.

Theology and global technology

Configuring the divine–human nexus in an age of science and hyper-techno-science brings with it a certain conceit: a hubris that we had finally conquered nature.

Probing the outer limits of our vast cosmos together with finding the arrow of time in evolutionary biology within two centuries can often show a picture of human vanity. So when the next generation of cutting-edge physics and biology comes on stream in the form of nanotechnology, genetic reproduction, human embryonic stem-cell research, enhancement, and germline therapies, our humanity is saddled with the hubris of a post-human age coupled with a surge in anxiety and trepidation about our capacity to self-implode. It is at this stage that we are confronted with major questions about the viability of our collective future. Newer installments of techno-science raise new questions for ethics and challenge the philosophical frontiers of thinking about the human as we know the species. Our reality, accelerated by biotechnology, is one where our bodies and our technologies enframe and act upon each other in unprecedented ways. And we are always already acting and shaping our biotechnical reality, just as we are being shaped by it. With the advance of a new generation of biotechnologies, some of the earlier bioethical qualms surrounding organ transplantation and brain death suddenly sound remote, if not passé, though not entirely.

On the face of it, biotechnology tends to have a semblance of being global. But it is possibly the best candidate for the term "glocal," an awkward neologism that connects the global to the local, or the local to the global. What might appear to be global vestiges are actually connections forged between numerous global elites and consumers of biotechnology around the world. Concurrently there are also entire, if not larger, global networks of people who are deprived of the fruits of biotechnology. Economically deprived and less visible communities in both developed and developing countries might receive only the dregs of such global dispersal of expensive and intensive biotechnological therapies. For some of the poor in the world, the low fruits are what they enjoy of biotechnology, such as immunization, HIV-AIDS tests and, if they are extremely lucky, basic healthcare. That might be the sum total of the benefits of biotechnology the largest segment of human beings in the world currently enjoy. At the same time, for the affluent of the world, biotechnology can bring the benefits of organ transplantation and super-advanced surgeries, give access to anti-retroviral drugs that can restore a viable life to AIDS sufferers, and offer advance reproductive and fertility treatments for those who desperately want offspring. The key moral question is the following: Can biotechnology be democratized and made accessible to the most deprived? Would this not be one of the moral determinants about the viability and future of this technology? Is biotechnology on the same democratic trajectory as, say, computer and cyber technology? If so, such considerations could be a game-changer.

For most Muslims, and Muslim-majority societies, questions of biotechnology intersect with at least three large sets of issues. The first are socio-economic and political realities. These socio-economic and political realities are immensely diverse across different Muslim contexts: they either facilitate, or impede access to, advanced science, or otherwise distort access along lines of privilege and class. The second are biocultural and psycho-social questions. By this I mean the way science and technology produced in the West are translated and received within the social imaginaries of individual Muslims and collectivities, and how biotechnologies ultimately become enacted in their lived reality. The third cluster of issues relate to

Muslim moral philosophies and theologies that are, by their very nature, complex examples of work in progress. For multiple reasons not easily distilled here, there remains within Muslim cultural settings an urgent but unattended debate about a cluster of burning epistemological questions: Whether representations of reality are both legitimate, theologically and culturally speaking; and accurate, scientifically speaking. For a whole host of reasons – resulting from colonization, postcolonial blues, and globalization questions such as epistemic dislocations – fractures and contestations over knowledge within many Muslim societies both exacerbate and impact debates affecting Muslim ethics (Rees 2010).

Biotechnology as a field of modern moral inquiry offers a window to our struggle, as humans, with the big questions of life. It brings us face-to-face with questions such as: How do divine intentions and purposes play out in relation to human will, agency, and freedom? How do we, as humans, flourish alongside the natural and inanimate resources that enclose us? When are we treating and medicating ourselves, and at what moment are we enhancing ourselves to the point of playing God, with an excess of vanity on our part? How do we judge our flourishing to be wholesome and responsible, and how do we know our actions are destructive and irresponsible? When does consumption turn into a fit of self-gratification that adds to the depletion of natural resources, making us complicit in possibly bequeathing a scorched Earth to our not-too-distant posterity?

When biotechnology is linked to concerns about justice, it takes the debate to those thought processes and practices that animate our perceptions of what is moral. Justice might appear to be a neutral category, but it is not. Even in a common culture, justice might only barely have a common sensibility, if people share a political and economic system that has attained a modicum of moral consensus. Otherwise, notions of justice and moral truths are as fractured and relativistic as the multiple audiences that "justice" serves. In a cross-cultural and comparative religious perspective, questions of justice become even more compounded, making the search for common understandings more challenging, but there is surely no need to despair. Despair sets in only if one is locked into a singular understanding of the issues, and in the search of singular solutions. Hope lies in appreciating the diversity of the challenges and the complex ways in which humans appreciate the issues.

Technology and bioethics in the mirror of tradition

Contestations between the bearers of the modern traditions, such as those who have access to advance science, modern social science, and the humanities, versus positions advanced by proponents of traditional forms of learning and culture, serve as two extreme polarities. Often, reality is marked by the in-between positions navigating these two extreme boundaries, since reality is never neatly sliced. Biotechnology surely poses major challenges for Muslims living in Europe, North America, and those prosperous parts of the Muslim world such as the oil-rich Gulf region, where medical infrastructures resemble those in developed societies. Yet for Muslims living in rural Mali or the slums of Jakarta in Indonesia, biotechnology might be thinkable only to the extent that artificial fertilizers and genetically modified seeds bring with them new hazards in agriculture and food integrity, compared with a time when farmers used natural compost and people consumed food grown from unmodified agricultural seeds.

Debates about the next generation of biotechnological issues under the impact of heightened Darwinian impulses, ranging from molecular genetics through stem cells and regenerative medical technologies, arrive at a time when Muslim ethicists are barely coming to grips with an earlier generation of biotechnology: transplantation surgery, brain death, artificial enhancements. Let's examine practices of transplantation surgery in places such as Egypt and Pakistan in order to review the fascinating responses. In Egypt, momentous and highly publicized and mediatized disagreement on transplantation surgery has created high levels of confusion among healthcare practitioners and sections of the religious establishment about the permissibility of such procedures in terms of Islamic law (Hamdy, 2006). Ironically, some former transplantation surgeons have publicly renounced their involvement in transplantation surgery, explaining that the body is sacred and that their surgical procedures involved mutilation and an affront to the integrity of the body (*ibid.*). Given disagreement among religious authorities as to whether brain death constitutes an acceptable definition of death in terms of Muslim ethics and law, the topmost jurisconsult (*mufti*) of Egypt, Shaykh Ali Jumu'a has declared live transplantation to be impermissible. Relying on the expert opinion of the physicians, Jumu'a has argued that his opposition was premised on the disagreement among medical experts and physicians themselves as to whether brain death qualifies as an indicator of death. Jumu'a hints that if the medical experts gained greater consensus on brain death, then he might review his own view on the subject. Ironically, these debates, which surfaced in the late 1990s, were preceded decades earlier by official rulings by Egyptian religious authorities about the permissibility of organ transplantation procedures (Moosa 1999). With an active professional community engaged with transplantation practices, bioethical issues not only become complicated and ambiguous, but they also connect to lived reality. Nevertheless, cornea transplantation is popularly accepted from cadaver donors, possibly because its materiality is different from the transplantation of, say, a kidney or a heart, even though the principal objection to transplantation should be valid in this case, too.

In Pakistan, the gulf between healthcare professionals and the religious authorities on crucial bioethical issues has remained as wide as ever (Moazam 2006). According to ethnographic studies, families and patients do demonstrate a sense of altruism in donating organs. However, there is little evidence that religious authorities are consulted in many of the bioethical deliberations taken by medical professionals. In 2010, Pakistan passed a law regulating transplantation and human tissue donation, even though the practice has been in vogue for some time. Meanwhile, religious authorities have yet to validate or proscribe transplantation surgery in terms of Islamic ethics. The partition between stakeholders in transplantation surgery, such as physicians, and the religious authorities in Pakistan is so polarized that conversations between those sectors are limited (Moazam 2006). In the absence of a national ethics forum, from the outside it appears that the incommensurability in world-views held by the various stakeholders might be the reason for the deadlock, although this might in itself not truly reflect the full and complex reality of Pakistani society.

Surely people in the Muslim world do encounter a new generation of biotechnology in one form or the other. Enthusiasm for the novel clearly is a factor. Often debates about technological transfer occur without adequate discussion about cultural adaptation and moral domestication of such practices. Another factor is that governance of both politics and medical politics inhibits contestation and debate about the merits and demerits of biotechnologies. Some of these tensions arise from what might on the surface appear to be irreconcilable differences. When Cole-Turner (Chapter 39 in this volume) argues that a whole new generation of biotechnological innovations form part of a Darwinian template of evolutionary science, then such discussions would certainly raise the theological red flag for some Muslims and give them pause. In many Muslim societies, Darwinism has had an uneven reception, being subject to mistranslation and suspicion, and has mostly been met by rejection (Elshakry 2003). One of the paradoxes, however, is that while many Muslim thinkers and professionals might resist the *philosophy* of Darwinism, there is very little attention to the glaring contradiction that people profit from research and technologies that are the products of evolutionary modes of thinking.

Darwinism was viewed to be part of a naturalistic philosophy that made nature autonomous and independent of divine intentions, with an open-ended, if not undetermined, *telos*. But, more significantly, naturalism challenged inherited Muslim theological precepts that were part of a speculative philosophical tradition. Many precepts and concepts, especially about nature, gender, sexuality, and race, were treated as essences in the speculative tradition. Now these concepts were being challenged, and for all practical purposes were supplanted by the rationality of empirical science. For some Muslim thinkers, this open-ended idea of nature threatened their *telos*-driven theological doctrines, centered on two crucial aspects: firstly, a purposive notion of nature; and secondly, a belief in a fixed and permanent human nature. Both aspects were once viewed as the ontological pyramid that gave coherence to a body of knowledge that supported certain theological beliefs. Among such beliefs were the twin ideas of divine creation and the finitude of the material world.

Not long ago, Muslim theologians in the Middle East and South Asia, important men such as Shaykh Hussain al-Jisr, Jamal al-Din al-Afghani, and Ashraf Ali Thanvi, scrutinized both naturalism and Darwinism in the late nineteenth and early twentieth centuries. They latched on to the evolutionary aspect of the emerging philosophy of science, and used it as a catchphrase to debunk, if not discredit, the philosophy of modern science, labeling it as materialistic and diabolical in its essence, especially when the narrative of science lacked any reference to a creator deity. Despite being vilified as ungodly and materialistic, both science and technology took off in the modern Muslim world with gusto, with no-one able to shut the floodgates. Religiously motivated Muslim critics cultivated an ambivalent relation to modern science: many critics condemned the evolutionary philosophy of science but welcomed its practical fruits. Some correctly claimed that, historically, Islamdom was no stranger to an empirical tradition of inquiry. And, theologically speaking, intellectuals generally separated the practice of science and its applications from its underlying philosophy. Yet strong theological opposition to evolution has effectively stifled any meaningful debate about the subject in Muslim circles, even as techno-science moves into higher gear, and both engulfs and shapes the reality of Muslim societies.

Resurgent scripturalism for most of the twentieth century foreclosed serious debate about Muslim theology. A sclerotic, scripture-based theology mined scientific truths from the teachings of the Qur'an – an apologetic venture made popular by authors such as the Egyptian Tantawi Jawhari, who related scientific discoveries to the Qur'an's observations of nature and its allegedly scientific features, supplemented more recently by the work of a French convert to Islam, Maurice Bucaille. All of these efforts tried to show that the Qur'an's observations of nature did not contradict scientific fact. Many Muslim traditionalists criticized this approach, arguing that, in the end, it made science the touchstone of validating scripture, but it did not put an end to the wildly popular enterprise of proof-texting the validity of science from scripture. Thoughtful thinkers asked: What would happen to the authority of scripture if scientific observations were altered? Would such change imply that the scriptural evidence was now wrong too? Despite many calls to found a Muslim theology that was compatible with modern science, such efforts invariably ran aground in apologetics mired in pseudo-science and pseudo-theology. A good example is the well heeled anti-evolution campaign waged by the Turkish popular preacher Harun Yahya (2010). The creationist and intelligent design gospels promoted in the West, especially in the United States, are harnessed to bolster Yahya's and other similar campaigns among Muslims.

But more often, these occasional stirrings and search for an Islamic approach to science were spurred by impulses to marry knowledge, including knowledge of science, to religious identity. It was believed that Muslim faith-claims also offer a unique view of empirical reality. Yet one cannot rule out that it could also be a strong case of wearing tinted glasses. The boundary between the facts of knowledge and the meaning of such knowledge, it seems, might have been blurred. Such initiatives went by the label "Islamization of knowledge" (al-Faruqi 1982) This venture had a brief flutter in the 1980s but had petered out by the 1990s, even though it is still fostered in some circles. Shrouded in triumphalist garb, Islamization meant that Islam's revelation would always be vindicated by science, provided science, in its own self-understanding, also yielded to certain Islamic theological propositions, especially in the realm of values and axiology. Sound reason, it was claimed, would always square with revelation if the latter was properly understood. Other thinkers advanced a new theology of science premised exclusively on Qur'anic foundations, which amounted to a crude scripturalist account of science but which, like its Islamization counterpart, was largely still-born (Nadvi 1989 [1409]).

Crisis of epistemology in Muslim ethics

What all these efforts cumulatively do signify is that there is a great deal of anxiety in dealing with emerging knowledge traditions. However, it also shows that very few Muslim thinkers and institutions recognize that the epistemological grounds of understanding the world from a believer's perspective have shifted, and that the premodern theologies require recasting and updating. While this desideratum is frequently upheld as a pious hope, it is perhaps often done in a piecemeal, *ad hoc* fashion. More often, these pious hopes surface in the domain of ethical deliberations over new generations of techno-science, where such theologies are practically enacted, instead of when theoretical debates about the theology of science are entertained. Muslim discourse on the bioethics of science is often steeped in an ethical pragmatism about the permissibility or impermissibility, and the beneficence or malfeasance, attached to the discoveries of techno-science. What is lacking, and remains elusive, is a critical and informed discourse about the philosophical grounds that underpin a contemporary Muslim moral and ethical vision in a prospective manner.

Anxiety-ridden sentiments mixed with theological undertones often surface strongly in encounters with biotechnological practices. Anxieties peak in discussions over genetics, where incredible as well as intimidating feats of techno-science potentially lie in store. Let's for the sake of convenience use the rubric "genetics" to cover a host of issues related to the transfer, use, manipulation, and experimentation of genetic materials. In dealing with some of these issues, many Muslim authorities frequently deploy a text of the Qur'an as a proof-text in these debates and wave it as evidence of prohibition of the use of genetic therapies. The verse in question goes back to a conversation between God and Satan before the latter's expulsion from Eden for refusing to honor Adam (Fadel 2001). At that moment, Satan promises God that he will avenge his expulsion on the children of Adam, striving henceforth to "disfigure the creation of God." Generations of Muslim exegetes understood that phrase to mean Satan threatening to sponsor the moral corruption of Adam's offspring and to disfigure their moral selves. However, in a post-Darwinian era, techno-science meets crass scripturalism to give that very same verse a completely new application and meaning: now it means Satan will enable humans to molest the genetic composition of their bodies! What better illustration of grotesque disfigurement of the body than messing with genes? In the view of many Muslim ethicists of a traditionalist, and even those of a revivalist, bent, this Qur'anic verse serves as a cautionary tale of the physical disfigurement of creation that awaits humanity experimenting with evil and profane science.

Two principal objections are frequently made against genetic engineering. Firstly, this brand of techno-science opens the door to asexual reproduction (Ahmad 2003). Secondly, it is argued that, in its essence, genetic engineering is a violation of human dignity and as such scoffs at the sanctity of life. More generally, many Muslim religious authorities view genetic engineering procedures as a frontal assault on the structure of the Muslim family, where the notion of paternity is upheld as a central artifice. Paternity in terms of Islamic law is established only within a heterosexual marriage. Asexual reproduction threatens the biological architecture that informs classical Islamic law. Intergenerational inheritance of property occurs along the lines of kinship associations in Islam, and therefore the hype of biotechnology surrounding genetic engineering threatens that specific narrative of kinship relations the way we know it. Genetically engineered offspring, it is feared, will find themselves in a legal and ethical no-man's-land in terms of existing Islamic criteria, challenging the entire system. One concern most religious experts voice is that asexual reproduction will promote discrimination between different *kinds* of offspring: children with naturally reproduced genetic make-up who will be subject to one set of rules versus children bearing artificially engineered genetic make-up who will be subject to a different set of norms. In short, what they dread is discrimination coupled with normative anarchy.

Much of the reaction to genetic engineering on the part of Muslim traditional jurists and ethicists points to the cloning of the sheep named Dolly as an indicator of the malevolent trajectory of techno-science (Sachedina 2009). Most fear that human cloning would be the ultimate perversion of reproduction the way we know it, and fears of its sinister consequences abound. While a very few scholars are unconditionally open to the possibility of therapeutic uses of genetic engineering, the majority of views canvassed and reviewed by Abdulaziz Sachedina on this topic expressed extreme caution blended with suspicion about the purposes of such techno-science (Sachedina 2009). Others in south Asia, especially in Pakistan, were outright dismissive of the merits of therapeutic uses of genetic engineering (Madani 2003, 2005a).

Critical changes in the construction of knowledge have created a crisis in Muslim epistemology. Since the seventeenth century, the new ideal of knowing is through *doing*, or knowing by *construction* (Funkenstein 1986). This definition of knowledge is the one that principally informs techno-science. In the view of Muslim traditionalists, the only knowledge worth pursuing was that which led to knowing God. All other modes of knowledge fell in the ancillary category of necessary, but secondary. As long as the dissonance in the social imaginaries fostered by techno-science and Muslim ethics persists, the communicative deficit between these two ethical regimes will remain high, for they, in effect, speak different languages.

Issues and trajectories in Muslim ethics

In a constantly mutating futuristic techno-science context, a backward-looking casuistic logic of the deontological *fiqh*-tradition of Muslim ethics is less helpful. Hence I propose the need to develop broad normative principles that are tightly hinged to a philosophical–theological narrative which begins to tease out the potential moral quandaries of social existence in which techno-science is part of our knowledge system.

Two kinds of traditionalists often respond to Muslim ethical issues. The first are traditionalist clerics, who provide a perspective from Islamic law and the canonical authority of the tradition. Another type of traditionalists self-identify with what I would call metaphysical traditionalists. The French thinker René Guénon's views on science often inform this perspective. Science, in this view, is portrayed as a "profane science" that had violated the principles of a "sacred science," namely metaphysics. Until this metaphysical breach in modern life is mended by a return to sacred science, and its propositions restored, this crisis will endure (Guénon 2001). Seyyed Hossein Nasr channels this perspective in his many works on science, faith, and ethics in Islam (Nasr 1993, 2006). Modernist perspectives in Islam range from those who try to bind science to some crass version of scripturalism, to more nuanced views, but neither is satisfactory (Sardar 1985; Hoodbhoy 1991). Here, too, there is an absence of a rigorous and robust engagement with both the juridical and theological traditions of Islamdom and a critical philosophical approach to techno-science and its globalization through economies of scale.

Often, traditionalist clerics view moderns and their lifestyles to be uncritically in the thrall of modern science and hence panglossian – a demeanor of being unwaveringly or unrealistically optimistic about anything, and in this case being enamored by the wonders of techno-science. Often, traditionalist concerns sound as if they are informed by the pessimism that authors such as Dominique Janicaud, Renée Fox, and Judith Swazey have voiced about biological futures in their many writings (Fox and Swazey 1992, 2002; Janicaud 1994). In my view, the traditional clerical views (barring exceptions, of course) are often poorly informed about science, and hardly have intimate experience with practices of science and life worlds premised on science, save as consumers of medicine or modern high-tech communications, from cell phones to the internet. Yet most clerical or metaphysical traditionalists often resist calls to revise Muslim theology in the light of newer developments in science, technology, and human experience. Underlying such reluctance is an assumption that pre-existing, pre-modern metaphysics and its compliant theologies are magical elixirs that would kick in as remedies if only we returned to traditional epistemology.

Among the clerical traditionalists, there is a predisposition for what I call the hyper-juridification of Muslim law and ethics. The default mode in ethics in the realm of modern scientific developments is to approve of new technologies by way of a vague and almost intuitive account of either beneficence (*maslaha*) or maleficence (*mafsada*). Or, if the scales between the two are balanced, then there is a predisposition to err on the side of the precautionary principle (*al-darar yuzal or la darar wa la dirar*). Both these aphorisms, that "maleficence ought to be eradicated" or, "do not inflict harm nor reciprocate with harm," equivalent to the "no harm, no harassment" principle in secular ethics, stem from a universe when Muslim epistemology was largely entrenched in a rational speculative mode with a commensurate ethical tradition. Harm and good in a world governed by social scientific and empirical rationalities require very different indices of measurement. Contemporary Muslim ethicists can no longer be content in quantifying beneficence or maleficence by an intuitive measure, or by the lights of scriptural reasoning, but rather they will require concrete empirical indicators in addition to other indices. If the measure of good and harm remains some abstract quality, then it is inevitable that the dissonance between the instrument of measurement and the measured thing is going to be at considerable variance. This is also the area in which Muslim bioethics specialists will be required to deliver innovative solutions.

References

Ahmad, N. Á. (2003) "Istinsakh (Cloning) *ka sa'insi 'amal*," *Muhaddis* 35: 53–69.

Dallal, Ahmad (2000) "Science, Medicine, and Technology: The Making of a Scientific Culture," in *The Oxford History of Islam*, John L. Esposito (ed.), New York: Oxford University Press, 155–213.

Elshakry, M. (2003) "Darwin's Legacy in the Arab East: Science, Religion and Politics, 1870–1914," PhD thesis, Princeton University.

Fadel, M. (2001) "Islam and the New Genetics," *Saint Thomas Law Review* 13: 901–9.

al-Faruqi, I. R. (1982) *Islamization of Knowledge: The Problem, Principles, and the Workplan*, Islamabad: National Hijra Centenary Committee of Pakistan.

Fox, R. C. and Swazey, J. P. (1992) *Spare Parts: Organ Replacement in American Society*, New York: Oxford University Press.

——(2002) *The Courage to Fail: A Social View of Organ Transplants and Dialysis*, New Brunswick, NJ: Transaction Publishers.

Funkenstein, A. (1986) *Theology and the Scientific Imagination from the Middle Ages to the Seventeenth Century*, Princeton, NJ: Princeton University Press.

Guénon, R. (2001) *The Crisis of the Modern World*, Ghent, NY: Sophia Perennis.

Hamdy, S. F. (2006) "Our Bodies belong to God: Islam, Medical Science, and Ethical Reasoning in Egyptian Life," PhD thesis, New York University.

Hoodbhoy, P. (1991) *Islam and Science: Religious Orthodoxy and the Battle for Rationality*, London and Atlantic Highlands, NJ: Zed Books.

Janicaud, D. (1994) *Powers of the Rational: Science, Technology, and the Future of Thought*, Bloomington, IN: Indiana University Press [electronic resource].

Madani, H. H. (2003) "Cloning *ka 'amal kya hai? Ghair sa'insi alfaz main*," *Muhaddis* 32: 70–71.

——(2005a) "*Islam main nasab awr nasal ka tahaffuz: ithbat-i nasab main qayafa wa qara in aur DNA ki test waghayra ki haythiyat*," *Muhaddith* 7.

——(2005b) "*Islam main nasab wa nasl ka tahaffua*," *Fikr-o nazar* 37: 2–34.

Moazam, F. (2006) *Bioethics and Organ Transplantation in a Muslim Society: A Study in Culture, Ethnography, and Religion*, Bloomington, IN: Indiana University Press.

Moosa, E. (1999) "Languages of Change in Islamic Law: Redefining Death in Modernity," *Islamic Studies* 38: 305–42.

Nadvi, M. A. S. B. N. (1989 [1409]) *Jadid 'ilm-i kalam Qur'an aur sa'ins ki raushni men*, Bangalore: Furqaniyah Ikadimi Trust.

Nasr, S. H. (1993) *The Need for a Sacred Science*, Richmond, UK: Curzon Press.

——(2006) "On the Question of Biological Origins," *Islam & Science* 4.

Rees, M. (2010) "Scientific Horizons: Lecture 1: The Scientific Citizen," *The Reith Lectures*.

Sachedina, A. A. (2009) *Islamic Biomedical Ethics: Principles and Application*, Oxford and New York: Oxford University Press.

Sardar, Z. (1985) *Islamic Futures: The Shape of Ideas to Come*, London and New York: Mansell.

Yahya, H. (2010) *The Collapse of Darwinism in Europe*, Harunyahya.com, www.harunyahya.com/presentation/collapse_in_europe/index.html.

Further reading

What a more fully fledged Muslim bioethics would look like remains a work in progress, yet some rudimentary outlines are clearly demarcated. Debates in Muslim bioethics are often framed in a discourse of juridical theology marked by the polarities of either pragmatism or idealism, lacking a nunaced and reflective middle space. Perhaps Abdulaziz Sachedina's *Islamic Biomedical Ethics: Principles and Application* (cited above) most adequately captures some of the intra-Muslim debates while making some comparative evaluations with secular and Christian ethical traditions. Apart from a plethora of writings in the vernacular languages of West Asia and South Asia on this topic, these views were often distinguished for their defensiveness of traditional Muslim doctrines rather than engaging biotechnology and science. At best, a few essays address the topic substantively in a preliminary fashion.

Mohammad Fadel, "Islam and the New Genetics," addresses some of the challenges posed by genetic technology, as does Sachedina's previously mentioned book. However, Muslim bioethicists have as yet to write about biotechnology in the light of larger ethico-philosophical questions, where the mutations between life and politics and the boundaries between molecular biopolitics and human vitality are being reconfigured, apart from a modest attempt on my part in Ebrahim Moosa, "Neuropolitics and the Body," in *Religion and Society: An Agenda for the 21st Century*, Gerrie ter Haar and Yoshio Tsuruoka (eds) (Brill, 2007) and "Languages of Change in Islamic Law: Redefining Death in Modernity" (cited above). Farhat Moazam's *Bioethics and Organ Transplantation in a Muslim Society: A Study in Culture, Ethnography, and Religion*, along with a few dissertations that might soon appear as monographs, map the history and journey of science and biotechnology in Muslim societies. Notable among the latter are the PhD studies of Marwa Elshakry, "Darwin's legacy in the Arab East: Science, religion and politics, 1870–1914" and Sherine Hamdy, "Our bodies belong to God: Islam, medical science, and ethical reasoning in Egyptian life".

42
BIOTECHNOLOGY AND JUSTICE
Roman Catholic perspectives

B. Andrew Lustig

Catholic anthropology and moral methodology

As Ronald Cole-Turner observes in his scientific introduction (Chapter 39 in this volume), ours is an era of rapidly emerging new technologies, with developments in biotechnology, nanotechnology, robotics, and informatics that challenge us to think anew about the scope of human responsibility for interventions into, and alterations of, nature and the natural world. The complexity of the issues raised is compounded by current and prospective developments to alter the physical substratum of human nature itself, especially in the areas of genetics and reproductive technology. Such developments are occurring in a culture wherein consumer preferences and desires are increasingly being "medicalized." Widespread use of pharmaceuticals has extended medicine's traditional curative commitments to include the use of drugs to alter mood, change behavioral tendencies, and enhance performance. Such "off-label" drug use, much like the widespread recourse to cosmetic surgery for non-medical conditions, reflects consumer trends that are likely to intensify with the rapid expansion of biotechnological possibilities.

Dr. Cole-Turner also notes the fundamental issues that the convergence of technologies (biotechnology, informatics, robotics, and perhaps even human–machine incorporation technologies) raise concerning our attitudes about "human nature" and the appropriate relations between humans and the natural world. For Catholics and other Christians, such issues are linked to fundamental themes of religious anthropology and to basic questions about the moral norms that should inform our assessments of particular technologies. Consequently, perspectives on nature and human nature developed in non-religious discourse cannot be the starting points for Roman Catholic approaches to anthropology or moral method. From the first, concepts of nature and human nature are transformed by the basic belief in God as Creator of the natural world and of human persons. In addition, the fuller context of Roman Catholic moral deliberations necessarily includes an eschatological dimension. All human goods find their ultimate fulfillment in the final end of *beatitudo* (beatitude), or union with God. While various "natural" goods – such as life and love, community and mutuality – are central features of Catholic moral reflection, they reach their completion or perfection only in the fullness of God's time and redemptive purposes.

Roman Catholic moral theology

Roman Catholic moral theology arose as a distinct discipline in the sixteenth century. At its core, in contrast to Protestant theological ethics, Roman Catholicism embodies a relatively positive appraisal of natural moral insight available to persons as a function of God's grace in creation. In the formulation of Thomas Aquinas, human beings share in God's Eternal Law by virtue of their rational nature (*Summa Theologica* I–II, 79–85).

From the time of High Scholasticism until the Second Vatican Council (1961–65), Roman Catholic moral method emphasized natural law as a source of moral knowledge in principle available to all persons. The primary natural law directive in Catholic thought, available to moral reason in a process called "synderesis," is to "do good and avoid evil." In light of that general precept, human reason, according to Aquinas and later Scholastics, reflects on certain natural inclinations as "givens." In the process, certain basic goods of human flourishing become obvious as appropriate ends of action.

Both nature and human nature are teleologically suffused in Catholic thought (*telos* = purpose or end). All reflective human choices and actions aim at certain practical ends – the natural law goods that are identified in the process of practical deliberation. While original sin has distorted human capacity to know and to do the good, Catholic moral method is distinguished from Protestantism by its greater confidence in our natural moral capacity to discern the good and in our natural ability to do the good (at least partially). At the same time, though often underemphasized in Catholic moral theology, Special Revelation (Scripture and Church Tradition) functions crucially in two respects: first, to illuminate and empower human beings to know and to realize their supernatural end of final union with God; and second, to bring greater clarity to the conclusions of natural moral knowledge.

Thomas Aquinas' approach to moral reasoning remains influential in Catholic thought. According to Aquinas, our human capacity to reason empowers men and women, upon reflection, to understand the ends and purposes of the created order, including the ends and purposes of human life. For Thomas, the basic goods of human flourishing that are transparent to reflection (*per se nota* truths) are self-preservation, the begetting and education of children, the good of community, and knowledge of and communion with God.

More recent natural law discussions (e.g. Grisez 1970; Grisez and Boyle 1979) have underscored the requirement that one should never choose *directly* against any of the basic goods accessible to practical reason. For example, the official Catholic position on abortion forbids termination of the life of the fetus as a direct choice against the good of personal life. However, some actions that result in fetal death – for example, a hysterectomy in the case of a pregnant woman with a cancerous uterus – are justified under the so-called rule of "double effect," whereby one distinguishes between the good effect one directly intends (removing the cancer) and the evil effect (death of the fetus) that, while foreseen, is unintended and therefore indirect.

The foregoing example of double effect reveals another characteristic feature of Catholic moral method – its employment of casuistry. Casuistry involves the application of general principles to particular cases, but it does so in a way that is attentive to the dialectic between general maxims and their interpretation and specification in particular circumstances. For example, in complex cases, the meaning of a general principle's terms may be unclear, or it may emerge in conflict with another norm. In other circumstances, a situation may pose novel features that require a reassessment of moral conclusions drawn from earlier paradigm cases. While casuistry is often judged harshly by its critics as a form of moral quibbling or sophistry (especially by much of the Protestant tradition), it is an important shared emphasis in Roman Catholic moral theology, Jewish rabbinical ethics, and Islamic reasoning (*sharia*). Indeed, in the judgment of two recent commentators, casuistry, when properly deployed, is an especially powerful method for deliberating about concrete dilemmas that arise in such areas as legal ethics and clinical medical ethics (Jonsen and Toulmin 1988: 304–43).

Since the Second Vatican Council (1962–65), natural law thought has been subject to critical scrutiny and major efforts at reformulation, with three new emphases emerging. First, a stress on historicism has challenged an earlier, largely static model of individuals and society. While the primary directive of natural law – to do good and avoid evil – retains its general, largely formal, force, many recent discussions point to the variability of cultural and historical values in the specification and application of "secondary" natural law directives in particular circumstances. To be sure, natural law method remains a bulwark against moral relativism, but the possibilities for genuine development in moral doctrine are now affirmed (Noonan 1993; Curran 1995).

In that light, critical studies, especially feminist approaches, have explored the ways in which past interpretations of nature and human nature have often confused cultural prejudices with religious norms, especially in relation to issues of sexuality, gender, and parenting, often to the detriment of women in particular settings (e.g. Cahill 2005b, 2005c). More broadly, critics have noted a so-called "physicalism" at work in the natural law tradition. Following the Council of Trent (1545–63), detailed penitential books were developed (so-called "manuals") to prepare seminary students for their future role as confessors. These manuals, often in exhaustive detail, classified "family trees" of sin according to objective categories in order to aid priests in assigning appropriate penances to individuals (Mahoney 1987: 1–36). However, especially in matters of sexual ethics, such "manualism" often devolved into "physicalism" by tending to emphasize the biological structure of acts to the exclusion of broader concerns about person-centered agency or intentionality. According to such critics, the official Catholic teaching against artificial contraception continues to reflect a preoccupation with the physical aspects of each act of sexual intercourse, rather than a more holistic appreciation of marriage as a sacramental relationship (Curran 1995).

As a second emphasis since the time of Vatican II, Catholic moral theology has increasingly adopted the approach and language of "personalism." This perspective has significantly broadened the focus of earlier natural law discussion. Human beings are naturally constituted to live in community; indeed, sociality is a constitutive dimension of personhood. Moreover, the goods of human embodiment – individual, sexual, and communal – are now understood in more dynamic and less deductive terms, with human flourishing now considered in terms of the overall good of persons (Fitzgerald 2005). The extent to which personalism's broader focus amplifies or alters moral judgments based on traditional natural law grounds remains the subject of ongoing debate.

A third emphasis in the recent tradition has been a renewed interest in, and appreciation for, the place of Scripture in moral reflection. Scripture retains its central place in virtually all forms of Protestant moral reflection; thus this recent Scriptural turn in Catholic moral theology has been a welcome ecumenical development. At the same time, despite the increased prominence of Scripture in Catholic discussions, its influence of moral reasoning and judgment remains primarily at the level of motivation and disposition. In practice, official Roman Catholic moral theology tends to retain its reliance on human reason, natural law, and the teachings of the magisterium.

Roman Catholicism is perhaps most distinct from other traditions in its official understanding of the magisterium as its central teaching authority. As defined by the First Vatican Council (1869–70), the term "magisterium" refers to the centralized teaching authority of the Church's hierarchy, headed by the Pope. The topics of magisterial teaching are matters of faith and morals. While natural law remains a fundamental source of moral insight, the magisterium as central authority embodies the Church's ecclesiological self-understanding: that the Pope claims the legacy of Peter as first pontiff in guarding and transmitting the "deposit of faith." This understanding claims the power of the Holy Spirit in aiding the Pope to provide unique insights about the essentials of the Catholic faith and fundamental implications of natural law.

Such confidence about the magisterium's role in clarifying moral conclusions that remain, in principle, derivable from natural law flows from Catholicism's traditional confidence in the mutuality between Revelation and natural moral insights. Nonetheless, the role of the magisterium in the Catholic Church has also been subject to significant misinterpretation. While the Church claims to teach infallibly (without the possibility of error) on certain matters of dogma, such pronouncements are in fact rare. Most Church pronouncements, especially on moral matters, assume the form of authoritative but non-infallible teaching. Thus, while deference is owed to magisterial authority, other sources of moral insight – natural law and human experience broadly construed – are increasingly brought to bear on the discussion by Catholic moral theologians of a number of conflicted questions, especially regarding sexual morality. Given the various sources available for moral reflection in Catholic moral theology, including relevant data from the natural and social sciences, there is clear room in the tradition, at least in principle, for change and development in moral teaching (Noonan 1993).

The implications of Catholic moral theology for issues in biotechnology

The theological basis for scientific and technological research

In the Catholic Christian tradition, the fundamental theological warrants for science and technology as appropriate human pursuits are twofold: God is the Creator of the world and humankind, and we are made in his image and likeness. The meanings associated with humans as made in the image of God in the Christian tradition include capacities that, in limited fashion, mirror attributes ascribed to God and, at the same time, reflect our distinct status in the created order. Central to these interpretations are two dominant strands: our rationality as self-conscious and free creatures, and our dominion over creation. Both emphases provide the warrant for science as an activity to explore the created world, as well as to derive appropriate benefits from dominion over the world and its resources (Cairns 1953: 110–20; Muckenhirn 1963; Childress 1986: 292–93; Hall 1986; Cahill 2005a). But both emphases are also problematic. Rationality is not, in the first instance, the mere capacity to reason about means to any and all ends. Theologically, judgments about appropriate means require a prior acceptance of, and reasoning about, God's creative and sustaining purposes, which provide the general framework for particular moral judgments, including judgments about science and technology. And the concept of dominion is often misconstrued as the exercise of mastery or control, whereby nature is reduced to the merely manipulable object of human desire. The value of nature, however, while not independent of human agency and judgment, is not thereby reducible to its instrumental use by humans. Instead, a rational sense of dominion will include an appreciation and affirmation of the integrity of all creation, which maintains its own "goodness" as an aspect of God's creating and sustaining will.

Within an expressly theological context, science emerges as our rational inquiry into the patterns of God's order, as well as our partnership with God as stewards and cultivators of the natural world. One finds, classically in Augustine and Aquinas, and notably in the writings of believing scientists since the seventeenth century, a strong affirmation of what has come to be called the "Two Books" tradition about the sources of our knowledge of God (Barbour 1997). In Scripture, the first book, God provides, through the history of Israel and the coming of Christ, His self-revelation as Father, Son, and Spirit. The second book, the Book of Nature, also provides its own witness to the patterns of God's creative, ordering, and sustaining will as revealed in nature and its regularities. This natural knowledge of God, available to all persons of good will, is a major theme in Jewish Wisdom literature and is also reflected in Paul's judgment (Romans 1) about the universal moral accountability of all human beings. Pre-eminently in the Scholastic tradition, Aquinas spoke of certain naturally available facts about the word that bespeak God as Creator and Orderer as "preambles to faith," accessible to all persons.

Catholic perspectives on reproductive technologies

Official Roman Catholic teaching on new reproductive technologies is based on what has been called the "inseparability principle": the goods of conjugal intimacy and openness to procreation should not be separated in any act of marital intercourse. On that basis, official Catholic teaching continues to reject artificial contraception as an illicit separation of conjugal intimacy from its procreative potential. On the same basis, official teaching rejects *in vitro* fertilization (IVF) as an illicit separation of conception from the act of sexual intercourse. Official teaching also rejects pre-implantation diagnosis on two grounds: that it involves extra-corporeal conception, and that it entails the destruction of those embryos that are not implanted. More broadly, official teaching condemns as intrinsically immoral acts all forms of manipulation (including embryonic stem cell research) that involve destruction of embryos. But in other areas of biotechnology, including the use of alternative sources of stem cells that do not involve the destruction of embryos, the Catholic tradition is deeply supportive of appropriate therapies in service to the basic goods of life and health.

Many Catholic moral theologians question official Church teaching on reproductive issues in ways that bear directly on judgments about various forms of biotechnology. With regard to the ban on artificial contraception, these critics propose as an alternative to the traditional act-centered analysis a broader "relationship-oriented" approach to the goods of marriage. From this perspective, while conjugal intimacy and procreative potential are, obviously, marital goods, it is far less clear that the latter must be expressed in every act of intercourse, rather than in the marital relationship as a whole. Moreover, for these commentators and most non-Catholic Christians, the "artificiality" of some forms of contraception (in contrast to so-called "natural family planning") fails to constitute, in itself, a morally decisive feature in choices about responsible parenting.

In light of the foregoing critique, many commentators also question the application of the inseparability principle to all cases of IVF. Richard McCormick, for example, observes that official Church teaching emphasizes the "natural perfection" of sexual intercourse as it occurs normally between loving spouses. McCormick focuses instead on the typical case of infertility between spouses that involves the lack of such natural perfection. It is precisely because of a natural deficit in such a case that alternative means are sought. McCormick argues that an aesthetic standard is here being confused or conflated with a moral norm. He calls, instead, for a broader understanding of the intention of IVF, not as a "substitution for sexual intimacy but as a kind of prolongation of it, and therefore as not involving the total severance of the unitive and procreative" goods of marriage (McCormick 1989: 348).

Other critics raise questions about the moral status of the early embryo in ways that bear directly on judgments about embryonic stem cell research as well as pre-implantation diagnosis. In *Donum Vitae*, the Vatican reaffirmed its position that the embryo must be respected as a person from the moment of conception (The Holy See 1987). Some moral theologians, however, point out that, for up to two weeks after conception (until the appearance of the so-called "primitive streak"), a single embryo may spontaneously become twins or a twinned embryo may recombine into a single organism. On that basis, they suggest that true biological individuality should not be equated with conception, that the early embryo does not yet warrant the status of "personhood," and that certain types of embryonic testing and research may therefore be justified (Shannon and Wolter 1993; Farley 2001: 116; Hansen and Schotsman 2005).

Genetic interventions: therapy and enhancement

Roman Catholic moral theology remains quite open in principle to medical interventions that are therapeutic in nature, though within clear constraints (for example, as we have seen, the *direct* taking of innocent human life is always forbidden). Official Catholic teaching, while allowing somatic cell genetic therapies that occur *in vivo*, reject all forms of genetic therapy, including so-called "therapeutic cloning," that involve the destruction of embryonic human life. Moreover, only cautious acceptance of prenatal genetic diagnosis is voiced, because such testing performed with the intention to abort an abnormal fetus is expressly forbidden (The Holy See 1987). Still, despite such negative judgments on certain matters, simplistic conclusions about Catholic teaching as being "against" biotechnology are inaccurate and misleading. Assessments of different interventions are neither uniformly positive nor negative; they vary depending on the application of general norms to concrete cases.

What, then, of so-called "enhancements" from a Catholic perspective? In broad terms, enhancements are, by definition, non-therapeutic in nature, and are therefore viewed with significant caution and reservation. In perhaps the most representative magisterial discussion of genetics, John Paul II, in an address entitled "The Dangers of Genetic Manipulation," affirms the therapeutic commitment to healing or to restoration of normal function as a core value, so long as it is directed to "the true promotion of the […] well-being of persons." (Interestingly, here the distinction between somatic and germline interventions is not seen as dispositive. For example if, in the future, the risks and uncertainties currently associated with therapeutic interventions into the germline could be adequately addressed, such interventions would appear to be warranted as especially effective forms of therapy.) At the same time, John Paul voices caution for any genetic intervention that cannot be described in therapeutic terms. Such enhancements must be assessed according to several broad principles: first, that "the biological nature of each person" must be safeguarded as a requirement of individual dignity; second, that such interventions must not "infringe" on the origin of human life (no use of reproductive technologies such as IVF and no destruction of embryos); third, that such interventions not be merely "materialist" or "reductionist" in their orientation; and fourth, that such interventions should not lead to new forms of social marginalization (between the enhanced and the unenhanced). Taken together, John Paul's four constraining principles appear fairly conservative in their implications for the moral legitimacy of genetic enhancements, as well as enhancement technologies more generally, in marked contrast to his more positive appraisal of interventions that are clearly therapeutic in their intent (Pope John Paul II 1983).

In contrast to John Paul's conservatism, other voices in Catholic moral theology reflect greater openness to both health- and non-health-related enhancements, although such openness is expressed at the level of broad anthropology rather than judgments about specific cases or traits. The work of Kevin Fitzgerald exemplifies this approach. Drawing on anthropological categories developed by systematic theologian Karl Rahner, Fitzgerald seeks to shift the terms of the discussion to a more dynamic understanding of human meaning and possibility. According to Rahner, our "nature" is largely defined by our own cultural activities throughout history, and may not be presupposed as a categorical, fixed quantity (Rahner 1972). Rahner's open-ended perspective on human nature leads Fitzgerald to recommend that the moral focus shift from the rather static distinction between therapy and enhancement to "more fundamental questions concerning human nature and human flourishing as the key to self-determination" (Fitzgerald 2005: 92). In a similar vein, James Keenan offers a largely positive assessment of the current and prospective enhancements within a framework that focuses primarily on certain fundamental *virtues* rather than on the first principles of natural law (Keenan 2005).

Biotechnology, justice, and the common good

As Dr. Cole-Turner emphasizes in his introductory survey (Chapter 39 in this volume), issues of justice are central to recent theological assessments of biotechnology. Catholic discussions provide an especially rich context for assessing the justice implications of biotechnological developments, because modern Catholic social teaching affirms both the dignity of individual persons and the reality of the common good, thereby linking notions of liberty and community in a way that is distinct from many secular conceptions of persons and society. In contrast to individualistic theories, a fundamentally social understanding infuses Catholic social thought, with the language of the common good pointing to the realities of human dependence and interdependence.

Beginning with the papacy of Pius XI (1922–39), the common good has also been linked with the concept of social justice. Pius XI invokes the notion of social justice in order to identify the institutional and structural dimensions of social relations. As societies develop and medicine progresses, institutions, especially at the governmental level, are morally required to mediate the claims of human dignity and to shape the content of human rights, including the right of access to basic medical care. More recently, Catholic social teaching has also emphasized a so-called "preferential option for the poor." In service to that value, institutions are required to respond to those inequities between and among individuals that particularly threaten the dignity of the most disadvantaged in society (Lustig 1998).

In light of this trinity of values – the common good, social justice, and the preferential option for the poor – Catholic social teaching may be invoked to raise the more pointed and concrete questions of distributive justice. Distributive justice, in more focused fashion than the language of social justice, considers two questions: how shall we distribute fairly the benefits of healthcare (including the potential benefits of biotechnology); and, with as much specificity as possible, which benefits should assume priority or be viewed as "basic"? (Keane 1993). According to Lisa Cahill, such issues are seldom central to discussions of biotechnology in the context of global capitalism. As she pointedly poses the question, "Does it serve the global common good to devote billions to new genetic interventions while more basic health needs are so dire and while great gaps in other basic needs […] bring early death to so many?" (Cahill 2005c: 215). In light of the central themes developed in recent Catholic social teaching, the answer would appear to be no. Developments in biotechnology may hold great promise for those who are already privileged, but Cahill's troubling query remains. Will the benefits of biotechnology be broadly shared, or will a market-driven, merely technological progress be more likely to reinforce or exacerbate current inequities? The Catholic response to that challenge will be uttered in the language of justice, solidarity, and the common good. But in order for justice to be done, prophetic rhetoric will need to be matched by effective and sustained commitment to action in a global context.

References

Barbour, Ian (1997) *Religion and Science: Historical and Contemporary Issues*, San Francisco, CA: HarperOne.

Cahill, Lisa (2005a) "Creation and Ethics," in *The Oxford Handbook of Theological Ethics*, G. Meilaender and W. Werpehowski (eds), New York: Oxford University Press, 7–24.

——(2005b) "Genetics, Theology, Common Good," in *Genetics, Theology, and Ethics: An Interdisciplinary Conversation*, L. Cahill (ed.), New York: Crossroad, 117–36.

——(2005c) *Theological Bioethics: Participation, Justice, Change*, Washington, DC: Georgetown University Press.

Childress, James (1986) "Image of God (*Imago Dei*)," in *The Westminster Dictionary of Christian Ethics*, J. F. Childress and J. Macquarrie (eds), Philadelphia, PA: The Westminster Press, 292–93.

Curran, Charles (1995) "Roman Catholicism," in *Encyclopedia of Bioethics, Volume Four* (revised edn), W. Reich (ed.), New York: Simon & Schuster/Macmillan, 2321–31.

Farley, Margaret (2001) "Roman Catholic Views on Research Involving Human Stem Cells," in *The Human Embryonic Stem Cell Debate: Science, Ethics, and Public Policy*, S. Holland, K. Lebacqz and L. Zoloth (eds), Cambridge, MA: MIT Press, 113–18.

Fitzgerald, Kevin (2005) "The Need for a Dynamic and Integrative Vision of the Human for the Ethics of Genetics," in *Genetics, Theology, and Ethics: An Interdisciplinary Conversation*, L. Cahill (ed.), New York: Crossroad, 79–96.

Grisez, Germain (1970) *Abortion: The Myths, The Realities, and the Arguments*. New York: Corpus Books.

Grisez, Germain and Joseph Boyle (1979) *Life and Death with Liberty and Justice: A Contribution to the Euthanasia Debate*, Notre Dame, IN: University of Notre Dame Press.

Hall, Douglas (1986) *Imaging God: Dominion as Stewardship*, Grand Rapids, MI: Eerdmans.

Hansen, Bart and Paul Schotsman (2005) "Stem Cell Research: A Theological Interpretation," in L. Cahill (ed.), *Genetics, Theology, and Ethics: An Interdisciplinary Conversation*, New York: Crossroad, 15–52.

The Holy See (1987) *Donum Vitae. Instruction from the Congregation of the Doctrine of the Faith*, Vatican, February 27.

Jonsen, Albert and Stephen Toulmin (1988) *The Abuse of Casuistry: A History of Moral Reasoning*, Berkeley, CA: University of California Press.

Keane, Phillip (1993) *Health Care Reform: A Catholic View*, Mahwah, NJ: Paulist Press.

Keenan, James (2005) "What Does Virtue Ethics Bring to Genetics?" in *Genetics, Theology, and Ethics: An Interdisciplinary Conversation*, L. Cahill (ed.), New York: Crossroad, 97–113.

Lustig, B. Andrew (1993) "The Common Good in a Secular Society: The Relevance of a Roman Catholic Notion to the Healthcare Allocation Debate," in *On Moral Medicine: Theological Perspectives in Medical Ethics* (2nd edn), S. Lammers and A. Verhey (eds), Grand Rapids, MI: 1998, 960–73.

Mahoney, John (1987) *The Making of Moral Theology: A Study of the Roman Catholic Tradition*, New York: Oxford University Press.

McCormick, Richard (1989) *The Critical Calling: Reflections on Moral Dilemmas Since Vatican II*, Washington, DC: Georgetown University Press.

Muckenhirn, Sister M. Charles Borromeo (1963) *The Image of God in Creation*, Englewood Cliffs, NJ.

Noonan, John (1993) "Development in Moral Doctrine," *Theological Studies* 54: 662–77.

Peters, Ted, *et al.* (2008) "Religious Traditions and Genetic Enhancement," in *Altering Nature, Volume Two: Religion, Biotechnology, and Public Policy*, B. A. Lustig, B. Brody and G. McKenny (eds), New York: Springer, 109–59.

Pope John Paul II (1983) "The Ethics of Genetic Manipulation: Address to the World Medical Association," address to members of the World Medical Association, October 29, 1983, www.ewtn.com/library/PAPALDOC/JP2GENMP.HTM

Rahner, Karl (1972) "The Problem of Genetic Manipulation," in K. Rahner, *Theological Investigations* 9, New York: Herder & Herder, 225–52.

Shannon, Thomas (2008) "The Roman Catholic Magisterium and Genetic Research: An Overview and Evaluation," in *Design and Destiny: Jewish and Christian Perspectives on Human Germline Modification*, R. Turner (ed.), Cambridge, MA: 51–71.

Shannon, Thomas and Allan Wolter (1990) "Reflections on the Moral Status of the Pre-embryo," *Theological Studies* 52: 603–26.

Further reading

There are numerous sources that are useful for placing Roman Catholic perspectives on particular bioethics issues in a broader conceptual and historical context. John Mahoney, in *The Making of Moral Theology: A Study of the Roman Catholic Tradition* (cited above), discusses the major historical sources and influences in the development of Roman Catholic ethics, critiques the rigidity of the earlier natural law tradition, and offers a number of suggestions for reform and renewal. Charles Curran, in his *Catholic Moral Theology in the United States: A History* (Georgetown University Press, 2008), surveys the development of Catholic moral theology in the United States and pays particular attention to the critical responses by US Catholic scholars to *Humanae Vitae*, the 1968 encyclical that reaffirmed the traditional ban on artificial contraception. Curran also provides a broader survey of recent themes and topics, one which includes European discussions, in *The Catholic Moral Tradition Today: A Synthesis* (Georgetown University Press, 1999). Catholic feminists have also made vital contributions to recent debates. Especially noteworthy are Lisa Cahill's *Sex, Gender, and Christian Ethics* (Cambridge University Press, 1996), Margaret Farley's *Just Love: A Framework for Christian Sexual Ethics* (Continuum, 2008), Maura Ryan's *Ethics and Economics of Assisted Reproduction: The Cost of Longing* (Georgetown University Press, 2003), and Christina Traina's *Feminist Ethics and Natural Law* (Georgetown University Press, 1999).

43

JUSTICE IN THE MARGINS OF THE LAND

Jewish responses to the challenges of biotechnology

Laurie Zoloth

> Never before in the history of nature has one species seemed poised to modify the natural world so radically and so quickly […] It is no wonder that many today find themselves worrying whether our technology now poses an unmanageable risk to nature and to our own kind. If technology controls nature, who or what controls technology?
>
> (Ronald Cole-Turner, Chapter 39 in this volume).

Consider the way that we write about biotechnology and nature. On the one hand, science is driven by the idea that the world, as other than self, can be understood progressively, and hence used creatively to change human fate. There is both an ontological and a teleological aspect to the narrative, for we tell the story of biotechnology as it "writes" us. The human being is a creation of technology as surely as we are creators of technology. This has been true since our species turned from foraging to cultivation. It is just as true now. In fact, for the theologian who is a watcher of science, it is immediately striking that the sentiments expressed by Cole-Turner above could have been expressed with as much veracity in the fifth century BCE, or the seventeenth century CE, or the middle of the twentieth century, as surely as in the summer of 2010 when this book was composed. This essay is based on the premise that the problems of new technology – its horizons, uncertainties, and power – are endemic, perennial, and foundational. If the making of the world is an ontological constancy, surely the question of meaning and making is a constancy as well. It is for this reason that we turn to the texts and traditions that are part of the human response. It is my contention that while, as Cole-Turner notes, "Technology is growing in its power to transform nature, and nature itself provides little or no guidance about the goal of our transformations," (Chapter 39), we are far from incapable of understanding and creating normative guidelines. For Jewish tradition, and for Jewish communities, the problem of just acquisition and the modalities for enhancing and sharing the goods of the world is at the core of the faith itself.

Making justice in an unjust and unfinished world is the commanded task of the Jew who lives a commanded life.

Biotechnology is the heir of three critical human revolutions that sought to make the world of nature fit human needs more closely. The first, agriculture, was based on the idea that plants could be made more useful and high-yielding via breeding. It was the insight of the Industrial Revolution that it was better to make things with machines than by individual human hands; and it is foundational to biotechnology that manipulation at the cellular and molecular levels allows delicate and efficient self-assembly. As in the Industrial Revolution, the central notion is that knowledge and production can be understood best by describing the structure and function of the smallest possible unit, rather than by describing principles of the whole.

For theologians and moral philosophers, it is this aspect of biotechnology that alerts us to the partiality of its vision. We are led to ask: what is left out of a narrative told in this way? Further, the vision of science, as Cole-Turner notes, is of one of faith – that the progressive narrative of human history is led by empirical research toward a better world. For reasons both epistemic and teleological, science and religion share some terrain, and it is on this contested ground that we meet and reflect on each new biotechnology that is introduced. The specifics of the technology vary in form, but not in intent, nor in the shared ideas noted above.

Theologians and moral philosophers drawn to the debate, and, I would argue, Jewish theologians in particular, have a complex duty. First, like all who comment on biotechnology, we must reflect on core issues of safety, integrity, and clarity about the particular experiments and applications. But second, we have a duty to raise the question of justice, a particular concern for Jewish tradition. The ethical issue in the first case, that of safety or risk, concerns our fears of the science somehow going wrong, but the ethical issues in the second case are all about success and its implications. The ethical issues are ones of just distribution, especially for those at the margins, the classic problem of normative Judaism.

The most recognizable aspect of this narrative of emerging science is the idea that human puzzles can be solved by careful empirical methods, which lead to new stuff. Yet for theologians, the very acquisition of new objects of knowledge and new materials for human use creates the possibility of error. The idea of new technology that claims to transform science is powerful. Yet in the debates about biotechnology, as in the first debates about recombinant DNA technology, the essential unknowability of the social and ethical implications creates a daunting challenge. What is left to be said is largely about the dangers of what is known, and how we might protect against the physical dangers that we can contain and measure.

We are witness to research that is embedded in a particular social narrative: big science, transformative possibilities, and the new logical positivism of our twenty-first century. It is being done at a specific time in history, under certain constraints, norms, and institutions, toward certain goals. It is a time in which such research suggests a trajectory – hypothesis, experiment, evidence, and application. Usually, our field of bioethics is devoted to the questions of *whether* the research is ethical, when judged in terms of its impact on our world. While typically, and historically, this means ascertaining whether it is dangerous, in the case of rDNA (for example) it meant insisting the first decade of research took place only in level 4 containment facilities. I will argue that that path is inadequate, in large part because it seeks to use either the precautionary principle or classic risk–benefit analysis. This approach assumes that biotechnology is one thing, a commodity to be contained, while biotechnology in fact is not a thing at all. It is a new means of industrial production. In large part, standard bioethics is inadequate because the actual risks are extraordinarily difficult to calculate and the benefits can vary; and their calculation is itself a matter of the scope of the market and recognition of the debt owed to the poor.

A new bioethics of biotechnology requires two primary philosophic arguments. First, we will need new principles in bioethics beyond autonomy, beneficence, and non-maleficence. I propose in this paper a theory of fidelity, or faithfulness to relationships in the fact of the reality of uncertainty. Second, we will need a theory of justice that goes beyond marketplace negotiations. I propose a theory of hospitality, or justice based in a theory that science accrues a debt to the poor that demands attention to their needs.

Hard to nail down: justice and the complete unknown

Let me begin with the first problem: the limits on our ability to balance a deep contemporary fear of new technology with our need for repair of a broken world by technological solutions. There is a long-standing moral unease about the inadequacy of the current principles of bioethics, based in autonomy of the individual self, to address the issue. There are two ways to think about the problem of biotechnology and the ethical duties of a polity. The first is the precautionary principle; the second, older standard, is risk–benefit, which is based on the principle of utility or public beneficence. I suggest a third way, which I call a "principle of fidelity."

The European responses to emerging technologies and bioscience in general, from genetic modification to stem cells to nanotechnology, have been based in the precautionary principle. This "principle" has newly emerged in the late twentieth century as an articulation of the need for control over events and forces that may well be entirely uncontrollable.

The precautionary principle requires that new technologies be *proved* safe – and in some formulations, *entirely safe* – before they are used in human populations. If there is doubt, it is argued, it is better to avoid the development of the technology altogether. It is, critics argue, a standard that would have cancelled much of science's advances in transportation, medicine, and engineering. Advocates of the precautionary principle argue for the need for precautionary language because of the magnitude of error, and thus of the scope of harm, that is possible in the new technologies. There are covert moral appeals you get with precaution: that "natural" is good; that "nature" is normative; that moral agency is linked to action, but not inaction; that the future can be known; that the world, thus and so, is good, and will continue in this good and normative manner, only if we do not interfere with it. These premises are problematic, and they not only understand the nature of moral activity incorrectly (inaction is just as powerful as action), but they make the assumption that what we have come to know as "nature" is inevitable, which contains within it deeper assumptions about one's social location. Finally, others note that without due precautions, a market-driven economy will seize every opportunity for profit at the expense of the health and welfare of citizens.

We need to move beyond "precaution" and "utility" to "fidelity"

The second, American approach is to rate new science using tools of risk analysis. There are covert appeals with risk analysis as well: that risks can be known and quantified (when science and experience tell us this is not fully true), that mistakes are not inevitable, that membership in affected groups is chosen and can be decided against, and that markets are logical. These premises are problematic, especially in the case of biotechnology, when some interventions assume that entire societies are affected by each choice. Under these circumstances, several aspects of risk arise. There is risk to bodies now, and to bodies and persons yet to exist, my body now and later, my progeny's body, and hers, and so on. There is risk to my local river, or to my nation, or to other nation states and to the individual bodies within them. And each risk category exists if you proceed, or desist from proceeding, with biotechnology.

A principle of fidelity takes into account these problems in both methods. It recognizes that a risk exists both for doing and not doing. Here we can reference the case of genetically modified corn, boycotts of corn, and famines that exist when seeds of boycotted corn are not planted, or epidemics that emerge when vaccines are not given, etc. As Pogge reminds us, it is an accident of history that we in the West, making the technology, are here, while others are elsewhere; this context creates duties to those others. We must proceed with some constraints, because of the principle of fidelity, fidelity to the neighbors with whom we share the world. A principle of fidelity means several things. First, it means that we have to treat safety testing as the first question of justice, recognizing that justice asks us to consider equally both those who get the benefits of the new technology and those who take on the risk. Second, a principle of fidelity suggests a contract or covenant between science and the polity that both takes the risk and reaps the benefits. For a justice theorist, to whom consent, and how it is obtained, are important, this contract or covenant must provide for a joint undertaking, a mutual agreement. Risks are correlative to goods, and rights are correlative to duties, the duties to others that arise from situations they have not chosen. A principle of fidelity, as opposed to precaution, motivates as a central concern the relationship between bioethics, health and safety, and the larger debates about global justice. Fidelity means that the burden of risk will be borne by the holders of the goods.

Fidelity also demands a commitment to the entire range and scope of the project at hand. This is true, by the way, for both action and inaction – the body that regulates and decides, and that profits from a policy decision, is accountable to repair any harms that occur. Unlike precaution, which takes no responsibility for the negative consequences of inaction, a principle of fidelity means that ill effects must be addressed and paid for, and this payment is part of the price of the decision. Unlike risk analysis, which assumes that failure was a risk "paid for" in advance, as it were, by the acceptance of benefits, a principle of fidelity would take into account the responsibility for repair in response to any harm, beyond even the compensatory benefits that the technology might have already created. In a world in which every exchange takes place on a global scale, in which our actions may affect vulnerable others in continents and times we cannot know, only the principle of fidelity reminds us we are responsible for the enormity of now, and the infinity of the world to come. It is unknowable what will occur – hence we commit only to what has occurred – our relationship to the other, who is our neighbor. This, I argue, must be understood by any one who offers leadership in biotechnology.

Now we address a final problem in the consideration of the unknowable – that of justice. It is the contention of this essay that the rich traditions of Jewish thought contain some of our strongest arguments for the necessity of justice as a pre-condition for biotechnology.

Texts of justice in the Jewish canon: how to make a theory of justice

After considering the complexities of negation, protection, and regulation of biotechnology, we need to reflect on the nature, goal, and meaning of the application of that biotechnology. First, *which* research project should proceed first? Which should receive our public support? Second, *how* is the research done? Under what conditions of moral restraint, and under what regulations as administered by what group, is it done? Third, and finally, *to whom* is the research aimed? Who bears the risk and who reaps the rewards? Finally, what are we to make of research conducted in a world of desperate, abject poverty?

It is my contention that in many debates about faith and science, a careful reading of texts, and a broad inclusion of interpretive possibilities within the tradition, can be useful in finding answers to these critical questions, in establishing the norms that Cole-Turner (Chapter 39) seeks from "nature" alone. The texts that comprise the Jewish canon – which spans the centuries from the reception of the Hebrew Scripture, through the formative rabbinic period (roughly 200 BCE to 600 CE), the medieval commentary, to the modern debates on enlightenment science – frequently contest questions and arguments about the moral life, and the question of nature and its fated, determinative norms. While there are clearly some aspects of Jewish arguments that lift up observations from nature as normative (for example, in Maimonides reflections on animal behavior), the more morally worthy argument turns from the world as it is, to the world as it must be, if the positive laws given at Sinai are enacted. Nature is not inherently just, nor a source for descriptive etiology for human events. Nature is largely the amoral location where humans struggle for justice. In fact, it is largely because the agriculturalists who heard the Hebrew Bible understood the realities of loss that the need for justice is so apparent, and so justice became a central concern of the Torah. Widows, orphans, and the poor haunt the abundance of the promised Land, and the world is so structured, even with God's presence and promise, to need sacrifice always, for community and fidelity to the poor.

Our problem – how to create a just world when the goods we make are not a harvest of barley, but a harvest of synthetically derived useful organisms, or stem cells, or nanobots – is precisely the same. Let us now turn to a consideration of Deuteronomy 22, which speaks of hunger, production, limits, and rules about to make the world of material production a just one. "You shall not watch your brother's ox or his sheep go astray, and hide yourself from them; you shall in any case bring them again to your brother [...] You shall make fringes upon the four quarters of your cloak, with which you cover yourself."

What occurs there? The text in full is a quotidian list of seemingly minor details about production of commodities, done in a community with neighbors and brothers near and far. We can use animals and land, people and things – but within rules, and importantly, the moral agent (the "you") must cover your "self" with the reminder of law itself – the blue-braided fringes that remind you that the body is bound-ligated-as in *ligio*, the root of the word religion, to God.

The people are assembled, remembering when they received the Law at Sinai. Moses re-reads the Law, making some changes from the reading in Leviticus. The verse that we are looking at is in the midst of a list of prohibitions, beginning with the case of restoration of lost property that is one of the proof texts for healing and medicine, for if you must return a lost ox or coat to your kinsman, surely, you would restore his lost health to him if you could! The prohibition on seeds is more specific – you have a vineyard, a permanent sort of field, and you cannot sow it with seeds. For the seeds cannot mix, fruit and fruit. Or is it that you can have a vineyard, and sow it with seeds of one kind, then another? It is not entirely clear, nor is the defilement explained. Then we are told of two other prohibited mixings – you cannot plow with an ox and an ass, you cannot wear wool and linen, you cannot look entirely like other peoples, but must be visibly marked, each corner of your outer garment, on the edges of your outer garment, marking your own edges.

In later texts of the Tenach, this biblical passage is recalled by the prophet Isaiah. "And when you reap the harvest of your land, you shall not reap to the very corners of your field, nor shall you gather the gleanings of your harvest." In Isaiah, we have a curious re-reading of the re-reading in Deuteronomy. The prophet considers the prohibitions of harvest and deepens them, linking their observance not only to the sanctification of God's name, but to the need for social and economic justice. The laws of harvest stress the point that the poor are an intrinsic part of the productive process – the land belongs to God, and the landholder is merely using a part of it for his family – he must set up production so that the poor also have access to their part of the land – the corners of the field and the gleanings are their entitlement, not dependent on the charity of the landowner. Can it be that the rule about the mixing of seeds is directed to the same end? Clearly, something interesting is hinted at by the careful delineation of the fact that, indeed, one can mix crops in some way: here is the barley and there the spelt and here the wheat in rows, the black seeds of sesame and the cumin thrown about? Clearly the instructions for this order are also non-stochastic – they are given by God, and the order of seed mixing is clearly a large part of the production valorized here as a farm in line with the divine order of creation itself.

The final re-reading is a midrashic one: Midrash Rabbah – Deuteronomy VI: 4

> If you have a field and you have gone to plough therein, the precepts accompany you, as it is said, Thou shalt not plough with an ox and ass together (Deuteronomy XXII: 10); if you are about to sow it, the precepts

> accompany you, as it is said, Thou shalt not sow thy vineyard with two kinds of seed (*ibid.*: 9); and if you reap it, the precepts accompany you, as it is said, When thou reapest thy harvest in thy field, and hast forgot a sheaf in the field (Deuteronomy XXIV: 19). God said: "Even if you are not engaged on any particular work but are merely journeying on the road, the precepts accompany you."

In this Midrash, we are back in the vineyard, and you have to carry your Law with you. Even in the most mundane and quotidian of tasks – farming – your actions have to correspond to the law.

In this account, and in others that link the carried Law to covenantal love, we see the fullest examination of the problem, and the hints at the elements of concern. The people's distinctiveness is the Covenant and the Land – but the land is complex, because cultivation, unlike nomadic wandering, requires an estate, crops that take years to mature, gains and losses, and the need for debt and forgiveness. Gleaning is a part of this – yet to glean requires a particular sort of crop – it requires a cessation and a pause in the productive process. One cannot, as it is tempting to do in a mild mediterranean climate, simply keep sowing seed to overlap harvest on harvest, for one must make room for the poor to glean in the interstitial, liminal space: "after the harvest" of one crop and before the fruition of the next. Thus crops may be mixed if they do not compete, and if the poor can glean without destroying the growth of the next crop. If the land "owner" felt that the poor destroyed his crop, he might be tempted to shut them out – and he is entitled to first pick. But this production is limited and shaped not only by his own hunger, but by the hunger of the Other, silently coming to interrupt the use of the land with her need and her right. One's self, one's daily work, a thing as small as a seed! All will matter in how the harvest – the core of the world itself – is made.

Belovedness – the covenant and promises that make Israel and God lovers – is interwoven, quite literally, with great specificity in the rhythm of the text, with rules, borders, and limits. In later texts that comment on this issue, from the Sifra and Sifre, collections of Midrash that expand on other books of the Hebrew Scripture, the rabbis re-read the spareness of the Law into the richness of the commands toward the poor, linking the two so that ontological and moral meaning is made. Not mistaking, not carelessly throwing the very promise of the future – one's seed crop – around, but planting it with utter intentionality. This care is what makes the "world acts" true "word acts," and hence ties action to the sacred nature of human things. It is precisely the non-natural, deliberative quality of this Law that concerns our commentators.

Conclusion: the poor at surrounding the field

Such are the concerns, I have argued, that might guide a thoroughly defensible Jewish response to the core problem of justice in biotechnology. It is not an answer to science-fiction concerns, or to the possibility of utter failure, or to the scenarios that vexed Hans Jonas in the 1970s (citation); it is an answer to a world right now, with the poor, right now, waiting for their turn at harvest. The textual midrashic answer is consonant with the Halachic one: genetic engineering is not prohibited in Jewish law, and in many cases, is defensibly required if done with correct attention to the actual command one might think prohibits it: the rules about how to act in the natural world and what we owe the poor that they might harvest decently.

We are – perhaps – blessed to exist at this time, not because of the newness of scientific discovery, but because humans continue to find extraordinary promise in the utterly large and not-yet-known world. Biotechnology projects, in this way, are like seeds themselves. For the entire effort could fail utterly, defeated unless watched carefully, nurtured through a risky start and harvested in careful accordance to the laws of justice and responsibility. For Jewish scholars who watch these beginnings, the challenge is not whether the technology is good – in itself it is not, of course – it is to accept the cloak that you must wear as you use the technology – the very clothes that cover you remind you to be bound by justice. When we plow the field, you must take the Law with you.

The readings of the texts of production are linked by this idea of the cloak-which-covers-the-self. Consider the critical texts about the relationship between obligation and redemption:

20. You shall not wrong a stranger, nor oppress him; for you were strangers in the land of Egypt. […]
25. If you take your neighbor's cloak as a pledge, you shall deliver it to him by sundown;
26. For that is his only covering, it is the garment for his skin; Where shall he sleep? and it shall come to pass, when he cries to me, that I will hear; for I am compassionate.

Here again the cloak: this time it is the neighbor's, and we understand, because of the other texts, how critical it is to one's very being. Even legitimate debt negotiations are limited by human need. It is this cloak that directs our attention to the larger theory of justice, the logic of debt that drives the organization of redistribution in the Scriptural account. "You" produce wealth because moral agents use the land given by God, work it and tend it, and create abundance, and you thus are in debt to a theo-economic system that works only if each moral agent understands the contingency of her/his place. If you, as the world of objects/nature/human creativity, allow productivity, then a portion of this – gleanings, margins, and corners – actually is already due to the poor. The debt to God is repaid by understanding this and not blocking their righteous taking of it. If the neighbor is in need, which will occur, of course, because of the inherent unfairness of the "natural" world and its limits and losses, then her/his neediness also has a limit beyond which no-one shall cause its increase. You cannot take the neighbor's cloak, because it is that which allows one to live as a Jew. The law covers the nakedness of being.

Let us bring this religious idea into the fields of biotechnology, to be the basis of the theory of justice that is authorized by the principle of fidelity. In other work, I have called this a theory of hospitality, because the demands of justice are inadequate to describe the sacrifice implied by such a theory, one that will need faith beyond all the power of the marketplace and its seductions and exchanges.

The manipulated world is not ours alone, nor are scientists and the watchers of scientific actors without an audience; for the moral world is fundamentally and ultimately transparent. The goods of biotechnology, should they come to us, are already pre-assigned in the patterns of Law. Only we must recognize and enact our duty to the Law to see it. Then, the poor become visible and we perceive that we are surrounded by observable margins and limits. It is the limit on our taking that is set by what is owed to the others at the margins, and thus the fragile fringes that edge the very garment of our being remind us to see the contingency at the edge of the big claims of bioscience. The place of the theologian and moral philosopher in bioethics, and in this volume, may be to raise this question and this witness. It is justice, only justice, that limits and defines human technology, the "doubled thought" of what is broken, and what yet could be healed.

References

Fagenblat, Michael (2010) *A Covenant of Creatures*, Palo Alto, CA: Stanford University Press.

Friedman, Thomas (2005) *The World is Flat: A Brief History of the Twenty-first Century*, New York: Farrar, Straus and Giroux.

Nagel, T. (1977) "Poverty and Food: Why Charity Isn't Enough," in *Food Policy*, P. Brown and H. Shue (eds), New York: Free Press, 54–62.

O'Neil, Onera (2001) "Agents of Justice," in *Global Justice*, Thomas Pogge (ed.), Malden, MA: Blackwell, 188–203.

Pogge, Thomas (2010) *Politics As Usual: What Lies Behind the Pro-Poor Rhetoric*, Malden, MA: Polity Press.

——(2001) (ed.) *Global Justice*, Malden, MA: Blackwell Publishing.

——(2008) *World Poverty and Human Rights*, 2nd edn, Malden, MA: Polity Press.

Walzer, Michael (1983) *Spheres of Justice: A Defense of Pluralism and Equality*, New York: Basic Books.

(iii) Non-human cognition: animal cognition and artificial intelligence

44
ECCE PAN
Primate theory of mind and the notion of awe

David Harnden-Warwick and Jesse M. Bering

Introduction

How a species interprets the world around it will always rely upon the unique nexus of selective pressures encountered during its evolution. For the evolutionary scholar working from an adaptationist perspective, it makes little sense to ask whether one species is "smarter" or "more intelligent" than another. Natural selection optimizes every species for one thing: to capitalize on biological and psychological traits in a way that leads, over time, to genetically profitable outcomes. The brain of each individual must therefore function over time to maximize reproductive fitness in response to specific ecological challenges. In the case of human ancestors, one very real challenge was other people. In the present chapter, we present the case that the unique social selective pressures encountered by our ancestors may have led to the evolution of our species' religious sentiments. More specifically, we show how one particular cognitive capacity – the capacity to attribute mental states to other natural agents – was co-opted by natural selection when it was extended to reasoning about the minds of supernatural agents.

Like any other product of natural selection, brains are subject to what evolutionary theorists refer to as an "environment of evolutionary adaptedness" (hereafter, EEA). John Tooby and Leda Cosmides define an EEA as "the statistical composite of selection pressures that caused the design of an adaptation" (Cosmides and Tooby 1997). Since no two species shared exactly the same ancestral climatological, geographical, biological, and social pressures during their evolution, selection pressures vary tremendously. An individual disadvantaged by a cognitive architecture unable to cope with these pressures would quickly find their genes doomed to extinction.

Fortunately, the brains of every species living today *did* find a way to navigate the hurdles of their respective EEAs. The challenge for cognitive scientists is to respect both the convergences and divergences between species that emerged due to these separate arenas of competition. By observing the psychological and behavioral similarities – and differences – between two species to infer shared – or distinct – selection pressures in their ancestral pasts, fresh light can be shed upon the unique abilities and limitations of each.

It therefore should come as no surprise that great apes have been an important focus of research for scientists interested in the evolution of the human mind. For example, chimpanzees and human beings share a common evolutionary ancestor that lived approximately 5–7 million years ago. If we were to compress the 4.5-billion-year age of our planet into one calendar year, chimpanzees and humans split roughly around noon on December 31. Although not identical, much of our respective mental architectures emerged from the very same EEAs.

This similarity is why our exploration of non-human cognition will focus upon our closest genetic relatives. Why? Because it is precisely this intimate genetic and evolutionary relationship that makes chimpanzees outstanding subjects for attention, not only to better understand our own place among life on Earth, but also to unravel the fascinating workings of the chimpanzee mind itself. Understanding how the brutal calculus of natural selection produced two species similar in so many ways, yet utterly different in others, is of inestimable value to both chimpanzee and human alike.

Our faces, our selves

In 1970, psychologist Gordon G. Gallup developed an experimental test that literally changed the way simians across the world viewed themselves (Gallup 1970). Gallup was interested in determining whether species other than human beings were able to think of themselves as selves – that is, whether they have a conception of their existence apart from that of others. While Gallup's chimpanzee subjects were put under a harmless general anesthesia, a red dye was applied to a place on their body visibly accessible only in a mirror, such as their eyebrow ridge. Upon reawakening, the chimpanzees were presented with a mirror and their reactions to the red dye recorded. The chimpanzees quickly recognized the anomalous nature of the red dot and touched the point on their face where the dot had been placed by the experimenters. The conclusion drawn by Gallup was that the chimpanzees could only react in such a manner if they understood that the reflected image was, in fact, an isomorphic representation of themselves. Otherwise, he reasoned, they might touch the mirror itself or react to the image as if it were another animal, perhaps a pitiably strange chimpanzee with a blemish on its face.

The results were shocking to many. If the results were, in fact, being properly interpreted, the implications would transcend ethological and psychological boundaries. Human uniqueness had long been a hallmark of philosophy, theology, anthropology, and linguistics, to name but a few disciplines. Thus the finding that an animal other than *Homo sapiens* could "recognize" itself in a mirror – and thus, many assumed, they must possess a "self-concept" – posed a challenge to traditional ways of thinking about humanity's place in the world. For example, advocates of animal rights argued that if chimpanzees understood themselves as individuals, then should they not also feel pain and suffer as humans do too?

Years of refinement and continued experimentation with Gallup's basic design have continued without pause. Dozens of species have been tested for mirror self-recognition (hereafter, MSR). Chimpanzees repeatedly have been shown to pass the test. They are not alone, but they remain in select company. In a 2008 review of the literature, primatologist Frans de Waal concluded that "strong indications for MSR have been obtained only for the four great apes, bottlenose dolphins, and Asian elephants" (de Waal 2008). Repeatable results like these have led to wide citation in academic journals and popular accounts of scientific research. In fact, for many readers of this volume, the MSR test may be their only acquaintance with the field of non-human cognition.

However, the MSR test is not without its critics. Neuroscientist V. S. Ramachandran has pointed out that human patients with certain neurological impairments can pass Gallup's test while absolutely unaware that the person in the mirror is them. They make no identification of "self" even though they move towards and immediately recognize the experimental marking (Ramachandran 2007). It is also possible that simple proprioception is at work. Proprioception refers to the sense an organism has of where its body and bodily parts reside in space. Movement towards the spot of red dye could be an unconscious behavior wholly unrelated to self-awareness.

But, given its implications for our understanding of human social evolution, let us assume that the MSR test *does* demonstrate that chimpanzees see themselves as selves. This would, as we have acknowledged, be of enormous significance. To know oneself as an individual is no doubt of great selective value. Yet primates are first and foremost creatures who have lived, with few exceptions, in groups for tens of millions of years. Regardless of how chimpanzees or humans conceive ourselves individually, as primates we are embedded within a complex web of interaction with conspecifics that must be navigated by sophisticated cognitive modeling. This view has been most notably articulated by British evolutionary biologist Robin Dunbar (1998). Dunbar points out that our ancestors lived in situations where getting along with others was paramount to survival. There are enormous advantages available to the individual living harmoniously with others: access to food, protection, and warmth being paramount among them. Efficient cooperative action translates into greater reproductive fitness and opportunities to pass along more pro-social genes.

The problem is that the social fabric is under constant threat from defectors and cheaters who would undermine the advantages of group living for personal gain. Their detection is of the utmost importance. Since the duplicitous rarely announce their intentions to cheat and offend, an individual needs access to the inner thoughts and intentions of those around them. Furthermore, over evolutionary time scales, as cheaters become easier to detect, they "raise their game" and embrace more subtle and complex methods of deception. Those who would censure the cheater must then become better at detection, fueling an ever-escalating cognitive arms race. For our ancestors, being content with "knowing thyself" would have been a road to oblivion.

Natural psychologists

In the mid-1970s, Nicholas Humphrey, then a young Cambridge researcher working with gorillas alongside the late Dian Fossey, became fascinated by this problem of how we deal with other minds. In a 2003 interview, he restates the idea that had first taken hold three decades before:

> We humans – and to a lesser extent maybe gorillas and chimps too – have evolved to be "natural psychologists." The most promising but also the most dangerous elements in our environment are other members of our own species. Success for our human ancestors must have depended on being able to get inside the minds of those they lived with, second-guess them, anticipate where they were going, help them if they needed it, challenge them, or manipulate them. To do this they had to develop brains that would deliver a story about what it's like to be another person from the inside.
>
> (Humphrey 2003)

Humphrey's realization that humans are endowed with an affinity for reasoning about what's going on inside other heads seems obvious. But the ramifications are enormous.

Two comparative psychologists, David Premack and Guy Woodruff, were among the first to grasp the importance of Humphrey's observation. They formalized Humphrey's "natural psychologist" construct by redefining it as a *theory of mind*. "A system of inferences of this kind," they wrote, "is properly viewed as a theory, first, because [mental] states are not directly observable, and second, because the system can be used to make predictions, specifically about the behavior of other organisms" (Premack and Woodruff 1978).

For most of us, we have no problem imagining what it's like to have a belief or desire. For example, you may be *wishing* that this sentence would get quickly to the point, you might be *hoping* that your friends don't forget your birthday, and you could be *intending* to go to a party after finishing this chapter. It's also trivially easy to intuit these states in other people around you. We call this taking an intentional stance towards others, described by philosopher Daniel Dennett in his influential book *The Intentional Stance* (Dennett 1987). Dennett argues that our theory of mind – in his terminology, our understanding of intentionality, which is essentially the "aboutness" of others' behaviors – is the default social cognitive world-view of *Homo sapiens*. We cannot help but see minds behind all kinds of things and events, even when they are absent entirely.

This ability comes so naturally that we intuitively see intent in inanimate, non-living things. For example, imagine the car that breaks down on the way to an important meeting, or the computer that decides to shut down forever, all your vital data irretrievably lost. Of course the car didn't sabotage your career on purpose, nor did the computer maliciously delete your files. Yet anger and resentment would no doubt characterize many reactions. These reactions seem silly once reflected upon. But that's the point: it takes *reflective* thought to overcome a *reflexive* intuition. Our original impulse is to see behaviors driven by purposeful, conscious agency. The rejection of intentionality requires great cognitive effort. Theory of mind acts as a filter through which our social cognitive systems interpret – and sometimes over-interpret – events and actions in terms of meaning and purpose.

Intentionality makes a theory of mind possible because intentional states are inherently recursive. This means that an individual can add layer upon layer of complexity to the ascriptions of beliefs and desires in other minds. If you think to yourself, "I *suspect* the man stole the food," that would express one level of intentionality. But you can add to that: "I *suspect* the man *intends* to steal the food" which would represent two levels of intentionality.[1] You could even mull over "I *wonder* if the man *knows* that I *suspect* that he *wants* me to *believe* that he *never intended* to steal the food," a six-level exercise in tracking mental states that stretches the limits of our social cognitive processing power.

If thinking about that last example gave you a headache, not to worry. Most humans cannot represent more than four to five levels of intentionality before reaching a frustrating bottleneck (Stiller and Dunbar 2007). Fortunately for our purposes, we are only concerned with second-level intentionality, the capacity to articulate ideas such as "I *believe* that he hates me because she *knows* I was late yesterday," or, "I *suspect* he *believes* I have a crush on him." This is the minimum requirement for having a theory of mind, and it appears around four years of age in human children. If you can mentally hold a thought, idea, belief, desire, or intention about someone else's thought, idea, belief, desire, or intention, then welcome – you're a member of the club.

Being able to infer the psychological causes of another's behavior by reasoning about their hidden mental states provides enormous strategic advantages. The man who thinks his affair with another man's wife has effectively been kept a secret might be shocked to see said cuckold approaching his home with a loaded shotgun. But his state of shock would not prevent him from instantly knowing why the man is there: "I *believe* he finally *realized* that I'm having an affair with his wife."

At issue for the past four decades has been the question of whether human beings are alone on this planet in possessing the ability to reason about other minds. Now that we have gone over in some detail what theory of mind is, and we have a sense of the evolutionary importance of this capacity to think about unseen psychological causes, let us examine the evidence for its presence beyond our species.

A *theory of mind*

In 1978, Premack and Woodruff published a classic article entitled "Does the Chimpanzee Have a Theory of Mind?" (Premack and Woodruff 1978). They were interested in the question of whether chimpanzees, like humans, have the capacity to reason about the beliefs, desires, and knowledge that make up the inner world of those around them. In one set of experiments reported by the authors, an American Sign Language-trained chimpanzee named Sarah was shown a video sequence of a person inside a cage trying to escape. She was thereafter given several objects to choose from, including a key. In each of these scenarios, Sarah chose the object that matched the actor's intentions in the scene, presumably indicating her ability to take the actor's subjective perspective. But critics have pointed out that Sarah had ample exposure to locks and keys prior to these trials and was likely drawing on associations from memory. A closer look at the original data, combined with various innovations in behavioral research, has tempered the original optimistic interpretation that Sarah's results were unambiguously indicative of a functioning theory of mind.

How can such a straightforward ability produce decidedly conflicting results and interpretations? Resolving this conundrum is central to our understanding of cognitive evolution. Enormous amounts of time, effort, and funding have gone into the effort. Indeed, two well known and independent primate research centers, one in the United States, the Cognitive Evolution Group in New Iberia, Louisiana; the other in Germany, the Max Planck Research Institute for Evolutionary Anthropology in Leipzig, exist more or less entirely to determine whether human beings are alone in our capacity to reason about mental states.

The Cognitive Evolution Group is led by comparative psychologist Daniel Povinelli. Povinelli is known for his uncompromising theoretical position that theory of mind is a human cognitive specialization that evolved sometime *after* human beings last shared a common ancestor with chimpanzees. Despite our similar appearances and our shared behavioral heritage, Povinelli maintains that our closest living relatives are in fact without even a kernel of this social cognitive capacity. Tightly controlled experiments with both chimpanzees and human children have generally supported Povinelli's argument. In the most frequently cited of these studies (Povinelli and Eddy 1996), a trained group of research chimpanzees were tested individually, one at a time, in a small room. Each animal was faced with two human research assistants who were standing side-by-side behind a Plexiglas partition. One of the assistants was alert and watching the chimpanzee, whereas the other had their vision compromised in some manner or was looking elsewhere. The latter assistant's eyes were closed, or had their back turned to the animal, or even had a bucket placed over their head. Unlike two-year-old children, the apes failed to differentiate between the person who could "see" them and the one who could not. In other words, when forced to choose between the two research assistants, the chimps were just as likely to insert their hands through a hole in the partition and beg for a coveted food reward from one versus the other. Povinelli and his colleagues discovered that, after several such trials, the chimpanzees eventually comprehended the task and began preferentially soliciting the rewards from the sighted person. However, the investigators interpreted this eventual success as being based on a learned behavioral heuristic (e.g. "pick-person-with-frontal-aspect-showing") rather than an appreciation of that person's actual "seeing."

Without this basic appreciation of perspective, the explanatory option of theory of mind is off the table. The implication of Povinelli's research is that what appears to be a theory of mind in other species is more likely the product of trial-and-error learning. And when it comes to doing research with a highly intelligent species like chimpanzees, Povinelli argues, such association learning is so subtle, speedy, and sophisticated that it can easily lead even the sharpest investigator into falsely concluding that theory of mind is present when appropriately rigorous controls have not been included in the study's design. After all, psychological scientists are still human beings who cannot help but interpret others' behaviors by appealing to their own evolved theory of mind.

Predictably, Povinelli's findings have not gone unchallenged. At the Max Planck Institute for Evolutionary Anthropology in Leipzig, comparative psychologist

Michael Tomasello and his colleagues Josep Call and Brian Hare have criticized Povinelli's interpretations on several grounds. They point out that we cannot assume that chimpanzees will display a theory of mind on ersatz tasks foreign to their nature. Being confronted with a cooperative human being, or one wearing a blindfold over their eyes, or one with a bucket over their head may all appear equally contrived from the cumulative perspective of the chimpanzees' cognitive EEA. In addition, they argue, chimpanzees that have been raised in sterile laboratory settings such as those in New Iberia are unrepresentative of the species in general; perhaps chimpanzees have the potential for a theory of mind, but the actualization of this capacity does not have a chance to materialize when raised in an inappropriate social milieu. The comparative analogue for humans would be that of a feral child who grows up in the wild without recourse to normal human enculturation. This deprived youngster might display a perfectly representative brain, but their psychological capacities would hardly reflect the cognitive benchmark of *Homo sapiens*.

To address these concerns, Tomasello's Leipzig-based research team has sought to conduct controlled experiments with non-deprived chimpanzees, such as those from lively sanctuaries in Africa. In doing so, Tomasello seeks ecological and experimental validity by replicating, or at least closely approximating, the species' natural environment. In one such study (Hare *et al.* 2001), subordinate chimps were pitted against dominant chimps for access to a strategically placed food reward. The subordinates could see the item from their vantage point, whereas the dominant animal could not. Under these conditions, the subordinate animal will act as though nothing is there. The subordinate will avert its gaze from the object, or "act natural" without giving away its coveted prize – until the dominant chimp leaves the scene. The investigators argued that the subordinate must therefore apprehend the dominant's mental state of "seeing/not seeing" in order to pull off the acquisition. Recalling what we said earlier about a species' unique EEA, these experiments suggest that competition over scarce resources, rather than contrived interactions with humans, can expose the chimpanzee's theory of mind.

Unfortunately, despite these tantalizing findings, more recent testing by the Max Planck group suggests a more conservative view might be in order. Like Povinelli, Tomasello and company have found that chimpanzees have difficulty reasoning about others' mental states, underperforming even thirty-month-old human children (see Call and Tomasello 2008). Although a chimpanzee might understand a rival being able to observe or not observe a coveted piece of food, there is no incontrovertible evidence that they understand that the act of seeing is linked to an inner set of beliefs and desires. Thus, while no doubt artful, and clever, and well adapted to the specific mental challenges of their evolutionary milieu, chimpanzees have not been shown to irrefutably meet the criteria for a theory of mind envisioned by Premack and Woodruff (Call and Tomasello 2008).

It seems a debate unlikely to be settled anytime soon. Some comparative psychologists believe that the best evidence lies not in chimps, but rather dogs, dolphins, or even scrub-jays (for a review see Emery and Clayton 2009). Yet, although the jury is still out on whether we're entirely unique in being able to conceptualize unobservable mental states, there's absolutely no question that we're uniquely good at it in the whole of the animal kingdom. In fact, we're exquisitely attuned to the unseen psychological world. Theory of mind is as much a peculiar trademark of our species as is walking upright on two legs, learning a language, and raising our offspring into their teens.

In awesome wonder?

Many of you reading this have arrived here from backgrounds in religion and theology. Those who ever watched one of those ubiquitous nature programs on television might have heard about cases of chimpanzees behaving in strange ways around water and even performing "rain dances." If you have, your natural curiosity as scholars of religion or as theologians of faith might prompt you to wonder how this alleged behavior fits into our overall consideration of the chimpanzee mind. An examination of the alleged evidence for chimpanzee spirituality is not only interesting on its own merits, but it provides a superb opportunity to explore the relevance of ideas and experiments so far discussed.

What is the "rain dance"? It certainly ranks among the most striking phenomena ever reported in the ethological literature: adult male chimpanzees performing intricate display rituals when confronted by the sight and sound of rushing water. Legendary primatologist Jane Goodall first witnessed these proceedings among the chimpanzees of Gombe four decades ago, and others, including photographers, have independently documented them. Goodall explains in detail:

> Deep in the forest are some spectacular waterfalls. Sometimes as a chimpanzee – most often an adult male – approaches one of these falls his hair bristles slightly, a sign of heightened arousal. As he gets closer, and the roar of falling water gets louder, his pace quickens, his hair becomes fully erect, and upon reaching the stream he may perform a magnificent display close to the foot of the falls. Standing upright, he sways rhythmically from foot to foot, stamping in the shallow, rushing water, picking up and hurling great rocks. Sometimes he climbs up the slender vines that hang down from the trees high above and swings out into the spray of the falling water. This "waterfall dance" may last for ten or fifteen minutes.
>
> (Goodall 2005)

Goodall then makes a remarkable claim:

> Is it not possible that these performances are stimulated by feelings akin to wonder and awe? After a waterfall display the performer may sit on a rock, his eyes following the falling water. What is it, this water? It is always coming, always going – yet always there. What unseen strength suddenly produces the great claps of thunder, the torrential downpour, the savage gusts of wind that bend and sway the chimpanzees clinging to their nests at night? If the chimpanzees had a spoken language, if they could discuss these feelings among themselves, might not they lead to an animistic, pagan worship of the elements?
>
> (*ibid.*)

One of the problems with this interpretation is the fact that alpha males are the ones most likely to exhibit this type of display. Threat displays are used to intimidate rivals and consolidate power within the group. Because of the formidable strength of chimpanzees and the ever-present potential for severe or fatal injury in direct combat, the most successful displays are the ones that prevent open conflict from ever arising in the first place. It would not be unparsimonious to conclude that the one member of the group most tasked with maintaining order and meeting novel challenges to group cohesion is also most likely to rage against the uncomprehended terrors of natural phenomena. However, the fact remains that chimpanzees besides alpha males do perform. Not many, but a few.

So let us return to Goodall's basic argument: chimpanzee displays toward raging waterfall; the display is one born of wonder and awe, or feelings quite similar; and if the chimpanzees only had a spoken language, they could articulate this feeling into organization. It is certainly not an unreasonable conjecture based on the closeness of human and chimpanzee evolutionary development. But it is almost certainly wrong.

If the experimental evidence we have reviewed has been correctly interpreted, then it is extremely doubtful that chimpanzees intuit the beliefs and desires of other agents. They do not seem to know that others can have intentions. Yet worship is a state of receptiveness predicated upon the very notion that divine forces have something to communicate (Bering 2001). Indeed, the animism spoken of by Goodall assumes the ensoulment of natural forces with conscious awareness. The chimpanzees would need to understand that the wind and water *wanted* to vex them, that these "unseen strengths" within the elements *intended* the Jobean provocation of their already volatile psyches. They would need that second level of intentionality we read about earlier. Without it, the forces of nature would remain forever silent to them. Language could not put in what the mind had left out.

Epilogue

No other ability molded by natural selection determined the fate of our genus as did the surfacing of a theory of mind. While theory of mind obviously does not exhaust the wide range of topics covered under the rubric of cognition, it is hoped that readers now understand why it served as the focus of our discussion on non-human cognition. The kinds of comparisons most people wish to make when considering the minds of our fellow animals stem from an interest in social and interpersonal aptitudes. Less frequently does the questioner have in mind qualities such as bipedal locomotion or stereoscopic vision. As we have seen, human beings cannot help but want to know what's going on in the other fellow's head.

As our closest living relative, the chimpanzee is a logical subject for these reflections. Their incredible social systems and amazing cognitive competencies are to be respected on their own terms. In no way does the failure so far to uncover a theory of mind in chimpanzees diminish them – and neither does it exalt us. Our differences are ones of adaptation, not value. Furthermore, nothing we have claimed in this chapter precludes the possibility of future experiments with novel protocols providing definitive proof of theory of mind in these creatures. Nevertheless, the present evidence points to *Homo sapiens* being the only surviving species since the chimpanzee–human split to possess a theory of mind.

It is up to the reader to make of that what they will.

Note

1 The written expressions of these intentional stances should be seen as representations only. Literal linguistic articulation of these states, while perhaps helpful at higher levels, is not necessary in order to hold them in mind. While a person can certainly think "out loud" in their head and say to themselves, "I *believe* he *wishes* to hurt me," most judgments involving intentionality and theory of mind are done non-verbally and without reflective effort.

References

Bering, J. (2001) "Theistic Percepts in Other Species: Can Chimpanzees Represent the Minds of Non-Natural Agents?," *Journal of Cognition and Culture* 1: 107–37.

Call, J. and M. Tomasello (2008) "Does the chimpanzee have a theory of mind? 30 years later," *Trends in Cognitive Science* 12: 187–92.

Cosmides, L. and J. Tooby (1997) "Evolutionary Psychology: A Primer," http://cogweb.ucla.edu/ep/EP-primer.html.

Dennett, D. (1987) *The Intentional Stance*, Cambridge, MA: MIT Press.

Dunbar, R. (1998) "The Social Brain Hypothesis," *Evolutionary Anthropology* 6: 178–90.

Emery, N. J. and N. S. Clayton (2009) "Comparative Social Cognition," *Annual Review of Psychology* 60: 87–113.

Gallup, G. G., Jr. (1970) "Chimpanzees: Self Recognition," *Science* 167: 86–87.

Goodall, J. (2005) "Primate Spirituality," in *Encyclopedia of Religion and Nature*, Bron Taylor (ed.), London and New York: Continuum, 1303–6.

Hare, B., J. Call and M. Tomasello (2001) "Do chimpanzees know what conspecifics know?," *Animal Behavior* 61: 771–85.

Humphrey, N. (2003) "A Self Worth Having," Edge.org, www.edge.org/3rd_culture/humphrey04/humphrey04_index.html.

Povinelli, D. J. and T. J. Eddy (1996) "What young chimpanzees know about seeing," *Monographs of the Society for Research in Child Development* 61(2): 247.

Premack, D. and G. Woodruff (1978) "Does the chimpanzee have a theory of mind?," *Behavioral and Brain Sciences* 1: 515–26.

Ramachandran, V. S. (2007) "The Neurology of Self-Awareness," Edge.org, www.edge.org/3rd_culture/ramachandran07/ramachandran07_index.html.

Stiller, J., and R.I.M. Dunbar (2007) "Perspective-taking and memory capacity predict social network size," *Social Networks* 29: 93–104.

de Waal, F. B. M. (2008) "The Thief in the Mirror," *PLoS Biology* 6: 1621–22.

45
ANIMALS AS RELIGIOUS AND SOTERIOLOGICAL BEINGS

A Hindu perspective

Ellison Banks Findly

The question raised for this essay is whether animals are religious beings, that is, whether we can know if animals have self-conscious experiences we can call "religious." We respond to this from the Hindu perspective, by arguing that it's impossible for us to know exactly what kinds of experiences animals have. We can, however, argue that animals are included in the overall Hindu understanding of soteriology, that is, the science of religious salvation by which all species in the system are guaranteed liberation from the imperfect world that we know through everyday, sense-based experience. To pursue this argument, we need to address what we mean by religious experience, notions of the uniqueness of human consciousness and the "other mind," the evidence Hindus use to develop answers to these issues, as well as the anecdotal and systematic theories regarding animal behavior by which Hinduism includes animals in systems of soteriology.

Animals and religious experience

On religion

Defining religion is a tricky business, tackled most often from the point of view of those religions a person knows best. Moreover, other terms besides religion – spirituality, world-view, faith – need to be considered in order to get true precision. Most often, the response to "what is religion?" is answered by some reference to the transcendent – a god, a higher force, an unknowable other. The experience of such transcendence is famously discussed in Rudolph Otto's *The Idea of the Holy* (1968 [1923]), in which the experience, that of the *numinous*, is "awe-full," full of both wonder and terror simultaneously. Such experience requires an understanding of religion defined in terms of transcendence, and such a definition, while it works for the Abrahamic traditions, does not work for many traditions born of Asian culture, particularly, in the present case, much of Hinduism. In these traditions, students of religion turn to issues of immanence, experiences that involve internal evolution and radical change as the true "self" emerges.

For this reason, we will use a different definition of religion here, one put forward by Frederick Streng and colleagues in *Ways of Being Religious* (Streng *et al.* 1973). As they frame it, religion is "the means towards ultimate transformation," with "transformation" suggesting internal change from an imperfect to a more perfect state (sinful to sinless, ignorant to wise, attached to unattached, etc.). This transformation is "ultimate" in that it is not incidental and temporary, like getting a haircut, but permanent, involuntary, irreversible, and all-consuming. And religious systems provide the "means" to such a change through belief systems that alter mental outlook and behavior – myth, theology, ethics, art, ritual, and contemplative practices. In this way, by focusing on ultimate transformation, we can be inclusive of the great variety of religious behaviors and experiences.

The uniqueness of human consciousness: Hindu views

The foundational structure of Hindu thought is the notion that living creatures have multiple lives, and that their souls transit from body to body within a round of rebirth known as *samsara*. The term *samsara* means to "revolve around together," suggesting either the accumulated lifetimes of a single individual making up rich and complex personal history, or the interdependence of all individual life forms as they weave their way together through rebirths to perfection. It is the latter sense that pertains here, for Hinduism proposes a unity of all life forms, life forms that constitute a continuum of living things, from the most simple (plants) to the most sophisticated (humans). It proposes, as well, the notion that it is only when the soul inhabits a human body, with a mind capable of full self-reflection and knowledge of its intentions, and a developed ability to employ that knowledge in the discipline of spiritual progress, that the individual soul can be liberated from *samsara*.

The unity of life is reflected in early views about the cyclical course of water and food moving around through living beings invigorating and enlivening them. The Taittiriya Upanishad (2.2.2) states: "From food […] are produced whatsoever creatures dwell on earth […] by food alone they live. And also into it they pass at the end" (Radhakrishnan 1953). The cosmological structure issuing from this cycle is contained in a Manavadharmashastra myth (1.57) about the creator god Brahma who, in his sleeping, waking, and sleeping again, brings into being each round of *samsara*. When Brahma rises out of his sleep, he breathes out new souls and they enter into vegetable, animal, and human seed and assume appropriate new corporeal forms; the cycle of rebirth ends with Brahma's return to the state of *pralaya*, or dissolution. Within any given waking period of Brahma, the lives of all creatures are governed by two themes: (1) each creature endures the "always terrible constantly changing circle (*samsara*) of births and deaths" (Buhler 1886), and (2) the continuum of births that a creature endures is a consistent one, with immovable beings (plants) at the lowest extreme and the highest movable beings (humans) at the uppermost extreme, with animals occupying a large middle range.

Thus, while categories of living beings are clearly identified, these categories do not have stable populations, but fluid ones; that is, there is no radical separation among types of living beings. This places the Hindu view of beings squarely in opposition to traditions that might be called "speciest," in which living beings belong to separable categories with impermeable boundaries, and in which one species is privileged over others. As Peter Singer (1990: 6–7) notes, speciesism "is a prejudice or attitude of bias in favor of the interests of members of one's own species and against those members of other species," and as Paul Waldau (2002: 38–39) refines this: "Speciesism is the inclusion of all human animals within, and the exclusion of all other animals from, the moral circle." In Hinduism, there is no real "other," as all life forms are bound in an interlocking web, figuratively expressed in the idea of "Indra's net," where the interconnectedness of the universe is like the net of the Vedic god Indra with multifaceted jewels at each juncture, each jewel reflecting and reflected in all of the other jewels. We argue here that, for Hindus, animals belong to a continuum of life in which variations of consciousness, based on karmic activity, can move fluidly among all life forms.

The problem of the "other mind:" the Hindu response

Given this fluid rebirth process for all living beings, the question arises as to whether we can have any knowledge of activity in an "other mind." The answer to this allows us to confirm or deny the interlinking of beings according to mental experience involving such things as intentional behavior, the cultivation of internal states of "self," and the openness to radical transformation. One Hindu answer to this derives from the empirical process: while we may attribute various degrees of consciousness to the full range of these beings, we have no absolute test of their having any such consciousness. Since modern experiments by Hindu scientists give results similar to those of non-Hindu scientists, we must rely instead on what Hindus traditionally rely on for the development of the *samsaric* theory, that is, the observed behavior of non-human beings. The assumption of the following material, then, comes from observing what animals "do," and making comparisons between these observations and what humans "do," known also by observations of other humans, but through serious and thorough reflection upon oneself as well. Such a method might proceed as follows: "I know the dog is feeling hungry/angry/respectful because it behaves like I do when I'm hungry/angry/respectful."

Many philosophical attempts have been mounted to explain why we can, or cannot, know what's happening in the other mind. In Hinduism, the banner is taken up early on by Samkhya, a system detailing the evolution of the world of sentient experience as it devolves from contact between the eternal individual spirit (*purusha*) and matter (*prakriti*). According to Samkhya, the real world is perceived to be distinct from, or external to, the body of the perceiver. But the experience of externality is, in fact, a function of the body and, as Bhattacharyya (1956: 159–60) notes, the "perceived world has no manifest reality apart from the percipient's felt body." In other words, for Samkhya, the "external world is *nothing manifest apart* from the perceiving body or bodily consciousness, being manifest through it as distinct from it" [my italics]; and the "entire manifest aspect of this world, spatial and qualitative, is an appearance projected by the feeling body." We cannot, then, ever get out of experience as the process of perception. The question of "the other mind" follows: "the other person I see before me is nothing more than my perception and every time I try to verify that person's existence I find that there is nothing more than compounded perceptions." To try to find out what that other person is experiencing, then, would be futile, for there is not a point in Samkhya at which an "aha!" moment occurs verifying that the interior perception connects to reality.

Samkhya, then, provides some basis for a pragmatic Indian approach to knowing "the other mind:" that is, making judgments about animal cognition or consciousness based on observation of their behavior and comparing it with what is known of human behavior. Thus, even though, in an *absolute sense*, we can't know what takes place in any other mind – whether of animal, plant, or human – we can, in an *ordinary sense*, make best guesses based on behavioral attributes.

Animals and the soteriological enterprise

Animals as conscious in Hindu folklore: projection of human traits

Animals are everywhere in popular Hinduism. Although their place in the Hindu pantheon is as vehicles for the gods, animals are most importantly presented in moral and didactic literature, where they appear with decidedly human characteristics. One of the most common traits animals take on is human speech, and the "talking goose" is one of the earliest humanoid animals in Hindu literature. The best known example is in the Nala and Damayanti story, where a talking goose is the go-between who facilitates the love between these two. Once, Nala grabs the goose and it shouts out: "I'm not to be killed by you […] I will do you a favor," and that favor is to intercede for him with Damayanti. In her presence, the goose, "making a human voice, then spoke" to her of the wondrous qualities of her future husband and she succumbed, resulting in a future union (Lanman 1884: 3).

The projection of human characteristics onto animals often catalyzes the movement of a narrative or makes a moral or instructive point. In the Ramayana, a troop of monkeys is in the service of the exiled prince Rama. Sugriva, the monkey general, is upset with Rama and treats him poorly. Rama calls Sugriva "vicious" and a monkey lieutenant (Hanuman) steps in, sooths Sugriva and offers him advice: "Remembering [Rama's] former service, it doth not behoove thee […] to excite his wrath [… nor] to neglect even in thought [… his] behests" (Dutt 1987: 2.783, 790). This encounter reflects the significant range of human traits attributed to the monkeys in this setting: a capacity for feelings of insult, anger, revenge, and empathy, a need for good judgment, and an ability to negotiate compromise and reconciliation.

In his work on the animal fables of the Pancatantra, P. Olivelle notes: "The human perception of animal behavior and character determines the choice of animal characteristics to play various human roles," and the use of animals to represent types of humans permits the author to highlight human social groupings and behavioral styles, as seen more clearly in animal analogues. Paraphrasing Olivelle (1997: xvii–xxv), for example, animals exemplify qualities known among humans:

boar – strength and ferocity
heron – greed, cunning
cat – cunning
jackal – greed, cunning
crocodile – hidden danger lurking
leopard – cunning, danger
crow – intelligence and curiosity
lion – nobility, bravery
deer – charm and innocence
monkey – playfulness
dog – uncleanliness and greed
owl – ferocity
dove – innocence
ox – strength, loyalty
elephant – nobility, strength
ram – strength
goose – the pure soul of a human being
snake – fickleness and duplicity

Finally, in Beck *et al.*'s (1987) compilation of Indian folk tales, the range of human-like animal behavior is especially broad: animals and birds can talk, they help each other out, they take turns doing social chores, they need to be praised, they see humor in things, they have social institutions like marriage, they take revenge on each other, they feel pain such as at the loss of children, they can be prideful, they can be seduced by compliments, and they can lay blame on each other. These stories about animals indicate at least two things: first, that Hindus observe animal behavior very carefully and note familiar characteristics that they match with their own behavior; and, second, that the kinds of characteristics authors project onto animals presuppose a view that animals possess fairly high mental and emotional capabilities, that is, a conscious life if not exactly like that of humans, then fairly close to it.

Animals in Hindu soteriology: graduated levels of consciousness

In the central Hindu ethic, that of non-violence or *ahimsa*, it is not only humans who must be spared as objects of violence, but animals and plants as well. This view is an outcome of the concept of the unity of life embedded in the notion of *samsara*, and it is the Jains who first insisted upon a strictly non-violent ethic, and who helped make *ahimsa* a standard by providing a rationale for its use by Hindus of the time, with whom they shared ideas about the soul, *karma*, and rebirth. This rationale is a schema for arranging living beings according to how many, and which, senses they have. In arranging beings according to their degree of sentience, all those who use this schema make the assumption that every being is alive because it has at least one sense.

(1) one sense (touch): plants, and earth-, water-, air- and fire-bodies
(2) two senses (touch, taste): e.g. worms, leeches, mollusks

(3) three senses (touch, taste, smell): e.g. ants, fleas, plant lice, cotton-seed insects, termites, centipedes
(4) four senses (touch, taste, smell, sight): e.g. bees, wasps, flies, gnats, mosquitoes, butterflies, moths
(5) five senses (touch, taste, smell, sight, hearing): e.g. fish, birds, quadrupeds

(Findly 2008: 117)

And Larson and Bhattacharya (1987: 59) list the final six evolutes of living beings (*bhuta-sarga*) in Samkhya as follows:

(1) realm of humans
(2) realm of domestic animals: from cows down to mice
(3) realm of birds: from Garuda down to gnats
(4) realm of wild animals: from lions down to jackals
(5) realm of reptiles: from serpents down to worms
(6) realm of plants: trees and grasses

The doctrine of non-violence necessarily attunes a practitioner to how many senses a sentient being has, and to the notion that all living beings have some kind of consciousness, since the senses are gateways for receiving and responding to external information. As the system behind the power of injunctions not to harm living sentient beings, *samsara* is fueled by the *karma* inherent in the rebirths of sentient beings. A peculiar mark of the karmic nature of *samsara* is that it is a singular and individual process. As Manu (4.240) notes: "Single is each being born; single it dies; single it enjoys (the reward of its) virtue; single (it suffers the punishment of its) sin" (Buhler 1886: 166). This, then, is the orthodox position: that the self is the agent propelling and experiencing the cycle of rebirths, and that each self can take rebirth in every type of womb and, by extension, may very well experience all types of rebirth by the end of its *samsara* cycle.

Consciousness impelling, and reflected in, rebirth

What, then, is the mechanism by which rebirth takes place, and what place does the mind or consciousness have in the transference of karmic quality from one body to another? First, we should note that *karma* is generated by three activities: thought, speech, and action. These activities are *karma*-bearing (a seed deposited to produce fruit later), in that *karma* is measured by the intention (*cetana*) of the act, such that one is morally responsible for any thought, speech, or deed, and therefore will bear its fruit, because these activities were born out of a conscious decision to think, say, or do this very thing, and not some other one. Thus, as Manu (12.81) notes, "with whatever disposition of mind [*yadrishena bhavena*] [one] performs any act, he reaps its result in a [future] body endowed with the same quality" (Buhler 1886: 501). In that all sentient beings are karmic, they operate with some kind of mental process, and S. K. R. Rao (1987: 151) notes, from Hindu medical literature, that while plants have only interior or hidden consciousness (*antahsamjna* or *avyakta-cetana*), those higher on the scale, such as animals and humans, have external and internal consciousness (*bhair-anta-cetana*). While the exact dimensions of this distinction remain unclear in the literature, what is clear is that, karmically speaking, plants can only experience the effects (*phala*) of their previous actions, but not sow new seeds, while animals and humans can both deposit new seeds and experience the fruition of seeds. That is, animals, using intention, can actively change their karmic field.

While the view of rebirth mechanism differs from one Hindu system to another, we take a example from Samkhya to suggest the degree to which consciousness and the activity of the mind are proposed to propel the cycle of rebirth. In Samkhya, there are two categories that help explain rebirth: the *linga* and the *bhavas*. The *linga* is the collection of thirteen of the twenty-five "evolutes" of the person that make up the trans migration body: the higher mind, the "I" maker or individuality, the lower mind, the five senses, and the five organs of actions. The first three are the internal organs that operate over past, present, and future, and the other ten are the external components that function only in the present. While the five senses give "bare awareness" and the five modes of action give speech, grasping, motion, excretion, and orgasm, the higher mind, the individuality function, and the lower mind have functions, respectively, of determination, self-awareness, and differentiation or discrimination. The highest function among them is that of the higher mind, which serves the soul in the quest for salvation. Finally, the *linga* is supported by the five subtle elements that "make up a kind of sheath or body which accompanies the *linga* in its transmigration from life to life." The *linga* body, then, is the transmigrating entity that includes both the thirteen-part instrument and the five subtle elements (Larson 1969: 206–8).

Moreover, in Samkhya, the transmigrating entity of the subtle *linga* body is helped by the force or power of the *bhavas*, the "dispositions" that reside in the higher mind. These eight dispositions come in pairs: virtue/vice, knowledge/ignorance, non-attachment/attachment, and power/impotence, and represent the "fundamental strivings in the innermost core of man's nature," carrying the being "along in the various phases and dimensions of the manifest world" and leading to continuing life through rebirth (Larson 1969: 210–11). This description from Samkhya is intended to underscore the complicated nature of one system's understanding of *samsara*, and that here, as elsewhere, rebirth involves causative elements in the transmigrational carriers of *karma* and consciousness. While Larson's discussion describes this process for humans, it assumes by design an application to the rebirth processes of all sentient beings.

Where can one be reborn? In Jainism, Buddhism, and Hinduism there is a traditional hierarchy of five or six births called *gatis*. They are as follows:

(1) *deva* – the realm of the gods
(2) *manussa* – the realm of humans
(3) *preta* – the realm of the ancestors, or hungry ghosts
(4) *tiryanca* – the realm of animals (and, for Jains, plants as well)
(5) *niraya* – the realm of various hells or purgatories

A sixth *gati* is often added between numbers (3) and (4), that of *asura*, or the realm of demons; when this *gati* is not mentioned in the list, it is included in the *preta* realm (McDermott 1980: 172).

The normative understanding of these levels is as a scale of "awareness" such that the beings with the lowest awareness are those in one of the hells, and those with the highest are in the realm of the *devas*. The same kind of ordering occurs within the animal or *tiryanca* category based upon the number of senses the animal has: at the top is the lion with five senses, and at the bottom are plants with only one. Because it is the only category where the full span of senses is represented, the span of reflective capabilities is broader and more differentiated among the animals. And among those animals that have five senses, some have a high quality of consciousness, while others with fewer senses have a lower one (Jaini 1980: 222–23).

The notion of realms of rebirth is augmented by another system, one that focuses on the physical nature of the types of birth. These categories appear in various combinations and usually number three or four. From the Aitareya Upanishad (3.3), for example, is a four-part schema:

(1) *andaja* – "egg-born;" oviparous; birds, snakes, crocodiles, fish, tortoises, and similar terrestrial and aquatic animals
(2) *udbhinnaja* – "sprout-born;" coming out of the earth; vegetal
(3) *jaruja/jarayuja* – "womb-born;" viviparous; born with an embryonic skin, placenta or foetal membrane; cattle, deer, livestock, antelopes, carnivorous animals or beasts of prey, demons, men
(4) *svedaja* – "sweat-born;" abiogenous; or born from moisture and warmth, from wet heat, hot warmth; stinging and biting insects, lice, flies, bugs and other creatures of this kind

(Radhakrishnan 1953)

Whatever the specific animal assigned to the specific birth type, it is clear that the Hindu tradition understands that all animals are living beings subject to birth and the ongoing cycle of *samsara*. Given that self-evolution in *samsara* is a function of the transference of *karma*/consciousness, whose quality is understood by an initial intention (*cetana*), we argue that the attribution of some kind of conscious life to animals must be assumed, as all of these kinds of lives occur within a karmically bound system.

What do you have to do to be born as an animal? Usually it is something demeritorious, and the law books give us some hints. Below are some animal rebirths that are attained by stealing:

steal grain, one becomes a rat
cow, an iguana
yellow metal, a goose
molasses, a flying fox
water, an aquatic bird
fine perfume, a muskrat
honey, a stinging insect
leafy vegetables, a peacock
milk, a crow
fire, a crane

juice, a dog
horse, a tiger
meat, a vulture
fruits and roots, a monkey
salt, a cricket
woman, a bear
linen, a frog
vehicle, a camel
cotton, a heron
cattle, a goat.

(Rocher 1980: 72–75)

Rebirth as an animal can come about for innumerable other offenses as well: if one slays a Brahman, one becomes a dog, pig, ass, camel, cow, goat, sheep, deer, or bird; if one is a Brahman and drinks liquor, one becomes a large insect, moth, bird, or destructive beast; if one is a Brahman and steals gold, one becomes a spider, snake, lizard, or aquatic animal; if one violates a teacher's bed or enjoys harming living things, one becomes a carnivorous animal; and if one eats forbidden food, one becomes a worm. On the other hand, animals can be born in higher rebirths, as noted again by Manu (12.54–67; 5.44; 11.241): "cattle, birds, and (other) animals that have been destroyed for sacrifices, receive (rebirth) in higher existences;" and "insects, snakes, moths, bees, (and) birds […] reach heaven by the power of austerities" (Buhler 1886: 175–76, 478, 496–98).

Finally, the process of rebirth results from the shifting nature of the "qualities" that make up a person at any given time. These qualities, the three *gunas*, completely pervade all existences, and follow every individual movement of *karma*, helping to shape the attendant aspects of psyches in each new life form. The three *gunas* are as follows:

(1) *sattva*: goodness, the dominant state of the gods
(2) *rajas*: passion, energy, the dominant state of men
(3) *tamas*: dullness, the dominant state of animals and plants

Beings in whom the *guna* of *tamas* prevails (e.g. plants and animals) are characterized by inertia, laziness, drowsiness, dullness, inability to discern, excessive love of pleasure, and excessive aversion to pain (Zaehner 1969; Bhagavad Gita 18). For Manu (12.26–44), *tamasic* beings have ignorance, delusion, irrationality, covetousness, sleepiness, timidity, cruelty, and inattentiveness, and fall into three levels: (1) the lower: plants, insects, fish, snakes, tortoises, cattle, and wild animals; (2) the middle: elephants, horses, lions, tigers, and boars; and (3) the highest: large birds of prey (Buhler 1886: 490–94). The attribution of *gunas* to animal life confirms that Hindu thinkers understand animals to have "character," with varying degrees of excellence or difficulty. And that the understanding of *tamas* as including ignorance, delusion, irrationality, and inability to discern clearly suggests that, though conscious, animals, are conscious in weak and aberrant forms.

Finally, we address the attribution of religiosity or spirituality to animals. Using examples from the Ramayana, the Bhagavata Purana, the Pancatantra, and the

Jatakas, Jaini concludes that, according to Indian views, animals clearly have a capacity for moral and spiritual development. Of the Jatakas, he says

> This spiritual capacity of animals is indicated by the fact that in almost all fables where the Bodhisattva appears as an animal-manifestation, he not only leads an exemplary life in practicing the perfections of charity and moral-discipline, but even preaches the dharma to human beings.
>
> (Jaini 1987: 170)

In one story, for example, a cow offers her life to a tiger if the tiger would allow her to return home for a moment to feed her calf. Overcome by the cow's truthfulness and the calf's devotion to its mother, the tiger spares them both. This, for Jaini (*ibid.*: 172), is a special feature "of the 'religious' behavior that was considered well within the scope of animals" by Indian authors. And the possibility for spiritual development and behavior is a capstone example for viewing animals as consciousness-bearing beings.

References

Beck, Brenda E. F., Peter J. Claus, Praphulladatta Goswami and Jawaharlal Handoo (eds) (1987) *Folktales of India*, Chicago, IL: University of Chicago Press.

Bhattacharyya, Gopinath (ed.) (1956) *Studies in Philosophy*, Calcutta: Progressive Publishers.

Buhler, Georg (trans.) (1886) *The Laws of Manu*, Oxford: Clarendon Press.

Dutt, Manmath Nuth (trans.) (1987) *The Ramayana*, Vol. 2, Patna, India: Eastern Book House.

Findly, Ellison Banks (2008) *Plant Lives: Borderline Beings in Indian Traditions*, Delhi: Motilal Banarsidass.

Jaini, Padmanabh S. (1980) "Karma and the Problem of Rebirth in Jainism," in *Karma and Rebirth in Classical Indian Traditions*, Wendy Doniger O'Flaherty (ed.), Berkeley, CA: University of California Press, 217–38.

——(1987) "Indian Perspectives on the Spirituality of Animals," in *Buddhist Philosophy and Culture*, David J. Kalupahana and W. G. Weeraratne (eds), Colombo, Sri Lanka: N. A. Jayawickrema Felicitation Volume Committee, 169–78.

Lanman, Charles Rockwell (1884) *A Sanskrit Reader*, Cambridge, MA: Harvard University Press.

Larson, Gerald James (1969) *Classical Samkhya: An Interpretation of Its History and Meaning*, Delhi: Motilal Banarsidass.

Larson, Gerald James and Ram Shankar Bhattacharya (eds) (1987) *Encyclopedia of Indian Philosophies*, Vol. IV: *Samkhya*, Delhi: Motilal Banarsidass.

McDermott, James P. (1980) "Karma and Rebirth in Early Buddhism," in *Karma and Rebirth in Classical Indian Traditions*, Wendy Doniger O'Flaherty (ed.), Berkeley, CA: University of California Press, 165–92.

O'Flaherty, Wendy Doniger (ed.) (1980) *Karma and Rebirth in Classical Indian Traditions*, Berkeley, CA: University of California Press.

Olivelle, Patrick (trans.) (1997) *The Pancatantra: The Book of India's Folk Wisdom*, New York: Oxford University Press.

Otto, Rudolf (1968 [1923]) *The Idea of the Holy*, London: Oxford University Press.

Potter, Karl (ed.) (1981) *Encyclopedia of Indian Philosophies*, Vol.III: *Advaita Vedanta up to Samkara and His Pupils*, Delhi: Motilal Banarsidass.

Radhakrishnan, S. (ed. and trans.) (1953) *The Principal Upanishads*, London: George Allen & Unwin.

Rao, S. K. Ramachandra (1987) *Encyclopaedia of Indian Medicine*, Vol. 2, Bangalore: Dr. V. Parameshvara Charitable Trust.

Rocher, Ludo (1980) "Karma and Rebirth in the Dharmashastras," in *Karma and Rebirth in Classical Indian Traditions*, Wendy Doniger O'Flaherty (ed.), Berkeley, CA: University of California Press, 61–89.

Singer, Peter (1990) *Animal Liberation*, New York: Random House.

Streng, Frederick J., Charles L. Lloyd, Jr. and Jay T. Allen (1973) *Ways of Being Religious*, Englewood Cliffs, NJ: Prentice-Hall.

Waldau, Paul (2002) *The Specter of Speciesism: Buddhist and Christian Views of Animals*, New York: Oxford University Press.

Zaehner, R. C. (trans.) (1969) *The Bhagavad-Gita*, London: Oxford University Press.

Further reading

Further discussion of animals and rebirth can be found in two publications by Christopher Key Chapple, "Animals and Environment in the Buddhist Birth Stories," in *Buddhism and Ecology*, Mary Evelyn Tucker and Duncan Ryuken Williams (eds) (Cambridge, MA: Harvard University Press, 1997), and *Nonviolence to Animals, Earth, and Self in Asian Traditions* (Albany, NY: SUNY Press, 1993). A third discussion appears in James P. McDermott's article, "Animals and Humans in Early Buddhism," *Indo-Iranian Journal* 32(2) (1989): 269–80). All three of these sources explore the connection of animals, non-violence, and rebirth in Hinduism, Jainism, and Buddhism. For a particularly Buddhist approach, see discussion of Ashoka's rock and pillar edicts in N. A. Nikam and Richard McKeon's rendition of *The Edicts of Asoka* (Chicago, IL: University of Chicago Press, 1959). For discussions of the particular issue of *karma* and animal rebirth, see three articles in the O'Flaherty collection on *karma* (cited above): by Wilhem Halbfass, "Karma, *Apurva*, and 'Natural Causes';" Gerald James Larson, "Karma as a 'Sociology of Knowledge';" and Bruce J. Long, "Human Action and Rebirth in the Mahabharata."

46
ANIMALS AND CHRISTIANITY

Gregory R. Peterson

David Harnden-Warwick and Jesse Bering, in their review of primate cognition (Chapter 44 in this volume), throw down a gauntlet of sorts, daring the theologian to see significance in the gap between primate and human abilities to think about the thoughts of others, commonly rendered in the literature as possessing a "theory of mind." This ability to theorize the contents of other minds, to mind-read, would seem to be one central component of the capacity to act morally. Further, they suggest, our propensity to mind-read and to attribute mentality and agency to even inanimate objects suggests a causal explanation of our religious beliefs as well – we believe because we have a biological propensity to do just that, to see spirits where none exist. Other animals, lacking such propensities, presumably live in a far different reality, one incapable of thinking of others as others, though having different intellectual gifts of their own. Intelligence, on their account, is not one thing, but a range of things, and while we have one species of intelligence, other animals have others. What should a theologian make of this?

Harnden-Warwick and Bering's clear distinction between human beings and other animals is congenial to traditional theological frameworks that emphasize a theologically and morally significant difference between human beings and other animals. Yet their arguments take place against a wider scientific and philosophical backdrop that is relevant for any theological reflection. Further, we might note that the starting point of theology is importantly different. Harnden-Warwick and Bering ask, given what we know about other animals and human psychology, what are the implications for religious belief? Theology asks, given the reality of God, how should we understand our relation to other animals and the rest of creation? These are very different questions. Understanding both, and understanding what both science and theology bring to the table, is important for understanding the answers that are available, as well as the questions that remain.

What's at stake?

It is standard to see the history of religion and science as one of unremitting conflict. The truth, however, is far different, and while it is indeed the case that conflict over particular issues abounds presently and can be found in centuries past, the historical tale turns out to be much more complicated. Without a doubt, religion and science have been in conflict historically, but, just as often, the relation has been one of peaceful coexistence or even mutual enrichment (Barbour 1997; Lindberg and Numbers 1986). Further, historians will point out that, while it now seems clear what counts as religion and what counts as science, this has not always been the case, with the result that we often retroject our own apparent clarity to previous periods when such clarity did not exist (Cantor and Kenny 2001).

When considering animal cognition research, conflict is one possibility. If it were the case that the denial of consciousness or self-consciousness to other animals was a central tenet of Christian theology, and the scientific research showed otherwise, this would be a damaging blow to the intellectual credibility of Christian thought. Yet other possibilities exist. Advances in scientific research may encourage theologians to move away from views that did not have much justification, theological or otherwise, in the first place, or they may encourage theologians to reconsider or explore themes that have previously been marginal to the tradition. Conversely, theological frameworks or perspectives may, from time to time, inspire scientific research, something that is often portrayed negatively but which has sometimes played an important role in the development of science, mainly at the level of motivation (Brooke 1991). Robert Russell has argued persuasively for an understanding of the relation of theology and science in terms of creative mutual interaction, an approach that encourages dialogue and fruitful exchange (Russell 2008). It is this potential for creative interaction that will be the focus here, with primary consideration given to questions concerning the implications of contemporary research in animal cognition for theological reflection, rather than the reverse.

Indeed, the essay by Harnden-Warwick and Bering (Chapter 44) raises two kinds of issues. The first concerns questions of ontology and ethics. If other animals are capable of experience, and if they are capable of richer forms of cognition, including the capacity to think about the thoughts of others, this raises issues of how we are to relate to other animals ethically. The second kind of issue is theological, for the capacity of animals to experience, to know, and hence to suffer, raises issues of God's goodness and traditional understandings of redemption. That there is a cognitive gap between humans and other animals may also suggest implications for how we consider these issues with respect to humans and to other animals. The questions are, of course, related, since theology informs ethics, and moral experience can inform how we think about theology.

Animals in creation: historical perspectives

Creation as a category of reflection has historically been an important and sometimes prominent element of reflection in Christian theology. This comes as a surprise to some, since it has sometimes been asserted that Christianity is a root cause of modern environmental problems (e.g. White 1967). Three decades of scholarship on theology and the environment have served to correct this misperception, demonstrating that Christianity has important resources for addressing environmental issues, and noting that the history has been more complex than commonly portrayed (Santmire 1985; McFague 1993; Rasmussen 1996).

That other animals have not figured as prominently in the history of Christian reflection and story can appear to be something of an understatement. A survey of those writings that have been most influential for Christian thought will show that reflection on other animals has varied from modest to non-existent. Christian theology has typically been focused on God and God's relation to human beings, and the central disputes of Christian doctrine have been those that impact, either directly or indirectly, our understanding of human redemption and salvation.

This impression, however, can be misleading, for it is certainly the case that consideration of animals, both independently and as a part of creation, has been an element of the tradition, and in some ways an important one. One trajectory of reflection concerns the doctrine of the image of God, first found in Genesis 1, and the recipient of much subsequent theological attention. Curiously, the language of the image of God occurs only three times in the Old Testament (Genesis 1: 26–28, 5: 1–3, 9: 6), with the clear primary referent being the initial account of creation that opens the Bible, where both man and woman are said to be created in the image of God. Despite this modest source material, the concept of the image of God has been an almost constant source of reflection, likely due to the conceptual fecundity of the term itself. On the one hand, to say that human beings are in the image of God is to say that they are like God in some important respect. On the other, that only human beings are explicitly designated as being in the image of God suggests that other creatures are not in the image of God. Put this way, the question naturally arises, what quality makes human beings like God while at the same time it distinguishes them from all other creatures?

In the ancient world, the answer came readily enough: the capacity to reason. More than three centuries before the birth of Jesus, this was the answer that Aristotle gave, and it was an answer that seemed widespread by the time Christian theologians began to reflect on the question (Aristotle 2000). Already in the second century, we see Irenaeus making a distinction between humans and other animals in terms of the capacity to reason, and the link between reason and the image of God is made explicit in the thought of Thomas Aquinas, among others (see Irenaeus, *Against Heresies* IV.37.6, Aquinas, *Summa Theologica* I.93.6).

In twentieth-century theology, these substantive interpretations came to be challenged by a relational one, primarily due to the influence of Dietrich Bonhoeffer and Karl Barth. Although Barth was not insensitive to the possible theological import of other animals, he insisted that human beings alone are in the image of God, and are so by virtue of their capacity for relation with one another and with God. It is in this relationality and in the relation itself that the image can be found (Barth, *Church Dogmatics* III.2–4; also Bonhoeffer 1997). Barth's view continues to be championed by contemporary scholars such as Noreen Herzfeld (2006), but has also been complemented by alternative views, with Wentzel van Huyssteen reviving an interpretation that the image of God is to be taken more literally to include the human physical form (van Huyssteen 2006). In recent decades, scholars of the Hebrew Bible seem to have arrived at some consensus on the meaning of the Genesis phrase in its original context, suggesting that the phraseology of the image of God was a play on ancient Near Eastern kingship language: for the king to be in the image of god was to accept the responsibilities to govern on behalf of the god; the genius of the writers of Genesis was to democratize this notion, assigning responsibility to all humans (cf. Hamilton 1990). In its original context, then, the language of the image of God seems to support a functional interpretation, having little to do with setting an ontological demarcation between humans and other animals, but rather an assigning of relationship and responsibility between humans and the world.

Independent of the concept of the image of God, many narratives, sayings, and injunctions of the Bible concern other animals, either directly or indirectly. Most notably, there are many references to meat-eating in the Old Testament, as well as guidelines in the legal texts as to which animals may be consumed and the proper means of preparation. The same is true for animal sacrifice, which is enjoined in the legal texts (e.g. Exodus 29). Although animal sacrifice is not commanded in the New Testament, and indeed seems to have been swept away, in part due to the understanding of Jesus' own sacrifice, meat-eating persists and is not roundly condemned. Whether Jesus himself ate meat is not well attested, and the only direct reference is Luke 24: 41–43, where the resurrected Jesus is said to eat fish.

One might conclude from this that no valuation is given to other animals at all, but this would be misleading. Many passages testify to the beauty and goodness of the created world and, in places, to God's providential care (e.g. Luke 12: 6). More importantly, some of the images of paradise and of the eschatological world to come are strongly suggestive of a more harmonious and egalitarian relationship. Thus in Genesis 2 we find Adam searching among the other animals for a companion; and Isaiah 65: 25 envisions a future where the wolf lays down with the lamb. Similarly, in his letter to the Romans, Paul speaks of the groaning of creation, suggesting that the Christian understanding of redemption is cosmic in scope (Romans 8: 18–22). These passages present strong possibilities, the only question being how to relate their promise to the countervailing trajectories suggestive of the uniqueness and centrality of human beings, as well as to the deeper themes of the gospel and Christian doctrine. Here, the kind of lives that other animals are capable of can become relevant. If other animals are just "dumb brutes," as has often been held, then it makes little sense to see other animals being of theological concern except in their broader participation in creation. If other animals are more than this, that opens the possibility that the lives of other animals do need to be considered within a theological framework, even if the role they play is understood to be different from that of human beings. It is here that the real theological work begins.

Animals, self, and soul

From a theological perspective, what would matter most about other animals is if they can be said to be, to use a phrase employed by Tom Regan, subjects of a life (Regan 1983). If animals were not subjects of a life, and if their activities fell below the level of conscious awareness, their lives would be of no more significance than plants, fungi, or other organisms. Such a view has been, and continues to be, endorsed by some, and René Descartes in particular is well known for his argument that other animals should be considered to be sophisticated but mindless machines (Descartes 1968). But if other animals are subjects of a life, the situation potentially changes, and can do so quite significantly, since it raises the possibility that other animals are due ethical regard in a way different from other organisms. Further, that other animals are subjects of a life raises the possibility that they deserve theological consideration as well, for questions of suffering and redemption normally considered solely in the human sphere become potentially expanded to other creatures as well.

It is here that the empirically oriented questions of animal cognition and relationality loom large, and it is these qualities that have played an important role in philosophical thinking on the matter, particularly in relation to contemporary ethical battles over animal rights and welfare, and it is relevant to consider the relation between claims of animal cognition and arguments about duties towards other animals. On some accounts, the fact that other animals are conscious at all is enough to confer moral consideration on them. Utilitarian philosopher Peter Singer argued for such a position in his early influential work on animal rights, and in doing so he was consistently applying a line of utilitarian reasoning dating back to Jeremy Bentham, one of its founding figures (Singer 1975; Bentham 2008). Equally long-standing is a tradition of reflection that ties moral consideration to the capacity to reason, an argument that is classically associated with Immanuel Kant, among other sources (Kant 1993). Part of the reason for this may stem from the claim that consciousness, the capacity to experience anything at all, is not dissociable from the capacity to reason. This seems to have been the view of Descartes, who saw the capacity of reason and language as indicators of the presence of a soul, and thus consciousness itself, and it is not implausible that this was Kant's view as well. For both Kant and Descartes, it may be added that the kind of rational capacity being primarily considered is one that is inclusive of self-awareness, such that the very capacity to be conscious would require the capacity to reflect on the contents of one's consciousness. Views that argue for the importance not only of reason, but of a particular kind of reason or structuring of the mind, continue to find endorsement among such philosophers as Daniel Dennett (1991) and Peter Carruthers (1986). Nevertheless, there is plenty of dissent, and Tom Regan has developed what is, in essence, a version of Kant's original view, but modified to be inclusive of at least mammals and similarly sophisticated animals, based on the capacity to have beliefs and desires (Regan 1983).

It is with these debates in the background that the literature surveyed by Harnden-Warwick and Bering (Chapter 44) takes on special prominence, for whether or not other animals have the capacity to mind-read (to possess a theory of mind, in the more standard locution) makes a difference for some of the ethical positions discussed. As they note, the evidence that other animals are capable of mind-reading is modest and limited, at best, to a few cognitively advanced animal species, notably including the great apes, Asian elephants, and bottlenose dolphins. Chimpanzees demonstrate some capacity to mind-read other chimpanzees, but fail at detecting false belief (Call and Tomasello 2008). If one includes field observations and not only experimental data, there is reason to believe that mind-reading might be more widespread, but not by much (e.g. Cheney and Seyfarth 1992). Further, while the mirror test may not provide clear evidence for the capacity for self-knowledge or mind-reading, failure to pass the mirror test, at least in visually oriented organisms, would seem to provide strong grounds to deny self-awareness or the capacity to mind-read, although Marc Bekoff (2003) provides a notable and interesting dissenting view. At best, self-recognition and some form of self-awareness in a philosophically relevant sense is limited to a few species of animals, mainly and perhaps exclusively including social mammals. At worst, mind-reading and self-awareness exists only in humans, making us indeed unique on our planet, and perhaps in the cosmos.

That other animals cannot mind-read, however, does not necessarily preclude them from theological consideration, since it is conceivable that other animals possess conscious awareness and so are capable of experiencing pain and pleasure. Since other mammals share a fair amount of our biology, and have analogous, if not identical, patterns of pain behavior and physiological responses to pain, it seems probable that they also have the corresponding capacity for conscious awareness. These analogues are most obvious for the social mammals that are most like us, less so for those organisms more distantly related to us. The great apes (gorillas, chimpanzees, bonobos, and orangutans) in particular demonstrate significant cognitive ability and social acumen. Although often exaggerated in popular presentations on the subject, efforts to teach apes some form of language have demonstrated the capacity to use abstract signs for purposes of communication and limited cooperation (Savage-Rumbaugh *et al.* 1993; Savage-Rumbaugh and Lewin 1994). Similarly, chimpanzees and bonobos in particular live in complex social groups, forming reciprocal relationships and, especially in the case of chimpanzees, leading to coalitions and hierarchies of power that can alter due to shifting allegiances (de Waal 1997, 2007).

From the ethical perspective, it is potentially of some importance where the line between those organisms capable of pain and those without conscious experience and sensation be drawn. For broader theological questions, this is less true. What matters is that pain exists at all, even if we are not sure which animals are capable of it.

It is sometimes observed that the capacity to experience pain is different from the capacity to suffer, implying that the latter is theologically and ethically relevant, but not the former. Certainly, the human capacity for pain and pleasure is, in some important respects, much expanded from that of other animals. Human beings can anticipate their own deaths and can experience dread from not only near but also distant harms, and the human capacity to engage in rich forms of social bonding carries with it the corresponding capacity to experience forms of grief, loss, rejection, and betrayal that go beyond similar expressions found in social mammals, and that seem to be not at all present in non-social animals. Without the capacity for language and mind-reading, the conscious experience of most other animals may include inchoate, episodic flashes of past events, but unlikely anything more than that. More probably, most other animals capable of conscious experience exist in a kind of eternal present, with limited ability to systematically probe the past or peer into the future. If so, this would seem to mitigate, but not eliminate, the capacity to suffer. A rabbit may not experience anxiety over its own capacity to die, or gloomily anticipate the likelihood that most of its young will not survive into adulthood, but a rabbit that gets its leg caught in a trap certainly experiences pain, and such pain, when prolonged without the possibility of escape, would seem to be enough to constitute suffering.

With respect to the social mammals, the capacity for such suffering would appear to be greater. Wolves and dogs seem to express something like joy when they greet fellow members of the pack, and elephants caress the bones of their deceased conspecifics (for anecdotal accounts of such behavior, see Masson and McCarthy 1996). Absent the capacity to mind-read, it is difficult to interpret the significance of such events, but they suggest a capacity greater than those found in non-social animals in ways that may bear on ethical, if not specifically theological, questions. Not all animals are alike, and it is not without merit to consider that different kinds of moral obligations extend to different kinds of creatures (for a particularly strong version of this view, see Cavalieri and Singer 1996).

Animals, ethics, and redemption

From the Christian perspective, then, consideration of other animals presents two kinds of primary issues, the first concerning the need to reconcile animal suffering with the goodness of God, the second concerning ethical frameworks for understanding human relationality to other animals. The two questions are clearly linked, for understanding how to reconcile God's goodness with suffering in general suggests something about how we ourselves should act in relation to other animals. If, for instance, causing and allowing suffering under any condition is wrong, this would place quite stringent boundaries around what constitutes right action, while also making it quite difficult to reconcile God's goodness with such suffering.

As the history of discourse concerning the image of God demonstrates, Christian scriptures provide resources for theological reflection on other animals, even though the broad trajectory of theological inquiry has been inclined to make a clear distinction between humans and other animals in a way that suggest that other animals are not a major theological concern, and in many instances to suggest that they are not a concern at all. Even so, there is nuance to this story. Descartes, writing as a philosopher but also a Christian thinker, represents an extreme when he argued that other animals are devoid of consciousness and so can be understood as sophisticated machines. Even Aquinas, who argued that the purpose of all of creation, including that of other animals, is to serve human beings, nevertheless retained Aristotle's view that animals have a soul, albeit one devoid of reason. Greater sympathy we find in Saint Francis of Assisi in his "Canticle of the Sun," as well as in some of the Greek fathers, notably John Chrysostom and Basil the Great, with the latter suggesting that salvation extends to other animals as well as humans (Armstrong *et al.* 1999; for an overview, see Passmore 1975). Yet these positions were developed prior to our much more extensive understanding of animal cognition as well as evolutionary history, and it is only recently that this kind of material, together with a greater interest in the theological status of animals generally, has led to more concentrated theological attention on the subject.

Two works illustrate this trend. Andrew Linzey, who has reflected for several decades on issues of animal rights and the theological status of animals, has consistently argued that Christian theology, properly understood, leads to an ethical stance against meat-eating and animal experimentation (Linzey 1994, 2009). Twin starting points for Linzey are the doctrine of the incarnation, that Christ became flesh to redeem the fallen creation, and the call to servanthood found at the core of the gospels. Although it is typically the case that it is God's taking on of *human* form that is seen to be theologically significant, Linzey suggests that it is God's taking on of bodily form more generally that is important. Nevertheless, Linzey retains the traditional argument for human exceptionalism. Humans, being uniquely made in the image of God, are different from all other creatures, but it is precisely because of this difference that we as human beings are held to a higher moral standard. Linzey notes that the gospels call us to a life of service on behalf of the weak and powerless, categories that include all other animals.

In support of his argument, Linzey draws on those biblical texts, some of which have already been noted, that suggest that divine concern is not limited to human affairs but includes all of creation, including other animals. Linzey recognizes, however, that the capacity to suffer raises issues of divine justice, and if other animals are capable of suffering, this potentially accentuates the difficulty of consistently affirming the goodness of God. To address this, Linzey affirms the traditional doctrine of the Fall, but widens it to include all of creation. Predation itself is evidence of the fallenness of creation, and so, rather than being seen as a natural and therefore good element of creation, Linzey views it as evidence of the need for redemption on the part of creation as a whole. Thus creation itself needs to be redeemed, and just as the Christian faith expresses hope in the resurrection to come for human beings, so too does it look forward to a day when creation is renewed. The afterlife is not the exclusive domain of humankind.

While he shares many of the same concerns as Linzey, an alternative view has been developed by Christopher Southgate (2008). Unlike Linzey, whose primary focus is ethical, Southgate's emphasis is on the question of theodicy and animal suffering. Southgate notes that the acknowledgement that other animals suffer raises significant challenges for affirming the goodness of God, and that this task is made all the more difficult by an appreciation of the amount of deep time required for the process of evolution to take shape. Indeed, not only does a study of geology and the fossil record demonstrate that the Earth has been home to living organisms for most of its 4.5 billion years, but also an understanding of evolutionary theory forces the realization that suffering is woven into natural selection itself. Borrowing an image from Holmes Rolston (1992), it is the claws of the cheetah that promote the swiftness of the impala, and without such competition and conflict the evolution of higher organisms would never have occurred.

It is this recognition of the deep history of evolution, with its attendant millennia of suffering, that leads Southgate to reject the concept of the Fall as a satisfactory explanation of animal suffering, for the idea of the Fall would seem to imply that there existed a time prior to such suffering, and no such obvious time between "pre-Fall" and "post-Fall" can be found. For different reasons, Southgate also rejects another solution, one that employs the doctrine of kenosis or self-emptying, to explain animal and human suffering. On a kenotic account, it is God's emptying of God's self that allows the space for creation to unfold, and it is precisely God's inactivity that allows the good in creation to develop alongside the evil. Nevertheless, God does not simply look on at a distance, but co-suffers with the creation, even in its darkest moments.

Southgate embraces God's co-suffering with creation and other animals, but he rejects the claim that a kenotic account by itself is sufficient to reconcile God's goodness with the extent of animal suffering. Rather, Southgate endorses what he calls the "only way" view, that the goodness found in creation, including the rich cognitive and spiritual capacities found in human beings, could only have come about through an evolutionary process. Thus the suffering found in creation was a necessary condition for the development of the intrinsic goods found there as well. Like Linzey, Southgate joins this with the hope of a cosmic redemption, including the hope that other animals can experience an afterlife, as difficult as that may be to conceive. These considerations lead Southgate to a different kind of animal ethic than that of Linzey. For Southgate, much of our experience of other animals takes the form of an I–it relationship, especially as manifested in modern, mechanized animal agriculture. Southgate endorses forms of human–animal community which do not exclude traditional forms of animal agriculture that allowed such I–thou relations to develop, and which require respect and care for domestic animals on the part of their human counterparts.

Linzey and Southgate provide just two examples of contemporary theological approaches that take animal subjectivity seriously, and do so in a way that is consistent with scientific understandings of animal cognition; it is important to note that there are many others (see McDaniel 1989; Rolston 1994; Russell 2008). In the context of Harnden-Warwick and Bering's interpretation of the evidence that the capacity for mind-reading is unique to human beings, it is noteworthy that both Linzey and Southgate retain the traditional Christian emphasis on human exceptionalism in a rather strong way, while nevertheless reinterpreting it to embrace other animals as thous, and not its.

Does this lend support to Harnden-Warwick and Bering's stronger suggestion that this separation might be taken for evidence of a creator? It is doubtful. Left out of their analysis is the whole history of human evolution itself, and if we had that before us, with its many intermediate stages and, as we are increasingly aware, meandering paths, the seemingly clear distinction between human abilities and those of our fellow animals may look different. Equally important, from a theological perspective, what counts most is the affirmation of God's goodness and creativity, which in and of itself does not dictate a particular path of evolution, but does suggest that such a God would create the kind of cosmos that would lead to fully relational beings, capable of both the love and suffering that is demonstrated on the cross.

Conclusion

Traditionally, Christian thought has neglected consideration of other animals, even though the scriptures provide hints and resources for thinking of the activity of God beyond the narrow confines of human failings and ultimate destiny. As is often the case, the sciences have gifted theology an opportunity to re-explore and reconsider these issues, and recent decades have seen a quiet but important re-evaluation of how to think about animals theologically. These developments are, at this point, best characterized as exploratory and tentative, delving into territory that has yet to be thoroughly thought through. This is fortunate, for there is much science yet to discover, which raises the possibility that theology and science can mutually engage and even inform one another in a way that spurs insight and generates greater understanding than what we now have. As the research on mind-reading reveals, what we learn about other animals reveals much about our own relationships with them, as well as revealing something about ourselves.

References

Aristotle (2000) *Nicomachean Ethics*, Roger Crisp (ed.), Cambridge: Cambridge University Press.

Armstrong, Regis, Wayne Hellman and William J. Short (eds) (1999) *Francis of Assisi: Early Documents*, New York: New City Press.

Barbour, Ian (1997) *Religion and Science: Historical and Contemporary Issues*, San Francisco, CA: HarperSanFrancisco.

Bekoff, Marc (2003) "Consciousness and Self in Animals: Some Reflections," *Zygon: Journal of Religion and Science* 38(2): 229–45.

Bentham, Jeremy (2008) *An Introduction to the Principles of Morals and Legislation*, New York: Barnes & Noble.

Bonhoeffer, Dietrich (1997) *Creation and Fall; Temptation: Two Biblical Studies*, New York: Simon & Schuster.

Brooke, John Hedley (1991) *Science and Religion: Some Historical Perspectives*, New York: Cambridge University Press.

Call, J. and M. Tomasello (2008) "Does the Chimpanzee Have a Theory of Mind? 30 Years Later," *Trends in Cognitive Sciences* 12(5): 187–92.

Cantor, Geoffrey and Chris Kenny (2001) "Barbour's Fourfold Way: Problems with His Taxonomy of Science–Religion Relationships," *Zygon: Journal of Religion and Science* 36(4): 765–81.

Carruthers, Peter (1989) "Brute Experience," *Journal of Philosophy* 86(2): 258–69.

Cavalieri, Paola and Peter Singer (1996) *The Great Ape Project: Equality Beyond Humanity*, New York: St Martin's Griffin.

Cheney, Dorothy L. and Robert M. Seyfarth (1992) *How Monkeys See the World: Inside the Mind of Another Species*, Chicago, IL: University of Chicago Press.

Dennett, Daniel (1991) *Consciousness Explained*, Boston, MA: Little, Brown & Co.

Descartes, Rene? (1968) *Discourse on Method and the Meditations*, F. E. Sutcliffe (trans.), New York: Penguin Books.

Hamilton, Victor (1990) *The Book of Genesis: Chapters 1–17*, Grand Rapids, MI: William B. Eerdmans.

Herzfeld, Noreen (2002) *In Our Image: Artificial Intelligence and the Human Spirit*, Minneapolis, MN: Fortress Press.

van Huyssteen, J. Wentzel (2006) *Alone in the World?: Human Uniqueness in Science and Theology*, Grand Rapids, MI: William B. Eerdmans.

Kant, Immanuel (1993) *Critique of Practical Reason*, 3rd edn, Lewis White Beck (trans.), Upper Saddle River, NJ: Prentice Hall.
Lindberg, David C. and Ronald L. Numbers (eds) (1986) *God and Nature: Historical Essays on the Encounter Between Religion and Science*, Berkeley, CA: University of California Press.
Linzey, Andrew (1994) *Animal Theology*. Chicago, IL: University of Illinois Press.
——(2009) *Why Animal Suffering Matters: Philosophy, Theology, and Practical Ethics*, New York: Oxford University Press.
McFague, Sallie (1993) *The Body of God: An Ecological Theology*, Minneapolis, MN: Fortress Press.
Masson, Jeffrey Moussaieff and Susan McCarthy (1996) *When Elephants Weep: The Emotional Lives of Animals*, New York: Delta.
McDaniel, Jay (1989) *Of God and Pelicans: A Theology of Reverence for Life*, Louisville, KY: Westminster John Knox.
Passmore, John (1975) "The Treatment of Animals," *Journal of the History of Ideas* 36(2): 195–218.
Rasmussen, Larry L, (1996) *Earth Community Earth Ethics*, Maryknoll, NY: Orbis Books.
Regan, Tom (1983) *The Case for Animal Rights*, Berkeley, CA: University of California Press.
Rolston III, Holmes (1992) "Disvalues in Nature," *Monist* 75(2): 250–81.
——(1994) "Does Nature Need to be Redeemed?" *Zygon: Journal of Religion and Science* 29: 205–29.
Russell, Robert John (2008) *Cosmology: From Alpha to Omega*, Minneapolis, MN: Fortress Press.
Santmire, H. Paul (1985) *The Travail of Nature: the Ambiguous Ecological Promise of Christian Theology*, Philadelphia, PA: Fortress Press.
Savage-Rumbaugh, E. and Roger Lewin (1994) *Kanzi: The Ape at the Brink of the Human Mind*, New York: Wiley.
Savage-Rumbaugh, E. S., J. Murphy, R. A. Sevick, K. E. Brakke, S. L. Williams and D. M. Rumbaugh (1993) "Language Comprehension in Ape and Child," *Monographs of the Society for Research in Child Development* 58(3): 1–222.
Singer, Peter (1975) *Animal Liberation: A New Ethic for our Treatment of Animals*, New York: Random House.
Southgate, Christopher (2008) *The Groaning of Creation: God, Evolution, and the Problem of Evil*, Louisville, KY: Westminster John Knox.
de Waal, Frans (1997) *Good Natured: The Origins of Right and Wrong in Humans and Other Animals*, Cambridge, MA: Harvard University Press.
——(2007) *Chimpanzee Politics: Power and Sex Among Apes*, Baltimore, MD: Johns Hopkins University Press.
White, Lynn, Jr. (1967) "The Historical Roots of Our Ecological Crisis," *Science* 155: 1203–7.

Further reading

A number of works are now available concerning the history and contemporary Christian understandings of other animals. Aspects of the history are covered in Ingvild Saelid Gilhus' *Animals, Gods and Humans: Changing Attitudes to Animals in Greek, Roman and Early Christian Thought* (Routledge, 2006), and a valuable comparative perspective can be found in Paul Waldau's *The Specter of Speciesism: Buddhist and Christian Views of Animals* (Oxford University Press, 2002). Contemporary theological reflections sometimes treat animals separately, but often within broader frameworks that include considerations of the environment, such as John Haught's *God After Darwin: A Theology of Evolution* (Basic Books,

1999). Theological reflection on other animals draws on, and is related to, not only scientific studies of animal cognition and behavior, but also relevant work in philosophy of mind and ethics. Two volumes that are representative of the range of inquiry are Robert W. Lurz's (ed.) *Philosophy of Animal Minds* (Cambridge University Press, 2009) and Cass R. Sunstein and Martha C. Nussbaum's *Animal Rights: Current Debates and New Directions* (Oxford University Press, 2004).

47
DOES THE BUDDHA HAVE A THEORY OF MIND?
Animal cognition and human distinctiveness in Buddhism

Jonathan C. Gold

Not the only moral animal

Before his enlightenment and liberation, the being that was going to be the Buddha – called the Bodhisattva – lived countless lives, being reborn again and again like all other beings in cyclic existence. Stories of the Buddha's previous lives are called *Jataka* tales, and in many of them, the Bodhisattva was born as an animal. *Jataka* tales resemble Aesop's fables, with talking animals and explicit morals. Indeed, the two collections seem to have drawn from the same treasury of story. Thus, even as an animal, the Bodhisattva is able to speak and exhibit his exemplary self-possession and compassion. In all his dealings, he is strikingly eloquent and unfailingly polite.

This is not ordinary animal behavior, and we should not imagine that these stories represent some failure of observation or rationality on the part of the Buddhist tradition. What these stories do represent, however, is a tendency among Buddhists to downplay the differences between humans and animals, whether in behavior, potential, or moral significance. After an analysis of the stories, I will lay out what I take to be their philosophical basis, which resonates with several issues in contemporary cognitive science.

Sometimes *Jataka* tales play humans against animals self-consciously. The great fourth-century Sanskrit poet Aryasura was particularly skillful at enlivening such play in his masterpiece, the *Jatakamala* (Arya Sura 2006). For instance, in one story the Bodhisattva is born as a hare, and is frustrated that he is unable to give any gift of worth, since his only practical ability (aside from preaching to other animals) is to nibble and cut grass. Finally, he figures out that he can offer up his own body as a gift to feed a Brahmin, and he jumps onto a pile of hot coals so as to simultaneously commit suicide and prepare himself as a meal. Aryasura asks, If a mere animal is capable of such generosity, what excuse can humans have for not being generous? This is apparently a joke on human speciesism.

In another story, the Bodhisattva is king of the geese, and he and his loyal general, Sumukha, are so beautiful and their flock so remarkable that their reputation attracts the attention of the just and righteous (human) king of Benares, Brahmadatta. Brahmadatta and his ministers put a plan into action so that the king might get to see these wonderful geese. To lure the geese, they build a magnificent man-made lake. (Here the Sanskrit poet excels: "Swarms of bees hovered in excitement, attracted by the lotuses that seemed to be laughing as they swayed to the rocking of the waves," *ibid.*: 142) The king's hope is that the geese will hear about their marvelous lake, and come to visit. It works. Against Sumukha's better judgment, the Bodhisattva assents to his subjects' agitations, and the geese resettle at this remarkable new lake.

After a time, even the Bodhisattva loses his skepticism, and he steps into a trap set by the king's fowler. At this point, Sumukha becomes the hero of the story, because when all of the other birds fly away out of fear, he never abandons the Bodhisattva, even at the latter's urging. Sumukha's loyalty impresses the fowler and convinces him to release the Bodhisattva. Once freed, the two grateful birds offer to follow the fowler back to meet king Brahmadatta, who had never intended them harm in any event, but only wanted to see them. The two wise kings – bird and human – then engage in a remarkably amicable conversation, and the story ends with Brahmadatta taking on the magnificent goose Bodhisattva as his teacher.

Let us return, though, to the protests against moving to the new lake that were voiced by the wise goose general Sumukha, close companion to the Bodhisattva. It is there that Aryasura provides a charming and ironic exposition on the differences between humans and animals:

> When men appear to have tender compassion in their hearts, it is usually deceptive. They affect charming ways and say nice things, but underneath it all you find a thoroughly nasty character. Just consider, my lord: birds and beasts express what they feel by their cries. Only human beings are clever enough to express the opposite. Of course their language is sweet and smooth and disarming. But, then, merchants also risk some outlay in the expectation of gain.
>
> (*ibid.*: 144)

Humans are thus distinguished from animals by the cleverness that makes them capable of deception. The sweetness of language is seen to be central to its instrumentality – humans do not give, even in their words, without expectation of some return on their investment. Sumukha is aware that, as Harnden-Warwick and Bering have explained (Chapter 44 in this volume), human distinctiveness is concomitant with our ability to second-guess, anticipate, and manipulate others' behavior.

An irony here is that, although the king has posted signs outlawing harm to animals, the most significant deception appears not in words, but in the form of an alluring, peaceful lake, which leads even the Bodhisattva into complacency. A further irony is that the goose Bodhisattva later speaks eloquently with the king in explicitly human language. Yet, as a bird (and a Bodhisattva), his language is superior to the politeness of ordinary courtiers because it is non-deceiving. The fact that the righteous king of Benares (in this story) is still a deceiver, with much to learn from the Bodhisattva as a goose, is a humorous, but still paradigmatic lesson. The spontaneous, unaffected honesty and unselfish generosity that is a goal of the Buddhist path is modeled not only by enlightened beings such as Buddhas and Bodhisattvas, but by animals as well.

This lesson is subtly expressed in yet another *Jataka* tale, the famous one in which the Bodhisattva, this time born as a man, throws himself off a cliff to provide his body as a gift to feed a starving tigress. Again, Aryasura contemplates the differences between humans and animals. Before encountering the tigress, the Bodhisattva is described as a wise and peaceful renunciant living in the forest:

> There, with a detachment and serenity made perfect by wisdom, he seemed almost to reproach mankind, whose persistent wrongdoing bars it from the wise man's peace of mind. His kindly presence had a calming effect on the wild beasts, who stopped preying on each other and began themselves to live like hermits. Because he was so transparently good, so self-disciplined, content, and compassionate, even strangers felt affection for him, just as he felt affection for them.
>
> (6)

In the wild, animals as well as humans are attracted and calmed by his goodness as by a kind of natural force. This spontaneous natural affection is contrasted with the ordinary world of men, in which wrongdoing is ceaseless.

The tale goes on to tell how the Bodhisattva encounters a tigress who has just given birth. She is so worn out that she is unable to hunt, and as her hunger grows, she contemplates eating her new cubs. It is this unnatural violation of a mother's love that moves the Bodhisattva, as he declares:

> Starvation forces this beast to break the laws of affection. Here she is, ready to devour her own offspring. Oh! how fierce is the instinct for self-preservation, such that a mother can be willing to eat her own young. How can one allow this scourge to continue unabated – this self-love which prompts such atrocities?
>
> (7)

This is what motivates the Bodhisattva first to send his disciple in search of meat, and then, after a moment's further thought, to sacrifice himself. That he has sent his disciple in search of meat, and that his intent is to restore a potentially man-eating tiger to health, suggest that the Bodhisattva's worry is not that the tigress will kill, but that she will kill her own offspring. This is a violation of nature, and far more dangerous, karmically, than the killing for food that is the tiger's natural behavior. The Bodhisattva's self-sacrifice is thus performed not principally to save the cubs, but to restore the natural state of love between mother and offspring.

Over countless lifetimes, Bodhisattvas are said to cultivate an equanimious universal compassion that is explicitly modeled on the spontaneous compassion and loving-kindness a mother shows for her babies. Buddhist teachings on the meditative cultivation of loving-kindness and compassion often begin with the instruction to think of one's own mother, and to realize that one owes her a debt of gratitude for her selfless, spontaneous care and protection. Reciprocating this feeling of love toward one's own visualized mother, the meditator then reasons that through endless time *every living being* has been one's mother at least once, and has thus provided one with selfless care one time or another. The gratefulness and compassion toward all beings that such a visualization practice seeks to engender is the basis for Buddhist rules against harming and killing animals, and its sometimes advocacy of vegetarianism (Shabkar 2004).

For our purposes, this visualized moral equivalence is simply another instance of a wider Buddhist tendency to downplay human distinctiveness. Yet, while there may be other species that experience the emotion of loving-kindness without selectively directing it toward one being or object, it is safe to say that only through human linguistic signs can such a generalization of an emotion be *cultivated*.[1] From the perspective of evolutionary science, the mother's emotional attachment has obvious benefits for her genetic heritage, but the meditative cultivation practice takes this emotion in a new direction. It is for this reason that human life, with its access to the lies and deceptions of human language, turns out, for that very reason, to be judged more valuable than any other.

Overcoming the language instinct

I mentioned above that the Bodhisattva, encountering the tigress, seemed more concerned with the *karmic* result of the violation of motherly loving-kindness than with the this-worldly, pragmatic goal of saving the lives of the cubs. This may seem callous if we read it as an instance of the Buddha favoring the tigress over her cubs (though, of course, he saves both), but it makes sense in a wider Buddhist worldview, in which one life is only a segment of the karmic continuum that must be taken into consideration.

The Buddha taught that after death, living beings are reborn into new lives that accord with the character of their previous morally significant actions (their *karma*). Rebirth comes in several physical and mental body types. Among beings with physical bodies, there are six main types (in descending order of pleasantness): Gods, demigods, humans, animals, hungry ghosts, and hell beings. The line between what are called the "fortunate births" and the "unfortunate births" is drawn between humans and animals – a significant divide, but as we have already seen, not as significant as we might expect. Humans are the least fortunate among the "fortunate," and animals are the most fortunate of the "unfortunate." Gods and demigods essentially live in blissful satisfaction of all of their desires, and hell beings and hungry ghosts are nearly always wracked with pain and suffering. Humans and animals share the wide middle, in which life can be alternately pleasant and unpleasant.

Yet a human birth, though less pleasant than life as a god, is often considered the most fortunate of all, from a very important perspective: Humans are the beings most capable of practicing the Buddha's teachings, the *dharma*. It is, consequently, only from the human realm that it is possible to attain *nirvana*, liberation from the endless cycle of rebirths. Most other beings are too distracted by passions and pains to turn their attentions to the Buddhist path of morality and meditative cultivation.

Gods are too pleased with the enjoyments of the heavenly realms to consider adopting the arduous practice of personal cultivation. Demigods are too obsessed with jealous competition. Hell beings and hungry ghosts, for their part, are too wrapped up in their own suffering to see beyond the immediate moment.

Animals, too, are often overwhelmed by their hunger or fear of predators, or, if domesticated, by being painfully exploited by humans. But even when they are not so distracted and have the gift of leisure time, animals are said to lack the necessary intellectual resources for the path. If we set aside the Bodhisattva's extraordinary animal accomplishments, the tradition tends to emphasize the life of animals as guided principally by ignorance: "Stupid and ignorant, they have no comprehension of what to do and what not to do" (Patrul 1994, 76). Animals have no sense of the moral context in which they exist; they do not realize that, when they kill one another, they condition themselves to be reborn again as animals. Humans are thus the only beings that are both intelligent enough to understand the Buddha's teachings, and not too distracted to practice them.

Yet, for all our intellectual resources, we are still motivated primarily by desire, hatred and, above all, ignorance. Like animals, we tend to perceive, conceive, and act out of habit alone. An accurate moral and cognitive frame is provided in the Buddha's teachings, but while many humans have the capacity, few have the opportunity, to study them. This general fact about the preciousness of our human life (living, as we do, in a rare period during which a Buddha's teachings survive) is noted by Buddhist teachers as motivation for the necessity of practice (of course), but also for the importance of cultivating compassion for all. Since all living beings act out of ignorance and ultimately suffer for it, there is no reason to hate one's enemies for their evil deeds, or to be jealous of them for their achievements, as the case may be. Anger, for Buddhists, is always irrational, like, as Harnden-Warwick and Bering explain, the anger one feels at a computer for losing one's files. We are asked to set aside, or ignore, the "intentional stance" with regard to *humans*. Actions performed without the Buddha's guidance are blind – caused as much by anger itself as by reasons. Better to blame the sword that cuts you, which is real, than the imagined projection of an intentional agent.

From the perspective of contemporary cognitive science, this may seem rather absurd and negative, worthy of outright dismissal as mere religious superstition. The reader is free to her own judgment. But the reasoning behind such a view rests upon and extends the conclusions of a belief in the conceptually constructed nature of the self. That is, the Buddhist view of the unreality of the self may be likened to what Dennett (1991) termed the "narrative self," which is a mainstream view in cognitive science today.

For mainstream Buddhists, the foundational ignorance is the positing of self, and every form of moral failure is, in one way or another, premised on the clinging and selfishness that such ignorance generates (Duerlinger 2003). The universality of this kind of ignorance means that, for Buddhists, even animals must be said to have, at least in a rudimentary way, what contemporary cognitive scientists call a "theory of mind" – that is, belief in one's own independent identity and perspective, if not that of others. Yet Buddhism turns contemporary cognitive science on its head by first, suggesting that animals *must* share with humans the tendency to view themselves as an enduring, living being; and second, suggesting that this shared tendency is the fundamental *mistake* that causes our shared suffering.[2] What distinguishes humans is not our ability (our habitual tendency) to see ourselves as *selves*, but on the contrary, our ability to use the Buddha's teachings to *free ourselves of this view.*

The purpose of Buddhist thought, quite explicitly stated, is to provide the tools necessary for us to know and perceive the truth behind our ordinary, false conceptions, and thereby to decide what among our beliefs identify real events and what are merely conceptually constructed fictions. As the great fifth-century Indian philosopher Vasubandhu explains, metaphysics (*abhidharma*) frees us from the false conception of self and the mass of cognitive hindrances that such a concept places upon us. Liberated from its spell, we may begin at last to base our actions not on ignorance, but on wisdom. Given the centrality of this Buddhist critique of the notion of the self, it is unsurprising that Buddhist philosophers in India understood the connections noted by Harnden-Warwick and Bering (Chapter 44) between perspective-taking, the ascription of intentionality, and conceptualization. Contemporary cognitive science and medieval Indian Buddhists are in agreement that all of these are embedded within our habitual conceptual construction of self, which provides them with their "narrative center."

While these issues appear in different forms across Buddhist texts, they are easiest (for me, at least) to identify in the Yogacara philosophical tradition (see Gold 2006, 2007 for a fuller treatment). Yogacarins believe that our ordinary experience of a distinction between perceptual organs (eyes, ears, noses, etc.) and their perceptual objects (sights, sounds, smells, etc.) is a mistake – indeed, a crucial mistake. The Yogacarin view is that the world in which we take ourselves to be living is an illusion, something like *The Matrix*. Here is not the place to lay out the arguments in favor of this view, or to analyze the texts that expound it. As a shortcut, perhaps the reader will forgive me for modernizing it into the comparatively realistic view that the brain generates a virtual world of experience, which we use to navigate the real world. (In fairness, it is disputed whether Yogacarins believe in a "real world" out there beyond the illusory one, and Yogacarins certainly do not believe that the mind is generated by the brain.)

The first issue, then, is the status of the perceptual organs and their objects *within* the virtual world. A moment's thought will show that they cannot but be deceptive. If the world as a whole is generated three-dimensionally by the brain, any locus of perception provides an inherently misleading impression of perspective. The visual experience I have that suggests to me that the world is stable as I move through it (for instance) is convenient and very likely adaptive, but it provides the basis for a false conceptualization – namely, my own reification of self. I think that "I" am the one into which the visual and auditory signals are coming, and that "I" am therefore distinct from the visual and auditory signals that come in. The mistake is that the visual and auditory signals are actually *part of me*, because they are aspects of my own brain's world-making project. Granted, the project is for my benefit (it gives new meaning to being "self-centered"), but it works by my fooling myself into ignoring the illusory nature of self-construction. The sensory world that I experience as "out there" is actually a world that is *my brain's representation of the outer world* (if there is an outer world). The world *as it is* can never be part of my virtual world.

The self–other distinction is therefore an illusory bifurcation of the virtual world, which the Yogacarins call a false "duality."

In addition to generating this false *perceptual* duality, there is another bifurcation that takes place when the mind generates *concepts*. The Buddhist epistemologists Dignaga and Dharmakirti explain conceptual construction as a process of "exclusion" (*apoha*). The idea is that concepts divide up the [virtual] universe, which is itself "non-dual," into categories: bowl and non-bowl, green and non-green, and so on.[3] This is difficult to wrap one's mind around, but these categories are also understood to be part and parcel of the mind's construction of self. A bowl to a person may be a bathtub to a bird. To conceptualize something as a "bowl" is to impose a human world-view. All of language, in this way, constructs a particular perspective – one's own self-centered perspective – as though it were natural.

Finally, the ascription of intentionality, in turn, depends upon language. Indeed, when Harnden-Warwick and Bering discuss the minimum criterion for intention-reading, they use propositions ("I suspect he believes I've slept with his wife") to represent the supposed intentions. Surely the ability to name such intentions is a cognitive capacity with massive utility. But, though useful, it can be misleading. Here the mistaken "duality" is the distinction between action and agent, which can have only a conventional, linguistically generated reality (Goodman 2009). The action is a conceptual–linguistic event; the agent is the "I" of the linguistic act, which simple observation shows us is also linguistic – the grammatical subject of "I suspect." But we reify it into something existing outside language.

Upon enlightenment, the ascription of intentionality dissolves in the face of a direct perception of the lack of reality of the intending "self." This does not mean, necessarily, that a Buddha no longer has access to the ordinary human (mistaken) conceptualizations that generate a "theory of mind." For most Buddhists, it would be difficult to accept that a Buddha could give teachings without himself having an understanding of his students' mental dispositions.[4] Yet he is no longer bewitched by language into reification of the self. The mind theorized to be acting intentionally is an adaptive theory, but one that is only a useful illusion.[5]

In addition to being adaptive (and so of pragmatic use), human language is a useful tool (for Buddhists) precisely because it can interrogate its own constructions. Second-order reflection, the bare minimum necessary to turn concepts into tools for manipulating others, is also the minimum necessary to allow language to identify, reflexively, the self's mode of construction. Once identified, the constructed self may be critiqued, and its processes of repair and reconstruction curtailed through meditative practice. If language is to accomplish this, though, it must to some degree undermine itself. This does not mean that a Buddha does not speak; but it does mean that he must have a different relationship to his linguistic utterances from that of ordinary beings. He cannot be fooled by, or attached to, the implicit reifications.

This is perhaps why Aryasura has the goose general Sumukha criticize humans for the deceptiveness of language, idealizing animals as models of Buddha-like spontaneity. Perhaps a Buddha's achievement means being able to speak human words, but through guileless, spontaneous cries. But animals are not Buddhas. If the Yogacara tradition is correct that the "duality" between sensory organs and objects causes living beings to reify the self, it would seem that animals ought to be subject to the same kind of self-construction. And if a Buddha is not fooled into reifying his own perceptual perspective, then his mental state would be quite unlike an animal's. The achievement of a Buddha, furthermore, is the result of his having learned and contemplated the fruits of that learning. Language is essential for such cultivation, and for this reason liberation is unavailable to animals. Still, most of us are not Buddhas, and if the animals are trapped in their false imagination of selfhood, that only means that they are no better off than the rest of us. But at least they don't pretend to be. The animals, unlike us, are unencumbered by the false projections and self-serving lies of human language.

Notes

1 The importance of mother visualization in this kind of meditative cultivation is supportive of Ostow's psychoanalytic theory that locates the origins of "religious" feeling in the bond between mother and child (Ostow 2007, 69). Yet if the experience has an instinctive source in infancy, the mechanisms of its intentional replication (which here include philosophical reasoning based in the nature of rebirth) still require explanation.

2 Human suffering takes many forms, but suffering that is directly related to the false conception of self arises when we fail to live up to our image of ourselves, for instance when we experience ourselves aging or dying. When we eliminate the false projection of the permanent self, we free ourselves from the fear of death.

3 It is called "exclusion" because the mind forms categories by excluding dissimilar entities. See Hayes (1988) and Dunne (2004) on the *apoha* doctrine in Dignāga and Dharmakīrti, respectively.

4 In truth, Buddhist traditions differ over whether Buddhas have access to conceptual constructs. See Eckel (1994); Griffiths & Urban (1994); Dunne (1996).

5 This view is similar to that advocated by Wegner (2003).

References

Arya Sura (1989) *Once the Buddha Was a Monkey: Arya Sura's Jatakamala*, Peter Khoroche (trans.), Chicago, IL and London, UK: University of Chicago Press.

Dennett, D. (1991) *Consciousness Explained*, Boston: Little, Brown & Co.

Duerlinger, J. (2003) *Indian Buddhist Theories of Persons: Vasubandhu's "Refutation of the Theory of Self"*, London: RoutledgeCurzon.

Dunne, J. (1996) "Thoughtless Buddha, Passionate Buddha," *Journal of the American Academy of Religion* 64: 525–56.

——(2004) *Foundations of Dharmakirti's Philosophy*, Studies in Indian and Tibetan Buddhism, Somerville, MA: Wisdom Publications.

Eckel, M. (1994) *To See the Buddha: A Philosopher's Quest for the Meaning of Emptiness*, Princeton, NJ: Princeton University Press.

Gold, J. (2006) "No Outside, No Inside: Duality, Reality, and Vasubandhu's Illusory Elephant," *Asian Philosophy* 16: 1–38.

——(2007) "Yogacara Strategies Against Realism: Appearances (*akrti*) and Metaphors (*upacara*)" *Religion Compass* 1: 131–47.

Goodman, C. (2009) "Vasubandhu's *Abhidharmakosa*: The Critique of the Soul," in *Buddhist Philosophy: Essential Readings*, W. Edelglass and J. Garfield (eds), New York: Oxford University Press, 297–308.

Griffiths, P. and Urban, H. (1994) "What Else Remains in Sunyata? An Investigation of Terms for Mental Imagery in the *Madhyantavibhaga*-Corpus," *Journal of the International Association of Buddhist Studies* 17: 1–25.

Hayes, R. (1988) *Dignaga on the Interpretation of Signs*, Studies of Classical India 9, Dordrecht: Kluwer Academic.

Ostow, M. (2007) *Spirit, Mind and Brain: A Psychoanalytic Examination of Spirituality and Religion*, New York: Columbia University Press.

Shabkar (2004) *Food of Bodhisattvas: Buddhist Teachings on Abstaining from Meat*, Padmakara Translation Group (trans.), Boston, MA: Shambhala Publications.

Wegner, D. (2003) *The Illusion of Conscious Will*, Cambridge, MA: MIT Press.

Further reading

Two articles from Philip Zelazo, Morris Moscovitch and Evan Thompson (eds), *The Cambridge Handbook of Consciousness* (Cambridge University Press, 2007) provide helpful background to the above discussion. The first, George Dreyfus and Evan Thompson, "Asian Perspectives: Indian Theories of Mind," 89–114, provides a good entry point to Buddhist philosophy of mind. The second, Antoine Lutz, John Dunne and Richard Davidson, "Meditation and the Neuroscience of Consciousness," 499–551, addresses methodological issues of relevance in bridging Buddhism and cognitive science. Both provide useful source lists as well.

It is rare to see Buddhist philosophy of mind hashed out with specific regard to animal cognition. More common, and also relevant here, is the discussion of animals as objects of compassion and non-violence, as in Christopher Chapple, *Nonviolence to Animals, Earth and Self in Asian Traditions* (SUNY Press, 1993) and Luis Gomez, "Nonviolence and the Self in Early Buddhism," in *Inner Peace, World Peace: Essays on Nonviolence and Buddhism*, Kenneth Kraft (ed.), (SUNY Press, 1992). Philosophical introductions to the no-self doctrine and Yogacara may be found in Mark T. Siderits, *Buddhism as Philosophy* (Hackett, 2007) and Paul Williams and Anthony Tribe, *Buddhist Thought: A Complete Introduction to the Indian Tradition* (Routledge, 2000). For further reading on specific topics, see the references listed above.

(iv) Aging and life extension

48
PROSPECTS FOR THE BIOMEDICAL POSTPONEMENT OF AGING

Technical context for a theological debate

Aubrey D. N. J. de Grey

Summary

The topic of combating aging is an emotive one, on which it seems that everybody has an opinion. By and large, although there is no objection to modest postponement of age-related ill-health, the prospect of more dramatic intervention elicits a wide variety of negative reactions, often arrived at with undue haste. Those who concern themselves with the religious and philosophical implications of such a prospect and its relationship to traditional religious claims are a key group of opinion-formers, whose pronouncements are likely to influence many in the wider world. It is thus essential that such scholars address these issues in the context of an accurate, albeit necessarily lay, understanding of the biomedical realities of aging – today's reality, that of the near future, and the range of possibilities for the longer term. To that end, in this introductory essay I outline what is and is not known about the biology of aging and its biomedical malleability, with emphasis on certain points that non-biologists are particularly prone to misunderstand.

The body is a machine that accumulates damage

Aging is popularly viewed as in some way biologically mysterious, not amenable even in principle to medical intervention. In fact, however, biogerontologists now understand the essentials of aging quite well, and are almost all agreed that it is not mysterious at all. Like any machine, the human body incurs damage as a side-effect of its normal operation. Again like any machine, this damage is initially harmless, because the body possesses inherent resilience that allows it to operate even in the presence of a certain amount of this damage. But, again like any machine, the damage accumulates as the body continues to function, and eventually the simple quantity of damage begins to impair organ and organismal function and finally causes death (Kirkwood 2005).

Two features of this process are probably paramount in blurring so many people's understanding of this altogether mundane reality. The first is that most of the types of accumulating damage that contribute to aging are, until at least middle age, not only harmless but invisible. They consist of molecular and cellular alterations – microscopic changes, in other words – that have essentially no impact on the body's outward appearance (other than in ways that are clearly of only marginal relevance to health, such as diminishing elasticity of the skin). The second reason is that the body is well known to incorporate a plethora of highly sophisticated, automatic "self-repair" systems that repair molecular and cellular damage as it arises. In combination, these two facts lead many people to two incorrect conclusions about the human body: firstly that aging doesn't happen at all until middle age or so, at which point some mysterious switch flips and the automatic repair processes cease to keep up with the creation of damage; and secondly that the body isn't really a machine at all, because human-made machines' self-repair capacity is so slight as to be negligible. (Other reasons for not viewing the body as a machine, involving the nature of consciousness, the soul and so on, are more appropriate topics for the essays that follow this one, so I shall not address them here.) In fact, the latter distinction is purely a matter of degree: Yes, we have far more sophisticated auto-repair systems than any human-made machine, but auto-repair of a primitive form certainly exists, such as in the case of humidifiers, freezers etc. that perform a regular cleaning cycle. And the former is an illusion; what actually happens is that our auto-repair processes are imperfect from the start of life, totally eliminating some types of damage but not addressing others, and the latter types eventually build up to a point where they impair the whole of the metabolism, including the formerly fully effective repair processes.

Long ago, it was suspected that aging is indeed "programmed" into our bodies – that it is in some sense good for the species that individuals not survive too long (Weismann 1891). But this is now almost universally agreed to be incorrect: Aging happens by default, just like the aging of human-made machines.

Being frail is risky, and it always will be

Once the idea that aging cannot even in principle be tackled by medicine has been dispelled, a follow-up concern arises so often that it has even acquired a name in the sociology literature: the Tithonus error (de Grey 2008). It has been eloquently cited by all manner of supposedly careful thinkers over the years; possibly the best known in contemporary literature is Francis Fukuyama's warning that the postponement of aging would create a "global nursing home" (Fukuyama 2002).

In the Greek myth named after him, Tithonus was a warrior who won the heart of the goddess Eos. Eos, being immortal, did not look forward to her consort's decline and death, but being a junior deity she lacked the ability to grant him immortality. She therefore asked Zeus to do this. Unfortunately for all parties, she "forgot" to ask that Tithonus also be rendered eternally youthful. As a result, Tithonus underwent a decline in health and functionality on schedule, but did not die – he just continued to become frailer and frailer, until in her despair Eos was eventually forced to turn him into a grasshopper.

Myth though it be, this story has been embraced with unrestrained credulity by extraordinary numbers of non-biologists. Perhaps the belief that the postponement of aging will entail the elongation of the less enjoyable end-stage of life, rather than the prime of life, is in some ways a corollary of the assumption that aging is qualitatively distinct from other types of ill-health. In fact, however, the reverse is true: since the dysfuction of aging is no more nor less than a type of ill-health, amenable in principle to medical intervention just like any other, its postponement will feature the same spectrum of difficulty that specific diseases do. In particular, postponing aging will be easier if it is done sooner rather than later: like any disease, the further it progresses, the faster it advances and the harder it is to address. Indeed, this is, in a real sense, even more true of aging than of specific diseases: Because aging is so complex and pervasive, with its various components exacerbating each other in innumerable interactions, a late-onset intervention that merely preserved the frail state rather than rejuvenating it would be astronomically complex. And finally (and, quite probably, most decisively), the fact that aging confers progressively increased susceptibility to extrinsic threats to life, such as infectious diseases and accidents, means that the mortality rate of frail people is never going to be as low as that of healthy people.

Finally, it is apposite to note that being frail is no fun. Thus, even in the unlikely event that therapies did emerge that extended the frail period at the end of life rather than healthy life, they would be of limited interest to society as compared with therapies that extend healthy life, so the effort to develop the latter would undoubtedly proceed unabated. The same applies to a common variant of the Tithonus error in which it is assumed that medicine might be able to keep the body youthful, but could not do the same for the brain. Accordingly, and especially in view of the options available for health-extending therapies discussed below, any "Tithonus scenario" would be short-lived, even in the outlandish event that it emerged.

The Tithonus error is, therefore, unequivocally an error. If we ever do succeed in postponing death and extending longevity by medical interventions, it will be by postponing the onset of frailty or by restoring the frail to youth, and not by extending frailty.

Geriatric medicine is a losing battle

A related issue arises when we consider the ability of geriatric medicine to address aging. First of all, a definition of what I mean by "geriatric medicine" is in order. It is best defined as the targeting of the clinically definable pathologies of old age, in contrast to "gerontological medicine" which, if it yet existed, would be defined as the targeting of the metabolic precursors of that pathology. (In the next section I return to "gerontological medicine" in more detail.)

There is abundant, and entirely appropriate, awareness in society that medical care for the elderly comprises the large majority of expenditure in healthcare, in terms of both provision of existing therapies and development of new ones. Things were not ever thus; historically, when fewer individuals survived long enough to experience the debilities of old age, correspondingly fewer resources were allocated to that age range. It is therefore perhaps unsurprising that many observers (and commentators) make the presumption that medical expenditure will continue along this same trajectory, with ever more complex and expensive – and quixotic – therapies being applied to the diseases and disabilities of aging.

This scenario is, in fact, immensely unlikely. Essentially as a result of the considerations mentioned above, geriatric medicine suffers from the phenomenon of diminishing returns – there is a decelerating, indeed logarithmic, or possibly even asymptotic relationship between the sophistication of geriatric medicine and its impact on life expectancy. Moreover, since geriatric medicine is intrinsically doomed to extend the frail part of lifespan (to the limited extent that that may be possible at all), rather than the healthy part, it will always be relatively unattractive to society and correspondingly under-supported in terms of resources.

Cleaning up metabolism (much) will probably be really difficult

The points summarized in the previous few sections have been fully taken on board, for many decades, by biogerontologists – those who study the biology of aging. The very reasonable conclusion that has been reached is that the only feasible option for substantially combating aging is to follow the age-old dictum that prevention is better than cure. Accordingly, when biogerontologists have concerned themselves with seeking interventions (as opposed to merely understanding aging ever better), they have focused on influencing the earliest stage of the chain of events that leads from metabolism to pathology: in other words, on retarding metabolism's ongoing creation of the side-effects (the "damage") that eventually cause age-related ill-health.

This focus has been greatly encouraged by the discovery of various quite simple ways in which this "cleaning-up" of metabolism can be substantially achieved in the laboratory. The first such intervention to be discovered (McCay *et al.* 1935), and by far the most robust and best studied to this day, is calorie restriction – the provision of a diet with substantially lower energy content than the animal desires, but (in its modern form) proportionately enriched in micronutrients. A reduction of calories by one-third relative to a rodent's *ad libitum* consumption typically confers a one-third increase in lifespan. Moreover, as predicted by the considerations outlined earlier, the additional life is healthy – the period of functional decline at the end of life is not stretched and may even be slightly compressed.

However, optimism concerning the translation of this intervention into a corresponding therapy for humans must be tempered. Three main issues arise.

First of all, substantial calorie restriction is – for most people, anyway – severely prejudicial to quality of life. For every person who practises calorie restriction there are many who have tried it and rapidly capitulated. Much effort is currently under way to develop calorie restriction "mimetics" – pharmaceuticals that essentially trick the body into thinking it is receiving fewer calories than it is – but at this stage such interventions are highly experimental (though they may be effective against particular conditions, especially diabetes).

Second, there are both strong evolutionary arguments and diverse (albeit somewhat soft) data indicating that calorie restriction confers a much smaller proportional postponement of aging in longer-lived species, such as humans, than in rodents – indeed, to a first approximation probably only a comparable absolute postponement (de Grey 2005). Any postponement is better than nothing, to be sure, but the quality-versus-quantity issue just mentioned is thrown into that much starker relief by this fact. And calorie-restriction mimetics are not expected ever to exceed the performance of *bona fide* calorie restriction, so this issue applies to them too, even if they can be made to work.

Third, and perhaps most importantly, calorie restriction at best retards aging by the same proportion whenever in life it is initiated, which means that the absolute period of postponement of ill-health will be even less for most people than indicated above, since they will only initiate the protocol in middle age (Dhahbi *et al.* 2007). And this, too, is anticipated also to apply to mimetics.

The particular gravity of the point just mentioned is that it is very likely to apply not only to calorie restriction, but also to any putative intervention that slows the creation of the eventually pathogenic side-effects of metabolism. Such interventions, by definition, cannot remove damage that has already been laid down; thus they can only postpone aging substantially if either they are initiated early in life, or else they alter metabolism very profoundly.

Well, so, what's so daunting about altering metabolism very profoundly? There is a simple answer to this: our ignorance. The human body is undoubtedly a machine, but it is not distinguished from human-made machines only by its complexity; another, even more dramatic difference is the extent to which we understand its operation. The depth of our ignorance of biology is hard to overstate. Of course, we know many times more now than we did fifty, or even twenty, years ago, but it is painfully apparent to all biologists that the stuff we know is utterly dwarfed by the astronomical amount that we don't know – even neglecting the probably even greater amount that we don't even know that we don't know. And "tuning" (for that is what I am describing here) a machine whose mechanics we understand so very poorly is as good as guaranteed to be impossible; any tweak we might perform is essentially certain to do more harm than good.

The phenomenon of life extension via calorie restriction might initially seem to be a refutation of what I have just stated – but this is an illusion. Calorie restriction works for the same reason that any simple intervention beneficially affects a complex system: because the complex system is already constructed so as to respond to that intervention in that way. In this case, evolutionary theory can easily explain the calorie restriction phenomenon, because famines happen in the real world as well as in the laboratory, and it is useful for organisms to be able to adjust their metabolic priorities in a famine to defend against aging (thus improving their chances of surviving the famine) rather than to procreate (creating offspring that starve in infancy). Thus organisms have evolved to possess whatever complexity of genetic machinery may be necessary to deliver this postponement of aging. Unfortunately, this does not alter the conclusion mentioned above that calorie restriction will work poorly on long-lived organisms such as humans.

Comprehensive preventative maintenance may be feasible

The previous two sections are in danger of giving solace to those who feel, in their hearts, that the successful postponement of age-related ill-health is a prospect whose drawbacks outweigh its attractions. This section will not.

I have explained that aging consists, in its most abstract description, of a two-stage process: metabolism ongoingly generates accumulating damage; and damage eventually causes pathology. I have outlined two candidate approaches to delaying that pathology: to retard the creation of damage; or to retard the progression of the pathologies themselves. I have gone on to explain why neither of these options shows any promise. But is there a third way?

It turns out that there is. In a nutshell, it can be described as the application of regenerative medicine to the problem of aging. Rather than retarding either of the processes that sequentially comprise aging, regenerative medicine targets their intersection – the damage itself. In this paradigm, we seek to repair damage after it has been created, thus delaying the point at which its level reaches the threshold that causes pathology to emerge. Regenerative medicine, in other words, is preventative maintenance for the human body (de Grey *et al.* 2002).

Regenerative medicine has been developed for use against much simpler conditions than aging – and indeed, only now are biogerontologists even beginning to take seriously the idea that it could be applied to aging. However, for the reasons discussed above, there is no *a priori* reason why aging should be intractable to the influence of therapeutic modalities that work against specific diseases and conditions. The only difference – a daunting one, to be sure, but rather clearly not an eternally insurmountable one – is that in order to apply regenerative medicine to aging, one must administer a panel of therapies in unison, rather than just a single intervention.

It must, however, be stressed that regenerative medicine will not defeat aging on its own. My own view is that it will be the cornerstone of the anti-aging interventions of the future, but it will undoubtedly be ramified in its efficacy by the impact of both the geriatric approach and the gerontological, "metabolic tuning" approach. Without the help of traditional geriatric medicine, regenerative medicine can be of only limited help to the very elderly; conversely, without the help of metabolic tuning, some people who might have "made the cut" for anti-aging regenerative medicine will be too frail to benefit by the time it arrives.

Maintenance cannot deliver infinite longevity

Having surveyed the various ways in which we might postpone age-related ill-health with future medicine, it is appropriate to remind ourselves of the fundamental limits of these measures. In the previous three sections, I have outlined some of the technical pros and cons of the various approaches to postponing aging, concluding that the "preventative maintenance" approach is the likely fulcrum, but ultimately my comments have addressed only the relative difficulty of achieving a goal that all the various approaches could achieve in principle. What is that goal – the pinnacle of what medicine could theoretically achieve for longevity?

The reason why this question is important in the present context is that there is a remarkable tendency to presume that there is no limit to what could be achieved: that medicine could, in due course, deliver immortality. It is, therefore, necessary to clarify why that is incorrect.

First, it is quite clear that foreseeable regenerative medicine will only incompletely address the accumulating damage of aging. That damage comes in many forms, some of them much easier to repair than others – and some of them very difficult indeed. It is impossible even to estimate, let alone place a time limit on, how long we will take to develop therapies that repair absolutely everything.

Second, even though progress in improving the comprehensiveness of such therapies is likely to occur at a pace sufficient to keep many people alive today healthy indefinitely (the concept of "longevity escape velocity"), such interventions affect only age-related mortality, and have no effect on causes of death that kill young adults. Thus, though lifespan may be rendered potentially indefinite by such therapies, it will not be rendered infinite.

Third, and perhaps most importantly from a theological or religious point of view, such therapies maintain only health, not life. Put simply: God can just as easily strike you down with a thunderbolt, however fit you are. This truism needs stating because of the extraordinarily pervasive tendency to equate aging with death, indefinite lifespans with infinite ones, and so on. Unbounded youth does not mean unbounded life. The term "immortality" is the purview of religion, and no biomedical progress will ever change that, however many journalists use the term in their articles about such research.

Deprioritizing elder care: shifts in the economic pros and cons

Finally, it may be useful to place anti-aging interventions in an economic context, so as to give the necessary background to considerations of whether such therapies can be introduced without violating norms of social justice.

At present, while medicine is essentially ineffective against aging, geriatric medicine is a tragedy of triage. It cannot really cure the ailments that it addresses, so it does the best it can, but it acknowledges that that is not very much at all. When geriatric medicine goes head-to-head for funding against specialities that benefit the young, therefore, the argument that the older patient has less to gain from treatment is essentially unassailable. This logic is powerfully reinforced by the fact that the sick elderly typically support it: they tend to resign themselves to their fate and meekly endorse the preferential provision of medical care to the young.

Should we acquiesce in this reality? If there were no prospect of substantive progress in alleviating the ill-health of the elderly, I would be inclined to feel that we should. But, as I hope I have made clear above, there is indeed such a prospect.

Sophisticated medicine is expensive to administer, and – essentially by definition – it always will be. But "sophisticated" has a shifting definition, in medicine as in all areas of technology. There is no reason to anticipate that medical treatments to postpone age-related ill-health will deviate from the norm of progressive reduction in cost.

This matters – a lot. Since such a high proportion of medical expenditure is devoted to caring for the frail elderly, the elimination (or even modest reduction) of age-related frailty would reduce the economic burden of healthcare by a massive amount.

It may be useful to spell out the relevance of this rather prosaic economic argument to theologians and religious thinkers. The relevance is quite straightforward: it comes down to the fact that money rules most people's lives. Sociological considerations can never be divorced from theological and religious ones, since morality is ultimately rooted in individuals' experience at the hands of their fellows. The other essays in this section will surely address such issues, so I will say no more.

Conclusion

If something can be done, and a lot of people badly want it to be done, it eventually will be done. The radical postponement of aging satisfies these criteria. It is, therefore, only a matter of time before much longer healthy lives become a reality. Theologians and religious thinkers, like any group tasked with developing thinking and/or policy in relation to the society of the future, are therefore duty-bound to apply themselves to this question: partly to the issue of whether we should seek to hasten the postponement of aging; and partly to the issue of how to manage it when it inevitably occurs whether they like it or not. In this essay I have touched on a number of the popular misconceptions surrounding the science of postponing aging, in the hope that theological and philosophical debate will thereby be enabled to be more relevant to what the future will hold. I look forward to such debate with great interest.

References

Dhahbi, J. M., H. J. Kim, P. L. Mote, R. J. Beaver and S. R. Spindler (2004) "Temporal Linkage Between the Phenotypic and Genomic Responses to Caloric Restriction," *Proceedings of the National Academy of Sciences USA* 101: 5524–29.

Fukuyama, F. (2002) *Our Posthuman Future: Consequences of the Biotechnology Revolution*, New York: Farrar, Straus and Giroux.

de Grey, A. D. N. J. (2005) "The Unfortunate Influence of the Weather on the Rate of Aging: Why Human Caloric Restriction or its Emulation may only Extend Life Expectancy by 2–3 Years," *Gerontology* 51: 73–82.

——(2008) "Combating the Tithonus Error: What Works?," *Rejuvenation Research* 11: 713–15.

de Grey, A. D. N. J., B. N. Ames, J. K. Andersen, A. Bartke, J. Campisi, C. B. Heward, R. J. M. McCarter and G. Stock (2002) "Time to Talk SENS: Critiquing the Immutability of Human Aging," *Annals of the New York Academy of Sciences* 959: 452–62.

Kirkwood, T. B. (2005) "Understanding the Odd Science of Aging," *Cell* 120: 437–47.

McCay, C.M., M. F. Crowell and L. A. Maynard (1935) "The Effect of Retarded Growth upon the Length of Life Span and upon the Ultimate Body Size," *Journal of Nutrition* 10: 63–79.

Weismann, A. (1891) "Essays upon Heredity and Kindred Biological Problems," 2nd edn, Vol. 1, Oxford: Clarendon Press.

Further reading

The application of regenerative medicine to the problem of aging is a new concept, about which few overviews have yet appeared. For the educated non-specialist, a starting-point that cuts no scientific corners, but provides abundant background and minimizes technical jargon, is de Grey and Rae's *Ending Aging: The Rejuvenation Breakthroughs that Could Reverse Human Aging in our Lifetime* (St Martin's Press, 2007). For those with biology training, a compendium encompassing the major themes within this emerging area is *Strategies for Engineered Negligible Senescence: Reasons Why Genuine Control of Aging May be Foreseeable* (New York Academy of Sciences, 2004), which is the proceedings volume of the inaugural conference in a series focused on this area. As yet, authoritative treatments of "biomedical rejuvenation" from a philosophical, theological, sociological, economic, or political perspective have not emerged.

49
RESPONSE TO AUBREY DE GREY FROM THE PERSPECTIVE OF BUDDHISM

Derek F. Maher

Aubrey de Grey's lively and enthused advocacy for prolongevity (Chapter 48 in this volume) is compelling and contagious. He envisions a not-too-distant future in which advanced biomedical therapies enable people to postpone the detrimental effects of living a long time by repairing the accumulated physical damage that constitutes aging. He expects that a broad array of therapies, which would address various sorts of diminished cellular performance, would serve to rejuvenate the recipients, rendering them biologically more youthful, even as they gather years in a chronological sense. As new advances are developed, de Grey supposes that patients would periodically visit clinics to receive the latest therapies and to repeat those they had utilized in the past, thereby continually bumping the biological clock back in time. His confidence that realistic headway could be made in postponing aging arises largely from his conviction that there are only a limited set of categories of change that occur in the human body to contribute to its usual and, until now, relentless decline (de Grey *et al.* 2002). Hence, as solutions are found to mitigate each of these limited types of problems, people will repeatedly be restored to a more youthful state of health, even as they grow older chronologically.

One of the most fascinating dimensions of de Grey's thought is embodied in his concept of longevity escape velocity (de Grey 2004). Assuming fairly conservative rates of scientific advancement, he shows that some people alive today can be expected to live dramatically extended lifetimes, perhaps hundreds of years long, or even indefinite. All this requires, he says, is that in the next few decades, therapies are developed that repair some types of damage such that individuals can be made to live, on average, another thirty years. The realistic nature of this claim is evident for those who have already lived long enough to see lifespans prolonged across a broad range of the public. This trajectory of therapeutic effectiveness would mean that, by the time such a person had once again drawn closer to the new expected time of death, further developments would have come along to extend their anticipated lifespan all over again. Although some people would continue to die of accidents, murders, wars, and other causes, a subset of the population would continue to enjoy the healthy lives of the physically vital. While such people would not attain immortality *per se*, he asserts that radically extended lives would become practical realities for many people.

de Grey is as optimistic about the prospects for the advances in longevity science that would make this vision possible as he is about the likelihood that society will make the decisions and allocate the resources needed to bring it into reality. In Chapter 48 in this volume, he remarks, "If something can be done, and a lot of people badly want it to be done, it eventually will be done." Elsewhere, de Grey concludes that "defeating aging – and progressively defeating other causes of death too – is God's work" and ought to be pursued as a moral imperative (de Grey 2009). He describes these biomedical advances as inevitable.

The reactions of the world's major religions are likely to be quite diverse, and we get a foreshadowing of this in a recent collection of responses from adherents of the major religions (Maher and Mercer 2009). It seems that suspicion of technologies aiming to extend human life radically is at its most acute among the Abrahamic religions (Judaism, Christianity, and Islam), although opinions among the adherents of each religion assuredly vary as well. A number of religions that emerged in Asia, in contrast, include narratives, doctrines, and practices that embrace the possibility of physical immortality, or at least extreme longevity. Daoist sages are said to have achieved immortality in the past, and their paradigms continue to animate contemporary practice. Hindus and Buddhists employ yogic, tantric, and other techniques intended to realize extreme longevity (*ibid.*).

Buddhists in particular have long maintained an array of beliefs that humans lived dramatically enduring lives long in the distant past. Based on canonical texts, it has been maintained that human beings on the continent of Jambudvīpa – the area of the world system that humans are thought to occupy even still – used to live to the age of 1000 years, but that this number has been diminishing by virtue of the corruption of our time, the decline of the moral virtue of humans, and cosmic forces. Eventually, it is maintained, human lifespans will reach a low point of a mere ten years before they begin to increase again in the future (Pruden 1988: Vol. 2). Relatedly, Buddhist cosmological accounts assert that there is an enormous variance in the lifespans of other beings born within cyclic existence (*saṃsāra*), which consists of the Desire Realm, the Form Realm, and the Formless Realm. Among the six levels of the Desire Realm, many hell beings, hungry ghosts, gods, and jealous gods live very long lives, ranging into the tens of thousands of years. It is only humans and animals that live the comparatively brief lives with which we are familiar. According to the sources, beings in the Form Realm and beings in the Formless Realm – the latter class lack a physical body – can live for hundreds of millions of years (Lati Rinbochay *et al.* 1983).

Thus it is generally accepted among Buddhists in a traditional context that the duration of normal lifespans might be significantly variable, for humans and indeed all sentient beings. This attitude has meant that Buddhists have been more disposed towards believing in radically extended lives, and more active in pursuing them, than advocates of many other major religions. Some Buddhists have felt motivated to seek greatly prolonged lifetimes while in a human form. For example, many practitioners of Vajrayana Buddhism propitiate White Tárā, a female bodhisattva who is thought to bestow a variety of blessings, including a long life. Others endeavor to extend their lives through medical practices, and there are several distinct forms of medical practice that appear throughout the Buddhist world, each embedded in Buddhist ideology, language, and narratives. Purificatory practices are thought to be beneficial in the quest for long life, both by removing medical impediments to good health and in cleansing one's *karma*; the distinction I make between these two categories here is for the sake of explanation and would be less natural within traditional Buddhist contexts.

In broad terms, it is felt by most Buddhists that the term of one's life is partly defined by the combination of the positive and negative actions (*karma*) one has accumulated throughout previous lifetimes through performing beneficial or detrimental actions. However, it is maintained that behavior in the present lifetime can also impact the duration of this life. Thus, in explanatory comments accompanying a ritual intended to prolong the human lifetime, Lama Zopa Rinpoche described some of the actions that could be expected to have such a result:

> You could live longer if you did the methods to purify, to purify the obstacles, purify the negative karma, so the various means to have long life, to prolong the life, reciting long-life mantras or reading texts or the long-life tsa-tsas making, long-life deities' thangka or tsa-tsa, liberating animals or even, not only animals but also helping people, people who are sick and people who need food and shelter, however, medicines, helping those people, serving people, taking care of people, old people, sick people, those are also for long life, cause of long life (Zopa Rinpoche 2009).[1]

Lama Zopa is declaring that meritorious actions can extend life by mitigating negative *karma* that would otherwise cut one's lifetime short. Most commonly, however, the idea of living radically long lives comes up for Buddhists in the context of a future incarnation in another form, rather than while in a human form. It is asserted that the advanced cultivation by human beings of certain meditative practices, called the concentrations and the formless absorptions, can lead to a rebirth as a god in the Form and Formless Realms, mentioned above (Lati Rinbochay *et al.* 1983). Through familiarizing the mind with such cognitive patterns in this lifetime, a being can predispose their mind stream to take on that form in the next life. Once reborn in these two upper realms, beings can remain utterly focused on advancing towards Buddhahood.

In other contexts, advocates of Pure Land Buddhism recite aspirational prayers in the hopes that they will be reborn in Sukhāvatī Heaven, the special realm inhabited by the Buddha called Amitābha (Infinite Light) or Amitāyus (Infinite Life). Practitioners of Pure Land devotionalism, which is most prominent among East Asian Buddhists, perceive the world as so corrupted and in decline that they consider it particularly difficult to gain enlightenment in the here and now; hence they feel their quest for the realization of their status as a Buddha can meet with success only if they take rebirth in the presence of a Buddha. Once there, the key Pure Land sūtras report, practitioners will have a far easier time making the sort of spiritual progress they seek because Sukhāvatī Heaven is an ideal realm blessed with all sorts of special characteristics that make it perfect for spiritual practice. For example, the voices of all the birds proclaim Buddhist virtues, and the tinkling bells that fill the Pure Land serve only to remind beings of the Buddha.

Amitābha Buddha, who realized his own enlightenment in part through an aspirational vow in the past, grants his devotees entry to his heavenly realm by virtue of their solemn and earnest commitment to him. When they are born into his heaven, they come under his protection. As a result of these factors, Pure Land devotees claim, they will be certain never to be reborn again. Instead, they will experience radically prolonged lives in which they are under the tutelage of Amitābha himself, and the 100 billion buddhas and bodhisattvas who attend him. With such potent guidance in such an idealized environment, it is believed, they are certain to attain Buddhahood themselves (Gomez 1996).

In broad terms, then, Buddhists are open to the concepts of radically prolonged lives, they employ practices directed to attaining them, and they hope to achieve long lives, either as humans or in their next lives in Pure Lands or other high realms. But what justification would a Buddhist offer for seeking a dramatically prolonged life? After all, aren't Buddhists supposed to be unattached to their body, the self, and the affairs of this life? Wouldn't an attachment to their own body be the very height of the materialism so thoroughly critiqued by the Buddha and subsequent generations?

For Buddhists, the spiritual path is a process that unfolds over numerous lifetimes, and each particular sort of rebirth presents characteristic opportunities and challenges in the quest for the perfection they seek. If in one particular lifetime, a practitioner is able to overcome afflictive emotions, desist from negative and harmful behavior, serve other beings, engage in meritorious activities, and cultivate wisdom – in short, if the being is able to employ their lifetime to achieve the goals of Buddhism – then that being would be regarded as living a life that would advance their progress towards Buddhahood. It would be thought among Buddhists that such a being, therefore, should seek to prolong that lifetime in whatever fashion they could. Ritual practices, supplicatory prayers, or indeed biomedical interventions would all be regarded as legitimate and commendable routes to that worthy objective (Maher 2009).

On the other hand, if some being was living a selfish life dedicated to harming others, or was otherwise squandering the rare and precious human lifetime[2] they had achieved, no similar urgency for longevity would be felt. Moreover, if, in a given lifetime, some being was living a malevolent and harmful life and they could reasonably be expected to continue harming others, generating negative *karma* for themselves, it has – in some highly specialized circumstances – occasionally been argued that it might be meritorious to terminate that being's life as an act of mercy for the person committing such wrongs. Thereby, that harmful being would be compassionately preserved from generating more negative *karma* that would enslave them in negative rebirths in the future (Maher 2008). In sum, Buddhists do not value long lives in their own right, but only if they are directed at achieving other salutary goals. In contrast, de Grey seems to value prolonged lifetimes as an intrinsic good.

Clearly, through their common advocacy of longevity, bridges of agreement and understanding could be built between some of the Buddhists described above and de Grey. However, there are a variety of points on which they would part company. For example, de Grey would find few Buddhists who agree with his mechanistic conception of the body. His observation above that "the human body is undoubtedly a machine" would be met with much skepticism, both by Buddhist philosophers and within Buddhist medical traditions. Tibetan medicine, for example, which is based in both Indian Aryavedic and Chinese medical systems and is animated by Buddhist tantric and yogic models, would reject the mechanistic view of the body and the mind–body dualism in which that viewpoint is embedded. Instead, Tibetan medicine is a holistic blending of ritual practices, the utterance of prayers, psychiatrically acute insights, mysticism, and an exceptionally diverse and highly effective pharmacopeia. The physician, who would traditionally have been a monk as well, treats the patient as a complete person, addressing their emotional lives and their spiritual progress in addition to their physical well-being (Clifford 1994 [1984]), and their treatments are based on the assumption that some dimensions of illness, healing, and well-being transcend merely physical mechanisms. Buddhist longevity practices, in particular, move beyond the strictly physical realm, relying upon contemplative visualization practices, the recitation of mantras, and the manipulation of yogic physiology.

Moreover, Aubrey de Grey's views on the practicality and advisability of longevity science reflect a world-view that is culturally embedded and conditioned by presumptions that are sometimes quite Western, sometimes quite "first world," and often both. These facts lead him to see the role of science and the relationship between science and religion in a narrow form that claims a universality it does not possess. He supposes that longevity therapies, and biomedicine in general, are both (1) driven primarily by rational market forces, and (2) ought to be supported by religious people since they would "save lives, just as holy scripture seems rather unanimously to advise we do" (de Grey 2009). He seems to believe that, since therapies that combat aging would save lives, and since religious traditions all advocate saving lives, religious people should all automatically be in favor of these therapies that radically extend life. Yet this line of argument fails to address the real situation in which we find ourselves.

While there is universal access to healthcare in many industrialized nations, within the United States, tens of millions of people lack access to basic medical care due to being uninsured, a situation that may be remedied to an extent with evolving healthcare policy debates still unfolding in early 2010. However, in many developing nations, there is not even a question of universal access to medical care. Instead, people are more concerned with a lack of food security, clean water, basic sanitation, or the most rudimentary medical care. Recently, the United Nations estimates that 25,000 people die of hunger or hunger-related causes each day, and nearly a billion people suffer from malnourishment or hunger (Holmes 2008). In many places in the world, people lack access to early twentieth-century medical technologies.

Already, in the present time, the very poor lack access to cheap and cost-effective measures to purify drinking water; despite the low cost, hundreds of millions of people are still not able to buy simple antibiotics. The disparities between the world's wealthy and the very poor are such that some people are profligate consumers of medical care, food, energy, and other natural resources, while others have only very limited access to these things. So this is not just some speculation on the future cost curve of expensive gene therapies. It is already evident that a very large number of the world's poor will not have access to twenty-first-century innovations.

Thus, if religious people are uniformly driven by their scriptures to preserve lives in the abstract, as de Grey supposes, they may seek to do so by alleviating the relatively inexpensive needs of the many, rather than endorsing for a comparatively small number of wealthy people the provision of costly procedures that divert the limited attentions of medical researchers and providers. This is likely to be particularly true for Buddhists, since that religion prevails in places where there are a lot of poor people. Similar things could be said about Hindus, Muslims, and others. In Chapter 48 in this volume, de Grey remarks, "Sophisticated medicine is expensive to administer, and – essentially by definition – it always will be." Meanwhile, the United Nations Conference on Trade and Development has defined the level of poverty as the condition of living on less than two dollars a day, and extreme poverty as the condition of living on less than a dollar a day (Blount 2002). Given these fiscal realities, it is unlikely that many Buddhists, religious people in general, or ethicists, for that matter, would be induced to advocate for radical life extension as a means to save the lives of their fellow humans. There would be far more effective and efficient ways of achieving that result than by providing expensive therapies to the privileged. So, while de Grey may be correct that the development of such therapies is inevitable, I would argue that most religious people would not be motivated to support those expenditures, at least not on the basis of the argument that it would be the best way to save lives.

The actual conditions experienced by people outside of the highly industrialized wealthy countries seem absent from his narrative. His account fundamentally has meaning only when considered in the context of those dwelling in the technologically advanced lands of western Europe and the United States, in addition to a few localized populations in other parts of the world, such as Japan. For the vast majority of people in the world, the basic conditions of poverty mean that any discussion of spending money to radically extend the lives of the citizenry makes no sense at all. The people who find themselves on the unfortunate side of this issue include almost all Buddhists in the world. Throughout most such poor lands, nobody is wondering about how to allocate medical resources when, as de Grey would have it (Chapter 48), "Geriatric medicine goes head-to-head for funding against specialties that benefit the young". In the bleak world of the very poor, the lottery of poverty sorts out who will make it to the age of five, and something they would consider to be a radical extension of life would be achieved by the utilization of the World Health Organization's immunization protocols and the boiling of water, thereby increasing lifespans from the thirties into the sixties. Similarly, for a large percentage of the world's people, "calorie restriction" is not a method they choose consciously with the objective of extending their lifespans, as de Grey describes at length; it is a consequence of the food insecurity or outright starvation that threatens to abbreviate their lives, much against their will. The issues of social justice and universal access to medical care remain the most vexing unanswered questions to be resolved by de Grey and his colleagues.

As a religion scholar, I cannot claim a position from which to adjudicate de Grey's scientific claims, and he returns the favor by pointing out that he lacks the training to provide insight as anything more than what he calls a "recreational theologian" (de Grey 2009). In that capacity, de Grey remarks in Chapter 48 in this volume:

> Theologians and religious thinkers, like any group tasked with developing thinking and/or policy in relation to the society of the future, are therefore duty-bound to apply themselves to this question: partly to the issue of whether we should seek to hasten the postponement of aging; and partly to the issue of how to manage it when it inevitably occurs whether they like it or not.

He further glosses the scholars he hopes to inform as being engaged in a theological and philosophical debate.

It will be instructive to distinguish between the scholarship that is undertaken by theologians and scholars of religious studies, a difference that is not evident in de Grey's comments on the use of science by religion scholars. As these terms are employed in the United States, scholars engaged in the discipline of religious studies attend to a critical examination of the ways in which religious adherents create meaning for themselves and live within the matrices of narrative, doctrinal, ritual, and other dimensions that constitute their religion. Their work is descriptive rather than prescriptive. In contrast, theologians are believers within a tradition who inhabit the world-view they are engaged in studying and accept the truth claims the religion makes for itself. Some Europeans employ the word "theologian" for both of these distinct roles, and it may be that this lack of clarity in terminology has induced de Grey to presume religion scholars have an active role to play in the development of social attitudes. As the terms are employed in the United States, scholars of religious studies are not tasked with developing policy intended to shape the future, although some theologians may play a role like that. Instead, scholars of religious studies see themselves as primarily engaged in descriptive analysis of previous or current religious phenomena. It is only occasionally, as in a book I recently edited, and to which de Grey contributed a chapter (Maher and Mercer 2009), that such scholars can be induced to adopt a speculative posture about future developments.

The fact is that Aubrey de Grey, as chairman of the Methuselah Foundation and an innovative scientist at the bleeding edge of developments in life-prolonging therapies, is probably correct. Biomedical developments that make it possible for people to live radically longer lives probably are inevitable, just as advances in the twentieth century lengthened the average lifespan and prevented many childhood diseases for most people in the world. The appeal of these new technologies probably means that they will be funded, just as complex and expensive heart and brain surgeries came into common use in industrialized nations in recent decades.

It is also probably inevitable that individual people will come to grapple with these developments in diverse personal ways that they couch within their values and world-views, both religious and otherwise. Indeed, this process has already begun. As some of those sundry views gain currency and earn broader acceptance, they will come to be integrated within particular existing ideological structures, including religious traditions. As this unfolds, such phenomena will come under the scrutiny of scholars of religious studies, and they will write and publish critical appraisals of how people are making religious sense out of the new science.

In contrast to the notion that science and religion are in competition, the two domains appear to be in a dynamic conversation; reflective people on either side of the divide ponder how the other's approach to truth might foster a broader and more coherent account of the world. It is evident that de Grey seeks to advance that dialogue. While many Buddhists would likely take issue with the specific points raised by de Grey, as I have endeavored to outline above, there is a strong basis for such an ongoing conversation. Many contemporary Buddhists are, in fact, quite fascinated with science. This is partly because of the importance of theories of causation within Buddhism, and also because many intellectuals regard the tradition as non-dogmatic. The present Dalai Lama, for example, continually engages with physicians, physicists, brain scientists, and others as he seeks to learn things that will inform his own religious outlook. Many scientists, likewise, seem interested in exploring how religious traditions might help them to complicate some of their own unproven assumptions about the world. It is a discussion worth having.

Notes

1 *Tsa-tsas* are small relief images of Buddhas or bodhisattvas. *Thangkas* are scroll paintings of sacred images.

2 A human lifetime is considered to be the one most suitable for spiritual practice. Humans have enough intelligence to reflect meaningfully on their lives, and enough suffering that they bother to make a priority of developing themselves through religious practice. The human lifetime is therefore regarded as precious. It is thought to be rare because it takes much good *karma* to be reborn as a human being, and it is so difficult to gain that good *karma* in the other states of cyclic existence. Thus one should make the most of having become a human being.

References

Blount, Elizabeth (2002) "UN Prices Poverty at Two Dollars," *BBC News, World Edition*, June 18, http://news.bbc.co.uk/2/hi/2052187.stm.

Clifford, T. (1994 [1984]) *Tibetan Buddhist Medicine and Psychiatry: The Diamond Healing*, Newburyport, MA: Samuel Weiser; reprinted Delhi: Motilal Banarsidass.

de Grey, A. D. N. J. (2004) "Escape Velocity: Why the Prospect of Extreme Human Life Extension Matters Now," *PLoS Biology* 2(6): 723–26.

——(2009) "Radical Life Extension: Technological Aspects," in D.F. Maher and C. Mercer (eds), *Religion and the Implications of Radical Life Extension*, New York: Palgrave Macmillan, 13–24.

de Grey, A. D. N. J., B. N. Ames, J. K. Andersen, A. Bartke, J. Campisi, C. B. Heward, R. J. M. McCarter and G. Stock (2002) "Time to Talk SENS: Critiquing the Immutability of Human Aging," *Annals of the New York Academy of Sciences* 959: 452–62.

Gomez, L. O. (1996) *The Land of the Bliss: The Paradise of the Buddha of Measureless Light*, Delhi: Motilal Banarsidass.
Holmes, J. (2008) "Losing 25,000 People to Hunger Every Day," *UN Chronicle Online*, www.un.org/wcm/content/site/chronicle/lang/en/home/archive.
Lati Rinbochay, Denma Locho Rinbochay, Leah Zahler and Jeffrey Hopkins (1983) *Meditative States in Tibetan Buddhism*, London: Wisdom Publications.
Maher, D. F. (2008) "The Rhetoric of War in Tibet: Towards a Buddhist Just War Theory," *Political Theology* 9(2): 179–91.
——(2009) "Two Wings of a Bird: Radical Life Extension from a Buddhist Perspective," in *Religion and the Implications of Radical Life Extension*, D.F. Maher and C. Mercer (eds), New York: Palgrave Macmillan, 111–21.
Maher, D. F. and Mercer, C. (eds) (2009) *Religion and the Implications of Radical Life Extension*, New York: Palgrave Macmillan.
Pruden, L. M. (1988) *Abhidharmakośabhāṣyam*, four volumes, Berkeley, CA: Asian Humanities Press.
Zopa Rinpoche, Lama (2009) "Talk at Long-Life Puja," www.lamayeshe.com/index.php?sect=article&id=594.

Further reading

For accounts of the likely reactions of major religions of the world to biomedical advances that radically prolong life, see Derek F. Maher and Calvin Mercer, eds, *Religion and the Implications of Radical Life Extension* (cited above). This collection of essays includes one by Aubrey de Grey, one from another scientist, and various chapters written by scholars of particular religions. Calvin Mercer, my colleague and co-editor of that collection, maintains a comprehensive and updated bibliography of sources on the scientific and social dimensions of radical life extension at www.ecu.edu/religionprogram/mercer.

50
COSMIC ALIVENESS
Nurturing life in the Daoist tradition

Livia Kohn

The current scientific view on aging, as outlined in Chapter 48 in this volume, is that it happens by default, as a form of natural entropy that affects everything. In other words, nothing lasts forever – things decay, affairs decline, trees wither, people age. It occurs gradually, as the metabolism slows and changes, eventually giving rise to pathology. However, this process can be retarded and, with more scientific progress, in the long run maybe even prevented, leading not only to long life, but to immortality.

Retardation of the aging process at this stage can occur at several points: by working with the metabolism before the onset of pathology (preventive medicine); by diagnosing and repairing the damage done after pathologies have manifested (geriatric medicine); or at the junction when the metabolism first starts to develop pathologies (regenerative medicine). The likelihood is that Western societies, driven by economic needs to reduce expenditure for the infirm and an overall cultural refusal to deal with issues until they have become blatantly obvious and scream for attention, will work with the second and third models, leaving the intervention rather late. They will also most likely continue to work dominantly with the biomedical model that sees the body as a mere machine, and use massively invasive methods, such as radical calorie restriction, massive injections of human growth hormone, and/or the cloning of organs to be ready for implantation as and when the old ones give out. All this, of course, does not deal with untimely death through accidents, violence, or suicide – which are really not issues of aging, but problems of fate and a general social inadequacy.

Aging postponed

The key questions raised in Chapter 48, then, are: (1) Should aging be postponed?, and (2) How do we manage once it is postponed? To that I might add, from the Daoist perspective: (3) What is the best way of going about this postponement?

The answer to the first question is moot, aging already is being postponed more every year, so that a child born in an industrialized society today has a life expectancy of well over 100 years, and rising. There has also been a long-standing advocacy for the radical extension of life by the so-called immortalists, a group of scientists who believe that old age is a disease to be cured and that human beings, with the help of genetic engineering and medical techniques, can live for several hundred years. The immortalist movement began in the 1960s with Wilson Ettinger, a professor of physics at the University of Michigan, who was injured in the Second World War. Hospitalized for three years, he had ample opportunity to confront his death and decided that he wanted to live forever, then set out to find the means to do so. He wrote *The Prospect of Immortality* (Ettinger 1964) to outline his vision, thereby beginning a cultural trend that is still flourishing. Today, after Ettinger's passing, this trend is most prominently represented by Alan Harrington, author of *The Immortalist* (1969).

The immortalists' argument against the naturalness of old age and death grows from the continuous increase in life expectancy over the past millennia. After all, in ancient Greece people on average only lived for twenty-two years, and even 100 years ago the median life expectancy was forty-six, as opposed to the eighties in industrialized countries today. Of course, these numbers reflect a high infant mortality rate in earlier centuries, and individuals even in traditional cultures made it to sixty, seventy, or eighty. But this does not deny the fact that people today live longer and stay young into older years, and that the fastest-growing segment of the population in the industrialized world are the centenarians – in the UK, Queen Elizabeth II, who writes a personal note to every one of her subjects who celebrates his or her 100th birthday, wrote only about 300 cards a year just twenty years ago. Now she, or rather her staff, have to send out several thousand annually, and the numbers are rising – leading, potentially, to the demise of the practice.

Immortalists, bolstered by these statistics, embrace the idea is that there is an inbuilt clock of aging in every person. They strive to discover its location and mechanism, then work to slow it down or stop it altogether. The recent mapping of the human genome has given them much support, as have studies on human growth hormones, the effect of very low-calorie diets on mice and men, and the increasing health benefits of work-outs in Western society. Immortalists hope to see everyone attain a very long life and eventually grow into immortality. They argue that survival is a key feature of nature; that the death of cells is very slow, and can and should be slowed down even more.

Addressing the second question above, the immortalists make long-lived people part of normality as they see our entire society growing into advanced old age of as many as several hundred years, finding this a very positive development, indeed. After all, with people living longer and remaining youthful and active, wouldn't the problems of the planet and society stand a much better chance of solution, considering that people will be around long enough to see the disastrous impact of present-day decisions? Wouldn't there be more balanced moral values, since people living for long periods would have to realize that doing things that are good for oneself had better also benefit others? Wouldn't people take fewer risks and move with more caution, since they would have so much more life to lose? And wouldn't we all have so much more fun, so much more freedom, and a great deal less urgency to get things done?

These attitude changes aside, a longer-lived population, as we are already starting to experience, at least in the short run, means a drastic increase in population. More pollution, diminishing resources, less social security money, retirement benefits stretched to the limit. Except, of course, that retirement wouldn't happen at sixty-five or seventy any more, people would work far into their eighties and nineties – taking jobs away from younger folks who, too, expect to have *very* long and fruitful careers. The latter, come to think of it, could be eased by creating a whole new life cycle: be young and in education for the first sixty years (attend college for ten or twenty years instead of four), go to work for the next sixty, and spend another sixty in retirement – or any number of years: eighty, 100, 200.

Society would change. With so much time to live, people would not have one or two families, but – given the divorce rate – three or four, adding enormous complexity to relationships and family structures. In the longer run, birth control would become essential, and new arrivals on the planet would have to be strictly limited, bringing society into a state of managed care, as described in Aldous Huxley's *Brave New World* with its official predestinators, and as already practiced in Communist China, where couples have to have a permit to get pregnant. At the other end of life, with people not dying naturally any more, exit strategies would need to be developed, as again is already happening through various end-of-life organizations such as Final Exit Network in the USA and Dignitas in Switzerland. After all, it is always possible that someone, even presented with the opportunity to go on forever, might not want to and needs a way out. Or that society, following the model of some prehistoric groups described in myths and tales, makes the decision for them: you've been around long enough, time to make room. Whether it's an automatic death sentence at a certain age, or a form of euthanasia by sifting out weaker and less productive specimens, death would have to be controlled – or, in the case of true immortality, birth would have to be prohibited.

Immortalists are not scared by these scenarios. They claim that consciousness will adjust to the new realities and develop new standards. People will grow older while remaining healthier, they will work longer years and be more productive, and methods of replacing body parts, cloning oneself, and deep-freezing the body until science is ready for the new you will happen anyway as research goes on. We are on the fast track to radical life extension and immortality, and nothing will stop us. How, then, to come back to the third question: What is the best way of going about it? This is where the Daoists have most to offer.

The Daoist take

Daoists are very much immortalists, and have traditionally embraced the firm conviction not only that aging is unnecessary, but also that a longer-lived and even immortal society will be beneficial for the planet and is ultimately the only true way to live. To this end they have created a complex vision of the energetic functioning of the body, which sees it as identical with the greater universe through a bio-energy known as *qi*.

Qi is the foundational energy of the universe, the basic stuff of Dao, the life force in the human body, and the basis of all physical vitality. Tangible in sensations and pulses, visible as vapor and breath, audible in sighs and sounds, it is what we are as physical, embodied beings. Yet it is also the material energy of Dao, the underlying force of the greater universe, the power that makes things happen in the cosmos. The body consists essentially of this cosmic *qi*, which is only one but comes in two major forms: a basic primordial or prenatal *qi* that is received in limited amounts at birth and connects people to the cosmos; and a secondary, earthly or postnatal *qi* that is replenished by breathing, food, and human interaction, and helps the body survive in everyday life. Both forms of *qi* are necessary and interact constantly with each other, so that primordial *qi* is lost as and when earthly *qi* is insufficient, and earthly *qi* becomes superfluous as and when primordial *qi* is complete – as is the case with the embryo in the womb (see Kaptchuk 1983).

People, once born, start an interchange of the two dimensions of *qi*, and soon begin to lose their primordial *qi* as they interact with the world and acquire a tendency toward shallow breathing, improper nutrition, emotional outbursts, sensory overloads, and intellectual tensions. All these are signs of wayward *qi* (*xieqi*), when *qi* has become disorderly and dysfunctional and creates change that violates the cosmic order, no longer supporting the dynamic forces of change. In this state, the *qi*-flow can turn upon itself and deplete the body's resources. The individual loses his or her connection to the universe, no longer operates as part of a greater system, and is increasingly out of tune with the basic life force. This, in due course, results in irritation: mental irritation that appears as negative emotions, and physical irritation that shows up as metabolic dysfunction and bodily discomfort, and eventually leads to pathologies and aging (Kohn 2005: 12).

In the face of this, Daoists propose radical prevention. They claim that it is possible to keep primordial *qi* intact by reaching and maintaining a state of "proper *qi*" (*zhengqi*), that is, a strong vital energy and a smooth and harmonious interaction with the world. The ideal is to have *qi* flow freely, creating harmony in the body and a balanced state of being in the person, which in turn radiates into nature, where proper *qi* means regular weather patterns and the absence of disasters, and into society, where it is the peaceful coexistence among all social units – in other words, the state of Great Peace.

To reach this state, it is essential to catch the harmful tendencies as they emerge, intervening with medical means (acupuncture, massages, diets, herbs) a long time before any acute illness manifests itself. Individuals and physicians are thus trained to spot the initial signs of an illness, which may still be very subtle and perceived merely as a slight irregularity. Only if these are not treated do specific symptoms appear, which cause physical discomfort and disruption of life's activities. They require a more serious intervention and longer-term treatment plus major changes in lifestyle. The third level of disease – the actual appearance of aging – in this understanding is a complex syndrome, a more encompassing pattern of disharmony that has taken over the individual's life. Daoists make great efforts to never even get close to this stage, catching irregularities before they have a chance to make any serious inroads.

Having attained good health and vitality by restoring the patterns of proper *qi*, Daoists further retard the aging process and extend life by increasing primordial *qi* to the level they had at birth and even above it. To do so, they follow a slew of so-called longevity techniques (see below) to control their *qi*-exchange with the environment and cultivate their physical and mental integrity.

Going beyond long life, the ultimate goal of Daoists is immortality, which raises the practices to a higher level, working to refine *qi* to ever subtler levels until all *qi* has become primordial. This *qi* eventually turns into pure spirit, with which practitioners increasingly identify to become transcendent beings. The path there goes beyond ordinary physicality and involves intensive meditation and trance training as well as more radical forms of diet and exercise. Immortality implies the overcoming of the natural tendencies of the body and its transformation into a different kind of *qi*-constellation. The result is a bypassing of death, so that even the end of the body has no impact on the continuation of the spirit-person. Rather than the mere retardation of the aging process, which is achieved on the longevity level, this implies the overcoming of the human condition as we know it and the unfolding of a celestial, otherworldly dimension (Kohn 2005: 5).

Immortality stands behind much of Daoist practice, but other than for theoretical appreciation, it is neither necessary nor particularly helpful if one is mainly interested in radical life extension. What really makes a major difference to one's enjoyment of life and the retardation of the aging process – as has been experienced by generations of Daoists and can be seen in practitioners of *taiji quan* and *qigong* even today – is the serious, continued practice of the various longevity techniques.

Longevity techniques

To actively attain a state of proper *qi*-flow and prevent aging and decline, Daoists over the millennia have developed a plethora of so-called longevity techniques (*yangsheng*) which address the issue at the metabolic and thus preventive level, and assure that one lives for an extended span and attains old age while yet remaining full of vigor.

Body cultivation

Their first demand is that one should live in close adaptation to the natural cycles of day and night and the changes of the seasons. The fourth-century *Yangsheng yaoji* (*Essential Compendium on Nourishing Life*) notes:

> The method of nourishing life consists mainly in not doing harm to oneself. Keep warm in winter and cool in summer, and never lose your harmony with the four seasons – that is how you can align yourself with the body. Do not allow sensuous beauty, provocative postures, easy leisure, and enticing entertainments to incite yearnings and desires – that is how you pervade all.
>
> (Kohn 2008: 70)

The most important advice for the beginning practitioner is to remain moderate in everything, since any excess will harm the inner organs: to eat and drink with control, to stay away from various luxuries that lead to a weakness of *qi*, and to keep speech and laughter within limits. In other words, no stress – sound familiar?

On the basis of a healthy and well adjusted lifestyle, practitioners then conform to a Daoist diet, which essentially means eating moderately (never to complete satiation) and in natural balance by partaking of all the different food groups, matching foods to the seasons, and supplementing regular foodstuffs with herbal and mineral substances. Over time they wean themselves from solid food, replacing it with raw vegetables, fruits, and nuts – not unlike some extreme low-calorie diets today, but without the radicality: Daoists move back and forth between lesser and heavier diets as their internal energy and social context demands. Yet they also may increase herbal supplements, liquid nourishment, and internal guiding of *qi* – the Daoist equivalent to growth hormone treatments – to the point where they no longer need food but live entirely on *qi*. This process is called "abstention from grain" (*bigu*). It lightens the body's structure in favor of subtler energies and cosmic awareness (see Arthur 2006; Kohn 2010).

Another way of opening and lightening the body is through healing exercises (*daoyin*), first outlined in medical manuscripts of the second century BCE, then adapted and expanded by Daoists. Not unlike yoga and *qigong* increasingly practiced in modern societies, these exercises consist of slow movements and careful stretches combined with deep breathing and conscious awareness. Releasing stress, alleviating heaviness, aiding digestion, and improving circulation, they open the energy channels, balance yin and yang, and activate a subtler dimension of being (Kohn 2008).

To sublimate the body's energies further, Daoists also engage in breathing techniques without body movements. For example, they exhale with specific lip positions and throat movements that release tensions from the inner organs, balance heat and cold, and enhance oxygen absorption. This is known as the Six Healing Sounds. They also hold the breath for several minutes to allow pulsation to slow and the heart to rest. And they practice "guiding *qi*," which involves breathing in deeply, mixing the breath with saliva, then swallowing it and directing it to different parts of the body. All this helps to develop another level of energetic awareness, nourish the organs, and open the energy channels (Despeux 2006).

Beyond all this, there is also the refinement of sexual energy or essence (*jing*). Emerging from the body's primordial *qi*, it is present in people from birth in limited amounts and centers in the Ocean of *Qi* (abdomen) in men and in the Cavern of *Qi* (chest) in women. Essence governs the kidneys and reproductive organs as well as the bones, marrow, teeth, brain, and body energy; it easily diminishes through sexual engagements. As a result, both medical and Daoist practitioners conserve the stock they have and replenish what is lost.

People conserve essence by limiting the frequency of its loss through ejaculation and menstruation, as well as by using massage techniques that keep the *qi* flowing. They replenish it by working on its "return" or "reversion" into primordial *qi* with the help of both partner and solo practices. These involve developing a state of excitement and then, instead of allowing the *jing* to flow out of the body, mentally and with the help of self-massages make it move up along the spine and into the head, guiding it along a cycle within the torso (microcosmic orbit) and thus enhancing vitality (Wik and Wik 2005; Winn 2006).

Meditation

Meditation is the inward focus of attention while ego-related concerns and critical evaluation are suspended in favor of perceiving a deeper, subtler, and possibly divine flow of consciousness. It is an essential tool not only for stress control and bodily integrity – as well known these days – but also to create the mind-set necessary for the more global responsibility and vision that comes with extended life. Daoists engage in all the classical forms of meditation, notably concentration, observation, and visualization.

Concentration is one-pointedness of mind. It involves complete control of attention and the absorption in a single object – a sound, a visual diagram, a concrete entity, or the breath – with the goal of calming the mind and quieting internal chatter. Daoists focus on breathing or the inner flow of *qi* and strive to gain a mental centering, a withdrawal of the senses, and a reduction of mental input. The goal is to reach a deep, calm quietude and thus a profound alignment with the natural transformations.

Observation – also called insight, mindfulness, or awareness meditation – encourages openness to all sorts of stimuli and leads to a sense of free-flowing awareness. It works through the detached apperception of physical sensations and sensory reactions. Daoists use this practice to see the body as a microcosmic replica of the starry heavens above, full of palaces and chambers, gods and deities. This cosmic body, moreover, is governed by the force of spirit – primordial, formless, and ever-changing – which works through the human mind and governs life perfectly. Instead of trying to follow sensory impressions, make judgments, and develop critical evaluations, Daoists practice to release from all stress and tension, rest in their original cosmic nature, and let the spirit guide them (Kohn 1989).

Visualization is the most common form of Daoist meditation. It involves complete mental focus on a specific scene or sequence of events, such as energy flows, deities, cosmic patterns, saints' lives, or potential future events. The scenes are either seen with detachment or involve the participation of the practitioner. In either case, visualization opens consciousness to subtler levels, allowing the unconscious to manifest and bringing new dimensions to life.

Also called creative imagination, visualization is an important method used today in a variety of contexts, from sports training to business presentations. In the Daoist world, it is called "actualization and imagination," and applies both internally and externally, that is, it serves as a form of intensified concentration to enhance the health and empowerment of the body, and also as a means to travel ecstatically to the otherworld and engage with the deities. Early visualization involved seeing lights of different colors in the body, matching the energies of the five phases with their directions and related inner organs.

An expanded version appeared in the middle ages as "Absorbing the Five Sprouts," the subtle, germinal energies of the five directions. After some purification and preparation, practitioners seat themselves to face a certain direction, then visualize its color, for example green in the east or yellow in the center. A general mist in the beginning, it gradually forms into a ball, like the rising Sun, then, through further concentration, shrinks in size and comes closer to the adept.

Eventually the size of a pill, the sprout can be swallowed and guided to the corresponding organ (green to the liver, yellow to the spleen). A suitable incantation anchors it firmly, and gradually the body is infused with cosmic energy.

The most advanced form of Daoist visualization is ecstatic excursions, an adaptation of shamanic soul travel. In trance, practitioners envision themselves taking a tour around the far reaches of the Earth, then move on to imitate the planets' movements, especially of the Sun and the Moon. Eventually they reach out to visit the higher spheres of heaven, where they engage with gods and immortals to learn cosmic secrets and receive instructions. Becoming more divine, they turn into denizens of the otherworld, often finding their heavenly life more real than their existence on Earth and thus preparing for life in their permanent celestial abode. Transition to the latter, moreover, in the middle ages was often achieved by taking an immortality elixir (*dan*, cinnabar), a divinely inspired but highly poisonous brew of arsenic and mercury. Called ritual suicide by some, it was a method of transcendence for Daoists, and can be considered the precursor of modern exit strategies (Robinet 1989).

Conclusion

From moderation of living through diet, exercise, breathing, and sexual control to various forms of meditation, Daoists thus have developed an extensive repertoire of longevity techniques that allow people to be comfortable in the body for many decades, if not centuries, while reaching out to greater cosmic spheres. Contrary to the Western machine model, they see the body as a conglomeration of dynamic, living *qi*-energy in various forms and levels of subtlety, which can be abused or enhanced, obstructed or expanded. The more enhanced the energetic structure, moreover, the healthier and happier one lives and the longer one can maintain life, even to the point of living forever. Generally agreeing with modern life-extension specialists and immortalists, Daoists strongly favor the preventive model, emphasizing the need for a complete lifestyle make-over in favor of extended living. While this does not imply eschewing pleasures or reducing social contacts, it does mean being careful in lifestyle choices and selective in relationships while developing a high degree of internal energetic awareness.

References

Arthur, Shawn (2006) "Life Without Grains: *Bigu* and the Daoist Body," in *Daoist Body Cultivation*, Livia Kohn (ed.), Magdalena, NM: Three Pines Press, 91–122.

Despeux, Catherine (2006) "The Six Healing Breaths," in *Daoist Body Cultivation*, Livia Kohn (ed.), Magdalena, NM: Three Pines Press, 37–67.

Ettinger, Robert C. W. (1964) *The Prospect of Immortality*, Garden City, NY: Doubleday.

Harrington, Alan (1969) *The Immortalist*, New York: Random House.

Kaptchuk, Ted J. (1983) *The Web that Has No Weaver: Understanding Chinese Medicine*, New York: Congdon & Weed.

Kohn, Livia (1989) "Taoist Insight Meditation: The Tang Practice of *Neiguan*," in *Taoist Meditation and Longevity Techniques*, Livia Kohn (ed.), Ann Arbor, MI: University of Michigan, Center for Chinese Studies Publications, 191–222.

——(2005) *Health and Long Life: The Chinese Way*, Cambridge, MA: Three Pines Press.

——(2008) *Chinese Healing Exercises: The Tradition of Daoyin*, Honolulu: University of Hawai'i Press.

——(2010) *Daoist Dietetics: Food for Immortality*, in cooperation with Ute Engelhardt, Dunedin, FL: Three Pines Press.

Robinet, Isabelle (1989) "Visualization and Ecstatic Flight in Shangqing Taoism," in *Taoist Meditation and Longevity Techniques*, Livia Kohn (ed.), Ann Arbor, MI: University of Michigan, Center for Chinese Studies Publications, 157–90.

Wik, Mieke and Stephan Wik (2005) *Beyond Tantra: Healing through Taoist Sacred Sex*, Forres UK: Findhorn Press.

Winn, Michael (2006) "Transforming Sexual Energy with Water-and-Fire Alchemy," in *Daoist Body Cultivation*, Livia Kohn (ed.), Magdalena, NM: Three Pines Press, 151–78.

Further reading

Daoist views of the body in essence match those of traditional Chinese medicine, and any textbook on acupuncture will provide the details. I tend to rely on two main works, Ted Kaptchuk's *The Web That Has No Weaver* (cited above), and Livia Kohn and Stephen Jackowicz, *Health and Long Life: The Chinese Way* (Three Pines Press, 2005). Studies on Daoist ways of life extension appear in two collected volumes, both edited by myself: *Taoist Meditation and Longevity Techniques* (University of Michigan, Center for Chinese Studies Publications, 1989) and *Daoist Body Cultivation* (Three Pines Press, 2006). For more specific information on Daoist exercises, see Kenneth S. Cohen's *The Way of Qigong* (Ballantine Books, 1997) and my *Chinese Healing Exercises* (cited above). Daoist sexual practices are discussed very nicely in Douglas Wile's *Art of the Bedchamber* (SUNY Press, 1992), while information on dietary techniques is available in my *Daoist Dietetics* (cited above). For the basic forms of meditation in Daoist from a comparative context, see my *Meditation Works* (Three Pines Press, 2008). More specifically, on Daoist forms of visualization and shamanic soul travel, there is Isabelle Robinet's *Taoist Meditation* (SUNY Press, 1993), while forms of absorption and insight practice are discussed in my *Sitting in Oblivion* (Three Pines Press, 2010).

51
A CHRISTIAN THEOLOGICAL RESPONSE TO AUBREY DE GREY'S PROSPECTS FOR THE BIOMEDICAL POSTPONEMENT OF AGING

Or: What does it mean to live long and prosper?

Ann Milliken Pederson

Introduction and context

In the 2009 remake of *Star Trek*, the Vulcan salute "Live long and prosper" (memorialized by Mr. Spock) recalls America's longing to vanquish the ills and scourges of aging and death in order to experience immortality. Like the original television series, the vision of modernity is that progress, reason, and the advances of science and technology will help to bring about this sought-after salvation. The legacies of the Enlightenment are both promising and problematic to cultures and people who, while hoping for progress and prosperity, simultaneously are never satiated and deny their own limitations and finitude. Early into the twenty-first century, the Western world, particularly those in Europe and the United States, live in the light of the progress of technology and in the shadow of its dangers. Advances in medicine and biotechnology, such as antibiotics and *in vitro* fertilization, have changed the way we come into the world, how we live, and when and how we shall die. But we also live with the haunting cries of those killed in the wake of genocides, of those who still do not have clean drinking water and healthy food, and those who are the victims of violence and poverty. Aubrey de Grey's research on the biomedical postponement of aging (see Chapter 48 in this volume) must be interpreted and evaluated in this context of possibilities and promises of technological enhancement, and the problems and perils of a world's population that is rapidly growing and does not have adequate access to the basics of food and water in order to survive.

In a culture where Enlightenment notions of individual rights take priorities over responsibilities, and dollars over common sense, it is no wonder that de Grey's ideas are appealing. The "disease" of aging takes a financial toll on individuals and society. Healthcare is bankrupting individual families and countries. Indeed, if life could be extended in a way to short-circuit the cost of aging, the payoff would appear attractive, at first glance. Most people would find de Grey's idea of living in a "robust and youthful fashion" for a long time an appealing one. We want scientists and physicians to be the high priests who cure our disease of frailty and finitude, and usher in the Valhalla of immortality. This ambiguous legacy of a consumerist and individualistic cultural milieu shapes both the problems and promises of de Grey's research program, and the response of Christian theologians who are also inheritors of the same Enlightenment culture. As well, a Christian response to de Grey reflects the tensions in the Christian tradition between the imperative to heal and the realization that death is finally not in human control; that humans are both created by God and ones who create with God; that the Christian gospel begins not from the wealthy and powerful but from lives of the poor and outcast; that longevity and immortality are not the same as resurrection and life abundant in God. A closer examination of de Grey's science, world-view, and ethical framework is needed in order to offer a theological response.

The science, world view and ethics of Aubrey de Grey

Aubrey de Grey's training and education in computer science, engineering, and artificial intelligence shape his descriptions of the human body as a machine that needs to be "fixed," or at least needs a major tune-up. de Grey's view of the body, and of nature, takes firm root in the mechanistic world-view of the Enlightenment and in many cases is still the world-view from which modern medical science research and practice takes place. Many people still experience visits to the doctor, in which the physician diagnoses the part that needs to be "fixed." While this viewpoint is changing within the realm of healthcare, the mechanistic model of the body also reigns in much of our popular culture's view of health and wellness. People want a quick fix to the problem so they can keep up a lifestyle that resists mortality. However, in recent years much of the research of modern science and evolutionary biology challenges this mechanistic view and insists, like the Hebraic view in Jewish and Christian scriptures, that people are whole beings – mind, body, spirit in one person. Parts do not equal the sum total of the person. Aubrey de Grey's view of the human body and human person emphasizes aging as the function of cells – parts of our body that can be regenerated and fixed. While his views are not simplistic reductionism, they seem dangerously close.

de Grey's picture of the human body reflects his Enlightenment values of autonomy and individual rights. Individualism is precariously tied to consumerism. What people want, they buy. And many of the fruits of medical science and biotechnology are driven by this pairing – people want perfection and immortality now, and they will pay for it at any price. In this setting, de Grey's views of the human person seem naïve at best and dangerous at worst. Choice is not simply what an individual wants, or has the right to want; choice must be defined in the context of relationships and interpreted within a dialectic of freedom and responsibility, community, and individual.

de Grey's philosophy and ethics about the human person and the purpose of life and death obviously shape his scientific research about aging. He is out to wage war on Public Enemy Number One: the disease of aging. The casualties of aging take a toll upon the infrastructure of healthcare, cost societies a great deal of money that could be spent in other areas, and ravage the human body and spirit. One hardly needs to look far to realize that those at the beginnings of life (such as babies in the neonatal intensive care unit) and those at the end of life use up a disproportionate amount of healthcare dollars in "first world" countries such as the United States. The mission of de Grey's not-for-profit group is to defeat aging and help cut the costs associated with it. Other groups, like the Methuselah Foundation, support and share his goals both in their research and in their outreach.

But the battle he engages over the disease of aging might contain some hidden costs about which he seems unaware. It is precisely those who are invisible in our world who suffer and die early as a result of the expensive lifestyle of a wealthy few. Many people in developing nations are more concerned about living until tomorrow, and not for 1000 years. Frailty is not a result of aging, but is caused by basic issues of malnutrition and lack of access to healthcare. And the basic necessities in life are either not available, or the cost is too great. The argument I have about de Grey's work is not with science *per se* or the notion that the nature of what it means to be human is changing. My critique centers on the way his science and technology are used to determine who and what is of value, and consequently how those ultimate values shape his notion of personhood. My commitment to Christianity's idea that to love the neighbor means taking care of society's least, lost, and last requires that other costs be taken into account when the priorities of healthcare are evaluated and when the value of persons is calculated. de Grey realizes that, while aging is the enemy to be defeated, science and technology cannot finally control everything. Death will still happen, but in very different ways. Humans all meet the same fate, eventually.

So, to address my concerns about de Grey's science and world-view from a Christian perspective, I must consider ways in which both my Christian response and his views are rooted in the culture's myths and stories in which we live, the current science and practices of medicine and biotechnology, and the challenges that postmodernity brings to our Enlightenment world views. To do so, I will engage the work of Donna Haraway, biologist and philosopher of science, as my guide through the maze of culture, science, and technology. Specifically, I find her understanding of the body and technology helpful for framing a postmodern notion of personhood. Hardly a Luddite or a sentimentalist, Haraway embraces the ambiguity of how the sciences and technologies shape the human person. She writes, "Technologies are not mediations, something in between us and another bit of the world. Rather, technologies are organs, full partners, in what Merleau-Ponty called 'infoldings of the flesh.' I like the word *infolding* better than *interface* to suggest the dance of world-making encounters. What happens in the folds is what is important. Infoldings of the flesh *are* worldly embodiment. […] Interfaces are made out of interacting grappling devices. […] Worldly embodiment is always a verb, or at least a gerund. Always in formation, embodiment is ongoing, dynamic, situated, and historical." (Haraway 2008: 249) When technologies fold in, with, and under the body, the nature of what it means to be human changes.

Haraway's language of embodiment, relationship, and encounter is radically different from de Grey's descriptive metaphor of machine (Chapter 48 in this volume). She envisions a dance taking place between technology, nature, and humans, a kind of choreographed relationship in which the boundaries between partners erode and implode. Haraway's critique of the Enlightenment and its ensuing descriptions of the human person are in many ways analogous to what many contemporary (and classic) Christian theologians also find problematic. As humans become body-selves, they learn what life is about by interpreting their life journey with and through others around them. Speaking of embodiment is ultimately narrative or artistic work – to be a body self is to tell a story, to compose a work of art. Embodiment is not "about" being a body, but is the act itself of becoming body-self. Body is the locus of our coming into the world, living out our lives, and leaving this world in death. This view of the body is congruent with the way that narrative shapes Christian theology and the story of the gospel in Jesus Christ told through the Christian tradition. We need to bring a new understanding of nature, informed by the modern sciences, into the domain of our Christian faith and practices by focusing on how we interpret our bodies as the Incarnation of God. In our bodily existence, we are, in our human-finite bodies, God's way of being God in the world. I find that Haraway's categories, when viewed through the Christian theological lens of incarnation, raise challenges to de Grey's notions of human personhood and embodiment.

Humans as body-selves: being and becoming in life

Old age, according to de Grey, is the technical failure of our cells which we can repair. On the one hand, this research will benefit many people whose lives are shortened by cancer and other degenerative diseases. On the other hand, those in wealthy countries spend thousands and millions of dollars "fixing" the aging process. Young girls get new breasts. Advertisements for Viagra run during scheduled Monday night football games. Older women cut and paste their figures through cosmetic surgery. Is this just a failure of our cells, or is it a failure of our culture to not accept anyone who isn't "perfect" and "young?" There is more to human personhood than extending or fixing aging cells. Life itself is not simply an extension of years. How we live shapes how we die. And surely how we are dying shapes how we are living, fearfully so.

The body is the access point, or the medium, through which we understand ourselves as both being and becoming through the relationships with those around us. Many of the new reproductive, regenerative, and trans-humanist sciences and technologies challenge the boundaries, borders, and ways in which humans experience their bodies. For example, there are multiple ways to be a parent: a sperm donor, the gestational mother, the surrogate mother, the adoptive father, the biological father, and the list goes on. Does personhood begin with conception? Does it end with brain death? Boundaries of death and life are changed as bodies live in, with, and under the borders of technologies. de Grey's trans-humanist science challenges our familiar boundaries of what personhood is, and the meaning of life and death. For that, Christian theologians need to be grateful. Too often Christians run from the sciences as if what they will learn will diminish their faith. The opposite should be true. When Christians turn living ideas into stones of faith, the tradition is rendered idolatrous. de Grey and others are partners with all in the world who seek to understand more fully, and celebrate, the human body. We may just do it in different ways.

To understand the human body more fully, those educated as physicians study the body in its final act – as the form of the cadaver. Understanding the history and nature of the corpse helps physicians gain insight into the living body. Taking a scalpel to the body is a rite of initiation that only some can appreciate first-hand. But such a rite instills both an intimacy and an abhorrence of the body that is so prevalent in our culture. In her book, *Body of Work: Meditations on Mortality from the Human Anatomy Lab*, Christine Montross, a young medical student, takes the reader on a journey to understand the living by studying the dead. She writes: "The dead body harbors the great mysteries of creation and humanity: the hidden beauty and intricacy of function, the insistence of individuality, the inevitability of decline, the incontrovertibility of death set up against the ill-defined boundaries of life." (Montross 2007: 2) Profound lessons about life inhabit the bodies of the dead. We learn best when we learn with our bodies, not apart from them. Many physicians who teach in medical schools challenge de Grey's notion that the human body is simply a machine. Like de Grey, they study the parts, but they also realize that the human person is much more, and that this mystery of the more is what makes us human. Physicians learn not only the practice of medicine, but also its art. And the composition of the human body is the *magnum opus*.

Literally, the composition of the human body and our interpretation of the meaning of the composition change along the frontiers of medicine and biotechnology. Telling stories about body-selves in a postmodern, scientific, and technological age requires new metaphors and new roadmaps. For example, new studies in sexuality and gender reveal that we can no longer identify sex and gender in typical dualisms, but we need new images that reveal the spectrum of diversity within the human being – a kind of rainbow of multiplicity. And so what we view and value as "normal" or "acceptable" human bodies also changes. What exactly does it mean to be accepted as normal? Will those in our society who are most vulnerable, those who are not seen as "normal," be those who are at our disposal? We already ostracize those who are frail and feeble in "homes," where they are out of sight and mind. We might need to revisit our history that is linked with eugenics, ostracizing those considered "savage or primitive," and quarantining others who do not fear the norms of society. The problems associated with aging are not just ones of economics. Not all those who are frail are elderly. Many in our world are frail because of other problems: disabilities, chronic illness, no access to basic healthcare, mental illness.

When we can face our mortality and no longer deny our death, then the prospect of longer life will be more meaningful. The promise of an extended lifespan must offer more than just a longer experience of the same. How we face death in our culture tells much about how we live. In American culture, we hide the dying in institutions and pay thousands to have funerals that disguise the mortality of our loved ones. At the end of the nineteenth century, most people died at home. Today, most people will die in a healthcare institution. We are embarrassed and frightened by mortality. That is why the promises of these regenerative and life-extending technologies are so appealing. We must ask: Who will benefit from this new science and engineering of regeneration? Most likely those who can afford and have access to such technological advances would benefit from the sciences of those like de Grey. The long-term consequences of extending the human life span indefinitely need to be adequately thought through for the long haul, not only for humans, but also for the entire ecosystem of our planet. Again and again, we must look at how the way we live shapes the way we will die.

Clearly, de Grey's science and world-view raise profound questions about life and death, and the mysteries of what it means to be human. Science and technology plunge humans into the human quest for meaning, which is the matrix of religion and spirituality. So, what does religion, specifically Christianity, offer about what the meaning of being human in a scientific and technological age? A Christian perspective about the science of extending human life span and ending aging welcomes the advances of medicine and biotechnology that offer healing and hope to those whose lives are cut short by debilitating disease and suffering; claims the reality that life and death are not in the ultimate control of humans; and affirms the Christian promise of a God who becomes flesh and experiences the very bodily nature of what it means to be human. So how, then, shall we live?

A Christian response to de Grey

For both Christian theologians and de Grey, the trappings of the Enlightenment can frame unrealistic expectations about the progress and hope that we place in science and our own limits, or lack thereof. Aubrey de Grey's view of nature is trapped in Enlightenment world-views of parts – reductionism. But many Christian views of the natural world are also snared by the Enlightenment outlook: Nature is simply the stage on which the drama of human salvation is carried out. Nature is not intrinsically important; humans are completely different from, or other than, the rest of the natural world. What both de Grey and many Christian theological views of nature lack is the complexity and nuance of a description and interpretation of nature that moves beyond the Enlightenment dualisms and hierarchies to one that celebrates nature as the mysterious revelation it shows itself to be. Christian theologians interpret the natural world as the created order in which God's saving and creating grace are revealed. And yet, in this natural world, suffering and death distort and destroy life, and it can be difficult to discern the will of God.

Some suffering in life is simply a result of being created. Life and death are part of the cycle of being alive, of being creatures. Those are limits we cannot escape.

However, Christian theologians would agree with de Grey that some kinds of suffering that take away one's personhood must be challenged and overcome. So, what do we say about aging? Is it something that is simply part of who we are as creatures? Or is it a disease that must be defeated and overcome? I believe that the process of aging must be interpreted within the theological picture of our lives as creatures of God – that we are dust, and to dust we shall return. And what do we say about those people who experience such agonizing suffering that it destroys their value as person? For example, people who have a physical disability can suffer at the will of other people who see "them" only as their physical handicap. While the American Disability Act is intended to help and empower people whose bodies are disabled to experience their personhood in a more accessible and full way, our culture continues to erect barriers because we are either ignorant of, or uncomfortable with, people who do not fit the limits of what "normal" bodies and thereby "normal" persons are able to do. We fall into the same trap – we reduce people to their body parts. This example about disability offers a challenge to both de Grey and Christian theologians. What would happen if both scientific researchers and Christian theologians started from the bodily experiences of those who experience such suffering as personal, that is, as inflicted upon them by others in such a way as to take away or demean their dignity. Not all suffering, or frailty, or deficit is easily categorized as something simply to be "overcome" by technology and progress through the sciences. If we begin with those persons whose voices are constrained by our culture, then the results of our research, the values we share, and the praxis of our lives will change drastically.

Finally, to consider what it means to be a body-self from a Christian theological perspective, one must ask: What does it mean to be created in the image of God? To be created in the image of God is to be a body-self and to serve God in the world by creating a world in which all life thrives. Humans fulfill their creaturely vocation when they transform the world so that all may have life abundant. The source of human creativity comes not from the self, but is indeed a gift of God's gracious love. To be created in the image of God is to experience the undeserved grace and love given in relationship by God, to be in community with self, God, and other. Like other creatures, we depend on God for life.

To say the least, Christianity has had an ambiguous understanding of the human body. Christian theologians have often followed cultural values which claimed that the body was the source of evil, and that the purpose of life was to flee the body for another world (heaven or immortality of the soul). Concomitant with this notion of the body is that Jesus only appeared to be human. His body was the shell or casing for his divine self. And yet, at the heart of the Christian narrative is the Incarnation: that the Word has become flesh, human flesh. God is in the world as human flesh. Can Christianity rehabilitate its own theological devaluing of the human body? Can the Christian myth offer a different hope for what it means to be human? The science of extending the human life span feeds the human's longing for immortality. But for Christians, this isn't enough. The resurrection of the body and the promise of eternal life through Christ are about the now and the not yet, about this world and the next. The human person is not a set of component parts that "fail," that needs to be fixed. Much of modern bio-gerontology, as well as some popular Christian pieties, pictures the body as either that which needs to be fixed or the "outer shell" which will be cast off when immortality is achieved. According to these views, the body is ultimately the problem. If it can be fixed or escaped, salvation is found. But the Christian doctrine of resurrection of the body challenges both views. Christianity claims that there will be a new Earth and a new heaven – not just an extension of more of what we already have. But something truly new, something given to us from the One who created us. Indeed, according to Colossians, all are made new – the whole person and the whole community. The human body-self will be transformed into something new […] a different kind of life.

References

Haraway, Donna (2008) *When Species Meet*, Minneapolis, MN: University of Minnesota Press.

Montross, Christine (2007) *Body of Work: Meditations on Mortality from the Human Anatomy Lab*, New York: Penguin.

Further reading

For other Christian theological responses to technology and human personhood, I suggest Philip Hefner, *The Human Factor* (Fortress Press, 2000) and *Technology and Human Becoming* (Fortress Press, 2003). Specific theological discussions about embodiment and disability can be found in Sharon Betcher's *Spirit and the Politics of Disablement* (Fortress Press, 2007) and in Nancy Eiesland and Don E. Saliers' *Human Disability and the Service of God: Reassessing Religious Practice* (Abingdon Press, 1998). Stephanie Paulsell's *Honoring the Body: Meditations on a Christian Practice* (Jossey-Bass/Wiley, 2002) provides a helpful pastoral approach to embodiment. Other helpful works of Donna Haraway's include *The Haraway Reader* (Routledge, 2004) and *Modest_Witness@Second_Millennium. FemaleMan_Meets_Oncomouse* (Routledge, 1997).

(v) Transhumanism and artificial intelligence

52
TRANSHUMANISM AND COGNITIVE ENHANCEMENT

Daniel S. Rizzuto and Joshua W. Fost

An introduction to transhumanism

Humanity is a work in progress. The evolution of all species, including *Homo sapiens*, continues today just as it has for the past several billion years. If this fact goes unappreciated, perhaps it is because the time scale for visible evolutionary change is typically – but not always – much longer than the typical human attentional focus on the coming hours, days, and years.

Evolution is guided by natural selection, takes place at the level of the population, and is measured by statistical changes in the frequencies of particular genes. Because gene frequencies are aggregate numbers applicable to groups but not individuals, individuals do not evolve, no matter what biological changes they may undergo in their lifetime. At the same time, however, individuals do contribute to the evolution of their species through their actions, with some actions being more important than others. A female chimpanzee's selection of a sexual partner, for instance, will probably make a greater impact on gene frequencies than will her choice of food, unless that food is contaminated and leads to death before reproduction. Even something as simple as deciding to climb one tree versus another may have a genetic consequence: decisions beget more decisions, actions lead to other actions, and an ever-lengthening chain of cause and effect impacts survival and reproduction in unpredictable ways.

This ability to steer evolution by conscious choice is greatly magnified in humans. We are uniquely cognitive animals. That cognition provides for the development of language, a rich and pervasive culture, and a collection of technologies that affects the distributions of human genes. In fact, it may be fairly said that cultural and technological forces, rather than natural forces, are the greater determinant of human gene frequencies. Birth control and *in vitro* fertilization, for example, have changed gene distributions across the population by providing women and men with greater control over their reproductive processes. Medicine allows many who would otherwise have died to survive and reproduce. These and other tools provide us with unprecedented control over the evolution of our species, even to the extent that it makes sense to talk about *cultural selection* as an evolutionary force falling under the more general heading of *natural selection*.

Transhumanism is a philosophical movement that affirms the human ability and right to fundamentally influence our own evolution, guided by the highest ethical principles and values. It is an extension of humanism, and correspondingly, it values human life and supports the application of reason to solve human problems. Transhumanists tend to view sickness, aging, and death as unnecessary burdens to be overcome. They seek to extend human physical and intellectual capabilities beyond their current limits, and to develop technologies that accelerate the pace of progress on these fronts. The transhumanist movement also focuses upon the ramifications of technological development and attempts to predict potential future scenarios, some of which appear indistinguishable from science fiction, often to both scientists and non-scientists alike.

Like most people, transhumanists support the development of medical technologies to alleviate human maladies, the creation of artificial body parts to replace worn-out bones and joints, and the improvement of tools to diagnose and treat disease. They also advocate, however, the evaluation of technologies for *non-medical* applications such as the amplification and extension of human capabilities beyond "normal" functioning. Some in the field point to the accelerating pace of discovery in biology, genetics, neuroscience, nanotechnology, robotics, and artificial intelligence as evidence that humanity is on the cusp of a leap forward in our ability to re-engineer ourselves. The possibilities associated with that power are impressive: drugs to prevent and reverse aging (de Grey 2003); the replacement of red blood cells with nanodevices allowing a person to sprint for several miles or to remain underwater for hours (Freitas 1998); neuropharmaceuticals to dramatically improve attention and memory (Bostrom and Sandberg 2009); neurochips allowing us to control external devices using our thoughts (Lebedev and Nicolelis 2006) and providing wireless "telepathic" connections to other people (Thompson 2008); and the uploading of one's mind to non-biological substrates (such as silicon computer chips), overcoming once and for all the spectre of biological death (Sandberg and Bostrom 2008). Some of these abilities are already present to some extent in other mammals, while others represent a fundamentally new kind of cybernetic being: *Homo excelsior*.

Where would the application of such powers lead us? Perhaps the most grandiose answer is: to the Singularity (Kurzweil 2006). One of the central pillars of the Singularity is a technological bootstrapping process wherein the first intelligent machines develop even more intelligent machines, and the first tiny, autonomous robots build even tinier robots. As each generation of new technology serves to further extend our senses and abilities, repair microscopic damage to our tissues, and make available to our web-enabled minds the ever-growing encyclopedia of human knowledge, we may reach a critical point, a discontinuity, beyond which all subsequent development would be subsumed by, and contained within, one great superintelligence. Some futurists imagine an entity that could be embodied either in human form via a dramatic upgrade and accessorizing of our normal bodies, or in a purely man-made form via electrical engineering, robotics, and artificial intelligence. To some, this is a vision of a dream come true. To others, it is a dystopian techno-nightmare; indeed, there is a subfield of artificial intelligence research dedicated to ensuring that the first superintelligence that we create is sympathetic toward "mere" human beings (Goertzel 2001).

As should be clear from the above, the fulfillment of transhumanist goals depends upon scientific discoveries. But it is misleading to portray the majority of transhumanist thought as a branch of science. Rather, its statements and hypotheses belong to the gray area between science and science fiction, simply because so many of them are presently untestable. This has not, however, prevented passionate debate over the ethical dimensions of transhumanist hypotheses and aims.

Can we alter human nature?

Certain critics of transhumanism have proposed a complete ban on the use of biotechnology for enhancement purposes (Fukuyama 2003). These arguments revolve around the claim that enhancement technologies will change the basis of human nature, leading to differences in equality and legal protection between enhanced and non-enhanced persons. Such arguments can be intuitively attractive, but ultimately rely upon the assumption that there is a mysterious human "essence" that is somehow changed during the process of enhancement.

The assumption that there is a fixed human nature runs contrary to the findings of evolutionary biology and genetics, which have observed that the genetic basis of our species (like all species) is constantly in flux. Gene frequencies change every time a new human being is born, and mutations occur spontaneously and regularly without our intervention. Consider two hypothetical individuals. One experiences a naturally occurring mutation at conception, leading to slightly altered biochemistry in her brain's emotional centers. As a result, she enjoys an above average sense of well-being compared with her peers, and has a lower chance of developing major depression. In contrast, another baby is born without the mutation but undergoes elective gene therapy later in life, resulting in the same change to her DNA and a corresponding increase in her mood and quality of life. Would anyone argue that either of these individuals is not a human being, or lacks some essential human quality?

Some may accept the essential equivalence of these two end-states, but still hesitate about the wisdom of intentional intervention in the latter. Is that hesitation justified? To be sure, any elective procedure carries risks, but this is true of all of medicine. We choose to take an antibiotic that might save our life, knowing that we might have an undiagnosed allergy to that medication. Few would suggest that such intervention is unethical. Some may feel that the involvement of changes to DNA is what is troubling – but no, the genetic changes are the same in both cases […] only the means by which the change was produced varied. What we might call the *argument from mutation* points to this central question: What could be our basis for believing that the first woman, the one with a naturally occurring mutation, is simply lucky, while the other has crossed some ethical line or done something unseemly? What is the ethical basis for embracing an improvement to our lives only as long we have had no hand in bringing it about?

If science is able to determine that, to the best of our knowledge, a given technology can improve our lives, then our argument is basically this: Why forsake it? Because the science is incomplete? Science is always incomplete. This does not stop us from dispensing present-day genetic counseling in which, for example, people with the gene for Huntington's disease or Tay–Sachs disease are advised as to the dire prognosis for their offspring. The science leading to such counsel is also incomplete, but we are sufficiently confident in it that we believe we are providing more benefit than harm.

A key feature – perhaps the key feature – of the transhumanist program is the use of technology to move beyond treatment and into enhancement, that is, to extend our faculties beyond anything that has occurred (so far) naturally. From arguments like the above, a consensus is emerging that arguing the merits and demerits of enhancement technology *in general* is rather pointless, partly due to the fact that we already utilize so many enhancements in our daily lives, but also because the risk–benefit trade-off is unique to each technology (e.g. Savulescu and Bostrom 2009). What are the side-effects of the technology in question? What are the actual (as opposed to hypothetical) costs and benefits? These are focused questions with answers that can vary widely from case to case. In the following section we consider just one of these debates: that of *cognitive* enhancement. As we will see, this particular debate is especially timely because, unlike some of the more exotic possibilities expressed by transhumanists (such as the artificial intelligence-mediated Singularity), several means of cognitive enhancement are already available and in widespread use.

Cognitive enhancements are here to stay

One of the readiest examples of a cognitive enhancer is caffeine. Because it is so common, it hardly appears controversial, but if natural caffeine-containing preparations were discovered today and promoted as alertness aids, they would almost certainly be regarded with the same suspicion as other herbal substances, such as nicotine, kava, or ephedra. In any case, caffeine is undeniably used by many people as a pharmacological manipulation of natural alertness levels.

An edgier example, one that has elicited controversy, is the use of synthetic psychoactive compounds by people with no diagnosed cognitive impairment. The most frequently discussed of these is Ritalin (methylphenidate). Normally prescribed to patients with attention deficit disorder (ADD) or attention deficit hyperactivity disorder (ADHD), Ritalin increases attention span and the duration of mental focus. This has been noticed by the general population, especially students, who, in increasing numbers, use it as a study aid (Maher 2008). The effects of the drug appear to be nearly entirely reversible, lasting only until it is metabolized or excreted, and as such this is a relatively weak form of transhumanist intervention. It does not, for example, have any connection with a permanent or even long-lasting modification of the brain. Nonetheless, the elective use of Ritalin qualifies as a contemporary application of a purely synthetic technology to extend the natural capacities of our minds. Should we be troubled?

In his recent book *The Ethical Brain*, Michael Gazzaniga (2005) argues that the decision to enhance our cognition using synthetic drugs should be a matter of personal choice. And, in some sense, we already use technology to enhance our cognitive apparatus every day. Through education, conversation, and exposure to culture, our minds become something other than what they would have been if left alone. We consider these cognitive enhancements "natural" because we are social creatures and the effects of such exposure are generally so benign. Note, however, that these enhancements also use technological means to achieve their ends. Education includes books, films, television, and many other artifacts of civilization. In fact, some philosophers argue that our cognitive capacity is a result of coupling between our physical brain and our environment, and thus that cognitive operations are not restricted solely to the brain (Clark and Chalmers 1998). But if technologically mediated cognitive enhancement is so conventional, then what is it about Ritalin use that furrows our brows? Why the difference?

Perhaps what is disconcerting about the Ritalin example is that it is *organic*. Unlike external tools (books, films, television, etc.), neuropharmaceuticals go inside our bodies and affect our physiology. Perhaps we are tuned in to some risk unique to the modification of our own chemistry. Perhaps. But consider another completely mundane feature of daily life: food. No-one would deny that poor nutrition handicaps our cognitive abilities. Correspondingly, good nutrition could be considered cognitive enhancement – our minds function better if we eat healthfully. Because good food, or at least decent food, is generally available to most people in industrialized nations, we don't usually consider it enhancement *per se*. But is this fair? How would an average resident of an earlier time – thirteenth-century Europe, say – regard the cornucopia of a twenty-first-century wholefoods grocery store? Such stores serve precisely those individuals who eat not only to stay alive, but also to enhance their health and performance. Eating lemons in Helsinki or salmon in Chicago requires a widespread technological infrastructure including refrigeration and transportation. Wouldn't it be reasonable for a thirteenth-century peasant to conclude that we moderns were enhancing our cognitive abilities through technology?

What we might call the *argument from nutrition* suggests a reassessment of one of the objections to cognitive enhancement: that it achieves its ends via "unnatural" means. Obviously the meaning of the word "unnatural" is the fulcrum in this objection, but that meaning is fuzzy at best. We are, at our core, tool-using, technological creatures. Even the diets of medieval Europeans or Paleolithic hunter-gatherers were obtained through the use of engineered devices such as scythes and rakes, digging sticks and hand axes. For 400,000 years, since *Homo erectus* at least, most of our necessities, and almost all our luxuries, have come to us via applications of technologies that were, at their inception, revolutionary. On this basis, we should be wary of opposing transhumanist goals merely on the grounds that they represent some new means of tinkering with our bodies or minds.

A call for evidence-based decision-making

None of this is to say that the elective use of Ritalin, or any other drug, is *advisable*. Questions of side-effects, short-term and/or long-term costs, complications, compensatory changes in neural function, etc. would all have to be answered by carefully controlled studies, just as they have been for non-enhancement medicines. By this argument, we merely wish to clear the way for such studies to be undertaken. It surely could be the case that Ritalin, on balance, has more disadvantages than advantages – only through scientific investigation will we be able to answer that question. But to the extent that new technologies can improve our lives, and do so without adding especially onerous burdens to our quest for a sustainable civilization, they should be investigated carefully and applied judiciously. To refrain from doing so because those technologies are more organic than the steel and silicon products of the industrial and electronic revolutions, whose benefits we thoroughly enjoy, does not seem either grounded in defensible argument or well advised.

As a society, we should allow, indeed insist, that the science comes before the legislation, thereby ensuring that any policies we develop are based on facts and not just on pre-existing bias. Moreover, there is a compelling need to perform such scientific enhancement research as soon as possible: Neuropharmaceuticals are currently being used off-label not just by students seeking an edge (Maher 2008), or transhumanists exploring the frontier, or octogenarians seeking to compensate for an aging brain, but also by professionals in medicine (Meier 2008) and the military (Emonson and Vanderbeek 1995), where the need for sustained attention even while sleep-deprived is paramount. Prescriptions in such off-label cases are legal and entirely at the physician's discretion. This kind of practice is not unique to cognitive enhancement: Many medical specialties such as dermatology, sports medicine, and plastic surgery have changed from a simple disease-treatment model into one that also seeks to improve the quality of life of healthy individuals. Still, these drugs, most notably Adderall, Ritalin, and ProVigil, were approved by the US Food and Drug Administration only to treat diseases such as ADHD and narcolepsy. We should know more about their use outside those patient populations. At the moment, informed decision-making on the part of physicians, legislators, and potential users is impossible because comprehensive studies of their effects on healthy volunteers have not been undertaken. Doing so requires the collaboration of psychometricians to evaluate their enhancement properties and neurologists to evaluate their safety, as well as oversight by institutional review boards to ensure adequate protection of human research volunteers. Once available, the data from these studies will make it easier for society to develop guidelines for their use.

In addition to questions of individual safety, we may wish to consider questions of larger-scale societal impact. People are inter-dependent, and the choices that each of us makes can affect our neighbors, our co-workers, our children, and even people in other countries. Will students who use enhancements have an unfair advantage over their non-enhancing peers? Will workers who use enhancements indirectly pressure their non-enhancing co-workers to do the same? Will expensive and powerful enhancements increase the gap between the haves and have-nots? Will nations that support cognitive enhancement research have a competitive advantage over those that do not?

These issues are more complex than the relatively simple question of whether a given enhancement has an acceptable risk/benefit trade-off for an individual, and must be addressed through rational debate and the development of policies at the level of schools, businesses, medical organizations, and governments. However, in contrast to Fukuyama (2003), we advocate a progressive approach to cognitive enhancement regulation in which the rights of individuals are balanced with the need for society to promote legal and economic justice. Greely *et al.* (2008) propose four mechanisms to balance these interests: (1) research into the risks and benefits of neuropharmaceuticals; (2) the development of cognitive enhancement guidelines from educational and physicians' associations; (3) broad dissemination of the results of cognitive enhancement research; and (4) careful and limited legislative action to maximize societal benefit and social justice.

Additional legislation may be needed to regulate the use of pharmaceuticals for enhancement purposes, as existing regulations focus primarily upon medical use. However, banning these technologies outright is not a viable option. A recent poll published in the journal *Nature* found that 25 per cent of college students have used some form of pharmaceutical cognitive enhancement in the past year, and 79 per cent of respondents were in favor of making cognitive enhancements available to healthy individuals (Maher 2008). Regulations prohibiting the use of enhancement technologies will not decrease this demand, but will instead force the marketing and distribution networks underground, where they are resistant to government oversight and regulation. It is our belief that a complete ban will lead to greater societal harm than closely studying and regulating their use.

How do we make wise decisions about technology?

All technology is ethically neutral. Only the decision to use a particular technology determines its ethical implications. Tubal ligation can provide women with safe and effective birth control, but it was also once used in the forced sterilization of vulnerable populations and minorities. The internet can be used to break down cultural barriers and generate great societal wealth, but it is also used to spread malicious software and foment hatred. Cardiac pacemakers and deep-brain stimulators can be used to treat disease and improve a patient's quality of life, but they are also susceptible to hackers intent upon doing bodily harm (Denning *et al.* 2009). In a similar fashion, future enhancement technologies promise to improve the quality of life for individuals and for society as a whole, but they will assuredly have dangerous uses as well.

Wisdom, both individually and societally, is needed to ensure that the decisions we make are skillful – that they are more helpful than harmful. With respect to transhumanist technology or any other domain, good decision-making requires balancing our rational, intellectual capacities with our intuitive, empathic capacities. In the 1927 case of *Buck v. Bell*, US Supreme Court Justice Oliver Wendell Holmes, Jr., writing the majority opinion, made a rational argument for the forced sterilization of mentally disabled persons. While this argument was superficially rational, it lacked a fundamental respect for human beings and self-determination, and would not satisfy most people today as being ethical or wise. Indeed, the ability to internalize the emotional experiences of others (empathy) may provide the ultimate basis for judgments of human rights (Hunt 2008). The nurturing and development of this ability allows us to see past the obvious facts that everyone is unique and that aptitudes are spread unequally, to arrive at concise and effective principles such as the Golden Rule and the statement that "all men are created equal."

Principles such as these have been known, though not always applied, for a long time. In a promising development, modern neuroscience research is beginning to discover the neural basis of wisdom and empathy, which seems to comprise a disparate network of brain regions, including dorso-lateral prefrontal areas that support executive processing and decision-making; medial pre-frontal and insular cortices that support emotional and empathic processing; and anterior cingulate areas that support conflict-detection (Singer *et al.* 2006; Meeks and Jeste 2009). Further characterizing these brain regions and their interactions may even support the development of technologies that are capable of enhancing wisdom – just as it may be possible to extend our physical capabilities and enhance our intellectual capacities, so too might we enhance our emotional competence and empathic understanding to become better decision-makers. How would we receive a transhumanist Solomon?

Conclusion

Humanity is evolving, whether we like it or not. The transhumanism movement recognizes this fact and seeks to take responsibility for the transformation rather than leaving it to chance. Technologies to extend the human senses and exceed our biological limitations fall within a vision for the future that promises a better quality of life for individuals and for society. Pharmaceutical cognitive enhancement is the most immediate example of a transhumanist technology and seems to be widely acceptable but current versions of these drugs require much closer scientific scrutiny for physicians, consumers, and regulators to make informed decisions about how best to use them. Society also needs to make better decisions about how to use technologies in general, and this requires the development of wisdom and the balancing of intellectual and empathic skills on the personal level. To achieve the maximum fulfillment of our potential, as transhumanists wish, we should pursue enhancements not only to our senses, intellects, and life spans, but also to our emotional intelligence, empathy, and capacity for balanced decision-making. This is an important point, as the interplay between these capacities may very well determine the direction in which we evolve.

References

Bostrom, N. and A. Sandberg (2009) "Cognitive Enhancement: Methods, Ethics, Regulatory Challenges," *Science and Engineering Ethics* 15: 311–41.

Clark, A. and D. J. Chalmers (1998) "The Extended Mind," *Analysis* 58: 7–19.

Denning, T., Y. Matsuoka and K. Tadayoshi (2009) "Neurosecurity: Security and Privacy for Neural Devices," *Neurosurgical Focus* 27: E7.

Emonson, D. L. and R. D. Vanderbeek (1995) "The Use of Amphetamines in U.S. Air Force Tactical Operations during Desert Shield and Storm," *Aviation, Space, and Environmental Medicine* 66: 260–63.

Freitas, R. A. (1998) "Exploratory Design in Medical Nanotechnology: A Mechanical Artificial Red Cell," *Artificial Cells, Blood Substitutes, and Immobilization Biotechnology* 26: 411–30.

Fukuyama, F. (2003) *Our Posthuman Future: Consequences of the Biotechnology Revolution*, New York: Picador Press.

Gazzaniga, M. (2005) *The Ethical Brain*, New York: Harper Perennial.

Goertzel, B. (2001) "Creating Friendly AI 1.0: The Analysis and Design of Benevolent Goal Architectures," white paper, Palo Alto, CA: Singularity Institute.

Greely, H., B. Sahakian, J. Harris, R. C. Kessler, M. Gazzaniga, P. Campbell and M. J. Farah (2008) "Towards Responsible Use of Cognitive-enhancing Drugs by the Healthy," *Nature* 456: 702–5.

de Grey, A. D. (2003) "Challenging but Essential Targets for Genuine Anti-Ageing Drugs," *Expert Opinion on Therapeutic Targets* 7: 1–5.

Hunt, L. (2008) "Inventing Human Rights: An Empathetic Understanding," in eJournal USA (a publication of the US State Department) 13(11), www.america.gov/st/hr-english/2008/November/20081119113936xjyrrep0.858349.html

Kurzweil, R. (2006) *The Singularity is Near: When Humans Transcend Biology*, New York: Penguin.

Lebedev, M. A. and M. A. Nicolelis (2006) "Brain–Machine Interfaces: Past, Present and Future," *Trends in Neuroscience* 29: 536–46.

Maher, B. (2008) "Poll Results: Look Who's Doping," *Nature* 452: 674–75.

Meeks, T. W. and D. V. Jeste (2009) "Neurobiology of Wisdom: A Literature Overview," *Archives of General Psychiatry* 66: 355–65.

Meier, M. (2008) "The End of Impairment?," ScienceProgress.org, September 30, www.scienceprogress.org/2008/09/the-end-of-impairment.

Moreno, J. D. (2006) *Mind Wars: Brain Research and National Defense*, New York: Dana Press.

Sandberg, A. and N. Bostrom (2008) "Whole Brain Emulation: A Roadmap," Technical Report #2008-3, Oxford: Future of Humanity Institute, Oxford University.

Savulescu, J. and N. Bostrom (eds) (2009) *Human Enhancement*, Oxford: Oxford University Press.

Singer, T., B. Seymour, J. P. O'Doherty, K. E. Stephan, R. J. Dolan and C. D. Frith (2006) "Empathic Neural Responses are Modulated by the Perceived Fairness of Others," *Nature* 439: 466–69.

Thompson, M. (2008) "The Army's Totally Serious Mind-control Project," *TIME Magazine*, September 14, www.time.com/time/nation/article/0,8599,1841108,00.html.

Further reading

The British Medical Association's discussion paper *Boosting your Brainpower: Ethical Aspects of Cognitive Enhancements* is an approachable consolidation of perspectives from practitioners in a variety of disciplines, including law, medicine, and ethics (www.bma.org.uk/ethics/health_technology/CognitiveEnhancement2007.jsp). Hava Tirosh-Samuelson's article "Facing the Challenges of Transhumanism: Philosophical, Religious, and Ethical Considerations" offers a broad historical context and critiques the transhumanist approach to happiness and its subtle utopianism (www.metanexus.net/magazine/tabid/68/id/10169/Default.aspx). Nick Bostrom penned a nice response to Francis Fukuyama, entitled "Transhumanism: The World's Most Dangerous Idea?" (www.nickbostrom.com/papers/dangerous.html). The Extropy Institute publishes a wide variety of transhumanist resources available for free on its website, including the Transhumanist FAQ (http://extropy.org), and *H+* magazine covers the technological, scientific, and cultural trends that provide a foundation for the transhumanist vision (http://hplusmagazine.com).

53
CYBORGS, ROBOTS, AND ETERNAL AVATARS
Transhumanist salvation at the interface of brains and machines

Robert M. Geraci

Introduction: The making of a cyborg

In a rapidly spreading cultural shift, the human species is becoming a species of cyborgs. The religious implications of this depend upon what we mean by a cyborg, of course, and to what extent the transformation of humankind progresses. But while it remains an open question as to whether we will be only minimally cyborg (and hence remain fundamentally still human) or find ways to fully and thoroughly integrate our selves with machines, many technology advocates have found an eager audience for claims that we will soon transcend the limitations of bodily life. Indeed, the belief that we will merge our minds with machines, perhaps even "uploading" our consciousness into robotic bodies and living forever, now echoes loudly off the walls of popular culture and political advocacy. Although the champions of such ideas tend toward atheism or agnosticism, and generally reject traditional religious communities (asserting that their approach is "scientific" rather than "based upon faith"), they nevertheless offer a new religion for modernity, one that merges concepts and practices from science, technology, and religion.

That we have become cyborgs in a broad sense will be obvious to even casual observers. The word "cyborg" was coined in reference to the prospects for mechanically augmented human beings who might have the ability to maintain life support in space (Clynes and Kline 1960). Today, the word generally refers to an individual whose life or lifestyle is dependent upon the integration of mechanical or electrical devices with his or her body; more and more, we find that technology penetrates our lives and even our senses of self, thus broadening what it might mean for technology to be "necessary" for life. Upon losing a cell phone, for example, many members of developed nations find themselves at a total loss because their access to information and communication with other people is increasingly mediated by texting, telephone conversations, and the internet (especially social networking sites). The integration of technology into our personal sense of subjectivity has been apparent for decades (Haraway 1997; Turkle 1997; Clark 2004), but as yet most of us retain an irreducible separation from our machines. While we may think of ourselves, and relate to ourselves and others, in and through technology, especially computers, it is still the case that we can be physically taken away from them. Those with pacemakers, electronic prostheses, cochlear implants, neural implants for epilepsy or Parkinson's disease, and similar devices are, of course, the exception. These individuals are physically cyborgs as a way of overcoming physical handicaps, but as technology improves, even the hardiest and most intelligent among us might benefit from implants to improve strength, speed, endurance, memory, or learning. If this happens, we will go from cyborgs in spirit to cyborgs in flesh as well.

The most radical claims – that we shall either become cyborgs with vastly expanded physical and mental powers, or we shall go beyond even this and transfer our conscious minds entirely into machines, departing our biological existence altogether – are the stories told and retold through mainstream media. First disseminated through science fiction, these promises of transhumanist technosalvation have become the principal public narratives surrounding brain–machine interfaces.

Of minds and machines

Philosophy of transhumanism

The desire to become powerful cyborgs or uploaded minds is a brand of transhumanism. Transhumanism is the desire to transcend the human condition through the use of science and technology, achieving long, happy, healthy, potentially immortal lives. Considerable variation exists among transhumanists as to how our transhuman future will unfold and to what extent we might wish to go beyond our present biology. For example, should we feel satisfied with eliminating disease, or should we pursue eternal youth? Should we upgrade our bodies and brains with robotic and computer replacements, or genetically engineer smarter people? Should we go so far as to depart human life altogether by uploading our minds into robots or into virtual reality landscapes? Thus, while all transhumanists share a certain mindset, they do not agree upon exactly what constitutes an ideal future outcome. For example, bioethicist Gregory Stock believes that human beings will enhance ourselves through genetic engineering (Stock 2003), while roboticist Kevin Warwick advocates using computer implants to become cyborgs (Warwick 2004), and AI pioneer Ray Kurzweil believes we will upload our minds into virtual reality and depart biological life altogether (Kurzweil 1999, 2005).

Transhumanist thinking has spread throughout developed countries, even though transhumanism as an explicitly philosophical or theological ideology has not. Philip Hefner, a distinguished theologian and scholar of religion and science, has argued that we ought to think of transhumanism both as a proper noun and as an improper noun (Hefner 2009). As a proper noun, Transhumanism refers to those individuals who explicitly advocate transhumanist principles and work toward a post-human future. But for every person who calls him or herself a "Transhumanist," there are literally thousands of others who do not so label themselves, yet whose actions and hopes remain pointed squarely toward transhumanist outcomes. As Hefner explains, the desires for a long, disease-free life, youthful beauty, and superior intellectual powers are different from the hopes of transhumanists only in degree, or in the choice of technologies expected to realize those ends. Using prescription pharmaceuticals to improve concentration and, thereby, enhance school or work performance does pretty much the same thing as genetic engineering to improve IQ. Botox and face-lifts look unambitious compared with stem cell rejuvenation of our skin, but are otherwise part of the same overall project.

Some futurists defend explicit transhumanism as the natural outcome of our cultural evolution. Oxford philosopher Nick Bostrom, for example, argues that transhumanism has a long history in our culture, with antecedents as far back as the *Epic of Gilgamesh* (Bostrom 2005). In Chapter 52 of this volume, Daniel Rizzuto and Joshua Fost argue that we should not reject transhumanist objectives as new and different from the ways in which human beings have enhanced themselves with technology throughout our tool-using history. They describe how therapeutic technologies have already given way to technologies of cognitive enhancement through neuropharmacology, and this shift can be ethically managed by an attentive culture. Ray Kurzweil, who, though not the originator of it, is nevertheless the world's most significant champion of the belief that we will upload our minds into machines, has repeatedly claimed that technological evolution is a continuation of biological evolution (Kurzweil 1999, 2005). By presenting transhumanism within the context of cultural and even biological evolution, these authors provide a providential aura for transhumanism, which begins to look like an inevitable historical outcome.

While advocates of transhumanism have claimed that the movement reflects a natural, evolutionary process, their beliefs are fundamentally different from early religious beliefs. Bostrom is correct in pointing out that Gilgamesh seeks immortality in his eponymous epic, and that Greek myths laud the power of Daedelus to build clever inventions, but it is nevertheless true that only in the past few centuries have science and technology been conceived as capable of fulfilling the most powerful goals of religious life. Indeed, there were no meaningful religious problems that Daedelus sought to solve because the ancient Greeks lacked the kind of aspirations that transhumanists presently hold. Certainly, Gilgamesh did share with modern transhumanists a desire for eternal youth, but he sought to reach this goal through magical rather than technological means. That transhumanists trust science and technology to provide happiness, immortality, and "angelic" bodies and minds marks the distinguishing feature of their tradition.

The idea that science and technology should fulfill traditionally religious objectives emerged in science fiction, which has both nurtured and normalized transhumanist ideas. Francis Bacon (1561–1626), justly famous for his contributions to the scientific method, also penned what is perhaps the first science fiction book, *The New Atlantis* (Bacon 1951 [1626]).[1] In it, he describes a society using technology to complete the divine creation, including the extension of human life spans. In the twentieth century, science fiction authors have likewise distributed transhumanist goals widely. Although many of transhumanism's key concepts can be traced to the claims of scientists, such as J. B. S. Haldane (1923), science fiction has done far more to popularize such ideas. Of course, many technologies have a grim presence in science fiction, such as the use of mind-altering drugs in Aldous Huxley's *Brave New*

World (1932). Other authors have, however, glorified technology and its power to benefit human life. Arthur C. Clarke, for example, influenced many in the 1960s and 1970s with his claim in *2001: A Space Odyssey* (1968) that humanity would and should evolve to god-like powers, and his description of copying minds and cloning bodies in *The City and the Stars* (2001 [1956]). Other authors, such as Roger Zelazny in *Lord of Light* (1967), explicitly connect transhumanist technologies such as cloning and mind uploading with a religious system. More recently, popular authors such as Cory Doctorow (2003) and Charles Stross (2005) have developed their storylines around transhumanist thinking. While these authors do not present transhumanist technologies as unambiguously good, choosing instead to drive their plots through the complexities of a transhumanist future, they portray such technologies as culturally significant and, indeed, likely inevitable.

Technologies of transhumanism

The technologies of transhumanism are in their infancy, but many promise significant growth in the twenty-first century. A variety of biotechnologies could provide considerable benefits, but the convergence of robotics, artificial intelligence, and neurophysiology gives transhumanists hope of a truly post-human salvation.

Doctors and patients alike look forward to the benefits of pharmacology, stem cell research, and genetic engineering, all of which could reduce the burdens of illness, injury, and old age. Stem cells offer considerable promise for stroke patients or for rejuvenating damaged organs or skin. Meanwhile, prescription drugs (especially if tailored to the user's genotype to reduce side-effects) could reduce dysfunctional mental or physical conditions to an even greater extent than they do at present. Ultimately, changing our genetic inheritance might vastly improve human potential if it can be done safely.

Although contemporary biotechnologies hold considerable promise for a transcendent future, many commentators already believe that most of these technologies will be far too limited for humankind to settle with them. A few leaders in robotics and artificial intelligence have prompted a growing awareness that we might integrate machines into our bodies and eventually transfer our minds from bodies into machines entirely.

By the early twenty-first century, humanity looks ready to reap substantial rewards from research into brain–machine interfaces. Researchers have developed systems by which people wired to a computer can move robotic arms by thinking about it (Associated Press 2009), control an entire robot moving around a room by thought alone (Physorg 2009a), drive a wheelchair controlled by relatively simple (and non-invasive) brain-scanning technology (Dillow 2009), and use limited language processors that the user can control with his or her thoughts, thus permitting stroke patients to speak again (Physorg 2009b). One group is even working on an artificial hippocampus that they hope will assist stroke and Alzheimer's patients in forming memories (Locklear 2003). Research is ongoing to allow "telepathic" communication, information transfer directly to human brains, improved sensory powers, and more. In 2009, Hasbro and Uncle Milton Industries launched consumer toys that take advantage of brain–computer interfaces to levitate balls. Though simple, these toys can track brain waves using a variant of an electroencephalography (EEG) system and use the data to instruct an air compressor to flow with greater or lesser strength. The benefits of this kind of technology for the handicapped and elderly cannot be ignored. For example, John Donoghue's research team at Brown University has developed a technology that enables quadriplegics to read e-mail, control a television, turn lights on and off, and play video games using their minds (Ward 2005). Eventually, even those of sound body might benefit from the ease of instructing machines, by thought alone, to prepare food or coffee, start an automobile, or turn on lights.

Not just transhumanists, but the scientists behind this kind of research, enjoy predicting the marvels that await us. For example, in conjunction with Ray Kurzweil's Singularity University, the Massachusetts Institute of Technology's X Prize Lab hosted a two-day seminar called "Brain–Machine Interfaces: Igniting a Revolution" intended to debate artificial vision, thought-controlled bionic arms, "super-charged" digital RAM memories, and more (Massachusetts Institute of Technology 2010). Scientists across the United States have joined the chorus of praise for brain–machine interface technologies, which hold out so much promise to satisfy our wants and needs. "We don't know what the limits are yet […] Nothing is out of the realm of possibility," says Melody Moore Jackson, director of Georgia Tech University's BrainLab, and "anything can happen," says Michael Crutcher of Emory University (both quoted in Hammock 2009).

The roboticist Kevin Warwick has made headlines by implanting simple electronic devices into his body and declaring himself the world's first cyborg, admittedly ignoring everyone with a pacemaker, cochlear implant, or other electronic prosthetic. He believes that humankind will inevitably upgrade itself with increasingly sophisticated computer interfaces until the day comes that our mental and physical powers vastly outstrip those of the present (Warwick 2004). Already, our thinking and interaction with the world is increasingly out-sourced from our bodies and brains thanks to our personal digital assistants (PDAs), cell phones, and the internet. As advocates of the "extended mind" hypothesis have argued, cognition is done in and through the environment, not in some isolated mental space divorced from the real world; our digital enhancements are simply one more (though vastly powerful) way in which our minds extend out into the world (Clark and Chalmers 1998; Clark 2004). Perhaps one day soon, instead of turning to our phone, we will gather information from the internet through a computer interface installed directly into our brain.

Not every computer enthusiast believes that supplementing our limited body and brain with machines will end the alienation of human experience; instead of adding to our body, some theorists desire to replace our biological body entirely with computers. Hans Moravec, former research scientist at Carnegie Mellon University's Robotics Institute, is the ideological prophet who recast the science fiction portrayal of uploading minds into machines as a legitimate scientific prospect available in the near future. After an early essay published in the science fiction magazine *Analog* (Moravec 1978), Moravec subsequently published two popular science books on robotics that claim we shall soon see biological life give way to mechanical life after we invent intelligent robots and join them in a transcendent future by copying our minds into robot bodies (Moravec 1988, 1999).

Moravec believes that human minds can be duplicated outside of the human body in a process of pattern replication. If the human mind is nothing but a pattern of electrochemical activity, then it could be copied in a different substrate that mimics the brain's organization (such as a computer), creating a perfect replica of the individual's personality (Moravec 1988: 117). Such a copy would gain all the benefits of a computer (easy learning, enormous memory with rapid recall, fast computation, etc.) and would be, in some sense, immortal because it can be backed up and transferred to a new medium. Moravec envisioned a robot slowly slicing into a human brain, recording the pattern of activity and copying that pattern into a computer as it proceeds. Subsequent theorists have been more enthusiastic about non-invasive brain-scanning technologies, for obvious reasons: Moravec's vision is a bit too close to murder for many people to appreciate. Lest we immediately jump to the conclusion that such a copy would necessarily be a different person, however, Kurzweil recommends a thought experiment where we slowly replace one person's biological parts with machine parts. If we replace one part of Jack's brain with a computer, we still have Jack, do we not? What if we replace another? Why would replacing Jack's entire brain at once be morally or scientifically different from replacing it one part at a time over a multi-year period? In the end, Jack has a computer brain either way. Because, like Moravec, he defines identity as the neural pattern, Kurzweil wonders why anyone would challenge that we still have Jack if he swaps his biological brain for a digital computer (Kurzweil 1999: 52–53).

Although Moravec anticipates a relatively early shift into robotic bodies (he has predicted this to take place in the mid- to late twenty-first century), he believes that we will not settle for robot bodies lumbering about in our traditional conception of the world. Moravec thinks a "Mind Fire" will sweep throughout the universe, converting everything in its path into computers hosting infinite worlds populated by AIs doing wondrous and worthwhile things. The "inhabited portions of the universe will be rapidly transformed into a cyberspace, where overt physical activity is imperceptible, but the world inside the computation is astronomically rich" (Moravec 1999: 164). The Mind Fire, which will spread outward from the Earth in the late twenty-first century, is the ultimate outcome of evolutionary history (Moravec 1988: 116).

Moravec's scientific defense of mind uploading gained traction in the 1990s, especially upon its adoption and dissemination by Ray Kurzweil, a leading innovator and entrepreneur in AI technologies. Kurzweil's *The Age of Spiritual Machines* (1999) is, essentially, a re-presentation of Moravec's ideas with a heavier emphasis upon describing the wonders of uploaded life. Kurzweil promises that we will be healthier, more intelligent, more spiritual, and even have better sex lives. His focus upon evangelical conversion, combined with exhaustive efforts to prove that history moves inexorably toward the Mind Fire, allowed Kurzweil to become the foremost champion of mind uploading and our post-biological future in early twenty-first-century life. His efforts have seen him rewarded by the World Transhumanist Association (now Humanity+) and led to invitations to speak before the United States Congress on technological matters.

According to Kurzweil, evolution is accelerating toward the day when human minds have saturated the entire computational universe. Technologically, we are nowhere close to creating vastly intelligent cyborgs or uploading our minds into robots. Nevertheless, argues Kurzweil, the speed at which our technologies improve is, itself, speeding up. Calling this the law of accelerating returns, Kurzweil says that in ordered systems, the time between salient events decreases exponentially, meaning that progress will increase at an exponential rate (as has, for example, the speed of our computers – approximately every eighteen months we double the number of transistors that we can put on an integrated chip). Kurzweil and other transhumanists believe that this means we will see unprecedented progress over the next thirty to forty years, literally accomplishing what would have, at past rates of technological progress, taken centuries. The Singularity, first defended by mathematician and science fiction author Vernor Vinge in a 1993 presentation at the VISION-21 Symposium (Vinge 2003 [1993]), is the moment where the exponential curve of technological progress reaches the point where enormous, unpredictable changes take place in the blink of an eye. Thus we are allegedly but decades from a total understanding of the human mind, from integrating machines into our bodies, and, eventually, from uploading our minds into cyberspace. And shortly afterward, "the Singularity will ultimately infuse the universe with spirit" (Kurzweil 2005: 389).

Already, with virtual reality in a primitive stage, belief that we can upload our minds into it has rapidly spread, helped along by a consensus that virtual worlds enable powerful new ways of living. If Hefner (2009) is correct that transhumanist thinking has spread throughout mainstream culture, we will have to accept that this is doubly true for virtual world residents. Those who regularly experience life in virtual environments have described themselves as "virtually empowered avatars" (Merlin 2007), "angels" (Stengers 1991: 52; Davis 1996), and "elemental spirits" (Davis 1996); the environment as the "landscape of rational magic" (Novak 1991: 226), as a liminal place of mystical knowledge (Tomas 1991: 40–41), and "alchemy," based upon "magical thinking" (quoted in Aupers 2009), and the experience as "Dionysian" (Reingold 1991: 385). In such an environment, it comes as no surprise that transhumanist communities have sprung up in the online world of *Second Life*. These groups seek new converts, and believe they or their children might upload their minds into virtual worlds such as *Second Life* and *World of Warcraft* (Geraci 2010). Feelings of transcendence are common for online gamers and virtual world residents, just as Moravec and Kurzweil seem to predict.

Moravec and Kurzweil have given transhumanists a powerful world-view, but, perhaps more importantly, they have also changed our culture. Moravec provided the first technoscientific defense of ideas formerly perceived as science fiction, and Kurzweil championed this apocalyptic vision, buttressing it with additional arguments. This work has been of profound significance in Euro-American culture. Kurzweil has tirelessly promoted the Singularity and, in doing so, has made it a part of our political, scientific, and economic landscapes (Geraci 2010). The mere possibility that we might become cyborgs in Warwick's vision, or disembodied intellects in Moravec's and Kurzweil's, has led to political debate in the United States Congress (as in the 21st Century Nanotechnology Research Act of 2001 and a 2007 report by the US Joint Economic Committee, both of which cite the possibility of a Singularity and massively intelligent computers to come). Kurzweil has been featured in major pop culture venues such as *Rolling Stone* magazine (Kushner 2009) and has founded a for-profit university (Singularity University) with support from NASA and Google. Thanks to a combination of clever articulation and breathless gushing, cyborg and mind-upload technologies look to increasingly bridge the gap between Philip Hefner's upper-case Transhumanism and lower-case transhumanism.

The sacred life of cognitive enhancement

Transhumanists generally define their system of belief in opposition to religion, but their hopes for cognitive enhancement inevitably lead them to a religious faith. Max More's influential Principles of Extropy, for example, define Extropy as (among other things) the search for perpetual progress through "reason" rather than "blind faith," and through "questioning" rather than "dogma." Likewise, the Order of Cosmic Engineers (a transhumanist group founded in 2008) declares itself to be "emphatically […] *NOT a religion*. The OCE is not a religion, not a faith, not a belief, not a church, not a sect, not a cult. We are not a faith-based organization. We are a *convictions based organization*" (Order of Cosmic Engineers 2008, emphasis original). Despite these claims, transhumanism – most especially transhumanism based upon brain–machine interfaces – is religious. Transhumanism is a variation on religious naturalism, an attempt to acquire the traditional goals of religion without recourse to supernatural entities.

Distributed sanctity

Modern religion exceeds the traditional boundaries of the sacred; contrary to the hopes of some secularists, religious beliefs and practices have not disappeared from our culture, but many have, in fact, been camouflaged in seemingly secular enterprises. Culture is thus infused with an attitude of religious naturalism, an expectation that we can, through wholly naturalistic means, accomplish our religious ends. The transhumanist ideology surrounding brain–machine interfaces is a clear example of this phenomenon.

In the middle of the twentieth century, perhaps in response to secularist claims that religion was in its death throes (that it no longer served any functional purpose in society), the great historian of religions Mircea Eliade argued that religion is actually integral to our psychology and our culture, and that the basic aims of religious belief remain with us. In his analysis of modern art, Eliade claims that secular art – art that is not about gods and has no explicitly religious imagery – is religious (Eliade 1985). This should come as no surprise now, when we have recognized that secularist impulses in modernity simply do not do away with religion, but are far more likely to result in religious innovation (Stark and Bainbridge 1985: 2), but Eliade's essays were originally published in the 1960s, at a time when secularist theory remained strong.

Religion is the "negotiation of what it means to be human with respect to the superhuman and the subhuman" (Chidester 2005: vii–viii). In other words, human beings are devoted to the task of meaning-making; we devise beliefs and practices to live by and institutions within which to live that allow us to perceive meaning in the world and our lives with reference to powers or beings greater and lesser than humanity. Any system of beliefs, practices, and institutions engaged in this agenda of developing meaning with respect to superhuman or subhuman forces and entities is, by this definition, religious. We could have philosophical systems of meaning-making that are not religious if they "negotiate what it means to be human" without regard for the superhuman and subhuman forces that are the basis of religious reference points but, as we shall see in the following section, transhumanism – especially that concerned with brain–machine interfaces – does not meet such a definition; transhumanism is unquestionably religious.

We must keep in mind that the superhuman and/or subhuman entities and forces essential to our definition of religion need not be supernatural. Unidentified flying object (UFO) cults, for example, are decidedly religious despite the (generally) naturalistic explanations for UFOs and their pilots. In fact, a broad swath of religious systems occurs without supernatural entities. Some authors have argued that phenomena as widely disparate as baseball (Chidester 2005) and nationalism (Marvin and Ingle 1996) provide religious experiences.

Apocalyptic visions of transhumanism – grounded in the desire to become cyborgs, robots, or uploaded minds in virtual reality – are authentically religious despite the fact that they deny the existence of supernatural powers. David Chidester uses the term "authentic fakes" to label systems wherein non-supernatural, initially non-sacred entities, practices, institutions, and persons take on the powers and aura of the sacred. Authentic fakes are fraudulent practices that do real religious work – they provide access to a sense of transcendence, promote the creation and maintenance of communities, establish morality, and guide human activity (Chidester 2005: vii). These "frauds" are not lies or scams; they are dishonest only in that they are not expected, at first glance, to be sacred, yet accomplish the same ends as if they were. Despite the fact that no gods have emerged to guide our human interface with machines, the transhumanist move toward such interfaces is a religious enterprise – an authentic fake.

The religious life of mind–brain interfaces

The belief that we might attain happiness and immortality, resolve the alienation that makes biological life painful, and make life more meaningful by becoming cyborgs, robots, or software avatars living in a virtual world is religious. Indeed, most likely all versions of transhumanism are religious, regardless of whether or not they deny the existence of supernatural entities and reject all of the traditional religions of humankind. For example, while the Order of Cosmic Engineers denies the existence of supernatural entities, it claims that through the interface of our minds with our machines (in virtual worlds) we have the potential to become gods (Order of Cosmic Engineers 2008). The Order recognizes the powerful connection to religious life by referring to itself as an "UNreligion," the perfect name for an authentically fake religious group.

Transhumanism assigns values, advocates practices, and describes the world by situating human life in a continuum from the earliest levels of evolution through a future in which our minds will transcend the limits we presently experience, becoming like angels or gods. As such, there can be no question that transhumanism is religious, no matter what its practitioners claim (and not all deny this fact).

Transhumanists have infused mind–brain interface technologies with authentic religious fakery. These technologies are given the power to do all of the things that we might once have required divine powers to do. This means that these technologies slide easily into our Western salvation history. The sociologist of religion (and transhumanist) William Sims Bainbridge has argued that religion arises out of the need for exchange partners who can provide human beings with goods that cannot be had from other people. From this "religiogony" (birth story of religion), we can see how the apocalyptic ideology surrounding brain–machine interfaces parallels religious ideology precisely. According to Bainbridge, human beings naturally trade with one another to gain goods and services that are not readily at hand for them, but eventually find that there are goods which no other person can provide, such as immortality or perfect happiness. Bainbridge believes that people subsequently invent gods as exchange partners so as to at least have some vague hope of getting the things they desire (Bainbridge 1995). Religious promises are, in his word, "compensators," because they compensate for our inability to acquire what we truly desire. As Bainbridge seems to have noted (Bainbridge 2006: 206), if brain–machine interfaces allow us to modulate our moods, acquire and learn what we want, and live forever, then they will provide the very things that religion was allegedly invented to help us cope without. As such, promises of a transcendent human-machine future have entered a competitive religious marketplace (Amarasingam 2008).

Many transhumanists, but especially those who follow Moravec, Kurzweil, and their Apocalyptic AI allies, share the common religious perspective that salvation is not just inevitable, but imminent. Faith in the Singularity essentially precludes believing that cyborg immortality is centuries away. The exponential curves drawn by Moravec and Kurzweil – and theorized by Kurzweil in a law of accelerating returns – demand that centuries-worth of technological progress (as we have known it) will take place in the next few decades. For Kurzweil, all ordered systems are subject to the law of accelerating returns and will thus experience exponential growth. In *The Singularity is Near* (Kurzweil 2005), he applies this logic to computational speeds, brain-scanning technologies, virtual reality development, and other, related technologies to "prove" that the Singularity will occur right around the year 2029. Other theorists give the time frame up to ten years more, but agree that our techno-salvation is fast approaching. Just as apocalyptic Christians have believed (for millennia) that Jesus will return in the very near future, advocates of the AI apocalypse look forward to a rapid onset of cyborg bodies and the Mind Fire.

Conclusion

Cyborg technologies, especially as combined with religious thinking, have the power to radically shape our culture. Even when transhumanists label their movement as "philosophical," as with Rizzuto and Fost (Chapter 52 in this volume), the movement remains deeply religious. Transhumanism is not just in "the gray area between science and science fiction" (Chapter 52); it is a search to renegotiate human meaning and transform human lives into superhuman ones. Those who believe that we will soon have the ability to become cyborgs, robots, or free-flowing software avatars in virtual reality are religious practitioners. Such shifts would presage a new future for religious life, as they would be easily implicated in our millennia-long search for transcendence, for perfect happiness, for freedom from alienation and pain, and for immortality. The view that cognitive enhancements through brain–machine interfaces promise any of these things is relatively common and is unquestionably religious. As the early transhumanist Robert Ettinger has written, technology "is an essential part of our salvation" (1989 [1971]: 31). The future remains open and, as yet, no-one has proved that we will succeed in becoming vastly intelligent and powerful cyborgs, robot bushes, or disembodied cyberspace minds. Nevertheless, the religious inclination of humankind is strong; thus many transhumanists take solace in the belief that we will accomplish these things and, in so doing, find a final solution to our religious hopes and dreams.

Note

1 Johannes Kepler's *Somnium* (written and elaborated between 1600 and 1630; published 1634) may have equal or greater claim to the title of "first science fiction story." For more on the *Somnium*, see Christianson (1976).

References

Amarasingam, Amarnath (2008) "Transcending Technology: Looking at Futurology as a New Religious Movement," *Journal of Contemporary Religion* 23(1): 1–16.

Associated Press (2009) "Researchers Claim Robotic Hand Controlled via Mind." CBS News (December 2), Available: http://cbs2chicago.com/technology/robotic.arm.thoughts.2.1345404.html (accessed January 10, 2010).

Aupers, Stef (2009) "'The Force is Great': Enchantment and Magic in Silicon Valley," *Masaryk University Journal of Law and Technology* 3(1): 153–73.

Bacon, Francis (1951 [1626]) *The Advancement of Learning and New Atlantis*, London: Oxford University Press.

Bainbridge, William Sims (1995) "Neural Network Models of Religious Belief," *Sociological Perspectives* 38(4): 483–95.

——(2006) "Cognitive Technologies," in *Managing Nano-Bio-Info-Cogno Innovations: Converging Technologies in Society*, William Sims Bainbridge and Mihail C. Roco (eds.), Dordrecht, The Netherlands: Springer, 203–26.

Bostrom, Nick (2005) "A History of Transhumanist Thought," *Journal of Evolution and Technology* 14: (1): 1–25.

Chidester, David (2005) *Authentic Fakes: Religion and American Popular Culture*, Berkeley, CA: University of California Press.

Christianson, Gale E. (1976) "Kepler's *Somnium*: Science Fiction and the Renaissance Scientist," *Science Fiction Studies* 3(1): 79–90.

Clark, Andy (2004) *Natural-Born Cyborgs: Minds, Technologies, and the Future of Human Intelligence*, New York: Oxford University Press.

Clark, Andy and Chalmers, David (1998) "The Extended Mind," *Analysis* 58(1): 7–19.

Clarke, Arthur C. (1968) *2001: A Space Odyssey*, New York: New American Library.

——(2001 [1956]) *The City and the Stars and The Sands of Mars*, New York: Warner Books.

Clynes, Manfred E. and Kline, Nathan S. (1960) "Cyborgs and Space," *Astronautics* (September): 26–27 and 74–76.

Dillow, Clay. (2009) "Toyota Unveils Wheelchair Propelled by Thoughts Alone," Fast Company.com (June 29), Available: http://www.fastcompany.com/blog/clay-dillow/culture-buffet/mobility-mind-control-toyota-unveils-wheelchair-propelled-thoughts-a (accessed January 10, 2010).

Doctorow, Cory (2003) *Down and Out in the Magic Kingdom*, New York: Tor.

Eliade, Mircea (1985) *Symbolism, the Sacred, and the Arts*, Diane Apostolos-Cappadona (ed.), New York: Crossroad.

Ettinger, Robert (1989 [1971]) *Man into Superman*, available: http://www.cryonics.org/book2.html.

Geraci, Robert M. (2010) *Apocalyptic AI: Visions of Heaven in Robotics, Artificial Intelligence, and Virtual Reality*, New York: Oxford University Press.

Haldane, J.B.S. (1923) "Daedalus, Or Science and the Future," Presented to the Heretics Society, Cambridge, U.K. (February 4), available: http://www.cscs.umich.edu/~crshalizi/Daedalus.html.

Hammock, Anne (2009) "The Future of Brain-Controlled Devices," *CNN.com*, available: http://www.cnn.com/2009/TECH/12/30/brain.controlled.computers/index.html (accessed January 5, 2010).

Haraway, Donna (1997) *Modest_Witness@Second_Millennium.Female_Man©_Meets_Oncomouse™*, New York: Routledge.

Hefner, Philip (2009) "The Animal that Aspires to be an Angel: The Challenge of Transhumanism," *Dialog: A Journal of Theology* 48(2): 164–73.

Huxley, Aldous (1932) *Brave New World*, London: Chatto and Windus.

Kurzweil, Ray (1999) *The Age of Spiritual Machines: When Computers Exceed Human Intelligence*, New York: Viking.

——(2005) *The Singularity is Near: When Humans Transcend Biology*, New York: Penguin Books.

Kushner, David (2009) "When Man and Machine Merge," *Rolling Stones* 1072: 56–61.

Locklear, Fred (2003) "Hippocampus on a Chip," ArsTechnica.com (March 12), available: http://arstechnica.com/old/content/2003/03/476.ars (accessed January 10, 2010).

Marvin, Carolyn and Ingle, David W. (1996) "Blood Sacrifice and the Nation: Revisiting Civil Religion," *Journal of the American Academy of Religion* 64(4): 767–80.

Massachusetts Institute of Technology (2010) X Prize Lab Events Page, available: http://web.mit.edu/deshpandecenter/xprizelab/events.html (accessed January 9, 2010).

Merlin, Qyxxql (2007) Blog comment, May 20, on "A Crisis of Faith," by W. James Au, New World Notes [weblog], May 18. http://nwn.blogs.com/nwn/2007/05/avatars_of_unch.html (accessed June 5, 2007).

Moravec, Hans (1978) "Today's Computers, Intelligent Machines and Our Future," *Analog* 99 (2): 59–84. Reposted by the Field Robotics Center at Carnegie Mellon University's Robotics Institute, available: www.frc.ri.cmu.edu/~hpm/project.archive/general.articles/1978/analog.1978.html (accessed August 5, 2007).

——(1988) *Mind Children: The Future of Robot and Human Intelligence*, Cambridge, MA: Harvard University Press.

——(1999) *Robot: Mere Machine to Transcendent Mind*, New York: Oxford University Press.

Novak, Marcos (1991) "Liquid Architectures in Cyberspace," in *Cyberspace: First Steps*, Michael Benedikt (ed.), Cambridge, MA: MIT Press, 225–54.

Order of Cosmic Engineers (2008) "Prospectus," available: http://www.cosmeng.org/index.php/Prospectus.

Physorg (2009a) "New Robot 'Steered by Human Thought': Honda," PhysOrg.com, available: http://www.physorg.com/news157703000.html.

——(2009b) "Machine Translates Thoughts into Speech in Real Time," PhysOrg.com, available: http://www.physorg.com/news180620740.html.

Stengers, Nicole (1991) "Mind is a Leaking Rainbow," in *Cyberspace: First Steps*, Michael Benedikt (ed.), Cambridge, MA: MIT Press, 49–58.

Stross, Charles (2005) *Accelerando*, New York: Ace.

Stock, Gregory (2003) *Redesigning Humans: Choosing Our Genes, Changing Our Future*, New York: Houghton Mifflin Company.

Tomas, David (1991) "Old Rituals for New Space: *Rites de Passage* and William Gibson's Cultural Model of Cyberspace," in *Cyberspace: First Steps*, Michael Benedikt (ed.), Cambridge, MA: MIT Press, 31–47.

Turkle, Shery (1997) *Life on the Screen: Identity in Age of the Internet*, New York: Simon & Schuster.

Vinge, Vernor (2003 [1993]) "Technological Singularity," rev ed., available at www-rohan.sdsu.edu/faculty/vinge/misc/WER2.html.

Ward, Logan (2005) "2005 Popular Mechanics Breakthrough Awards," *Popular Mechanics*, November.

Warwick, Kevin (2004) *I, Cyborg*, Urbana, IL: University of Illinois Press.

Zelazny, Roger (1967) *Lord of Light*, Garden City, NY: Doubleday.

Further reading

Studies in transhumanism and in neural prostheses are proliferating as technology advances. To begin studies in this field, a new reader ought to consider early work such as Ferodouin Esfandiary's *Up-Wingers* (Popular Library, 1973), as well as more recent titles such as Hans Moravec's *Robot* and Ray Kurzweil's *The Singularity is Near* (both cited above). The wide array of contributors to the February 2009 edition of the Metanexus Institute's *Global Spiral* (www.metanexus.net/magazine) provides helpful starting points to understand transhumanism in the words of many contemporary figures. Finally, science fiction works such as those by Neal Stephenson (*Snow Crash*, Bantam, 1992), Vernor Vinge (*True Names*, Tor, 2001), Cory Doctorow (*Down and Out in the Magic Kingdom*, Tor, 2003), and Charles Stross (*Accelerando*, Tor, 2005) provide imaginative insight into what a transhuman future might look like, and such books have been influential among transhumanist thinkers.

54
HUMAN-DIRECTED EVOLUTION
A Christian perspective

Noreen Herzfeld

Genesis 1 notes that on the sixth day of creation, after God created human beings, He pronounced his creation "very good." Could modern technologies such as genetic engineering, cloning, pharmaceuticals, robotics, and nanotechnology – technologies that hold the prospect of not just temporarily alleviating human ills, but of altering our very nature as a species – make us better than "very good"? Transhumanists believe they can. Though defined in a number of different ways, most transhumanists share a belief in the power of technology to enhance our mental and physical abilities. While some take a minimalist approach, looking for relief from the enemies of pain, sickness, and aging, others hope to overcome the ultimate enemy, death itself. They see the primary goal of technology not in terms of immediate therapy or enhancement, but as an instrument through which we humans can deliberately direct the evolution of our species, transcending our fallible bodily platform for a new one of our own design.

Do scientists find these hopes either feasible or desirable? Responses vary. In an article in *Wired*, Bill Joy, then chief executive officer of Sun Microsystems, warned that human beings may be contributing to our own extinction through the rapid and unconsidered development of technology. In particular, Joy expresses concerns about possible future interactions between nanotechnology, robotics, and genetic engineering. Joy foresees the potential for several problems, including the development of an artificial intelligence that sees no use for human beings, or the development of self-replicating machines at the nanometer scale that somehow escape our control or, worse, are set loose as weapons of mass destruction. He calls for scientists to slow down research in robotics and nanotechnology until we are assured that self-destruction by such technologies could be avoided (Joy 2000).

On the other hand, renowned physicist Stephen Hawking believes human beings must actively pursue genetic engineering in order to stay ahead, intellectually and physically, of future artificial intelligences (Odenwald 2001). Hawking is joined by computer scientists Rodney Brooks of MIT, and Ray Kurzweil, in suggesting that, rather than seeing them as portents of our demise as a species, we should view artificial intelligence, nanotechnology, and genetic engineering as possible avenues to saving the human species, so as to adapt to an ecologically threatened planet or to move beyond our planet into space. Hans Moravec of Carnegie Mellon suggests that artificial intelligence will be the next step in evolution, that the "goal" of evolution is not humanity *per se*, but intelligence. Genetic engineering and the interrelated computer technologies of nanotechnology, artificial intelligence, and robotics provide possible new directions for a post-human species (Moravec 1988).

Is human-designed evolution playing God in a way that should not be ours, or is it simply the living out of our destiny as created co-creators with God? Should we go full steam ahead, as Hawking suggests, or proceed only with caution, as Joy suggests? The Christian response, though mixed, leans more toward Joy than Hawking. While we are called by Jesus to heal the sick and help the suffering (Luke 9), there are several reasons, both scientific and theological, for us to be extremely wary of the self-designed evolution of a post-human species as a reasonable solution either to the pains of the human condition or to our current ecological crises.

From a scientific standpoint, evolution is clearly the theory of the day, the basis of modern biology as well as much current sociological and psychological research. However, it must be noted that human-designed evolution would differ radically from that based on natural selection, as described by Darwin. Natural selection produces new species with features generated by chance, selected for by reproductive or survival advantage over long periods of time. Despite the use of the term "selection," natural selection is the antithesis of conscious improvement. It moves slowly, produces endless variation, and makes no judgments of good or bad.

No species heretofore has designed its own successor. The claim that we are capable of doing so, and coming up with something better than "very good," runs up against four tenets central to Christian thought: reverence for the human body in the incarnation; our final destiny in the resurrection; our creation in the image of God; and the ubiquity of sin as part of the human condition. These tenets make the prospect of human-directed evolution dubious at best, and at worst dangerously hubristic, threatening what matters most to us as humans.

Incarnation and the body

Transhumanists do not find the human body to be "very good." The transhumanist understanding of the human person is unabashedly dualistic, dismissive of the physical body. While many hope simply to enhance the body through technological means such as genetic engineering, implanted chips, or pharmaceuticals, thereby making us stronger, smarter, or longer-lived, there is a strong strain within transhumanism that seeks to escape or supplant the human body altogether. It suggests that, though emerging out of matter, what constitutes the essence of the human person is information, the pattern of one's thoughts, memories, and experiences. According to molecular biologist Francis Crick: "You, your joys and your sorrows, your memories and your ambitions, your sense of personal identity and your will, are in fact no more than the behavior of a vast assembly of nerve cells and their associated molecules […] You're nothing but a pack of neurons" (Crick 1994: 3). The contents of these neurons, notes astronomer Robert Jastrow, need not remain on a biological platform: "A bold scientist will be able to tap the contents of his mind and transfer them into the metallic lattices of a computer […] liberated from the weakness of the mortal flesh" (Jastrow 1983: 166). Unlike Jastrow, Moravec views the computer not as a vehicle for personal liberation from the body, but as the next step in human evolution. He hopes that mind itself might be "rescued from the limitations of a mortal body" and we might pass on our intelligence to our "unfettered mind children" (Moravec 1988: 122). Whether general or particular, all of these views have in common a disdain for the bodies in which we currently find ourselves.

Christianity faced a similar disdain for the physical in ancient Gnosticism, which taught that the physical body, as part of the material world, was evil and unredeemed, a source of limitation to the spirit, which was immortal. Only secret knowledge, given to the few, would release the spirit from the body and lead to redemption. The early Church Fathers, particularly Irenaeus and Tertullian, rejected these claims. Irenaeus notes that the human being is "a mixed organization of soul and flesh, who was formed after the likeness of God, and moulded by His hands, that is, by the Son and Holy Spirit" (*Against Heresies*: IV, Preface). He sees the body not only as a vital part of being human, but as one that has been sanctified through Jesus' incarnation into human form:

> Since the Lord thus has redeemed us through His own blood, giving His soul for our souls, and His flesh for our flesh, […] attaching man to God by His own incarnation, and bestowing upon us at His coming immortality, durably and truly, by means of communion with God, all the doctrines of the heretics fall to ruin.
>
> (*ibid.*: V.1.1)

This affirmation of the physical body is continued through the Christian practice of the Eucharist, "for, even as the blessed Paul declares in his Epistle to the Ephesians, that 'we are members of His body, of His flesh, and of His bones' he does not speak these words of some spiritual and invisible man, for a spirit has not bones nor flesh; but [he refers to] that dispensation [by which the Lord became] an actual man, consisting of flesh, and nerves, and bones, that which is nourished by the cup which is His blood, and receives increase from the bread which is His body" (*ibid.*: V.2.3).

The Word became flesh. Our finite bodies are an integral part of who we are. And our God, in saving us, took on that nature. If God did not disdain having a human body, should we?

Resurrection or eternal life

Our God, in human form, also died on the cross. While the Gnostics were right in noting that the body can be at times an uncomfortable source of pain, limitation, or temptation, the ultimate enemy is death. Downloading our thought patterns to a computer seems to provide a solution. Kurzweil writes:

> Up until now our mortality was tied to the longevity of our hardware. When the hardware crashed, that was it […] As we cross the divide to instantiate ourselves into our computational technology, our identity will be based on our evolving mind file. We will be software, not hardware […] As software, our mortality will no longer be dependent on the survival of the computing circuitry [… as] we periodically port ourselves to the latest, ever more capable "personal" computer […] our immortality will be a matter of being sufficiently careful to make frequent backups.
>
> (Kurzweil 1999: ch. 6)

The philosopher Valentine Turchin notes that dreams of an existence in cyberspace lift the concept of resurrection out of the conceptual sphere of religion into something more concrete. He deems some concept of immortality to be necessary if life is to have meaning: "The decline of traditional religions appealing to metaphysical immortality threatens to degrade modern society. Cybernetic immortality can take the place of metaphysical immortality to provide the ultimate goals and values for the emerging global civilization" (Turchin 1997). How does eternal life through computation compare with the Christian view of eternal life through the resurrection?

First, cybernetic immortality denies the importance of the body, yet, unlike the Gnostics, ties immortality to the material world. It promises more time on this Earth, albeit in a different form. This differs considerably from the Christian resurrection. Theologian Reinhold Niebuhr writes: "The Christian faith insists that the final consummation of history lies beyond the conditions of the temporal process," even though "the consummation [in the resurrection] fulfills, rather than negates, the historical process" (Niebuhr 1992b: 291). Cybernetic immortality posits a future that cannot be everlasting. No matter what physical platform is used to instantiate information, it would remain a finite creation within a finite universe. Even scientists agree that "heaven and earth will pass away" (Mark 13: 31). In other words, cybernetic instantiation promises not immortality, but simply a longer life span; the Sun will some day go nova, our galaxy will eventually burn out. Any life in this material realm must inevitably end.

Second, consider the underlying premise that the human being is ultimately the information held in one's brain. Such a view is sadly individualistic, isolating each one of us in our own perceptions and experiences. Theologian Karl Barth posits a view of humankind that is quite different. According to Barth, we image a triune God, a God who embodies relationship in God's very self, by being in relationship first with God, and secondarily with one another. Our true humanity is thus never experienced as individuals. It is a cultural entity in the sense that we image God corporately, the image lying in the act of our relationships themselves, of which the information in our brains is only a pale reminder (Barth 1958: 184–85).

The resurrection Christians hope for is not simply more time on this Earth. It is not a life span greatly lengthened. Nor is it a transmigration of one's soul away from the body, but a raising up of both soul and body into a new creation. The three creeds of Christianity, Apostles', Nicene, and Athanasian, are emphatic that the resurrection is "of the body." Third-century theologian Minucius Felix likens this to the reappearance of the same plants each spring: "See, too, how for our consolation all nature suggests the future resurrection. […] Flowers die, but come to life again. After their decay shrubs put forth leaves again; not unless seeds decay does their strength return. A body in the grave is like the trees in winter: They hide their sap under a deceptive dryness." (Minucius Felix 1978: 34.11–12). The *Catechism of the Catholic Church* (1994: 265) states, "'We believe in the true resurrection of this flesh that we now possess' (Council of Lyons II). We sow a corruptible body in the tomb, but he raises up an incorruptible body."

Better than the image of God?

While the goal of a truly eternal life through technology must elude us, a more modest goal of better health, of stronger, more capable bodies and minds seems obtainable. Modern medical technology has already lengthened our life span, and holds the promise of therapies or cures for a variety of illnesses we have heretofore found intractable. In the book of Mark, one of the most frequent activities Jesus engages in is to heal the sick. In Luke 9: 2 the disciples are commanded to do likewise. Clearly the use of healing technologies lies well within this purview. However, many of these same technologies can also make us better than well, enhancing our bodies or our minds. If human-directed evolution does not make us immortal, might it at least make us a better species?

Consider the case of neuropharmaceuticals, drugs that hold the prospect not only of curing mental illness and dysfunction, but also of improving the functioning of our minds and/or our perceived quality of life. According to the US Centers for Disease Control, antidepressants were the most frequently prescribed class of drugs in 2005, with a total of 118 million prescriptions. These drugs, selective serotonin reuptake inhibitors (SSRIs), block the reabsorption of serotonin, thus increasing the amount available to the brain. Serotonin is one of the primary chemicals that the brain uses to transfer signals between neurons and plays a major role in regulating mood, appetite, anger, sleep, sexuality, and body temperature.

The advent of SSRIs and other psychotropic drugs reflects the rapid advances that have been made in understanding the physical and biochemical structure of the brain. While depression has long been associated with troubling thoughts and emotions, or even certain personality types, we now know that it is truly a disease, associated with nerve-cell atrophy in the brain that is cumulative over time. Depression also harms the heart, endocrine system, and skeletal structure, and can be life-threatening should it lead to suicide. The advent of new medications to treat this illness is clearly a step forward in healing the sick and helping the suffering.

Yet many remain troubled. Psychiatrist Peter Kramer notes that after the publication of his book *Listening to Prozac* (2005), in which he describes the almost miraculous transformation of many of his patients, he was frequently asked the question "what if Prozac had been available in van Gogh's time?". The unease that underlies this question is twofold. First, is all suffering bad? Might widespread usage of such a drug deprive us of some of the world's most insightful art, music, or literature? Would its widespread use remove a necessary aspect of the human condition? Second, Prozac, and other psychotropic drugs have the potential to radically alter a patient's personality. Is our personality strictly biochemical and alterable at will? If so, who, then, are we?

Irish psychiatrist Maurice Drury, in an essay entitled "Madness and Religion," describes a Catholic priest for whom saying the mass no longer held any meaning. This man felt he had lost his faith, was having trouble sleeping and eating, and experienced odd physical pains. While the latter are classic symptoms of clinical depression, the priest found meaning for his state in the former; he attributed his malaise to the realm of the spirit (Drury 2003: 116–17). The struggle with faith is a recurring theme in religious literature. We need only think of St John of the Cross's "dark night of the soul." Or consider the psalmist, crying out:

> How long, O Lord? Will you forget me forever?
> How long will you hide your face from me?
> How long must I bear pain in my soul,
> And have sorrow in my heart all day long?
>
> (Psalm 13)

Tolstoy writes of a similar time of spiritual darkness: "I can call this by no other name than that of a thirst for God. This craving for God had nothing to do with the movement of my ideas, in fact, it was the direct contrary of that movement, but it came from my heart. It was like a feeling of dread that made me seem like an orphan and isolated in the midst of all these things that were so foreign" (James 1961: 135). It was this search, this time of despair, that led Tolstoy to change his entire way of life. Gordon Allport (1950: 73) notes that "the mature religious sentiment is ordinarily fashioned in the workshop of doubt." The maturing of the individual necessitates some pain that we might not want to be too quick to alleviate.

Another frequently prescribed neuropharmaceutical is Ritalin, the trade name for methylphenidate, a stimulant in the same family as methamphetamine and cocaine. Ritalin is prescribed to over 3.5 million children and adults around the world to treat the syndrome known variously as attention deficit disorder or attention deficit hyperactivity disorder (ADHD). ADHD is diagnosed through its symptoms, which include restlessness, hyperactivity, difficulty concentrating, and impulsive behaviors. The striking thing is how rapidly the number of diagnoses of ADHD has risen. In 1990, 900,000 children were using Ritalin. By 1997 it was 2 million, and by 2000 5 million were using Ritalin or other related stimulants (Diller 1998: 35). Why such a rapid rise? Some authors suggest that ADHD is not really a disease at all, but a diagnosis for a collection of normal childhood behaviors. Others point to the speed and availability of sensory stimulation in our culture as a source of hyperactivity. Children whose minds are conditioned by the rapid-fire world of MTV and video games find themselves uncomfortable in the absence of such stimuli.

Whatever its source, and whether or not the diagnosis of ADHD is accurate in most cases, what we see is a move toward a biological understanding of human behavior. The President's Council on Bioethics describes the problem inherent in this:

> A medical diagnosis of ADHD […] implies or claims the presence of a malfunction in the child's brain. If impulse control is the behavioral product

> of combining an impulse-to-do and the will-to-restrain, one can then imagine Ritalin as acting to reduce impulse-to-do rather than strengthen the will-to-restrain. In contrast, the traditional tools of teaching young children "good" and "bad" behavior, involves praise and blame from parents and teachers […] A central moral question about treating hyperactive children with Ritalin is now apparent: Is it desirable to substitute the language and methods of medicine for the language and methods of morals?
>
> (President's Council on Bioethics 2002)

Advances in neuroscience have led in general toward locating the source of mental difficulty in the individual's brain chemistry. This is a view that lends itself to a technological fix. Change the chemistry in the brain with the appropriate drug, and the problem is solved. Or is it? Just as taking an aspirin might alleviate a headache without getting at the initial cause, so taking Prozac or Ritalin changes an individual's behaviors or emotions without necessarily addressing the cause of those behavior or emotions.

Finally, just as Prozac might be used as a tool for personality enhancement by those who are not clinically depressed, Ritalin is increasingly used by adults or college students to enhance mental performance. Recent campus surveys show that as many as 20 per cent of college students have at one time used Ritalin to boost concentration for writing a paper or taking an exam (Anon. 2005: 1). As with the question of where a person's true personality lies, Ritalin use raises the question of what is a true measure of one's mental abilities – those measured on or off Ritalin? However, as Michael Gazzaniga points out, our fears likely outstrip the potential of these drugs. Most students are not interested in using Ritalin as more than an occasional study aid, and memory-enhancing drugs are unlikely to be used as more than an aid to the natural memory loss that comes with aging (Gazzaniga 2005: 74).

Steroids make sports no longer a contest, but an exhibition. Ritalin does the same for mental performance. Doping dissolves the limits that have long defined what a normal person can do. Does this matter? Some think not, so long as the option is available to all. According to David Malloy, who teaches sports ethics at the University of Regina: "I don't think the average person cares that players are on steroids. I think they just want to see them hit the ball a mile out of the park" (Longman 2007).

This quotation highlights the dilemma of using pharmaceuticals for mental or physical enhancement. Both demonstrate an obsession with performance and with quantitative measurements – higher batting averages, faster race times, higher test scores. Even Kramer's patients on Prozac evaluated their happiness quantitatively, in terms of the number of dates they were asked on, or whether they received a raise in salary at work. This obsession with performance shifts our understanding of ourselves from who we are to what we do. But doing is a never-ending task. The philosopher Jacques Ellul notes the end result: "There is no longer respite for reflecting or choosing or adapting oneself, or for acting or wishing or pulling oneself together […] Life has become a racecourse […] a succession of objective events which drag us along and lead us astray without anything affording us the possibility of standing apart, taking stock, and ceasing to act" (Ellul 1964: 330). On such a racecourse, one can never be satisfied with oneself "as is." The President's Council on Bioethics agrees:

> In wanting to become more than we are, and in sometimes acting as if we were already superhuman or divine, we risk despising what we are and neglecting what we have. In wanting to improve our bodies and our minds using new tools to enhance their performance, we risk making our bodies and minds little different from our tools, in the process also compromising the distinctly human character of our agency and activity […] In seeking brighter outlooks, reliable contentment, and dependable feelings of self-esteem in ways that bypass their usual natural sources, we risk flattening our soul, lowering our aspirations, and weakening our loves and attachments.
>
> (President's Council on Bioethics 2003)

A 2002 Vatican document, *Communion and Stewardship: Human Persons Created in the Image of God* echoes this concern. While accepting technology for therapeutic use, noting that restoring the body or mind to full functioning respects God's original design and the organic unity of body and soul, the document's authors warn us not to fundamentally change our nature:

> The idea of man as "co-creator" with God could be used to try to justify the management of human evolution […] But this would imply that man has full right of disposal over his own biological nature. Changing the genetic identity of man as a human person through the production of an infra-human being is radically immoral […] The uniqueness of each human person, in part constituted by his biogenetic characteristics and developed through nurture and growth, belongs intrinsically to him and cannot be instrumentalized in order to improve some of these characteristics. A man can only truly improve by realizing more fully the image of God in him by uniting himself to Christ and in imitation of him.
>
> (International Theological Commission 2002)

Can we trust our own design?

While transhumanists seek to surmount or improve on our finite bodies, Reinhold Niebuhr sees our inability to accept our bodily limitations as a source of sin:

> Man is ignorant and involved in the limitations of a finite mind; but he pretends that he is not limited. He assumes that he can gradually transcend finite limitations until his mind becomes identical with universal mind. All of his intellectual and cultural pursuits, therefore, become infected with the sin of pride.
>
> (Niebuhr 1992a: 178–79)

One of the ways pride manifests itself is through what Niebuhr calls the sin of insecurity, a sin "of those, who knowing themselves to be insecure, seek sufficient power to guarantee their security, inevitably of course at the expense of other life" (*ibid.*: 190). And here we come back to scientists Stephen Hawking and Bill Joy. Hawking's call to embrace new technologies uncritically is rooted in his fear that climate change and other ecological crises might make the Earth unlivable. Joy notes that we pursue genetic engineering, nanotechnology, and artificial intelligence because the proponents of these technologies have told us that they will result in new cures, lengthened life spans, and increased material prospects. In our insecurity when faced with sickness and death, we grab hold of these promises, and in doing so we fail ourselves and the rest of nature in three ways. First, we do not give thought to the fact that the down-side of any given technology has equal probability of occurring as the up-side, even though history tells us this is true. So we blithely ignore warnings of what could go wrong and we ignore collateral damage to nature that happens along the way.

However, away from the realm of the potential and in the realm of the here and now, there is a second more insidious evil, namely, that the promises these technologies hold out dazzle us with possible, rather fantastic, but also unlikely outcomes and, in so doing, blind us to other, more practical options. The ecological options of lowering consumption, of conservation and true stewardship of our resources, just don't look as sexy. The day-to-day work of providing care for the sick, or hospice for the dying, is not so exciting.

Third, we do damage to ourselves spiritually when we look for a technological escape from the human condition. Niebuhr notes that our "arrogant sense of independence and greedy effort to overcome the insecurity of nature's rhythms" results in the destruction of our "sense of dependence upon nature and [our] reverent gratitude toward the miracle of nature's perennial abundance" (Niebuhr 1992a: 190–91). This loss of reverence extends beyond nature to a loss of reverence for what it means to be human, and a loss of reverence for the creator God. We put our energy into the futile task of trying to fix nature, to extend our lives, and thereby risk missing exactly what makes our lives meaningful.

Technology is not going to save us from our human condition. Nor are technologies intrinsically evil. As Christians, we recognize the potential of new technologies to heal the sick and help the suffering while simultaneously being aware of the potential of every technology to do ill as well as good. The dreams of transhumanism, from a Christian perspective, are precisely that – dreams. Yet we recognize that, in these dreams, transhumanists share with Christians the understanding that our world and our existence are not yet perfect; that, as the apostle Paul writes: "we know that the whole creation has been groaning as in the pains of childbirth right up to the present time. Not only so but we ourselves, who have the first fruits of the Spirit, groan inwardly as we wait eagerly for our adoption as sons, the redemption of our bodies" (Romans 8: 24). We know things are not yet as they should be.

Evolution will continue, but we must exercise care in deciding that we know how it should continue. As Christians, we must always remember that we were created by God, in His image, and that he has already pronounced that creation "very good." We may not always see the goodness when life presents us with suffering, pain, or death. Yet we place our hope in the events recorded in scripture, in the incarnation, death, and resurrection of our Lord Jesus Christ, and therefore of ourselves.

References

Allport, Gordon (1950) *The Individual and His Religion*, New York: Macmillan.
Anon. (2005) "College Life: The Ritalin Advantage?," *New York Times News Service*, August 1.
Barth, Karl (1958) *Church Dogmatics*, Volume 3, G. W. Bromiley and T. F. Torrance (eds), J. W. Edwards, O. Bussey and Harold Knight (trans.), Edinburgh: T& T Clark.
Catechism of the Catholic Church (1994) Collegeville, MN: Liturgical Press.
Crick, Francis (1994) *The Astonishing Hypothesis: The Scientific Search for the Soul*, New York: Charles Scribner's Sons.
Diller, Lawrence (1998) *Running on Ritalin: A Physician Reflects on Children, Society, and Performance in a Pill*, New York: Bantam.
Drury, Maurice (2003) *The Danger of Words*, Bristol: Thoemmes.
Ellul, Jacques (1964) *The Technological Society*, New York: Alfred Knopf.
Gazzaniga, Michael (2005) *The Ethical Brain*, New York: Dana Press.
International Theological Commission (2002) *Communion and Stewardship: Human Persons Created in the Image of God*, Vatican: International Theological Commission, www.vatican.va/roman_curia/congregations/cfaith/cti_documents/rc_con_cfaith_doc_20040723_communion-stewardship_en.html
Ireneaus (n.d.), *Against Heresies*, www.newadvent.org/fathers/0103.htm.
James, William (1961) *The Varieties of Religious Experience*, New York: Macmillan.
Jastrow, Robert (1983) *The Enchanted Loom*, New York: Simon & Schuster.
Joy, Bill (2000) "Why the Future Doesn't Need Us," *Wired* 8: 04.
Kramer, Peter (2005) "There's Nothing Deep About Depression," *The New York Times*, April 17.
Kurzweil, Raymond (1999) *The Age of Spiritual Machines: When Computers Exceed Human Intelligence*, New York: Penguin.
Longman, Jere (2007) "The Deafening Roar of the Shrug," *The New York Times*, July 29.
Niebuhr, Reinhold (1992a) *The Nature and Destiny of Man: A Christian Interpretation*, Volume 1, Louisville, KY: Westminster John Knox.
——(1992b) *The Nature and Destiny of Man: A Christian Interpretation*, Volume 2, Louisville, KY: Westminster John Knox.
Minucius Felix (1978) *Octavius*, G. W. Clarke (trans.), New York: Paulist.
Moravec, Hans (1988) *Mind Children: The Future of Robot and Human Intelligence*, Cambridge, MA: Harvard University Press.
Odenwald, Michael (2001) "Ich könnte mit Einstein und Newton pokern," *Focus* 36.
President's Council on Bioethics (2002) "Human Flourishing, Performance Enhancement, and Ritalin," www.bioethics.gov/background/humanflourish.html.
——(2003) "Beyond Therapy: Biotechnology and the Pursuit of Happiness," www.bioethics.gov/reports/beyondtherapy/index.html.
Turchin, Valentine (1997) "Cybernetic Immortality," http://pespmc1.vub.ac.be/CYBIMM.html.

Further reading

For differing views, both scientific and theological, of the concept of resurrection, see Ted Peters, Robert Russell and Michael Welker's *Resurrection: Theological and Scientific Assessments* (Grand Rapids, MI: Eerdmans, 2002). A fuller theological assessment of several modern technologies can be found in Noreen Herzfeld, *Technology and Religion: Remaining Human in a Co-Created World* (West Conshohocken, PA: Templeton, 2009), and in Greg Peterson, *Minding God: Theology and the Cognitive Sciences* (Minneapolis, MN: Fortress, 2003). Albert Borgmann provides a more philosophical assessment in *Power Failure: Christianity and the Culture of Technology* (Grand Rapids, MI: Brazos, 2003).

55
AMERICAN INDIANS, TRANSHUMANISM AND COGNITIVE ENHANCEMENT

Thurman Lee Hester, Jr.

Elements of culture affecting acceptance

Though it is impossible to speak of American Indian culture monolithically, there are several cultural norms that are almost universally held, though they may manifest in different ways from nation to nation. These foundations of American Indian culture have endured through generations of boarding schools, missionaries, and government policies that have sought to "Americanize" them. While American Indian people have bent with the winds, they have not broken. The depth and breadth of practices maintained varies from individual to individual, and from nation to nation, but the fundamental core is still vibrant in many communities and only slowly fading in others. On a very basic level, American Indian people continue to be both pragmatic and what Euro-American philosophers might call "mystical." For American Indians, everything is both mundane and spiritual. To live, we must eat. This is a very practical fact. To eat, we might kill a deer or raise corn. On one hand we take a life and on the other we nurture it, but both have profound spiritual overtones and consequences. In every element of life there are both practical answers and unfathomable mysteries. In providing the practical answers, American Indian people are very pragmatic, and well known for adopting the answers of other cultures in a kind of syncretism that often skips any attempt at reconciliation of belief. This is, in part, because belief plays a much less important role in Native American culture. Orthopraxy, among other things, provides the group cohesion and identity that orthodoxy gives most European cultures. So, American Indian nations and people are very likely to adopt emerging technologies that fill a practical need unless these conflict with other practices that are more central to their cultures. While ideas presented here are generally true, it should be remembered that there are literally hundreds of American Indian Nations and thus specifics will certainly vary.

In approaching life's mysteries, American Indian cultures have responded, like all human cultures, with the full range of tools that human ingenuity could provide. Everything from philosophical enquiry, through religion and on to altered states of consciousness has been used by all cultures facing the infinite. The differences have really been in each culture's emphasis. Among American Indian people, altered states of consciousness have been a more common response throughout history than they ever were among Europeans. Though one can argue that one of the most widespread methods of mind-altering, and certainly the most widespread chemical method – alcohol use – is a European institution, the extent of its use to truly alter perception is unclear. Liquor as an institution among Europeans may involve loving cups, stirrup cups, toasts, and all the rest, but these are now more nearly rituals than purposeful attempts to enter another state of consciousness. Though any of these instances may extend to mind-altering, they typically end with a single drink. Non-ritual alcohol use in European cultures certainly extends to altered consciousness, but it seems more a "social lubricant" or a "recreational use" than any response to the infinite. Among Native peoples, peyote use, the Sundance, sweat lodges, and many other institutions can, and do, lead to altered consciousness that is a direct response to the great mysteries. Though they also fulfill a social role, their aim is the infinite. Thus we would expect that those technologies that might enhance, alter, or interconnect the human mind would find ready acceptance unless they ran afoul of more central practices or institutions.

The two main elements of culture that might conflict with adoption of new technologies and ideas are what we might term "respect" (Cheney and Hester 2000 have respect as a recurring theme, as do many others) and "circularity" (Fixico 2003 devotes an entire book to this; also see Norton-Smith 2010: ch. 7). Both of these are complex and highly textured notions that are at the core of most American Indian practices. Most, if not all, American Indian cultures respect *all things*. Everything plays a role in existence; all are part of a web of interdependence and mutuality that constitutes existence. In this context it is impossible to speak of a hierarchy. A Christian God might grant "dominion" to man, but Indian people are struck by the fact that they live and die; they eat and are in turn, eaten; they affect things around them while striving toward their goals and they are likewise affected by all around them. Dominion is absurd when one stumbles from a cliff or faces a tiger bare-handed. Humans are an element of existence, no more or less so than animals, plants, mountains, or oceans. Each has its nature or role, and each must be respected for their role. Thus respect for the identity, the *integrity* of each entity is key.

On this view, humans are not of a different kind, nor do they have a superior position or role. Indeed, if anything, modern humans are often thought to have lost touch with this basic truth, and thus at a fundamental level are often considered inferior to other animals. Other animals are often considered our older siblings, since they have roamed the Earth longer than we have. While European evolutionary theory might say this means humans are at the pinnacle, Indians recognize that it means other animals have survived the test of time, while we have yet to prove ourselves. So technologies and philosophies that fail to respect all things, or that elevate humans disrespectfully, would be immediately suspect to American Indian people. Despite this, there are many cases in Native American history where individuals and even nations have elevated their own petty desires ahead of even the basic welfare of others. There are clearly times when the fur trade, for example, was so lucrative as to entice Indian trappers and hunters to take unsustainable numbers of animals. So the standard of respect has certainly been ignored at times, probably more so than the other traditional practices and norms. Though American Indian societies have many institutions that help inculcate an awareness and appreciation for communal and other higher goods over personal goods, personal gain can still sometimes win out. However, the norm of respect and appreciation for all things, even at one's own expense, is so great that its violation is certainly a cause of shame.

So far I have stressed respect for non-human animals and other entities primarily because this is less prevalent in European philosophies. This is a strong point of difference. But it does not mean that American Indian people do not respect humans and human societies. On the contrary, the colonizing of America by Europeans and the subsequent attempted destruction of Native lifeways and sovereignty is a prime example of disrespect that will never be forgotten by Native people. So technologies and ideas that might be taken as "colonizing" would provoke an immediate and sharply negative response, both because they are not respectful, and as a visceral expression of anguish over history and loss. Feelings run so deep on this that writers such as Taiaiake Alfred reject not only many of the technologies, but even the very knowledge and world-view of colonization as well as that which has been foisted off on Natives by the colonizers. As Alfred (2005: 280) says, "Decolonization, to make the point again, is a process of discovering the truth in a world created out of lies. It is thinking through what we think we know to what is actually true but is obscured by knowledge derived from our experiences as colonized peoples." But Native American appreciation for other cultures would be strong even without the experience of colonization. When American Indians from different Nations meet, they seek to know each other by exchanging information on who their people are, particularly things that are considered key elements of culture, including extended family history, place, and beliefs. Contrast this with two Euroamericans, who would typically discuss their occupations first, and might even avoid subjects like religion or other deeply held beliefs. So respect for *all* things, human and non-human, cultural as well as physical, would be a part of any American Indian approach.

This is also true of circularity. The idea of "circularity," as described here, has some correspondence with Western philosophical notions, though Western views are mainly linear. Circularity is partly a recognition of the cyclical nature of so many elements of the world. Its importance in American Indian culture is manifest in the many and varied circles present in the culture that are meant as a metaphor or recapitulation of natural cycles. Going in and out of the sweat lodge, we travel in a rough circle around both the outer fire and the heated rocks inside the lodge. To enter and exit, we must crawl as we did when we were babies and as we will again before we die, completing the circle. The great ceremonial dances are almost all done in circles, and ceremonial grounds as well as pow-wow grounds are arranged in circles. Traditionally, one may not cut across a ground, one must circle it, and the direction of the circling (clockwise or counterclockwise) is tribally dependant. When children first begin to dance, in many cultures they are admitted to the circle in an often elaborate ceremony involving giveaways and speeches. The birth–death cycle and the cycle of the seasons are probably the two most fundamental cycles at the core of these practices. The correspondence of this notion to European notions lies both in content and in how it is held. Among other things, it is clearly related to various dialectic notions. Opposites give meaning to each other, define and inform each other. We could not appreciate any one opposite without the other. Possibly because the practices associated with circles are so widespread, they are not merely practiced, but also remarked upon by the practitioners themselves. Here is a "truth" that goes beyond orthopraxy and approaches orthodoxy.

Circularity also involves reciprocity, which is further strengthened by the notion of respect mentioned above. Perhaps the most fundamental example of this is in the recognition of the cycle of life, in which the eater is, in turn, eaten. Many American Indian cultures exposed the bodies of their dead in various ways, such as the scaffold burials in which flesh-eating birds, among other beings, would partake of the flesh. In such cultures, only the bones would be kept, and even they would often be returned to the Earth. This contrasts with Euroamerican traditions that bury dead in coffins and even in concrete vaults to deny any return to other animals, often with the bodies preserved by chemicals that seek to deny even bacteria any benefit. Though local laws ban many traditional practices, and some Christians' views of a bodily resurrection have taken root among many Indian people, reciprocity and the notion of circularity behind it are still of great importance.

Transhumanism and American Indians

Transhumanism as an ideology, set of beliefs, or philosophy is immediately problematic for American Indian people because it is more nearly orthodoxy than orthopraxy. It is highly likely that most Native Americans will adopt some of the technologies associated with transhumanism for a variety of pragmatic reasons, but few if any will know about transhumanism, and fewer will profess it. Of course, this is not really that different from the reaction of most European societies to philosophical ideologies. Though orthodoxy may be at the heart of European culture, the orthodoxies adopted by the masses are generally religious, economic, or political in nature. Euro-Americans may profess to be Southern Baptist, Free-Market, Capitalists (often with capital letters), but postmodern deconstructionists they are not, though they may unwittingly act in that way. Even within the ideologies they profess, they will often not know the specific doctrines. Few Christians would know what the Pelagian or Albigensian heresies were, and even if you were to cite the doctrines violated by these heresies, only a few more would have any real knowledge of the doctrines themselves. So the real question for each group would more nearly be the extent to which they would disagree if they understood the position and, given that both are likely to adopt the technologies, the extent to which they adopt the technologies despite the transhuman position.

In addition to the problem of orthodoxy, American Indians are predisposed against some elements of transhumanism. If the transhumanist position requires a belief that humans have a "right to fundamentally influence our own evolution"

(Rizzuto and Fost in Chapter 52 of this volume), this may cause problems for Native Americans. Though Indian people arguably conducted the most extensive controlled breeding program in human history to create corn, and conducted only slightly less extensive projects with other plants, the human role in shaping plants and other elements of the environment does not necessarily translate to a belief that humans should have a role in shaping their own evolution. Given that we have shaped other plants and animals to fulfill our needs, shouldn't it be the case that we accept being shaped to fulfill their needs as well? Besides fitting in with circularity and specifically with reciprocity, as discussed above, it fits in with the notion of respect as well as the interrelatedness and interdependence of all things. Though we shape, we are in turn shaped. This is as it should be.

Besides this problem based on respect, there are other problems rooted in culture and history, if not in philosophy. American Indian people are among the poorest in the United States, largely due to a history of repression and dispossession by the incoming Europeans. Their shared poverty is a tangible expression and ongoing reminder of this history. American Indian people who "succeed" by breaking into the working, middle, or higher classes are often viewed as "sellouts". Even before the advent of Europeans in North America, too high a relative standard of living was considered "selfish". Giveaways or "potlatches," in which one gave away large numbers of possessions, were a source of great pride and standing within the community. Great leaders were not those who accumulated wealth, but rather those who saw to the welfare of their tribe, often at their own expense. Thus both culturally and due to historical forces, relative poverty is almost an essential element of identity. So even those who succeed in ways that make it clear they haven't sold out often find themselves cut off from their people anyway. Success often involves physical removal, since most American Indian communities and reservations are economically depressed areas. Thus the high-paying jobs and entrepreneurial opportunities will be "off-rez," usually far distant from Indian communities. If the transhumanist's "fundamental influence" on human evolution or the various technologies involved either require or exacerbate social differences, then most American Indian people would probably not be a part of the movement. A couple of quick illustrations can make this clear. If the enhancements, either genetically or technologically, cost any significant amount of money, then the fact that one had the money to receive the enhancement would automatically set one apart. Similarly, even if the enhancements were free, if their presence were enough to ensure a significant competitive advantage, then most American Indian people would probably forgo them, or possibly get them and then stay in jobs where they were effectively underemployed to ensure they were not cut off from their family, friends, community, and even identity. So, unless the benefits of transhumanism were available more or less across the board, so that people were rewarded equally and thus retained their relative position in society, many Native Americans would opt out. Perhaps more fundamentally because American Indian societies tend not to be hierarchical, if any of these technologies promoted hierarchies they would be extremely unwelcome (Cordova 2003: 177 explains how fundamental a non-hierarchical view is to American Indians).

American Indians and the technologies of transhumanism

Differences in adoption of technology by Native Americans as opposed to transhumanists would depend upon exactly which technologies the transhumanist would adopt. Rizzuto and Fost mention various technologies, but focus on cognitive enhancement. They do this partly because they assume that some of the other technologies are relatively non-controversial. As they put it, "Like most people, transhumanists support the development of medical technologies to alleviate human maladies, the creation of artificial body parts to replace worn-out bones and joints, and the improvement of tools to diagnose and treat disease" (Chapter 52 in this volume). They go on to say that what sets transhumanists apart is their willingness to use such technologies to extend human capacities beyond what is normal, which would include cognitive enhancement. But their assertion that this somehow sets transhumanists apart seems rather far-fetched. The whole point of a tool is to extend human capacities. Humans are tool-using animals, and humans of all cultures are well aware of this. While some, like the Mennonites, may eschew the use of particular technologies, their lives are far from technology-free. American Indians may revere the time-tested technologies of their ancestors but they pragmatically accept new technologies that fit their culture quite readily. Even more to the point American Indians recognize that humans are, by nature, tool-using animals. Various American Indian teaching stories and sayings hinge on the fact that we aren't particularly speedy, don't have long teeth or claws, and don't have fur or armored skin. Instead, we have intelligence. It is fitting and proper, even inevitable, that humans use their intelligence to extend their capacities, since their capacities are so limited otherwise. The other animals have special capacities, while we have only our brains to make up for a lack in all other areas. Most humans, and American Indians in particular, wish to use tools to extend human capacities beyond what is normal. The real difference in the transhumanist position is that they seem more willing to change the human organism itself, which is perhaps why cognitive enhancement plays such a key role in Rizzuto and Fost's essay. Though the transhumanist's position arguably does not differ quite as radically as they claim, there would still be some differences between Native Americans and the transhumanist, even in some of the supposedly uncontroversial areas.

In healthcare, the acceptability of various technologies for Native Americans would depend on the extent to which they respect the rest of existence and fit in with the circular nature of existence. This is mediated to some extent by the natural desire to survive, which undoubtedly motivated Rizzuto and Fost's claim that these are relatively uncontroversial. So, even though American Indian people desire to survive and thrive like all other peoples, if a technology conflicts too much with circularity or respect, then it is likely to be rejected or be of limited use. Things such as artificial body parts and replacement joints would indeed enhance quality of life and don't appear to conflict with these principles. On the other hand, technologies that extend life indefinitely may be unwelcome because they interfere with the natural cycle of birth and death. Additionally, most American Indian people believe the world to be overcrowded with humans as it is. There is not enough room for the other animals and plants, whose claim to this world is as great as, or possibly even greater than, ours. Whether the "instinct" for survival would overcome deeply held views is unclear. But the fact that it would be a real issue among American Indian people would come as a surprise to the majority of Americans, for whom immortality would be a top goal.

Among the technologies mentioned by Rizzuto and Fost that would almost certainly be welcomed by American Indians is the ability to read minds or communicate telepathically. Group harmony is among the main goals of all American Indian societies. Many major practices, including important ceremonies, are specifically set up to promote harmony. Indeed, it seems likely that such technologies would form the basis of new ceremonies that would be passed on for generations to come.

More generic forms of "cognitive enhancement" are problematic, and in some cases the outcome of American Indian views might be the opposite of what Rizzuto and Fost might consider "mainstream" and be somewhat more in line with the views of the transhumanist, at least for people who are usually considered cognitively average. Perhaps the key example of this might be the use of Ritalin (methylphenidate) examined in Chapter 52. Its use to treat attention deficit disorder and similar cognitive disorders is considered mainstream; however, the transhumanist would not only use it therapeutically, but would also consider its use on people with no impairment for the possibility of enhancing their abilities. Here the difference with American Indians is striking. The use of a psychoactive compound by an "average" person would not be unusual for Native Americans, as the example of peyote mentioned earlier would suggest. On the other hand, a very traditional American Indian person might very well question its therapeutic use on a person with a supposed impairment. That person's "impairment" sets them apart where the average person's cognitive ability is unremarkable. Thus the "impaired" person's identity is, in part, their purported impairment. While this is also true to some extent for people with missing limbs and other non-cognitive medical problems, the centrality of cognition to identity is clear in most human societies, including Native American societies. Thus among American Indians the therapeutic use of Ritalin might well be more questionable than its use for cognitive enhancement. Respect for the integrity of the individual would certainly give pause, and respect for their freedom would normally require that they accept the treatment for it even to be considered. While social and cultural dynamics outside the scope of this essay might cause an adult patient or the parents of a younger patient to "accept" treatment, covert non-compliance could result. However, for cognitive enhancement, chemicals would certainly be an option for Native Americans if they should prove to be efficacious. Among American Indian populations, the use of drugs like Ritalin for such enhancement might become more frequent than therapeutic use if it were legal.

Other results that might seem paradoxical to the non-Indians would be in cognitive enhancements that are caused by implanted hardware rather than chemicals, and those whose effects would include an enhanced memory for certain "facts." Implanted hardware is problematic again because of respect for the integrity of the individual. While chemicals may alter us, that is part of the natural cycle of things. We are what we eat. Though chemicals such as Ritalin are "synthetic," as Rizzuto and Fost point out, very little of what we eat is unchanged by humans. Whether it be as simple as cooking or as complex as the long-term breeding program that created corn, humans create their food. Though the synthetic nature of some drugs might be slightly problematic for some American Indians, hardware would be much more so. While an individual's choice to receive such an implant would be respected, and the implant would then be considered a part of the individual, such a choice would not be made lightly.

Enhancements to human memory are among those that most people would consider very useful. However, one version that will likely become available provides what we might term "facts" rather than the memories of our "experience." Imagine an implanted link to the internet. The implant would certainly help us to remember "facts," like the range of wavelengths in visible light, or the year that the Treaty of Dancing Rabbit Creek was signed, but it would not help us remember our "experience" of a rock we touched last week. The problem lies in just what purported "facts" are made available and in how their availability affects our relationship to them. Taiaiake Alfred's indictment of the knowledge of colonizers, quoted above, weighs heavily here. The internet may provide facts as known to European science, but they are a part of a world-view often at odds with that of Native Americans. While the facts may be of interest and may be useful, they are not and cannot be used by Native Americans as a substitute for their own indigenous knowledge. The mere availability of "facts" from a European world-view is relatively unproblematic, but if their presentation were such that they might supplant indigenous views, then they would likely be rejected. A parallel here can be seen with the boarding schools to which so many Indian children were subjected in the late 1800s and early 1900s. The problem with those schools was not just that they were often brutal, or even that the families were coerced or even forced to make their children attend. The real problem was that the schools sought to "Americanize" the American Indian. Modern American Indian parents have fewer objections to the current public school system, since they can offset many of the acculturating elements of these schools. So, depending on just how a memory enhancement affected people, it might or might not be considered appropriate. If an enhancement made certain facts more readily available, thus causing the person to be more likely to accept them, then the enhancement would likely be rejected.

Conclusion

The pragmatism and syncretism of American Indian societies will certainly allow for the adoption of many future technologies, particularly those involving cognitive enhancement by chemical means. However, the technologies will be weighed against a variety of values including respect and circularity. Though much of the technology developed historically has been used to the detriment of American Indians, "After several centuries of technologies that foster control and manipulation through military might, we may be entering an era in which modern information technology liberates rather than controls situations"(Grinde and Johansen 1995: 274). American Indians can be expected to be technologically savvy in the future, and may even be early adopters of some technologies that are accessible and culturally acceptable.

References

Alfred, T. (2005) *Wasáse: Indigenous Pathways of Action and Freedom*, Peterborough, ON, Canada: Broadview Press.

Cheney, J. and L. Hester (2000) "Ceremonial Worlds and Environmental Sanity," *Strategies: Journal of Theory, Culture and Politics* 13(1): 77–87.

Cordova, V. (2003) "Ethics: The We and the I," in *American Indian Thought*, A. Waters (ed.), Malden, MA and Oxford: Blackwell, 173–81.

Fixico, D. (2003) *The American Indian Mind in a Linear World*, New York: Routledge.

Grinde, D. and B. Johansen (1995) *Ecocide of Native America: Environmental Destruction of Indian Lands and Peoples*, Santa Fe, NM: Clear Light Publishing.

Norton-Smith, T. (2010) *The Dance of Person and Place: One Interpretation of American Indian Philosophy*, Albany, NY: SUNY Press.

Further reading

Though no single work could ever provide a comprehensive overview of American Indian philosophy, there are a variety of books that provide insights into portions of it. John F. Boatman's book, *My Elders Taught Me: Aspects of Western Great Lakes American Indian Philosophy* (American Indian Studies, University of Wisconsin-Milwaukee, 1991) provides a nice combination of traditional stories and thoughtful observations, and is a good example of a work on a particular nation or group of nations. The journal *Ayaangwaamizin: The International Journal of Indigenous Philosophy* has been a forum for a variety of informative articles. Finally, Vine Deloria Jr. is widely recognized as the leading American Indian thinker in recent years, and any work written by him will be worthwhile and thought-provoking.

INDEX